Taxation of Derivatives and Cryptoassets

Series on International Taxation

VOLUME 52

Series Editors

Prof. Ruth Mason, University of Virginia School of Law
Prof. Dr Ekkehart Reimer, University of Heidelberg

Introduction & Contents

The Series on International Taxation deals with a wide variety of topics in the global tax arena. The authors include many of the field's leading experts as well as talented newcomers. Their expert views and incisive commentary have proven highly useful to practitioners and academics alike.

Objective

The volumes published in this series are aimed at offering high-quality analytical information and practical solutions to international tax practitioners.

Readership

Practitioners, academics and policy makers in international tax law.

Frequency of Publication

2-3 new volumes published each year.

The titles published in this series are listed at the end of this volume.

Taxation of Derivatives and Cryptoassets

Second Edition

Oktavia Weidmann

Wolters Kluwer

Published by:
Kluwer Law International B.V.
PO Box 316
2400 AH Alphen aan den Rijn
The Netherlands
E-mail: lrs-sales@wolterskluwer.com
Website: www.wolterskluwer.com/en/solutions/kluwerlawinternational

Sold and distributed by:
Wolters Kluwer Legal & Regulatory U.S.
920 Links Avenue
Landisville, PA 17538
United States of America
E-mail: customer.service@wolterskluwer.com

ISBN 978-94-035-2383-5

e-Book: ISBN 978-94-035-2405-4
web-PDF: ISBN 978-94-035-2384-2

To my family

About the Author

Oktavia Weidmann is a barrister in England and Wales and teaches at the Dickson Poon School of Law of King's College London in the *International Financial & Commercial Law* and *International Tax Law* LLM programmes. For several years, she led the modules *Derivatives in a Legal Context* and *Risk Management and Law* at the Centre of Commercial Law Studies, Queen Mary University of London.

The author held front-office positions in derivatives teams of several investment banks and worked as a Chief Risk Officer in a Swiss investment management company during her previous finance career.

In 2019, the author co-wrote the General Report on investment funds for the IFA Congress in London. She has been a member of the Advanced Diploma in International Taxation (ADIT) Examination Sub-Committee since 2020.

The author qualified as a German and English lawyer and holds law degrees from the University of Trier, the State of Bavaria, a Bachelor of Civil Law from the University of Oxford, and a Master of Laws (Taxation) and Doctor of Philosophy from Queen Mary University of London.

Table of Contents

About the Author vii

Foreword xxvii

Preface to the Second Edition xxix

Acknowledgements xxxi

Introduction xxxiii

Reference Sources and Effective Date xxxvii

List of Abbreviations xxxix

CHAPTER 1
Taxing Derivatives and Cryptoassets – An Introduction 1
§1.01 The Methodology 2
§1.02 The Taxation of Derivatives and Cryptoassets 2
§1.03 The Scope: Chapter by Chapter 4

CHAPTER 2
Basic Economic Concepts of Derivatives and Cryptoassets 7
§2.01 Economic Properties of Derivatives and Cryptoassets 8
[A] Classification of Derivatives According to Their Type 8
[B] Categorisation of Derivatives According to Their Underlying Variable 11
[C] Cryptoassets as a New Underlying Asset Class 12
[D] ESG as a New Underlying Variable for Derivatives? 17
§2.02 Basic Terms: Replication, Hedging of Derivatives and Leverage 21
[A] Economic Replication 21

[1] Static Replication of Derivatives Using the Put-Call Parity Formula 22
[2] Replication of Options by Means of Dynamic Replication 26
[B] Hedging of Derivatives/with Derivatives 26
[C] Valuation of Options 27
[D] Definition of Leverage 29

CHAPTER 3
Problems in the Context of Taxing Derivatives and Cryptoassets 31
§3.01 Problem 1: Defining Derivatives for Tax Purposes 31
§3.02 Problem 2: Accounting Standards Applying to Derivatives and Cryptoassets and Their Alignment with Tax Rules 33
§3.03 Problem 3: A Special Taxation Regime Versus the Application of General Tax Rules to Derivatives and Cryptoassets, and the Distinction of Income and Capital, and Equity and Debt 34
[A] Specific Taxation Regime Versus the Application of the General Tax Rules 34
[B] The Taxation Rules for Income and Capital Gains Applying to Derivatives 34
[C] The Taxation Rules for Equity and Debt and Their Application to Derivatives 36
§3.04 Problem 4: Taxation of Derivatives and Cryptoassets in the Context of Hedging Transactions 38
§3.05 Problem 5: Taxation of Structured Products and Hybrid Instruments 39
[A] Defining Structured Products for Tax Purposes 40
[B] Problems in the Taxation of Structured Products and Hybrid Instruments 40
§3.06 Problem 6: Derivatives in a Cross-Border Context 41
[A] Derivatives in the Context of Withholding Taxes 42
[B] Ownership Issues 44
[C] Cross-Border Qualification Conflicts and Hybrid Instruments 47
§3.07 Problem 7: Tax Avoidance Relating to Derivatives and Cryptoassets and Applicable Anti-avoidance Legislation 47

CHAPTER 4
Defining Derivatives for Tax Purposes 51
§4.01 Framing the Problem 51
§4.02 Common Approaches in Defining Derivatives for Tax Purposes 52
§4.03 Definitions of Derivatives for Tax Purposes in the UK and Germany 53
[A] The UK Corporate Tax Definition Applying to Derivative Contracts 53
[1] Relevant Contract 54
[a] Futures 55
[b] Options 56

[c] Contract for Differences 57
[2] Accounting Conditions 59
[3] Underlying Subject Matter Test 61
[B] Evaluation of the UK Approach to Defining Derivative Contracts 65
[C] The German Definition Applying to 'Derivative Contracts' for Tax Purposes 66
[1] Definition of Derivative Contract Applying to Private Individuals 67
[2] Definition of 'Derivative Contract' Applying to Business and Corporate Taxpayers 71
[D] Evaluation of the German Approach to Defining Derivative Contracts 73
§4.04 Other Definitional Approaches 75
[A] Different Approaches to Defining Derivatives in Other Countries 75
[B] Definition of Derivatives for Tax Purposes in the Academic Tax Literature 75
§4.05 The Accounting Definition of Derivatives and Its Suitability for Taxation 77
§4.06 Solution to Problem 1: Designing a Suitable Definition of Derivatives 79
[A] The Task 79
[B] Definitional Criteria for Defining Derivatives for Tax Purposes 80
[1] Economic Criterion of Contingency 80
[2] Deterministic Dependence on Stochastic Underlying Variables 81
[3] Limited Term of a Derivative 83
[4] Replication 83
[5] Summary of a Tailor-Made Definition for Tax Purposes 86
[C] Application of the Definition to Existing Derivatives 87
[1] Income Streams and Payoffs as Underlying Variables 87
[2] Credit Derivatives 88
[3] Crypto Derivatives 95
[a] Should Cryptoassets/Cryptocurrencies Be Qualified as Derivatives for Tax Purposes? 97
[b] Do Crypto Derivatives Qualify as Derivatives for Tax Purposes? 99
[4] ESG Derivatives 102
[a] Weather Derivatives 102
[b] Catastrophe Derivatives 104
[c] Sustainability-Linked Derivatives 105
[d] ESG-Related Credit Derivatives 107
[e] ESG-Related Exchange-Traded Derivatives 108

[f] Derivatives Based on Carbon Allowances and Carbon Offsets 109
[g] Renewable Energy and Renewable Fuel Derivatives 109
[D] Introduction of a Definition of Derivatives in Tax Treaties 110

CHAPTER 5
Accounting Standards Applying to Derivatives and Cryptoassets 113
§5.01 Accounting Methods Applying to Derivatives as a Basis for Taxation 114
§5.02 Alignment of Accounting Standards and Tax Rules Applying to Derivatives in the UK 116
[A] IFRS and UK GAAP Alignment 116
[B] Accounting Methods in the UK Applying to Financial Instruments 120
[1] FRS 102, Sections 11 and 12 Applying to Financial Instruments 121
[2] IAS 39 Applying to Financial Assets and Liabilities 124
[3] IFRS 9 Applying to Financial Instruments 127
[4] Differences Between FRS 102, Sections 11 and 12, IAS 39 and IFRS 9 128
[C] FRS 102, Sections 11 and 12, IAS 39 and IFRS 9: Application to Derivatives 131
[1] FRS 102, Sections 11 and 12 Applying to Derivatives 132
[2] IAS 39 Applying to Derivatives 133
[3] IFRS 9 Applying to Derivatives 134
[a] Change in Value of the Derivative in Response to the Change of the Underlying Asset/Variable 134
[b] No or Little Net Investment 135
[c] Settled at a Future Date 135
[d] Financial Liabilities 136
[e] Challenges 136
[D] State of Alignment of Accounting Standards and Taxation Rules Applying to Derivatives 136
§5.03 Alignment of Accounting and Tax Rules Applying to Derivatives in Germany 140
[A] German GAAP as a Basis for Taxation 140
[B] German GAAP Applying to the Taxation of Derivatives 141
§5.04 Comparison of the State of Alignment of Accounting and Tax Rules in the UK and Germany 143
§5.05 Accounting of Cryptoassets, with Focus on Cryptocurrencies 145
[A] Accounting of Cryptoassets under IFRS 146
[1] Classification of Cryptoassets under IFRS 146
[a] IAS 32/IFRS 9 147
[i] 'Digital Cash'? 147
[ii] Cash Equivalent? 151

[iii] Contractual Right? 152
[b] IAS 38: Intangible Assets 152
[i] Identifiable 152
[ii] Non-monetary Asset? 153
[iii] Without Physical Substance? 154
[2] Measurement of Cryptoassets under IFRS 154
[B] Accounting of Cryptoassets under UK GAAP 155
[1] Classification of Cryptoassets under FRS 102, Section 18 155
[2] Measurement of Cryptoassets under FRS 102, Section 18 157
[C] Accounting of Cryptoassets under German GAAP 159
[D] Accounting of Cryptoassets in Other Jurisdictions 161
[1] US GAAP 161
[2] Australian Accounting Standards Board 168
§5.06 Accounting of Crypto Derivatives 169
[A] Accounting of Crypto Derivatives in the UK 170
[1] Accounting under FRS 102 171
[a] A Derivative Is a Financial Instrument or 'Other Contract' 172
[i] Is a Crypto Derivative a Financial Instrument? 172
[b] The Value Changes in Response to the Change of an Underlying, Provided in the Case of a Non-financial Variable That the Variable Is Not Specific to a Party to the Contract 175
[c] It Requires No or Little Net Investment 176
[d] It Is Settled at a Future Date 176
[e] Explicit Exception of FRS 102, Paragraph 12.5 176
[2] Accounting under IAS 39 and IFRS 9 176
[B] Accounting of Crypto Derivatives in Germany 178
[C] Policy Outlook 178
§5.07 Accounting of ESG Derivatives 179
§5.08 Solutions on the Alignment of Accounting and Taxation Rules and the Application of Fair Value Accounting for Tax Purposes 181
[A] Aligning Financial Accounting Rules with Taxation Rules? 181
[B] Application of Fair Value Accounting of Derivatives for Tax Purposes? 184

CHAPTER 6
The Special Regime Approach Versus the Integrative Approach, the Distinction of Income and Capital, and Equity and Debt 187
§6.01 A Special Taxation Regime Applying to Derivatives Held by Companies in the UK 188
§6.02 The Distinction Between Income and Capital, and Between Equity and Debt in the UK 190

§6.03 The Integrative Approach Applying to Derivatives Held by Companies in Germany 195
§6.04 The Distinction Between Income and Capital, and Between Equity and Debt in Germany 196
§6.05 The UK Taxation Rules on Derivative Contracts Entered into by Companies 198
[A] The General Taxation Principles for Companies 198
[B] Taxation of Derivatives Income 199
[1] Analysis of Historical Change of Rules and Policy Background 200
[2] Taxation of Derivative Contracts under CTA 2009, Part 7 204
[a] Derivative Contracts Entered into for Trading and Non-trading Purposes 205
[b] Profits and Losses of Derivative Contracts under CTA 2009, Section 595(3)(a) 207
[c] Expenses Incurred in Relation to Derivative Contracts 209
[d] FX Gains and Losses in Relation to Derivative Contracts 210
[e] Taxation of Specific Derivative Contracts over Land 213
[f] Equity Derivatives 214
[i] Taxation of Plain Vanilla Equity Options or Futures 214
[ii] Taxation of Equity Swaps 215
[3] Taxation of Derivative Contracts That Are Excluded by Virtue of Their Underlying Subject Matter 216
[a] Options and Futures over Intangible Fixed Assets: Cryptocurrencies 216
[b] Certain Equity Derivatives 221
[i] Quoted Options to Subscribe for Shares 222
[ii] Derivatives That Hedge Shareholdings, CTA 2009, Section 591(3) 222
[iii] Derivatives to Acquire Substantial Shareholdings, CTA 2009, s. 591(5) 223
[iv] Derivatives Entered by a Life Insurance Company 224
[c] Units of a Unit Trust Scheme 224
§6.06 German Taxation Rules Applying to Derivatives Entered into by Companies 224
[A] General Taxation Principles for Companies 224
[B] General Accounting Principles as a Basis for German Business Taxation 226
[C] Taxation of Derivatives Held by Companies 226
[1] Tax Treatment of a Derivative Contract During Its Term 227

[2] Taxation of Derivatives Held by Corporate Investors at Maturity 227
[a] Taxation of Futures, Forwards and Swaps 227
[b] Taxation of Options 230
[i] Taxation of Long Positions and Short Positions 230
[ii] Taxation of Equity Options 237
[c] Taxation of Equity Swaps 238
[i] Taxation of the Equity Performance Seller (Protection Buyer) 238
[ii] Taxation of the Equity Performance Buyer (Protection Seller) 240
§6.07 Comparison of the UK and German Corporate Taxation Rules Applying to Derivatives 241
[A] Comparison of the Special Regime Approach Applied in the UK with the Integrative Approach Applied in German Corporate Tax Law 241
[B] Abolition of the Income and Capital Divide in the UK and German Corporate Taxation Rules 242
[C] The Equity and Debt Divide in the UK and German Corporate Tax Legislation 242
§6.08 Taxation of Cryptoassets 243
[A] Taxation of Cryptoassets in the UK 243
[B] Taxation of Cryptoassets in Germany 245
[C] Outlook 246
§6.09 Solution to Problem 3: Coherence in Domestic Tax Rules 247
[A] The Integrative Approach 247
[B] The Special Regime Approach 248
[C] Coherent Solutions: Integrative Versus Special Regime Approach 248
[1] Achieving Coherence in Applying an Integrative Approach? 248
[2] Achieving Coherence in Applying a Special Regime Approach? 249
[3] Special Regime Approach as the More Appropriate Solution 250

CHAPTER 7
The Taxation of Derivatives and Cryptoassets in the Context of Hedging Transactions 253
§7.01 The Economic Background of Hedging Approaches 253
§7.02 The Accounting and Tax Treatment of Hedging Relationships Involving Derivatives 256

[A] Hedge Accounting and Its Tax Treatment During the Term of the Transaction 256
[B] Treatment of Hedging Relationships from a Post-tax Perspective 257
§7.03 Treatment of Hedging Transactions until Maturity in the UK and Germany 258
[A] Derivatives Hedging Transactions in the UK 258
[1] Treatment Hedging Transactions for Accounting Purposes 258
[a] Hedge Accounting under FRS 102, Section 12 258
[i] Hedged Item 259
[ii] Hedging Instrument 259
[iii] Hedge Accounting Conditions 260
[iv] Types of Hedges Permitted 260
[b] Hedge Accounting under IAS 39 262
[c] Hedge Accounting under IFRS 9 264
[i] Hedged Items 265
[ii] Hedging Instruments 265
[iii] Types of Hedges under IFRS 9 266
[2] Treatment of Derivatives Hedging Transactions for Tax Purposes 268
[a] Summary of the Current UK Disregard Regulations Applying to Hedging Transactions 271
[i] Purpose and Background 271
[ii] Mechanism of the Disregard Regulations 272
[B] Derivatives Hedging Transactions in Germany 275
[1] Treatment of Hedges for Accounting Purposes 275
[2] Treatment of Hedging Transactions for Tax Purposes 277
[C] Comparison of Tax Hedge Accounting Approaches in the UK and Germany 277
§7.04 Pre- and Post-tax Hedging Approaches 278
[A] The Policy Aim of Tax Neutral Post-tax Hedges 278
[B] Approach Towards Pre- and Post-tax Hedging in the UK 279
[C] Approach Towards Pre- and Post-tax Hedging in Germany 283
[D] Comparison of Approaches Towards Pre- and Post-tax Hedging in the UK and Germany 284
§7.05 Problem 4: Solutions on How to Tax Hedged Positions and Post-tax Hedging Schemes 285
[A] Solutions in the Context of General Hedge Accounting Provisions 285
[B] Solutions in Respect of the Tax Treatment of Hedges on a Post-tax Basis 287
§7.06 Hedging Relationships with Cryptoassets and Crypto Derivatives 288

[A] General Considerations: Hedge Accounting of Cryptoassets in the Banking Sector 289
[B] Accounting and Tax Considerations: United Kingdom 291
[1] Accounting Considerations 292
[a] FRS 102, Section 12 292
[i] Hedge Accounting Conditions 292
[ii] Types of Hedges Permitted 296
[b] IAS 39 297
[c] IFRS 9 299
[2] Taxation 301
[a] Group 1a, 1b and Group 2a Cryptoassets and Their Derivatives 301
[b] Application of the Disregard Regulations? 302
[C] Accounting and Tax Considerations: Germany 305
[1] Accounting Treatment in Germany 305
[2] Treatment of Crypto Hedging Transactions for Tax Purposes 306

CHAPTER 8
Taxation of Structured Products and Hybrid Instruments 309
§8.01 Defining Structured Products 310
[A] Development of a Definition of Structured Products for Tax Purposes 310
[B] Application of the Definition to Structured Products 311
[1] False Friends I: Put-Call Parity Combinations 311
[2] False Friends II: Legally Separable Combinations 312
[3] False Friends III: Combinations of Two or More Derivative Contracts 313
[4] Reverse Convertible Bonds as an Example of Structured Products 314
§8.02 Bifurcation of Structured Products 314
§8.03 Defining Hybrid Instruments 316
§8.04 No Bifurcation of Hybrid Instruments 316
§8.05 Bifurcation Versus Integration Approaches in the UK 320
[A] Historical Accounting Treatment of Hybrid Instruments under Old UK GAAP 321
[B] Accounting Treatment of Structured Products and Hybrid Instruments under IAS 32 and IAS 39 322
[1] The Basic Rules 322
[2] Definitional Criteria under IAS 39, Paragraph 11 as an Indicator for Bifurcation 324
[C] Accounting Treatment of Structured Products and Hybrid Instruments under IFRS 9 326
[1] Summary of the Rules 326

[2] The Reasons for Moving from Bifurcation to Integration: From IAS 39 Towards IFRS 9 328

[D] Integration Versus Bifurcation of Structured Products and Hybrid Instruments under FRS 102, Sections 11 and 12 331

[1] Holder of Plain Vanilla Convertible Bonds (Hybrid Instruments) 332

[2] Issuer of Plain Vanilla Convertible Bonds (Hybrid Instruments) 333

[a] FRS 102, Section 22/IFRS 9: Split Accounting 336

[b] IAS 39: Bifurcation 337

[3] Issuance of Other Instruments 338

[4] Holder of Structured Products (Reverse Convertible Bonds) 338

[5] Issuer of Structured Products (Reverse Convertible Bonds) 339

[E] Evaluation of the Bifurcation Approach for Structured Products and Hybrid Instruments under IAS 39, IFRS 9 and FRS 102, Schedules 11 or 12 339

[F] Treatment of Structured Products and Hybrid Instruments under UK Tax Law 340

[1] Summary of the Rules 340

[a] Cases of Non-bifurcation 340

[b] Cases of bifurcation: CTA 2009, sections 584-586 341

[i] Hybrid Derivatives with Embedded Derivatives 341

[ii] Loan Relationships with Embedded Derivatives 341

[iii] Other Contracts with Embedded Derivatives 341

[iv] Tax Treatment of the Embedded Derivative Contract as Capital Gains 342

[v] Issuer of Structured Products and Hybrid Instruments 342

[2] The UK Tax Treatment of Structured Products and Hybrid Instruments in Detail 343

[a] Embedded Derivatives under CTA 2009, Sections 584-586 343

[i] Hybrid Derivatives with Embedded Derivatives 343

[ii] Loan Relationships with Embedded Derivatives 345

[iii] Other Contracts with Embedded Derivatives 349

§8.06 Bifurcation Versus Integration Approaches in Germany 349

[A] Accounting of Structured Products and Hybrid Instruments under German GAAP 349

[1] Bifurcation Versus Integration for Structured Products under German GAAP (IDW View) 350

[a] Accounting Treatment of the Holder of Structured Products 351
[b] Accounting Treatment of the Issuer of Structured Products 353
[2] Bifurcation Versus Integration for Hybrid Instruments under German GAAP 354
[a] Accounting Treatment of the Holder of Hybrid Instruments 354
[b] Accounting Treatment of the Issuer of Hybrid Instruments 354
[B] Taxation of Structured Products and Hybrid Instruments in Germany 355
[1] Taxation of Structured Products: Holders and Issuers 355
[2] Taxation of Hybrid Instruments 357
[a] Taxation of the Holder of Hybrid Instruments 357
[b] Taxation of the Issuer of Hybrid Instruments 358
§8.07 Comparison of the Taxation Rules for Structured Products and Hybrid Instruments in the UK and Germany 359
§8.08 Solution to Problem 5: Bifurcation for Structured Products and Integration for Hybrid Instruments? 360
[A] Hybrid Instruments 362
[B] Structured Products 362
[1] Solution 1 for Structured Products: Bifurcation 362
[2] Solution 2 for Structured Products: Integration 362
§8.09 Crypto Structured Products and Cryptoassets with Embedded Derivatives 364
[A] The Economic Properties of Crypto Structured Products 364
[B] Accounting of Crypto Structured Products 369
[C] Taxation of Crypto Structured Products 370
[1] UK Taxation of Crypto Structured Products 371
[2] German Tax Treatment of Crypto Structured Products 371
§8.10 ESG-Linked Structured Products 371
[A] What Are ESG-Linked Structured Products? 372
[B] Regulation 373
[C] Categories of ESG-Linked Structured Products 375
[D] Accounting of ESG-Linked Structured Products 377
[1] IFRS S1 and S2 377
[2] Accounting Treatment of ESG-Linked CLOs and ABS and Other ESG-Linked Securitised Products 378
[3] Accounting of Structured Products Based on Carbon Credits 379
[4] Outlook 380
[E] Taxation of ESG-Linked Structured Products 380
[1] UK Tax Treatment of ESG-Linked Structured Products 380

[a] Tax Treatment of ESG-Linked CLOs and ABSs and Related Structured Products 380
[b] Tax Treatment of Structured Products with Embedded Carbon Credits or Carbon Credit Derivatives 381
[2] German Tax Treatment of ESG-Linked Structured Products 382
[3] Outlook 382

CHAPTER 9
Derivatives in a Cross-Border Context: Beneficial Ownership and Withholding Taxes 383
§9.01 Withholding Taxes on Derivatives in the UK and Germany 384
[A] Withholding Taxes on Derivatives in the UK 384
[B] Withholding Taxes on Derivatives in Germany 385
[C] Withholding Tax Rules in the UK and Germany Applying to Dividend Swaps and Equity Swaps 386
[1] The UK Dividend Withholding Tax Regime 386
[2] The German Dividend Withholding Tax Regime 388
§9.02 Beneficial Ownership and the Use of Derivatives 388
[A] The Domestic Beneficial Ownership Concept in Relation to Derivatives 389
[B] The UK Domestic Concept of Beneficial Ownership 389
[C] The German Domestic Concept of Economic Ownership 390
[D] Interpretation of the Term 'Beneficial Owner' at the Tax Treaty Level 392
[1] Interpretation of the Treaty Term 'Beneficial Owner' in UK Tax Law 392
[2] Interpretation of the Treaty Term 'Beneficial Owner' in German Tax Law 393
[3] Interpretation of the Treaty Term 'Beneficial Owner' by the OECD 393
[E] Broad Versus Narrow Interpretation of the Treaty Term 'Beneficial Owner' by the Courts 398
[1] The Spanish Cases 398
[2] The Swiss Cases 399
[a] The Swiss Swaps Case 400
[i] The Decision of the Lower Swiss Federal Administrative Court 400
[ii] The Decision of the Swiss Federal Supreme Court 402

[iii] The *Swiss Swaps* Case in Light of the OECD Model Commentary on Article 10, Paragraph 12.4 410
[b] The SMI Futures Case 414
[i] The Facts of the Case 415
[ii] The Reasoning of the Federal Administrative Court 416
[iii] The Reasoning of the Federal Supreme Court 417
[iv] Critical Analysis of the Federal Supreme Court's Decision in the SMI Futures Case 423
[c] The Single Stock Futures Case 425
[i] Facts of the Case 425
[ii] Domestic Tax Law Background of the Case 428
[iii] The Decision of the Federal Administrative Court 429
[iv] The Decision of the Swiss Federal Supreme Court 433
[v] Critical Discussion of the *Single Stock Futures* Case 437
[d] A Plc v. Federal Tax Administration 440
§9.03 Solutions for the Treatment of Derivatives in Cross-Border Transactions 440
[A] Solution 1: Alternative Definition of 'Beneficial Owner' in Domestic Law and in the Tax Treaties 440
[1] Objective Criteria to Determine Beneficial Ownership 441
[a] Market Risk with Regard to the Share Price Movement 441
[b] Market Risk with Regard to the Dividends 442
[c] Market Risk with Regard to the Lending Amount Received 443
[B] Solution 2: Equalisation of Corporate and Withholding Tax Rates on Dividends 443
[C] Solution 3: Application of a Withholding Tax on Derivatives 444

Chapter 10
Countering Tax Avoidance: Derivatives and Cryptoassets 447
§10.01 Anti-avoidance Legislation in the UK Applying to Derivatives 447
[A] Specific Anti-avoidance Legislation Applying to Derivative Contracts 448
[1] Derivative Contracts for Unallowable Purposes 449
[2] Non-arm's Length Derivative Contracts 452
[3] Value Shifting to Connected Companies with Option Contracts 452
[4] Derivative Contracts with Non-residents 452

[5] Amounts Not Fully Recognised for Accounting Purposes 453
[6] Debts Arising from Derecognition of Derivative Contracts 454
[B] Provisions Concerning the Counteracting of Avoidance Arrangements (Regime Anti-avoidance Rules) 455
[C] Hybrid Mismatch and Hybrid Capital Instrument Rules 457
[1] BEPS Action 2: Hybrid Mismatch Arrangements 457
[2] The UK Hybrid Mismatch Rules 463
[3] The Hybrid Capital Instruments Rules 465
[a] The Issuer of the Loan Relationship Is Entitled to Defer or Cancel Interest Payments 467
[b] The Loan Relationship Has No Other Significant Equity Features 467
[c] The Issuer Has Made an 'Irrevocable Election into the New Rules Within Six Months of Issue of the Debt Instrument' 468
[D] UK General Anti-avoidance Legislation Applying to Derivatives 469
[1] The Disclosure Rules 469
[a] Mandatory Disclosure Rules (MDR) 470
[b] Disclosure Rules Applying to Direct Taxes 471
[2] The UK GAAR 472
[a] The Basic Design of the GAAR 472
[b] Procedural Requirements for HMRC to Apply the GAAR 473
[c] Critical Analysis of the UK GAAR 474
[3] Pillar Two 476
[E] Case Law Concerning Derivative Arrangements 478
[1] Griffin (Inspector of Taxes) v. Citibank Investments Ltd [2000] STC 1010 478
[2] HSBC Life (UK) Ltd v. Stubbs [2002] STC (SCD) 9 479
[3] IRC v. Scottish Provident Institution [2004] UKHL 52 479
[4] HBOS Treasury Services Plc v. R&C Commissioners [2010] SFTD 134 479
[5] Abbey National Treasury Services Plc v. R&C Commissioners [2015] SFTD 929 480
[6] Bristol & West Plc v. R&C Commissioners [2016] STC 1491 480
[7] Greene King Plc v. R&C Commissioners [2016] EWCA Civ 782 480
[8] Union Castle Main Steamship Company Ltd v. R&C Commissioners [2016] UKFTT 0256 (TC) 480
§10.02 Anti-avoidance Legislation in Germany Applying to Derivatives 480
[A] Specific Anti-avoidance Legislation Applying to Derivatives 481
[1] The Derivatives Loss Ring-Fencing Rule 481
[2] Ring-Fencing of Losses from Tax Deferral Models 481

[3] Re-qualification of Income on the Basis of Section 20(1) No. 7 ITA 482
[4] Treaty Switch-Over Clauses 482
[5] Anti-treaty Shopping Rule of Section 50d(3) ITA 483
[B] Anti-Hybrid Mismatch Rules: EU ATAD Implementation 483
[C] The General Anti-avoidance Rule Applying to Derivatives 485
[D] Pillar Two 486
§10.03 Comparison of the Effectiveness of Anti-avoidance Legislation in the UK and Germany 487
§10.04 Tax Avoidance and Cryptoassets 487
[A] The UK 487
[1] Cryptocurrencies and Impairment Losses 487
[a] Cost Model 488
[b] Taxation Follows the Financial Accounts 488
[2] Tax Avoidance and Crypto Derivatives 490
[B] Germany 490
[1] Tax Avoidance and Cryptoassets 490
[2] Tax Avoidance and Crypto Derivatives 490
[3] EU Reporting Requirements for Cryptoassets 490
§10.05 Solutions to Problem 7: Tackling Tax Avoidance Effectively 491
[A] Improvement of the General Design of the Tax System 492
[1] Specific Taxation Rules Versus the Application of General Taxation Rules 493
[2] Accounting and Taxation Alignment as a Way to Counter Tax Avoidance? 493
[3] Hedging Approaches and Tax Avoidance 494
[4] Hybrid Instruments and Tax Avoidance 495
[5] Structured Products and Tax Avoidance 495
[6] Hybrid Instruments and Qualification Conflicts in Cross-Border Transactions 496
[B] Improving the Design of Anti-avoidance Legislation and Similar Measures 497
[1] Introduction of Specific or General Anti-avoidance Rules 497
[2] Implementation of Disclosure Rules 498
[3] The Principles-Based, the Purposive and the Formal Approach in the Application of Tax Rules 500
[a] The Formal Approach 500
[b] The Principles-Based Approach 501
[c] The Purposive Approach 502
[d] The Coherent Principles Approach 502
[e] Evaluation of the Approaches as Possible Solutions to Counter Tax Avoidance Schemes 503
[i] Evaluation of the Purposive Approach 503

[ii] Evaluation of the Principles-Based Approach 504
[iii] Evaluation of the Coherent Principles Approach 505
[iv] Evaluation of the Formal Approach 506
[v] Proposed Solution 506
[4] Implementing Broader Rules That Tackle the Overall Tax Behaviour of Certain Taxpayers 506

CHAPTER 11
Conclusion 509
§11.01 Final Thoughts 509
§11.02 Problems Identified in the Taxation of Derivatives and Cryptoassets 510
§11.03 Summary of Solutions Adopted by the UK and Germany and Solutions Proposed by the Author Regarding the Taxation Problems Posed by Derivatives and Cryptoassets 510
[A] Problem 1 and Its Solution 511
[1] Definitions of Derivatives in the UK and German Tax Legislation 511
[2] Solution to Problem 1: Abstract Definition of Derivatives in the Domestic Tax Legislation 512
[B] Problem 2 and Its Solution 512
[1] Solution to Problem 2: Introduction of a Different Set of Taxation Rules Instead of Complete Alignment of Accounting and Taxation Rules 512
[C] Problem 3 and Its Solution 514
[1] The Influence of the Distinction Between Income and Capital, and Between Equity and Debt on the UK and German Taxation of Derivatives 514
[2] Solution to Problem 3: A Special Taxation Regime Applying to Derivatives and Cryptoassets 515
[D] Problem 4 and Its Solutions 516
[1] Solutions in the UK and Germany: Tax-Efficient Hedging and Post-tax Hedging Approaches 516
[2] Solutions to Problem 4: Tax-Efficient Hedging Provisions and the Implementation of Anti-avoidance Legislation 517
[E] Problem 5 and Its Solution 518
[1] The UK and German Solutions for Taxing Structured Products and Hybrid Instruments 518
[2] Solution to Problem 5: Striking the Balance Between Integration and Bifurcation for Tax Purposes 518
[F] Problem 6 and Its Solutions 519

[1] Solutions Adopted by the UK and Germany to Deal with Cross-Border Derivatives Transactions 519
[a] Withholding Tax Regimes Applying to Derivatives 519
[b] The Beneficial Ownership Concept in Cross-Border Transactions 520
[2] Solutions to Problem 6: Adjustment of Withholding Tax Provisions, Amendment of the 'Beneficial Owner' Definition or Introduction of a New Definition of Derivatives at Tax Treaty Level 520
[G] Problem 7 and Its Solutions 521
[1] The UK and German Solutions in Tackling Tax Avoidance 521
[2] Solutions to Problem 7: Improving the General Design of the Tax System and Introducing Effective Anti-avoidance Legislation 522
§11.04 Outlook 523

Bibliography 525

Table of Cases and Decisions 567

Table of Double Taxation Conventions, OECD and UN Model Conventions and Other OECD and UN Materials 573

Table of Financial Accounting Standards and Other Materials 579

Table of ISDA and BCBS Documents 587

Table of National Legislation and EU Materials 591

Table of Statutory Instruments, Legislative Material and Other Official Documents 597

Index 605

Foreword

This work climbs methodically through the foothills and slopes until it reaches the summit of its subject. It is thereby able to take a broad synoptic view, which lifts the reader to the same height.

This book first saw the light of day in the form of the author's doctoral thesis. A doctoral thesis needs to satisfy three requirements: it must (i) display excellence in scholarship, (ii) be an original contribution to knowledge, and (iii) be of publishable quality. It was plain to the examiners (of which I was one) that her work fulfilled these three requirements. However, it was so much more. The author displays a conceptual grasp of the subject, which transcends and organises the mass of detail, and writes with a verve which vivifies the otherwise dry and technical nature of the subject.

She is able and qualified to achieve this because her professional and academic experience in the subject matter seeks its equal. She is an English and German lawyer. She has worked in this field for leading banks. She has worked in leading law firms, nationally and internationally. She is loaded to the Plimsoll line and beyond with academic qualifications and distinctions.

This is a work which honours the writer, the reader, the world of commercial finance with which it deals and the legal and accounting systems in which it is set.

David Southern KC
Field Court Tax Chambers
5 Field Court
Gray's Inn

Preface to the Second Edition

If you cannot explain something in simple terms, you don't understand it.

—Richard Feynman, Physicist

Derivatives exist in great variety and complexity, and many of us believe they are incomprehensible, so we do not think further about them. The often-overlooked truth, however, is that no man-made subject is too difficult to understand if we have the will to learn its details and find someone who can explain it to us in clear and concise terms.

The first edition originated from the author's doctoral research, which gives the work its unique structure by identifying seven issues in the taxation of derivatives and developing viable policy solutions to solve them. The second edition has been updated and expanded to encompass accounting developments, legislative changes, recent case law, and the emergence of new financial instruments and asset classes.

While researching for the second edition, the author became increasingly aware of the importance of cryptoassets as a new asset class. Their creation process, valuation methodologies and associated derivatives pose unique challenges not only for tax authorities but also for tax advisers. The author believes that one must think in new, and sometimes very different, ways to tax cryptoassets and the recently emerged crypto derivatives appropriately. Consequently, the title of this second edition had to be amended to reflect the extensive thought process of analysing the taxation of cryptoassets and their derivatives.

A new challenge is already on the horizon: the taxation of ESG[1] derivatives, including derivatives over Verified Carbon Credits (VCCs) and ESG-linked structured products. While the author has analysed their basic economic properties and accounting treatment and developed some initial thoughts on their taxation, the tax questions raised by ESG financial instruments will undoubtedly inspire further publications.

Finally, with this new edition, the author hopes to convey new insight to the reader and, more importantly, offer some enjoyment in reading it.

1. ESG is an acronym that stands for 'environmental, social and governance'.

Acknowledgements

In 2019, the author co-wrote, together with Mr Sung Hwang, the General Report on Investment Funds for the IFA London Congress. The second edition not only profits from the experience of this joint research endeavour but also from a pupillage at Field Court Tax Chambers. The author is greatly indebted to Philip Baker, KC, OBE, for the encouragement to write the book's second edition and for guiding her professionally. In the same way, David Southern, KC, convinced the author to share her knowledge about derivatives in the form of a second edition, and the author is indebted to him for the productive discussions about the accounting and tax treatment of derivatives and cryptoassets.

The author also wishes to thank several past classes of LLM students whom she taught at the Centre of Commercial Law Studies at Queen Mary University of London. Their intellectual engagement and curiosity to understand the topic of derivatives inspired the author to enhance the second edition's clarity and readability, particularly when analysing the economic and financial properties of derivatives and cryptoassets.

The author would like to thank the two editors of the Series on International Taxation, Professor Ruth Mason and Professor Dr Ekkehart Reimer, for their valuable suggestions. The author wishes to thank the professional teams of Kluwer Law International and NewGen, and also Laura Findley, LLM student at King's College London for their valuable support in turning the manuscript into a printed book. Last but not least, the author thanks her friend Gerry for reading through the manuscript and providing valuable points of critique.

Introduction

Derivatives in and of themselves are not evil. There's nothing evil about how they are traded, how they're accounted for, and how they're financed, like any other financial instrument, if done properly.

— James Chanos, *Q&A with James Chanos, Part I: Greece Is A Prelude*

This work analyses corporate taxation issues arising in domestic and cross-border transactions involving derivatives or cryptoassets. It identifies and examines seven major problems that derivatives or cryptoassets may create from a taxation perspective; each is dealt with in a separate chapter.

The book contains eleven chapters. Chapter 1 introduces the topic of derivatives and cryptoassets and explains the methodology used in this work. Chapter 2 explains the economic properties of derivatives and their underlyings. In this context, the author has introduced a discussion of cryptoassets as they not only constitute a new asset class but are also eligible underlyings for the recently emerged crypto derivatives. Further, the recently emerged ESG investment category is discussed, including ESG derivatives and ESG-linked structured products. In Chapter 3, the author identifies the various taxation issues that derivatives and cryptoassets may create domestically and cross-border.

Chapters 4 to 10 are specific 'problem chapters' where the seven issues identified in Chapter 3 are addressed. After evaluating the advantages and disadvantages of the tax policy solutions implemented by the UK and Germany, the author suggests, at the end of each chapter, policy solutions that domestic tax legislators, as well as international bodies like the OECD and the UN, may implement to solve these problems coherently and comprehensively. The last chapter summarises the author's evaluation of the UK and German legislative approaches to the various taxation problems discussed in the previous chapters and the policy solutions advanced by the author to achieve coherent taxation rules for derivatives and cryptoassets in the corporate tax environment.

As this work aims to contribute to a wider policy discussion, both at domestic and international level, it analyses the taxation problems posed by derivatives and cryptoassets in detail by comparing UK tax legislation with German and sometimes Swiss legislation and cases. The use of real-life examples permits an analysis of the issues and some available solutions for legislators to consider when drafting and implementing legislation concerning the taxation of derivatives and cryptoassets.

Based on its general principles, the book provides a tool kit for domestic policymakers and those working for international organisations on how to effectively solve those issues when designing a comprehensive taxation system for derivatives and cryptoassets. In the same way, this publication is relevant to UK, German and Swiss practitioners and academics alike due to an in-depth analysis of the legislation applying to derivatives and cryptoassets.

This work focuses only on major problems in the taxation of derivatives and cryptoassets entered into by companies. The taxation issues in a private or non-corporate context (e.g., individuals, partnerships, charities, pension funds, etc.) cannot be comprehensively discussed in this publication without compromising the depth of the analysis.

For the same reason, specific topics, such as the taxation of derivatives and cryptoassets held by all forms of investment funds or other vehicles, go beyond the scope of this work. For readers interested in the taxation of investment funds, their managers and fund investors, the 2019 *IFA General Report on Investment Funds* will provide a valuable source of information.[1]

Derivatives do not pose entirely new problems in the context of transfer pricing and the attribution of profits to a permanent establishment.[2] Rather, particular difficulties may arise for tax administrations at a practical level as they have to determine how to allocate profits from the global trading books of banks, both from proprietary trading and customer transactions.[3] As a discussion of these practical problems falls outside the scope of this book, these topics have not been considered.[4] Further, an analysis of thin capitalisation rules, which apply to groups of companies,[5] and a discussion of controlled foreign companies (CFC) legislation will not be part of this book.

---

1. Sung Hwang and Oktavia Weidmann, *General Report: Investment Funds*, International Fiscal Association, 2019 London Congress in: Cahiers de Droit fiscal international, volume 104.
2. Victor Thuronyi, 'Taxation of New Financial Instruments' (2001) 24 Tax Notes International 261, 265.
3. John Neighbour, 'The Taxation of Global Trading of Financial Instruments' (1998) 16 Tax Notes International 1269; Thuronyi (2001a) 265.
4. The OECD has dealt comprehensively with the attribution of profits and losses of derivatives in the context of global trading activities of financial institutions in two reports: OECD, *Report on the Attribution of Profits to Permanent Establishments* (OECD Centre for Tax Policy and Administration, 2008) and its revised version: OECD, *2010 Report on the Attribution of Profits to Permanent Establishments* (2010).

   The findings of the 2010 OECD Report resulted in a new version of Art. 7 OECD Model and a revised Commentary. *See* OECD Model Tax Convention on Income and on Capital, Condensed version (2010), Commentary on Art. 7, paras 8 and 9.

   An update of the Commentary to Art. 7 OECD Model followed in 2017, *see* OECD Model Tax Convention on Income and on Capital, Condensed version (2017), https://read.oecd-ilibrary.org/taxation/model-tax-convention-on-income-and-on-capital-condensed-version-2017/commentary-on-article-7_mtc_cond-2017-10-en#page1 (accessed 3 August 2023).
5. For a summary of the debt cap provisions in the context of the BEPS Action Plan, *see* OECD/G20, *Base Erosion and Profit Shifting Project, Limiting Base Erosion Involving Interest Deductions and Other Financial Payments, Action 4, 2016 Update inclusive Framework on BEPS.*

In light of the continuing discussions on tax avoidance schemes and the introduction of more comprehensive anti-avoidance rules globally, some anti-avoidance aspects, such as specific anti-avoidance rules applying to derivatives, regime anti-avoidance rules, and the application of General Anti-Abuse Rules (GAARs) in the context of derivatives, have been evaluated in Chapter 10. Likewise, EU initiatives like the EU Anti-tax Avoidance Directives (ATAD I and II) and the OECD's Pillar Two Model Rules[6] have been touched upon briefly.

A thorough analysis of the OECD/G20's Inclusive Framework on Base Erosion and Profit Shifting (BEPS) would go beyond the framework of this book. The BEPS Project engages in broader policy and anti-avoidance discussions rather than dealing specifically with the tax treatment of derivatives. Even a discussion of the enacted legislative changes in the UK and German legislation as a result of the BEPS Project exceeds the scope of this work as those matters rather concern the general tax system.[7] Some rules, like the UK and German rules applying to hybrid mismatches and hybrid capital instruments, have been briefly touched upon in Chapters 6, 8 and 10 insofar as they are relevant to the taxation of derivatives.

Further, a detailed discussion of tax reporting and the automatic exchange of information has not been discussed in this work, although the new tax transparency rules for service providers facilitating cryptoasset transactions (DAC8) have been briefly mentioned. In the absence of specific anti-avoidance provisions applying to cryptoassets, the author discusses the challenges that cryptoassets may pose in terms of tax avoidance and asks if it is desirable to introduce targeted anti-avoidance legislation applying to cryptoasset transactions.

Finally, it should be noted that each chapter of this book can also be read independently.

---

6. Those rules are also referred to as 'Global Anti-Base Erosion' or 'GloBE' rules.
7. Works by the OECD/G20 include, among others: OECD/G20 Base Erosion and Profit Shifting Project (2021) Tax Challenges Arising from the Digitalisation of the Economy – Global Anti-Base Erosion Model Rules (Pillar Two): Inclusive Framework on BEPS.

   Excellent books and articles have been written on all aspects of the BEPS Project and the BEPS 2.0 reform package with its two-pillar approach, so the author does not need to repeat those findings here. Among others, the books recommended to further engage in the topic of the BEPS project are: Richard S. Collier and Joseph L. Andrus, *Transfer Pricing and the Arm's Length Principle after BEPS* (OUP 2019); Félix Daniel Martínez Laguna, *Hybrid Financial Instruments, Double Non-taxation and Linking Rules* (Series on International Taxation, Wolters Kluwer 2019); Michael Lang, Alfred Storck and Raffaele Petruzzi, *Transfer Pricing in a Post-BEPS World* (EUCOTAX Series on European Taxation, Wolters Kluwer, 2016) Volume 50; Leopoldo Parada, *Double Non-Taxation and the Use of Hybrid Entities: An Alternative Approach in the New Era of BEPS* (Series on International Taxation, Wolters Kluwer, 2018); John Abrahamson, *International Taxation of Banking* (Series on International Taxation Wolters Kluwer, 2020); Kerrie Sadiq, Adrian Sawyer and Bronwyn McCredie, *Tax Design and Administration in a Post-BEPS Era: A Study of Key Reform Measures in 18 Jurisdictions* (Fiscal Publications 2019); Joanna Wheeler, *The Aftermath of BEPS* (IBFD 2020).

   The following article provides a good summary of BEPS 2.0 and Pillar One and Two: Christos Theophilou, 'Deconstructing Pillar Two—Impact on Multinational Enterprises' Bloomberg Tax 2022, https://news.bloombergtax.com/daily-tax-report-international/deconstructing-pillar-two-impact-on-multinational-enterprises, accessed 30 July 2023.

Reference Sources and Effective Date

Sources used in this work are mainly the UK and German tax legislation and statements of both countries' tax authorities, such as HMRC manuals and statements of practice, and letter rulings by the German Revenue. Likewise, the opinions of leading tax practitioners and academics in this field brought forward in textbooks, manuals, loose-leaf commentaries and articles have been considered, discussed, analysed and sometimes criticised.

This work also considers decided cases in this field insofar as they are necessary to illustrate specific problems that arise in the context of derivatives and cryptoassets taxation. Lastly, the author's professional experience found a place in the more technical aspects of derivatives economics and taxation.

The cut-off date for new legislation is 1 August 2023, although some new proposals and recent developments concerning cryptoassets, ESG investments and Pillar Two have been discussed in this work beyond this date.

List of Abbreviations

ABS	Asset-Backed Security
AC	Appeal Cases
ADIT	Advanced Diploma in International Taxation
AI	artificial intelligence
All En	All England Law Reports
ALM	Asset Liability Management
art/arts (Art/Arts)	article/articles (Article/Articles)
ASB	Accounting Standards Board (UK)
AUKCA	Approved United Kingdom Collecting Agent
AUKI	Authorised United Kingdom Intermediary
BB	*Betriebs-Berater*
BEPS	Base Erosion and Profit Shifting
BFH	*Bundesfinanzhof* (Federal Fiscal Court)
BFHE	*Bundesfinanzhof-Entscheidungen* (Federal Fiscal Court decisions)
BGB	*Bürgerliches Gesetzbuch* (General Civil Law Act)
BilMoG	*Gesetz zur Modernisierung des Bilanzrechts* (Accounting Law Modernisation Act)
BIM	Business Income Manual
bp/bps	basis point/basis points
BR	*Bundesrat*
BStBl	*Bundessteuerblatt* (Federal Tax Gazette)
BT	*Bundestag*

BTR	British Tax Review
C	call option
CA	Court of Appeal
CA	Companies Act
CBDC	Central Bank Digital Currency
CBT	Centre for Business Taxation (Oxford University)
CCCTB	Common Consolidated Corporate Tax Base
CCP	Central Counterparty
CDO	credit default option
CDS	credit default swap
CDU	*Christlich Demokratische Union*
CFC	Controlled Foreign Company
CFD	contract for differences
CFM	Corporate Finance Manual
CG	Capital Gains Manual
Ch./Chs	chapter/chapters
CIOT	Chartered Institute of Taxation
CJEU	Court of Justice of the European Union
cl/cls	clause/clauses
CLA	Commercial Law Act (*Handelsgesetzbuch – HGB*)
CLN	credit linked note
CLO	collateralised loan obligation
Co	company
col/cols	column/columns
CRS	Common Reporting Standard
CSA	Credit Support Annex
CSD	Credit Support Deed
CSO	credit spread option
CSU	*Christlich Soziale Union*
CTA	Corporation Tax Act
CTM	Company Taxation Manual
DAX	*Deutscher Aktienindex*
DB	*Der Betrieb* (tax journal)
DCO	Derivatives Clearing Organisation
Dir	Directive

Div	dividends
Drs	*Drucksache*
DStR	*Deutsches Steuerrecht* (tax journal)
DTC	double taxation convention
EBITDA	Earnings Before Interest, Taxes, Depreciation and Amortisation
ECJ	European Court of Justice
ECR	European Court Reports
ED	exposure draft
ed./eds	editor/editors
edn	edition/editions
EFRAG	European Financial Reporting Advisory Group
ESG	environmental, social and governance
EStG	*Einkommensteuergesetz* (Income Tax Act)
ETH	Ethereum
EURIBOR	European Inter-bank Offered Rate
EWCA	England and Wales Court of Appeal (UK)
FA	Finance Act
FB	Finance Bill
ff	and following
FG	*Finanzgericht* (Fiscal Court)
fn/fns	footnote/footnotes
FATCA	Foreign Account Tax Compliance Act
FASB	Financial Accounting Standards Board (US)
FRC	Financial Reporting Council
FRS	Financial Reporting Standard
FRSSE	Financial Reporting Standard for Smaller Entities
FSMA	Financial Services and Markets Act
FVTOCI	fair value through other comprehensive income
FVTPL	fair value through profit or loss
GAAP	generally accepted accounting principles
GAAR	general anti-abuse rule
GloBE	Global Anti-Base Erosion
GTA	General Tax Act (*Abgabenordnung - AO*)
H/H/R	*Herrmann/Heuer/Raupach* (legal commentary)
HGB	*Handelsgesetzbuch* (Commercial Law Act)

hist perf	historical performance
HL	House of Lords
HM	Her Majesty's Treasury
HMRC	Her Majesty's Revenue and Customs
HNW	High-Net-Worth
IAS	International Accounting Standards
IASB	International Accounting Standards Board
ICAEW	Institute of Chartered Accountants in England and Wales
ICTA	Income and Corporation Taxes Act
IDW	*Institut der Wirtschaftsprüfer* (Institute of Public Auditors)
IF	Inclusive Framework
IFA	International Fiscal Association
IFRIC	International Financial Reporting Interpretations Committee
IFRS	International Financial Reporting Standards
IFSC	International Financial Services Centre
IIR	Income Inclusion Rule
IHTM	Inheritance Tax Manual
INTM	International Manual
IRC	Internal Revenue Code (US)
ISDA	International Swaps and Derivatives Association
ISIN	International Securities Identification Numbers Organisation
IStR	*Internationales Steuerrecht* (journal on international taxation)
ITA	Income Tax Act
ITEPA	Income Tax (Earnings and Pensions) Act
ITLR	International Tax Law Reports
ITR	International Tax Review
ITTOIA	Income Tax (Trading and Other Income) Act
K	strike price
KB	King's Bench division
KStG	*Körperschaftsteuergesetz* (Corporation Tax Act)
LIBOR	London Inter-bank Offered Rate
Ltd	Limited
MREL	minimum requirement on own funds and eligible liabilities
MOD	Manufactured Overseas Dividend
MTM	mark-to-market
NFI	new financial instruments

no/nos (No./Nos)	number/numbers
NZ	New Zealand
NZCA	Court of Appeal of New Zealand
OECD	Organisation for Economic Cooperation and Development
OECD Model	OECD Model Tax Convention on Income and on Capital
OECD-MA	*OECD-Musterabkommen* (OECD Model)
OEIC	Open-Ended Investment Company
OJLS	Oxford Journal of Legal Studies
OTC	over-the-counter
OTM	out of the money
OUP	Oxford University Press
P	put option
P&L account	Profit and Loss account
P&L	profit and loss
para./paras	paragraph/paragraphs
PE	permanent establishment
PPA	power purchase agreement
PPL	profit participating loan
pt/pts	part/parts
PV	present value
QCB	qualifying corporate bond
r/rr	rule/rules
RBS	Royal Bank of Scotland
reg/regs	regulation/regulations
RECs	renewable energy certificates
REIT	Real Estate Investment Trust
RFH	*Reichsfinanzhof*
RFS	renewable fuel standard
RIN	Renewable Identification Number
RStBl	*Reichssteuerblatt*
S	underlying asset
s/ss	section/sections (Section/Sections)
sch/schs (Sch/Schs)	schedule/schedules (Schedule/Schedules)
sent	sentence
SI	statutory instrument

SME	Small and Medium-sized Entities
SMU Law Review	Southern Methodist University Law Review
SOCIE	statement of changes in equity
SOFR	Secured Overnight Financing Rate
SONIA	Sterling Overnight Index Average
SP	Statement of Practice
SpC	Special Commissioners
SPD	*Sozialdemokratische Partei Deutschlands*
SPV	special purpose vehicle
STA	Securities Trading Act (*Wertpapierhandelsgesetz - WpHG*)
STC	Simon's Tax Cases
STRGL	Statement of Total Recognised Gains and Losses
Sub	subsidiary
TAAR	targeted anti-avoidance rules
TC	Tax Cases
TCGA	Taxation of Chargeable Gains Act
TFEU	Treaty on the Functioning of the European Union
TIOPA	Taxation (International and Other Provisions) Act
TNI	Tax Notes International
TOFA	The Taxation of Financial Arrangements
tr/trs	translator/translators
TRS	total return swap
UCITS	Undertakings for Collective Investments in Transferable Securities
UITF	unit investment trust fund
UK	United Kingdom
UKHL	House of Lords (UK)
UKSC	Supreme Court (UK)
UN Model	United Nations Model Double Tax Convention Between Developed and Developing Countries
UNPAN	United Nations Public Administration Network
UNSW Law Journal	University of New South Wales Law Journal
US	United States
USDT	USD Tether
UTPR	Undertaxed Profits Rule (Undertaxed Payments Rule)

VaR	Value at Risk
VAT	Value-Added Tax (VAT)
vol/vols	volume/volumes
WM	*Wertpapiermitteilungen* (legal journal)
WP-Handbuch	*Wirtschaftsprüfer-Handbuch* (handbook for certified auditors)
yr/yrs	year/years
Γ	gamma
Δ	delta
Θ	theta
ρ	rho
V	vega

Chapter 1
Taxing Derivatives and Cryptoassets – An Introduction*

In order to know an object, I must know not its external but all its internal qualities.

— Ludwig Wittgenstein, *Tractatus Logico-Philosphicus*

Nowadays, derivatives and structured financial products exist in such a variety and complexity that even experts working in financial institutions may not have an in-depth knowledge of the whole universe of those instruments.[1] New forms of derivatives and combinations of pre-existing forms have been frequently invented based on newly emerged risk categories and the need of banking clients to invest in or hedge these risks.[2] Hence, tax legislators need to find credible answers for taxing those instruments.

In recent years, the emergence of cryptoassets and associated derivatives and structured products has further contributed to the heterogeneity of the derivatives markets. Cryptoassets have enabled the rise of new market players and the establishment of decentralised trading platforms that challenge traditional payment systems because the blockchain framework enables instant, cheap, reliable and anonymous transfer of items of value.

In an almost parallel development, the growing importance of carbon credit transactions and the increased investor interest in ESG products have spurred the innovation of various ESG derivatives and ESG-linked structured products.

---

* Translations of the legislation and statutes from foreign languages into English used in the course of this work are unofficial translations, unless stated otherwise.

References to the OECD Model or UN Model refer to the latest version of the Model, unless stated otherwise.

1. Derivatives experts, such as quantitative analysts, financial engineers and derivatives traders will typically be focused on analysing, structuring, or trading derivatives on a single underlying asset class.
2. John Hull, *Options, Futures and Other Derivatives* (9th edn, Pearson 2018) 1.

The following chapter outlines the basic methodology of this work, explains the challenges that derivatives and cryptoassets pose in terms of their taxation due to constant financial product innovation, and provides a detailed chapter-by-chapter outline of this book.

§1.01 THE METHODOLOGY

In the course of this work, the above epigraph quoting *Wittgenstein's Tractatus*[3] serves as a guiding principle which reminds us that the best outcomes can be achieved when we understand the true nature of things. Applying this logic to derivatives and cryptoassets means that when we classify instruments for tax purposes, we need to consider not only their external form but also their economic substance. In the context of the taxation of derivatives and cryptoassets, we should, therefore, acknowledge their specific role in the transaction, their mode of operation and their payoff profile.[4]

The author, therefore, proposes to apply this general principle of logic when taxing complex derivatives, hybrid instruments, structured products and cryptoassets, as their internal structure is often neither easy to determine nor visible at first sight.

In a more general sense, this observation by *Wittgenstein* may also be seen as a guiding principle for carefully formulating the wording of tax legislation.

§1.02 THE TAXATION OF DERIVATIVES AND CRYPTOASSETS

Although derivatives have existed for more than 2,000 years,[5] their exploding use in the past decades has created challenges for tax authorities to deal with these instruments comprehensively.[6]

The borders between capital gains and ordinary income, realised and unrealised gains, dividends and interest have become obliterated because derivatives can be used to economically convert one category of income into another category[7] due to the means of static or dynamic replication.[8] Additionally, a derivative itself might be

---

3. Ludwig Wittgenstein, *Tractatus Logico-Philosphicus* (CK Ogden tr, Kegan Paul, Trench, Trubner & Co Ltd 1922) para. 2.01231.
4. In the author's view, economic substance should not be seen statically, but the context must be considered in which a financial instrument is used and which role it plays in the scope of a larger transaction.
5. Charles Kindleberger, *Manias, Panics and Crashes, A History of Financial Crises* (5th edn, Wiley 2005) 23-24; Alfred Steinherr, *Derivatives, The Wild Beast of Finance* (Wiley 1998) 3. Others trace back the use of derivatives to Babylonian times and the old Greeks, *see* Robert Whaley, *Derivatives: Markets, Valuation, and Risk Management* (Wiley 2006) 11, with two examples from the *Code of Hammurabi* (approx. 1750 BCE) and Aristotle's *Politics* (350 BCE).
6. John Neighbour, *Taxing Financial Innovation in a Global Economy* (in: Report of the Ad Hoc Group of Experts on International Co-operation in Tax Matters; UNPAN Conference Documents, 2001) 1; Victor Thuronyi, 'Taxation of New Financial Instruments' (2001) 24 Tax Notes International 261.
7. Thuronyi (2001a) 261.
8. For a definition of the terms, *see* Ch. 2 §2.02[A][1] and [B].

attributed to various categories of income depending on whether its external form or its economic content is decisive for classification purposes in the respective tax system.[9]

Tax experts of the OECD, the UN, tax practitioners and academic scholars have been debating for some time to what extent existing tax systems should be reformed in order to ensure that they can cope effectively with the rapid pace of product innovation in the field of derivatives.[10]

While some tax systems have introduced reforms to integrate the taxation of derivatives within existing tax rules,[11] others decided to implement a separate set of rules in order to cope with the constantly evolving variety of instruments.[12]

A closer look at the taxation rules applying to derivatives in various countries, however, suggests that, so far, none of the countries has fully addressed the issues posed by derivatives and structured products, nor has the OECD or UN Model been revised to deal with these financial instruments adequately.[13] Further, the OECD/G20 Base Erosion and Profit Shifting (BEPS) Project has not dealt with derivatives in a comprehensive manner. Four action points, however, have some relevance in the context of derivatives, namely tax treaty abuse (Action 6), hybrid mismatch

---

9. OECD, Innovative Financial Transactions: Tax Policy Implications (A Report by the Special Sessions on Innovative Financial Transactions of the OECD) (Ad Hoc Group of Experts on International Cooperation in Tax Matters, UNPAN conference documents, 2001) paras 51 and 96.
10. The following books and articles are a small selection that discuss the need for reforming tax legislation to cater for the issues posed by derivatives in national and international tax law: Conlon & Aquilino: Principles of Financial Derivatives: U.S. & International Taxation (WG&L), Looseleaf, latest issue: March 2022; Tim Edgar, *The Income Tax Treatment of Financial Instruments: Theory and Practice* (Canadian Tax Foundation 2000); Ghosh, Johnson and Miller (2022), Looseleaf (Tolley, LexisNexis 2009 with updates through issue 28, December 2022); Edward Kleinbard, 'Designing an Income Tax on Capital' (Conference on Taxing Capital Income, Brookings Institution, Washington, 23 September 2005); Antti Laukkanen, *Taxation of Investment Derivatives* (Doctoral Series, vol. 13, IBFD 2007); Neighbour (2001); Günter Reiner, *Derivative Finanzinstrumente im Recht* (Deutsches, Europäisches und Vergleichendes Wirtschaftsrecht, Band 24, Nomos, 2002), https://www.nomos-elibrary.de/10.5771/9783845287164/derivative-finanzinstrumente-im-recht, accessed 14 July 2023 (DOI: 10.5771/9783845287164); David Schizer, 'Balance in the Taxation of Derivative Securities: An Agenda for Reform' (2004) Columbia Law and Economics Working Paper No. 247; David Southern, *Taxation of Loan Relationships and Derivative Contracts* (10th edition, Bloomsbury 2017); Jeff Strnad, 'Taxing New Financial Products: A Conceptual Framework' (1994) 46 Stanford Law Review 569 DOI: 10.2307/1229102; Thuronyi (2001a); Alvin Warren, 'Financial Contract Innovation and Income Tax Policy' (1993) 107 Harvard Law Review 460 DOI: 10.2307/1341780.

    Reports of the OECD include: OECD, Taxation of New Financial Instruments (OECD Publishing, 1994); OECD, The Taxation of Global Trading of Financial Instruments (1998); OECD (2001) at fn. 15; OECD, Report on the Attribution of Profits to Permanent Establishments (OECD Centre for Tax Policy and Administration, 2008); OECD, 2010 Report on the Attribution of Profits to Permanent Establishments; OECD, Aggressive Tax Planning based on After-Tax Hedging (2013); OECD, Limiting Base Erosion Involving Interest Deductions and Other Financial Payments, Action 4 – 2016 Update.
11. The German legislator decided on an approach that applies the traditional taxation rules also to derivatives entered into by companies; *see* Ch. 6 §6.03.
12. The UK legislator opted for a separate and extensive set of rules in CTA 2009, Part 7 to deal with the taxation of derivatives held by companies; *see* Ch. 6 §6.01.
13. Thuronyi (2001a) 261.

arrangements (Action 2), interest deductions and other financial payments (Action 4) and risk transfers (Action 9).[14]

Although legislative approaches may be different, tax administrations need to ensure that they develop rules which allow capital markets to function efficiently and also promote financial innovation by eliminating artificial tax barriers.[15]

At the same time, tax administrations should protect their countries' tax base from tax avoidance schemes utilising derivatives.[16] Among other approaches, many countries have chosen to incorporate targeted anti-avoidance rules and disclosure rules into their legislation to counter tax arbitrage opportunities arising in the context of derivatives transactions.[17]

Cryptoassets as a new underlying asset class and financial product innovation in the context of associated derivatives and structured products have created further challenges that domestic legislators have to face in terms of taxation and tax reporting.[18]

Similarly, ESG investments, including ESG derivatives and ESG-linked structured products, require tax legislators to find appropriate solutions for their taxation and reporting.

§1.03 THE SCOPE: CHAPTER BY CHAPTER

Various taxation issues posed by derivatives and cryptoassets used in domestic and cross-border transactions will be discussed in this work. Approaches that tax legislators may adopt to solve these problems are explained, analysed, criticised, and compared by using the example of the two most important domestic tax systems in relation to derivatives in Europe: the UK[19] and Germany.[20]

---

14. For a comprehensive summary on the relevance of the BEPS Project for derivatives, *see* Richard Collier, DFI 2014, 247-252 and David Southern, Taxation of Loan Relationships and Derivative Contracts, Supplement to the 10th Edition (Bloomsbury Professional 2020), Chs 1 to 6.
15. Neighbour (2001) 2.
16. John Neighbour, 'Innovative Financial Instruments Challenge the Global Tax System' (1997) Tax Notes International 931, 933; Thuronyi (2001a) 265.
17. In the United States, Australia and the UK extensive avoidance, anti-arbitrage and disclosure rules have been introduced to also tackle tax arbitrage opportunities arising from the use of derivatives.
18. The new Council Directive amending Directive 2011/16/EU on administrative cooperation in the field of taxation (DAC8), https://data.consilium.europa.eu/doc/document/ST-10215-2023-INIT/en/pdf, accessed 20 October 2023, requires the reporting of cryptoasset holdings and transactions by cryptoasset service providers and an automatic exchange of information between tax authorities on revenues from transactions in cryptoassets and on advance tax rulings for the high-net-worth (HNW) individuals. DAC8 is based on the OECD's Crypto-Asset Reporting Framework (CARF) which is scheduled to come into force in 2026. *See* OECD, Crypto-Asset Reporting Framework and Amendment to the Common Reporting Standard (2022), https://www.oecd.org/tax/exchange-of-tax-information/crypto-asset-reporting-framework-and-amendments-to-the-common-reporting-standard.pdf, accessed 20 October 2023.
19. Within the past thirty years, London has established itself as a globally important market for derivatives. Even after Brexit, one can so far conclude that it did not diminish the importance of the City of London as a hub for derivatives innovation. Although a brain drain was predicted by

This work contains eleven chapters. The chapter-by-chapter scope of this book is as follows:

While Chapter 1 provides a general introduction to the topic and explains the methodology, Chapter 2 outlines the economic definition of derivatives and explains the concepts of replication and hedging. Chapter 2 also deals with the economic analysis of cryptoassets and acknowledges them as a suitable underlying asset for crypto derivatives, which are discussed in Chapter 4. Further, ESG investments are discussed, as not only ESG factors but also carbon credits can provide the basis for the recently emerged ESG derivatives. Beyond this, it should be noted that the various taxation problems which arise in the context of those instruments are discussed in the chapters throughout the book.

Chapter 3 categorises and explains the various problems in the context of taxing derivatives and cryptoassets in order to provide a framework for the later analysis.

In Chapter 4, the author identifies the definition of derivatives for tax purposes as a key factor in dealing efficiently with taxation issues arising in domestic and cross-border derivatives transactions. After analysing and comparing the approaches to defining derivatives in the UK and German tax legislation, the author suggests a new definition of derivatives for tax purposes that is able to solve common problems of classification of derivatives income both at a domestic and a tax treaty level. The definition of derivatives for tax purposes is not only tested in relation to traditional derivatives, such as credit derivatives, but also in the context of crypto derivatives and ESG derivatives.

Chapter 5 analyses the alignment of accounting standards and tax law in the UK and Germany and discusses challenges that arise for taxpayers and tax authorities if fair value accounting is applied in the context of derivatives taxation. Possible solutions on whether to align accounting standards and taxation rules and also introduce a fair value approach for taxation purposes are discussed. In addition, the accounting treatment of cryptoassets, crypto derivatives and ESG derivatives is addressed in this chapter.

In Chapter 6, the author compares the application of the special tax regime for derivatives in the UK to the German approach that applies general taxation rules to

---

many, this has largely not happened due to the lack of alternative centres of derivatives trading in the EU. Neither Paris, Frankfurt or Dublin could establish themselves as the new hubs for derivatives trading so far due unfavourable tax regimes for businesses and employees, and the lack of trading infrastructure that only the City of London seems to provide so reliably. In the light of the new challenges and looming recession, a robust and reliable regime for the taxation of derivatives is still key to foster the economic growth in the UK.

20. Approximately 30,000 German companies are dealing in over-the-counter (OTC) derivatives in Germany. *See* Nicola Benatti and Francesco Napolitano, European Central Bank, Irving Fisher Committee on Central Bank Statistics, Ninth IFC Conference on 'Are post-crisis statistical initiatives completed?' Basel, 30-31 August 2018, *An insight into the derivatives trading of firms in the euro area*, https://www.bis.org/ifc/publ/ifcb49_20.pdf, accessed 3 August 2023. In particular, foreign exchange forward transactions and OTC interest rate derivatives have seen a strong growth recently, Deutsche Bundesbank, Press Release, *Foreign exchange trading and derivatives transactions in Germany, see significant growth in activity*, 27 October 2022, https://www.bundesbank.de/en/press/press-releases/foreign-exchange-trading-and-derivatives-transactions-in-germany-see-significant-growth-in-activity-899262, accessed 3 July 2023.

derivatives. In addition, the taxation of derivatives gains and losses in the dichotomy of income versus capital and equity versus debt is analysed through the example of the UK and German corporate tax legislation dealing with derivatives. In addition, the application of the current rules of the UK derivative contracts regime to crypto derivatives is discussed.

Chapter 7 analyses how the UK and Germany deal with the question of hedge accounting and its impact on the taxation rules for derivatives. In addition, the problem of pre- and post-tax hedging and its impact on taxation is explained, and possible solutions on how to deal with hedging in the tax legislation are suggested. In subchapter §7.06, hedging relationships with cryptoassets and crypto derivatives are discussed.

In Chapter 8, the author explains the problem of bifurcation and integration with regard to structured products and hybrid instruments. After analysing the UK and German tax legislation on these financial instruments, feasible solutions are suggested. Subchapters §8.09 and §8.10 discuss crypto structured products and cryptoassets with embedded derivatives as well as ESG-linked structured products.

Chapter 9 deals with issues in the context of cross-border derivatives transactions and analyses specifically the problem of withholding taxes and the attribution of income due to the application of the beneficial ownership concept. In this context, the various Swiss beneficial ownership cases in relation to hedged derivatives transactions will be discussed.

In Chapter 10, the author discusses certain aspects of tax avoidance in relation to derivatives and cryptoassets and evaluates the existing UK and German anti-avoidance approaches in their effectiveness to counter tax avoidance schemes that utilise derivatives. Chapter 10 also outlines how the OECD BEPS Project influenced the anti-avoidance legislation concerning derivatives. The UK hybrid mismatch and hybrid capital instrument rules, Pillar Two and the UK case law concerning derivative arrangements, as well as the German anti-treaty shopping rules and the EU ATAD implementation, are discussed.

Chapter 11 summarises the major conclusions and proposed solutions developed in this work.

CHAPTER 2

Basic Economic Concepts of Derivatives and Cryptoassets

> *The derivatives genie is now well out of the bottle, and these instruments will almost certainly multiply in variety and number until some event makes their toxicity clear. Central banks and governments have so far found no effective way to control, or even monitor, the risks posed by these contracts. In my view, derivatives are financial weapons of mass destruction, carrying dangers that, while now latent, are potentially lethal.*
>
> — Warren Buffett, *Excerpt from the 2002 Annual Report, Berkshire Hathaway*

Although derivatives have not vanished since Buffett's statement in 2002, we have experienced the Global Financial Crisis of 2007-2009, partly driven by the wrong evaluation of credit risks by banks but mainly fuelled by a crumbling US housing market. Fifteen years later, investors fear another substantial economic downturn, leading to declining house prices in the UK and elsewhere caused by swiftly rising interest rates and a simultaneous decline in real household disposable income due to high inflation and difficult overall economic circumstances[1] after more than a decade of cheap money during the quantitative easing (QE) policies employed by central banks globally.

Still, there is some optimism not only with the promises of economic prosperity caused by the rise of artificial intelligence (AI) applications in the financial sector and beyond but also with the increasing use of cryptoassets and the attempts by several central banks to introduce Central Bank Digital Currencies (CBDCs).

In this chapter, the author will discuss the basic economic properties of derivatives and cryptoassets, as only an understanding of their economics will allow a proper analysis of their tax treatment.

1. Daniel Harari et al., Rising Cost of Living in the UK, House of Commons Library, 24 November 2023, https://researchbriefings.files.parliament.uk/documents/CBP-9428/CBP-9428.pdf, accessed 6 December 2023.

In relation to derivatives, Chapter 2 explains the basic economic concepts of derivatives, such as their economic definition, replication techniques, the put-call parity, hedging and leverage.

Cryptoassets, as a new asset class, have unique features due to their entirely digital existence. Those will be outlined in Chapter 2, while crypto derivatives, i.e., derivatives with cryptocurrencies as underlyings, will be discussed in Chapter 4.

§2.01 ECONOMIC PROPERTIES OF DERIVATIVES AND CRYPTOASSETS

In the economic literature, a derivative is defined as 'a financial instrument whose value depends on the value of other, more basic, underlying variables'.[2] Derivatives are 'contingent claims' as their payoffs are contingent upon the value of an underlying variable.[3] The settlement of a derivative contract is always at a future date.

One can classify derivatives either based on their forms as options, forwards, futures and swaps,[4] or their underlying variables as equity derivatives, fixed income derivatives, currency derivatives, credit derivatives, commodity derivatives, insurance derivatives and so forth. A classification has to be made in both categories in order to value and price them.[5]

[A] Classification of Derivatives According to Their Type

An *option* is an agreement which gives the holder of the option the *right*, but not the obligation, to buy ('call option') or to sell ('put option') an underlying asset or underlying variable *by* ('American option') or *on* ('European option') a certain specified date in the future for a certain specified price.[6]

A *forward contract* is an agreement to buy ('forward purchase') or to sell ('forward sale') an underlying asset or variable at a certain specified 'delivery price' at a certain specified time in the future.[7] In contrast to options, a *forward* assumes an obligation to buy or sell for both contracting parties.[8]

2. John Hull, *Options, Futures and Other Derivatives* (9th edn, Pearson 2018) 23; *also* Frank Fabozzi et al., *Foundation of Financial Markets and Institutions* (3rd edn, Prentice Hall 2002) 496; Mark Rubinstein, *Rubinstein on Derivatives* (Risk Books 1999) 1-3; Whaley (2006) 3.
3. Rubinstein (1999a) 1.
4. Hull (2018) 23; *also* Tim Edgar, 'The Taxation of Financial Arrangements (TOFA) Proposals: A Modest and Defensible Agenda of Reform' (2000) 23 UNSW Law Journal 288, 290.
5. A valuation of a derivative will require knowing to which category of derivative the instrument belongs and knowledge of the price, volatility and other parameters of the underlying.
6. Hull (2018) 30-31; Fabozzi et al. (2002) 517; John Hull, *Introduction to Futures and Options Markets* (Prentice Hall 1997) 6; Sheldon Natenberg, *Option Volatility and Pricing* (McGraw-Hill 1994) 1; OECD (2001) para. 23; Mark Rubinstein, *Derivatives: A PowerPlus Picture Book*, vol. 1 (In-The-Money 1999) 138ff; Warren (1993) 464; Paul Wilmott, *Derivatives* (Wiley 2000) 22.
7. Hull (2018) 28; *also* Fabozzi et al. (2002) 502; OECD (2001) para. 20; Whaley (2006) 3; Wilmott (2000) 16.
8. Wilmott (2000) 21.

Example 1:

Company A purchases a one-year forward contract over Barclays shares and pays a pre-set delivery price of GBP 100 per share.

Scenario 1: Barclays shares have risen to a value of GBP 110 at maturity of the forward. Company A makes a gain of GBP 10.

Scenario 2: Barclays shares have dropped to a value of GBP 90 at maturity. Company A makes a loss of GBP 10.

A forward contract pays the difference between the price of the underlying asset at maturity and the pre-determined delivery price.[9] Commonly, at the time the contract is entered into, the delivery price is chosen so that the present value of the forward contract to both parties is zero.[10] That means that it costs nothing at inception to either take a 'long' forward purchase position or a 'short' forward sale position.

A forward is a bespoke, over-the-counter[11] (OTC) private agreement between either two financial institutions or financial institutions and their clients.[12]

Nowadays, the parties either clear OTC derivatives via a central counterparty (CCP) in Europe, the derivatives clearing organisation (DCO) in the US, or bilaterally.[13] A central counterparty acts in a similar way compared to an exchange's clearing house and 'stands between the two parties to the derivatives transaction so that one party does not have to bear the risk that the other party will default'.[14] If both parties clear the transaction bilaterally and no collateral is agreed or provided, both counterparties are usually exposed to the credit risk of the other because either party may default on its obligation.[15]

Futures are somewhat similar to forward contracts as they also involve the buying or selling of an underlying asset at a certain time for a certain price. In contrast to forward contracts, futures are traded on an organised exchange, and the contract terms are standardised by that exchange.[16] The counterparty of the futures contract is the exchange itself that matches and intermediates opposite contracts via its adjunct clearing house. Hence, the credit risk of the futures buyer or seller is only against the exchange's clearing house.[17] Gains or losses on futures positions are determined each day by the exchange, the so-called *marking to market*. Gains and losses are credited or

9. Payoff = S (underlying asset price at delivery date) – K (strike price). *See* Rubinstein (1999a) 89.
10. The strike price (K) is set initially, so that the $PV0$ $(S - K) = 0$. *See* Rubinstein (1999a) 89.
11. OTC contracts are contracts that are directly traded between two or more parties, and not traded on an exchange.
12. Hull (2018) 28; *also* Fabozzi et al. (2002) 502.
13. Hull (2018) 25.
14. *Ibid.*
15. Fabozzi et al. (2002) 502.
16. Hull (2018) 30; *see also* OECD (2001) para. 22; Wilmott (2000) 16.
17. Fabozzi et al. (2002) 498; Hull (2006) 29.

debited to a margin account, which has to be set up with a member of the exchange, usually a bank or financial institution.[18]

Swaps are agreements between two parties to exchange a series of cash flows in the future according to a pre-arranged formula, which is calculated by reference to a notional principal amount that is usually not exchanged.[19]

Caps and floors are agreements consisting of a series of options.[20] Under a cap, the short position holder receives a premium for giving up the upside price movement of an underlying asset[21] or payment stream (e.g., interest rate).[22] In contrast, the long position holder receives periodic payments[23] if the underlying index, price of an underlying asset or variable moves above the strike level during specified periods. Common caps and floors are interest rate caps or floors.[24]

Example 2:

Company A wants to protect against rising interest rates above a level of 3%. It purchases a one-year interest rate cap at 3%, under which the interest rate is periodically reset to EURIBOR. The tenor of the reset is quarterly, and payment, if triggered, is made quarterly. Company A pays a premium for the cap to Bank B. The cap provides for a payment to Company A if the then three-month EURIBOR rate goes above 3%, being the difference between the three-month EURIBOR at each reset date and 3% over a period of one year. Hence, if the three-month EURIBOR interest rate is 3.5% at reset date 1 (after three months), 3% at reset date 2 (after six months), 2.5% at reset date 3 (after nine months) and 4% after reset date 4 (after twelve months), Company A will receive 0.5% at date 1, 0% at date 2 and 3 and 1% interest at date 4, thereby effectively protecting the Company against interest rates rising above 3%. No payment is made to Company A by the counterparty of the cap if interest rates fall below 3%.

A cap effectively limits the maximum price of the underlying or the level of the index for the short position holder of the cap. For the long position holder of the cap, it effectively provides insurance against rising interest on a floating rate note or swap interest above a pre-agreed cap level (cap rate).[25]

18. For details of how the marking to market of the futures position and the margin account management works: Hull (2018) 51-54; Whaley (2006), 6.
19. Hull (2018) 174-175; *also* OECD (2001) para. 25.
20. Hull (2018) 713; OECD (2001) para. 27.
21. For example, price movements in an equity position.
22. The position in a short cap equals the position in a short call option position, receiving option premium, but paying out the holder of the long call position, if the price of the underlying moves above the strike price.
23. In case of caps over the price of an underlying equity, the payment can also be a one-off payment at maturity.
24. Hull (2018) 713-718.
25. *Ibid.*, 713; *also* Wilmott (2000) 450 (at the example of interest rates as an underlying).

In contrast, a floor agreement provides downside protection, and payments will be made to the holder of the long floor position[26] if the price of the underlying asset, index or rate falls below a pre-agreed value.

A collar agreement is 'a combination of a long position in a cap and a short position in a floor'.[27] Alternatively, it could be seen as a combination of a short call option and a long put option over an underlying index, asset, or other variable, where a lower and upper strike price is agreed upon.

For example, in case of interest rate collars, A makes periodic payments to B if the interest rate rises above the specified upper level,[28] whereas B makes periodic payments[29] if the interest rate drops below the pre-agreed lower level.[30] The interest rate collar is a combination of an interest rate cap and an interest rate floor.[31]

An equity collar hedges against share price losses below a certain minimum price (put strike), whereas the investor can still participate in the share price appreciation up to the level of the call strike.

Similarly, a put spread can be used as a limited hedge against falling pricing of the underlying assets, for example, shares. A put spread is a combination of a long put option with a high strike price and a short put option with a lower strike price. Investors can simultaneously buy a put option to protect themselves from the downward movements of the underlying asset and sell another put option at a lower strike price to partly finance the option premium paid under the first put option. The initial downside protection of the first put is thus limited to the strike price of the second put option.

By combining and amending these basic forms of derivatives, financial engineers have developed a great variety of derivatives with exotic features. In many cases, these exotic derivatives have been incorporated into structured products to meet the investment objectives and risk features required by financial institutions and corporate investors.[32]

[B] Categorisation of Derivatives According to Their Underlying Variable

Derivative contracts can also be categorised according to their specific *underlying asset* or *underlying variable*.[33] Basic forms of derivatives based on their underlying are equity derivatives, fixed income derivatives, commodity derivatives, currency derivatives and credit derivatives.

26. This position is effectively a portfolio of put options on interest rates.
27. Hull (2018) 714.
28. Which equals the short call position for A.
29. Which equals the short put position for B.
30. Natenberg (1994) 265; OECD (2001) para. 27.
31. Hull (2018) 714.
32. Edgar (2000b) 290 considers the aspect of combining derivatives as critical for tax policy purposes.
33. For the distinction between the term underlying asset and underlying variable, *see* Ch. 4 §4.06[B][1].

Equity derivatives are all derivatives which are derived from the price of an underlying equity asset, a basket of equities, an equity index, or from the value of the payment streams of the equities, i.e., the dividends.

Fixed income derivatives are all derivatives that are derived from either the price of bonds, baskets of bonds or bond indices, or from interest rates.

Currency or FX derivatives are those derivatives which have the price of one or more currencies as the underlying variable.

Commodity derivatives are derived from the price of physical commodities, such as silver, wheat, soya, crude oil, etc.

Credit derivatives are derivatives whose payoffs depend on the probability of a credit event in relation to government, corporate or other bonds or a credit event occurring in relation to a defined creditor.

[C] Cryptoassets as a New Underlying Asset Class

In order to understand crypto derivatives, one has to understand their underlying: cryptoassets. The following subchapter, therefore, deals briefly with the economics of cryptoassets. In recent years, cryptoassets have emerged as a new asset class. In line with this new asset class, various crypto derivatives have been created and traded.

Southern and the author of this work published an article in the British Tax Review, Issue 1, 2023, on the taxation of cryptoassets with a specific focus on the location of cryptoassets for tax purposes and the tax treatment of impairment losses.[34] The author refers to this article for a deeper understanding of those taxation issues.

Cryptoassets can be divided into cryptocurrencies and (crypto) tokens, which can be further subdivided into non-fungible tokens (NFTs), security tokens and utility tokens.[35] All those tokens have different economic properties.[36] *Stablecoins* are a subcategory of cryptoassets which are referenced – or pegged – to a traditional currency.

It has been suggested by *Southern* and the author in the above-mentioned article that cryptocurrencies may melt in the digital wallets of their users like snow in the sun.[37] That happened in 2022. While one Bitcoin had a value of above USD 60,000 at the beginning of November 2021 and April 2022, it had dropped to below USD 17,000 by the end of 2022.[38]

During the Bitcoin downturn, which also concerned all other major cryptocurrencies, the warnings about cryptocurrencies of Luke Ellis, CEO of Man Group, came to mind: 'There is no inherent worth in it whatsoever. It's a tulip bulb.'[39]

34. David Southern and Oktavia Weidmann, 'Cryptotaxation: A Guide to a Brave New World', (2023) British Tax Review, Issue No. 1, 68-96.
35. Southern and Weidmann (2023), 69.
36. *Ibid.*
37. *Ibid.*, 96.
38. Google Finance, https://www.google.com/finance/quote/BTC-USD, accessed 28 July 2023.
39. Jamie Crawley, *Coindesk*, 2021, https://www.coindesk.com/markets/2021/07/26/tulip-bulb-crypto-has-no-inherent-worth-man-group-ceo-says/, accessed 28 July 2023.

Warren Buffett agreed with Ellis and suggested: 'It's ingenious and blockchain is important but Bitcoin has no unique value at all, it doesn't produce anything. You can stare at it all day and no little Bitcoins come out or anything like that. It's a delusion basically.'[40]

One year later, Buffett insisted that '[c]ryptocurrencies basically have no value, and they don't produce anything. They don't reproduce, they can't mail you a check, they can't do anything, and what you hope is that somebody else comes along and pays you more money for them later on, but then that person's got the problem. In terms of value: zero'.[41]

If one considers the economic properties of cryptoassets in general and cryptocurrencies more specifically, one must go back to their beginnings: the emergence of Bitcoin. Anonymous 'person(s)' who called themselves Satoshi Nakamoto published a White paper called: 'Bitcoin: A Peer-to-Peer Electronic Cash System'[42] amidst the 2007-2009 Global Financial Crisis. This White paper describes a way individuals could digitally 'hold, send, and receive "electronic cash" without a trusted intermediary in the middle'.[43]

The revolutionary idea of Bitcoin is that it cuts out the middleman in those value transfers, meaning that no bank or any other payment processor stands between the persons sending and receiving cryptocurrencies, and no central register exists that records or holds them – nor are any intermediaries interposed through which the transactions pass through.[44] The software that enables processing Bitcoin transactions was released at the beginning of 2009, which allowed the first Bitcoin to be minted.[45]

40. CNBC, February 2019, https://www.youtube.com/watch?v=m4vDTAelhCM, accessed 23 July 2023.
41. CNBC, February 2020, https://www.youtube.com/watch?v=d6yqrwOZVjY, accessed 4 January 2024.
42. Satoshi Nakamoto, *Bitcoin: A Peer-to-Peer Electronic Cash System*, 2008, satoshin@gmx.com, www.bitcoin.org, https://bitcoin.org/bitcoin.pdf, accessed 7 July 2023. For readers in the UK, the White paper can be accessed via the weblink: Bitcoin.com, Bitcoin Whitepaper, Satoshi's archive. https://www.bitcoin.com/satoshi-archive/whitepaper/, accessed 1 December 2023.
43. Satoshi Nakamoto, *Bitcoin: A Peer-to-Peer Electronic Cash System*, 2008, Abstract, https://bitcoin.org/bitcoin.pdf, accessed 4 July 2023.
44. *Ibid.*, 2. Nakamoto states in this respect: 'What is needed is an electronic payment system based on cryptographic proof instead of trust, allowing any two willing parties to transact directly with each other without the need for a trusted third party. Transactions that are computationally impractical to reverse would protect sellers from fraud, and routine escrow mechanisms could easily be implemented to protect buyers. In this paper, we propose a solution to the double-spending problem using a peer-to-peer distributed timestamp server to generate computational proof of the chronological order of transactions. The system is secure as long as honest nodes collectively control more CPU power than any cooperating group of attacker nodes.' *Compare also* Southern and Weidmann (2023), 73.
45. Matt Hougan and David Lavant, CTA Research Foundation, *Cryptoassets, The Guide to Bitcoin, Blockchain and Cryptocurrency for Investment Professionals* (2021), 2.

It is important to understand that cryptocurrencies like Bitcoin can be traded or exchanged, one for another. 'They are held and managed in the form of a blockchain on numerous linked computers as fungible electronic units.'[46]

In contrast, other cryptoassets like NFTs are held through a single computer and can only be accessed by an encrypted personal electronic key.[47] NFTs are sometimes defined as 'unique pieces of software, powered by smart contracts, stored on a blockchain'.[48] NFTs have unique identification codes that distinguish them from each other. Unlike cryptocurrencies, they cannot be traded or exchanged at equivalency.[49]

NFTs are a digital representation of physical assets, like artwork, sports cards. rarities and even real estate.[50] There are currently no crypto derivatives on NFTs, although that may change in the future. One should not mistake NFT derivatives for crypto derivatives on NFTs, however. 'NFT derivatives are NFT collections that pull attributes and styles from popular NFT projects. Besides bearing a strong visual resemblance to the original NFT, a derivative will also have a similar name.'[51] That means those NFT derivatives are not derivatives in a financial sense but alternative NFT underlyings which resemble original NFTs.

In the same way, the financial market has not seen any derivatives on digital in-game items, although this market will reach an estimated volume in excess of USD 150 billion in 2023.[52] Virtual or digital gaming items usually belong to a different category than NFTs (although there are exceptions to NFTs used in games). In-game items are commonly called Skins. Skins primarily give weapons 'special looks' that gamers admire in games, but they can also be other digital goods, such as special clothes used in games. Skins change the look of an item in a computer game. For example, an object in an online game can have different Skins, which inevitably make the object look different.

In terms of taxation, cryptocurrencies are of foremost importance for tax administrations worldwide due to their sheer size and rapid expansion. This work will, therefore, focus on cryptocurrencies as the most important class of cryptoassets.

---

46. Southern and Weidmann (2023), 70.
47. *Ibid.*
48. Ian Bradley, EY, *How Taxes on Cryptocurrencies and Digital Assets Will Soon Take Shape*, https://www.ey.com/en_gl/tax/how-taxes-on-cryptocurrencies-and-digital-assets-will-soon-take-shape, accessed 20 July 2023.
49. Investopedia, What Are Non-fungible Tokens? https://www.investopedia.com/non-fungible-tokens-nft-5115211, accessed 12 February 2023.
50. For example, OpenSea is the largest marketplace for buying and selling NFTs. *See* OpenSea, *Discover, Collect, and Sell Extraordinary NFTs*, https://opensea.io, accessed 21 July 2023.
51. Binance, Binance Blog, Everything You Need To Know About NFT Derivatives, 8 December 2022, https://www.binance.com/en/blog/nft/everything-you-need-to-know-about-nft-derivatives-821805022347323l524, accessed 12 January 2023.
52. Caleb Naysmith, Gamers Making Thousands Selling Gaming Skins And Assets: Gameflip's Bold Vision For The Future Of Gaming Commerce (2023), https://www.benzinga.com/startups/23/05/32168043/making-thousands-selling-gaming-skins-and-assets-gameflips-bold-vision-for-the-future-of-in-game-com, accessed 1 September 2023.

The following example of a Bitcoin transaction demonstrates the basic mechanics of cryptocurrency transactions in the blockchain network:[53]

(1) A intends to send 10 Bitcoins to B. To do so, A puts the following message in the Bitcoin database, 'A wants to send 10 Bitcoins to B.' That message is sent to all computers that run a copy of the current Bitcoin database. A has a unique password, which is called a 'private key', which lets her sign the message so that the network knows the message is coming from her and not someone else.[54]

(2) The computers are all part of the Bitcoin network. The other computers can confirm that A has 10 Bitcoins in her possession, which she has the right to send because they each have a copy of the current database.[55]

(3) The transaction has only been proposed at that point, and no computer has updated the distributed ledger. The transaction is in the so-called waiting room, where it awaits confirmation. The system can rapidly distribute the message to ensure that every participant is aware of it because it is not settled yet. At the time when A proposes her transaction to the network, other participants are also sending messages. They also want to send their Bitcoins to various recipients.[56]

(4) At that point in the process, the 'miners'[57] enter the network. The so-called miners are computers around the world which aggregate groups of valid new transactions. Those groups of transactions are commonly called 'blocks'. The miners propose those blocks for settlement. Many miners compete at any given time for the right to settle the next block. To receive the right to settle this next block, the miners need to solve a mathematical puzzle before all other miners and post the correct solution to the other miners within the Bitcoin network in order to be successful in that competition. One can imagine that mathematical puzzle as a list of characters which represent the computer's output. The task involves finding the correct input. If the correct input is submitted, resulting in the correct output, the puzzle is solved.[58]

(5) Only if they solve the puzzle can a miner propose a new block for settlement. For successfully adding a block to the blockchain, the miner receives a reward, which currently reflects the amount of 6.25 Bitcoins. It is that payment which incentivises the miners to perform the necessary work to verify transactions and maintain the database.[59]

---

53. A detailed description of how Bitcoin and the mining process works can be found in: Hougan and Lavant (2021), 4–7. Compare Southern and Weidmann (2023), 73-74 for a similar example taken from Hougan and Lavant.
54. Hougan and Lavant (2021), 4.
55. *Ibid.*, 5.
56. *Ibid.*
57. Coinbase, *What Is Mining?* https://www.coinbase.com/learn/crypto-basics/what-is-mining, accessed 14 July 2023.
58. Hougan and Lavant (2021), 5. *Compare also* Southern and Weidmann (2023), 73-74.
59. Nakamoto (2008) 4.

(6) If one of the miners solves the puzzle, it can post the solution and propose a block of transactions to the network. Other participating miners then check the work and validate it.[60]

(7) If the transactions are valid and the solution is correct, the network participants update their copy of the database to reflect the new transactions, such as the transaction between A and B. At that point in time, the transaction between A and B is considered settled.[61]

To sum it up, cryptocurrencies are entirely self-contained, and they do not go back to anything outside themselves.[62] Cryptocurrencies themselves do not represent any real value, but this value is only an attributed value based on their perceived scarcity. They neither represent the value of an ongoing business, a debt obligation, physical assets, a concept which may produce practical results, nor a design.[63] Instead, cryptocurrencies only reflect the value that the buyers and sellers attribute to them at a specific moment in time. Or, as Buffett puts it: 'The attributed value can only be maintained if more people want to hold them than holders want to monetise them.'[64]

Formulated even more pointedly, it means that cryptocurrencies 'have no spatial reference and are purely electronic. [They] are simply a form of electronic communication combined with human hope or ambition'.[65]

Furthermore, as a peer-to-peer 'exchange of value' system, cryptocurrencies:

> are not attached to any state or jurisdiction or entity. There is no central point of control. They are not governed by a central bank, a board of directors, an issuing authority or physical constraints. [...] There is no central register of the existence or ownership of cryptoassets. There is no land register, share register, bank account or public document which tells you that a cryptoasset exists and who owns it. Those holding them do so in a wholly anonymised way.[66]

Frequent crypto crashes, crypto heists, and crypto scams like the rise and fall of *OneCoin*, the collapse of the Bahamian digital asset exchange company *FTX Trading Ltd*[67] and the collapse of the Luna crypto network, which alone wiped out USD 60 billion,[68] show the fragility of the cryptoasset world. Those collapses and crypto scams

60. Hougan and Lavant (2021) 5; *compare* Southern and Weidmann (2023), 74.
61. Nakamoto (2008) 3.
62. Eswar Prasad, *Five Myths about Cryptocurrency*, OP-ED, Brookings, 24 May 2021, https://www.brookings.edu/opinions/five-myths-about-cryptocurrency/, accessed 4 July 2023. *Compare also* Southern and Weidmann (2023), 70.
63. *Ibid.*
64. Warren Buffett in CNBC Interview, February 2019, https://www.youtube.com/watch?v=m4vDTAelhCM, accessed 2 July 2023.
65. Southern and Weidmann (2023), 70.
66. *Ibid.*
67. Carol Alexander, The Guardian, https://www.theguardian.com/commentisfree/2022/nov/23/ftx-binance-crypto-market, 23 November 2022, accessed 24 July 2023. *Compare* Southern/Weidmann (2023), 69.
68. Forbes, What Really Happened to LUNA Crypto? (20 September 2022), https://www.forbes.com/sites/qai/2022/09/20/what-really-happened-to-luna-crypto/?sh=2c2428d14ff1, accessed 1 July 2023.

frequently occur because of a lack of regulatory oversight.[69] Nevertheless, cryptoassets exist as a new asset class and, thus, can also serve as an underlying for derivatives.

[D] ESG as a New Underlying Variable for Derivatives?

The term ESG stands for *environmental, social and governance*. Investments in various forms of ESG products have become increasingly popular in recent years. Thus, one needs to understand the purpose behind those ESG investments and what they represent.

Beyond this literal meaning of the three words, ESG is, first and foremost, a concept. ESG is sometimes defined as a framework that is 'used to assess an organization's business practices and performance on various sustainability and ethical issues'.[70]

The factor 'environmental' describes a company's 'overall impact on the environment and the potential risks and opportunities it faces because of environmental issues'.[71] The factor 'social' evaluates how 'a company treats different groups of people: employees, suppliers, customers, community members and more'.[72] The factor 'governance' focuses on 'internal controls and practices to maintain compliance with regulations, industry best practices and corporate policies'.[73]

In terms of investments, the fulfilment or non-fulfilment of ESG criteria is a way to measure business opportunities or risks in the ESG realm. Thus, some investors use ESG criteria and ratings to evaluate a company's ESG performance and make investment decisions accordingly.

ESG ratings should guide investors towards companies and investments which are perceived by the market as environmentally or socially responsible or companies with high internal governance standards. Thus, ESG investments are often seen as 'ethical' investments and companies that (1) are environmentally friendly, (2) fulfil desirable social purposes, and (3) apply practices, procedures and controls to govern themselves in an effective manner and comply with the law and fulfil stakeholder needs.[74]

However, those ESG criteria are sometimes lofty, and the ratings combine the criteria of 'environmental', 'social' and 'governance' so that often ESG ratings do not appear to be accessible by way of common sense.

For example, Tesla was recently added to an ESG index. Tesla is regarded as the global pioneer for electric cars and mobility. The disturbing fact, however, is that Tesla received a significantly lower ESG rating compared to tobacco companies and oil

69. Southern and Weidmann (2023), 75-76.
70. Sandra Mathis and Craig Stedman, What is environmental, social and governance (ESG)?, TechTarget, March 2023, https://www.techtarget.com/whatis/definition/environmental-social-and-governance-ESG, accessed 1 September 2023.
71. *Ibid.*
72. *Ibid.*
73. *Ibid.*
74. Witold Henisz, Tim Koller, and Robin Nuttall, Five Ways That ESG Creates Value, 14 November 2019, McKinsey Quarterly, https://www.mckinsey.com/capabilities/strategy-and-corporate-finance/our-insights/five-ways-that-esg-creates-value, accessed 16 July 2023.

companies in the same index. Similarly, S&P Global gave Tesla Inc. a rating of 37 out of 100,[75] while Philip Morris International Inc. received an overall rating of 84 out of 100,[76] with an 'environmental' rating of 87 out of 100.[77]

In the same way, the London Stock Exchange gave British American Tobacco plc (BAT)[78] a rating of 94, while Tesla earned a meagre rating of 65.[79] Some authors argue that such high ratings are incomprehensible when common sense is applied, as tobacco companies are responsible for the death of millions of people worldwide due to their products.[80] For example, BAT revenues in 2022 were 83% or 23 billion, while more than 10% were contributed by modern 'vaping' and heating products, which are largely seen as starter drugs for children and teens due to the sweet taste of many of those products, leading to a ban of vaping products in some countries.[81]

One may ask if those ratings accurately reflect the underlying notion that ESG investments involve ethically responsible companies or investment products.

Nowadays, even some cryptoassets are branded as ESG-friendly, but that may be considered 'greenwashing'. *Greenwashing* is when companies want to appear more environmentally friendly and/or socially responsible than they actually are because they hope for a more positive public image or higher recognition among investors.[82]

75. S&P Global, S&P Global Inc. ESG Score, https://www.spglobal.com/esg/scores/results?cid=4574287, accessed 12 June 2023.
76. *Ibid.*
77. Allen Root, Tesla Got Added to an ESG Index. But Oil and Tobacco Firms Scored Higher, Barron's, 1 June 2023, https://www.barrons.com/articles/tesla-chevron-stock-sp500-esg-score-index-bf95e0fe, accessed 13 February 2024.
78. BAT, 'Delivering Transformation' Combined Performance and ESG Summary, https://docs.publicnow.com/viewDoc?hash_primary=A80FFDEB57CEC9FE68700F643978CB1487232384, accessed 12 June 2023.
79. Aaron Sibarium, How Tobacco Companies Are Crushing ESG Ratings, The Washington Free Beacon, 13 June 2023, https://freebeacon.com/latest-news/how-tobacco-companies-are-crushing-esg-ratings/, accessed 1 August 2023.
80. *Ibid.*
81. Darryl Rigby, Where Is Vaping Banned? Countries with Strict E-Cig Laws, https://vapoholic.co.uk/2022/02/11/where-is-vaping-banned-countries-with-strictest-e-cig-laws/, accessed 14 June 2023.
82. Greenwashing is 'the act or practice of making a product, policy, activity, etc. appear to be more environmentally friendly or less environmentally damaging than it really is', *see* Merriam Webster Dictionary, definition of greenwashing, https://www.merriam-webster.com/dictionary/greenwashing, accessed 12 April 2023.

    For example, cryptoassets can be seen as bad for the environment as tons of computer equipment and graphic cards are used to perform the mining of cryptocurrencies as that requires substantial computer power.

    In fact, cryptocurrencies stand for the misallocation of energy resources and a lack of sustainability. For example, the annualised total Bitcoin footprint is as follows: Bitcoin mining has an annual carbon footprint of 97 MT CO2 which is comparable to the carbon footprint of Kuwait, miners use combined electrical energy of 204.5 TWh which is comparable to the power consumption of Thailand, and electronic waste is produced of 65.01 kilotons (kt) which is comparable to the small IT equipment waste of the Netherlands; *see* Digiconomist 'Bitcoin Electronic Waste Monitor' (2023), https://digiconomist.net/bitcoin-electronic-waste-monitor/, accessed 1 September 2023. Yet, no country is seriously targeting this absurd energy misallocation through crypto mining.

It should be noted that 'tax' itself has become an ESG factor. The 2020 World Economic Forum 'has outlined "total tax paid" as a reportable metric to reflect a corporation's contribution to public finances through direct and indirect tax, [and] "to disclose their progress in the ESG areas of people, planet, prosperity and governance"'.[83]

Consequently, some investors factor in the 'total tax paid' in deciding whether to (or continue to) invest in a company or not.[84] For example, a report from KPMG highlights that:

> Institutional investors are starting to use this information to make informed investment decisions. [...] A group of Danish pension funds have developed and signed a Tax Code of Conduct to help support goals of responsible tax behavior in their investments and through their investment partners. Actions like these underscore the public approach investors are taking in supporting tax as a critical component of ESG.[85]

The author believes that particularly those multinationals which pay little or no tax and have been targeted by recent anti-BEPS initiatives, such as the OECD's Pillar One and Two, will come under more scrutiny from ESG-inspired investors. Indeed, investors may start distinguishing between *ESG-compliant companies*, which are those that are transparent in their tax dealings and pay their fair share of tax, and *non-ESG-compliant companies*, being those which employ aggressive tax optimisation strategies as described in the OECD's/G20 BEPS project. Thus, the author predicts that the ESG factor of 'governance' will gain increased importance within the ESG-triad in the future.

ESG investments consist broadly of ESG investment funds, ESG derivatives and ESG-linked structured products.

To better understand ESG investments, and in particular ESG derivatives, one may ask the following question:

Are ESG simply derivatives over some environmentally, social or governance-friendly investments, or is ESG a new asset class that can be compared to crypto assets?

With the increasing popularity of ESG-related investments, the financial markets have devised a multitude of products containing not only ESG derivatives but also green bonds and various sustainability-linked products, which fall under the umbrella term of ESG-linked structured products. In addition, a whole range of investment opportunities relating to carbon credits and associated derivatives have been devised by the financial institutions and sold to their customers.

The author cannot conclusively answer the question of whether ESG investments already constitute a whole new asset class or not. Still, derivatives over various ESG-related underlyings are a fact, and many investors are interested in investing in them for various reasons, so this work will categorise them and determine how they should be accounted for and taxed.

83. KPMG, ESG and Tax: Increasing Importance to Institutional Investors, 2021, https://assets.kpmg.com/content/dam/kpmg/xx/pdf/2021/09/esg-and-tax.pdf, accessed 2 September 2023.
84. *Ibid.*
85. *Ibid.*

One might argue that investment products with the label 'ESG' may not be regarded as an entirely new asset class like cryptoassets. Many ESG derivatives contain only some ESG element or feature but are, in fact, derivatives over traditional underlyings. This position is, however, not without debate, and there are arguments to regard 'ESG' as an entirely new asset class. For instance, the New York Stock Exchange and the Intrinsic Exchange Group announced in 2021 that they have developed a 'new class of sustainable publicly traded assets'.[86]

The legal framework for some ESG derivatives already exists with the International Swaps and Derivatives Association (ISDA)'s recent publication of the 2022 ISDA Verified Carbon Credit Derivatives Definitions and the US Renewable Energy Certificate (REC) Annex to the ISDA Master Agreement,[87] which allows 'market participants to more easily trade in renewable energy certificates'.[88]

In 2021, ISDA produced a report which outlines the various forms of ESG derivatives.[89]

Conventional derivatives, like interest rate swaps and credit default swaps (CDSs), can be used to hedge exposure to so-called green bonds.[90] However, those interest rate swaps and CDSs are traditional instruments and are not further discussed in the ISDA report.[91] The ISDA report instead categorises ESG derivatives and investments as follows: 'sustainability-linked derivatives; ESG-related CDS indices; exchange-traded derivatives on listed ESG-related equity indices; emissions trading derivatives; renewable energy and renewable fuels derivatives; and catastrophe and

86. ESG Investing, NYSE launches new sustainable asset class, 15 September 2021, https://www.esginvesting.co.uk/2021/09/nyse-launches-new-sustainable-asset-class/, accessed 15 June 2023.
87. ISDA US Renewable Energy Certificate Annex, https://www.isda.org/book/isda-u-s-renewable-energy-certificate-annex/, accessed 12 July 2023.
88. Richard Kelly, Garret Farrelly and Alan Bunbury, ESG Derivatives: A Look at Their Use and Regulation (2021) https://www.matheson.com/insights/detail/esg-derivatives-a-look-at-their-use-and-regulation, accessed 28 July 2023.
89. ISDA, Overview of ESG-Related Derivatives Products and Transactions, January 2021, https://www.isda.org/a/qRpTE/Overview-of-ESG-related-Derivatives-Products-and-Transactions.pdf, accessed 23 July 2023.
90. 'A green bond is a debt security that is issued to raise capital specifically to support climate-related or environmental projects.' *See* World Bank, What Are Green Bonds?, 1 December 2015, https://documents1.worldbank.org/curated/en/400251468187810398/pdf/99662-REVISED-WB-Green-Bond-Box393208B-PUBLIC.pdf, accessed 12 April 2023.
    The ISDA Report, Overview of ESG-related Derivatives Products and Transactions (2021), Glossary, 16, defines green bonds as follows: 'green bonds are a type of bond instrument where the proceeds will be exclusively applied to finance or refinance, in part or in full, new and/or existing eligible green projects and are aligned with the four core components of the green bond principles (GBP). Green projects contribute to environmental objectives such as climate change mitigation, climate change adaptation, natural resource conservation, biodiversity conservation, and pollution prevention and control, referring to the International Capital Market Association (ICMA) Green Bond Principles', https://www.icmagroup.org/assets/documents/Regulatory/Green-Bonds/Green-Bonds-Principles-June-2018-270520.pdf, accessed 12 August 2023.
91. ISDA, Overview of ESG-related Derivatives Products and Transactions (2021), 1.

weather derivatives'.[92] In total, the report identifies seven categories of ESG derivatives, which are further outlined in Chapter 4 of this book. If one, however, looks at the structure of those derivatives more closely, one will recognise that many of them are traditional derivatives, such as options, futures, forwards, swaps or credit derivatives, which have some link or element of ESG. In addition, ESG-linked structured products have been promoted by banks in recent years. They are bonds and derivatives combinations that contain some ESG element.

The author will investigate in Chapter 4 of this work if the various types of ESG derivatives fall under the definition of derivatives for tax purposes developed by the author and discuss in Chapter 8 the economic properties and the accounting and tax treatment of ESG-linked structured products.

§2.02 BASIC TERMS: REPLICATION, HEDGING OF DERIVATIVES AND LEVERAGE

[A] Economic Replication

Replication, in general, means that at any time during the term of the derivative it is possible to replicate the total sum of the payoffs of the derivative by entering into a trading strategy using other financial instruments, including basic underlying assets, cash and other derivatives.[93]

A derivative can be replicated by entering into other financial instrument(s) if, at maturity of the derivative, the financial instrument(s) which replicate the derivative have in sum the same *payoff* as the derivative, meaning the sum of all cash flows[94] of the financial instrument(s) used in the replicating portfolio must have the same present value as all cash flows of the derivative itself.

Although the replicating portfolio mirrors the changes in value and risks of the derivative, it is neither necessary nor possible that the cash flows of the derivative at any time of its term equal the cash flows of the replicating portfolio.

Thus, one can speak of 'replication' if, independently from the parameters which determine cash flows, the economic value of the derivative is identical to the value of the portfolio of replicating instruments.[95]

Example 3:

A future can be replicated with a forward contract, although the cash flows of a futures contract and a forward contract are not identical during the term of the

92. *Ibid.*
93. Rubinstein (1999a) 71-72 and 179-192. *See* OECD (2001) paras 31-41 for a general discussion of the concept of replication and its importance in the context of tax law.
94. Cash flows of a derivative are one or more payments, which at certain points in time during the term of the derivative either inflow or outflow; *see* Peter Newman, Murray Milgate and John Eatwell (eds), *The New Palgrave Dictionary of Money and Finance* (Macmillan 1992).
95. Rubinstein (1999b) 22.

instruments. Futures contracts require the payment of an initial margin and further maintenance margin payments to be made during the term of the contract. Thus, a fraction of the purchase price is paid at inception and adjusting margin payments are made during the term to reflect the value of the futures contract. By contrast, forward contracts require payment of the strike price only at maturity, assuming that the value of the forward is zero at inception.[96] Thus, a future and a forward do not have identical cash flows but identical payoffs and, therefore, can be replicated with each other.

In terms of valuation and pricing, one must distinguish between *static replication* and *dynamic replication*.

[1] Static Replication of Derivatives Using the Put-Call Parity Formula

Static replication means the combination of financial instruments to create the payoff of a different financial instrument or portfolio, thereby duplicating its economic substance. To statically replicate a financial instrument or portfolio, a replicating portfolio in one or more other financial instruments is built up once at inception, for example, by purchasing or selling the underlying asset or another derivative on the underlying asset.[97]

Thus, a one-off buy-and-hold strategy can be used to create the desired payoff.[98] This strategy is then sufficient to replicate the payoff profile of a derivative or other financial instrument. If the replication strategy is completely debt-financed, it exactly equals in its payoff profile the derivative or financial instrument which gets replicated.[99]

Further changes or adaptations in a static replication strategy are not necessary during the term of the financial instrument/portfolio since the replicating portfolio has the same payoff as the replicated financial instrument, no matter in which direction the price of the underlying asset moves.

Example 4:

A ten-year German government bond (*Bundesanleihe*) can be statically replicated by setting up a cash account that pays overnight *Eonia* interest plus the purchase of a *Bund future*. The interest paid on the cash account plus the proceeds under the *Bund future* will have the same payoff as the *Bundesanleihe*. It thus can be used to statically replicate the *Bundesanleihe*, although they may not always have the same cash flows during the term.

96. In certain cases of prepaid forwards, the purchase price is paid at inception of the contract.
97. Hull (2018) 71 and 442.
98. Rubinstein (1999a) 96 and 188.
99. *Ibid.*, 102.

Payoffs of financial instruments can be replicated using different formulas for static replication. Derivatives' payoffs can also be statically replicated using the *put-call parity formula.*

The put-call parity formula describes the relationship between the price of a European call option and the price of a European put option with the same strike price and the same maturity.[100] It can be expressed in a simplified way as:

Call *(C) – Put (P) = Underlying Asset (S) – Strike Price (K)*[101]

The formula means that the value of a purchased (long) call option and a sold (short) put option equals, *at maturity* of the options, the value of the purchase of the underlying asset at the pre-determined strike price (K).[102]

Shortly before maturity, it would, therefore, make no difference whether the purchaser buys the underlying asset at the pre-determined strike price of, say, 100 or whether he buys a call with a strike of 100 and sells a put with the same strike.[103]

Before maturity of the options, it is necessary also to consider the financing costs for the purchase of the underlying assets, i.e., the financing costs for the payment of the strike price at maturity.

The present value for the payment of the *strike price*, therefore, equals the value of a *zero bond* with a nominal value equal to the strike price.

Furthermore, all income, such as dividends or coupons, and all costs (cost of carry or banking costs) which are related to the holding of the underlying asset during the term of the option must be considered to determine the value of the options.

Both the strike price for the purchase of the underlying shares at maturity and the income during the term must be discounted to determine the present value of these payments.

The put-call parity formula for determining the value of the options during their term can be expressed as:

$$C - P = S - PV\ (K) - PV\ (D)$$ [104]

whereas:
C = call option price
P = put option price

100. Hull (2018) 263.
101. The formula used above is a simplified formula, which is nevertheless mathematically correct. *See* for a more technical formula: Rubinstein (1999b) 147ff; Wilmott (2000) 34.
102. The put-call parity formula is often explained using European call options on traded shares. It, however, works for all tradable underlying assets.
103. For an example of a replication using the simplified put-call parity formula, *see* OECD (2001), Appendix I, Example 1.
104. Again, this formula is simplified to provide a better understanding of the core of the formula.

S = value of the underlying asset/variable
K = strike price
D = pay-out return of the underlying (dividends, interest, or other income from the underlying) minus costs[105]
PV = present value
PV(K) = present value of the strike price K
PV(D) = present value of the pay-out return of the underlying asset over the life of the option

The put-call parity formula is also a common tax structuring tool to replicate payoffs of one financial instrument or portfolio by the combination of other instruments in order to achieve the most attractive tax outcome. The author provides below basic examples of how the put-call parity formula can be used to statically replicate option contracts as well as underlying assets.

Example 5:

Synthetic replication of a call option
$C = S - PV(K) - PV(D) + P$

The remodelled formula means that the payoff of a call option can be synthetically replicated by buying the underlying asset, buying a put option, borrowing the present value of the strike price and paying the present value of the expected pay-outs (dividends or interest) of the underlying asset if any.[106]

In the same way, put options can be synthetically replicated using the put-call parity formula:

Example 6:

Synthetic replication of a put option
$P = C - S + PV(K) + PV(D)$

Here, the value of a put option is replicated by a portfolio of a purchased call option, a sold underlying, the purchase of a zero bond with a notional equal to

105. For simplification purposes, costs are not further considered in the following.
106. Rubinstein (1999b) 147.

the strike price and investing the present value of the expected pay-outs (i.e., dividends or interest) at the risk-free market interest rate.[107]

Similarly, an underlying asset can be synthetically replicated using the put-call parity formula.

> *Example 7:*
>
> *Synthetic replication of the underlying asset*
> $S = C - P + PV(K) + PV(D)$

The economic performance of an underlying asset can be synthetically replicated by buying a call option, selling a put option, buying a zero bond with a notional equal to the strike price, and investing the present value of the expected pay-outs (i.e., dividends or interest) at the risk-free market interest rate.[108]

Not only can options be replicated using the put-call parity formula, other derivatives can be as well. For example, using the put-call parity formula, the payoff of a forward contract can be replicated by a combination of buying a call option and selling a put option, with the same maturity equal to the delivery date of the forward and a common strike price equal to the forward price.[109] It can be expressed as:

> $F = C - P$ [110]
>
> whereas:
> F = value of the forward
> C = value of a European call option
> P = value of a European put option

More generally, the above examples show that the put-call parity formula allows expressing derivatives as a combination of its underlying variables and other derivatives by remodelling the formula. It can be applied to all underlyings, which are tradable assets.

Futures, forwards and swaps over equities, bonds, interest rates, currencies and commodities can alternatively be replicated using a simpler model, namely the forward-spot parity relation,[111] which uses static replication techniques.[112]

---

107. *Ibid.*, 148.
108. OECD (2001), Appendix I, Example 2.
109. Rubinstein (1999b) 154; OECD (2001), Appendix I, Example 3.
110. $F = S - PV(K) - PV(D)$; $S - PV(K) - PV(D) = C - P$; hence $F = C - P$.
111. The forward-spot parity is a variant of the put-call parity as C – P is substituted by F.
112. Rubinstein (1999b) 96 and 102.

> *Example 8:*
>
> A payoff of a forward contract can be replicated by entering into a portfolio containing one unit of the underlying asset if the purchase of the asset is entirely financed by borrowing the present value of the forward price.[113]

[2] Replication of Options by Means of Dynamic Replication

Options can also be replicated by means of dynamic replication. *Dynamic replication* of an option also requires the initial investment into the underlying, financed by borrowing. However, as the price of the underlying increases or decreases, the underlying asset holding is gradually increased by further purchases of the underlying, financed by additional borrowing, or decreased by reducing the holding in the underlying, using the proceeds to repay the borrowing.[114] Dynamic replication, therefore, means a constant change in the position held in the underlying asset.[115]

The value of the option during the term determines the delta of an option (Δ). The delta is the ratio of the change of the option price to the change of price in the underlying.[116] Thus, it determines the sensitivity of the option price in relation to the underlying asset or variable.

With the help of delta, it is possible to determine how many contracts in the underlying need to be bought or sold to replicate the option dynamically. Hence, 'the current option value equals the product of the current underlying asset times the delta minus the current amount of borrowing in the replicating portfolio'.[117] Thus, option valuation[118] and dynamic replication of options are directly intertwined.[119]

[B] Hedging of Derivatives/with Derivatives

Hedging means the neutralisation or reduction of risk components of a derivative or any other financial instrument.[120] 'The returns of a derivative can be perfectly hedged by following an offsetting replicating portfolio strategy'[121] as hedging means the opposite of replication. Different hedging strategies are applicable depending on the type of derivative. Corresponding to static and dynamic replication, one distinguishes between static and dynamic hedging of a derivative.

---

113. *See* Rubinstein (1999a) 99 for a numeric example of a synthetic replication of a forward contract.
114. *Ibid.*, 179.
115. Hull (2018) 847; Rubinstein (1999a) 71ff and 179; *also* OECD (2001) paras 31-41.
116. Hull (2018) 307.
117. Rubinstein (1999a) 179.
118. *See* Ch. 2 §2.02[C].
119. Rubinstein (1999a) 179.
120. Hull (2018) 71; OECD (2001) para. 115.
121. Rubinstein (1999b) 22.

Static hedging – or a *hedge-and-forget* strategy[122] – means that the derivative can be hedged at inception by entering into an initial hedging portfolio, which allows hedging the derivative over its term. The hedging portfolio will be terminated at maturity of the hedged derivative.[123] The hedging portfolio remains constant over the life of the hedge, with no adjustments being made to the hedging portfolio.[124] Forwards, futures or swaps can be statically hedged.[125]

In contrast, dynamic hedging requires a constant adjustment of the hedging portfolio to the current market price of the derivatives position during the term of the transaction.[126] Options ultimately must be *hedged dynamically* in order to achieve a complete hedge of the option.[127]

Example 9:

Company A wishes to hedge the purchase of an equity call option. Company A has two ways to hedge this call option: either Company A can enter directly into an offsetting position by selling a call option, or it can hedge the option by buying or selling the underlying shares according to the current market price of the option, thereby hedging the call option dynamically by replicating the offsetting position.

There is a recent discussion regarding the hedge effectiveness between hedging units of cryptoassets and crypto derivatives. The author will discuss this topic further in Chapter 7 of this book.

[C] Valuation of Options

The value of an option depends on the following parameters: the current market price of the underlying (S), the strike price (K), the time (T) until maturity of the option, the risk-free interest rate (r),[128] the volatility (σ)[129] and the date(s) and amount(s) of the dividend payment(s) (D), if any.[130]

122. Hull (2018) 71.
123. A derivative may be hedged by buying or selling the underlying, or by buying or selling other derivatives on the underlying variable.
124. Hull (2018) 71.
125. Rubinstein (1999b) 102.
126. Hull (2018) 424 and 847.
127. *Ibid.*, 425. If the hedge is complete, the delta of the hedging portfolio offsets the delta of the option position, with the position being delta neutral.
128. When purchasing or selling an option, one has to consider the risk/reward ratio. If an underlying is purchased for delivery at a future date, as it is the case for options, the yields of alternative investments must be considered when pricing an option.
129. Volatility is defined as the standard deviation of the returns provided by the price of the underlying asset per annum, 'when the return is expressed using continuous compounding'. It could also be described as the relative change in price of the underlying asset per annum. *See* Hull (2018) 347.
130. *Ibid.*, 256-260.

The value of an option is the sum of the 'intrinsic value' and the 'time value' of the option.[131] The intrinsic value equals the value of an immediate exercise, whereas the time value depends on the expectation of the volatility up until exercise or maturity.[132]

Different valuation models have been developed to calculate the price of different derivatives, depending on the type of derivative and the respective underlying. Without proper valuation models, mispricing of derivative contracts, meaning that the seller of the contract sells the instrument too cheap or the purchaser of the contract buys the instrument too expensive, is certain to occur and often arises in volatile market situations of the underlying assets.

The standard model for the valuation of European equity options is the *Black-Scholes model.*[133] Pricing models for other options, such as bond options,[134] commodity options and FX options,[135] are often derived from the basic Black-Scholes model of option pricing. Their basic principles, such as the option values' stochastic dependence on the underlying variables (parameters), are similar to the Black-Scholes model.

The AI industry develops at incredible speed. For example, a recent research project of the Pervasive Artificial Intelligence Research (PAIR) Labs in China 'applies various AI technologies in asset allocation, derivatives pricing and risk management'.[136]

In connection with derivatives pricing,

> the project is targeted to provide fast and accurate derivatives pricing methods to correctly evaluate the price and hedge ratio of derivatives. It enables financial institutions to issue derivatives in low risk with the proposed dynamic hedging principle and allows investors to invest more with the hedging tools. Mutually, it is expected that the economy will become more prosperous.[137]

It remains to be seen how derivatives pricing will be influenced by the AI industry and whether we will soon witness the rise of a new asset class: AI derivatives.

---

131. *Ibid.*, 242.
132. The intrinsic value of a call option is calculated as the maximum of the difference between the price of the underlying (S) and the agreed strike price (K) or zero if the difference is negative. This can be mathematically expressed in the formula $C = \max(S - K, 0)$.
    The intrinsic value of a put option is the maximum of the difference between the strike price (K) and the price of the underlying (S) or zero if the difference is negative. This is expressed in the formula $P = \max(K - S, 0)$.
133. Fischer Black and Myron Scholes, 'The Pricing of Options and Corporate Liabilities' 81 (1973) Journal of Political Economy 637-659 DOI: 10.1086/260062; Robert Merton, 'Theory of Rational Option Pricing' (1973) 4 Bell Journal of Economics and Management Science 141-183 DOI: 10.2307/3003143.
134. The standard model to calculate the price of bond options is the Black model. *See* Fischer Black, 'The Pricing of Commodity Contracts' (1976) Journal of Financial Economics 167-179 DOI: 10.1016/0304-405x(76)90024-6.
135. The standard model for currency options is the *Garman-Kohlhagen* pricing model, which basically extended the *Black-Scholes* model to cope with two interest rates, being one for each currency.
136. PAIR, Artificial Intelligence in Asset Allocation, Derivatives Pricing and Risk Management (2020), https://pairlabs.ai/en/portfolio-item/artificial-intelligence-in-asset-allocation-derivatives-pricing-and-risk-management-p-en/, accessed 17 April 2023.
137. *Ibid.*

[D] Definition of Leverage

Leverage means the loan-financing of investments. Whether the loan is taken outright, i.e., from a bank, or whether the loan is an integral part of a derivative, represents the same economic principle:

> Derivatives often permit much greater implicit leverage compared to buying or selling their underlying assets, even considering allowable margin borrowings; that is, with a smaller amount of money than the price of the underlying asset, derivatives can provide similar exposure to movements in the underlying asset price.[138]

If leverage is provided to an investor via a derivative, the provider of the derivative is, in fact, granting a loan to the holder of the derivative. In order to secure the loan, the derivatives provider might ask for 'collateral' in the form of cash or securities for some types of derivatives, i.e., futures and forwards. In the case of cash collateral, this is also called margin.

Example 10:

Investor A has GBP 100 initial capital and wants to buy shares in Company X. Each share costs GBP 10. If Investor A buys the shares directly, he would receive 10 shares. If the value of the shares declines 10%, Investor A would lose 10% of the invested capital when selling the shares, i.e., GBP 10. Investor B only has GBP 10 and wants to invest in Company X.

Instead of buying one share for GBP 10, Investor B opts for buying 10 forward contracts on the shares in Company X and makes a margin payment of GBP 1 for each contract. Hence, he agrees to buy 10 shares at a price of GBP 10 each at a future date. If the share price went down 10%, the shares would be worth only GBP 9 each. Investor B would not have lost only 10% of his investment but 100% (i.e., the whole GBP 10) because he would have lost GBP 1 on each of the 10 forward contracts.

Unless Investor B pays an additional margin to the seller of the forward contracts, the investment will end at this point with all capital lost.

On the other hand, if the share price went up 10%, Investor B would make a profit of GBP 10, which is nominally the same profit as Investor A would have made. Relatively speaking, Investor B would have made a profit of 100% of the capital invested compared to a profit of only 10% on the capital invested by Investor A.

One can see the advantages and disadvantages of the second trade: Investor B can achieve the same nominal profit when investing in Company X via derivatives with

138. Rubinstein (1999b) 36.

much less capital invested. On the other hand, if the investment decreases in value by 10%, the leveraged investor only has the choice of providing additional capital or a 100% loss on the capital invested.

CHAPTER 3
Problems in the Context of Taxing Derivatives and Cryptoassets

The time will come when diligent research over long periods will bring to light things which now lie hidden.

— Lucius Annaeus Seneca, *Natural Questions*

Chapter 3 highlights seven taxation issues in the context of derivatives and cryptoassets, each discussed in detail in Chapters 4 to 10. They include, among others, the problem of defining derivatives and cryptoassets for tax purposes, the determination of the character of income, the distinction between debt and equity, the timing and amount of income, the accounting and tax treatment of hedges, bifurcation or integration of structured products and hybrid instruments, and the use of derivatives and cryptoassets for tax avoidance purposes.[1]

Derivatives and cryptoasset transactions may also cause specific challenges at a cross-border level. Although the main focus of this work is on domestic taxation problems, significant international taxation issues, such as derivatives and withholding taxes, beneficial ownership and qualification conflicts in the context of hybrid instruments, will be discussed in Chapter 9 of this book.[2]

§3.01 PROBLEM 1: DEFINING DERIVATIVES FOR TAX PURPOSES

Tax systems may apply their general taxation regime to derivatives, or they adopt specific rules for the taxation of derivatives to deal with those instruments comprehensively.

1. OECD (2001) para. 47.
2. Derivatives and cryptoassets transactions between affiliated entities will not be discussed in this work; *see* Introduction.

If the general corporate tax rules apply to derivatives but do not contain a specific definition for the term 'derivatives', they may not be able to subject derivatives to tax in those cases where derivatives income does not fall within the traditional categories of income. Similarly, the general tax rules also applying to derivatives may be too unspecific in their application, thereby leading to overtaxation[3] or undertaxation[4] of certain income or gains.

In the case of a special tax regime applying to derivatives, problems may arise if the special regime is tailored only to existing derivatives and is not able to incorporate newly emerging instruments, thereby causing a time lag between the development of new financial products and the introduction of specifically targeted tax legislation.

Constant financial innovation of new types of derivatives, such as the newly emerged crypto and ESG derivatives, or the use of unusual underlyings, for example, the annual rainfall, may, therefore, challenge the ability of tax systems to define derivatives for tax purposes.[5]

A static definitional approach may lead to tax arbitrage opportunities as certain instruments may not meet the words or the interpretation of the existing tax legislation. Tax avoidance schemes may be designed to fall either inside or outside the scope of the derivatives definition, depending on the aim that the particular scheme is pursuing.[6] At the same time, a static definition may deter taxpayers from entering into derivatives transactions because of the unknown tax treatment of newly emerging instruments.

Different definitions of derivatives used by different countries can also pose a serious obstacle to their coherent taxation in cross-border transactions. The application of tax treaties in those transactions can create difficult legal issues of interpretation because derivatives and hybrid instruments[7] often cannot be classified unambiguously under the existing articles of double tax treaties.[8]

Treaty classification conflicts are likely to arise in cross-border transactions if one country attributes the income, gains or losses from derivatives to a different category

3. For example, a general tax system may not only tax net gains and losses under an interest rate swap, but all different payment streams under the swap without allowing the netting of those payment streams for tax purposes due to the application of general rules.
4. For example, undertaxation of certain derivatives income may occur in a general tax system if gains from cash-settled equity derivatives would fall under the normal taxation rules of debt gains and be fully taxable, whereas gains from the disposal of shares under physically settled equity derivatives would be tax-exempt under the general rules.
5. Neighbour (2001) 1; Strnad (1994) 569; Thuronyi (2001a) 261; Warren (1993) 461.
6. Thuronyi (2001a) 263.
7. For a definition of the term, *see* Ch. 8 §8.03.

   Emphasising the debt/equity character but applying it to a slightly broader range of instruments: Neighbour (1997) 932; Thuronyi (2001a) 262; Victor Thuronyi, *International Tax Aspects of New Financial Instruments* (in: Report of the Ad Hoc Group of Experts on International Cooperation in Tax Matters, UNPAN conference documents, 2001) 7, https://digitallibrary.un.org/record/44676, accessed 1 February 2024.
8. Thuronyi (2001a) 264; Thuronyi (2001b) 3; *also* OECD (2001) para. 63.

than the other country and, therefore, applies different taxation rules.[9] Thus, it may be uncertain in those cases under which article of the double tax treaty the income will fall, as neither the OECD Model nor the UN Model defines the term 'derivative'.

In the context of cryptoassets, domestic legislators need to decide (a) if they should incorporate a definition of cryptoassets into their tax legislation, and (b) if so, whether and how to define their subcategories. The problem of defining cryptoassets for tax purposes is interlinked with the question of whether the tax legislator decides to apply a special taxation regime to cryptoassets or not. It will, therefore, be discussed in Chapter 6 of this work.

§3.02 PROBLEM 2: ACCOUNTING STANDARDS APPLYING TO DERIVATIVES AND CRYPTOASSETS AND THEIR ALIGNMENT WITH TAX RULES

Derivatives and cryptoassets pose several challenges regarding timing. The time when income from derivatives or cryptoassets is taken into account depends on several factors.

First, tax legislators must decide if the country's tax rules or, at least, the tax rules applying to derivatives or cryptoassets should follow the accounting rules.[10] Alternatively, accounting rules may only serve as a starting point for determining the taxable profits or losses from derivatives or cryptoassets, or the tax rules applying to those instruments are entirely independent of accounting standards.[11]

Second, if accounting standards serve as a basis for the taxation of derivatives or cryptoassets, the legislator must decide which accounting standards to apply: domestic, international, or both.

Third, domestic legislators may choose accruals or fair value accounting to recognise income, gains or losses from derivatives or cryptoassets if they apply domestic accounting standards as a basis for taxation. When choosing an accounting method, domestic tax legislators implicitly have to decide if the realisation principle applies.[12] If international financial reporting standards (IFRS) are applied, the question of which accounting methods are applied will not arise, as IFRS provides detailed descriptions of which accounting method is to be applied to which assets and liabilities.

9. Thuronyi (2001a) 265.
10. *Ibid.*, 263 suggests that financial accounting rules 'may provide a basis of dealing sensibly with new financial instruments in such a way that there is not a significant threat to erosion of the tax base from use of such instruments'.
11. Judith Freedman, 'Defining Taxable Profits in a Changing Accounting Environment' (1995) 5 BTR 434, 434; Judith Freedman, 'Aligning Taxable Profits and Accounting Profits: Accounting Standards, Legislators and Judges' (2004) 2(1) eJournal of Tax Research 71, http://classic.austlii.edu.au/au/journals/eJlTaxR/2004/4.html, accessed 8 July 2023.
12. In favour of applying the principle of realisation: Edward A. Zelinsky, 'For Realization: Income Taxation, Sectoral Accretionism, and the Virtue of Attainable Virtues' (1997) 19 Cardozo Law Review 861, 861ff.

§3.03 PROBLEM 3: A SPECIAL TAXATION REGIME VERSUS THE APPLICATION OF GENERAL TAX RULES TO DERIVATIVES AND CRYPTOASSETS, AND THE DISTINCTION OF INCOME AND CAPITAL, AND EQUITY AND DEBT

[A] Specific Taxation Regime Versus the Application of the General Tax Rules

Derivatives can be seen as a third category beyond equity or debt.[13] Legislators may choose to design a separate taxation regime for derivatives,[14] or they may decide to apply the existing set of tax rules.[15] A third legislative approach is to apply a separate set of rules to derivatives but maintain the distinction between equity and debt in the context of those rules.[16]

In the context of all approaches, problems in the taxation of derivatives are likely to occur if tax systems distinguish 'in [the] taxation [rules] according to the *character* of income',[17] for example, if capital gains are subject to a more favourable tax regime or lower tax rates than other income.[18] Issues may also arise if the tax legislator treats returns from equity differently as compared to returns from debt, for example, privileges equity over debt capital gains or dividends over interest.

Newly emerging derivatives, such as crypto derivatives and ESG derivatives, have to be tested to determine if they can be appropriately captured by the general taxation rules or if special rules have to be introduced for those newly emerged derivatives.

In relation to cryptoassets, legislators need to decide if they want to introduce a special taxation regime for them or if the general taxation regime is sufficient to capture those instruments.

[B] The Taxation Rules for Income and Capital Gains Applying to Derivatives

Tax systems may distinguish between transactions that are entered into in the course of a trade or business and those with an underlying investment purpose.[19]

13. OECD (2001) para. 66.
14. In this scenario, the legislator would classify derivatives as a third category that is distinguished from equity and debt instruments and would treat them completely separately for tax purposes from equity and debt instruments.
15. Germany applies this approach to derivatives held by companies.
16. The UK taxes derivatives by applying a completely separate set of rules. Within the derivative contracts regime, a distinction between equity derivatives, which, in certain cases, are still taxed on a capital gains basis, and other derivative contracts, which are rather attributed to the debt category, is still being made. *See* Southern (2017) Ch. 13 paras 13.4-13.5.
17. Thuronyi (2001b) 1.
18. Thuronyi (2001a) 263; Thuronyi (2001b) 1.
19. Laukkanen (2007) 127; OECD (2001) para. 49; Thuronyi (2001b) 1.

Although capital gains belong to the normal corporate income tax base in many countries,[20] some countries still privilege capital gains. Often, countries apply preferred tax treatment to equity capital gains in the tax rules applying to corporates, for example through lower tax rates, deferral or an adjustment for inflation, and sometimes even complete exemption from tax.[21] Correspondingly, capital losses may not be offsetable against ordinary income or are not offsetable at all if a capital gains tax exemption applies.[22]

Both in domestic as well as in cross-border transactions, it can make a difference whether the national legislator distinguishes between income and capital. If such a distinction is applied, derivatives may pose a more significant and complex issue for the legislator than in tax systems where this distinction is not made.[23] Arbitrage opportunities may arise if taxpayers can convert income into capital gains to benefit from favourable tax treatment, or vice versa, capital gains into income to achieve deductibility of losses with the help of derivatives.[24]

A distinct feature of a derivative is that its payoff can be replicated by using combinations of other financial instruments and/or derivatives.[25] Vice versa, a combination of derivatives can be used to replicate the payoffs of traditional financial instruments.[26] Hence, if different tax rules are in place for ordinary income or capital gains, taxpayers may be able to convert ordinary income into capital gains, or vice versa, depending on which category has a preferable tax treatment, without bearing additional economic risk.[27] The same possibility arises if income generated from assets, such as interest, dividends and royalties, is treated differently.

Chapter 2 §2.02[A][1] describes how financial instruments and/or derivatives payoffs can be replicated by applying the put-call parity formula. Tax avoidance schemes may employ the mathematics of this formula to 'create' the desired legal form of any given payoff without changing its economic profile.[28]

Thuronyi argues that the possibility of static replication suggests that taxation based on an instrument's economic substance may not be an appropriate solution for the taxation of financial instruments and derivatives because 'any possible sets of equivalent combinations of instruments [are] an equally valid [economic] representation of the instrument in question'[29] due to the possibility of replication.

20. Both in Germany and the UK, capital gains form a part of the corporate income tax base.
21. OECD (2001) para. 49; Thuronyi (2001b) 1. *Also* Laukkanen (2007) 129 who provides examples of special capital gains rules in different countries.
22. OECD (2001) para. 49.
23. Thuronyi (2001a) 263; Thuronyi (2001b) 2 suggests that countries should abolish the distinction between income and capital in order to avoid issues posed by derivatives and other innovative financial instruments.
24. Thuronyi (2001a) 263; OECD (2001) para. 50.
25. For the definition and mechanics of replication, *see* Ch. 2 §2.02[A][1] and §2.02[A][2].
26. Warren (1993) 469; *also* OECD (2001) para. 72; Reiner (2002) 21.
27. OECD (2001) para. 51.
28. *Ibid.*, para. 40.
29. Thuronyi (2001b) 5.

The put-call parity formula may also be employed by taxpayers to replicate payoffs in the context of cryptoassets, crypto derivatives and associated structured products.

[C] The Taxation Rules for Equity and Debt and Their Application to Derivatives

Business activities can be financed through equity or debt. *Southern* provides an excellent summary of this distinction, stating:

> The distinction between debt and equity is best expressed in the German terms *Fremdkapital* ('external finance') and *Eigenkapital* ('internal finance'). The distinction is between proprietors' capital and creditors' capital. Debt is capital provided by third-party lenders, while equity is capital provided by shareholders.[30]

In the same way, one can distinguish the income streams arising from financial instruments: dividends arise from equity, whereas interest is paid as income on debt. This equity versus debt dichotomy particularly influences the taxation of (equity) derivatives. A tax system may face problems if derivatives are taxed by applying the traditional categories of equity and debt. Traditionally, tax systems provide for several fundamental differences in the tax treatment of financial instruments depending on whether they are qualified as equity or debt.[31]

In some countries, equity is generally privileged for tax purposes, either by way of tax exemption or preferential tax rates applying to both dividends and capital gains from the sale of the equities.[32] Other countries privilege only dividends over interest income but tax equity capital gains at the same tax rate as debt capital gains for corporation tax purposes. But even if the same tax rates apply, different taxation rules for equity and debt may lead to different taxation results in the context of derivatives.

There are various issues when equity and debt are treated differently for taxation purposes, but the existence of derivatives has brought a new dimension to those problems.

Tax legislators may choose different ways of treating derivatives for tax purposes. If a tax legislator privileges equity over debt, frictions are likely to arise if capital gains from the sale of equities are exempt, but gains from the settlement of equity derivatives are not. Tax legislators may also treat equity derivatives differently for tax purposes depending on their form of settlement. Gains from physically settled equity derivatives may be tax-exempt when exercised because the gains from the disposal of the equities

30. Southern (2017), Ch. 1, para. 1.25.
31. OECD (2001) 2, Executive Summary; Victor Thuronyi, *Taxation of New Financial Instruments* (in: Report of the Ad Hoc Group of Experts on International Cooperation in Tax Matters; UNPAN conference documents, 2001) 5, https://digitallibrary.un.org/record/453791, accessed 1 February 2024.
32. For example, Germany provides a 95% corporate tax exemption for equity capital gains and non-portfolio dividends. Section 8b para. 1, para. 2 and para. 4 CTA. With regard to German trade tax, equity capital gains from the disposal of shares are 95% tax-exempt. *See* for details: Ch. 5 §5.04.

are exempt, whereas cash-settled equity derivatives would be subject to tax at the full rate. Thus, taxpayers may choose a form of settlement which provides them with a favourable tax treatment.

Tax avoidance schemes may enable taxpayers to receive income or gains as tax-privileged dividends or equity capital gains, thereby avoiding non-privileged interest or debt. Vice versa, they may structure transactions to achieve fully tax-deductible debt capital losses instead of non-deductible equity losses. That is, however, only possible if equity capital gains and/or dividends are privileged over debt capital gains and/or interest and if no comprehensive anti-avoidance and disclosure regimes are in place that prevent this outcome.

Taxpayers have in the past (since the late 1980s) used the put-call parity and its reformulations to convert income that is fully taxed into other income that is subject to a preferential tax rate or tax-exempt.

Thus, the implications of the put-call parity will be important for tax systems that distinguish between equity and debt in their tax laws. Consequently, legislators should incorporate viable solutions in their tax legislation to deal appropriately with the problem of economic replication.

The equity and debt divide has been addressed by Action 4 of the BEPS Action Plan,[33] which 'recommends that an entity's net deduction for interest and economically equivalent payments should be limited to a percentage of the earnings before interest, taxes, depreciation, and amortisation (EBITDA) in a corridor of 10-30%'.[34] It is worth noting that the EU is further addressing the discrepancy between equity and debt taxation in a new EU Directive proposal concerning the so-called equity bias.[35]

The Directive proposal supports the financial neutrality of a tax system by limiting the tax deductibility of borrowing costs that exceed a so-called debt-equity bias reduction allowance (DEBRA).[36] The proposal aims to deal with the disparity between equity and debt financing by (1) introducing a tax-deductible allowance for equity investments, and (2) a further limitation of the ability to deduct the interest. It will be tied to the existing interest limitation rule under Article 4 of the EU's Anti-Tax Avoidance Directive (ATAD).[37]

---

33. OECD/G20 Base Erosion and Profit Shifting Project, Limiting Base Erosion Involving Interest Deductions and Other Financial Payments, Action 4 - 2015 Final Report; OECD/G20 Base Erosion and Profit Shifting Project, Limiting Base Erosion Involving Interest Deductions and Other Financial Payments, Action 4 - 2016 Update, *Inclusive Framework on BEPS*; OECD/G20 Inclusive Framework on BEPS: Progress Report September 2021-September 2022: all reports can be found at: OECD, https://www.oecd.org/tax/beps/beps-actions/action4/, accessed 3 February 2023.
34. Southern (2020) Ch. 1, para. 1.23.
35. European Commission, *Debt-equity bias reduction allowance (DEBRA)*, 11 May 2022, https://ec.europa.eu/info/law/better-regulation/have-your-say/initiatives/12995-Debt-equity-bias-reduction-allowance-DEBRA-_en, accessed 2 July 2023.
36. *Ibid.*
37. Council directive (EU) 2016/1164 of 12 July 2016, *Laying down rules against tax avoidance practices that directly affect the functioning of the internal market*, https://eur-lex.europa.eu/legal-content/EN/TXT/PDF/?uri=CELEX:32016L1164&from=EN, accessed 2 July 2023.

Even after Brexit, the proposal is also relevant to UK companies as the rules apply to taxpayers subject to tax in one of the EU Member States, which includes permanent establishments of non-EU head offices.

§3.04 PROBLEM 4: TAXATION OF DERIVATIVES AND CRYPTOASSETS IN THE CONTEXT OF HEDGING TRANSACTIONS

Taxation rules applying to derivatives may sometimes treat taxpayers differently with respect to the same transaction depending on the purpose of the transaction, such as arbitrage, speculation or hedging.[38] Companies often use derivatives to hedge or limit their share price risk on existing shareholdings, foreign exchange risks, commodity risks or counterparty risks.[39] The instruments commonly used are put options,[40] collars, put spreads and combinations of those instruments. Banks may use derivatives for hedging strategies that protect or limit various downside risks on their trading portfolios. High-net-worth individuals sometimes enter into derivatives in order to hedge their exposure in certain shareholdings or bonds.[41]

Generally, due to the exploding use of derivatives for risk management purposes, there had been a growing understanding among tax authorities and international policy organisations that tax rules should allow for efficient hedging strategies,[42] thereby enabling taxpayers to manage the various risks entailed in their portfolios and businesses on a tax-neutral basis.[43]

Thus, when derivatives positions or portfolios provide a hedge for certain risks and are economically offsetting with the risks arising from other financial instruments, including other derivatives, such economic effects should be taken into account by applying appropriate hedging provisions.[44] Missing or asymmetric tax hedging rules may partially destroy the hedging effect for the taxpayer.

---

38. OECD (2001) para. 80.
39. In the US, hedges by companies were also used to monetise shareholdings without the imposition of tax, for example by using 'contingent debt instruments', which is a structured product with the payoff consisting of a disposed underlying and a purchased 'bull spread' of call options. *See* Mark Fichtenbaum, 'Corporate Applications of Derivatives' in Frank J. Fabozzi (ed.), *The Use of Derivatives in Tax Planning* (Wiley, 2001) 267.
40. A put option is bought if the buyer wants to hedge against share price depreciation.
41. In some jurisdictions, individuals have used different 'hedging strategies' to monetise the appreciation in their shares without triggering a taxable capital gain; this applies, for example, to structures in the US prior of the introduction of IRC §1259. *See* Lewis R. Steinberg, 'Using OTC Equity Derivatives for High-Net-Worth Individuals' in Frank J. Fabozzi (ed.), *The Use of Derivatives in Tax Planning* (2001) 234.
42. OECD (2001) para. 80.

    Recently, the OECD has, however, shifted from a policy approach that requests tax-efficient after-tax hedging strategies for the taxpayer to an approach that primarily wants to tackle tax arbitrage schemes based on after-tax hedging instead of encouraging local tax authorities to remove tax mismatches between the hedge and the hedged item. *See* OECD (2013a) 13.
43. Neighbour (2001) 3.
44. OECD (2001) para. 81.

Example 11:

A tax system may treat gains on the underlying as taxable, but losses on the derivative that is hedging the underlying instrument as non-deductible or ring-fenced.[45]

In these cases, a pre-tax hedge may not provide a full hedge on a post-tax basis if the hedged item and the hedge are treated differently for tax purposes.[46] On the other hand, insufficient or asymmetric hedging provisions may also lead to unwanted tax arbitrage opportunities for taxpayers.[47] Hedging rules that only consider the pre-tax position of the taxpayer may lead to taxation results where the taxpayer profits from tax-free gains on an asset that are overcompensated by tax-deductible losses from the hedge. Thus, domestic tax legislators have to decide, from a policy point of view, whether hedging rules should look at transactions from a pre-tax perspective or from a post-tax perspective.

New issues arise in the context of hedging of cryptoassets with crypto derivatives, particularly in relation to the hedge effectiveness of the hedge. Those problems will be discussed in the context of Chapter 7 §7.06.

§3.05 PROBLEM 5: TAXATION OF STRUCTURED PRODUCTS AND HYBRID INSTRUMENTS

Apart from the issue of synthetic replication of financial instruments' payoffs by using derivatives, or vice versa,[48] derivatives challenge tax systems if they are components of structured financial instruments.

In Chapter 8 §8.01, the definition of structured products for tax purposes is discussed, and their distinction from other non-structured financial instruments, in particular, hybrid instruments, is highlighted. Chapter 8 §8.01 to §8.08, deals with the application of an integration approach versus a bifurcation approach to structured products and hybrid instruments for tax purposes.

Both problems will be formulated below under [A] and [B].

45. This is the case in Germany where losses from derivatives that are not hedging the ordinary business of the taxpayer are treated as ring-fenced losses that cannot be offset against other income. *See* s. 15 para. 4 sent. 3 to 5 ITA. The loss ring-fencing provisions, however, do not apply to banks, credit institutions and financial services, if the transaction forms a part of the regular business of the taxpayer.
46. *See* Neighbour (2001) 5, who explains the negative outcome of a pre-tax hedge at the example of a currency forward contract, where the tax authorities may tax an FX profit, although the taxpayer has incurred a net FX loss.
47. The taxpayer may be able to 'cherry-pick' and choose a 'non-hedging' tax treatment so that gains of the underlying shares are treated as tax-exempt and losses on the derivative that is hedging the shares are tax-deductible, while he would be able to apply symmetric 'hedging' tax treatment in case of losses on the underlying shares and gains on the derivative.
48. *See* Ch. 2 §2.02[B][1].

[A] Defining Structured Products for Tax Purposes

A definition of structured products for tax purposes is necessary to distinguish these products reliably from non-structured financial instruments, as they may have to be taxed differently. Their taxation treatment will largely depend on whether a tax system decides on an integration approach with regard to structured products, whether it opts for a bifurcation approach of structured products, or a mixture of both.

Consequently, the question of the definition of structured products will come before the question of whether to bifurcate structured products or not.

In particular, structured products have to be distinguished from:

- non-structured derivatives, which are disguised as structured products, sometimes in order to achieve a preferable tax treatment;
- other combinations of financial instruments which do not qualify as structured products; and
- hybrid instruments.

[B] Problems in the Taxation of Structured Products and Hybrid Instruments

Structured products and hybrid instruments pose a particular challenge to tax systems that are largely organised along the traditional categories of equity and debt as their 'derivatives element' makes them difficult to fit into these categories.

Structured products cause problems because they contain several financial instruments in one security that are often taxed differently as a single instrument compared to the taxation of their individual components.

Tax legislators have to decide whether they respect the legal form of structured products, allowing taxation according to their form or if they require a bifurcation into their basic components. If a tax system applies an approach which taxes according to the legal form and not the economic substance, taxation of those instruments according to their true economic content may not be possible.

If a tax system applies an approach which taxes the economic substance, it may be difficult to decide what qualifies as the basic component of such a structured product. Due to the application of the put-call parity formula, any 'possible sets of equivalent combinations of instruments [can be regarded] as an equally valid [economic] representation of the instrument in question'.[49]

Hybrid instruments are a particular challenge to tax systems, which are either fully or partly based on a distinction between debt and equity, as those systems usually incorporate a number of fundamental differences between the tax treatment of instruments qualified as debt or equity.[50] Hybrid instruments may also pose a challenge to tax systems that apply the IFRS (or the old IAS) accounting rules to hybrid

49. Thuronyi (2001b) 5.
50. OECD (2001) para. 64.

instruments for tax purposes but at the same time keep the traditional distinction between equity and debt in their taxation rules for those instruments.

Based on the distinction between equity and debt, tax systems may:

(1) tax dividends favourably compared to interest;
(2) allow tax deductions for debt financing but not for equity financing;
(3) tax interest based on an accruals basis but dividends on a realisation basis;
(4) provide favourable treatment for capital gains on shares compared to capital gains on bonds;
(5) impose withholding tax on dividends but no withholding tax on interest; and
(6) tax debt instruments on an accruals basis, equity instruments on a realisation basis and derivatives on a fair value basis.[51]

Hence, tax rules need to establish exact qualification criteria according to which hybrid instruments are treated as debt or equity for tax purposes. If those rules are insufficient or designed on an arbitrary basis, problems are likely to arise in a domestic as well as in a cross-border context. Those issues will be discussed in Chapter 8.

Crypto structured products and ESG-linked structured products also test if the existing tax legislation is able to cater to those instruments. A discussion related to those questions can be found in Chapter 8 §8.09 and §8.10.

§3.06 PROBLEM 6: DERIVATIVES IN A CROSS-BORDER CONTEXT

Cross-border derivatives transactions can raise various problems, both in the context of domestic tax legislation as well as in a double tax treaty context, as national tax rules and the rules in the respective double tax treaties[52] are often not advanced or detailed enough to deal with the taxation of derivatives in an international context.

This work focuses only on cross-border taxation problems where derivatives raise new issues. As transfer pricing issues are outside the scope of this work,[53] only cross-border derivatives transactions between unrelated parties will be discussed.

In outbound cases, domestic companies enter into derivatives with non-residents. As a resident company will normally be subject to tax on its worldwide income, tax issues may arise in the context of the calculation of this income and a possible limitation of an offset of domestic income against 'foreign source' losses.[54] Furthermore, where the source state retains its full or restricted right to tax derivatives income, domestic and/or tax treaty rules will determine whether the jurisdiction of

51. *Ibid.*
52. Many double taxation conventions between two states were signed more than thirty years ago and thus cannot deal sufficiently with the specific problems in the context of derivative contracts.
53. *See* Introduction.
54. Germany has introduced such a per-country limitation in its domestic tax law for the calculation of foreign source income in ss 34c and 34d Income Tax Act (ITA).

residence of the taxpayer is required to provide unilateral or double tax treaty relief from juridical double taxation either by way of credit[55] or exemption[56] on these payments.[57]

A discussion of these provisions would go beyond the scope of this work as these problems raise questions of a general nature and are not specific issues in the context of derivatives. That leaves three main issues to analyse in the taxation of derivatives in a cross-border context:

(1) allocation of taxing rights between the source and the resident state and the application of withholding taxes in the source country ('inbound cases');
(2) application of the 'beneficial ownership' concept in complex transactions that use derivatives to shift income or risks and rewards of assets; and
(3) international qualification conflicts arising in the context of hybrid instruments.

Cross-border taxation issues in the context of cryptoassets have not been dealt with in this work, partly because no withholding tax is applied to cryptoassets and partly because beneficial ownership issues and international qualification conflicts have not been widely reported in the context of cryptoassets. The author believes that those issues may become more prominent in the future when tax authorities start negotiating whether profits from cryptoassets should be attributed to the resident or the source country.

[A] Derivatives in the Context of Withholding Taxes

Cross-border derivatives transactions have raised several new issues with regard to the application of withholding tax rules in the source country.[58] Unilateral source tax rules will determine whether a country imposes withholding taxes on cross-border derivatives payments.[59]

Source taxation rules in double tax treaties will describe the ultimate limit up to which the source country will be permitted to impose withholding taxes on these payments.[60] In the residence state, these rules give guidance on whether a jurisdiction is required to provide relief from double taxation through credit or exemption.

Significant constraints exist at a cross-border level in imposing withholding taxes on income from derivatives.[61] In a domestic context, source countries usually tax

55. Article 23B OECD Model.
56. Article 23A OECD Model.
57. Philip Baker, *Double Tax Conventions: A Manual on the Model Tax Convention on Income and on Capital* (Sweet & Maxwell Release 23, December 2012) Art. 23, 23B.01; OECD (2001) para. 59.
58. OECD (2001) para. 59.
59. *Ibid.*, para. 59.
60. This is subject to the exception that the treaty is amended, replaced or overridden by the source state. *See* Baker (2012) B.10.
61. Thuronyi (2001a) 268.

non-residents only at a flat-rate withholding tax on traditional categories of payments, such as interest, dividends and royalties.[62] Withholding taxes usually do not apply to derivatives due to a lack of domestic tax provisions levying withholding taxes on derivatives.[63]

Absent of legislative provisions, national tax legislators will struggle to apply their domestic tax rules to payment streams received by taxpayers from derivatives as these payment streams can often not be categorised as falling under the traditional categories of income. Tax policy concerns exist on levying withholding taxes on income from derivatives as payments under some derivatives 'may not be closely correlated with the amount of income actually earned'.[64]

Thuronyi and *Neighbour* argue that if withholding tax was imposed on derivatives income, it may hinder taxpayers from entering into derivatives because of punitive taxation on this income.[65] Likewise, the OECD considers withholding on a gross basis inappropriate in these cases.[66]

In a cross-border context, source countries face problems as to whether they can tax derivatives income and gains under their treaties.[67] But even if they are permitted to levy withholding taxes on derivatives under their negotiated treaties, qualification conflicts on the specific income may still arise.

First, derivatives income may not be regarded as income from interest or dividends under the treaty.[68] For example, if the income arose from interest rate swaps or derivatives paying 'manufactured' dividend payment streams, such as dividends swaps, this income is likely to be attributed to capital gains, business income or other income.[69] Thus, withholding tax may not be levied by the source state as its right to tax would be denied because the treaty categories 'capital gains', 'business income' or 'other income' are generally taxable only in the resident country under the OECD Model, in the absence of any different provisions in the specific tax treaty.

Second, different tax legislators may interpret differently whether certain income from a derivative contract falls within the category of interest, dividends, capital gains, business income or other income in their domestic law. Thus, qualification conflicts in the context of withholding taxes may arise in cross-border transactions if one country

62. Richard Vann, 'Chapter 18, International Aspects of Income Tax' in Victor Thuronyi (ed.), *Tax Law Design and Drafting*, vol. 2 (International Monetary Fund 1998) 45.
63. OECD (2001) para. 60; Thuronyi (2001a) 270; Thuronyi (2001b) 3.
64. Thuronyi (2001b) 3.
65. *Ibid.*, 3; *also* Neighbour (2001) 6.
66. OECD (2001) para. 60.
67. OECD, *Addressing Base Erosion and Profit Shifting* (OECD Publishing, 2013) 41.
68. Explicitly with regard to interest rate swaps and other 'non-traditional financial instruments': Baker (2012) 11B-08; Neighbour (2001) 6; Thuronyi (2001b) 10-11; Klaus Vogel and Morris Lehner (eds), *Doppelbesteuerungsabkommen* (7th edn, 2021) Art. 11, para. 74.

    Differentiating: OECD, Model Tax Convention on Income and on Capital 2017 (Full Version), Commentary on Art. 11, II, para. 3, 21.1 suggesting that payments under an interest rate swap may – as an exception – qualify as 'interest' under Art. 11 OECD Model based on anti-avoidance considerations, such as the substance over form approach.
69. Thuronyi (2001a) 268ff.

qualifies the payments made as interest or dividends and the other country qualifies the same payments as derivatives income.[70]

Example 12:

Company A may enter into a loan in a foreign currency in order to buy products in this currency for its business. Under the loan contract, it has to pay an interest amount of, say, 5% per annum in foreign currency to Bank B, which is resident in another country. If unhedged, Company A bears the risks both with regard to a change in exchange rates as well as to a change in interest rates.

Company A may want to enter either into an interest rate swap with Bank B or a foreign third party to hedge the interest rate risk and a currency swap to hedge the currency risk in relation to the interest payments and the repayment of the redemption amount. Alternatively, Company A may enter into a cross-currency interest rate swap to hedge both risks with one instrument.

If the source state decides to qualify the payments received by Company A under the interest swap or even under the cross-currency swap as interest payments, this income may be subject to withholding taxes in the source state.

The residence state may not provide for unilateral relief or relief under the double tax treaty by disallowing a deduction for the foreign tax withheld in the source state. As a result, Company A may find itself in a position where the swap does not fully hedge the interest or currency risks under the loan on a post-tax basis. If double tax treaties come into effect, both countries might be able to solve the problem by finding a common understanding, by way of the Mutual Agreement Procedure, whether any form of derivatives payments should fall within the definition of interest or not.

Third, due to the difficulties in applying withholding taxes on derivatives, these instruments have been frequently used to circumvent withholding taxes on interest or dividends, with the counterparties entering into interest rate swaps, forwards or dividend swaps instead.[71]

[B] Ownership Issues

Both in a domestic and a cross-border context, it is essential to establish ownership for tax purposes in order to determine who is taxable in relation to certain income and who

70. Unsolved qualification conflicts when applying the tax treaty to derivatives income are in the author's view, less likely in cases where the respective article in the treaty provides for an exhaustive definition of income, such as Art. 11 OECD Model on interest, than in cases where no such exhaustive definition exists, as in the case of Art. 10 OECD Model (dividends).
71. OECD (2013b) 41.

can deduct the respective losses.[72] Profits and losses are usually recognised when a transfer of ownership takes place.

The question of beneficial ownership is intertwined with the question of withholding taxes. Under most countries' domestic tax rules and the OECD Model, the imposition of withholding taxes on income from dividends, interest and royalties is based on who the beneficial owner of the income is and where they are resident.[73]

Derivatives can upset the traditional criterion of beneficial ownership in certain scenarios.

First, derivatives make it possible to fully or only partly *transfer the risks and rewards* of economic ownership *without the actual transfer of the legal ownership*,[74] for example, by using equity swaps or total return swaps (TRS).

> *Example 13:*
>
> Company A holds foreign government bonds as an investment of surplus cash. As it believes that the bonds will not further appreciate in value as yields on the bonds have already been low, it hedges its exposure against the bonds with a three-year cash-settled TRS entered into with Bank B. Under the TRS, Company A pays Bank B any increase in the value of the bond and any interest received, and Company A receives from Bank B any decrease in the value of the bond and European Inter-bank Offered Rate (EURIBOR)- or Secured Overnight Financing Rate (SOFR)-based interest payments.[75]

Depending on the exact criteria applied, the question of whether the derivative is cash or physically settled may or may not be decisive for the purposes of determining the transfer of beneficial ownership.

> *Example 14:*
>
> As above, Company A enters into a physically settled TRS with Bank B, under which Company A pays Bank B any coupons received during the term and receives SOFR-based interest. At maturity of the swap, any appreciation or depreciation in the value of the bonds is settled due to the delivery of the bonds to Bank B.

In the above cases, both at the level of the domestic tax system and at the tax treaty level, criteria have to be established under which it can be determined whether

72. OECD (2001) para. 75.
73. In the OECD Model, Art. 10(2), Art. 11(4) as well as Art. 12(3) refer to the beneficial ownership concept.
74. OECD (2001) para. 77.
75. Hull (2006) 515.

and when beneficial ownership passes and whether the beneficial owner becomes taxable or whether the legal owner remains taxable until maturity of the derivative. Chapter 9 deals with the beneficial ownership issues in the context of derivatives and particularly discusses the Swiss beneficial ownership cases, namely the *Swiss Swaps* case,[76] the *SMI Futures* case,[77] the *Single Stock Futures* case[78] and also briefly the *A Plc v. Swiss Tax Administration* case.[79]

Second, in transactions where legal ownership of a financial asset or financial liability passed, derivatives can be used to ensure that economic exposure in relation to the financial asset or liability is retained.

Example 15:

Company A wants to transfer legal ownership of certain illiquid bonds to Bank B in order to optimise its tax position on the coupons. Company A sells the bonds to Bank B and receives cash.

As Company A wants to retain market exposure to the bonds, it enters with Bank B into a cash-settled three-year TRS under which it will receive coupons and any value appreciation in the bonds, and it will pay any depreciation of value in the bonds and a European Inter-bank Offered Rate (EURIBOR)-based interest payment to Bank B.

Bank B will receive the bond coupons free of withholding tax as it is resident in the country where the bonds are issued.

At maturity, Bank B will sell the bonds in a bilateral transaction - OTC - to Broker C. Company A will simultaneously buy the bonds from Broker C, thereby again ending up with the bonds after the swap has matured.

Again, criteria should be established at both the national and the tax treaty levels that determine whether Company A has retained the beneficial ownership of the bonds by selling the bonds and entering into the TRS with Bank B or whether both legal and beneficial ownership of the bonds has been transferred to Bank B.

---

76. Swiss Federal Supreme Court (Bundesgericht) decision of 5 May 2015, 2C_364/2012 and 2C_377/2012 (Swiss Swaps Case), Re Swiss Swaps Case I/A in 18 ITLR, 138; *see also* Oktavia Weidmann, *Beneficial Ownership and Derivatives: An Analysis of the Decision of the Swiss Federal Supreme Court Concerning Total Return Swaps*, (2016) 44(8 & 9) Intertax 620-641 DOI: 10.54648/taxi2016051.
77. Swiss Federal Supreme Court (Bundesgericht) decision of 5 May 2015, 2C_895/2012 (*SMI Futures* case), *see also* Oktavia Weidmann, *Beneficial Ownership and Derivatives: Has the Swiss Federal Supreme Court Decision in the SMI Futures Case Put an End to Cash-Futures Arbitrage?* (2017) 45(3) Intertax 229-253 DOI: 10.54648/taxi2017019.
78. *Swiss Federal Supreme Court (Bundesgericht) decision of 2nd October 2015, 2C_383/2013 (Single Stock Futures case)* (hereinafter: Federal Supreme Court, 2C_383/2013). For a brief description of the overturned decision of the Federal Administrative Court, *see* Ch. 9; *also* Peter Hongler, *New Swiss Court Decision on Hedged Equity Investments*, (2013) 71(2) Tax Notes International 155.
79. Swiss Federal Supreme Court, 2C_880/2018, decision of 19 May 2020, *A Plc v. Swiss Tax Administration* in 23 ITLR, 864.

Third, tax systems may apply different concepts to attribute income or losses, or have different domestic concepts of beneficial ownership, which they also apply when interpreting a tax treaty.[80]

For example, if one country applies the concept of legal ownership, whereas the other country applies a concept of beneficial ownership in its tax laws, qualification conflicts can arise, and it is possible that income or an asset is attributed to more than one owner.

[C] Cross-Border Qualification Conflicts and Hybrid Instruments

International qualification conflicts may arise in the context of hybrid instruments if those instruments are qualified as equity by the tax rules of one country and as debt by the other.[81] The jurisdiction of the issuer may look at the legal form of the hybrid instrument and treat it as debt, thus allowing an interest deduction that can be used to offset other income of the issuer.[82] In contrast, the jurisdiction of the recipient may treat the hybrid instrument as equity, which is given favourable tax treatment resulting in tax-free dividends or capital gains for the recipient,[83] either by way of domestic or treaty participation exemption for dividends.[84] In certain cases, these qualification conflicts are not solved by applying a tax treaty, for example, because the definition of dividend is not exhaustive in the treaty but is based on how the national tax law of the recipient state would treat the income.[85]

Thus, even if domestic tax systems make no distinction in the tax treatment of debt and equity, qualification conflicts may still arise in a cross-border context and may not be solved by a tax treaty, thus providing taxpayers with an opportunity to avoid taxes using hybrid instruments.

§3.07 PROBLEM 7: TAX AVOIDANCE RELATING TO DERIVATIVES AND CRYPTOASSETS AND APPLICABLE ANTI-AVOIDANCE LEGISLATION

The problem of efficient tax avoidance legislation applying to avoidance arrangements and abusive tax arbitrage schemes arises in the context of domestic and cross-border

80. *See* Art. 3(2) OECD Model on the general rule of interpretation of terms used in the Model but not defined therein; *also* Baker (2012) Art. 3, 3C.13.1.
81. Thuronyi (2001a) 265.
82. Example taken from: OECD (1994) Appendix II, 101ff.; *see also* OECD (2001) paras 64ff.; Thuronyi (2001b) 7; Thuronyi (2001a) 265.
83. Thuronyi (2001b) 7.
84. Thuronyi (2001a) 265.
85. In the OECD Model, coupons from convertible bonds are treated as interest within the meaning of Art. 11 para. 3. *See* OECD Model (2017), Commentary on Art. 10, para. 24; Baker (2012) Arts 10, 10B-21. In contrast, Germany treats coupons received from convertible bonds in most of its treaties as dividend income within the meaning of Art. 10 para. 3, thereby addressing the qualification conflict at a treaty level. *See* Franz Wassermeyer, *Doppelbesteuerung, Kommentar zu allen deutschen Doppelbesteuerungsabkommen*, vol. 1 (89th edn, Beck Verlag, August 2022) Art. 11 Zinsen, Eigene Kommentierung, para. 85 (158th issue).

derivatives transactions. Tax arbitrage is defined by the OECD as 'taking advantage of differences in the tax treatment, either of persons undertaking transactions or of the transactions themselves'.[86]

Tax arbitrage opportunities may arise either as a result of the asymmetries within the domestic tax system itself, as cross-border qualification conflicts between tax systems, or as a consequence of a special tax regime applying to persons entering into the transactions, such as banks or insurance companies.[87]

In the academic literature, international tax arbitrage has been defined as 'the exploit[ation of] differences between the tax system[s] of two different jurisdictions to minimise the taxes paid to either or both'.[88]

Derivatives provide a particular challenge to tax systems and expand opportunities for tax arbitrage.[89] Tax benefits can be achieved in various circumstances by taking advantage of differences in the tax treatment of persons or categories of income. Significant tax avoidance opportunities may arise in the following contexts:

(1) Conversion of normal business income or interest into capital gains:

Taxpayers may convert one form of income of a financial asset into another form of income or into capital gains by replicating the economic payoff of the financial asset or its income streams with the help of derivatives to achieve the tax-efficient outcome for their investment and its proceeds.

(2) Transactions that generate tax-free capital gains and tax-deductible losses:

By using and combining derivatives with other financial instruments, it may be possible in a domestic context to achieve a tax deduction on one leg of the structured transaction that can be offset against other income and, at the same time, generate tax-free income on the other leg of the transaction without having significant economic or financial effects apart from those tax benefits.

(3) Conversion of restricted losses into offsetable losses:

Taxpayers may be able to convert ring-fenced losses into fully offsetable losses by using derivatives strategies that create corresponding gains and losses but do not significantly increase the market risk of the taxpayer.

(4) Transactions that allow shifting market risk from the taxpayer to the Revenue:

Taxpayers may enter into risk transfer schemes that allow them to profit from tax-free gains on an asset that are overcompensated by tax-deductible losses from the hedge, thereby shifting the risk in the asset from the taxpayer to the Revenue.[90]

86. OECD (2001) para. 84.
87. *Ibid.*
88. Reuven Avi-Yonah, 'Commentary (Response to Article by H. David Rosenbloom)' (2000) 53 Tax Law Review 167, 167, referring to a definition provided by David Rosenbloom, International Tax Arbitrage, (2000) 53 Tax Law Review, 137.
89. OECD (2001) para. 85.
90. Risk transfer schemes will be discussed in Chs 7 and 10 of this work.

(5) Tax transactions benefiting from qualification conflicts:

It may be possible for a taxpayer to receive a deduction for the derivatives payments in his residence state and for the receiver of the payments to obtain the income tax-free because of a different qualification of that income in both states. Likewise, it may be possible to achieve tax benefits due to qualification conflicts arising in the context of hybrid instruments.[91]

(6) Dividend tax arbitrage using derivatives:

Cross-border derivatives transactions are often used as a means of tax arbitrage to avoid withholding taxes on interest and dividends because the legal form is decisive in the context of withholding taxes.[92]

Not only specific anti-avoidance rules, regime anti-avoidance rules and GAARs, as well as disclosure rules, but also the general design of a tax system will have an impact on whether a tax system can strike a balance between (1) dealing effectively with many forms of domestic and cross-border tax arbitrage,[93] and (2) providing taxpayers legal certainty with regard to their tax affairs by upholding the rule of law in dealing with those tax avoidance schemes.

In the context of cryptoassets, the problem of a deduction of impairment losses has arisen recently as the tax write-down is not rectified until the disposal of the cryptoassets, thus enabling taxpayers to enjoy a tax deferral of gains as those can be offset against cryptoasset impairment losses. Chapter 10 will deal with this tax avoidance issue.

91. *Neighbour* mentions qualification conflicts for hybrid instruments qualifying as debt in one country and equity in the other; *see* Neighbour (1997) 933; *also* Thuronyi (2001b) 7.
92. Thuronyi (2001b) 2.
93. OECD (2001) paras 149-154; Laukkanen (2007) 249.

CHAPTER 4
Defining Derivatives for Tax Purposes

Accordingly, the most important point to stress is that we should not, like sheep, follow the herd of creatures in front of us, making our way where others go, not where we ought to go.

— Lucius Annaeus Seneca, *Dialogs and Essays, On the Happy Life, To Gallio*

§4.01 FRAMING THE PROBLEM

Derivatives exist in a large variety of different forms, and new derivatives are frequently invented.[1] They often, however, do not fit easily into the definition of derivatives provided by the tax legislation.[2] Hence, national legislators need to develop a definition of derivative contracts that has the capacity to deal with newly emerging instruments, thereby giving certainty to the capital markets, but, at the same time, can prevent tax avoidance made possible by financial engineering techniques.[3]

For example, with the rise of cryptoassets, one has seen the emergence of crypto derivatives, including futures, options, contracts for differences (CFDs), perpetual swaps and swaps on cryptoassets.[4] They exist in an exchange-traded form or as OTC contracts.

Similarly, ESG derivatives have only emerged in recent years.

In this chapter, the author will first outline common concepts used to define derivatives for tax purposes.

1. Hull (2018) 1; Warren (1993) 461.
2. Thuronyi (2001b) 4, questions to which extent some 'new financial instruments' can be appropriately defined in the tax laws. David Weisbach, 'Colloquium on Financial Instruments: Tax Responses to Financial Contract Innovation' (2005) 50 Tax Law Review 491 suggests that 'tax rules cannot keep pace with the creation of new financial products'.
3. Edgar (2000b) 290; Neighbour (1997) 933; Thuronyi (2001a) 262.
4. Delta Exchange, *Home of Crypto Options*, https://www.delta.exchange, accessed 5 July 2023.

Second, the author will analyse and compare the specific definitions of derivatives used in the UK and German tax legislation.

Third, the different approaches that countries like Switzerland and the US have adopted to define derivatives for tax purposes will be summarised, and the suggestions made to define derivatives in the academic literature will be discussed.

Fourth, the author will investigate if the accounting definition of derivatives provided in IFRS 9 could be sufficient to define them for tax purposes.

Finally, in the solutions part of the chapter, the author will develop a comprehensive definition of derivatives for tax purposes and present it as an alternative to the existing domestic definitions in the UK and Germany. In the context of Chapter 4, the author also investigates how the legislator should categorise crypto derivatives and the recently emerged ESG derivatives for tax purposes.

§4.02 COMMON APPROACHES IN DEFINING DERIVATIVES FOR TAX PURPOSES

One can distinguish various approaches to defining derivatives in domestic tax legislation:

(1) the enumerative approach;
(2) the abstract or abstract-prescriptive approach;
(3) the policy-based or principles-based approach;
(4) the borrowing from other legislation approach; and
(5) the approach which applies the economic definition of derivatives.

(1) The *enumerative approach* does not define derivatives comprehensively based on established definitional criteria but simply states the various forms of derivatives, such as options, futures and swaps, and may also list the various underlyings to define the scope of the term.
(2) The *abstract or abstract-prescriptive approach* contains a specific list of self-contained requirements or features that must be met for a derivative to qualify; if such requirements are not met, the derivative would not be taxed under the specific tax legislation. The instrument may, however, fall into another taxation category.
(3) A *policy-based or principles-based approach* focuses on the intended outcome of the law.[5] The approach 'aims to produce law expressed in such principles', whereas the principle 'specifies the outcome rather than the mechanism that

5. Greg Pinder, 'The Coherent Principles Approach to Tax Law Design' (2005) Economic Round-Up, 75-90, at 78, https://treasury.gov.au/publication/economic-roundup-autumn-2005/the-coherent-principles-approach-to-tax-law-design, accessed 2 January 2023.
For a discussion of principle-based approaches in relation to UK tax law: Judith Freedman, 'Improving (Not Perfecting) Tax Legislation: Rules and Principles Revisited' (2010) BTR 717.

achieves it'.[6] The form of a contract is not overly important for an instrument to qualify as a derivative, but the economic substance of a transaction is decisive.

(4) The *borrowing from other legislation approach* simply borrows the definition of a derivative from other legislation, such as accounting or securities law, without considering any requirements or purposes of a definition of derivatives in the tax legislation.

(5) The *economic definition approach* simply uses the economic definition of derivatives to define these instruments for tax purposes. In many cases, this approach will be combined with the *borrowing from other legislation approach* and the *enumerative approach.*

§4.03 DEFINITIONS OF DERIVATIVES FOR TAX PURPOSES IN THE UK AND GERMANY

The following subchapter analyses and compares the different approaches adopted in defining derivatives in the tax legislation of the UK and Germany.

[A] The UK Corporate Tax Definition Applying to Derivative Contracts

With respect to corporate taxpayers,[7] the UK legislator has opted for an approach of integrating a separate set of rules into UK tax law to deal with the taxation of derivatives comprehensively.[8] CTA 2009, s. 571(1) states that 'all profits arising to a company from its derivative contracts are chargeable to corporation tax as income in accordance with [CTA 2009, Part 7]'.[9] The *derivative contracts regime* of Part 7 applies to both single derivative contracts and certain embedded derivatives which are bifurcated from a *loan relationship* host contract under UK GAAP[10] or international accounting standards.[11]

6. Pinder (2005) 78.
7. Only derivatives entered into by companies are subject to the provisions of CTA 2009, Part 7; CTA 2009, s. 578(1). *See* Ghosh, Johnson and Miller (2022) [E2.61] (issue 28); Southern (2017) para. 13.3.
8. Ghosh, Johnson and Miller (2022) [E2.34] (issue 28); Southern (2017) para. 13.3.
9. CTA 2009, s. 571(1).
   FA 2002, Schedule 26, formerly applicable to *derivative contracts* has been substituted by CTA 2009, Part 7 in the course of the Tax Law Rewrite project. It can be presumed that consolidation acts, such as CTA 2009 Part 7 do not change the pre-existing law as such.
   See Beswick v. Beswick [1968] AC 58 (HL) 73; HMRC, *Corporation Tax Act, Explanatory Notes* (2009): 'The Act does not generally change the meaning of the law when rewriting it.'; *also* Ghosh, Johnson and Miller (2022) [E2.27] (issue 28).
10. UK GAAP is the abbreviation for UK *Generally Accepted Accounting Practice,* as laid down in FRS 100 to FRS 102.
   'FRS 100 Application of Financial Reporting Requirements sets out a new financial reporting regime for UK entities effective from 1 January 2015. It explains which standards apply to which entity, when an entity can apply the reduced disclosure framework, and when an entity should follow a SORP.' *See* ICAEW, *FRS 100 Application of Financial Reporting Requirements,* https://www.icaew.com/technical/financial-reporting/uk-gaap/frs-100-application-of-financial-reporting-requirements, accessed 8 July 2023.

To qualify as a derivative contract under CTA 2009, Part 7, a contract must satisfy three tests under CTA 2009, Part 7:[12]

(1) It must be a 'relevant contract'.[13]
(2) It satisfies the 'accounting conditions' for the accounting period in question,[14] or if it does not meet the 'accounting conditions', it is a commodity-based derivative or certain type of contract for differences.[15]
(3) It must not be excluded from being a derivative contract by virtue of its underlying subject matter[16] or by any other provision of CTA 2009.[17]

[1] Relevant Contract

A derivative contract is a *relevant contract* within the scope of CTA 2009, Part 7 if it qualifies as an option,[18] a future[19] or a contract for differences (CFD).[20]

All three definitions have a wide meaning. The two conditions, namely the 'accounting conditions' and 'the exclusions', narrow down the scope of a derivative contract.[21]

One has to distinguish between options and futures, on the one hand, and CFDs, on the other, because there are differences in the taxation of those instruments.[22]

FRS 101 is a reduced disclosure framework that is available to 'UK qualifying subsidiaries and parent companies that otherwise apply the recognition, measurements and disclosure requirements of EU-adopted IFRS.' *See* ICAEW, *FRS 101 Reduced Disclosure Framework*, https://www.icaew.com/technical/financial-reporting/uk-gaap/frs-101-reduced-disclosure-framework, accessed 8 July 2023.

'FRS 102 is the principal accounting standard in the UK financial reporting regime. It sets out the financial reporting requirements for entities that are not applying adopted IFRS, FRS 101 or FRS 105.' *See* ICAEW, *FRS 102 The Financial Reporting Standard applicable in the UK and Republic of Ireland*, https://www.icaew.com/technical/financial-reporting/uk-gaap/frs-102-the-financial-reporting-standard, accessed 8 July 2023.

11. CTA 2009, s. 585(1)-(3). *See* Southern (2017) para. 13.2; Bramwell et al. (2023) H 1.2.4 (Release 41).
12. CTA 2009, s. 576(1)(a)-(c).
13. CTA 2009, ss 576(1)(a), 577(1).
14. CTA 2009, s. 579(1).
15. CTA 2009, s. 579(2)(a), (b).
16. CTA 2009, s. 589.
17. CTA 2009, s. 576(1)(a)-(c). *See* Ghosh, Johnson and Miller (2022) [E2.96]-[E2.120] (issue 28); Southern (2017) para. 13.12.
18. CTA 2009, s. 580(1).
19. CTA 2009, s. 581(1).
20. CTA 2009, ss 577(1), 582. *Compare* Bramwell et al. (2023) H 1.2.2. (Release 41).
21. Ghosh, Johnson and Miller (2022) [E2.96]-[E2.120] (issue 28) referring to the three tests for a derivative contract.
22. These differences occur, for example, in the context of excluded underlying subject matter, being intangible fixed assets, CTA 2009, s. 589(4). *See* Ch. 5 §5.06[C]. Furthermore, different accounting tests apply to options and futures on land, and CFDs on land. *See* Ch. 4 §4.03[A][2][b].

[a] Futures

A future is defined in the CTA 2009, Part 7 as:

> a contract for the sale of property under which delivery is to be made:
>
> - at a future date agreed when the contract is made; and
> - at a price so agreed.[23]

Again, this definition has a very wide scope and includes forwards, i.e., contracts which are non-standardised OTC transactions.[24] It contrasts with the economic definition of a future where a distinction between exchange-traded futures and OTC forwards is made.[25]

Because the scope of the definition is wide, one might argue that physically settled (equity) price swaps,[26] as well as physically settled total return (equity) swaps,[27] would fall under the wording of the definition of future under CTA 2009, section 581.

Example 16:

Party A enters into a physically settled total return equity swap with Party B over three years. The underlying shares are shares of Company Z. Under the swap, Party A will pay Party B any dividends when received, and Party B will periodically pay Party A interest payments.

At maturity, Party A will deliver shares in Company Z to Party B. Thus, Party B will be economically exposed to the price of the shares during the term of the swap without physically holding the shares until maturity of the swap.

One could provide the following arguments in favour of including a physically settled equity swap into the definition of a future under CTA 2009, section 581, namely:

(1) The physically settled equity swap would qualify as a future under CTA 2009, section 581(1) because, at inception, both the price of the shares and the date of delivery of the equities have been agreed upon.

23. CTA 2009, s. 581(1).
24. *See* Statement of Practice 03/02 which indicates the wide range of the term; *also* Ghosh, Johnson and Miller (2022) [E2.145] (issue 28); Southern (2017) para. 13.17.
25. Hull (2006) 6.
26. Under an equity price swap, one party owes any upside movement of the shares to the other party and has the right to get expensed for any downside movement of the shares. Because the swap is physically settled at maturity, the obligations are fulfilled by delivery of the underlying instrument. No dividend payments are made under a price swap.
27. Under a total return equity swap, not only the upside or downside movement of the shares is exchanged under the swap, but any dividends received and interest paid. Thus, even in case of physical settlement of the swaps, (manufactured) dividend and interest payments will be made periodically during the term of the swap.

(2) CTA 2009, section 581(3)(ii) only requires an instrument to be excluded from being a future if 'a cash payment in respect of all that party's obligations to the other under the contract [is made]'.

Thus, CTA 2009, section 581(3)(ii) would not preclude a physically settled equity swap from qualifying as a future, as only a cash payment with regard to dividends and interest is made, but no other payments with regard to price movements of the shares are made because the price fluctuations of the shares are not mirrored through a cash payment but by delivery of the underlying shares.

The *Corporate Finance Manual*[28] does not state whether a physically settled equity swap would qualify as a future or, rather, as a CFD.

Because of this uncertainty, taxpayers may, in practice, either prefer to enter into a cash-settled swap or try to document a physically settled total return equity swap as a forward under ISDA, with dividend payments and interest payments estimated upfront and included in the purchase price of the shares and an adjustment clause for the real dividends and interest.[29]

To avoid these uncertainties, it would, in the author's view, be preferable to redraft the definition of a future to explicitly exclude those physically settled equity swaps from the definition of a future under CTA 2009, section 581 and explicitly include them in the definition of a CFD.[30]

If that outcome is not preferred, the legislator could explicitly include physically settled swaps into the definition of a future or, as a further policy choice, incorporate an entirely separate definition of those instruments into the law.

[b] Options

The legislation does not define what an option is but only states that it includes a warrant.[31] Hence, the definition of an option will take its normal commercial meaning.[32]

---

28. HMRC, *Corporate Finance Manual* (2016).
29. Whether such documentation under ISDA as a forward instead of a swap really helps to clarify the tax analysis is doubtful. The main element of an equity swap, period dividend and interest payments can only be remodelled as a forward due to approximation of the payments and using an adjustment clause at maturity. In some cases, this may not be what the parties would want economically.
30. *See also* discussion below in Ch. 4 §4.03[A][2][a][iii].
31. CTA 2009, s. 580(1).

    A warrant is a financial instrument that gives the holder the right to subscribe for shares of a company.

    See Simon's Taxes, vol. 5 (Lexis Nexis UK, 2008, Looseleaf) D1.806 (issue 171, December 2022).

    Southern suggests that it 'is immaterial whether the shares or securities to which the holder of the warrant is entitled to subscribe exist or are identifiable', *see* Southern (2017) para. 13.16.
32. Ghosh, Johnson and Miller (2022) [E2.200] (issue 28); *also* Conlon & Aquilino: Principles of Financial Derivatives, *US and International Taxation* (WG&L, Thomson Reuters, Looseleaf, originally published 1999), D1.02[2] (issue December 2022); Southern (2017) para. 13.16.

[c] *Contract for Differences*

A contract for differences (CFD) is defined as:

> a contract for the purpose or pretended purpose of which is to make a profit or avoid a loss by reference to fluctuations in –
> 1. the value or price of property described in the contract, or
> 2. an index or other factor designated in the contract.[33]

The definition of a CFD has a wide meaning in CTA 2009, Part 7.[34]

In the author's opinion, the better arguments support the view that the definition of a CFD includes – in contrast to the definitions of options and futures – both cash- and physically settled CFDs.[35]

Southern suggests:

> FRS 102, paras 12.4-12.5 distinguish between (a) options, forwards and swaps which are to be settled by delivery, and (b) contracts where no delivery is intended. The former are not financial instruments. Hence, options and forwards which are intended to result in delivery of the underlying subject matter will be outside of FRS 102, Section 12 and so will not be derivative contracts, unless they are relevant contracts, which, although not classified as derivative financial instrument for accounting purposes, are, by way of exception to the general rule, brought within the derivatives contract rules.[36]

The Corporate Finance Manual remains silent as to whether the definition of CFDs also includes physically settled contracts.[37] If one would define CFDs only as cash-settled instruments, any physically settled derivatives that would neither qualify as an option nor a future would be excluded from being a 'relevant contract'. One could argue in favour of the idea that the term CFD includes only cash-settled contracts based on the wording of the term *contract for differences*.

The natural meaning of the word may imply that only contracts that pay a difference between the market price and the agreed price are included. However, the 'natural meaning' of the word would not necessarily exclude contracts that allow for physical settlement because the value of these contracts will also be determined by the difference between the market price of the underlying and its agreed settlement price.

The definition of a CFD, like many definitions used in CTA 2009, Part 7, has – in part – been borrowed from the Financial Services and Markets Act (FSMA) 2000

---

33. CTA 2009, s. 582(1).
34. Ghosh, Johnson and Miller (2022) [E2.121] (issue 28).
35. *Ibid.*, [E2.226]-[E2.230] (issue 28) suggest that 'the vast majority of the contracts which relate to indices or other factors will be cash settled even if there is an underlying subject matter which is capable of being delivered. That avoids the difficulties associated with delivering certain types of subject matter and is clearly essential for subject matters which are not capable of delivery. The author however does not stipulate that physically settled CFDs are per se excluded from the definition.
36. Southern (2017) para. 13.24.
37. HMRC, CFM50380.

(Regulated Activities) Order 2001 (SI 2001/544).[38] It has been suggested by the courts with regard to the definition of a CFD used in FSMA 2000 that CFDs only encompass cash-settled instruments and not physically settled contracts.[39] But this view of the courts with regard to the definition in FSMA 2000 does not also have to apply to the definition used in tax law.

In the author's view, it should be considered that the derivatives definition in FSMA and the tax definition in CTA 2009, Part 7 serve completely different purposes. Whereas the definition of a CFD in SI 2001/544 Article 85 serves the purpose of identifying investments,[40] the definition in CTA 2009, section 581(2) is concerned with determining what falls within the taxation base. Thus, the definitions used in both laws may encompass different meanings.

Furthermore, there are various other problems of borrowing from the FSMA 2000 definition when defining CFDs for tax purposes.

SI 2001/544 Article 85(1) refers to:

> rights under –
>
> (a) a contract for differences; *or*
> (b) any other contract the purpose or pretended purpose of which is to secure a profit or avoid a loss in –
>   (i) the value or price of property of any description; or
>   (ii) an index or other factor designated for that purpose in the contract.

The following problems arise:

First, a 'contract for differences' is only mentioned as a phrase in Article 85(1)(a) but not further defined in SI 2001/544 Article 85.

Second, the term 'contract for differences' used in Article 85(1)(a) is likely to be different from 'any other contract' that is defined in Article 85(1)(b).[41]

However, the definition used as a definition of a CFD for tax purposes in CTA 2009, section 582(1) is exactly the definition of 'any other contract' used in Article 85(1)(b) of SI 2001/544.

Third, SI 2001/544 Article 85(2)(a) explicitly excludes physically settled CFDs. The exclusion in Article 85(2)(a) is, however, not part of the definition of a CFD used in CTA 2009, section 582(1), where only the part of the definition in Article 85(1)(b) was truncated from SI 2001/544 and used as a tax definition.

38. *See* David Haworth and James Hollis, 'IFRS and Derivatives Taxation' [March/April 2010] Derivatives and Financial Instruments 23, 24-25; Southern (2017) para. 13.20.
    Although the UK operates an accounts-based system for the taxation of derivatives, the derivative contracts regime has more in common with the FSMA 2000 than with UK GAAP, given the number of divergences between the derivative contracts legislation and UK GAAP, such as the inclusion of commodities (CTA 2009, s. 579(1)(c)), open-ended investment companies and unit trusts (CTA 2009, s. 587) as underlying subject matters.
39. *See* Lord Donaldson in: *City Index Ltd v. Leslie* [1991] 3 All ER 180 with respect to a similar definition in the Financial Services Act 1986.
40. *See* an older version of: David Southern, *Taxation of Loan Relationships and Derivative Contracts* (8th edn, Tottel Publishing 2007) para. 16.17.
41. *See* the exact wording in SI 2001/544, Art. 85(1).

Thus, in contrast to SI 2001/544, the definition in CTA 2009, section 582(1) does not distinguish between cash and physically settled CFDs[42] – *argumentum e contrario* – which leads to the conclusion that the definition in the tax law encompasses both cash and physically settled CFDs.

Although HMRC suggests that the courts in tax cases should be guided by case law related to regulated activities,[43] the better arguments, in the author's view, support a wide tax definition of CFDs in CTA 2009, Part 7, which includes both cash- and physically settled contracts.[44]

In contrast, the definitions of options and futures include only contracts that *also* provide for physical settlement.[45] Accordingly, where the terms of an 'economic' option or future provide for cash settlement only, the contract will be treated as a CFD and not as an option or future,[46] except where the underlying subject matter is foreign currency.[47] In this case, the foreign currency is the property that falls to be delivered under the contract.[48]

As an option or a future is excluded by law from being a CFD,[49] options and futures, on the one hand, and CFDs, on the other, are mutually exclusive.[50]

[2] Accounting Conditions

A relevant contract is not a derivative contract under CTA 2009, section 576 unless it meets the accounting conditions set out in CTA 2009, section 579.[51]

This section narrows down the wide definition of a derivative contract as being a relevant contract by applying the accounting test.[52]

Principally, only those relevant contracts qualify, which are treated as derivatives for accounting purposes for that accounting period.[53]

In addition, certain financial contracts that fail the accounting test only because they require a certain initial net investment equal to comparable spot contracts, such as

42. CTA 2009, s. 582(1). This understanding is based on the natural meaning of the wording used in this section.
43. HMRC, CFM11110.
44. One might however argue that physically settled equity swaps are also caught within the definition of a futures contract (*see* discussion in Ch. 4 §4.03[A][2][a][i]). If one took this position, physically settled equity swaps would not fall under the definition of a CFD as 'futures' are excluded by law from being a CFD, CTA 2009, s. 582(2)(b). It seems however unlikely that this outcome was incorporated intentionally in the legislation by the draftsman of the *derivative contracts regime*. Thus, a clarification of the law seems desirable.
45. CTA 2009, ss 580(2) and 581(3). *See* HMRC, CFM11086; in an older edition *also* Southern (2007) para. 16.16.
46. Ghosh, Johnson and Miller (2022) [E2.211] (issue 28); Southern (2017) para. 13.18.
47. CTA 2009, ss 580(3) and 581(4).
48. HMRC, CFM13212.
49. CTA 2009, s. 582(2)(a), (b).
50. HMRC, CFM50400.
51. Because of the application of an accounting test, the amount being subject to tax under the *derivative contracts regime* mirrors the accounting profit or loss and thereby also its volatility. Whether such a volatility of the tax charge is desirable, is a question of tax policy.
52. Ghosh, Johnson and Miller (2022) [E2.302] (issue 28).
53. CTA 2009, s. 579(1)(a).

pre-paid forwards[54] or deep-in-the-money swaps,[55] are nevertheless included in the definition of a derivative contract under CTA 2009, section 579(1)(b).[56]

A financial contract is treated as a derivative for an accounting period if it is so treated for the purposes of the relevant accounting standard,[57] being FRS 102 or IFRS 9 (if IFRS accounting has been chosen and applied to accounting periods on or after 1 January 2018).[58]

FRS 102, Appendix I (IFRS 9, Appendix A; IAS 39, paragraph 9)[59] defines a derivative as:

> a financial instrument or other contract with all three of the following characteristics:
>
> (a) its value changes in response to the change in a specified interest rate, financial instrument price, commodity price, foreign exchange rate, index of prices or rates, credit rating or credit index, or other variable (sometimes called the 'underlying'), provided in the case of a non-financial variable that the variable is not specific to a party to the contract;
> (b) it requires no initial net investment or an initial net investment that is smaller than would be required for other types of contracts that would be expected to have a similar response to changes in market factors; and
> (c) it is settled at a future date.

The definition used in FRS 102 is identical to the definition of a derivative in IFRS 9, Appendix A and IAS 39, paragraph 9.[60] Hence, a contract that qualifies as a derivative under IFRS 9 or IAS 39 will also satisfy the accounting test under CTA 2009, section 579.

CTA 2009, section 579(2) deems certain relevant contracts to fall within the derivative contracts definition, notwithstanding whether they meet the accounting test of CTA 2009, section 579(1).[61]

Those relevant contracts, which may or may not be derivatives for accounting purposes, include any commodity derivatives[62] and CFDs over certain underlying subject matters, such as land, tangible movable property, intangible fixed assets, weather conditions and creditworthiness.[63]

54. Ghosh, Johnson and Miller (2022) [E2.317]-[E2.330] (issue 28).
55. Southern (2017) para. 13.26.
56. Bramwell et al. (2023) H 1.2.2. (Release 41); Southern (2017) para. 13.23.
57. CTA 2009, s. 579(3).
58. CTA 2009, s. 579(5). For accounting periods starting on or after 1 January 2015, FRS 102 is the relevant UK accounting standard for those companies not using IFRS, FRS 101 or FRSSE. *See* Ch. 6 §6.02[B]. *Compare also* Ghosh, Johnson and Miller (2022) [U1.11] and [B1.1D] (issue 28); Southern (2017) para. 13.23.
59. Southern (2017) 13.23.
60. *See* definition of IAS 39 in Ch. 4 §4.05.
61. Ghosh, Johnson and Miller (2022) [E2.341] (issue 28); Southern (2017) para. 13.26.
62. CTA 2009, s. 579(2)(a) includes commodity futures and options as well as commodity CFDs. Commodities are not defined in the law. Thus, one needs to apply its normal commercial meaning, being all forms of traded commodities, thereby including intangible commodities, such as electricity; *see* HMRC, CFM13086.
63. CTA 2009, s. 579(2)(b)(i)-(v). *See* Bramwell et al. (2023), H 1.2.2 (Release 41). Ghosh, Johnson and Miller (2022) [E2.341] (issue 28); Southern (2017) para. 13.27.

The policy behind the provision of CTA 2009, section 579(2), which includes in its definition derivative contracts over certain underlyings, notwithstanding their accounting treatment, is to ensure coherent taxation of those contracts, regardless of whether they are settled in cash or physically because the kind of settlement would not justify a different tax treatment. Consequently, the anti-avoidance provisions will also apply to those contracts that are physically settled.[64]

> *Example 17:*
>
> A meat-producing company enters into two commodity futures over pork bellies. One contract is to be settled in cash, the other physically. The cash-settled future would qualify as a relevant contract under CTA 2009, section 582(1), being a CFD and satisfying the accounting test as a derivative under FRS 102.
>
> The physically settled future would qualify as a relevant contract under CTA 2009, section 581, but it would fail the accounting test of FRS 102 because FRS 102 does not apply to derivatives that buy or sell non-financial assets when those contracts are held for the purpose of the receipt or delivery of those assets.[65] Hence, CTA 2009, section 579(2) ensures that also the physically settled pork-belly future qualifies as a derivative contract so that both commodity contracts are taxed in the same way.

The accounting tests must be met in each accounting period.[66] A derivative contract may cease being taxed under CTA 2009, Part 7, if it fails the accounting tests.[67]

[3] Underlying Subject Matter Test

In order to further narrow down the definition of derivatives for corporation tax purposes, CTA 2009, section 589 excludes certain derivative contracts[68] that would prima facie qualify as derivatives solely by virtue of their underlying subject matter.[69]

64. Ghosh, Johnson and Miller (2022) [E2.362] (issue 28).
65. FRS 102, Appendix I.
66. CTA 2009, s. 579(1).
67. CTA 2009, s. 662.
68. The exclusion of underlying subject matters has been substantially narrowed down since the introduction of the test by FA 2002, Sch. 26. The original definition in FA 2002, Sch. 26 was subject to several amendments by FA 2004, FA 2005, Statutory Instruments SI 2004/2201, SI 2004/3270, SI 2005/646 and SI 2005/2082, SI2005/3340 and SI 2006/3269. Those changes have effectively expanded the definition of derivatives for tax purposes and certain derivatives, previously excluded, were included in the definition of Sch. 26, such as *property derivatives* (including derivatives on land and tangible movable property) and *embedded derivatives* whose *underlying* subject matter are *shares* or tracking contracts whose *subject matter is land or listed ordinary shares*. Now only few contracts are excluded by the underlying subject matter test. *See* Ch. 6 §6.05[B][1].
69. Ghosh, Johnson and Miller (2022) [E2.381] (issue 28).

Underlying subject matter is defined in CTA 2009, section 583, using different definitions for options, futures and CFDs. Underlying subject matters for options and futures are the underlying property to be delivered,[70] or if a derivative contract is to be delivered, the underlying of this contract.[71]

Underlying subject matters of CFDs are the value of the underlying property[72] or where the payment is determined by reference to an index or factor, the matter by which the index or factor is determined.[73]

> *Example 18:*[74]
>
> A company buys a cash-settled future over the EURO STOXX 50. The value of the future will depend on the movement of the EURO STOXX 50. The contract will qualify as a CFD under CTA 2009, section 582(1) because it is cash settled. The EURO STOXX 50 is an equity index. The underlying subject matter will not be the EURO STOXX 50 index as such, but simply 'shares', being ultimately the matter by reference to which the index is determined (CTA 2009, section 583(4)(b)).[75]

Interest rates, weather conditions and creditworthiness are explicitly included as underlying subject matters of CFDs.[76] However, interest rates are carved out if the terms of a contract only refer to interest rates for the purpose of establishing an amount of money relating purely to the duration of the settlement payment, CTA 2009, section 583(6).[77] For some contracts, the underlying is difficult to determine if the price of the contract depends on more than one subject matter. A derivative contract can have more than one underlying subject matter.[78]

In relation to income from land, shares or unit trusts, the legislation provides that the contract has two underlying subject matters if the price of the derivative contract depends on both changes in the capital value of the underlying and income streams thereof.[79]

---

70. CTA 2009, s. 583(2)(a) and (3)(a).
71. CTA 2009, s. 583(2)(b) and (3)(b).

    In case of such a derivative on a derivative (e.g., an option on a currency option), the underlying will always be the ultimate underlying of the contracts. The derivative itself can never constitute an underlying as such.

    See HMRC, CFM50520; Ghosh, Johnson and Miller (2022) [E2.387] (issue 28).
72. CTA 2009, s. 583(4)(a).
73. CTA 2009, s. 583(4)(b).
74. *See* HMRC, CFM50550, Example 2 that provides an example of a commercial property price index.
75. Note that the cash-settled futures contract, qualifying as a CFD, may not be excluded from the derivative contracts regime unless it meets the conditions set down in CTA 2009, ss 589, 591.
76. CTA 2009, s. 583(5).
77. For example, if an option is to be settled after ten days and the price of the option is increased by applying an interest rate to it for these ten days.
78. HMRC, CFM50520.
79. CTA 2009, s. 583(7).

Example 19:

Company A enters into a forward contract over a total return real property index, whose value is determined both by the changes in the capital value of the real property as well as any rental income received. The underlying subject matters of the forward will be both land and rents in accordance with CTA 2009, section 583(7).[80]

The exclusion of a derivative contract from CTA 2009, Part 7 is based on an underlying subject matter test, which is only fulfilled if the underlying consists wholly of one or more excluded types of subject matter,[81] or if it is treated as consisting wholly of one or more excluded types of subject matter.[82] CTA 2009, sections 589(1)(b), 589(6), 590 also exclude those relevant contracts where the non-excluded underlying subject matter is subordinated or of small value compared to the excluded subject matter.[83]

Example 20:[84]

Company A buys a future over the DAX. The DAX is a total return equity index comprising both capital appreciation of the stocks and dividends. The dividends will constitute a subordinated or small subject matter.[85] Thus, the underlying will only be shares.[86] CTA 2009, section 589(1)(b) takes priority over CTA 2009, section 583(4) and (7).

In case of options or futures, where the underlying subject matter consists in part of excluded property and in part of non-excluded underlying subject matter, the legislation provides for a bifurcation into two contracts.[87]

80. Example taken from: HMRC, CFM50570.
81. CTA 2009, s. 589(1)(a).
82. CTA 2009, s. 589(1)(b).
83. Ghosh, Johnson and Miller (2022) [E2.493] (issue 28). As the terms 'subordinate' and 'small value' used in CTA 2009, s. 590(1)(b)(i) and (ii) are not defined in the legislation, guidance can be found in: HMRC, CFM50580 which states that if the value of the non-excluded underlying subject matter is 5% or less compared to the entire contract, it will be regarded as small.
84. For a similar example in respect to the DAX: HMRC, CFM50590.
85. CTA 2009, s. 589(1)(b).
86. The future may not be excluded from the derivative contracts regime unless it fails to meet the conditions set down in CTA 2009, ss 589 and 591.
87. CTA 2009, s. 593(1) and (2). *See* Simon's Taxes (2022), vol. 5, D1.828 (issue 171), which discusses an example governed by CTA 2009, s. 593, where neither subject matter is subordinate nor of small value. In this example, the contract is divided into its two elements and the amounts are being apportioned to one or the other underlying subject matter, leading to one part of the contract to be taxed under the *derivative contracts regime*, and the other part being taxed outside of it.

The law does not, however, require the bifurcation of the derivative contract if the contract is a CFD. Hence, physically settled options or futures will be treated differently compared to cash-settled options or futures, which would qualify as CFDs.

CTA 2009, section 589 provides the list of excluded contracts by virtue of their underlying subject matter, being:

(1) options and futures on intangible fixed assets;[88]
(2) certain equity derivatives on shares,[89] if they satisfy all conditions laid down in CTA 2009, section 589(2)(b), (3), (5); and
(3) derivative contracts on certain rights of a unit holder under a unit trust scheme.[90]

Only those equity derivatives which have already passed the accounting test of section 579(1) fall under the exclusion of CTA 2009, section 589.

Hence, certain equity derivatives will not qualify as derivative contracts because they already do not fall under the definition of FRS 102.11/IFRS 9, such as derivatives over an interest in a subsidiary and any financial instruments that are *issued*[91] by an entity that meets the definition of an equity instrument in FRS 102.11, including both options and warrants.[92]

Shares as an underlying subject matter are only excluded if they fulfil all of the following criteria, namely:

- one of the conditions A-E set out in section 591;[93]
- they are not designed to produce what is, in substance, a commercial rate of interest on the invested money;[94]
- they are not shares to which section 524 or 526 applies;[95]
- they are not shares in an OEIC to which section 490 applies.[96]

There are principally five main categories of equity derivatives excluded from CTA 2009, Part 7 by CTA 2009, section 591, broadly being:

- contracts that are entered into by an insurance company;[97]

88. CTA 2009, ss 589(2)(a), (4). CFDs on intangible fixed assets are not excluded. CFDs on intangible fixed assets fall under s. 579(2) and therefore will not need to satisfy the accounting definition of s. 579(1).
89. As defined in CTA 2009, s. 710, being 'shares of a company under which an entitlement to receive distributions may arise'. *Compare* Bramwell et al. (2023) H 1.2.2. (Release 41).
90. CTA 2009, s. 589(2)(c), if the unit trust scheme is not a scheme of holdings in OEICs, unit trusts and offshore funds.
91. That carve-out only applies to the issuer, not to the holder of the instrument.
92. Ghosh, Johnson and Miller (2022) [E2.432] (issue 28).
93. CTA 2009, s. 589(5)(a).
94. CTA 2009, s. 589(5)(b).
95. CTA 2009, s. 589(3)(a). CTA 2009, ss 524 and 526 were repealed by FA 2009, s. 48, Sch. 24, para. 8(c)(1) and replaced by Part 6, Chs 2A and 6A but the old reference has not been updated yet.
96. CTA 2009, s. 589(3)(b).
97. Condition A: CTA 2009, s. 591(2).

- contracts that hedge a holding of shares;[98]
- quoted options to subscribe for shares if held for non-trading purposes;[99]
- options or futures to acquire substantial shareholdings, if held otherwise than in the course of activities integral to a trade;[100] and
- contracts that hedge bifurcated loan relationships with embedded derivatives.[101]

[B] Evaluation of the UK Approach to Defining Derivative Contracts

For corporate tax purposes, the UK applies an advanced, yet quite static, approach to defining derivatives, which is based on a three-step test to determine if an instrument qualifies as a derivative contract.[102] However, although the UK definition in corporate tax law can cater for almost all of the existing derivatives, the current definition may, however, not fit newly emerging derivatives due to a mixture of enumerative and prescriptive elements in the definition of derivative contracts.

At first sight, the three-part test appears to suggest an abstract-prescriptive approach to defining derivative contracts. However, it fails in this respect because the abstract definitional criteria which might define a derivative contract for tax purposes are not, in fact, laid down in law.

The first test is simply an enumerative account of the type of derivatives but does not define what a derivative contract is based on more general and abstract definitional criteria. Although the definitions of the different types of derivatives, such as the definitions of the terms 'future' and 'CFD', are economic definitions of these instruments based on prescriptive criteria, they cannot describe the full spectrum of all instruments that may qualify under the term derivative contract. The accounting test simply narrows down the broad categories by asking whether the derivative contract qualifies as a derivative for accounting purposes[103] but does not establish sufficient criteria for defining derivatives for tax purposes.[104] The exclusion of the underlying subject matter simply narrows down the scope of the definition, again only by enumerating certain underlyings, resulting in an exclusion of these derivatives from the definition.

Thus, on the one hand, the various amendments of the derivative contracts legislation have been successful insofar as CTA 2009, Part 7 provides a framework to deal with the taxation of derivatives rather comprehensively. On the other hand, those amendments lead to very complex corporate tax legislation on derivatives due to the enumerative and descriptive character of the law.[105] The application of the different

98. Condition B: CTA 2009, s. 591(3).
99. Condition C: CTA 2009, s. 591(4).
100. Condition D: CTA 2009, s. 591(5).
101. Condition E: CTA 2009, s. 591(6) *See* Ghosh, Johnson and Miller (2022) [E2.437]-[E2.460] (issue 28).
102. *See* Ch. 4 §4.03[A][2].
103. *See* Ch. 4 §4.03[A][2][b].
104. *See* Ch. 4 §4.05 below.
105. *See* HMRC, *Modernising the taxation of corporate debt and derivative contracts* (Consultation document, 2013) para. 1.1, confirming that '[o]ver the years there have been many piecemeal changes to the legislation, arising from changes in commercial practice and accounting

income and capital gains regimes with regard to derivative contracts in the current tax legislation provides a further layer of complexity because it effectively maintains the distinction between income and capital.

The various sets of rules with their distinction between income and capital may potentially cause problems of legal qualification both in the context of domestic and cross-border derivatives transactions.[106]

> *Example 21:*
>
> A simple example is a total return equity swap sold by a UK company to a Swiss company. The swap is regarded as a derivative contract from a UK tax perspective whilst being regarded as a (synthetic) long equity position under Swiss tax law principles, as Switzerland applies an economic substance test.[107]

Further, the aim of the *Tax Law Rewrite* of making 'the direct tax legislation clearer and easier to use'[108] could not be achieved with regard to the derivative contracts legislation because the secondary legislation in the form of statutory instruments has not been incorporated into the CTA 2009, Part 7, and thus is in certain cases still applicable.[109]

The author, therefore, believes that the current rules in defining derivatives for corporate tax purposes should be amended to allow for an abstract-definitional approach which can not only cater to long-established derivatives but also to the recently emerged crypto derivatives, the various forms of ESG derivatives and any new forms of derivatives and underlyings that the market may devise in the future.

[C] The German Definition Applying to 'Derivative Contracts' for Tax Purposes

In Germany, tax authorities have dealt more comprehensively with the taxation of derivatives held by private investors as opposed to businesses and corporates.[110] As the

standards, and in responds to attempts to avoid tax. As a result, the regime has become ever more complex and less coherent'.

106. The possibility of using derivatives structures to take advantage of the differences of tax regulations in separate tax jurisdictions is also mentioned in: Hudson (2008) D1.03[4].
107. *See* Ch. 4 §4.04[A] below.
108. With regard to the Tax Law Rewrite project and its major achievements, *see* HMRC, *Tax Law Rewrite* (2011), https://webarchive.nationalarchives.gov.uk/20100202111102/http://www.hmrc.gov.uk/rewrite/index.htm, accessed 8 August 2023.
109. *Compare* HMRC, Corporate Finance Manual (16 April 2016, updated 20 July 2023), CFM76060 – Other tax rules on corporate finance: change of accounting basis: secondary legislation, https://www.gov.uk/hmrc-internal-manuals/corporate-finance-manual/cfm76060, accessed 8 January 2023, *also* Ghosh, Johnson and Miller (2022) [E2.24] (issue 28).
110. Conlon & Aquilino: Derivatives D 2.01 (issue December 2022).

definition for derivatives applying to private individuals and companies are interlinked, it is important to investigate in some detail how German tax law defines derivatives for individual and business tax purposes. For private individuals, a flat tax regime applies to gains and income from derivative contracts, gains and income from structured products[111] and option premiums received.[112]

[1] *Definition of Derivative Contract Applying to Private Individuals*

Section 20(2) sentence 1 No. 3 Income Tax Act (ITA) deals with the taxation of gains from derivatives held by private individuals. It contains two alternatives[113] but no definition of the term derivative contract. Thus, the concrete definition of the term is subject to an intense debate in the tax literature. It remains uncertain whether the term derivative contract has the same meaning as the term used in the German Securities Trading Act[114] (STA) or whether it has its own meaning for tax purposes.

Financial instruments qualify as derivatives (*Derivate*) within section 2(3) No. 1 to 5 STA if they fall into one of five categories:

1. firm contracts or option contracts in the form of purchases or swaps or in other forms that are to be settled at a future date and whose values are derived directly or indirectly from the price or dimension of an underlying instrument (forward transactions) relating to the following underlying instruments: a) securities or money market instruments, b) foreign exchange, to the extent that the transaction does not meet the conditions set out in Article 10 of Delegated Regulation (EU) 2017/565, or units of account, c) interest rates or other yields, d) indices of the underlying instruments specified in a), b), c) or f), other financial indices or financial measures, e) derivatives or f) allowances, emission reduction units and certified emission reductions within the meaning of section 3 numbers 3, 6 and 16 of the Greenhouse Gas Emissions Trading Act (Treibhausgas-Emissionshandelsgesetz), to the extent that they may be held in the EU emissions trading registry (emission allowances);
2. forward transactions relating to commodities, freight rates, climatic or other physical variables, inflation rates or other economic variables or other assets, indices or measures as underlying instruments, provided that they a) are cash-settled or grant the party to a contract the right to demand cash settlement without this right being contingent on default or another termination event; b) are entered into on an organised market or a multilateral or organised trading liability and are not wholesale energy products within the meaning of subsection 20 that are traded on an organised trading facility and must be physically settled, orc) that have characteristics of other derivative contracts within the meaning of Article 7 of Delegated Regulation (EU) 2017/565 and are not for commercial purposes, and are not spot contracts within the meaning of Article 7 of Delegated Regulation (EU) 2017/565;
3. financial contracts for differences;

111. For a definition, *see* Ch. 8 §8.01.
112. Section 20(1) No. 11 ITA.
113. These alternatives will be discussed in detail below.
114. *Wertpapierhandelsgesetz.*

4. firm contracts or option contracts in the form of purchases or swaps or in other forms that are to be settled at a future date and are used to transfer credit risk (credit derivatives);
5. forward transactions relating to the underlying instruments referred to in Article 8 of Delegated Regulation (EU) 2017/565 if they satisfy the conditions of number 2.

The definition in section 2(3) STA distinguishes between the term *Derivate* (derivatives) and *Termingeschäfte*. An appropriate translation of the German term *Termingeschäfte* used in the STA could be the term *derivative contracts*. The term *derivative contracts* used in section 2(3) includes forwards, futures, swaps and options, whereas the wider term derivative also entails financial contracts for differences (CFDs) and credit derivatives.

Haisch also suggests that financial CFDs are always derived from some basic underlying and settled at a future date and thus also have all properties of a derivative contract.[115]

The same applies to credit derivatives, where the underlying variable or reference parameter is the credit risk in relation to the specific reference asset.[116] As every derivative, even a financial CFD, would always also qualify as a derivative contract because of its properties, the author proposes that both terms can be used interchangeably.

It has been suggested that the term *Termingeschäft* (derivative contract) used in the tax legislation has been borrowed from section 2(3) STA.[117] But even if the term has been borrowed from capital markets law, the term used in section 2(3) STA may not have the same meaning as the same term used in section 20(2) sentence 1 No. 3a) and 3b) ITA because of different purposes and aims.[118]

Haisch suggests that:

> [even] if the tax law contains a term that has been borrowed from other legislation, it has to be determined by way of interpretation whether tax law follows the intent of the other law, or whether the borrowed term has to be interpreted independently from the other law based on the specific purpose of the tax law.[119]

---

115. Martin Haisch, 'Derivatebesteuerung im Privatvermögen ab 2009' (PhD thesis, Richard Boorberg Verlag 2010) 32.
116. *See* Ch 4 §4.06[C].
117. Haisch (2010) 28. The legislative material in the context of an earlier change in the wording of the previous sections dealing with derivatives suggests that the wording in this paragraph relies on the definition of 'derivative contracts' used in s. 2(3) STA. *See* BT-Drucksache 14/443 of 3 March 1999, 28ff. concerning former s. 23(1) sent. 1 No. 4 ITA.

    In contrast, explanatory legislative material that was concerned with the change to the new flat tax regime did not explicitly refer to the definition used in STA but only used similar wording as in section 2(3) No. 1 STA to explain the term. *See* Gesetzesentwurf der Bundesregierung, BR-Drucksache 220/07, 88.
118. Hans-Jürgen Feyerabend (ed.) *Besteuerung privater Kapitalanlagen* (C.H. Beck 2009) 315; Haisch (2010) 148; Martin Haisch and Marcus Helios, *Rechtshandbuch Finanzinstrumente* (C.H. Beck 2011) 311.
119. Haisch (2010) 148 with further references at fn. 832, referring to two decisions of the Federal Fiscal Court and the Constitutional Court.

The aim of capital markets law is to determine which instruments fall under the term *derivative contract* based on considerations of investor protection and market certainty, whereas tax law is concerned with determining what falls within the taxation base.[120]

Thus, the term *derivative contract* used in STA may provide guidance as to what are *necessary* definitional criteria for defining derivative contracts for tax purposes, such as that a derivative needs to be derived from the price or value of some basic underlying and is settled at a future date.[121] In the author's opinion, the STA, however, does not provide *sufficient* definitional criteria to define derivatives for tax purposes, as these have to be found based on the purpose of the tax law as a basis for the charge to tax. Hence, both terms should be interpreted independently from each other.[122]

With regard to the two alternatives of section 20(2) sentence 1 No. 3 ITA, it is uncertain whether the provisions apply to both physically settled and cash-settled derivatives or whether they are only applicable to cash-settled derivatives.[123] In the author's view, one has to carefully distinguish between the two alternatives of section 20(2) sentence 1 No. 3a) ITA and section 20(2) sentence 1 No. 3b) ITA based on their different wording.

Section 20(2) sentence 1 No. 3b) ITA subjects to tax any capital gains 'from the disposal of a financial instrument that is structured as a derivative contract'. Section 20(2) sentence 1 No. 3a) ITA also uses the general term derivative contract.

Thus, in the first step, it can be said that the term 'derivative contract' in both alternatives of section 20(2) sentence No. 3 ITA entails, in principle, both cash and physically settled derivative contracts similar to the term derivative contract used in section 2(3) STA.[124]

Section 20(2) sentence 1 No. 3a) ITA subjects to tax only those capital gains from derivative contracts, through which the taxpayer obtains a difference payment or a cash amount or advantage, which is determined by the value of a variable reference parameter.[125]

---

120. Haisch and Helios (2011) 263.
121. Haisch (2010) 148.
122. *Ibid.*, 148; Haisch and Helios (2011) 311; Sven-Christian Witt, '§ 15' in Carl Herrmann, Gerhard Heuer and Arndt Raupach (eds), *Einkommensteuer – und Körperschaftsteuergesetz, Kommentar* (2022) para. 1541; Friedrich Harenberg, '§ 20' in Carl Herrmann, Gerhard Heuer and Arndt Raupach (eds), *Einkommensteuer -und Körperschaftsteuergesetz Kommentar* (2013) paras 472 and 641; Feyerabend (2009) 315.
123. There has been some debate in the literature as to whether the old s. 23(1) No. 4 ITA (2008), which is similar in its wording to the new section 20(2) sent. 1 No. 3a) ITA (2009), only applied to income arising from cash-settled derivatives, or whether it also included physically settled derivatives. For a narrow interpretation under the old law to include only cash-settled derivatives, *see* Friedrich Harenberg, '§ 23' in Carl Herrmann, Gerhard Heuer and Arndt Raupach (eds), *Einkommensteuer – und Körperschaftsteuergesetz Kommentar* (21st edn, Verlag Dr Otto Schmidt KG 2003) para. 188.

    Other opinion Heinrich Glenk, '§ 23 EStG' in Bernd Heuermann (ed.), *Blümich, EStG, KStG, GewStG* (91st edn, Verlag Franz Vahlen München 2006) para. 79.
124. Haisch (2010) 36. For the settlement possibilities in STA: Heinz-Dieter Assmann and Uwe Schneider, *Wertpapierhandelsgesetz Kommentar* (6th edn, Dr Otto Schmidt Verlag 2012) § 2, paras 41-56.
125. Section 20(2) sent. 1 No. 3a) ITA.

The additional condition in section 20(2) sentence 1 No. 3a) 1st alt ITA determines that cash-settled derivative contracts, i.e., those which require a cash difference payment, will fall under the section.

It is, however, uncertain whether section 20(2) sentence 1 No. 3a) 2nd alt ITA will also include physically settled derivatives.

The majority view in the tax literature suggests that only cash settlement in kind or net share settlement[126] can be regarded as an *advantage* under section 20(2) sentence 1 No. 3a) 2nd alt. ITA.[127] The argument is that an *advantage* that is determined by reference to the *value* of an underlying parameter would not include the physical settlement of derivative contracts, where the underlying is delivered in order to *fulfil* the contract.[128] Thus, physically settled derivatives should not be subject to tax under the provision of section 20(2) sentence 1 No. 3a) 2nd alt. ITA.[129]

A letter ruling by the Ministry of Finance concerning private individuals seems to support that view as it maintains that the physical delivery of the underlying asset will lead to a non-taxable acquisition of the underlying, with taxable income arising only at the time when the underlying asset is disposed of.[130]

Any gains at the time of disposal of the underlying would then be subject to tax under the flat tax regime according to section 20(2) sentence 1 No. 1[131] or section 20(2) sentence 1 No. 7 ITA.[132]

The majority view of the literature, which suggests that physically settled derivatives do not fall under the wording of section 20(2) sentence 1 No. 3a) 2nd alt. ITA, is not compelling.

The wording of section 20(2) sentence 1 No. 3a) 2nd alt. ITA prescribes that the *advantage* (which is obtained by the taxpayer) is determined by the *value* of the underlying reference parameter.

---

126. Instead of a difference payment in cash, the same value is delivered in the form of shares or another underlying, i.e., the delivery is only a substitute means payment for cash but no physical delivery.
127. *See* Haisch (2010) 151-152; Haisch and Helios (2011) 312; Conlon & Aquilino: Derivatives D2.02[3][c][ii] (issue December 2022).
128. Haisch (2010) 152-153.
129. In favour of a narrow interpretation under the new section: Joachim Dahm and Rolfjosef Hamacher, 'Termingeschäfte und Abgeltungsteuer' DStR 2008 1910, 1912; Feyerabend (2009) 323; Matthias Geurts, '§ 20 EStG' in Arno Bordewin and Jürgen Brandt (eds), *Einkommensteuergesetz, Kommentar* (2009) paras 607 and 622; Haisch (2010) 152-153; Haisch and Helios (2011) 312 with further references in fn. 142; Harenberg *in H/H/R* (2013) *§ 20*, para. 472; Conlon & Aquilino: Derivatives D2.02[3][c][ii] (issue December 2022). *Other opinion:* Eckart Ratschow, '§ 20 EStG' in Peter Brandis and Bernd Heuermann (eds), *Blümich, EStG, KStG, GewStG, Kommentar* (2013) para. 369; Heinrich Weber-Grellet (ed.) *Schmidt Einkommensteuergesetz Kommentar* (31st edn, C.H. Beck 2012) § 20, paras 133 and 137.
130. BMF, *Schreiben vom 9 Oktober 2012, Einzelfragen zur Abgeltungsteuer* (IV C 1 - S 2252/10/10013), paras 22 and 36; *BMR, Schreiben vom 18. Januar 2016, Einzelfragen zur Abgeltungsteuer, Neuveroeffentlichung des BMF-Schreibens,* (IV C 1 - S 2252/08/10004:017), paras 22 and 36, https://www.bzst.de/SharedDocs/BMF/DE/Downloads/bmf_Schreiben_20160118_Einzelfragen_Abgeltungsteuer.html, accessed 9 January 2023.

    See also Conlon & Aquilino: Derivatives D2.02[3][c][ii] (issue December 2022).
131. Shares.
132. Any bonds and debentures.

One may argue that the *advantage* in the case of a physical delivery of the underlying asset is the fact that one receives an underlying asset for which one has to pay only the (lower) strike price agreed upon and not the current market price. Thus, the advantage is the difference between the strike price paid and the current market price of the underlying at maturity.

Example 22:

A buys from Bank B a physically settled equity call option with a term of one year and pays an option premium of 10. The strike price is 100. At maturity, the current share price has risen to 120. A receives delivery of the shares and pays a strike price of 100.

In *Example 22* above, A has obtained an *advantage* of 10. This advantage can be calculated as 120 (current price) minus strike price (100) minus option premium paid (10). Thus, the advantage is not the delivery of the underlying asset as such but the delivery of the underlying asset in exchange for the lower pre-agreed strike price instead of a purchase of the shares at the current market price. Hence, the wording of section 20(2) sentence 1 No. 3a) ITA would support the position that the provision applies to both cash-settled and physically settled derivative contracts.[133]

[2] Definition of 'Derivative Contract' Applying to Business and Corporate Taxpayers

Instead of providing a specific set of taxation rules for derivatives, German tax law applies the general business income tax and corporation tax rules for the taxation of derivatives. For business investors, the only reference to the term *derivative contract* (*Termingeschäft*) can be found in the derivatives loss ring-fencing provisions in section 15(4) sentences 3 to 5 ITA.[134] Under this section, derivatives losses cannot be offset against other income of the company but only against other derivatives gains.[135] For corporate investors, these provisions apply by way of reference to the business provisions of ITA.[136] Those provisions have to be further investigated to understand the scope of the German corporate tax legislation applying to derivatives.

133. When those gains from physically settled derivatives should be taxed (at delivery of the underlying asset or only at disposal of the underlying asset) has not been mentioned in this section, however.
134. This is the only provision incorporated in the business tax legislation dealing specifically and explicitly with the taxation of derivatives.
135. Section 15(4) sent. 1 and 3 ITA. The losses can also not be carried back or forward to set-off against other business income (ss 15(4) sent. 1 2nd part, sent. 3 and s. 10d(1) ITA). A loss carry-back or forward is only possible against positive derivatives gains (s. 15(4) sent. 2 and 3 ITA).
136. Section 8(1) CTA.

As with the case of private individuals, section 15(4) sentence 3 ITA does not define the term *derivative contract*.[137] The German Ministry of Finance took the view in two letter rulings issued in 2005 and 2007 that losses from physically settled derivatives would fall under the loss ring-fencing provisions of section 15(4) sentence 3 to 5 ITA.[138] These letter rulings were, however, discontinued due to a new letter ruling, which did not include those two letter rulings in a positive list of all rulings that continue to apply after 1 January 2010.[139]

So far, the German legislator has not explicitly clarified in the law whether section 15(4) sentence 3 ITA applies to both cash and physically settled derivatives or only to cash-settled derivatives.[140] The intention of the legislator in section 15(4) sentence 3 to 5 ITA was to avoid speculative losses from derivatives transactions being offset against ordinary business income and income from other schedules.[141]

If only losses from cash-settled derivatives were ring-fenced under section 15(4) sentence 3 ITA, whilst losses from physically settled derivatives were not caught, this would constitute an inequitable tax treatment solely based on the form of settlement.

As a consequence of such a mismatch between cash and physical settlement, taxpayers could easily use the form of physical settlement to avoid the application of the loss ring-fencing rule. Hence, one might argue from a pure policy point of view that both cash and physically settled derivatives should fall within section 15(4) sentence 3 ITA.

However, in the author's view, the wording of the law should be the decisive factor in interpreting a technical term rather than policy considerations.

Similar to the wording for private individuals, section 15(4) sentence 3 ITA only applies to those losses from derivative contracts, 'through which the taxpayer obtains a difference payment, or a cash amount or advantage which is determined by the value of a variable reference parameter'.[142] As in the case of private individuals, one may argue that the *advantage* could be regarded as the difference between the strike price and the current market price, thus leading to the conclusion that section 15(4) sentence 3 ITA would apply derivative losses from both physically and cash-settled contracts.[143]

137. Weber-Grellet *Schmidt, EStG* (2012) § 15 para. 902.
138. BMF, *Schreiben vom 23. September 2005, Verlustabzugsbeschränkung nach § 15 Abs. 4 Satz 3 EStG*, IV B 2 - S 2119 - 7/05, DStR 2005, 2269 and BMF, *Schreiben vom 12. Februar 2007* (IV B 2 - S 2119-10-5 - *unpublished*).
139. BMF, *Schreiben betr. Eindämmung der Normenflut; BMF-Schreiben, die bis zum 31. Dezember 2009 ergangen sind.* (Verwaltungsanweisung vom 23. April 2010 - IV A 6 - O 1000/09/10095, BStBl I 2010, 391ff.).
140. The German *Bundesrat* (second chamber of the German legislator) suggested in 2010 to include both forms of settlement explicitly into s. 15(4) sent. 3 ITA but the proposal has not been taken up by the German government. *See* BT-Drucksache 17/2823 of 27 August 2010, 10-11.
141. BT-Drucksache 14/443, 28.
142. Section 15(4) sent. 3 ITA.
143. *See* for the full argument: Ch. 4 §4.03[C][1].

This is, however, disputed by the prevalent view in the literature, which suggests that the delivery of the underlying in case of a physical settlement of the derivative will not qualify as such an advantage because the physical delivery of the underlying is not the advantage, but the fulfilment of the contract itself.[144]

The Federal Fiscal Court (*Bundesfinanzhof* – BFH) decided in 2016 that derivatives, which are intended for physical delivery of the underlying asset are not subject to the loss ring-fencing rules of section 15(4) sentence 3 ITA.[145] The decision explicitly overruled the Federal Ministry of Finance's (*Bundesfinanzministerium* – BMF) letter ruling of 2005.

[D] Evaluation of the German Approach to Defining Derivative Contracts

The German tax legislation applies a 'borrowing from other legislation' approach to defining derivative contracts. German income tax law simply refers to the term *derivative contracts* but does not contain a definition.[146] Similarly, the derivatives loss ring-fencing provision of section 15(4) sentence 3 ITA applying to business and corporate investors[147] does not define the term.[148] The term used in the tax legislation has been borrowed from the capital markets law.[149] Nonetheless, the term *derivative contract* used in capital markets law and tax law is thought to have a different meaning.[150]

In the author's view, the term *derivative contract* used in the tax legislation raises the following issues of definition and interpretation:

(1) The reliance and borrowing from the capital markets definition of section 2(3) STA is neither explicitly mentioned in section 20(2) No. 3a) ITA nor in section 15(4) sentence 3 ITA. Instead, the legislative material presumes that the term *derivative contract* used in the tax legislation is the same as the term used in

144. Hans-Jürgen Feyerabend, 'EStG § 15, Einkünfte aus Gewerbebetrieb' in Bernd Erle and Thomas Sauter (eds), *Körperschaftsteuergesetz, Die Besteuerung der Kapitalgesellschaft und ihrer Anteilseigner* (3rd edn, C.F. Müller, Heidelberger Kommentar 2010) 1992-1993; Haisch and Helios (2011) 265 at fn. 55 with further references; Intemann *in H/H/R* (2013) *§ 15*, para. 1542; Conlon & Aquilino: Derivatives D2.03[6] (issue December 2022).
Other opinion Walter Bode, '§ 15 EStG' in Bernd Heuermann and Peter Brandis (eds), *Blümich, EStG, KStG and GewStG Kommentar* (2013) para. 655; Wendt *in H/H/R, Steuerreform I* (2001) *§ 15* para. R16 (regarding the old law).
145. BFH, decision of 6 July 2016, I R 25/14, https://www.bundesfinanzhof.de/en/entscheidungen/entscheidungen-online/decision-detail/STRE201610211/, accessed 9 January 2023. Similarly, the court decided in respect to s. 20 ITA (private individuals), *see* BFH, decision of 20 November 2018 – VIII R 37/15 BStBl 2019 II S. 507, https://datenbank.nwb.de/Dokument/774727/, accessed 8 July 2023.
146. Section 20(2) No. 3 ITA.
147. Section 15(4) sent. 3 ITA.
148. Haisch (2010) 28.
149. BT-Drucksache 14/443, 27ff.
150. *See* Ch. 4 §4.03[C][1].

the STA.[151] A definition of *derivative contracts* based on the German STA without explicit reference in the Income Tax Act misses, in the author's view, a direct authorisation by the legislator creates uncertainty and cannot provide clear guidance on how to define derivatives for tax purposes.

(2) The scope of a crucial term, like derivative contracts, should have been decided upon by the tax legislator independently from its scope in other areas of law. For private individuals, the scope of the term defines which kinds of derivatives the flat tax regime applies to. For business and corporate investors, the term determines whether or not losses are treated as ring-fenced. Thus, a specific definition for tax purposes is desirable.

(3) Even if one would assume that the term *derivative contract* used in the ITA would be entirely based on the definition of *derivative contract* used in STA, this definition could, in the author's view, not constitute a sufficient definition for tax purposes. The definition of the term *derivative contract* in section 2(3) STA is exclusive[152] and relies on an enumeration of the underlying variables and does not provide abstract definitional criteria apart from the basic observation that a derivative is derived from underlying variables and is settled at a future date.[153] Because the definition is enumerative in terms of the types of derivatives and the underlying assets, it may not be sufficient to catch newly invented derivatives for tax purposes. Thus, borrowing from the capital markets legislation will not sufficiently serve the aim of defining derivative contracts for tax purposes.

(4) In Chapter 4 §4.03[C][1] and §4.03[C][2], the author has illustrated that an unambiguous determination of the exact scope of the term in relation to cash and physical derivatives is hardly possible because of the rather imprecise wording in the law, leading to different points of view in the German tax literature.

To avoid the uncertainty in the scope of the term *derivative contract* used in sections 20(2) sentence 1 No. 3a) and 15(4) sentence 3 ITA, it is imperative from a systematic point of view that the term is defined comprehensively and unambiguously both in the tax legislation for private individuals as well as in the tax legislation for business investors.[154] This will also allow corporate taxpayers to unambiguously determine (1) if the existing definition of derivatives captures the derivative contracts they enter into and (2) if newly emerging derivatives, such as crypto and ESG derivatives, will fall within the existing definition of derivatives for tax purposes.

151. Brandis/Heuermann (2023), para. 717.
152. Haisch (2010) 34.
153. Glenk in Blümich (2006) § 23 EStG para. 65; Haisch (2010) 33-34.
154. *Similar* H/H/R, EStG/KStG (2022) § 20, para. 641.

§4.04 OTHER DEFINITIONAL APPROACHES

[A] Different Approaches to Defining Derivatives in Other Countries

In the tax legislation of other countries, one can find different approaches to defining derivative contracts for tax purposes that can be categorised according to the criteria outlined in Chapter 4 §4.02 of this work.

Switzerland simply uses the economic definition of derivatives to categorise them for tax purposes, as there are no special rules for taxing derivatives in the legislation.[155]

The US legislator has not developed a comprehensive definition of derivatives for tax purposes. Instead, forwards, futures, options, swaps and similar financial products are subject to different sets of tax rules.[156] As the tax treatment can be substantially different, it is critical to determine which sets of rules are applicable to the particular transaction. In addition, the tax rules governing exchange-traded options and futures are very different from the rules that apply to non-exchange-traded forwards and options.

As the US income tax system has no single definition of derivatives, it deals with the different contracts enumeratively by way of statutes, rulings, and case law with the result that many inconsistencies arise and that, in many cases, the taxation does not reflect the underlying economics.[157]

Australia uses a broad definition of 'financial arrangement' in its Taxation of Financial Arrangement Rules (TOFA)[158] and applies the so-called coherent principles approach[159] when taxing this form of arrangement.[160] The TOFA rules, however, do not include a specific definition of derivatives in the legislation but instead define financial arrangements more generally.

[B] Definition of Derivatives for Tax Purposes in the Academic Tax Literature

Similarly, in the academic literature, many attempts have been made to define derivatives for tax purposes. Some authors merely define derivatives by way of enumeration of the basic building blocks and also include instruments like mortgage-backed securities, structured notes and hybrid securities.[161]

155. Conlon & Aquilino: Derivatives D5.01 (issue December 2022).
156. *Ibid.*, B1.01.
157. *Ibid.*
158. Income Tax Assessment Act (ITAA) 1997, Ch. 3, ss 230-245, 230-250 and Subdivision 230J.
159. Pinder (2005) 77. Under a coherent principles approach, the principle becomes an operative legislative provision; *see* Freedman (2010) 725.
160. Australian Treasury, Exposure Draft: Tax Laws Amendment (Taxation of Financial Arrangements) Bill 2008, Explanatory Material (2008) 1.19.
161. Conlon & Aquilino: Derivatives D2.01[3] (issue December 2022).

Zelinsky suggests that 'the term "derivatives", taken literally, is over-inclusive, describing some quite traditional form of investments' and proposes the use of the broad designation of *New Financial Instruments* instead.[162]

Other authors favour a policy-based approach, which tries to capture both existing and newly emerging derivatives. For example, *Thuronyi* argues in favour of a very broad concept of *New Financial Instruments* 'as tax law should be prepared to cover whatever financial instruments the market can devise'.[163] His argument in favour of such a policy-based approach is that:

> the inherent difficulty in defining NFIs [New Financial Instruments] should be kept in mind if an attempt is made to define new financial instruments or specific categories thereof, such as derivatives, in the tax legislation. [...]. A detailed definition, unless very carefully structured, can fall prey to tax planners who will parse the definition precisely and devise arrangements that fall outside the scope of the definition if it is in their interest to do so.[164]

Likewise, *Romer* proposes that tax rules 'need to evolve as new technologies arrive'[165] and suggests by referring to a statement of Myron Scholes[166] that:

> if there is a fixed set of rules in something like a tax code, clever opportunists will steadily undermine their effectiveness. They will do this, for example, by changing the names of familiar objects to shift them between different legal categories, or by winning judicial rulings that narrow the applicability of the existing rules. In sum, rules have to evolve in response to three distinct factors: new technologies, increases in the scale of social interaction and opportunistic attempts at evasion.[167]

The author agrees that the tax rules must be prepared to deal effectively with financial product innovation and cover newly developed derivatives in order to prevent tax avoidance.[168] In the author's view, however, the tax legislator should not define the term 'derivative' as broadly as possible but as comprehensively and precisely as possible based on abstract definitional criteria.

A definition from a pure policy point of view[169] cannot, in the author's view, provide the financial markets with the certainty needed with respect to the tax treatment of those instruments.[170] Therefore, abstract definitional criteria are necessary to deal with the challenge of taxing derivatives.

---

162. Zelinsky (1997) 947, at fn. 185.
163. Thuronyi (2001a) 262.
164. *Ibid.*, 263.
165. Paul Romer, 'Process, Responsibility, and Myron's Law', Chapter 12 in: In the Wake of the Crisis: Leading Economists Reassess Economic Policy, Olivier J. Blanchard, David Romer, A. Michael Spence and Joseph E. Stiglitz (eds.) Cambridge: MIT Press, 2012, 111, 112.
166. Romer attributes to Myron Scholes the statement: 'Asymptotically any finite tax code collects zero revenue', confirming that tax law needs to be abstract-prescriptive instead of enumerative.
167. *Ibid.*
168. OECD (2001) para. 87; *also* Neighbour (2001) 2.
169. Thuronyi (2001a) 262 suggests that a New Financial Instrument (NFI) 'should include any instrument or arrangement that does not fit neatly into existing categories of debt or equity'.
170. *Neighbour* suggests that 'a difficult balance needs to be struck between allowing markets to operate as efficiently as possible and guarding against tax avoidance and arbitrage', *see* Neighbour (2001) 2.

Neither descriptive definitions nor pure policy-based definitions can provide legal certainty due to constant financial innovation and new derivatives designs, as seen with the emergence of crypto derivatives and ESG derivatives. A tax legislator – when developing the abstract definitional criteria for derivatives – however, needs to find the exact balance between a definition that is too narrow (that may be used by tax planners to circumvent the tax legislation on derivatives) and a definition that is too wide for tax purposes (e.g., because it also includes non-derivative financial instruments when applying the abstract definitional criteria).

§4.05 THE ACCOUNTING DEFINITION OF DERIVATIVES AND ITS SUITABILITY FOR TAXATION

Financial accounting rules, including accounting principles, standards and procedures, together constitute the Generally Accepted Accounting Practice (GAAP). The relevant International Financial Reporting Standard (IFRS) applicable to derivatives is IFRS 9 Financial Instruments, which replaced IAS 39 in 2018.[171]

IFRS 9, Appendix A defines a derivative as:

> A financial instrument or other contract within the scope of this IFRS (see paragraph 2.1) with all three of the following characteristics.
>
> (a) Its value changes in response to the change in a specified interest rate, financial instrument price, commodity price, foreign exchange rate, index of prices or rates, credit rating or credit index, or other variable provided in the case of a non-financial variable that the variable is not specific to a party to the contract (sometimes called the 'underlying'),
> (b) It requires no initial net investment or an initial net investment that is smaller than would be required for other types of contracts that would be expected to have a similar response to changes in market factors, and
> (c) It is settled at a future date.[172]

Although the accounting definition in IFRS 9 is partly based on the common economic definition of derivatives (mirrored in the criteria (a) and (c)), an additional criterion (the provision of *leverage*)[173] has been introduced under (b) in order to define derivatives for the purposes of IFRS 9.

In the author's view, the definitional criteria of IFRS 9 cannot be regarded as sufficient criteria for defining derivatives for tax purposes, although they are sufficient for classifying a financial instrument as a derivative for accounting purposes.

---

171. 'IFRS 9 is effective for annual periods beginning on or after 1 January 2018'. IFRS, https://www.ifrs.org/issued-standards/list-of-standards/ifrs-9-financial-instruments/, accessed 8 January 2023. For the state of the application of IFRS 9 in the European Union and their relevance in the context of UK GAAP, *see* Ch 6 § 6.02 [C] at fn. 55.
172. IAS 39, Financial Instruments: Recognition and Measurement (2010) para. 8, refers to the term defined in IFRS 9, in the meaning specified in Appendix A, Defined terms: 'derivative' of IFRS 9 (2022).
173. *See* for a definition and explanation of leverage: Ch. 2 §2.02[D].

First, the possibility to provide leverage is a feature of many derivatives, which is often – but not always – fulfilled when categorising derivatives from an economic point of view. For example, financial instruments, like pre-paid swaps, where the full net investment in the contract is made at inception, can also be qualified as a derivative. However, a pre-paid swap misses the element of leverage that is required by IFRS 9.

Second, accounting principles, in general, whether IFRS or national accounting standards, do not always have the same purposes and requirements compared to taxation rules.[174] For example, IFRS 9 is concerned with the mere classification of an instrument. Thus, IFRS 9 determines whether an instrument can *also* be seen as a derivative based on its economic features and does not consider the question of *what* falls into a certain category of income.

Accounting standards are designed to provide information about the company to different users, such as existing shareholders, creditors, potential investors,[175] regulators and management.[176] They are tailored to and influenced by those different users' needs in relation to economic decision-making, especially in the context of providing resources to the entity,[177] making distributions,[178] accountability of management to shareholders[179] and control.[180] A great variety of users exist, and that may influence what information is provided and how it is provided in the commercial accounts.[181] Thus, not one true profit figure but a range of figures may be necessary to give a true and fair view of a company's state, current dealings and future potential of business.[182]

Tax law is primarily concerned with raising and equitably collecting revenues.[183] Additionally, tax law may also direct taxpayers to comply with certain economic or social policies due to specific tax advantages or tax breaks.[184] In contrast to accounting rules, tax law requires a single, statutorily derived figure to determine the liability to tax of the taxpayer.[185] Whereas different methods of preparing accounts can lead to equally acceptable results, those methods may not be equally acceptable for tax purposes as

174. Simon James, 'The Relationship between Accounting and Taxation' Paper 02/2009 https://core.ac.uk/download/pdf/12824388.pdf, accessed 14 January 2023, 4.
175. International Financial Reporting Standards (IFRS) (2022) Part A, Conceptual Framework, OB2.
176. Laukkanen (2007) 226. In the US case *Thor Power Tools Company v. Commissioner of Internal Revenue* 439 US 522 (1979) 522, 542, the different requirement of accounting and tax rules have been discussed.
177. *IFRS* (2022) Part A, Conceptual Framework, OB3.
178. Judith Freedman, 'Accounting Standards: A Panacea?' (2004) The Tax Journal, 18 October 2014, 9; Judith Freedman, 'The Role of Realisation: Accounting, Company Law and Taxation' in IFA Congress Seminar Series (ed.), *The Influence of Corporate Tax Law and Accounting Principles in Determining Taxable Income*, vol. 21b (1996) 29, 30.
179. OECD (2001) para. 100.
180. James (2009) 4.
181. OECD (2001) para. 100.
182. Freedman (2004a) 74-77 sums up the arguments for and against alignment of accounting and tax profits. The author agrees with the position of Freedman, who argues against complete alignment of accounting rules and taxation due to different objectives.
183. *Thor Power Tools Company v. Commissioner of Internal Revenue*, 522, 542.
184. James (2009) 7.
185. Geoffrey Whittington, 'Accounting Standards as a Basis for Taxation: The Case Against' (Tax law workshop on accounting principles and taxable profits, Queen's College, University of Cambridge, 16 January 2004); *also* Freedman (2004a) 75.

they can lead to taxation results which do not reflect the correct tax liability of the taxpayer. As tax law is concerned with the ability to pay at a current point in time, it has to be much more focused on the application of the realisation principle than IFRS accounting standards, which are designed to provide accurate financial information for investors and financial markets alike.[186] Thus, the needs for a definition of derivatives for accounting purposes on the one hand and for tax purposes on the other are different.

Freedman suggests that the different functions and objectives of accounting standards and tax legislation make it desirable that 'the rules for each one are not unduly influenced by the rules for the other'.[187] This is also true in the case of derivatives. Because of different objectives, the accounting definition under IFRS 9 can only provide *necessary* but *not sufficient* criteria for classifying income as derivatives income for tax purposes. Consequently, the legislator should incorporate in the tax legislation a definition for derivatives that is different from the accounting definition used in IFRS 9.

§4.06 SOLUTION TO PROBLEM 1: DESIGNING A SUITABLE DEFINITION OF DERIVATIVES

[A] The Task

Tax systems may adopt specific rules for the taxation of derivatives to deal with those instruments comprehensively. A major task for tax legislators will be to consider general tax policy goals when developing a derivatives taxation regime and strive to find a balance between these goals and highly targeted tax legislation.[188] Problems tend to arise if the special tax regime for derivatives is only tailored to existing derivatives and is not able to incorporate newly developed instruments, thereby causing a time lag between the development of new financial instruments and the introduction of specifically targeted tax legislation.

An enumerative definition may lead to tax arbitrage opportunities for taxpayers on the one hand and to legal uncertainty on the other, as the exact tax treatment of those newly designed derivatives is not prescribed in the law.[189]

From a general tax policy point of view, it is therefore desirable that a definition of derivatives for tax purposes can potentially apply to newly invented derivatives, whilst simultaneously incorporating precise definitional criteria to provide legal

186. Freedman (1996) 30.
187. Freedman (2004a) 76. *Other opinion:* Wolfgang Schön, 'International Accounting Standards – a "Starting Point" for a Common European Tax Base?' *European Taxation, Vol. 44, No. 10, 2004, 426-440,* https://papers.ssrn.com/sol3/papers.cfm?abstract_id=1603758 (Annual Conference of the European Association of Tax Law Professors, Paris, accessed 1 February 2024) 29.
188. Neighbour (2001) 2-3.
189. *See* Ch. 3 §3.01.

certainty for taxpayers in respect of the taxation of existing derivatives. In addition, a definition of derivatives should be robust to changes in other legislation.[190]

The criteria to be set out in a suitable tax definition should also be capable of distinguishing derivatives from other financial instruments that have no derivatives character. A remedy for the problems described above may be the introduction of an abstract definition of derivatives for tax purposes, which can also incorporate newly developed derivatives.

At the level of domestic tax legislation, a comprehensively formulated definition based on abstract definitional criteria could allow a clear determination of whether a financial instrument qualifies as a derivative or not.

Given the shortcomings of the existing definitions of 'derivative contracts' in the legislation of the UK and Germany, the aim of the following subchapter is to develop a comprehensive definition which will be able to deal with the classification issues arising in a domestic taxation context.

[B] Definitional Criteria for Defining Derivatives for Tax Purposes

[1] Economic Criterion of Contingency

A financial instrument qualifies as a derivative *if its value depends on the value of one or more independent underlying variables*. Derivatives are '*contingent claims* since their payoffs are "contingent" upon the outcome of an underlying variable'.[191]

Excursus:

The term 'underlying variable' or 'underlying parameter' has to be distinguished from the term 'underlying asset' or 'underlying'.

The term 'underlying asset' or 'underlying' should be used for the asset as such.[192] However, derivatives are – strictly speaking – not derived from the underlying asset as such but from an underlying parameter or underlying variable of the asset.

Hence, it is necessary to define from which underlying variable or parameter the derivative is derived, i.e., based on which variable or parameter the payoff of the derivative depends.

For example, if the underlying asset is the share of a company, the underlying variable on which the payoff of the derivative depends can either be the price of

190. *See* Erika Nijenhuis, 'New Tax Issues Arising from the Dodd-Frank Act and Related Changes to Market Practice for Derivatives' (2011) 2(1) Columbia Journal of Tax Law 1-99 DOI: 10.2139/ssrn.1611212.
191. John Hull, *Options, Futures and Other Derivatives* (3rd edn, Prentice Hall 1997) 1; Rubinstein (1999a) 3.
192. The term 'underlying asset' may be used in the context of replication and hedging, as the purchase or sale of the underlying asset will provide exposure to the 'underlying variables' of the asset, such as the price or the dividends of the asset.

the share,[193] the payment streams of the underlying (dividends),[194] or the value of the derivative depends on both.[195]

Neighbour relies on the basic economic definition to define derivatives for tax purposes.[196] In the author's view, a definitional approach that relies purely on the economic definition does not consider that the payoff of an underlying variable can also be derived from even more basic underlying variables. It could be said that the value of the shares of a company also depends in some way on the expected (future) profits and losses and the assets of that company. Likewise, the value of a bond also depends on the creditworthiness of the issuer.[197]

Therefore, the contingency of the payoff upon the underlying variable is merely a necessary but not sufficient criterion for defining derivatives for tax purposes.[198] In order to distinguish derivatives from their underlying assets on the one hand and from gambling on the other, additional definitional criteria have to be developed when defining derivatives for tax purposes.[199]

[2] Deterministic Dependence on Stochastic Underlying Variables

Ingersoll defines a derivative as 'one whose end-of-period payoff is *exactly determined* by the payoffs on one or more of the other assets, sometimes distinguished by the name *primitive assets*'.[200]

To qualify as a derivative, future payoffs have to be deterministically dependent on stochastic variables.

A *payoff* can be best described as an amount which is paid during the term or at maturity of a financial instrument and whose value depends on static or stochastic variables. A *variable* is *stochastic* if it has a random probability distribution or pattern that may be analysed statistically but may not be predicted precisely:[201]

> Any variable whose value changes over time in an uncertain way is said to follow a stochastic process. [...] Stochastic processes can also be classified as continuous variable or discrete variable. In a continuous variable process, the underlying variable can take any value within a certain range, whereas in a discrete-variable process, only certain discrete values are possible.[202]

---

193. An example would be an equity option or an equity futures contract.
194. An example would be a dividend swap.
195. An example of a derivative, which has two underlying variables, being the price of the equity and the dividends, is a total return equity swap.
196. Neighbour (1997) 932.
197. Zelinsky (1997) 947.
198. Reiner (2002) 21.
199. The distinction between derivatives and spread betting is a very subtle one and will be investigated in more detail below.
200. Jonathan Ingersoll, *Theory of Financial Decision Making* (Rowman & Littlefield Publishers 1987) 26 (emphasis added).
201. *The Concise Oxford English Dictionary* (10th edn, Oxford University Press 2002).
202. Hull (2006) 263.

In relation to derivatives, the term 'stochastic' means that *the payoff* depends in an uncertain way on the change in value of the underlying variables.[203]

Deterministically dependent means that the mathematical *payoff function* of the derivative as such is *pre-defined*. The *value* of the payoff, however, remains *uncertain* as it depends on uncertain variables.

Thus, whereas the payoff is dependent on the change in value of certain parameters of the underlying, for any given set of parameter values, there is *always one – and only one – payoff value* at maturity. Consequently, there is only one possible result for every constellation of variables.

The criterion of deterministic dependence on stochastic variables allows the exclusion of non-derivative financial instruments from the definition of derivatives.

> *Example 23:*
>
> One might argue that the payoff on the bond is uncertain because it depends on the creditworthiness of the bond issuer.[204] If the bond issuer defaults, the bondholder will not receive the full notional amount back at maturity but only an *uncertain recovery rate*, if any.
>
> Thus, the repayment of the principal, as well as further interest payments, are uncertain, as they depend *stochastically* on whether the bond issuer defaults or not.
>
> Nevertheless, there is no pre-defined dependence of the bond payments on variables such as creditworthiness, as there is no mathematical way of determining what the exact recovery rate will be before the event of default.

Thus, a fixed interest rate bond will not qualify as a derivative, as the *payoff* is not *deterministically dependent* on static or stochastic variables because there is no exact mathematical relation between the payoff in the event of default and the creditworthiness of the issuer.

The criterion of *deterministic dependence* also excludes shares from qualifying as derivatives. The price of shares does not depend deterministically on future profits and losses made by the company. No one could predict at any given time what the exact share price will be at a certain point of time in the future only based on the level of the profits or losses generated by this company.

---

203. *Ibid.*
204. The argument that a bond may also qualify as a derivative is used by *Zelinsky* to avoid defining the term *derivative* for tax purposes at all and instead use the broad concept of *new financial innovation* which would also include traditional instruments like plain vanilla bonds. *See* Zelinsky (1997) 947.

[3] Limited Term of a Derivative

A financial instrument can only be qualified as a derivative if it has some future date at which it will mature.[205]

In the academic literature, more precise definitions of derivatives also include the element of time:

> A financial contract is a *derivative security*, or a *contingent claim*, if its value at expiration date T is determined *exactly* by the market price of the underlying cash instrument at time T [...] Hence, at the time of the expiration of the derivative contract, denoted by T, the price F(T) of the derivative asset is completely determined by S_T, the value of the 'underlying asset'. After that date, the security ceases to exist.[206]

Hence, derivatives are contracts where the primary obligation (delivery of an underlying asset or cash payment) is due to be fulfilled at a future date.[207]

Underlying assets such as shares, currencies, commodities and property[208] can, therefore, be excluded from the derivatives' definition for tax purposes as no future date exists on which they mature. In contrast to derivatives, these underlying assets have an unlimited term.

[4] Replication

A financial instrument will only qualify as a derivative for tax purposes if it can be replicated during its term.

Replication means that, at any time during the term of the derivative, it is possible to replicate the sum of its payoffs by entering into a trading strategy using other financial instruments, including underlying assets, cash and other derivatives.[209]

Replication of a derivative does not necessarily require the replication portfolio to include the underlying variable.[210] It is sufficient that other financial instruments exist, for example, other derivatives on the underlying variable, that mirror the value of the underlying variable.

Reiner suggests in his thesis[211] that to replicate a derivative, it is necessary that the underlying asset itself is traded at a cash market.[212]

---

205. Fabozzi et al. (2002) 497.
206. Ali Hirsa and Salih Neftci, *An Introduction to the Mathematics of Financial Derivatives* (Academic Press, 3rd edn, 2013) 2.
207. Rubinstein (1999a) 3.
208. To avoid any misunderstanding, the exclusion from the derivatives definition for tax purposes concerns the underlying asset as such, not the derivative contracts over these underlyings.
209. *See* Ch. 2 §2.02[A].
210. Reiner (2002) 21.
211. *Ibid.*, 22.
212. A cash market is a financial market, where financial instruments or commodities are traded for immediate delivery. This includes both the exchange and the OTC market.

If such a criterion were necessary to define a derivative for tax purposes, a cash market would be required for the underlying, and thus fungibility[213] and liquidity[214] in the underlying variable.

The author does not agree with *Reiner*'s proposition. The pre-requisite of an underlying variable, which is traded in the cash market, cannot properly describe the term replication in the context of derivatives because the decisive issue is whether a derivative can be replicated during its term, rather than how the derivative is replicated.

Thus, neither *fungibility* nor *liquidity* in the underlying are necessary requirements in defining a derivative for tax purposes. Rather, it is necessary that the financial instruments which are used to replicate the derivative are fungible and liquid. Market liquidity in the replicating or hedging instruments is necessary to ensure the ability to hedge the position at a fair market price.[215]

Thus, it must also be ensured that the replicating portfolio or the mirroring *hedge* is tradable, which means it can be bought and sold in the market.

If no such fungible and liquid financial instruments exist that can be used to replicate the derivative, then and only then is it necessary that a tradable and liquid market exists for the underlying asset.[216]

Hence, derivatives over non-fungible underlying variables can be replicated, for example, weather derivatives, if another financial instrument on the underlying variable, not necessarily being the underlying variable itself, exists, which can be used to replicate the derivative, for example, a future.

From the perspective of the tax legislation, the inclusion of a replication criterion in the definition of derivatives ensures that derivatives can be distinguished from betting.

Betting should be excluded as a source of taxation[217] because gains should be treated as taxable income based on the principles of reciprocity and correspondence in taxation. Thus, if the tax legislator decides to tax gains from gambling and betting, it also has to make corresponding losses tax deductible.

A government would, however, take part in the gambler's risk regarding the outcome of the game if it allowed the deduction of these losses. Therefore, any losses from gambling and betting should not be tax deductible, and any gains should not be taxable (reciprocity and correspondence of taxation).

---

213. The value of the underlying variable can be monetised if another derivative or financial instrument exists that displays a certain supply and demand in the underlying variable.
214. Liquidity of an instrument means that a market for the financial instrument exists, on which financial instruments are traded and hence, where a fair market price can be determined for this instrument. Such a market can also be an OTC market.
215. For a definition of hedging, *see* Ch. 2 §2.02[B].
216. This is, for example, the case if a derivative contract over commodities is hedged and no other derivatives exists, which can be used to replicate the derivative contract.
217. In the UK, profits arising from gambling transactions are not subject to income tax as they do not constitute a trade and are also exempt under TCGA 1992, s. 51. *See* HMRC, *Business Income Manual* (2011) BIM22015-22020. This is also the position of the German tax legislation since 1921. *See* RFH, RFHE 21, 244 (1921) and RFH, RStBl 1928, 181.

A derivative can be distinguished from bets because a derivative can be replicated and hedged.[218] Whereas derivative traders in banks partly or fully hedge the risks of their portfolios, a gambler takes the full risk. Hence, derivatives and betting can also be distinguished by the existence of a final risk taker. In a betting transaction, both parties take some, not necessarily the corresponding risk of losing.

In contrast, in a derivatives transaction, both counterparties can have a trading position at maturity, with neither of them having lost on their position as both parties can hedge themselves.[219] If both counterparties can hedge the final payoff, no final risk taker is needed.

Example 24:

A sells Bund futures to B. A hedges this contract by purchasing the underlying German government bonds from C. B borrows the bonds from A and sells them short to C. At maturity, A, B, and C end up without any of them having entered into a net risk position.[220]

Hence, for any transaction or financial instrument to qualify as a derivative, it must be possible to replicate (and hedge) it.[221] Therefore, so-called spread betting transactions may qualify as derivatives in certain cases under the proposed definition of derivatives.

Excursus:

Spread betting means that one party pays another party a certain amount of money depending on the movement of a reference underlying.

Sports spread betting (e.g., on the outcome of a football game) is not regulated under the FSMA 2000, whereas spread betting on the price movement of a security (financial spread betting) constitutes a regulated activity because the dealing in securities as such is regulated.

---

218. *See* Ch. 2 §2.02[A].
219. For the definition of hedging, *see* Ch. 2 §2.02[B].
220. For the treatment of futures transactions and their distinction from pure gambling in the UK: *Cooper v. Stubbs* 2 KB [1925] 753. It was held in this case that the distinction between a speculator and the gambler is that the contract to buy or to sell the cotton is a very real one from the point of view of the vendor and gives rise to very real contractual rights whereas in a gambling transaction both parties regard the matter as a mere wager. As derivative contracts nowadays are often cash settled, the criterion of 'very real contractual rights' would not provide a sufficient distinction from gambling anymore.
221. *See* Ch. 2 §2.02[A].

In the author's view, sports spread betting transactions will not qualify as derivatives for tax purposes, whereas financial spread betting on securities should fall under the definition of derivatives for tax purposes.[222]

Whereas financial spread bets can be hedged by buying or selling the underlying securities, the outcome of a sports spread bet cannot be hedged as one party to the bet will lose, and the other will win.

In a sports spread bet, a final risk taker is needed, whereas in a financial spread bet, a final risk taker is not necessarily needed.

Example 25:

In a financial spread bet, A promises to pay B a spread at a future date. The spread is defined as the difference between the share price of share X at settlement date and a fixed reference price.

A hedges this spread bet by purchasing the underlying share from C immediately after entering into the contract with B. B again borrows the share from A and sells it short to C.

At maturity, all parties are hedged against the price movement of the underlying share. None of them has entered into a risk position.

[5] Summary of a Tailor-Made Definition for Tax Purposes

Based on the above considerations, an abstract, comprehensive and self-contained legal definition for tax purposes could look as follows:

A financial instrument qualifies as a derivative if (and as long as):

(1) its value depends on the value of one or more independent underlying variables,
(2) its payoff is deterministically dependent on stochastic variables, i.e., the payoff depends in an uncertain way on the value of the underlying variable, but the payoff function as such is pre-defined,
(3) it has some future date at which it will mature, and
(4) it is at any time during the term of the financial instrument possible to replicate the sum of its payoffs by following a trading strategy using the underlying asset(s), cash or other derivative(s).

222. In the context of CTA 2009, Part 7 regarding spread bets entered by companies, HMRC regards these spread bets as CFDs that are within the scope of the derivative contracts regime; *see* HMRC, CFM50380. Gains or losses from financial spread betting realised by individuals are however not subject to capital gains tax in the UK.

In Germany, the Federal Fiscal Court in BFH, decision of 8 December 1981, VIII R 125/79, BStBl II 1982, 618 regarded spread betting as non-taxable/non-deductible gambling with the argument that 'the taxpayer enters to the transaction and takes an excessive loss risk to satisfy his gambling ambitions'. In the author's view, this argumentation cannot add a valid criterion for the definition of derivatives because it is based on the subjective motive of the

[C] Application of the Definition to Existing Derivatives

All traditional types of derivatives, such as options, futures, forwards and swaps, will fall under the above definition. In particular, it makes no difference for the qualification under the definition whether the derivative is settled in cash or physically or whether it is sold or novated before maturity, as the different forms of settlement do not have an impact on its economic value. Hence, they should not be treated differently with regard to their qualification for tax purposes.[223] Furthermore, it does not matter from which underlying asset or variable the value of the derivative is derived as long as it is at any time during the term of the derivative possible to replicate its payoff.[224]

In the following, the author applies the above-developed definition to specific types of derivatives, like weather derivatives, credit derivatives, crypto derivatives and ESG derivatives, and determines in relation to each of these instruments whether they fall under the derivatives' definition or not.

[1] Income Streams and Payoffs as Underlying Variables

Underlying variables of derivatives can also be payoffs or income streams, such as interest and dividends. Interest payments in swap transactions are an example of those income streams. However, only derivatives with an underlying floating interest rate would qualify as derivatives because a necessary criterion of every derivative is the *stochasticity* of at least one payment stream.[225] If a fixed rate coupon would be the underlying variable from which a derivative is derived, this criterion could not be fulfilled, as no parameter exists that changes over time, i.e., which entails an uncertain payment stream. A fixed-for-floating interest rate swap where fixed-rate interest is exchanged against a floating-rate interest is an example of a derivative which derives from interest rates as an underlying variable.[226]

In the same way, interest reference rates, such as SOFR, SONIA or EURIBOR, qualify as eligible underlying variables for derivatives. Examples of such derivatives are plain vanilla interest rate swaps, which are commonly based on such reference indices. The reference index is calculated based on bonds in a pre-defined maturity range. As the maturity of the bond securities becomes less every day, a number of interest-bearing securities issued by various banks will be taken as a reference, and the mean of those interest rates will be determined to generate the reference interest rate for a certain maturity every day. Thus, notional interest payments of an in-reality, not existing bond, will be calculated. This calculation will

taxpayer and hence the qualification as a bet is more likely to be applied if the taxpayer makes losses.

223. The author, in this respect, agrees with the position of Reiner (2002) 341.
224. *See* Excursus of Ch. 4 §4.06[B][1] regarding the distinction between an 'underlying variable' and an 'underlying asset'.
225. *See* Ch. 4 §4.06[B][2].
226. Hull (2006) 150.

then represent the reference index, being an underlying variable for every swap contract with a certain maturity.[227]

An example of a derivative on income streams of (listed) shares is a dividend swap, which allows the exchange of annual, semi-annual, or quarterly actual dividends against a fixed interest rate. As the dividend payments under the swap are uncertain for future dates because they depend on the dividend payments made on the shares in the future, the criterion of *stochasticity* is fulfilled.

[2] Credit Derivatives

Credit derivatives are financial instruments which transfer credit risk in a loan, a bond, or a guarantee from one party to another party.[228]

Miller defines credit derivatives as:

> financial instruments for which payments are determined by reference to some adverse 'credit event' with respect to another financial 'reference asset'. Credit events typically include an actual default in payments on the reference asset or a downgrade in the credit rating of the issuer of the reference asset.[229]

Miller's definition precisely captures the two elements of a credit derivative: the default event and the underlying reference asset. For the purpose of determining whether credit derivatives fall under the proposed definition of derivatives for tax purposes, it is important to ascertain what exactly the underlying variable of the credit derivative is and whether the underlying variable can be hedged with other financial instruments or assets.

The first question to consider is whether the underlying variable of a credit derivative is the general credit risk of the issuer of the reference asset or whether it is the specific credit risk only in relation to this reference asset.[230] The author will investigate this through the example of *Credit Default Swaps* (CDSs), which are the most common credit derivatives. CDSs provide insurance against the risk of default of the issuer of the reference asset.[231]

Reference assets are typically government bonds, corporate bonds, or bonds issued by federal states and municipal entities.[232] CDSs are OTC contracts.[233]

227. EURIBOR, SOFR and SONIA and rates range from one to twelve months. Rates above twelve months are non-standardised 'swap rates' which will be quoted differently by different banks depending on their view of the market.
228. Definitions of credit derivatives can be found in: Jack Clark Francis, Joyce Frost and J. Gregg Whittaker, *The Handbook of Credit Derivatives* (McCraw-Hill, 1999) 3ff. *Also* Christian Neske, 'Grundformen von Kreditderivaten' in Hans-Peter Burghof et al. (eds), *Kreditderivate* (2nd edn, 2005) 46; Fabozzi (1997) 1049; David Miller, 'Overview of the Taxation of Credit Derivatives' in Frank Fabozzi (ed.), *The Use of Derivatives in Tax Planning* (John Wiley & Sons, 2001) 91; Wilmott (2000) 585.
229. Miller (2001) 91.
230. Thus, the question is whether a credit derivative protects against any credit risk of the issuer of the reference asset, or only against the credit risk tied to the specific reference asset.
231. Hull (2006) 507.
232. For example, in Germany, not only the central government issues government bonds, but also the sixteen federal states.
233. Over-the-counter contracts are contracts that are directly traded between two parties, and not traded on an exchange.

Under a CDS, the protection buyer pays a one-time or periodic premium to the protection seller.[234] The obligation of the protection seller depends on whether cash or physical settlement is agreed upon.

Under a physically settled CDS, the protection buyer has the right to sell (the protection seller has an obligation to buy) the reference bonds for their face value when a credit event occurs.[235]

Under a cash-settled CDS, the protection seller will compensate the protection buyer for any defaulted payments under the reference asset over the reference asset's remaining term.[236] Thus, a CDS allows the buying or selling of protection that hedges credit risk in relation to a specific reference asset, not necessarily in relation to the credit risks of all bonds, loans or guarantees of the issuer.

The underlying variable of a credit default swap is the credit risk in relation to the reference asset, not the general credit risk of the issuer of the reference asset.

Example 26:

Company A purchases a CDS with the aim to protect against the default of Greece. The CDS is referenced to a specific Greek government bond X, which has a term until maturity of one year. The CDS has a term of one year. In case a default event is triggered, the CDS pays the protection buyer an amount which equals any defaulted payments during the term of the CDS plus any defaulted amount on the repayment of the notional. If the Greek government defaults on other bonds but not on this specific bond, to which the CDS is referenced, a default event, in general, may be triggered under the CDS, but the protection buyer receives no payment under the CDS because no defaulted payments exist in relation to the reference bond.

To understand the functionality of credit derivatives, one has to consider the 'default event' or 'credit event' in the context of credit derivatives or, more specifically, in the context of a CDS. Under each individual CDS, the parties have to agree on a credit event, which triggers the payment under the CDS.

A 'credit event' can be broadly seen as any non-compliance with the exact specifications in terms of the reference asset in respect of payments under the contract.[237] The term 'credit event' has been standardised by the ISDA Credit Derivatives Definitions.[238] Under ISDA, there are nine different credit events defined, which are chosen individually by the parties of the credit derivative.[239] The terms of a CDS

234. Hull (2006) 507; Miller (2001) 104; Wilmott (2000) 585.
235. Hull (2006) 507; Neske (2005) 48.
236. Miller (2001) 104.
237. Wilmott (2000) 585.
238. ISDA, 2014 Credit Derivatives Definitions.
239. Under the ISDA Credit Derivatives Definitions, the following terms are defined as potential credit events: 'bankruptcy' of a non-government debtor, a sovereign credit event, failure to

often contain a clause that the 'credit event' is only triggered if the reference asset has substantially changed in value.

This 'materiality clause' ensures that a purely technical delay of payment without an adverse change of the credit rating of the debtor does not trigger a credit event. Otherwise, a payment delay of just one day could count as a credit event.

One could view a CDS as an instrument that contains three layers:

(1) The first layer is the 'credit event', which functions as a trigger for any payment under the CDS.[240] But even if a credit event occurs, it is still unclear whether any payment under the CDS has to be made.
(2) The second layer is the default in payments on the reference asset.[241] This layer ensures that payments under the CDS have to be made in principle.
(3) The third layer in a CDS is the recovery rate, which determines how much is paid out under the CDS.[242] Once a credit event occurs and the debtor defaults on the specific reference bond, an auction is made to determine the price of the reference bond.[243] The payment under the CDS will be determined as (1 – recovery rate in per cent).

One can illustrate the function of the first layer (credit event) and the second layer (reference asset) by the following example:

Example 27:

A wants to purchase protection from Bank B against the short-term default of the country Greece. Bank B offers a CDS to A that is referenced to a specific Greek government bond, being the underlying reference asset of the CDS. The CDS is not referenced to all Greek government bonds. The terms of the CDS will include a definition of the 'credit events' which would trigger the CDS to kick in.

Greece could trigger such a credit event by non-payment on any of the bonds it has issued, including bonds which do not function as a reference asset of this specific CDS. However, triggering the credit event only means that the protection under the CDS has, in principle, kicked in but does not say whether any payment is actually made under the CDS. A payment under the CDS will only occur if Greece defaults on the specific reference asset by not repaying interest or the principal under this specific reference bond. Hence, the kick-in of

pay, material adverse restructuring, cross acceleration, cross default, repudiation, a credit event upon merger, and rating downgrade.

240. Wilmott (2000) 585.

241. If no reference asset exists anymore, for example the reference bond has already matured and the CDS is still in existence, a *pari passu* clause ensures that a similar bond will be regarded as the reference bond.

242. The recovery rate is defined as 'the value of the bond immediately after default as a per cent of face value'. *See* Hull (2006) 509.

243. In certain cases, more than one bond functions as the reference asset. In such cases, the reference bond which is 'cheapest-to-deliver' will be regarded as the reference bond, based on which the recovery rate is calculated.

the trigger 'credit event' does not necessarily mean that the CDS actually pays out anything.

Also, in cases of non-government defaults, one can illustrate that the trigger of a credit event does not necessarily mean that payments are made under the CDS.

Example 28:

Company A delivers valuable goods to Company B for its car manufacturing business on a regular basis. Because the business of Company B decreases, Company A wants to protect against the possible default of Company B and purchases a CDS from Bank C.

The CDS is referenced to a corporate bond, which Company B has issued recently. Company B shortly afterwards defaults on its payment obligations for the goods that Company A has delivered. However, Company B does not go into insolvency and fulfils its obligations under the reference bond.

As Company B has defaulted on its obligation to pay for the goods in relation to A, a credit event was triggered. However, because Company B honours its obligation on the corporate bond, Company A will not receive any payments under the CDS from Bank C because the reference bond is paid back in full. Hence, by entering into the CDS, Company A was not necessarily protected against the default of Company B in relation to Company B's obligations against Company A.

The function of the third layer (recovery rate) can be illustrated by the following example:

Example 29:

Company A purchases a CDS from Bank B to protect against a default of Company C. The CDS is referenced to the corporate bond X (term until maturity of five years), which was issued by Company C. The CDS has a term of two years.

Company C goes bankrupt in year 1. The default under the CDS is triggered by the credit event 'bankruptcy' of Company C. As Company C will not repay its obligation under the bond, Company C defaults on the reference bond under the CDS.

An auction is held after the default of Company C to determine the recovery value of the corporate bond. In the auction, the bonds are sold at 40% of their notional value; thus, the recovery rate is determined at 40% of the notional value of the bond. Bank B will pay Company A 60% of the notional value of the bond X under the CDS (1%–40%).

CDSs and other credit derivatives only qualify as derivatives for tax purposes under the proposed definition if they can be replicated using other derivatives, the underlying asset or other financial instruments.[244]

Because a CDS is always referenced to a specific bond, the protection seller can replicate the assumed risk under the CDS by shorting the underlying reference bond.

Example 30:

Bank A sells protection in respect of the default of Company C to Company B under a CDS. The CDS pays out the notional value of 100 minus the recovery rate if Company C defaults on the reference bond X. The term of the CDS is two years, and Company B pays periodic interest payments to Bank A for default protection under the CDS.

Bank A borrows the reference bond from Bank D and sells the bond to Bank E in order to hedge its exposure under the CDS. If Company C defaults under the reference bond X, assuming a recovery rate of, for example, 20% in the auction, Bank A has the following position:

(1) Bank A pays Company B 100% - 20%, which equals 80% of the notional value of the reference bond.
(2) Bank A makes a gain of 80% of the notional value of the reference bond under the short position because it has sold a bond for 100 to Bank E. When returning the borrowed reference bond to Bank D, it simply purchases the bond at 20% of the notional value in the market because that is the value the bond has after default and closes its short position, thereby making a gain of 80% of the notional value of the bond.
(3) The gain under the short position offsets the loss under the CDS.

Hence, by entering into the short position, Bank A could perfectly hedge the risk of payment under the CDS.

The above example shows that a CDS referenced to an underlying bond qualifies as a derivative for the purposes of the definition of these instruments for tax purposes because of the possibility of replicating the above-mentioned CDS and, hence, hedging the risk position.

As CDSs are OTC contracts, the parties could also agree on the terms of a CDS, which is not referenced to a specific bond but where the 'reference asset' is a loan or a guarantee. In those cases, a CDS would not qualify as a derivative for the purposes of the tax definition as the protection seller could not hedge against the payment risk under the CDS. For loans or guarantees, no primary or secondary market exists on which the loan or guarantee can be traded during the term of the CDS. Thus, no

244. *See* Ch. 4 §4.06[B][4].

financial instrument, including the reference asset, exists that is fungible and liquid and, thus, could be used to replicate the CDS.

Hence, CDSs over loans or guarantees would not qualify as derivatives under the proposed tax definition because a replication or hedge of the CDS would not be possible. Instead, such CDSs over loans or guarantees would qualify as mere bets.

Other credit derivatives include Credit-Linked Notes (CLN), Total Return Swaps and Credit Spread Options.

Under a CLN,[245] the buyer of the CLN pays the notional amount of the CLN to the issuer at inception and receives periodic interest payments, which consist of interest payments on the capital invested and additional interest for the credit risk that the buyer of the CLN has assumed.

At maturity of the note, the issuer only pays back the notional value of the CLN if no credit event has occurred in the underlying reference asset(s) of the CLN.[246] Underlying reference assets of CLNs could be a specific loan issued by the seller of the CLN to a third party, a single reference bond or a whole portfolio of reference bonds or loans.[247]

CLNs are structured products,[248] as they consist of a bond plus short CDS(s).[249] Before the credit crisis, CLNs were popular instruments under which banks would pool the credit risks of various reference assets and sell those risks on to investors who obtained a yield pick-up for effectively assuming the credit risks of the underlying assets or portfolio as well as the credit risk of the issuer of the CLN.[250]

The CDSs contained in the CLNs only qualify as derivatives for tax purposes if the reference assets contained in the underlying asset portfolio were all tradable and liquid assets, thereby allowing the investor of the CLN to hedge the assumed risk. Because banks would often get rid of very illiquid or non-tradable assets by issuing a CLN, most CDSs contained in the CLNs would, in practice, not qualify as derivatives for tax purposes. Instead, the investor of a CLN could often be said to have entered into a bet because the CLN could not be properly replicated with fungible and liquid reference assets. However, if one imagined a scenario where those short CDSs contained in the CLNs could be hedged by using (a combination of) other (liquid, tradable and fungible) derivatives over the credit risks contained in those CLNs, underlying reference assets and cash, those CDSs contained in the CLNs should qualify as derivatives for tax purposes, and not as mere bets.

245. A credit-linked note can be regarded as a securitised CDS.
246. Hohl/Liebig in: Roland Eller, Walter Gruber and Markus Reif, *Kreditrisikomodelle und Kreditderivate* (1999) 508.
247. Scharpf and Luz (2000) 183.
248. *See* Ch. 8 §8.01. Similar: Moorad Choudhry, *An Introduction to Bond Markets* (3 edn, John Wiley & Sons 2006) 315.
249. The investor of the CLN holds a bond and at the same time enters into the position of the protection seller under a CDS. Hence, the payout under the CLN at maturity is the notional value of the bond minus any losses assumed under the position of the CDS on the reference basket of assets. If the basket of underlying reference assets is only worth 50% of the initial value of day 1, the CLN would pay a notional value of the CLN – 50% of the value of the reference basket at maturity.
250. Choudhry (2006) 315.

Under a Total Return Swap (TRS), the protection buyer pays the protection seller income from the reference asset as well as any increase in value of the asset and receives a fixed or floating interest rate and payment of any decreases in value of the underlying reference asset.[251] The increases or decreases in value of the reference asset can either be paid periodically during the term of the TRS or at maturity of the swap.[252]

Under the TRS, the protection seller effectively also assumes the credit risk of the bond or the equity over the term of the TRS, as the market price of the bond or the equity will depend on its respective credit risk.[253]

Underlings of a TRS are normally bonds or shares. Thus, a TRS qualifies as a derivative for tax purposes if it can be replicated with fungible and liquid underlying reference assets, which is usually the case if the underlying assets are bonds or shares.[254] By entering into a TRS, the protection seller assumes the position of a synthetic bond or equity[255] and thus can replicate the position with a purchase of the underlying bond or equity.[256]

A *Credit Spread Option* (CSO) is a financial instrument where the payment amount of the option depends on a reference credit spread, meaning that the payoff depends on the credit spread between two reference assets.[257] A CSO protects the protection buyer against the widening of the credit spread between two reference assets,[258] where the buyer receives a payment if the credit spread widens above the agreed strike price.

Example 31:

Company A wants to protect against widening credit spreads between Italian government bonds and German government bonds because it has Italian government bonds on its books and fears a deterioration of the credit rating of Italy.

Company A buys from Bank B a CSO under which Bank B is obliged to pay Company A the difference between the credit spreads between the Italian and German government bonds above a certain agreed strike price. Company A pays a premium to Bank B. If the credit spreads widen as Company A fears, and if the widening of the credit spreads is above the agreed strike price, Company A will receive from Bank B the credit spread minus the strike price. The CSO qualifies

251. Neske (2005) 51; *also* IDW, *RS BFA 1, Bilanzierung von Kreditderivaten* (2001) WPg 2002, 195ff; Hohl/Liebig in: Eller, Gruber and Reif (1999) 508; Häuselmann and Wagner (2002b) 2174.
252. Häuselmann and Wagner (2002b) 2174.
253. The price of the bond at maturity of the TRS will have declined if the credit rating of the issuer of the bond has deteriorated or if the issuer of the bond has defaulted.
254. In cases where the underlying of the TRS is a loan note, which is not fungible and liquid, the TRS would not qualify as a derivative contract for tax purposes.
255. Häuselmann and Wagner (2002b) 2174.
256. The protection seller can hedge the position by selling the underlying shares or bonds.
257. Hull (2006) 746.
258. Hohl/Liebig in: Eller, Gruber and Reif (1999) 509.

as a derivative for tax purposes because Bank B can replicate the CSO by dynamically trading in the spread position of the two underlying bonds.

[3] Crypto Derivatives

Reuters proposed in an article in July 2022 that the then volume of crypto derivatives 'makes up 69% of total crypto volumes, up from 66% in June'.[259] Although those numbers should be taken with caution, the fact is that crypto derivatives exist and that there are a variety of them. A recent *EY* report stipulates that:

> Commonly found digital asset-based derivative products on the market today include bitcoin and ether-based futures and options, such as those offered by Binance, FTX and Chicago Mercantile Exchange Group Inc. (CME). Overall, digital asset-based derivatives have experienced fast-paced growth that far exceeds the underlying cryptocurrency spot market, with global estimates of over $32 trillion in trading volume for just bitcoin and ether-based futures in 2021.[260]

Crypto derivatives are traded in the form of exchange-traded crypto options, exchange-traded futures, perpetual futures and perpetual swaps. One can distinguish exchange-traded and listed crypto derivatives, OTC crypto derivatives and derivatives on so-called Decentralised Finance (DeFi) markets.[261] According to *EY*, listed crypto derivatives in the US include:

(1) cash-settled CME Bitcoin Futures;[262]
(2) CME options on Bitcoin Futures;[263] and
(3) Bitnomial Bitcoin US Dollar Futures.[264]

259. Elizabeth Howcroft, Crypto derivatives volumes surge to $3.12 trillion in July – CryptoCompare, Reuters (12 September 2023), https://www.reuters.com/technology/crypto-derivatives-volumes-surge-312-trillion-july-cryptocompare-2022-08-11/, accessed 6 February 2024.
260. EY, Crypto derivatives are becoming a major digital asset class (2022), 1, https://assets.ey.com/content/dam/ey-sites/ey-com/en_us/topics/financial-services/ey-crypto-derivatives-pov_final4.pdf?download, accessed 11 July 2023.
261. *Ibid.*, 12: 'DeFi refers to a growing financial ecosystem that offers traditional financial services, such as derivatives, using public blockchain infrastructure and smart contracts to facilitate transactions. Decentralized derivative protocols (DDPs) facilitate the issuing, servicing, trading, and settlement of various digital asset-based derivatives using smart contracts.'
262. For the contract specifications of the Bitcoin futures *see* CME Group, Bitcoin Futures, https://www.cmegroup.com/markets/cryptocurrencies/bitcoin/bitcoin.contractSpecs.html, accessed 11 August 2023.
263. CME Group, Get to know options on Bitcoin futures, https://www.cmegroup.com/education/courses/introduction-to-bitcoin/get-to-know-options-on-bitcoin-futures.html, accessed 11 January 2023.
264. Bitnomial, Bitcoin US Dollar Futures, https://bitnomial.com/products/bitcoin-us-dollar-futures, accessed 11 January 2023; *compare business wire, A Berkshire Hathaway Company, Bitnomial Launches Margined, Physically Settled Bitcoin futures in the US* (15 November 2021) https://www.businesswire.com/news/home/20211115005890/en/Bitnomial-Launches-Margined-Physically-Settled-Bitcoin-Futures-in-the-US, accessed 23 February 2023.

As *EY* described, offshore exchanges like Binance, BTCEX and the now-bankrupt FTX[265] were 'market leaders in the offshore exchanges in listed digital asset futures and options'.[266] Binance explains that:

> Crypto futures contracts represent the value of a specific cryptocurrency at a specified time. These are agreements between traders to buy or sell a particular asset at a predetermined price on a specified date in the future. In a traditional futures contract, the holder of the position is under an obligation to buy or sell the underlying asset at the contract price at expiry.[267]

For example, 'Binance Futures offer traders the ability to trade quarterly and perpetual futures contracts. Quarterly futures contracts expire after three months, while perpetual futures contracts don't have an expiration date.'[268] Crypto options provide the holder with the right but not the obligation to buy or sell an asset at a pre-defined price and date.[269]

EY states that outside the listed crypto derivatives, there are further instruments, such as perpetual swaps and non-deliverable forwards.

Perpetual swaps, also called perpetuals, are:

> relatively similar to index or equity-linked swaps, [and] have become widely used for digital assets. These contracts are similar to a future but do not settle. Rather, the price of the contract generally mirrors that of the underlying asset (e.g., bitcoin) and has no fixed maturity. Perpetuals are not currently offered by US-regulated exchanges.[270] According to *EY*, those perpetual swaps 'represent a significant portion of all digital assets derivatives trading globally'.

EY proposes that those instruments:

> are attractive to investors as they provide the buyer with synthetic long exposure to a digital asset and the seller with short exposure to that same asset. Given there is no expiration, the swap provides both the buyer and seller with the ability to offset their risk and exposure indefinitely, or at least until the contract is terminated. While perpetual swaps are often compared with futures, the price does not converge to the index price in the way a cash-settled future does. Thus, perpetual swaps may compare more closely to an equity-linked swap in traditional equities markets.[271]

---

265. New York Times, 11 November 2022, Embattled Cryptoexchange FTX files for Bankruptcy, https://www.nytimes.com/2022/11/11/business/ftx-bankruptcy.html, accessed 11 January 2023.
266. EY, Crypto derivatives (2022), 9 referring to the website: Coingecko, Top Derivative Exchanges Ranked by Open Interest & Trade Volume, https://www.coingecko.com/en/exchanges/derivatives, accessed 11 January 2024.
267. Binance, Crypto Futures and Options: What Are the Similarities and Differences? (4 January 2023), https://www.binance.com/en/blog/futures/crypto-futures-and-options-what-are-the-similarities-and-differences-421499824684902074, accessed 12 January 2023.
268. *Ibid.*
269. *Ibid.*
270. EY, Crypto derivatives (2022), 9.
271. *Ibid.*, 9-10.

Non-deliverable forwards (NDFs) are another category of crypto derivatives.[272] They are like traditional forward contracts dependent on the price of an underlying – in this case, the price of a cryptocurrency – whether Bitcoin, Ethereum or similar. NDFs can be cash settled only. *EY* mentions in their report that Goldman Sachs has been offering Bitcoin-based NDFs to their clients.[273] To hedge themselves from the risk exposure, Goldman Sachs buys and sells Bitcoin futures in block trades on the CME Group Inc. exchange.[274]

A further category is contracts for differences over cryptocurrencies. They are 'cash-settled instruments that allow investors to trade on the price movement of cryptocurrencies without owning the underlying assets'.[275]

When we consider crypto derivatives, one needs to determine:

- if cryptoassets/cryptocurrencies could themselves be considered derivatives, and
- if their prices could be an eligible underlying asset/variable or if crypto derivatives qualify as mere bets for tax purposes.

[a] *Should Cryptoassets/Cryptocurrencies Be Qualified as Derivatives for Tax Purposes?*

To reiterate, a financial instrument qualifies as a derivative if (and as long as):

(1) its value depends on the value of one or more independent underlying variables;
(2) its payoff is deterministically dependent on stochastic variables, i.e., the payoff depends in an uncertain way on the value of the underlying variable, but the payoff function as such is pre-defined;
(3) it has some future date at which it will mature; and
(4) it is at any time during the term of the financial instrument possible to replicate the sum of its payoffs by following a trading strategy using the underlying asset(s), cash or other derivative(s).

The elements of a derivative (1) to (3) are already not fulfilled. Further, stochastic replication is a necessary element of a derivative.[276] Thus, according to the above-presented definition of derivatives for tax purposes, cryptoassets/cryptocurrencies do not qualify as derivatives.

272. Shanny Basar, NDFs could boost institutional crypto use, *Marketsmedia* newsletter, https://www.marketsmedia.com/ndfs-could-boost-institutional-crypto-use/, accessed 1 August 2023.
273. EY, Crypto derivatives (2022), 9.
274. *Ibid.*, referring to an article in Bloomberg Law (6 May 2021), Goldman Offers New Bitcoin Derivatives to Wall Street Investors, https://news.bloomberglaw.com/banking-law/goldman-offers-new-bitcoin-derivatives-to-wall-street-investors, accessed 11 July 2023.
275. *Ibid.*
276. *See* Ch. 4 §4.06[B][4].

Even if one applied the accounting definition of a derivative of IFRS 9, cryptocurrencies do not fulfil any of the elements outlined in IFRS 9/FRS 102, Appendix A.

IFRS 9 states that a derivative is a *financial instrument* or other contract with all three of the following characteristics:

(a) its value changes in response to the change in a specified interest rate, financial instrument price, commodity price, foreign exchange rate, index of prices or rates, credit rating or credit index, or other variable (sometimes called the 'underlying'), provided in the case of a non-financial variable that the variable is not specific to a party to the contract;
(b) it requires no initial net investment or an initial net investment that is smaller than would be required for other types of contracts that would be expected to have a similar response to changes in market factors; and
(c) it is settled at a future date.

If one applied this accounting definition to cryptocurrencies, none of the three criteria outlined from (a) to (c) are fulfilled because of the following reasons:

(a) There is no underlying of a cryptocurrency which changes in response to a specific value. The cryptocurrency is the underlying itself.
(b) If one purchases a cryptocurrency, the full cost of the net investment must be paid upfront.
(c) Cryptocurrencies are unlike derivatives, not settled at a future date, but upon purchase, the cryptocurrency is delivered immediately.[277]

Furthermore, cryptocurrencies are not financial instruments according to the majority view held in the accounting literature.

Southern and the author argued that '[a]ccounting cryptocurrencies as a financial asset at FVTPL in accordance with *IFRS 9* would have the policy advantage of having a ready system that measures cryptocurrencies in a timely manner. To be able to do so, cryptocurrencies must meet the definition of IAS 32'.[278]

IAS 32.11 defines a financial instrument as 'a contract that gives rise to a financial asset of one entity and a financial liability or equity instrument of another entity'.[279]

If one characterises cryptocurrency as a financial asset within IAS 32, it must be an asset that is:

(a) cash
(b) an equity instrument of another entity
(c) a contractual right
 (i) to receive cash or another financial asset from another entity; or
 (ii) to exchange financial assets or financial liabilities with another entity under conditions that are potentially favourable to the entity; or

277. Southern and Weidmann (2023), 81 with regard to the accounting treatment of cryptoassets in the context of IFRS 9.
278. *Ibid.*, 77.
279. IAS 32 Financial Instruments: Presentation, para. 11, https://www.ifrs.org/content/dam/ifrs/publications/pdf-standards/english/2021/issued/part-a/ias-32-financial-instruments-presentation.pdf, accessed 11 February 2023.

(d) a contract that will or may be settled in the entity's own equity instruments and is:
   (i) a non-derivative for which the entity is or may be obliged to receive a variable number of the entity's own equity instruments; or
   (ii) a derivative that will or may be settled other than by the exchange of a fixed amount of cash or another financial asset for a fixed number of the entity's own equity instruments. For this purpose, the entity's own equity instruments do not include puttable financial instruments classified as equity instruments in accordance with paragraphs 16A and 16B, instruments that impose on the entity an obligation to deliver to another party a pro-rata share of the net assets of the entity only on liquidation and are classified as equity instruments in accordance with paragraphs 16C and 16D, or instruments that are contracts for the future receipt or delivery of the entity's own equity instruments.[280]

Cryptocurrencies do not qualify as financial assets according to the majority view in the accounting world, although there are good arguments that cryptocurrencies can be seen as digital cash.[281]

Hence, according to the majority view, they are not financial assets, and thus, they can also not qualify as financial instruments. In summary, cryptoassets cannot be regarded as derivatives – neither for accounting nor tax purposes.

[b] Do Crypto Derivatives Qualify as Derivatives for Tax Purposes?

Cryptocurrencies, as such, might be an eligible underlying for a derivative contract. HMRC seems to support the view that cryptoassets can be eligible underlyings for derivative contracts and that crypto derivatives would fall under CTA 2009, Part 7.[282]

To determine if cryptoassets can be eligible underlyings, one must distinguish between gambling, which should be excluded as a source of taxation,[283] and derivatives over eligible underlyings.

To reiterate, gains should be treated as taxable income based on the principles of reciprocity and correspondence in taxation, meaning if a legislator makes gains from betting taxable, losses should be tax deductible.

From a policy point of view, gambling and betting should be excluded as a source of taxation because gains should be treated as taxable income based on the principles of reciprocity and correspondence in taxation. If the tax legislator decides to tax gains from gambling and betting, it also has to make corresponding losses tax deductible.

280. IAS 32.11.
281. Southern and Weidmann (2023), 79-80.
282. HMRC, Cryptoassets Manual, 30 March 2021 (updated 3 November 2022), CRYPTO10150 – Introduction to cryptoassets: derivatives over cryptoassets.
283. In the UK, profits arising from gambling transactions are not subject to income tax as they do not constitute a trade and are also exempt under TCGA 1992, s. 51. *See* HMRC, *Business Income Manual* (2011), BIM22015-22020. This is also the position of the German tax legislation since 1921. *See* RFH, RFHE 21, 244 (1921) and RFH, RStBl 1928, 181.

In the author's view, governments should not take part in the gambler's risk regarding the outcome of the game if they allow the deduction of these losses. Therefore, any losses from gambling and betting should not be tax deductible, and any gains should not be taxable.

Former NatWest Chair Sir Howard Davies goes as far as to support even a ban on cryptocurrency trading on the grounds that: 'It's gambling as far as I can see, with a sort of libertarian veneer on top of it. You should put a big sign on the door saying, Abandon Hope All Ye Who Enter Here', citing Dante's Inferno.[284]

Governments around the world have, however, largely taken a different stance and treat gains from cryptocurrencies as taxable and losses from them as tax deductible, or at least offsetable against cryptocurrency gains, and not as gambling.

To verify this position, one needs to investigate the definition of derivatives for tax purposes again. The author has stated above that 'a derivative is a derivative if it can be stochastically replicated by using combinations of other financial instruments, cash and/or derivatives'.[285]

According to *Hull*, a derivative is defined as 'a financial instrument whose value depends on the value of other, more basic, underlying variables'.[286]

From the perspective of the tax legislation, the inclusion of a replication criterion in the definition of derivatives ensures that derivatives can be distinguished from mere betting.

A derivative can be distinguished from bets because a derivative can be replicated and hedged.[287] Whereas derivative traders partly or fully hedge the risks of their portfolios, a gambler takes the full risk. Hence, derivatives and betting can also be distinguished by the existence of a final risk taker. In a betting transaction, both parties take some, not necessarily the corresponding risk of losing. In a derivatives transaction, both counterparties can have a trading position at maturity, with neither of them having lost on their position as both parties can hedge themselves.[288] If both counterparties can hedge the final payoff, no final risk taker is needed.

HMRC suggests that if transactions fall into the definition of gambling or are identified as a highly speculative activity, such transactions may not be taxable. In terms of cryptoassets, 'HMRC does not consider the buying and selling of cryptoassets as gambling.'[289] HMRC suggests, however, that all facts of a transaction involving

284. Daily Mail, 1 October 2021, Crypto traders should be warned 'abandon all hope', NatWest's boss declares, as he praises China for 'banning the damned stuff', https://www.dailymail.co.uk/news/article-10047803/NatWest-boss-Sir-Howard-Davies-applauds-China-banning-practice-crypto-trading.html, accessed 11 January 2023.
285. *See* Ch. 2 §2.02[A], referring to Rubinstein (1999a), 71-72 and 179-192.
286. Hull (2018) 1.
287. *See* Ch. 2 §2.02[A].
288. For the definition of hedging, *see* Ch. 2 §2.02[B].
289. HMRC, Crypotassets Manual, CRYPTO10450 – Introduction to cryptoassets: why HMRC does not consider buying and selling cryptoassets to be gambling, 30 March 2021, updated November 2022. https://www.gov.uk/hmrc-internal-manuals/cryptoassets-manual/crypto10450, accessed 11 January 2023.

cryptoassets need to be considered to conclude that the transactions classify as gambling. In practice, HMRC taxes cryptoassets in the hands of individuals, businesses and companies but also allows a deduction of capital losses from cryptoassets with certain recording and time limitations,[290] including the tax deduction for impairment losses.

To determine if crypto derivatives qualify as derivatives or mere bets, one needs to answer the following question:

Can crypto derivatives be hedged using fungible, liquid and tradable cryptocurrencies, other crypto derivatives and/or cash?

If that is the case, crypto derivatives would qualify as derivatives for tax purposes under the definition outlined above. However, if crypto derivatives cannot be sufficiently hedged (so that no final risk taker is needed), they would qualify as a gambling activity and should be outside the scope of (direct) taxation. In contrast, if crypto derivatives can be sufficiently hedged, they should be inside the taxation scope and would qualify as derivatives for tax purposes under the above-proposed definition.

Parallel to the discussions of credit derivatives and particularly CLNs, crypto derivatives only qualify as derivatives for tax purposes if the underlying reference assets are tradable, fungible and liquid assets or if other tradable, fungible and liquid crypto derivatives exist that allow hedging of the assumed cryptocurrency risks.

Crypto derivatives are predominantly instruments where the underlying variable is the price of a cryptocurrency. In order for them to qualify as derivatives for tax purposes under the above-mentioned definition, the underlying reference asset – here, the specific cryptocurrency – needs to be (i) tradable, (ii) fungible, and (iii) liquid for the crypto derivative over that cryptocurrency to qualify as a derivative for tax purposes.

There are crypto futures in existence on the largest cryptocurrencies, such as Bitcoin and Ethereum.[291] Thus, one can argue that as long as the markets for underlying cryptocurrencies (or other crypto derivatives over that cryptocurrency) provide sufficient liquidity, a crypto derivative on those cryptocurrencies should qualify as a derivative for tax purposes because such a crypto derivative could be hedged with a liquid, fungible and tradable cryptocurrency (or alternatively another crypto derivative over the same cryptocurrency) – or used as a hedge for the underlying cryptocurrency.

However, if – at some point in time – those crypto exchanges became dysfunctional, or if the cryptocurrency – and the crypto derivatives over that cryptocurrency itself ceases to become tradable, fungible and liquid, there are good arguments to maintain that crypto derivatives would at that point in time not qualify as derivatives for tax purposes according to the proposed definition but as mere gambling, with the result that any gains or losses would *not* be subject to taxation.

290. HMRC, Cryptoassets Manual (2021).
291. Binance, Ether Futures, https://www.binance.com/en/e/ether_futures, accessed 12 January 2023.

The author understands that this view, however, leaves the crypto derivatives investor/trader with the risk that crypto derivatives losses may not be tax deductible, although cryptocurrency gains were previously taxable. Nonetheless, this argument may be justifiable from a tax policy perspective, although it contradicts the principle of correspondence in taxation because it protects domestic tax legislators from potentially harmful erosion of their tax base if crypto (derivatives) losses are made deductible without any restrictions.

NFTs do not represent tradable, fungible and liquid assets, and thus, any potential derivatives over an NFT should not qualify as a derivative for tax purposes. As previously explained in Chapter 2, derivatives over NFTs should not be mistaken for NFT derivatives, which are simply NFT projects created using creative assets and intellectual property from existing projects.[292] Unlike cryptocurrencies, NFTs cannot be traded or exchanged at equivalency. This differs from fungible tokens like cryptocurrencies, which are identical to each other and, therefore, can serve as a medium for commercial transactions.[293]

[4] ESG Derivatives

As outlined in Chapter 2, ESG-related investments may not yet qualify as a new comprehensive underlying asset class in the same way as cryptoassets. The term ESG derivatives, however, encompasses a multitude of underlying variables with the result that some of them will qualify as derivatives for tax purposes while others more likely will not. Further, in many cases, the ESG component is a simple add-on which uses traditional derivative categories and combines them with some form of ESG element. The following discusses the various ESG derivatives categories and determines if they qualify as derivatives for tax purposes based on the definition outlined above.

[a] Weather Derivatives

There is a growing need for the use of the derivatives market to manage climate-related risks which result directly from the impact of climate change, a recent report of the Climate-Related Subcommittee, Market Risk Advisory Committee of the US Commodity Futures Trading Commission advised.[294] Weather derivatives have already existed

292. Mirijam Teiss, NFT Collections Explained (Dexterlab 2022), https://dexterlab.com/nft-derivatives/, accessed 1 September 2023.
293. Investopedia, What Are Non-fungible Tokens? https://www.investopedia.com/non-fungible-tokens-nft-5115211, accessed 12 February 2023.
294. Climate-Related Subcommittee, Market Risk Advisory Committee of the US Commodity Futures Trading Commission, Managing climate risk in the U.S. financial system, Report of the Climate-Related Subcommittee (2020), https://www.cftc.gov/sites/default/files/2020-09/9-9-20%20Report%20of%20the%20Subcommittee%20on%20Climate-Related%20Market%20Risk%20-%20Managing%20Climate%20Risk%20in%20the%20U.S.%20Financial%20System%20for%20posting.pdf, accessed 8 February 2024.

for many years, and the first OTC weather derivatives were introduced in 1997.[295] One could categorise those derivatives within the broad category of ESG derivatives.

As *Hull* puts it, '[m]any companies are in the position where their performance is liable to be adversely affected by the weather', mentioning that roughly one-seventh of the US economy is subject to weather risk.[296] A typical OTC weather derivative is an option or forward contract that provides a payoff that is dependent on the cumulative 'Heating degree days' (HDD) or 'Cooling degree days' (CDD) during a month.[297]

Also, exchange-traded weather derivatives exist, with the Chicago Mercantile Exchange beginning trading them in 1999, both 'weather futures and European options on weather futures'.[298]

The CME Group, where those futures and options are traded, confirmed that:

> the awareness of climate-related risk has contributed to increased activity in CME Group Weather futures and options trading volumes and the addition of new market participants in the space, including hedge funds and asset managers:
>
> - In 2020, futures volumes have increased 60 percent year-to-date with a notional value of $750 million, while options volumes increased 143 percent year-to-date with a notional value of $480 million.
> - September 2020 marked the highest volume month in over two years, with an average daily volume (ADV) of over 1,000 contracts.
> - As of December 2020, open interest (OI) was over 29,000 contracts, a 175 percent increase year-over-year.[299]

Weather derivatives will qualify as derivatives under the above definition only if another financial instrument, including another derivative, exists which can be used to replicate the payoff of the derivative.

Sunshine and rain are not physical assets which could be used to hedge the derivative, but they are underlying variables. However, no spot market exists for these underlying variables.[300]

Weather derivatives may nevertheless fall under the tax definition of derivatives if a liquid market on other weather derivatives exists that can be used to replicate the specific weather derivative.[301] Insofar as weather-swaps, -options, -floors, -collars, or

---

295. Hull (2018) 821.
296. *Ibid.*
297. *Ibid.*
298. *Ibid.*, 822.
299. Dominic-Sutton Vermeulen, Managing Climate Risk with CME Weather Futures and Options (20 January 2021), https://www.cmegroup.com/education/articles-and-reports/managing-climate-risk-with-cme-group-weather-futures-and-options.html, accessed 8 May 2023.
300. Helyette Geman, *Insurance and Weather Derivatives: From Exotic Options to Exotic Underlyings* (Risk Books, 1999) 3.
301. Vermeulen (2021), states:

> In order to construct a hedging strategy, it will become necessary to quantify the relationship between economic outcomes (such as sales revenues) and weather conditions (as implied in weather futures prices). In particular, one wants to find an appropriate hedge ratio (HR) that might balance the anticipated change in revenues (denoted as Δ Revenues) with the changing value of the subject derivatives contracts

-bonds are actively traded at a liquid OTC market,[302] or temperature-based index futures or options can be traded over the exchange,[303] weather derivatives could be replicated and hedged by another type of weather derivative.

Example 32:

A sunshine call or put option could be hedged with a sunshine futures contract, although the 'sun hours' are not tradable at a spot market.

[b] Catastrophe Derivatives

Catastrophe or CAT derivatives have been around for many years. CAT derivatives simply transfer the risk of a natural disaster between counterparties. For example, OTC catastrophe swaps are purchased by the protection buyer to protect against financial losses from significant natural disasters like cyclones, floods, tsunamis, and earthquakes. A premium is paid by the protection buyer to the protection seller (usually a bank).

Catastrophe derivatives are a type of insurance derivative.[304] Usually, a bank then transfers the risks of the catastrophe swaps to investors via catastrophe bonds, who are then the final risk takers of the CAT risk. Similar to credit default derivatives, CAT derivatives have the same function as reinsurance contracts or CAT bond insurance but without the complexity of the contracts. 'Catastrophe swaps allow countries to transfer some of their disaster risk exposure to insurance and capital markets without increasing their sovereign debt. A country pays a premium and in return receives a pay-out if a specified disaster event occurs.'[305]

Vice versa, the insurance industry also uses derivatives to hedge its exposure to CAT risks, such as the ones named above.[306] Those contracts are basically reinsurance contracts.

Hence, CAT derivatives qualify as derivatives under the definition for tax purposes as the banks can hedge their risks with the issuance of catastrophe bonds. It should, however, be noted that in contrast to weather derivatives, where an active market exists where those contracts can be traded, CAT derivatives are commonly bespoke OTC contracts. The CATEX is a Catastrophe Risk Exchange where one could also trade CAT swaps. The Catastrophe Risk Exchange is, however, not an SEC-registered exchange, so the counterparties bear the credit risk under the swap and not

(Δ Value of Futures). A statistical regression between revenues and weather conditions is frequently useful in assessing these quantitative relationships.

302. Geman (1999), 176.
303. CME Group, Weather Products, https://www.cmegroup.com/trading/weather/, accessed 8 May 2023.
304. Hull (2018) 823.
305. ISDA, Overview of ESG-related Derivatives (2021), 13.
306. Hull (2018) 822-823.

the exchange. As far as the author understands, the CATEX is a software solution which allows insurance and reinsurance companies to conclude OTC CAT swaps among each other.

Hence, as long as liquid and fungible instruments, for example, CAT bonds or other derivatives, exist that allow the party of the CAT derivative to hedge itself, CAT derivatives should qualify as derivatives for tax purposes under the definition provided above.

[c] Sustainability-Linked Derivatives

Sustainability-linked derivatives are simply derivatives that add some ESG pricing component to the conventional derivatives that are used for hedging purposes, such as interest rate swaps, cross-currency swaps and forwards.[307]

Many Sustainability-linked derivatives are traded OTC and are highly customised.[308] The aim of those derivatives is to 'reduce one counterparty's payment in the event it achieves some pre-agreed sustainability performance target. This mechanism provides market participants with a financial incentive for improved ESG performance'.[309]

Other derivatives simply pressure a derivatives counterparty to meet certain pre-determined ESG targets. 'If a company cannot meet its ESG target, it will have to compensate by supporting climate action sustainability projects',[310] the ISDA report explains. That means they are used to incentivise ESG performance, or they facilitate the support for 'sustainable projects'.[311] Sustainability-linked derivatives 'involve an ESG overlay added to a conventional derivative, such as an interest rate or cross-currency swap. This ESG overlay usually takes the form of an ESG target that is applied to one or both counterparties'.[312]

The ISDA report contains examples of banks that have executed tailor-made sustainability-linked derivatives.

There are sustainability-linked interest rate swaps.[313] The ISDA report mentions the example of ING bank, which 'executed the world's first sustainability improvement derivative (SID), designed to hedge the interest rate risk of SBM's[314] $1 billion five-year floating rate revolving credit facility. SBM pays a fixed rate on the swap and receives a floating rate'.[315]

---

307. ISDA, Overview of ESG-related Derivatives (2021), 3; *also* UN, Scaling Finance for sustainable development goals, 26, https://globalcompact.no/app/uploads/2020/01/Scaling-SDG-Finance.pdf, accessed 12 April 2023.
308. ISDA Future Leader in Derivatives, Sustainability-linked derivatives: Where to begin, paper (May 2022), 3.
309. ISDA, Overview of ESG-related Derivatives (2021), 3.
310. *Ibid.*
311. ISDA Future Leader in Derivatives, Sustainability-linked derivatives, 6.
312. *Ibid.*
313. Kelly, Farrelly et al. (2021).
314. SBM is a global supplier of floating production solutions to the offshore energy industry, *see* ISDA, Overview of ESG-related Derivatives (2021), 3.
315. *Ibid.*

In 2020, HSBC executed an interest rate swap with Siemens Gamesa, a supplier of wind power solutions 'that converted a €250 million tranche of a floating-rate syndicated loan, which was arranged in December 2019, into fixed-rate funding'.[316] It is important to understand how this swap works. Under the term of the swap, the 'fixed rate of the swap will not vary if Siemens Gamesa's ESG rating changes, but any change during the life of the swap will prompt charitable giving'.[317] In contrast, 'if Siemens Gamesa's ESG rating improves, HSBC will donate annually to projects of non-profit organizations. If the rating declines, Siemens Gamesa will donate'.[318]

One must agree that this kind of charitable giving through derivatives is something quite innovative as it positively encourages Siemens Gamesa to improve its ESG rating – in any case, charitable concerns always win.

In the space of FX derivatives, sustainability has also entered the derivatives market.[319] For example, in 2019, 'Société Générale executed a sustainable-development-goal-linked cross-currency swap[320] tied to a €1.5 billion bond.'[321] 'The swap enables Enel to hedge its exposure against the euro/dollar exchange rate and interest rate risk created by the different denominations of the bond repayments (US dollars) and the source of repayments (Euros).'[322] The sustainability element of this 'traditional' cross-currency swap is constructed as follows:

> Enel received a discounted rate based on its commitment to sustainability performance. Société Générale provided the discount as part of its commitment to the positive impact finance and based on Enel's positive contribution to one of the pillars of sustainable development (economic, environmental and social) and mitigation of any potential negative impacts to any of the pillars.[323]

It is interesting to note that Société Générale, a bank and privately owned company, provides another privately owned company, Enel, a discount based on Enel's commitment to positively contribute to one of the pillars of sustainable development. Société Générale, however, provides the discount as part of its own sustainability program.[324] Do good, and talk about it, as they say.

As one sees, those sustainability-linked interest rates and FX swaps are traditional derivative instruments that have a sustainability element linked to some form of

316. *Ibid.*
317. *Ibid.*
318. *Ibid.*
319. Kelly, Farrelly et al. (2021).
320. *Hull* defines a cross-currency derivative as 'an instrument where two currencies are involved. The payoff is defined in terms of a variable that is measured in one of the currencies and the payoff is made in the other currency', *see* John Hull and Sankarshan Basu, *Options, Futures and Other Derivatives* (Pearson, 11th edn, 2022) 734.
321. ISDA, Overview of ESG-related Derivatives (2021), 3.
322. *Ibid.*
323. *Ibid.*
324. Société Générale, Enel Electrifies Sustainability Market With Inaugural Green-Linked Bond And Swap (2019), https://wholesale.banking.societegenerale.com/en/news-insights/clients-successes/clients-successes-details/news/enel-electrifies-sustainability-market-with-inaugural-green-linked-bond-and-swap/, accessed 2 September 2023.

discount or incentive or require charitable giving if the ESG performance a company commits to under the swap is not reached.

However, if that ESG element is decisive for the pay-out, the author believes that the company entering that derivative may not be able to hedge itself against the achievement of the ESG goal (unless the contract specifies that it can buy itself out from reaching the ESG goals by for example buying carbon credits). In the author's view, sustainability-linked derivatives have more of a betting character than a derivative character – but this will depend on the specific terms of the sustainability-linked derivatives. The author, therefore, proposes that sustainability-linked derivatives are unlikely to qualify as derivatives for tax purposes under the definition proposed above.

[d] ESG-Related Credit Derivatives

Credit derivatives are financial instruments that transfer credit risks of a loan, a bond or a guarantee from one party to the other party of the credit derivative. *Miller* defines credit derivatives as 'financial instruments for which payments are determined by reference to some adverse credit event with respect to another financial reference assets'.[325] That means we have some kind of default event in relation to some reference asset.

ESG-related credit derivatives can be used to track those companies which are perceived as having a strong ESG focus.[326] Credit default swaps (CDSs) serve as an important indicator to price the credit risk of corporates. In this respect, 'ESG-related risks – and the disclosure of those risks – can impact on a corporate's risk profile.'[327] Furthermore, '[m]arket participants can use CDS to manage the credit risk of a counterparty or credit where its financial results may suffer because of climate change or where its viability might be threatened'.[328]

The ISDA report outlines that ESG-related CDSs serve two purposes, namely:

> (i) to *hedge future potential losses* that would be realised following the occurrence of a *catastrophic event* (that leads to bankruptcies/defaults); and (ii) to *hedge the risk of changes in the market value of ESG/sustainability-linked bonds/loans* resulting from market expectations of future potential losses/damages and other market factors.[329]

---

325. Miller (2001), 91.
326. Kelly, Farrelly et al. (2021).
327. *Ibid.*, referring to an article of Julian Koelbel et al., How Disclosing Transition and Physical Climate Risks Affect Credit Default Swaps (8 April 2021), https://www.unpri.org/pri-blog/how-disclosing-transition-and-physical-climate-risks-affects-credit-default-swaps/7418.article, accessed 13 April 2023; Rohit Mendiratta et al., How ESG Affected Corporate Credit Risk and Performance, Journal of Impact & ESG, https://www.msci.com/documents/10199/19248715/Foundations-of-ESG-Investing-in-Corporate-Bonds-How-ESG-Affects-Corporate-Credit-Risk-and-Performance + (002).pdf, accessed 13 April 2023.
328. ISDA, Overview of ESG-related Derivatives (2021), 7.
329. *Ibid.*

When pricing a CDS, banks can apply ESG screening to the underlying reference entities/bonds issued by those reference entities.[330] An article by authors employed by MSCI[331] suggests that there is a positive correlation between higher ESG ratings and lower credit risks of companies.[332] For example, *iTraxx MSCI ESG Screened Europe Index* – launched in May 2020 – tracks European corporates based on ESG factors.[333] The *MSCI ESG Screened Europe Index*[334] 'is a broad European *corporate CDS index* derived using ESG criteria. The index includes a basket of CDS contracts on companies that meet various sectoral, controversy and ESG risk criteria'.[335]

Those ESG-related derivatives qualify in the same way as other credit derivatives as derivatives for tax purposes under the proposed definition. The author, therefore, refers to the discussion on credit derivatives above.

[e] ESG-Related Exchange-Traded Derivatives

These are basically equity index exchange-traded futures and options contracts related to some ESG benchmarks.[336] 'Many of the major exchanges have also launched exchange-traded futures and options which track ESG indexes, such as CBOE S&P 500 ESG Index options or EURO STOXX 50 Low Carbon Index futures.'[337] The ISDA report summarises the major ESG index options and futures by major exchanges[338] and explains that:

> ESG futures and options enable institutional managers to better hedge their ESG investments, more efficiently implement their ESG investment strategies, and better manage cash inflows and outflows of their ESG funds. Using ESG futures and options allows funds to meet target allocation in a more cash-efficient way than investing directly in the underlying stocks.[339]

330. *Ibid.*
331. MSCI is an index provider. They are 'the world's largest provider of Environmental, Social and Governance (ESG) Indexes with over 1,500 equity and fixed income ESG Indexes designed to help institutional investors more effectively benchmark ESG investment performance and manage, measure and report on ESG mandates'. *See* MSCI, 30 Years ESG Indexes, https://www.msci.com/our-solutions/indexes/esg-indexes, accessed 12 April 2023.
332. Mendiratta et al. (2021).
333. Kelly, Farrelly et al. (2021).
334. MSCI, MSCI Screened Indexes, https://www.msci.com/our-solutions/indexes/esg-screened-indexes, accessed 12 April 2023: 'MSCI ESG Screened Indexes are designed to help institutional investors apply the most common exclusions to the underlying market-cap benchmark. They *exclude* companies associated with civilian and nuclear weapons, tobacco, palm oil and arctic oil & gas and other controversial products, deriving revenues from thermal coal power and fossil fuel extraction, not in compliance with the United Nations Global Compact principles, involved in very severe controversies including those related to biodiversity.'
335. ISDA, Overview of ESG-related Derivatives (2021), 7.
336. *Ibid.*; *also* Donna Davis and James Buffin, The Frontier Line, The How and Why of ESG Derivatives, Issue 182, September 2021, https://www.frontieradvisors.com.au, accessed 14 April 2023.
337. Kelly, Farrelly et al. (2021).
338. ISDA, Overview of ESG-related Derivatives (2021), 8.
339. *Ibid.*

Those exchange-traded derivatives fall under the definition of derivatives for tax purposes as they can be hedged with either underlying bonds over some ESG index or other exchange-traded ESG derivatives.

[f] Derivatives Based on Carbon Allowances and Carbon Offsets

In the context of emission trading, market participants can not only trade emission allowances but also derivatives on emission allowances, such as options and futures.[340] Emission trading schemes '(i) limit the amount of pollutants that companies can emit,[341] and (ii) allow companies to trade the unused portion[342] of their emission allowances'.[343] The ISDA report outlines that '[t]he limit declines on an annual basis, with the intention of reducing the overall amount of emissions'.[344]

Secondary trading of emission derivatives is possible via exchanges or OTC, where forward, futures or options contracts are traded.[345] ISDA templates exist for emission allowances,[346] and both the *ISDA US Emissions Annex* and the *ISDA EU Emissions Annex* provide wording for documenting swaps, options and futures in this sector.[347] 'Derivatives based on carbon allowances and carbon offsets enable companies [that are] subject to carbon cap-and-trade programs to meet obligations and manage their risk in a cost-effective way.'[348]

The author proposes that both exchange-traded derivatives, as well as OTC derivatives over carbon emissions, should qualify as derivatives under the proposed tax definition as the underlying - emission allowances - and other derivatives on emission allowances are actively traded in a liquid market. Hence, a carbon emission-linked derivative can be replicated with other instruments and also be hedged.

[g] Renewable Energy and Renewable Fuel Derivatives

Various kinds of derivatives exist to 'trade renewable energy and renewable fuels'.[349] They are described below:

Power Purchase Agreements (PPAs) are agreements for the purchase of renewable energy 'between a specific renewable energy generator (the seller) and a purchaser of renewable electricity (the buyer)',[350] with the renewable energy being mainly

340. *Ibid.*, 9.
341. This is the limit or cap on pollution.
342. Those tradable allowances authorise the allowance holder to emit a specific quantity of a pre-determined pollutant.
343. Kelly, Farrelly et al. (2021).
344. ISDA, Overview of ESG-related Derivatives (2021), 9.
345. *Ibid.*
346. Kelly, Farrelly et al. (2021).
347. ISDA, Overview of ESG-related Derivatives (2021), 9.
348. *Ibid.*
349. Kelly, Farrelly et al. (2021).
350. ISDA, Overview of ESG-related Derivatives (2021), 11.

generated from solar and wind resources.[351] 'PPAs are an important way for sellers of renewable energy to finance new projects and hedge the risks associated with market price volatility. They also allow energy purchasers to hedge market price risk, making green energy a more attractive proposition.'[352]

Financial PPAs are cash-settled fixed-for-floating commodity swaps. ISDA states in its report that in a PPA:

> [t]he buyer and seller agree to a strike price per kilowatt hour that the seller will receive for its delivery of electricity into the wholesale market. There is no physical delivery of energy. The cash difference between the strike price and the wholesale market price is exchanged between the buyer and the seller with the result that the seller receives the net strike price for the sale of electricity, which the buyer of the financial PPA usually receives so-called Renewable Energy Certificates (RECs).[353]

RECs 'represent the property rights to the environmental, social and other non-power attributes of renewable electricity generation'.[354] They are traded on the spot and futures market. For example, the Intercontinental Exchange (ICE) offers REC futures[355] 'for RECs issued by five state renewable portfolio standards (RPS) programs'.[356] Those contracts are physically settled by delivery of the RECs to the REC registry within a specific US State.

There are other products as well. For example, '[w]ind index futures are financial instruments that enable trading firms and companies operating in the energy industry to hedge against the risks associated with fluctuations in wind energy production'.[357] Renewable Identification Numbers (RINs) are credits that 'are used for compliance in the Renewable Fuel Standard (RFS) program in the US, which sets renewable fuel blending standards for fuel producers',[358] and several exchanges offer futures on RINs.

If those derivatives can be hedged with an underlying such as Renewable Energy Certificates or other derivatives that are fungible, tradable and liquid, they would also qualify as a derivative for tax purposes under the above definition.

[D] Introduction of a Definition of Derivatives in Tax Treaties

The problem of defining a derivative contract for tax purposes also appears at the level of double tax treaties.[359] The OECD Model definitions of interest, dividends, other income, business profits or capital gains may potentially also apply to derivatives income.[360]

---

351. *Ibid.*; *also* Kelly, Farrelly et al. (2021).
352. *Ibid.*
353. ISDA, Overview of ESG-related Derivatives (2021), 9.
354. *Ibid.*, 11.
355. ICE, All Products, https://www.theice.com/products/?filter=renewable%20energy%20certificate%20futures, accessed 13 April 2023.
356. ISDA, Overview of ESG-related Derivatives (2021), 12.
357. *Ibid.*
358. *Ibid.*, 13.
359. *See* Ch. 3 §3.01.
360. Thuronyi (2001c) 15.

In principle, payments or income from derivatives would normally qualify as other income, business profits or capital gains under the OECD Model and thus would be taxable only in the residence state.[361] However, it will depend on the specific terms of the derivative as well as on the wording of the articles in the applicable tax treaty, which article will apply to the respective derivatives payments.

Problems of classification of derivatives income or gains may arise because the definitions of *dividends* and *other income* are (as a rule) not conclusive in a double tax treaty. Thus, the interpretation of their scope will depend on the national tax law. In certain cases, domestic tax legislation may, for example, include income from dividend swaps and equity swaps in the category of dividends in their national law. Furthermore, interest, although comprehensively defined, may also include certain kinds of derivatives income based on the wide meaning of the definition in the OECD Model.[362] Thus, in certain cases, income from interest rate swaps may be treated as interest under the respective treaty.[363]

Therefore, the article of the double tax treaty that applies to the derivatives income must be determined on a case-by-case basis as no definition of derivatives income exists in the OECD Model. As a result, the treaty classification of derivatives income will largely depend on how a tax system classifies the income, gains, and payments from derivatives under its national law.[364]

Under the UN Model, *other income* may also be taxed in the source state. Where source countries follow the UN Model, they will be able to impose direct taxes on derivatives income if they qualify derivatives income as *other income* under their national law.[365]

In the author's view, a self-contained definition of derivatives, as suggested above, that is incorporated in domestic law could be used to establish whether income belongs to the category of *derivatives income* in the first place.

A definition of derivatives in domestic tax law can, however, only provide the basis for solving classification issues in a cross-border context if it is ensured that the qualification of derivatives in national law is consistent with the interpretation at the level of the double tax treaty.

Thus, one should consider whether a separate definition of derivatives in the OECD and UN Models would be of merit. This could be achieved by introducing a further article for income and proceeds from derivatives in the OECD and the UN Models that defines derivatives for tax treaty purposes and applies to common cross-border derivatives transactions. The OECD suggests a:

> need to complement existing standards that are designed to prevent double taxation with instruments that prevent double non-taxation in areas previously not

361. Articles 7(1), 13(5) and 21(1) OECD Model.
362. Thuronyi (2001c) 15.
    Swap payments could, for example, be treated as interest income under the treaty in cases where the specific tax treaty uses the language of Art. 11 of the OECD Draft Convention (1963) which refers to income that is treated as interest under the laws of the source state.
363. *See* Ch. 3 §3.06[A], Example 12.
364. OECD (2001) para. 62.
365. Thuronyi (2001c) 15.

> covered by international standards and that address cases of no or low taxation associated with practices that artificially segregate taxable income from the activities that generate it.[366]

So far, neither the OECD nor the UN has proposed an introduction of a definition of derivatives in the OECD Model. In the author's view, a comprehensive definition in a further article of the OECD and UN Model could provide certainty in the taxation of those instruments in a cross-border context. Hence, a tax treaty policy discussion regarding that question is of importance at the level of the OECD and the UN.

366. OECD, *Action Plan on Base Erosion and Profit Shifting* (OECD Publishing, 2013) 13, https://read.oecd-ilibrary.org/taxation/action-plan-on-base-erosion-and-profit-shifting_9789264202719-en#page4, accessed 2 February 2023.

CHAPTER 5

Accounting Standards Applying to Derivatives and Cryptoassets

Take derivative trading, with mark-to-market accounting, which degenerates into mark-to-model. Two firms make a big derivatives trade, and the accountants on both sides show a large profit from the same trade.

— Charles T. Munger, *Q&A: Legal Matters with Charles T. Munger* (2009)

The following chapter contains various topics relating to accounting standards applying to derivatives and cryptoassets and their relationship to the tax rules applying to those instruments. Those topics specifically include:

(1) the state of alignment of accounting standards with the tax legislation in the UK and Germany and discussion of advantages and disadvantages of a close alignment;
(2) the accounting standards applying to derivatives (IFRS 9, UK and German GAAP);
(3) the accounting standards applying to cryptoassets and crypto derivatives (IFRS, UK, German, US and Australian GAAP); and
(4) the accounting standards applying to ESG derivatives.

In the context of cryptoassets, it is essential to understand that they are a new asset class. Whereas one can find literature and guidelines for the accounting treatment of cryptoassets, crypto derivatives accounting has not been discussed in detail in the literature so far. The author, therefore, suggests solutions on how to account for crypto derivatives and discusses whether the accounting and taxation rules should be aligned. This chapter also deals with the accounting treatment of ESG derivatives. It should be noted that the suggestions made by the author are far from final, as the accounting of cryptoassets, crypto derivatives and ESG derivatives are emerging topics.

§5.01 ACCOUNTING METHODS APPLYING TO DERIVATIVES AS A BASIS FOR TAXATION

Accounting concepts are concerned with classifying the various financial and non-financial assets and liabilities of a company and measuring a company's profits or losses for a period of time, usually the company's business year.

Legislators, practitioners and academic authors sometimes use different terminology when describing accounting methods. Furthermore, the understanding of what the respective accounting method means may differ considerably.[1]

Legislators may choose to apply either accounting on a cash basis, accruals accounting or fair value accounting to derivatives.

Accounting on a cash basis means that income and expenses are only recorded at the time when a contractual right to payment becomes fixed,[2] i.e., when the payment is received or made.[3] This method is not appropriate for the accounting of derivatives held by corporate taxpayers as recognition of gains and losses is on a received or paid basis, and it is, therefore, difficult to match revenues received with expenses made.[4] Tax systems may apply this accounting method to sole proprietors or small, non-corporate businesses, which are not discussed in this work.

Accruals accounting, in a general sense, means that transactions and events are recognised when they occur, not necessarily in the accounting period when the cash (or its equivalent) is received or paid.[5] That means that income is recognised when it is earned, and expenses are recognised when they are incurred, not necessarily when they are paid.[6] Consequently, transactions are reported in the financial statements for the accounting periods to which they relate, 'even if the resulting cash receipts and payments occur in a different period.[7]

---

1. Laukkanen (2007) 100ff uses the term 'realisation method' and contrasts it with the accruals method at page 88ff, which he regards as a method that considers unrealised gains and losses as taxable income.

   Zelinsky (1997) 861ff also contrasts a realisation method with accruals or accretion methods.
2. OECD (2001) para. 52.
3. Laukkanen (2007) 101.
4. ACCA, Cash Accounting – the pros and cons, July 2013, https://www.accaglobal.com/gb/en/technical-activities/technical-resources-search/2013/july/cash-accounting.html, accessed 1 November 2023.
5. For a general definition: *IFRS*, Conceptual Framework for Financial Reporting, issued September 2010, revised March 2018, Ch. 1, 1.17., https://www.ifrs.org/content/dam/ifrs/publications/pdf-standards/english/2021/issued/part-a/conceptual-framework-for-financial-reporting.pdf, accessed 9 March 2023.

   Compare also Jeff Schmidt, 'Accruals Accounting' (updated 4 January 2023) Corporate Finance Institute, https://corporatefinanceinstitute.com/resources/accounting/accrual-accounting-guide/, accessed 16 February 2023.
6. *IFRS*, Conceptual Framework for Financial Reporting (March 2018), Ch. 1, 1.17.

   This is also confirmed in an older version of: David Southern, Tolley's Taxation of Corporate Debt, Foreign Exchange and Derivative Contracts (7th edn, LexisNexis UK 2004) para. 7.17.
7. Under old UK GAAP: FRS 18, para. 27, now: FRS 102, Section 10: Accounting Policies, Estimates and Errors, *see* ICAEW, FRS 18: Accounting Policies, https://www.icaew.com/library/subject-gateways/accounting-standards/uk-frs/frs-18, accessed 9 March 2023.

An *amortised cost basis of accounting* in relation to loan relationships is defined in the UK Corporation Tax Act (CTA) 2009, section 313(4) as 'a basis of accounting under which an asset or liability representing the loan relationship is measured in the company's balance sheet at its amortised cost using the effective interest method, but with that amortised cost being adjusted as necessary where the loan relationship is the hedged item under a designated fair value hedge'.[8]

Nguyen states:

> Amortization is the systematic recognition of an income or expense related to an accrual or other asset. Whereas accruals create assets or liabilities, amortizations create income or expense. Amortization is the method by which the amount of a common accrual, such as prepaid rent, is reduced gradually to zero over time so the expense is transferred to the profit and loss statement in the period that the company uses up the accrual. While both accruals and amortizations are used in accrual accounting, a company can have accruals without having amortizations.[9]

HMRC's Corporate Finance Manual outlines the differences between an accruals basis of accounting and an amortised cost basis of accounting. If an *amortised cost base of accounting* is applied, items are shown in the 'balance sheet at cost, adjusted for:

- amortisation of any discount or premium using the effective interest rate method, which takes into account fees incurred for borrowing (or received for lending) and similar amounts, and
- any impairment [...], repayment or release'.[10]

A *fair value accounting basis* 'means a basis of accounting under which –

(a) assets and liabilities are measured in the company's balance sheet at their fair value, and
(b) changes in the fair value of assets and liabilities are recognised as items of profit or loss'.[11]

Fair value accounting requires valuing the assets or liabilities at inception based on market prices or prices determined at arm's length. Any changes in value of the assets or liabilities during the life of the asset or liability are also based on market prices or prices determined on an arm's length basis between independent parties.[12] *Laukkanen* suggests that fair value accounting would be broadly similar to the former mark-to-market accounting[13] method.[14]

8. CTA 2009, s. 313(4).
9. Teresa Nyugen, 'Differences Between Amortizations and Accruals' *Chron*, https://smallbusiness.chron.com/differences-between-amortizations-accruals-62840.html, accessed 14 February 2023.
10. HMRC, Corporate Finance Manual, CFM33130 – Loan relationships: computational rules: GAAP: fair value and amortised cost accounting (updated 1 September 2022).
11. Compare the definition used in UK tax law in CTA 2009, s. 313(5).
12. Laukkanen (2007) 91; *also* Redson (2005-06) *Loan Relationships*, 6.
13. The term *mark-to-market accounting* has been substituted by the term 'fair value accounting'.
14. Laukkanen (2007) 91.

By determining the accounting method, the legislator also decides whether the principle of realisation should be applied when accounting and subsequently taxing derivatives.[15]

Realisation basis means that profits and losses are accounted for and taxed when they occur, not upon a fluctuation in the value of the asset, but upon the sale of the asset, and that income, such as interest and dividends, are accounted for and taxed upon receipt.[16]

Both cash accounting and the accruals method effectively honour the principle of realisation, as they only recognise profits or losses when they are realised.[17] In contrast, a fair value basis of accounting does not apply the principle of realisation.

For traditional financial instruments, the amount of income and the timing when profits or losses are taken into account are generally determined by way of accruals accounting.[18]

Some countries apply accruals accounting as a basis for the taxation of derivatives.[19] Other tax systems follow fair value accounting methods as a basis for taxation or simply follow IFRS 9[20] when determining taxable profits or losses arising from derivatives, thereby departing from the concept of realisation in tax law. Under IFRS 9, derivatives are accounted for and valued based on the fair value method as determined by IFRS 9, meaning they must be measured at fair value, with all changes in those fair values recognised immediately in the P&L account except in cases of hedge accounting.[21]

§5.02 ALIGNMENT OF ACCOUNTING STANDARDS AND TAX RULES APPLYING TO DERIVATIVES IN THE UK

[A] IFRS and UK GAAP Alignment

The UK accounting legislation has evolved for some time and continues to do so.

15. In favour of applying the principle of realisation: Zelinsky (1997) 861ff.
16. *Ibid.*, 861.
17. Southern (2012) para. 2.20.
18. *Other opinion:* OECD (2001) para. 52, suggesting that both the cash accounting method and the accruals accounting method are used when accounting for traditional instruments, such as bonds.

    In the author's opinion, many tax systems nowadays will rather apply the accruals method of accounting (sometimes modified by amortisation and impairments) instead of the cash method when accounting traditional financial instruments, for example by accounting and taxing discount and deferred interest returns in the financial accounting period to which they relate.
19. Those tax systems would apply their domestic tax rules as a basis for taxation, which would in many cases honour the principle of realisation.
20. The International Accounting Standards Board has replaced IAS 39 Financial Instruments: Recognition and Measurement with the new accounting standard: IFRS 9 Financial Instruments.

    Compare Deloitte, IFRS 9: Financial Instruments – high level summary (April 2016), https://www2.deloitte.com/content/dam/Deloitte/lu/Documents/audit/lu-IFRS-9.pdf, accessed 15 February 2023.
21. Deloitte (2016) 7.

Under Regulation EC No. 1606/2002, which applied directly into UK law before Brexit, UK incorporated publicly traded companies had to prepare their consolidated accounts in accordance with (EU-adopted) IFRS.[22] Both UK GAAP and (EU-adopted) IFRS were considered acceptable accounting standards for single company accounts in the UK.[23]

Thus, UK publicly traded companies were allowed, but not required, to prepare their individual accounts in accordance with IFRS.[24] In the same way, non-publicly traded companies were allowed to prepare their consolidated and/or individual accounts in accordance with IFRS.[25] If the company was a small company, the accounts were prepared under the Financial Reporting Standard for Smaller Entities (FRSSE).

The 'old UK GAAP' relevant in the context of derivatives were Financial Reporting Standards (FRS) 25, 26 and 29,[26] which aligned with IAS 32,[27] IAS 39[28] and IFRS 7 by way of incorporation of these IASs into UK GAAP.[29] Thus, even where the company prepared the accounts under those UK GAAPs, it effectively applied IAS 39 in relation to derivatives as FRS 26 incorporated IAS 39 into UK GAAP.

IAS 39 was replaced by IFRS 9 for accounting periods beginning on or after 1 January 2018.[30] Insurance companies could delay the implementation of IFRS 9 until 1 January 2023. The IASB states that in cases of hedge accounting, companies still have the choice of whether to continue to apply the 'old' hedge accounting provisions under IAS 39 or switch to IFRS 9.[31]

In this respect, the IFRS states that:

> IAS 39 was superseded by IFRS 9 subject to:
>
> - the accounting policy choice about whether or not to continue applying the hedge accounting requirements in IAS 39 in accordance with paragraph 7.2.21 or paragraph 6.1.3 of IFRS 9; and

---

22. Regulation (EC) No. 1606/2002 of the European Parliament and of the Council of 19 July 2002 on the application of international accounting standards, Arts 3, 4 and 6(2). *See also* Ghosh, Johnson and Miller (2022) [B1.13] (issue 28); Southern (2017) para. 2.9.
23. Companies Act 2006, ss 395-397. *See* Ghosh, Johnson and Miller (2022) [B1.23] (issue 28).
24. *Simon's Taxes, vol 5,* D1.843; Southern (2017) para. 2.25; *also* Ghosh, Johnson and Miller (2022) [B1.23] (issue 28).
25. CA 2006, s. 395. *See also* Bramwell et al., *Taxation of Companies and Company Reconstructions*, vol. 2 (9th edn, Sweet & Maxwell 2009, with updates through Release 41, January 2023), H1.4.5; Ghosh, Johnson and Miller (2022) [B1.23] (issue 28); Southern (2017) para. 2.25.
26. FRS 29 only applied to companies, which applied FRS 26. In those cases, FRS 29 replaced the disclosure requirements of FRS 25.
27. FRS 25 (IAS 32) Financial Instruments: Presentation (ASB, as amended in 2010).
28. FRS 26 (IAS 39) Financial Instruments: Recognition and Measurement (ASB, as amended in 2009).
29. FRS 25 (IAS 32) Financial Instruments: Presentation; FRS 26 (IAS 39) Financial Instruments: Recognition and Measurement; ASB, *Amendment to FRS 25 (IAS 32) 'Financial Instruments: Presentation', Classification of Rights Issues* (2010); Southern (2017) paras 2.14-2.16; HMRC, *Accounting Standards – the UK tax implications* (2006).
30. LucaNet, White paper, 'Key differences between IFRS and UK GAAP' (2022) https://www.icaew.com/-/media/corporate/files/insights/sponsored-content/key-differences-between-uk-gaap-and-ifrs-uk.ashx?la=en, accessed 1 March 2023.
31. IFRS, IAS 39, Recognition and Measurement, Standard 2022 Issued, About – on file with the author.

- the temporary exemption in paragraph 20A of IFRS 4 provides to some insurers a temporary exemption from applying IFRS 9 until they apply IFRS 17.[32]

However, the situation is more complicated in the UK due to the accounting choices that the 'new UK GAAP' provides its users.

In 2015, the UK GAAP underwent major changes with the introduction of the 'new UK GAAP', being FRS 100, 101 and 102 that substituted all other FRSs (except FRS 27) with these three standards 'for accounting periods beginning on or after 1 January 2015'.[33]

For those companies not using IFRS, FRS 101 or FRSSE, FRS 102 became 'mandatory for periods starting on or after 1 January 2015'.[34]

Ghosh, Johnson and Miller outline that:

> FRS 102 is a new comprehensive standard [which] [u]nlike the previous standards that it replaced [...] does not just deal with one subject, such as financial instruments or inventory, but with all aspects of accounting. Thus, it contains the provisions of relevance to the accounting for and taxation of debt and derivatives.[35]

In addition, FRS 103 applies to entities which want to issue insurance contracts in the UK or in the Republic of Ireland, while FRS 104 provides guidance for the preparation of interim financial reports for 'organisations which apply FRS 102'.[36] FRS 105 is the 'Financial Reporting Standard Applicable to the Micro-entities Regime'. Further, the Statements of Recommended Practice (SORPs) describe accounting best practices.

The Financial Reporting Council (FRC) states that '[t]he requirements in FRS 102 are based on the IASB's International Financial Reporting Standard for Small and Medium-sized Entities ("the IFRS for SMEs Accounting Standard"), with some significant amendments made for application in the UK and Republic of Ireland'.[37]

Ghosh, Johnson and Miller describe in this respect the origins of FRS 102 as follows:

> FRS 102 was based on the IASB's International Financial Reporting Standard for SMEs ('IFRS for SMEs') published in 2009. However, it is potentially available to a much wider range of companies than the IFRS for SMEs was designed for. In

32. IFRS, IAS 39 (2022).
33. FRS 102, The Financial Reporting Standard applicable in the UK and Republic of Ireland (March 2013) – old version, https://www.frc.org.uk/getattachment/2731d03d-1174-415b-aa40-a983a55a2dfb/FRS-102-2013.pdf, accessed 1 August 2023, para. 1.14; Deloitte, FRS 102, https://www.iasplus.com/en-gb/standards/uk-gaap/frs102, accessed 1 August 2023.
34. Ghosh, Johnson and Miller (2022) [B1.70C] (issue 28).
35. *Ibid.*
36. Indeed, A guide to accounting standards (UK GAAP and IFRS), (updated 7 December 2022), https://uk.indeed.com/career-advice/career-development/accounting-standards, accessed 17 February 2023.
37. FRC, FRS 102, The Financial Reporting Standards Applicable in the United Kingdom and the Republic of Ireland (2022), https://www.frc.org.uk/documents/4279/FRS_102_The_Financial_Reporting_Standard_applicable_in_the_UK_and_Republic_of_Ireland_ns2SqGY.pdf, accessed 1 September 2023.

> addition, FRS 102 includes some extra options for ways in which to account over and above the approach in IFRS for SMEs [...] because some very large companies will be able to use FRS 102.[38]

IFRS co-exists alongside UK GAAP, and 'since 1 January 2015 with the application of FRS 102, the substantial differences [between IFRS and UK GAAP] have been considerably diminished'.[39] The FRSSE has been withdrawn and replaced by section 1A of FRS 102 from 1 January 2016.[40]

Brexit has also brought changes to the accounting standards in the UK. The Financial Reporting Council issued together with the UK Department for Business, Energy and Industrial Strategy (BEIS) a letter in November 2020 which concerned the 'Accounting and Corporate Reporting after the End of the Transition Period'.[41] In this letter, it is explained that:

> All UK incorporated companies that are currently required to use EU-adopted IFRS will need to use UK-adopted international accounting standards for financial years that begin on or after 1 January 2021. On 1 January 2021, UK-adopted IFRS and EU-adopted IFRS will be identical.
>
> Companies with financial years ending on 31 December 2020 can continue to use EU-adopted IFRS as it stands at the end of the transition period for the 2020 financial year and UK-adopted international accounting standards for the next financial year.
>
> Where new or amended IFRS are adopted by the UK after the transition period, but before those companies file their accounts for the financial years that straddle the end of the transition period, they can choose to apply any new IFRS adopted by the UK in addition to EU-adopted IFRS as they exist at the end of the transition period. This also applies to companies with financial years ending before the end of the transition period but who do not file until after the end of the transition period. Where companies choose to make use of this option, they will need to disclose what standards they have used as part of the notes to their financial statements.[42]

This publication was withdrawn on 25 May 2021 after the end of the transition period.[43] That, however, only means that companies now either apply UK GAAP or

38. Ghosh, Johnson and Miller (2022) [B1.70C] (issue 28).
39. Southern (2017), para. 2.3.
40. 'The FRSSE is withdrawn from 1 January 2016, when it was replaced by Section 1A of FRS 102 The Financial Reporting Standard applicable in the UK and Republic of Ireland and FRS 105 The Financial Reporting Standard applicable to the Micro-entities Regime', *see* ICAEW, Old UK GAAP: The Financial Reporting Standard for Smaller Entities (FRSSE), https://www.icaew.com/technical/financial-reporting/uk-gaap/old-uk-gaap-standards/financial-reporting-standard-for-smaller-entities-frsse, accessed 23 February 2023.
41. FRC and BEIS, 'Accounting and Corporate Reporting after the end of the Transition Period' (November 2020), https://assets.publishing.service.gov.uk/government/uploads/system/uploads/attachment_data/file/937294/Letter_to_the_accounting_sector_preparing_for_1_January_2021.pdf, accessed 22 February 2023).
42. *Ibid.*
43. UK.Gov, Correspondence, UK accounting and audit framework from 1 January 2021, https://www.gov.uk/government/publications/uk-accounting-and-audit-framework-from-1-january-2021, accessed 23 February 2023.

UK-adopted IFRS.[44] In a way, the freezing of the EU-adopted IFRS at the state they existed at the end of the transition period can now be overwritten by new IFRS adopted by the UK.

There are some differences between UK GAAP and IFRS, which are summarised in the 2022 *LucaNet (UK) Limited* White paper called 'Key Differences between UK GAAP and IFRS'.[45] Those differences concern intangible assets, which are particularly relevant to the accounting of cryptoassets and crypto derivatives, which are discussed in Chapter 5 §5.06. There are also differences in the accounting treatment of financial instruments between FRS 102, Sections 11 and 12, and IFRS 9. Those differences, in particular in relation to impairments, are discussed below in Chapter 5 §5.02 [B][4].[46] Further, differences also exist in the context of hedge accounting. They are discussed in Chapter 7.

[B] Accounting Methods in the UK Applying to Financial Instruments

The following subsection discusses the accounting provisions and methods applied in the UK to financial instruments. The author focuses on FRS 102, IAS and IFRS and outlines the key differences of those standards for financial instruments. A discussion in respect of the accounting standards applying to derivatives can be found in Chapter 5 §5.02[C].

Under FRS 102, Sections 11 and 12, companies can choose from three options to recognise and measure financial instruments. FRS 102 (January 2022), para 11.2. explicitly states that:

> An entity shall choose to apply either:
>
> (a) the provisions of both *Sections 11 and Section 12 in full*; or
> (b) the recognition and measurement provisions of *IAS 39 Financial Instruments: Recognition and Measurement*, the *disclosure and presentation requirements of Sections 11 and 12*; or
> (c) the *recognition and measurement provisions of IFRS 9 Financial Instruments* and *IAS 39* (as amended following the publication of IFRS 9), the *disclosure and presentation requirements of Sections 11 and 12*;
>
> to account for all of its financial instruments. Where an entity chooses (b) or (c), it applies the scope of the relevant standard to its financial instruments. An entity's choice of (a), (b) or (c) is an accounting policy choice.[47]

44. Bramwell et al., *Taxation of Companies and Company Reconstructions*, vol. 2, H.1.4.5. state in this respect: 'For accounting periods beginning before 1 January 2021 where a UK parent company has securities that are admitted to trading on the UK regulated market as at its balance sheet date the consolidated group accounts are required to be prepared in accordance with UK-adopted international accounting standards.' *Compare also* Companies Act 2006, s. 403(1).
45. LucaNet, White paper, 'Key differences between IFRS and UK GAAP' (2022) https://www.icaew.com/-/media/corporate/files/insights/sponsored-content/key-differences-between-uk-gaap-and-ifrs-uk.ashx?la=en, accessed 1 March 2023.
46. *Ibid.*, 9-11.
47. FRS 102, The Financial Reporting Standards applicable in the UK and the Republic of Ireland (January 2022), para. 11.2.

That means although IFRS 9 superseded IAS 39, under FRS 102, UK companies basically still have three options to recognise and measure financial instruments.[48] They can either apply:

(1) FRS 102, Sections 11 and 12;
(2) IAS 39 *Financial Instruments: Recognition and Measurement*,[49] or
(3) IFRS 9 *Financial Instruments*.[50]

Factsheet 4, issued by the FRC, states that:

> [t]he choice to apply IAS 39 or IFRS 9 might be relevant to entities that previously applied FRS 26 (IAS 39) Financial Instruments: Recognition and Measurement or when the simplified accounting in FRS 102 means that certain options within IAS 39 or IFRS 9 are not available. As part of the triennial review of FRS 102, it was clarified that *the option to apply IAS 39 through FRS 102 continues to be available after IAS 39 has been superseded by IFRS 9 for IFRS reporters*.[51]

The *FRC Factsheet 4* confirms that '[a]s part of the triennial review of FRS 102 it was clarified that the option to apply IAS 39 through FRS 102 continues to be available after IAS 39 has been superseded by IFRS 9 for IFRS reporters'.[52] It further states that '[w]hichever choice is made, the disclosure requirements of FRS 102 will apply'.[53]

[1] FRS 102, Sections 11 and 12 Applying to Financial Instruments

Under FRS 102, Sections 11 and 12, there are, in principle, only two measurement options: amortised cost basis of accounting and fair value through profit or loss. Very occasionally, financial instruments can be measured at cost less impairment.[54]

48. LucaNet, White paper, 'Key differences between IFRS and UK GAAP', 16.
49. FRS 102, para. 11.2, footnote 47 states: 'Until IAS 39 Financial Instruments: Recognition and Measurement is fully superseded by IFRS 9 Financial Instruments (i.e., for all entities, including insurers), an entity shall apply the version of IAS 39 that is in effect at the entity's reporting date. When IAS 39 is fully superseded by IFRS 9, an entity shall apply the version of IAS 39 that applied immediately prior to IFRS 9 fully superseding IAS 39. A copy of that version will be retained for reference on the FRC website. Entities shall apply the so-called EU carve-out of IAS 39, which amended paragraph 81A and related Application Guidance in IAS 39.'
50. *Compare also* Ghosh, Johnson and Miller (2022) [B2.3A] (issue 28); FRS 102, Factsheet 4, Financial Instruments (December 2018), 1, https://media.frc.org.uk/documents/Fact_Sheet_4_-_FRS_102_Financial_Instruments.pdf, accessed 16 March 2023; LucaNet, White paper, 'Key differences between IFRS and UK GAAP', 9.
51. FRS 102, Factsheet 4, Financial Instruments (December 2018), 2, emphasis added.
52. FRS 102, Factsheet 4, Financial Instruments (December 2018), 2; *compare also* FRC, FRS Factsheet 1, Triennial Review 2017 Amendments, 5 https://www.frc.org.uk/getattachment/fad30eea-aa8f-4961-beda-a7d8128e3165/FS-01-FRS-102-Triennial-Review-2017-(Dec-2018).pdf, accessed 1 August 2023 which states that FRS 102, para. 11.2 contains a statement that 'the option to apply IAS 39 continues to be available to entities applying FRS 102 until FRS 102 is amended to reflect IFRS 9 Financial Instruments, or it is otherwise decided that no further amendments are to be made to FRS 102 in relation to IFRS 9. The IAS 39 EU carve-out continues to be available'.
53. FRS 102, Factsheet 4, Financial Instruments (December 2018), 2.
54. Coroner-I Navigate, Differences between FRS 102, IAS 39 and IFRS 9, https://library.croneri.co.uk/cch_uk/nuk102-02/ufs11-9-1a, accessed 2 May 2023.

Financial instruments under FRS 102 'include cash, trade receivables and payables, equity investments, borrowings and derivatives'.[55]

FRS 102 distinguishes between two categories of financial instruments: basic and complex.[56] FRS 102, Section 11 applies to basic financial instruments, and Section 12 'applies to other, more complex financial instruments and transactions'.[57]

Under FRS 102, paragraph 11.8, basic financial instruments include 'cash, certain debt instruments (such as a loan receivable or payable), and investments in non-derivatives (e.g., ordinary shares)'.[58]

The FRC states that:

> For debt instruments, [FRS 102] paragraph 11.9 sets out the conditions that must be met in order for them to be classified as basic. If any of the conditions are not met, the financial instrument is not basic unless it meets the principle-based description in paragraph 11.9A. Features of a basic financial instrument include it having a fixed return for the lender, or the return being a positive fixed or variable rate (i.e., linked to a single observable interest rate). Although many common loans will be classified as basic, just because an instrument appears to be common it cannot be assumed that it will be basic.[59]

Basic financial instruments are accounted for at an *amortised cost basis*. Those instruments are initially measured at the transaction price, adjusted by any transaction costs,

> except in the initial measurement of financial assets and liabilities that are subsequently measured at fair value through profit or loss) unless the arrangement constitutes, in effect, a financing transaction. [...] if the arrangement constitutes a financing transaction, the entity shall measure the financial asset or financial liability at the present value of the future payments discounted at a market rate of interest for a similar debt instrument as determined at initial recognition adjusted for transaction costs.[60]

That means that exceptions to an amortised cost basis of accounting – and the initial measurement at transaction costs, adjusted by the transaction price apply for financing transactions which 'shall be measured at present value of the future payments discounted at a market rate of interest for a similar instrument, adjusted for transaction costs. This means it should be measured as if it were a market-rate loan'.[61]

Subsequent measurement uses the *effective interest method*,[62] which 'allocates the interest (and transaction costs) over the life of an instrument at a constant rate,

55. FRS 102, Factsheet 4, Financial Instruments (December 2018), 2.
56. Coroner-I Navigate, Differences between FRS 102, IAS 39 and IFRS 9.
57. FRS 102, Factsheet 4, Financial Instruments (December 2018), 1; LucaNet, White paper, 'Key differences between IFRS and UK GAAP', 9.
58. LucaNet, White paper, 'Key differences between IFRS and UK GAAP', 9.
59. FRS 102, Factsheet 4, Financial Instruments (December 2018), 2.
60. FRS 102, para. 11.13, emphasis added.
61. FRS 102, Factsheet 4, Financial Instruments (December 2018), 2.
62. FRS 102, para. 11.14 a).

based on its carrying amount. Interest includes not just the coupon rate, but any other receipts/payments or changes in value that constitute interest'.[63]

FRS 102, paragraph 11.6 states:

> The effective interest method is a method of calculating the amortised cost of a financial asset or a financial liability (or a group of financial assets or financial liabilities) and of allocating the interest income or interest expense over the relevant period. The effective interest rate is the rate that exactly discounts estimated future cash payments or receipts through the expected life of the financial instrument or, when appropriate, a shorter period to the carrying amount of the financial asset or financial liability. The effective interest rate is determined on the basis of the carrying amount of the financial asset or liability at initial recognition. Under the effective interest method:
>
> (a) the amortised cost of a financial asset (liability) is the present value of future cash receipts (payments) discounted at the effective interest rate; and
> (b) in the absence of capital repayments, the interest expense (income) in a period equals the carrying amount of the financial liability (asset) at the beginning of a period multiplied by the effective interest rate for the period.[64]

Impairments are tested for financial assets measured at cost or amortised cost based on objective evidence.[65] Any impairment loss is immediately recognised in the P&L statement if there is objective evidence of impairment.[66]

The amortised cost basis of accounting using the effective interest method applies to *most basis financial instruments*; however, 'there is an ability to treat certain debt instruments on a *fair value through profit or loss* basis'.[67] FRS 102, paragraph 11.14 mentions those debt instruments which *can* be measured at fair value.

Financial instruments, which are dealt with under FRS 102, Section 12, i.e., non-basic financial instruments, must be measured at fair value through profit or loss.[68]

However, exceptions apply for:

(a) non-publicly traded equity whose fair value cannot be determined;
(b) hedging instruments; and
(c) where the law otherwise requires.[69]

'[T]he *holder* of a convertible loan note will not have to bifurcate it, and since it will not be a "basic financial instrument", will have to account for it at FVTPL.'[70] Those instruments are discussed in more detail in Chapter 8 in the context of hybrid instruments.

63. FRS 102, Factsheet 4, Financial Instruments (December 2018), 5.
64. FRS 102, para. 11.16.
65. FRS 102, para. 11.21; FRS 102, Factsheet 4, Financial Instruments (December 2018), 5.
66. FRS 102, Factsheet 4, Financial Instruments (December 2018), 5.
67. Ghosh, Johnson and Miller (2022) [B2.3A] (issue 28).
68. FRS 102, para 12.7.
69. FRS 102, para 12.8(a)-(c).
70. Ghosh, Johnson and Miller (2022) [B2.3A] (issue 28).

[2] IAS 39 Applying to Financial Assets and Liabilities

To reiterate, if a UK company makes the accounting choice of IAS 39 for recognition and measurement of financial assets, it can do so according to FRS 102, paragraph 11.2 as an accounting choice.[71]

The IAS 39, which then applies, is, in that case, the de facto EU-adopted accounting standard that was frozen on 31 December 2020. That is because IAS 39 will not have any changes after 1 January 2018 because IAS 39 was superseded by IFRS 9 at the level of IFRSs. Those standards are now de facto the IASs endorsed by FRS as an accounting choice under FRS 102, paragraph 11.2.

Under IAS 39, an entity shall initially measure financial assets and financial liabilities at its fair value through profit or loss.[72] In cases where a financial asset or financial liability is not measured at fair value through profit or loss, transaction costs are directly attributable to the acquisition or issue of the financial asset or financial liability.[73]

For classification and subsequent measurement purposes, IAS 39 required all *financial assets* to fall within one of four categories; they are categorised as:

(1) financial assets at fair value through profit and loss (FVTPL);
(2) held-to-maturity investments, measured at amortised cost (AC);[74]
(3) loans and receivables, measured at AC; and
(4) available for sale financial assets, measured at fair value through other comprehensive income (FVTOCI).[75]

The 'fair value through profit or loss' category further divides into those assets 'held for trading'[76] and those designated as 'fair value through profit or loss'.[77]

Under IAS 39, 'a financial asset or financial liability is classified as held for trading if:

(i) it is acquired or incurred principally for the purpose of selling or repurchasing it in the near term;
(ii) on initial recognition, it is part of a portfolio of identified financial instruments that are managed together and for which there is evidence of a recent actual pattern of short-term profit-taking; or

71. The FRC published comprehensive changes to the accounting standards on 27 March 2024 in the context of a period review, which could not be considered in this edition.
Those changes also include the '[r]emoval of the option to newly adopt the recognition and measurement requirements of IAS 39 Financial Instruments [...] Entities already applying the IAS 39 option are permitted to continue to apply it.'
The changes are effective for accounting periods beginning on or after 1 January 2026.
72. IAS 39, Financial Instruments: Recognition and Measurement, IAS 39.9, Definitions of four categories of financial instruments (2009).
73. IAS 39 (2009), para. 43.
74. *Compare also* LucaNet, White paper, 'Key differences between IFRS and UK GAAP', 10.
75. IAS 39 (2009), Definitions, para. 9.
76. IAS 39 (2009), Definitions, para. 9(a).
77. IAS 39 (2009), Definitions, para. 9(b).

> (iii) it is a derivative (except for a derivative that is a financial guarantee contract or a designated and effective hedging instrument)'.[78]

An entity may designate financial assets as fair value through profit or loss upon initial recognition.

> [A]n entity may use this designation only when permitted by paragraph 11A or when doing so results in more relevant information because either:
>
> (i) it eliminates or significantly reduces a measurement or recognition inconsistency (sometimes referred to as 'an accounting mismatch') that would otherwise arise from measuring assets or liabilities or recognising the gains and losses on them on different bases; or
> (ii) a group of financial assets, financial liabilities or both is managed and its performance is evaluated on a fair value basis in accordance with a documented risk management or investment strategy, and information about the group is provided internally on that basis to the entity's key management personnel (as defined in IAS 24 Related Party Disclosures), for example, the entity's board of directors and chief executive officer.[79]

IAS 39, paragraph 11A states:

> Notwithstanding paragraph 11, if a contract contains one or more embedded derivatives, an entity may designate the entire hybrid (combined) contract as a financial asset or financial liability at fair value through profit or loss unless:
>
> (a) the embedded derivative(s) does not significantly modify the cash flows that otherwise would be required by the contract; or
> (b) it is clear with little or no analysis when a similar hybrid (combined) instrument is first considered that separation of the embedded derivative(s) is prohibited, such as a prepayment option embedded in a loan that permits the holder to prepay the loan for approximately its amortised cost.[80]

For subsequent measurement, IAS 39 states in relation to financial assets:

> After initial recognition, an entity shall measure financial assets, including derivatives that are assets, at their fair values, without any deduction for transaction costs it may incur on sale or other disposal, except for the following financial assets:
>
> (a) loans and receivables as defined in paragraph 9, which shall be measured at amortised cost using the effective interest method;
> (b) held-to-maturity investments as defined in paragraph 9, which shall be measured at amortised cost using the effective interest method; and
> (c) investments in equity instruments that do not have a quoted price in an active market and whose fair value cannot be reliably measured and derivatives that

78. IAS 39 (2009), para. 9(a).
79. IAS 39 (2009), para. 9(b).
80. IAS 39 (2009), para. 11A.

are linked to and must be settled by delivery of such equity instruments, which shall be measured at cost (see Appendix A paragraphs AG80 and AG81).[81]

Financial liabilities are classified as either:

(1) financial Liabilities at FVTPL; or
(2) financial liabilities measured at amortised cost (AC) using the effective interest method.[82]

The subsequent measurement of *financial liabilities* under IAS 39 depends on whether they fall either within the category 'fair value through profit or loss' or 'amortised cost'.

IAS 39, para 47 states that:

> [a]fter initial recognition, an entity shall measure all financial liabilities at amortised cost using the effective interest method, except for:
>
> (a) financial liabilities at fair value through profit or loss. Such liabilities, including derivatives that are liabilities, shall be *measured at fair value except* for a derivative liability that is linked to and must be settled by *delivery of an equity instrument* that does not have a quoted price in an active market for an identical instrument (i.e., a Level 1 input) whose fair value cannot otherwise be reliably measured, which shall be *measured at cost.*
> (b) financial liabilities that arise when a transfer of a financial asset does not qualify for derecognition or when the continuing involvement approach applies. Paragraphs 29 and 31 apply to the measurement of such financial liabilities.
> (c) financial guarantee contracts as defined in paragraph 9. After initial recognition, an issuer of such a contract shall (unless paragraph 47(a) or (b) applies) measure it at the higher of:
>   (i) the amount determined in accordance with IAS 37; and
>   (ii) the amount initially recognised (*see* paragraph 43) less, when appropriate, cumulative amortisation recognised in accordance with IAS 18.
> (d) commitments to provide a loan at a below-market interest rate. After initial recognition, an issuer of such a commitment shall (unless paragraph 47(a) applies) measure it at the higher of:
>   (i) the amount determined in accordance with IAS 37; and
>   (ii) the amount initially recognised (see paragraph 43) less, when appropriate, cumulative amortisation recognised in accordance with IAS 18.[83]

Financial liabilities are derecognised 'only when [they are] extinguished, i.e., when the obligation specified in the contract is discharged, cancelled or expired'.[84]

81. IAS 39 (2009), para. 46.
82. LucaNet, White paper, 'Key differences between IFRS and UK GAAP', 10.
83. IAS 39 (2009), para. 47.
84. IAS 39 (2009), para. 39.

[3] IFRS 9 Applying to Financial Instruments

IFRS 9, as the successor standard of IAS 39, has to be adopted by companies that prepare their accounts in accordance with IFRS or that apply FRS 101 Reduced Disclosure Framework.[85]

IFRS 9 applies to all financial instruments, as defined in IAS 32.

A *financial asset within IAS 32* is an asset that is:

(a) *cash*;
(b) *an equity instrument* of another entity;
(c) *a contractual right*:
  (i) to receive cash or another financial asset from another entity; or
  (ii) to exchange financial assets or financial liabilities with another entity under conditions that are potentially favourable to the entity; or
(d) *a contract* that will or may be *settled in the entity's own equity instruments* and is:
  (i) a non-derivative for which the entity is or may be obliged to receive a variable number of the entity's own equity instruments; or
  (ii) a derivative that will or may be settled other than by the exchange of a fixed amount of cash or another financial asset for a fixed number of the entity's own equity instruments. For this purpose, the entity's own equity instruments do not include puttable financial instruments classified as equity instruments in accordance with paragraphs 16A and 16B, instruments that impose on the entity an obligation to deliver to another party a pro-rata share of the net assets of the entity only on liquidation and are classified as equity instruments in accordance with paragraphs 16C and 16D, or instruments that are contracts for the future receipt or delivery of the entity's own equity instruments.[86]

Under IFRS 9, all financial assets are measured at amortised cost, fair value through other comprehensive income or fair value through profit or loss,[87] 'depending on the *contractual cash flows* and the *business model* they are managed under'.[88]

That means that the determination of how a financial instrument is measured depends on

(1) how a company manages its financial instruments to generate cash flows, and
(2) the characteristics of the contractual cash flows.[89]

It should be noted that the company can have more than one business model. Further, the assessment of which business model is applied is done on a portfolio basis and not on a single asset basis.[90]

85. Ghosh, Johnson and Miller (2022) [B2.3B] (issue 28).
86. IAS 32, para. 11.
87. IFRS 9, para. 5.2.1; *compare* LucaNet, White paper, 'Key differences between IFRS and UK GAAP', 10.
88. LucaNet, White paper, 'Key differences between IFRS and UK GAAP', 10, emphasis added.
89. Ghosh, Johnson and Miller (2022) [B2.3B] (issue 28).
90. *Ibid.*

IFRS 9, paragraph 5.1.1 states that:

> Except for trade receivables within the scope of *paragraph 5.1.3*, at initial recognition, an entity shall measure a financial asset or financial liability at its fair value plus or minus, in the case of a financial asset or financial liability not at fair value through profit or loss, transaction costs that are directly attributable to the acquisition or issue of the financial asset or financial liability.[91]

IFRS 9, paragraph 5.1.2 mentions that even if an asset is subsequently measured at amortised cost, it is initially recognised at its fair value at the trade date.[92]

Upon subsequent valuation, financial assets shall be measured at:

(a) amortised cost;
(b) fair value through other comprehensive income; or
(c) fair value through profit or loss.[93]

For financial liabilities, IFRS 9, paragraphs 5.3.1 in conjunction with paragraphs 4.2.1 state that they shall be measured at amortised cost with the exceptions of:

(a) *financial liabilities at fair value through profit or loss*. Such liabilities, including *derivatives* that are liabilities, shall be subsequently measured at fair value.
(b) financial liabilities that arise when a transfer of a financial asset does not qualify for derecognition or when the continuing involvement approach applies [...]
(c) *financial guarantee contracts* [...]
(d) commitments to provide a *loan at a below-market interest rate*. [...]
(e) contingent consideration recognised by an acquirer in a business combination to which IFRS 3 applies. [...][94]

IFRS 9, paragraph 4.2.2 provides the option to designate a financial liability at fair value through profit or loss upon subsequent measurement.[95]

[4] Differences Between FRS 102, Sections 11 and 12, IAS 39 and IFRS 9

'Even though the classification differs conceptually between FRS 102, IAS 39 and IFRS 9, for non-financial corporations, the classification and thus the accounting treatment regarding initial and subsequent measurement will often be the same under all three standards.'[96]

91. IFRS 9, para. 5.1.1, emphasis added.
92. IFRS 9, para. 5.1.2.
93. IFRS 9, para. 5.2.1.
94. IFRS 9, para 4.2.1.
95. IFRS 9, para. 4.2.2.
96. LucaNet, White paper, 'Key differences between IFRS and UK GAAP', 10.

FRS 102, Sections 11 and 12 recognise the following accounting methods: *amortised cost basis of accounting* and *fair value accounting,* and very occasionally,[97] cost less impairment.[98] FRS 102, Sections 11 and 12 recognise two categories of financial assets, basic and others, and two categories of financial liabilities, basic (which are recognised at amortised cost) and others (recognised at FVTPL).[99]

Both IAS 39 and IFRS 9 have the measurement options of amortised cost of accounting and fair value – either through profit or loss or with changes in other comprehensive income. Again, occasionally, financial instruments are measured at cost less impairment under IAS 39,[100] whereas IFRS 9 requires all equity instruments to be measured at fair value,[101] although it also 'acknowledges that, in limited circumstances, cost may be an appropriate estimate of fair value for unquoted equity instruments'.[102]

Whereas IAS 39 has four categories of financial assets, IFRS 9 has only three, and both have two categories of financial liabilities (see above).

The accounting methods are defined in IAS 39, Appendix A to IFRS 9 and the Glossary to FRS 102, respectively.

'Accounting may adopt a transaction-based approach or a balance sheet-based approach.'[103] *Southern* describes both approaches as follows:

> A transaction-based approach works on the basis that there must be an event, a transaction with a third party, for a profit to be realised, a liability to be incurred, or an asset to be acquired. Accounting records the results of transactions. A

97. ICAEW, Technical Advisory Service, Fixed Asset Investments under FRS 102, https://www.icaew.com/-/media/corporate/files/helpsheets/technical/fixed-asset-investments-under-frs-102.ashx, accessed 2 August 2023. The helpsheet explains that the cost less impairments accounting method can be applied under FRS 102, Section 11 to investment in shares (other than investments in another group entity) in the following circumstances (emphasis added):
'FRS 102 paragraph 11.8(d) requires investments in non-derivative financial instruments that are equity of the issuer (e.g., most ordinary shares and certain preference shares) to be accounted for as basic financial instruments in accordance with Section 11 of FRS 102.
FRS 102 paragraph 11.14(d) requires such *investments to be measured at fair value, with changes in fair value recognised in profit or loss, if the shares are publicly traded or if the fair value can otherwise be measured reliably.* Even if the investments did not meet the definition of a basic financial instrument, the treatment would be the same under FRS 102 paragraph 12.8.
[...] *When it is not possible to measure their fair value reliably, these investments shall instead be measured at cost less impairment.*'
98. Coroner-I Navigate, Differences between FRS 102, IAS 39 and IFRS 9.
99. *Ibid.*
100. Deloitte, IAS 39, Recognition and Measurement, https://www.iasplus.com/en/standards/ias/ias39, accessed 2 May 2023, confirms that: 'Investments in equity instruments with no reliable fair value measurement (and derivatives indexed to such equity instruments) should be measured at cost.'
101. Coroner-I Navigate, Differences between FRS 102, IAS 39 and IFRS 9; Southern (2017) para. 2.68.
102. IFRScommunity.com, Measurement of financial instruments (IFRS 9), 21 September 2023, https://ifrscommunity.com/knowledge-base/ifrs-9-measurement-of-financial-instruments/, accessed 2 October 2023, referencing IFRS 9, B5.2.3-B5.2.6.
103. *Ibid.*

> balance sheet-based approach assumes that what goes on in the balance sheet is more important than whether transactions are completed, or profits realised.[104]

The transaction-based approach is mirrored by the *amortised cost basis of accounting*, while *fair value accounting* mirrors the balance sheet-based approach.

Both accounting methods - amortised cost and fair value accounting - are correspondingly the two methods recognised for the taxation of a company's profits.[105]

Under an *amortised cost basis of accounting*, any asset or liability is shown in the company accounts at cost, adjustments only to be made for accumulated amortisation[106] and any impairment.[107] This method principally takes into account only the profits or losses when payments are made or received, subject to adjustments made for accruals and write-downs (impairments).[108] Taking into account accruals means that revenues and expenses are recognised in the correct accounting period, with the elimination of cash flows which do not belong to that accounting period.[109]

Fair value accounting means 'a basis of accounting under which the assets and liabilities are shown in the company's balance sheet at their fair value'.[110] Thus, any changes in value of the asset or the liability, including all unrealised profits and losses, are already recognised at each balance sheet date and not only at the disposal of the asset or at maturity of the liability.

It should be noted that the impairment provisions under FRS 102, Sections 11 and 12 and IAS 39 are different from those provisions in IFRS 9.

Southern defines an impairment loss as 'an amount by which the carrying amount of an asset exceeds its recoverable amount'.[111]

Under old GAAP, FRS 12 or IAS 36, impairment losses were already recognised in the accounting period they occurred, even if the asset was not sold or the liability was still in existence. For tax purposes, a provision for impairment losses was held to be deductible when made.[112]

FRS 102, paragraph 11.21 states: 'At the end of each reporting period, an entity shall assess whether there is objective evidence of impairment of any financial assets that are measured at cost or amortised cost. If there is objective evidence of impairment, the entity shall recognise an impairment loss in profit or loss immediately.'

In FRS 102, paragraph 11.23, it is maintained: 'Other factors may also be evidence of impairment, including significant changes with an adverse effect that have taken place in the technological, market, economic or legal environment in which the issuer operates.'

104. Southern (2017), para. 2.68.
105. Before the changes in FA 2004, the two 'authorised' accounting methods as a basis for taxation were authorised accruals or authorised mark-to-market accounting.
106. Accumulated amortisation means accumulated depreciation of the asset through usage.
107. CTA 2009, s. 313(4).
108. Ghosh, Johnson and Miller (2022) [E3.114]-[E3.120] (issue 28); Southern (2007) para. 1.85.
109. Laukkanen (2007) 186.
110. CTA 2009, s. 313(5).
111. Southern (2017) para. 7.6.
112. *Compare Herbert Smith v. Honour (Inspector of Taxes)* [2000] STC 173.

FRS 102 and IAS 39 follow the 'incurred loss model', which means 'an impairment loss is only recognized when there is objective evidence that the financial asset is impaired. Both standards provide indicators for such objective evidence'.[113]

Under IFRS 9, 'a company is required to make a provision for *expected credit losses* on financial instruments that are measured at amortised cost, or at fair value through other comprehensive income'.[114] Under the expected loss model, the expected cash shortfalls in the future determine the allowance for losses.[115]

IFRS 9 applies a three-stage model, the so-called Expected Credit Loss (ECL) model, for impairments based on the changes in credit quality since initial recognition.[116] The ECL model applies a 'general approach' and contains two exceptions: a 'simplified approach' for certain financial assets like trade-receivables and 'a credit-adjusted approach for loans which are impaired at initial recognition'.[117] *PWC* outlines the three stages of the model as follows:

> Stage 1 includes financial instruments that have not had a significant increase in credit risk since initial recognition or that have low credit risk at the reporting date. For these assets, 12-month expected credit losses ('ECL') are recognised, and interest revenue is calculated on the gross carrying amount of the asset (that is, without deduction for credit allowance).
> Stage 2 includes financial instruments that have had a significant increase in credit risk since initial recognition (unless they have low credit risk at the reporting date) but that do not have objective evidence of impairment. For these assets, lifetime ECL are recognised, but interest revenue is still calculated on the gross carrying amount of the asset.
> Stage 3 includes financial assets that have objective evidence of impairment at the reporting date. For these assets, lifetime ECL are recognised, and interest revenue is calculated on the net carrying amount (that is, net of credit allowance).[118]

The details of the accounting treatment of derivatives under FRS 102, Section 12, IAS 39 and IFRS 9 are discussed below under [C]. Details regarding hedge accounting under FRS 102, Section 12, IAS 39 and IFRS 9 are discussed in Chapter 7, and embedded derivatives are discussed in Chapter 8 of this book.

[C] FRS 102, Sections 11 and 12, IAS 39 and IFRS 9: Application to Derivatives

FRS 102 contains provisions in Sections 11 and 12 that apply to derivatives.[119]

113. LucaNet, White paper, 'Key differences between IFRS and UK GAAP', 11.
114. Ghosh, Johnson and Miller (2022) [B2.3] (issue 28).
115. LucaNet, White paper, 'Key differences between IFRS and UK GAAP', 11.
116. *PWC*, IFRS 9, Expected credit losses (13 August 2014), https://www.pwc.nl/nl/banken/assets/documents/in-depth-ifrs9-expected-credit-losses.pdf, accessed 1 September 2023.
117. LucaNet, White paper, 'Key differences between IFRS and UK GAAP', 11.
118. *PWC*, IFRS 9, Expected credit losses (13 August 2014).
119. FRS 102, Sections 11 and 12.

As seen above, UK companies can choose between applying FRS 102, Sections 11 and 12, IAS 39 or IFRS 9 for the recognition and measurement of derivatives.[120] FRS 102, paragraph 11.2(c) provides that certain companies can adopt the provisions of IFRS 9 in relation to derivatives.

In the following, FRS 102, Section 12 (in conjunction with Section 11), IAS 39 and IFRS 9 are outlined, and it is described how they apply for the recognition and measurement of derivatives.

[1] FRS 102, Sections 11 and 12 Applying to Derivatives

FRS 102, paragraph 11.6 provides examples of complex financial instruments which are within the scope of Section 12, such as:

(a) asset-backed securities, such as collateralised mortgage obligations, repurchase agreements and securitised packages of receivables;
(b) derivatives, e.g., options, rights, warrants, futures contracts, forward contracts and interest rate swaps;
(c) financial instruments that qualify and are designated as hedging instruments in accordance with the requirements in Section 12; and
(d) commitments to make a loan to another entity and commitments to receive a loan if the commitment can be settled net in cash.[121]

Under FRS 102, Section 12, when a financial asset or financial liability is recognised initially, 'an entity shall measure it at its *fair value*, which is normally the *transaction price* (adjusted for transaction costs except in the initial measurement of financial assets and liabilities that are subsequently measured at fair value through *profit or loss*).[122]

Thus, FRS 102, Section 12 requires 'all derivatives to be regarded as held for trading and measured at fair value, with changes in the carrying amount being taken to income'.[123]

As *Southern* correctly points out:

> [o]ne of the difficulties in applying the legislation is whether to record profits on a contract-by-contract or a cumulative basis. Companies will normally run books of derivatives on a portfolio basis. The book is split into constituent cash flows and managed as one pool. This enables companies to manage – and if wanted – hedge specific risks or part of risks of derivatives that they don't want to take, for example, the interest rate risk, the currency risk or the credit risk.[124]

Under FRS 102, Section 12, financial instruments are subsequently measured at fair value, with any changes recognised in the P&L account.[125]

120. FRS 102, para. 11.2.
121. FRS 102, para. 11.6.
122. FRS 102, para. 12.7.
123. Southern (2017), para. 13.38.
124. *Ibid.*
125. FRS 102, Factsheet 4, Financial Instruments (December 2018), 8.

There are exceptions for the fair value subsequent measurement for:

(a) investments in non-derivative financial instruments that are equity of the issuer that are not publicly traded and whose fair value cannot otherwise be measured reliably and contracts linked to such instruments that, if exercised, will result in delivery of such instruments, shall be measured at cost less impairment;
(b) hedging instruments in a designated hedging relationship accounted for in accordance with paragraph 12.23 or 12.24; and
(c) financial instruments that are not permitted by the Small Company Regulations, the Regulations, the Small LLP Regulations, or the LLP Regulations to be measured at fair value through profit or loss shall be measured at amortised cost in accordance with paragraphs 11.15 to 11.20.[126]

Of those exceptions, only (b) in relation to hedging instruments in a designated hedging relationship is relevant in the context of derivatives. Under FRS 102, Section 12, fair value hedges, cash flow hedges, and hedges of a net investment in a foreign corporation as permissible,[127] and hedge accounting is optional.[128] For example, 'any interest rate swaps or forward foreign exchange contracts will be measured at fair value at each reporting date, with the change in fair value being recognised in profit or loss, unless the entity chooses to apply hedge accounting'.[129]

[2] IAS 39 Applying to Derivatives

To reiterate, IAS 39 can be applied as an accounting choice under FRS 102, paragraph 11.2, although it has been superseded by IFRS 9 since 2018.[130] This is a situation under the UK GAAP, which is - in the author's view - quite unsettling as a standard is applied under UK GAAP, which is no longer endorsed by the IFRS. Consequently, IAS 39 in relation to recognition and measurement is no longer found on the IFRS website but only on the UK FRC website.

If IAS 39 is applied, derivatives are, in principle, accounted at *fair value,*[131] with any changes going through the income statement as profit or loss.[132] However, certain equity derivatives over unquoted shares are, however, held at amortised cost because they cannot be 'designated by the entity as fair value through profit or loss'.[133]

126. FRS 102, para. 12.8.
127. FRS 102, paras 12.20-12.24.
128. FRS 102, Factsheet 4, Financial Instruments (December 2018), 8.
129. *Ibid.*
130. FRS 102, Factsheet 4, Financial Instruments (December 2018), 1. On 27 March 2024, the FRC issued amendments to FRS 102 that include the removal of the option to newly adopt the recognition and measurement requirements of IAS 39. They apply for accounting periods beginning on or after 1 January 2026.
131. For a definition of fair value accounting and the distinction to the amortised cost basis of accounting, *see* Ch. 6 §6.02[A].
132. HMRC, CFM16120. For exceptions if hedge accounting under IAS 39 is applied and effective, *see* Ch. 7 §7.03[A][1].
133. IAS 39, paras 9(b) sent. 2.

Ghosh, Johnson and Miller describe that situation as follows:

> The one exception to the FVTPL basket relates to equities and equity derivatives. In cases where the fair value cannot be reliably measured, they are to be held at cost. This treatment applies where an investment in an equity instrument [...] does not have a quoted market price in an active market and its fair value cannot reliably be measured[134] [...]. The same applies to derivatives that are linked to and must be settled by delivery of such unquoted equity instruments. In such cases, the equity instrument or derivative, as the case may be, must be measured at cost.[135]

[3] IFRS 9 Applying to Derivatives

Similar to IAS 39, IFRS 9, Appendix A defines a derivative as:

> a financial instrument or other contract within the scope of the Standard with all three of the following characteristics:
>
> (a) its value changes in response to the change in a specified interest rate, financial instrument price, commodity price, foreign exchange rate, index of prices or rates, credit rating or credit index, or other variable, provided in the case of a non-financial variable that the variable is not specific to a party to the contract (sometimes called the 'underlying');
> (b) it requires no initial net investment or an initial net investment that is smaller than would be required for other types of contracts that would be expected to have a similar response to changes in market factors;
> (c) it is settled at a future date.[136]

[a] Change in Value of the Derivative in Response to the Change of the Underlying Asset/Variable

IFRS 9, Appendix Application Guidance B2 gives examples of derivatives that fall under the definition. Under IFRS 9, BA.1, typical examples are mentioned, such as futures and forwards, swaps and option contracts.[137]

The underlying asset usually has a notional amount, and changes in the value of the derivative depend on the changes in the value of the underlying. For example, if the price(s) of the underlying equities are changing, the value of the derivative will change as well. That is why the author described in Chapter 2 of this book that the underlying is actually not the asset itself but the price or, sometimes, income stream of the asset.

In IFRS 9, it is stated that:

> A derivative usually has a notional amount, which is an amount of currency, a number of shares, a number of units of weight or volume or other units specified

134. This refers to IAS 39, para. 46(c).
135. Ghosh, Johnson and Miller (2022) [B2.28]-[B2.30] (issue 28).
136. IFRS 9, Appendix A.
137. IFRS 9, BA.1.

> in the contract. However, a derivative instrument does not require the holder or writer to invest or receive the notional amount at the inception of the contract. Alternatively, a derivative could require a fixed payment or payment of an amount that can change (but not proportionally with a change in the underlying) as a result of some future event that is unrelated to the notional amount.[138]

In the Application Guidance to IFRS 9, it is confirmed that 'such a contract is a derivative even though a notional amount is not specified'.[139] Also, non-standard contracts are included. For example, '[t]he definition of a derivative refers to non-financial variables that are not specific to a party to the contract. These include an index of earthquake losses in a particular region and an index of temperatures in a particular city'.[140]

[b] No or Little Net Investment

IFRS 9, BA.3 explains in this respect:

> One of the defining characteristics of a derivative is that it has an initial net investment that is smaller than would be required for other types of contracts that would be expected to have a similar response to changes in market factors. An option contract meets that definition because the premium is less than the investment that would be required to obtain the underlying financial instrument to which the option is linked. A currency swap that requires an initial exchange of different currencies of equal fair value meets the definition because it has a zero initial net investment.[141]

[c] Settled at a Future Date

One should note that a short term (usually two days) between the trade date and the settlement date of a contractual commitment does not give rise to a derivative contract.[142] Also, it is irrelevant if the derivative is gross or net settled.[143] The lapse of an option is also a form of settlement.[144]

---

138. IFRS 9, BA.1.; *compare also* IFRSCommunity.com, Derivatives and Embedded Derivatives: Definitions and Characteristics (IFRS 9), Blog, (updated 6 June 2023), https://ifrscommunity.com/knowledge-base/ifrs-9-derivatives-and-embedded-derivatives/, accessed 13 August 2023.
139. *Compare* IFRS 9, BA.1, *see* IFRSCommunity.com, Derivatives and Embedded Derivatives: Definitions and Characteristics (IFRS 9), Blog.
140. IFRS 9, BA.5.
141. *Ibid.*, BA.3.
142. *Ibid.*, BA.4.
143. *Ibid.*, BA.2.
144. IFRSCommunity.com, Derivatives and Embedded Derivatives: Definitions and Characteristics (IFRS 9), Blog.

[d] *Financial Liabilities*

IFRS 9, BA.7 states that financial liabilities held for trading 'include derivative liabilities that are not accounted for as hedging instruments'.[145]

[e] *Challenges*

Challenges occur in those cases where the definition of a derivative does not exactly match the words used in IFRS 9, Appendix A.

For example, such a mismatch may occur in case of prepaid contracts. Another example is a physically settled forward contract, which has a non-financial instrument as an underlying to be delivered and where there is no cash settlement option in the contract.

A physically settled forward contract to acquire, for example, real estate, falls outside the definition of a derivative under IFRS 9.[146] Yet, those instruments may be regarded as derivatives from an economic point of view – and perhaps should be considered as derivatives both from an accounting and taxation point of view.

Other examples of contracts falling outside of the definition of derivatives under IFRS 9 are physically settled options and futures over cryptoassets, which will be discussed below. In the same way, variable forward purchases may challenge the definitional criteria set out in IFRS 9.

The author cannot propose detailed solutions for those problems as that would exceed the scope of this work. It is up to the accountants and the IFRS standard setters to deal with those challenges in the accounting treatment of derivatives under IFRS 9.

[D] State of Alignment of Accounting Standards and Taxation Rules Applying to Derivatives

Within the last forty years, UK corporate tax legislation has been increasingly aligned with accounting standards up to the point where accounts based on these standards are now considered a basis for taxing a company's income.[147] This is codified for derivative contracts in CTA 2009, section 595(2), which is discussed below.

For corporate tax purposes, CTA 2010, section 1127(2)[148] confirms that '[i]n the Corporation Tax Acts "UK generally accepted accounting practice"—

---

145. IFRS 9, BA.7.
146. *PWC*, 2.4.2. Accounting for forward contracts and options to acquire real estate (13 December 2021, updated 1 February 2023), https://viewpoint.pwc.com/dt/ca/en/pwc/industry/industry_INT/industry_INT/real_estate__1_INT/Applying-IFRS-for-the-real-est/2_Acquisition_or_construction_of_real_estate/2_4_Asset_acquisitions_measurement_at_initial_recognition/2_4_2_Accounting_for_forward_contracts_and_options_to_acquire_real_estate.html, accessed 15 March 2023.
147. Southern (2017) para. 2.2; *also* Ghosh, Johnson and Miller (2022) [B2.3A] and [B7.1] (issue 28).
148. Former FA 2004, s. 50(1), (4) and ICTA 1988, s. 832(1).

(a) means generally accepted accounting practice in relation to accounts of UK companies (other than IAS accounts) that are intended to give a true and fair view, and
(b) has the same meaning in relation to—
  (i) individuals,
  (ii) entities other than companies, and
  (iii) companies that are not UK companies,
  as it has in relation to UK companies'.[149]

CTA 2010, section 1127(3) states that '[i]n relation to the affairs of a company or other entity that prepares IAS accounts, in the Corporation Tax Acts "generally accepted accounting practice" means generally accepted accounting practice in relation to IAS accounts'.[150]

Thus, accounts prepared according to UK GAAP[151] or IFRS/IAS[152] constitute an acceptable basis for computing taxable profits.[153]

---

149. CTA 2010, s. 1127 (2).
150. CTA 2010, s. 1127 (3).
151. CTA 2010, s. 1127(1) and (2). UK GAAP means 'generally accepted accounting practice in relation to accounts of UK companies (other than IAS accounts) that are intended to give a true and fair view', *see* CTA 2010, s. 1127(2)(a).
152. CTA 2010, s. 1127(3). This includes both original and modified IASs as long as they are now UK-adopted or EU-adopted with modifications, IFRS, *see* CTA 2010, s. 1127(5), (6) and (7).
CTA 2010, s. 1127(5) to (7) now reads:

(5) In the Corporation Tax Acts 'international accounting standards' has the same meaning as in Regulation (EC) No 1606/2002 of the European Parliament and the Council of 19 July 2002 on the application of international accounting standards.
(6) If an international accounting standard has been adopted by the United Kingdom or the European Commission with modifications, then as regards matters covered by that standard—
  (a) generally accepted accounting practice with respect to IAS accounts is to be regarded as permitting the use of the standard either with or without modifications, and
  (b) accounts prepared on either basis are to be regarded for the purposes of the Corporation Tax Acts as prepared in accordance with international accounting standards.
(7) In this section—

'adopted by the United Kingdom' means adopted for use within the United Kingdom by virtue of Chapter 2 or 3 of Part 2 of the International Accounting Standards and European Public Limited-Liability Company (Amendment etc.) (EU Exit) Regulations 2019,
'adopted by the European Commission' means adopted by the European Commission in accordance with Regulation (EC) No 1606/2002 of the European Parliament and the Council of 19 July 2002 on the application of international accounting standards (as it has effect in EU law),
'IAS accounts' means accounts prepared in accordance with international accounting standards, and
'UK companies' means companies incorporated or formed under the law of a part of the United Kingdom.

Compare also Ghosh, Johnson and Miller (2022) [B7.3]-[B7.4] (issue 28).

153. FRS 102 allows the application of IAS 39 or IFRS 9 for companies that account under FRS 102.
Compare Ghosh, Johnson and Miller (2022) [B2.3A] (issue 28).

The derivative contracts rules and the taxation of foreign exchange differences in derivative contracts[154] are almost entirely accounts driven.[155]

The computational rules of CTA 2009, ss 594-610, and, in particular, CTA 2009, section 595 have been subject to significant changes by virtue of Finance (No 2 Act 2015).[156]

CTA 2009, section 594 gives an overview of the chapter. CTA 2009, section 594A(1) states as a general rule that for the purposes of CTA 2009, Part 7, 'matters' that have to be brought into account 'in respect of a company's derivative contracts are—

(a) profits and losses of the company which arise from its derivative contracts and related transactions (excluding expenses), and
(b) expenses incurred by the company under or for the purposes of those contracts and transactions'.[157]

CTA 2009, section 595(2) determines that the amounts to be brought into account by a company 'are those which are recognised in determining the company's profit or loss for the period in accordance with generally accepted accounting practice'.[158]

Thus, section 595(2) effectively stipulates that the company's accounts are to be followed to determine the profit or loss from a derivative contract for tax purposes recognised with GAAP if they are drawn in accordance with 'generally accepted accounting practice',[159] i.e., if they are GAAP-compliant accounts.[160]

CTA 2009, section 597 now states, 'an amount recognised in determining a company's profit or loss for a period are to an amount that is recognised in the company's accounts for the period as an item of profit or loss'.[161]

HMRC explains in the Corporate Finance Manual:

> Before amendment, there was an expanded tax definition of an 'amount taken into account in determining a company's profit or loss' in section 597(1), as it then stood. This was primarily based on the statement in the account to which a debit or credit was taken, including the company's profit and loss account, income statement or statement of comprehensive income for that period, statement of total

154. From 1 October 2002 onwards, the rules applicable to foreign exchange differences have been incorporated into the loan relationship and derivative contracts rules and are treated the same way as any other profit or loss from loan relationships (CTA 2009, s. 328) or derivative contracts (CTA 2009, s. 606). *See* HMRC, CFM60010 and CMF61020.
155. Southern (2017) para. 1.20.
156. HMRC, CFM51005.
157. CTA 2009, s. 594A(1); HMRC, CFM51005.
158. CTA 2009, s. 595(2).
    HMRC, CFM51034 explains what is meant by generally accepted accounting practice, namely that GAAP: 'is defined in CTA10/S1127 as UK GAAP. Where a company prepares IAS accounts, UK GAAP will mean GAAP in relation to IAS accounts. IAS accounts are accounts prepared in accordance with International Accounting Standards and a standard may be applied in its current form at any particular time, or as adopted by the EU. (More recent international standards are entitled, International Financial Reporting Standards or IFRS, but these fall within the ambit of the statutory definition of IAS)'.
159. Ghosh, Johnson and Miller (2022) [E3.21] (issue 28).
160. HMRC, CFM51034.
161. CTA 2009, s. 597(1).

> recognised gains and losses, statement of recognised income and expense, statement of changes in equity or statement of income and retained earnings for a period. Numerous, often complex, special tax rules then limited the effect of this expanded meaning of profit or loss.[162]

Thus, following the company accounts for tax purposes under CTA 2009, section 595 means that the credits and debits are accounted for on a fair value basis and subsequently taxed on that basis. If the accounts are not drawn up at all, or if the accounts are not drawn up in accordance with UK GAAP or IFRS/IAS, the company will be treated as 'if they had been so recognised for accounting purposes'.[163]

In the following example, the author illustrates the application of fair value accounting under FRS 102, Section 12, IAS 39 or IFRS 9 in the context of the UK derivative contracts regime.

Example 33:

The taxpayer buys an option in year 1 and pays 10 as an option premium, which equals the market value of the option. The option has a term of two years. Due to increasing equity markets, the option becomes worth 30 at the end of business year 1, and the taxpayer has to pay tax on the gain of 20. In year 2, the equity markets sharply decline, and at maturity, the option will be worthless. In economic terms, the taxpayer has a loss of 10, i.e., the option premium. However, as the option has been 'fair valued' during the life of the transaction, the taxpayer will recognise a loss on the option of 30 in year 2.

As a result of fair value accounting through P&L, the option buyer will have to pay tax on an option which is deeply in the money but not exercised at the end of year 1 and will have an increased deduction in year 2, which is the difference between the market value of the option at the end of year 1 and the value at maturity.

The example shows that the taxation of derivatives, which follows fair value accounting through P&L, creates the following problems:

(1) The taxpayer has to suffer tax on gains which are not 'realised' by way of a sale or an expiry of the option.
(2) The taxpayer's ability to pay is not taken into account because the company may not have sufficient funds available to pay the tax in year 1.
(3) As the taxpayer is fully subject to the volatility of the assets underlying the option, the tax levied is directly linked to the volatility of the capital markets, although the company has not realised its investment(s).

162. HMRC, CFM51034.
163. HMRC, CFM51080.

§5.03 ALIGNMENT OF ACCOUNTING AND TAX RULES APPLYING TO DERIVATIVES IN GERMANY

[A] German GAAP as a Basis for Taxation

Applying the authoritative principle ('*Grundsatz der Maßgeblichkeit*'),[164] the German tax legislation regards the 'general principles of orderly accounting' (GAAP),[165] laid down in the German Commercial Code,[166] as a starting point for taxing income of non-corporate businesses and companies.[167] These 'general principles of orderly accounting' are also applicable for tax purposes unless the tax law provides for special rules.[168] As a consequence, the taxpayer is required to set up both financial accounts and tax accounts.

Even after the introduction of IFRS on a group accounts basis,[169] German GAAP[170] remains the *only* financial accounting basis for the determination of the tax base. IFRS are not considered valid accounting standards in the single company accounts on which taxation can be based.[171]

In the course of the reform of the accounting rules, the legislator has abolished the principle that tax law has, in some cases, 'reverse authority' over commercial accounts, i.e., that commercial accounts have to be brought in line with tax accounts. Hence, certain accounting choices, for example, in relation to the recognition and valuation of intangible assets,[172] can now be selected differently in commercial and tax accounts.[173]

In addition, the separate valuation norms for tax purposes have increasingly departed from the valuation norms for accounting purposes over time, leading to a gap between financial and tax accounts.[174] New valuation rules for tax purposes were introduced, which are designed to apply independently from commercial valuation

164. *See* §6.02[A][1] for further details.
165. *Grundsätze ordnungsgemäßer Buchführung.*
166. *Handelsgesetzbuch.*
167. Section 5(1) sent. 1 1st part German Income Tax Act (ITA) and section 8(1) German Corporate Tax Act (CTA).
168. Section 5(1) sent. 1, 2nd part ITA. *See* Conlon & Aquilino: Derivatives D2.03.[2].
169. Section 315a(1) Commercial Law Act (CLA).
170. In Germany, the abbreviation GAAP may refer to the '*Generally Accepted Accounting Principles*'. To avoid confusion with the UK term, being Generally Accepted Accounting Practice, I will use the term GAAP as referring to 'generally accepted accounting practice' in both countries.
171. IFRS can be used to prepare group accounts but not the single company accounts. *See* Wolfgang Blödtner, Kurt Bilke and Rudolf Heining, *Lehrbuch Buchführung und Bilanzsteuerrecht* (8th edn, nwb Verlag 2009) 554; *also* Conlon & Aquilino: Derivatives D2.03.[2].
172. Section 248(2) CLA.
173. BMF, *Maßgeblichkeit der handelsrechtlichen Grundsätze ordnungsgemäßer Buchführung für die steuerliche Gewinnermittlung* (IV C 6 – S 2133/09/10001, 12. März 2010) para. 13.
174. Wendt et al. *in H/H/R, Steuerreform I* (2001) *§* 6 paras R 13 and R 25; Jochem Schreiber, '§ 5 EStG' in Bernd Heuermann (ed), *Blümich, EStG, KStG, GewStG, Kommentar* (91st edn, Verlag Franz Vahlen 2006) § 5, para. 78.

rules.[175] Both reforms[176] emphasise that the German legislator follows the trend of non-alignment of accounting standards and tax rules. Financial accounting standards and taxation rules have been further dis-aligned over time, leading to a further disengagement of the tax accounts from the financial accounts.

[B] German GAAP Applying to the Taxation of Derivatives

German GAAP is mainly codified in the Commercial Code, sometimes also referred to as the *Commercial Law Act* (CLA). German GAAP does not contain comprehensive rules regarding the accounting treatment of derivatives. Instead, the general principles of orderly accounting, namely the prudence principle, the realisation principle, the imparity principle as a concretisation of the prudence principle, and the item-per-item valuation, apply to derivatives entered into by companies.[177]

The realisation principle means gains are only accounted for when realised.[178] The imparity principle maintains that all predictable risks and losses until the reporting date need to be taken into account.[179] The coexistence of both principles leads to a deliberately different recognition of gains and losses. Unrealised gains cannot be recognised at balance sheet date, whereas unrealised losses, in general, have to be recognised,[180] for example, in the form of reserves.[181] The *item-per-item valuation principle* postulates that the above principles are applied separately to each item shown in the balance sheet.[182]

Additionally, the historical cost principle,[183] the principle of consistency of valuation choices,[184] and the principle of non-accountability of gains in *pending transactions*[185] have to be applied as they are all expressions of an overarching prudence principle.

A transaction is regarded as a pending transaction if the payment or delivery obligation has not been fulfilled yet by the taxpayer or by both counterparties at the

175. Heinz Kußmaul and Nicole Klein, 'Überlegungen zum Maßgeblichkeitsprinzip in Kontext jüngerer nationaler sowie internationaler Entwicklungen' DStR 2001 546, 546ff.
176. This includes both the reforms in the context of the '*Steuerentlastungsgesetz 1999-2000-2002*', as well as the reforms in the context of the modernisation of the accounting law '*Gesetz zur Modernisierung des Bilanzrechts (Bilanzrechtsmodernisierungsgesetz – BilMoG) 2009*'.
177. Conlon & Aquilino: Derivatives D2.03[2].
178. Section 252(1) No. 4 sent. 1 2nd part CLA.
179. Section 252(1) No. 4 sent. 1 1st part CLA.
180. Conlon & Aquilino: Derivatives D2.03[2].
181. Section 249 CLA.
182. Section 252(1) No. 3 CLA. *See* Conlon & Aquilino: Derivatives D2.03[2].
The item-per-item valuation principle is a concretisation of the accounting principle of clarity. *See* Blödtner, Bilke and Heining (2009) 156.
183. Section 253(1) sent. 1 CLA: Assets can be valued in the accounts up to a maximum of their historical acquisition costs minus depreciation. No 'writing up' of the value of the assets in case of unrealised gains is possible.
184. Section 252(1) No. 6 CLA. The valuation methods used in former accounts should be applied.
185. Blödtner, Bilke and Heining (2009) 366; *also* Conlon & Aquilino: Derivatives D2.03[3]: 'unrealized gains from pending transactions must not be shown on the balance sheet (realization principle)'.

relevant balance sheet date.[186] Pending transactions are not usually shown in the accounts unless they currently carry a loss from the taxpayer's perspective.[187] In this case, a reserve for expected, unrealised losses has to be established in the commercial accounts.[188]

Although German GAAP has been 'modernised' in order to be more aligned with international accounting standards,[189] the structure of German GAAP and the general principles of orderly accounting, such as the prudence principle, the realisation principle and the imparity principle, have remained intact.

As a result, derivatives entered into by companies are still not accounted for on a fair value basis but on an *accrual basis* with the observance of the prudence and realisation principle.[190] The P&L accounted in such a way in principle then constitutes the basis for taxation.[191]

Futures, forwards and swaps are treated as pending transactions and, as such, are not shown in the accounts unless a reserve for expected, unrealised losses has been established.[192] In accordance with the financial accounts, any unrealised gains generated from derivatives during the term of the transaction are deferred until realisation for tax purposes.[193]

In contrast, reserves, established for unrealised derivatives losses under accounting principles, are denied in the tax accounts due to the explicit prohibition to recognise for tax purposes unrealised losses from pending transactions in section 5(4a) sentence 2 ITA.[194] The result of this accounting versus tax mismatch is that negative market movements cannot be deducted for tax purposes during the term of the derivative, although they are recognised in commercial accounts.

Special accounting rules, however, apply to securities and other financial instruments, including derivatives that are held in the trading book of a credit institution, bank or financial services institution.[195] Financial instruments attributed to the trading

186. Conlon & Aquilino: Derivatives D2.03[3]. *See* BFH, decision of 23 June 1997 – GrS 2/93, BStBl II 1997, 735, 737.
187. Section 252(1) No. 4. CLA (realisation and imparity principle).
Thus, any unrealised gains of 'pending transactions' are not shown in the accounts. *See* Conlon & Aquilino: Derivatives D2.03[3].
188. Section 249(1) sent. 1 CLA.
189. *Gesetz zur Modernisierung des Bilanzrechts* (BilMoG) of 25 May 2009 (BStBl I 2009, 650ff) – law regarding the modernisation of accounting law.
190. Conlon & Aquilino: Derivatives D2.03[2].
191. *Ibid.* Section 5(1) sent. 1 ITA applies as a general tax accounting rule also in respect of the tax accounting of derivative contracts.
192. Federal Fiscal Court cases concerning currency futures: BFH, decision of 4 July 1991 – IV R 29/88, BStBl II 1992, 76; BFH, decision of 5 March 1981 – IV R 94/78, BStBl II 1981, 658; BFH, decision of 19 February 1997 – IX R 1/96, BStBl II 1997, 399.
193. Section 252(1) No. 4 CLA, s. 5(1) sent. 1 ITA. *See* Conlon & Aquilino: Derivatives D2.03[3].
194. These losses can, however, also be recognised for tax purposes in the course of hedging transactions, *see* s. 5(4a) sent. 2 and 5(1a) sent. 2 ITA. *See* BMF, *Schreiben vom 25. August 2010, betr. steuerliche Gewinnermittlung bei der Bildung von Bewertungseinheiten* (IVC 6 – S 2133/07/10001, Der Betrieb 2010, 2024); *also* Conlon & Aquilino: Derivatives (Germany) D2.03[5][b].
195. Sections 340-340g CLA. For a detailed summary of these accounting rules, *see* Scharpf and Schaber (2009) 181ff.

book[196] have to be accounted for at each balance sheet date on a fair value basis.[197] Section 340e(3) CLA is an exception to the general accounting treatment of pending transactions under German GAAP, as the rule departs from the general realisation principle.

The legislator has, however, implemented a modified fair value method for financial instruments held in the trading book, which applies elements of the prudence principle because the fair value result has to be adjusted by a 'risk allowance'.[198] Additionally, section 340e(4) CLA requires a special item to be set up for general banking risks in every business year with an amount of at least 10% of the net income of the trading book.[199]

Special accounting provisions applying to a specific industry, such as banks, credit institutions or insurance companies, are normally not authoritative for tax purposes,[200] except where tax rules specifically allow or demand such a provision in the tax accounts. With regard to derivatives held in the trading book of a credit institution, bank or financial services institution, section 340e(3) sentence 1 CLA, which requires fair value accounting adjusted by the risk allowance, is also authoritative for tax purposes because section 6(1) No. 2b ITA specifically requires fair value accounting in the tax accounts.[201]

Thus, the general rule of non-recognition of losses from pending transactions under section 5(4a) ITA, which would normally disregard non-realised losses from derivatives transactions for tax purposes will not apply. Instead, these losses have to be recognised in the tax accounts of banks or financial services institutions at the end of each accounting year.[202] Correspondingly, according to section 6(1) No. 2b ITA, non-realised gains will have to be recognised for tax purposes, adjusted by the risk margin of section 340e(3) sentence 1 CLA.

§5.04 COMPARISON OF THE STATE OF ALIGNMENT OF ACCOUNTING AND TAX RULES IN THE UK AND GERMANY

The UK has moved from a corporate tax legislation, which was largely independent of accounting standards, to a taxation regime that is based on and aligned with the financial accounts. The derivative contracts regime relies on accounting standards as a

196. Section 340e(1) sent. 1 and 2 CLA determine whether financial instruments are attributed to the banking book or to the trading book.
197. Section 340e(3) CLA. *See* Scharpf and Schaber (2009) 182; *also* Mathias Schaber et al., *Handbuch strukturierte Finanzinstrumente, HGB – IFRS* (2nd edn, IDW Verlag 2010) 39; Frank Schmitz and Andreas Huthmann, *Bilanzierung von Finanzinstrumenten, IAS/IFRS und BilMoG* (1st edn, Gabler 2012) 92.
198. Section 340e(3) sent. 1 CLA. This risk allowance in principle mirrors a 'Value at Risk' allowance as calculated in accordance with the German Banking Act. *See* Scharpf and Schaber (2009) 199-201.
199. *Ibid.*, 182 and 202-204.
200. Conlon & Aquilino: Derivatives D2.03[2].
201. Section 6(1) No. 2b ITA. *See* Wolfram Scheffler, *Besteuerung von Unternehmen II, Steuerbilanz* (7th edn, C.F. Müller 2011) 267.
202. Section 6(1) No. 2b ITA.

basis for taxation and accepts fair value accounting methods applied by corporate taxpayers. Due to the introduction of fair value accounting for tax purposes, the recognition of gains and losses has moved away from realisation as a trigger for recognising income and gains.

In contrast, the German legislator is following a different route with respect to the alignment of accounting standards and tax rules. Although German tax legislation traditionally bases its tax accounts on the financial accounts, the introduction of IFRS at the level of consolidated accounts has opened a debate among German tax practitioners as to whether the German legislator should completely move away from the alignment of financial and tax accounts and the authoritative principle by introducing a separate set of tax accounts with different recognition rules.[203]

Some authors take the view that IFRS can provide a 'starting point' for the tax accounts in order to avoid solutions which are not in line with the EU's attempt to harmonise taxes and create a common consolidated corporate tax base.[204] Others do not see fair value accounting as an acceptable starting point for taxation because it does not recognise the realisation and ability-to-pay principles.[205] The German government has endorsed the second opinion in the 2008 German Corporate Tax Reform, thereby moving more closely to a separate accounting basis for tax purposes.[206]

As IFRS do not promote either the realisation principle or the ability-to-pay principle, fair value accounting may not be the most suitable approach for corporate taxpayers to determine if and when (unrealised) gains and losses are recognised for tax purposes.[207]

The academic literature on the alignment of accounting standards and taxation has suggested the introduction of 'some form of tax realisation principle [...] [which

203. Norbert Herzig, 'Steuerliche Gewinnermittung und handelsrechtliche Rechnungslegung' IStR 2006 557; Ulrich Prinz, 'Reform der deutschen Rechnungslegung – Gedanken und Anregungen an den Gesetzgeber zur Umsetzung der Mitgliedstaatenwahlrechte der IAS/IFRS-Verordnung aus Praktikersicht' DStR 2003 1359, 1364; Wolfgang Schön, *Steuerliche Maßgeblichkeit in Deutschland und Europa* (1st edn, Dr Otto Schmid KG Verlag 2005) 195-196. Against a separation of financial accounts and tax accounts in the case of a theoretical introduction of IAS/IFRS in the single company accounts: Rainer Buchholz and Bettina Weis, 'Maßgeblichkeitsprinzip ade? Zur inhaltlichen Vereinbarkeit der Gewinnermittlung nach IAS und EStG (Teil 1)' DStR 2002 512, 513.

204. Hans-Joachim Böcking and Marius Gros, 'IFRS und die Zukunft der steuerlichen Gewinnermittlung' DStR 2007 2339, 2341-2343; Herzig (2006) 557; Christoph Spengel, 'International Accounting Standards und Unternehmensbesteuerung in der Europäischen Union (Teil 1)' IStR 2003 29.

205. Wolfgang Schön, 'Arbeitskreis Bilanzrecht der Hochschullehrer Rechtswissenschaft' BB 2002 2379; Schön (2005) 194-195; *also* Lee Sheppard, 'New Analysis: Financial Accounting Conformity for European Corporate Taxation' (2004) Tax Notes International 1375, 1378-1379, summarising the view of Wolfgang Schön at the European Association of Tax Law Professors (4 June 2004).

206. 'Coalition Agreement between CDU/CSU and SPD' (11 November 2005) https://webarchiv.bundestag.de/archive/2008/0416/aktuell/archiv/2005/koalition/vertrag_en.pdf, accessed 25 October 2023.

207. Similar: Freedman (2004a) 76. Also recognising the problem of taxing unrealised gains: Neighbour (1997) 935.

may be] more closely linked to legal rights than to revenue recognition'[208] to deal with the challenges posed by the introduction of fair value accounting.

§5.05 ACCOUNTING OF CRYPTOASSETS, WITH FOCUS ON CRYPTOCURRENCIES

It is necessary to discuss the accounting treatment of cryptoassets in the context of this book not only because they are a new asset class but because they can be underlyings to cryptoasset derivatives, which are discussed in various chapters of this work. When a new asset class emerges, standard setters – and also investors for the valuation of their investments – should not rely on traditional accounting categories as those new instruments may not fit them. The author supports the position that new approaches to account for those newly emerged instruments may be necessary.

For example, *Barth* insists:

> Investors need and use information not contained in traditional financial statements. [..] Two issues on the horizon – accounting for digital assets and the effects of climate change – reveal how embracing this perspective could help avoid the 'Too Difficult' Box. These issues reveal pitfalls arising from trying to fit newly created assets into categories – and consequent accounting – designed for previously identified assets.[209]

In this subchapter, the author considers the IFRS accounting classification and measurement for cryptoassets and compares the differences and similarities with the UK and German accounting standards. Further, the US GAAP treatment of cryptoassets is discussed in detail as the *Financial Accounting Standards Board's* (*FASB's*) suggestions on the accounting of cryptoassets significantly changed in October 2022 and now diverts from the accounting treatment of cryptoassets under IFRS. The position on the accounting treatment of cryptoassets by the Australian Accounting Standards Board is also highlighted as it considerably deviates from IFRS. While discussing the various approaches adopted by the different accounting standard setters, the author considers the following questions:

(1) How are cryptocurrencies classified for accounting purposes, and why?
(2) How are cryptocurrency profits and losses measured for accounting purposes, and how is the impairment of cryptoassets treated in the financial accounts?

208. Freedman (2004a) 85.
209. Mary E Barth, Accounting Standards: The 'too difficult box' – the big accounting issue, August 2022, https://www.tandfonline.com/doi/full/10.1080/00014788.2022.2079757, accessed 14 August 2023 DOI: https://doi.org/10.1080/00014788.2022.2079757.

[A] Accounting of Cryptoassets under IFRS

The classification and measurement of cryptoassets has not been settled yet. The 2019 IFRS Interpretations Committee suggestions are only tentative,[210] and, for example, *PWC* suggests that there is 'no clear industry practice'.[211] In April 2022, EFRAG issued 'Recommendations and Feedback Statement on Accounting for Crypto-Assets (Liabilities)',[212] which deals with the accounting treatment of cryptoassets. Those recommendations closely align with those made by the IFRS Interpretations Committee.

The following analysis focuses on cryptocurrencies as they provide a significant challenge for tax authorities. Further, crypto derivatives have cryptocurrencies as underlyings, and thus, the accounting treatment of the underlying cryptocurrencies is relevant and will be discussed in this subchapter. For a general discussion of other cryptoassets, *see* Chapter 2 § 2.01[C].

[1] Classification of Cryptoassets under IFRS

In the White paper, Bitcoin: *A Peer-to-Peer Electronic Cash System*, which was published in 2009, the founder of Bitcoin, Satoshi Nakamoto, identifies the purpose of Bitcoin as follows:

> Commerce on the Internet has come to rely almost exclusively on financial institutions serving as trusted third parties to process electronic payments. [...] The cost of mediation increases transaction costs [...] *What is needed is an electronic payment system based on cryptographic proof instead of trust, allowing any two willing parties to transact directly with each other without the need for a trusted third party.*[213]

Thus, the inventor of the Bitcoin cryptocurrency intended Bitcoin to be a peer-to-peer *electronic cash system.*

For accounting purposes, the various characteristics of cryptocurrency are summarised by the IFRS Interpretations Committee as follows:

(a) a digital or virtual currency recorded on a distributed ledger that uses cryptography for security,

---

210. IFRS Interpretations Committee Meeting, Holding of Cryptocurrencies, Agenda Decision to finalise (June 2019) https://www.ifrs.org/content/dam/ifrs/meetings/2019/june/ifric/ap12-holdings-of-cryptocurrencies.pdf, accessed 1 October 2023, 1.
211. *PWC*, Cryptographic assets and related transactions: accounting considerations under IFRS (June 2021), GX In depth INT2021-06, https://viewpoint.pwc.com/dt/gx/en/pwc/in_depths/in_depths_INT/in_depths_INT/Cryptographic-assets-and-related-transactions-in-depth/2-Cryptographic-assets-held-by-an-entity.html#pwc-topic.dita_83fa5bac-4fe2-4141-956e-a173ee028d45, accessed 1 October, para 2.1.
212. EFRAG, 'Recommendations and Feedback Statement on Accounting for Crypto-Assets (Liabilities)' (April 2022, https://www.efrag.org/News/Project-585/EFRAGs-Recommendations-and-Feedback-Statement-on-Accounting-for-Crypto-Assets-Liabilities-, accessed 1 October 2023.
213. Satoshi Nakamoto, Bitcoin, A Peer-to-Peer electronic cash system, https://bitcoin.org/bitcoin.pdf, accessed 1 August 2023, emphasis added.

(b) not issued by a jurisdictional authority or another party, and
(c) does not give rise to a contract between the holder and another party.[214]

If one considers the accounting treatment without prejudice based on the economic properties of cryptocurrencies, the following choices should be considered: *IAS 7, IAS 32, IFRS 9, IAS 38 and IAS 40.*[215]

[a] IAS 32/IFRS 9

Accounting cryptocurrencies as a financial asset at FVTPL in accordance with *IFRS 9* would have the policy advantage of having a ready system that measures cryptocurrencies in a timely manner. To be able to do so, cryptocurrencies must meet the definition of *IAS 32*.

If a cryptocurrency is a *financial asset within IAS 32*, it must be an asset that is:

(a) cash
(b) an equity instrument of another entity
(c) a contractual right
  (i) to receive cash or another financial asset from another entity; or
  (ii) to exchange financial assets or financial liabilities with another entity under conditions that are potentially favourable to the entity; or
(d) a contract that will or may be settled in the entity's own equity instruments and is:
  (i) a non-derivative for which the entity is or may be obliged to receive a variable number of the entity's own equity instruments; or
  (ii) a derivative that will or may be settled other than by the exchange of a fixed amount of cash or another financial asset for a fixed number of the entity's own equity instruments. For this purpose, the entity's own equity instruments do not include puttable financial instruments classified as equity instruments in accordance with paragraphs 16A and 16B, instruments that impose on the entity an obligation to deliver to another party a pro-rata share of the net assets of the entity only on liquidation and are classified as equity instruments in accordance with paragraphs 16C and 16D, or instruments that are contracts for the future receipt or delivery of the entity's own equity instruments.[216]

[i] 'Digital Cash'?

As Nakamoto intended Bitcoin to be a peer-to-peer electronic payment system, one could see cryptocurrencies as digital or virtual cash. Further, the name

214. IFRS Interpretations Committee Meeting, Holding of Cryptocurrencies (June 2019), 1.
215. For an in-depth analysis of the various possible accounting treatments, *see* Southern and Weidmann (2023), 76-87.
216. IAS. 32.11.

'cryptocurrencies' seems to hint in this direction, and cryptocurrencies are in some investment publications referred to as digital currencies.[217]

Thus, it is worth considering if cryptocurrencies can be seen as 'cash', 'cash equivalent', 'currency' or 'digital money'.[218]

IAS 7 concerns *cash and cash equivalents,* but it does not define it. *IAS 32* 'Financial Instruments: Presentation' determines that '*currency* (cash) is a *financial asset* because it represents the medium of exchange and is, therefore, the basis on which all transactions are measured and recognised in financial statements'.[219]

(1) The case against digital cash

In a traditional currency system, money is anything the state orders to be, and the market accepts as being money. Consequently, a legal tender takes place, and central banks issue the countries' currency in return for securities.[220] The value of a currency is related to the general outputs of an economy, and the money supply expands and contracts as the economy grows and shrinks, depending on the policies of the respective central bank.[221]

'Traditional cryptocurrencies' like Bitcoin and Ether are not issued or backed by any government, and there is no legal tender.[222] This is in contrast to Central Bank Digital Currencies (CBDCs) like the *digital yuan,* which are issued by a government.[223] Traditional cryptocurrencies like Bitcoin only exist in a finite number of electronic units, and their value depends upon the operation of a market which brings buyers and sellers together.[224]

The IFRS Interpretations Committee states that 'it is not aware of any cryptocurrency that is used as a medium of exchange and as the monetary unit in the pricing of goods or services to such an extent that it would be the basis on which all transactions

217. Jake Frankenfield, Investopia, Cryptocurrency Explained with Pros and Cons for Investment, (updated 29 August 2023), https://www.investopedia.com/terms/c/cryptocurrency.asp, accessed 30 August 2023.
218. The words cash, currency and money are interchangeable in this respect.
219. IAS 32.AG3.
220. Southern and Weidmann (2023), 78.
221. *Ibid.*
222. *PWC,* Cryptographic assets and related transactions: accounting considerations under IFRS, December 2019, https://www.pwc.com/gx/en/audit-services/ifrs/publications/ifrs-16/cryptographic-assets-related-transactions-accounting-considerations-ifrs-pwc-in-depth.pdf, accessed 8 October, 2023, 5.
223. Southern and Weidmann (2023), 79; *compare also* Jennifer Conrad, 'China's Digital Yuan Works Just Like Cash – With Added Surveillance' (8 November 2022) *Wired, https://www.wired.com/story/chinas-digital-yuan-ecny-works-just-like-cash-surveillance/*, accessed 8 March 2023; Eric Dunne, 'China Doles Out Free Digital Yuan During New Year to Boost Adoption' (updated 6 February 2023) *inside bitcoins,* https://insidebitcoins.com/news/china-doles-out-free-digital-yuan-during-new-year-to-boost-adoption, accessed March 2023; Arendse Huld, 'China Launches Digital Yuan App – All You Need to Know' (22 September 2022) *China Briefing from Dezan Shira & Associates, https://www.china-briefing.com/news/china-launches-digital-yuan-app-what-you-need-to-know/*, accessed 1 March 2023.
224. Southern and Weidmann (2023), 79.

are measured and recognised in financial statements'.[225] The IFRS Interpretations Committee argues and suggests that cryptocurrency is not cash because it cannot be readily exchanged for any good or service.[226]

Similarly, *EY* maintains in a paper on the accounting of cryptoassets:

> The description of cash in IAS 32 suggests that cash is expected to be used as a medium of exchange (i.e., used in exchange for goods or services) and as the monetary unit in pricing goods or services to such an extent that it would be the basis on which all transactions are measured and recognised in financial statements (i.e., it could act as the functional currency of an entity). Currently, it is unlikely that any crypto-asset would be considered a suitable basis for measuring and recognising all the items in an entity's financial statements.[227]

PWC suggests in a similar way:

> Cryptocurrencies do not have some of the common properties of cash and currency, especially:
>
> - cryptocurrencies are not legal tender and mostly are not issued or backed by any government or state; and
> - cryptocurrencies are currently not capable of setting prices for goods and services directly. In other words, cryptocurrencies might be accepted to settle some transactions, but they are not directly related to the setting of prices for goods or services in an economy.
>
> The assessment [if the respective cryptocurrency qualifies as a currency under IAS 32] should consider the facts and circumstances for each cryptocurrency. At the time of writing (June 2021), we are seeing central banks launch pilot projects as they explore the use of Central Bank Digital Currencies (CBDCs).[228]

Thus, as tentatively interpreted by the IFRS Interpretations Committee[229] and by many accounting firms in the context of applying IFRS, cryptocurrencies are not

225. IFRIC Update March 2019, Holding of Cryptocurrencies, Agenda Paper 4, https://www.ifrs.org/news-and-events/updates/ifric/2019/ifric-update-march-2019/#1, accessed 6 October 2023.
226. Grant Thornton, 'IFRS Viewpoint, Accounting for cryptocurrencies – the basics' (May 2018), https://www.grantthornton.global/globalassets/1.-member-firms/global/insights/article-pdfs/ifrs/ifrs-viewpoint-9---accounting-for-cryptocurrencies--the-basics.pdf, 4, accessed 3 October 2023. *Compare* Southern and Weidmann (2023), 79.
227. *EY*, 'Applying IFRS, Accounting by holders of cryptoassets' (updated October 2021), https://www.ey.com/en_gl/ifrs-technical-resources/accounting-by-holders-of-crypto-assets-updated-october-2021, accessed 1 October 2023.
228. *PWC*, Cryptographic assets and related transactions: accounting considerations under IFRS (June 2021).
229. IFRIC Update (March 2019), Holding of Cryptocurrencies, Agenda Paper 4.
 The staff paper from June 2019 suggested to finalise the agenda decision based on the IFRIC Agenda Paper of March 2019 with some changes, but still maintains that intangible assets should be classified as intangible assets under IFRS 38. *See* IFRS, Interpretations Committee Meeting, 'Holding of Cryptocurrencies', Agenda ref 12 (June 2019), *https://www.ifrs.org/content/dam/ifrs/meetings/2019/june/ifric/ap12-holdings-of-cryptocurrencies.pdf*, accessed 1 October 2023, 14, para. 50.

regarded as cash because they are not backed by a government or central bank, and they are not legal tender in almost all jurisdictions.[230]

(2) The case for digital cash

There are a number of good arguments that cryptocurrencies can be seen as digital cash. They are as follows:

(a) The classification of cryptocurrency for accounting purposes is a moving target. For example, the legal tender argument does not apply to CBDCs like the *digital yuan* as they meet the criteria of currency and money.[231] More than a hundred countries, representing 95% of the global GDP, are at least exploring the launch of *Central Bank Digital Currencies* (CBDC).[232]
(b) Some merchants – in particular in the internet world – accept (or have accepted) cryptocurrencies as a payment means for their goods.[233] However, this acceptance has waned since the sharp decline of cryptocurrencies in 2022. Still, there are already signs that cryptocurrencies are seen as an alternative means to pay for goods and services.[234] Bitcoin was sold at ATMs in the UK and is sold at cash machines in Germany, which shows that the public perception of Bitcoin is that it is at least cash-like.[235]
(c) The old English proverb: 'If it looks like a duck, and swims like a duck, and quacks like a duck, then it probably is a duck' comes to mind if one takes a closer look at what Bitcoin stands for. The following facts speak for cryptocurrencies being 'the duck', aka cash-like:
    (i) The intention of the inventor of Bitcoin was to create a peer-to-peer electronic cash system. This supports its categorisation as cash.
    (ii) The behaviour of cryptocurrency can be seen as cash but without the backing of a government. The public sees it as something that symbolises monetary value. It is seen as a means of storing value outside of the traditional government and monetary system.
(d) Cryptocurrencies can be converted into cash at cryptocurrency exchanges or third-party brokers against a fee. Sellers can sell their cryptocurrencies at such

230. *Compare* Southern and Weidmann (2023), 79.
231. Sharecast, What does China's Digital Yuan mean for Bitcoin?, https://www.sharecast.com/promoted/cryptocurrencies/what-does-chinas-digital-yuan-mean-for-bitcoin.html, accessed 7 February 2023.
232. Atlantic Council, Central Bank Cryptocurrency tracker, https://www.atlanticcouncil.org/cbdctracker/
233. Rohit KVN, After Bitcoin, Tesla now accepts Dogecoin cryptocurrency for merchandise purchase, Deccanherald, https://www.deccanherald.com/business/technology/after-bitcoin-tesla-now-accepts-dogecoin-cryptocurrency-for-merchandise-purchase-1071023.html, access ed 20 February 2023.
234. Cointelegraph, Bitcoin as a payment method, https://cointelegraph.com/explained/who-accepts-bitcoin-as-payment, accessed 11 March 2023.
235. In the UK, a total of 85 Bitcoin cash machines, where people could buy cryptocurrency at an 'ATM'. The FCA shut down those unregulated 'cash machines' in March 2022, *see* BBC, Bitcoin cash machines ordered to shut down in UK, 11 March 2022, https://www.bbc.com/news/technology-60709209, accessed 10 March 2023.

a decentralised exchange and convert them into cash if a buyer is willing to pay the amount requested, although the prices are highly volatile.[236]

(e) The alternative to classifying cryptoassets as cash or cash-like is to classify them as intangible assets. In the author's view, that classification, however, does not fit the character of cryptocurrencies. Cryptocurrencies are highly volatile compared to goodwill, trademarks and copyrights, which have been built up in a business and contain a substantial economic value which was built up over years. In the author's opinion, cryptocurrencies behave more like high-risk financial assets or volatile currencies than intangible assets, such as trademarks, copyrights and goodwill.[237]

(f) If cryptocurrencies are something other than digital cash, that will also have consequences for their tax treatment. Classification of cryptocurrencies as financial assets could be beneficial from a tax policy point of view as the accounting and taxation rules applying to financial assets are a well-developed system. If they were to be classified as digital cash or financial assets, this classification could contribute to solving various taxation issues, such as the tax treatment of impairment losses, ring-fencing of losses and the use of cryptocurrencies in tax avoidance schemes.

Although the above arguments provide good grounds for treating cryptocurrencies as *digital cash*, the tentative position of the IFRS Interpretations Committee contradicts this position.

[ii] Cash Equivalent?

'Cash equivalents are short-term, highly liquid investments that are readily convertible to known amounts of cash and which are subject to an insignificant risk of changes in value.'[238]

It has been argued that because cryptocurrencies are highly volatile, they cannot be regarded as cash equivalent.[239] If one compares the maximal US Dollar against Turkish Lira volatility of 73% (according to the GARCH volatility analysis) against the maximum US Dollar against Bitcoin volatility of 423%, this argument seems valid.[240] However, as cryptocurrencies only came into existence in 2009, they may become less volatile over the years.[241]

236. Southern and Weidmann (2023), 80.
237. *Ibid.*
238. IAS 7.6.
239. Grant Thornton, IFRS Viewpoint, Accounting for Cryptocurrencies – the basics, https://www.grantthornton.global/globalassets/1.-member-firms/global/insights/article-pdfs/ifrs/ifrs-viewpoint-9---accounting-for-cryptocurrencies--the-basics.pdf, accessed 24 February 2023.
240. Volatility calculator, https://vlab.stern.nyu.edu/volatility/VOL.BTCUSD%3AFOREX-R.GARCH, accessed 12 December 2023.
241. Southern and Weidmann (2023), 80.

In any case, the emerging CBDCs, like the *digital yuan*, can be seen as cash-like as there is legal tender, and goods and services in China's retail sector can be bought with the digital yuan.[242]

[iii] Contractual Right?

Does cryptocurrency provide a contractual right:

(i) to receive cash or another financial asset from another entity; or
(ii) to exchange financial assets or financial liabilities with another entity under conditions that are potentially favourable to the entity?

If one considers *Bitcoin*, one will have to conclude that Bitcoin does not give any right to receive cash or another financial asset from another entity. The IFRIC Agenda Paper, therefore, concludes that traditional cryptocurrencies like Bitcoin do not give rise to a contractual right for the holder, and it is not a contract that will or may be settled in the holder's own equity instruments.[243]

[b] IAS 38: Intangible Assets

As cryptocurrencies do not fall in any other category, they are commonly regarded as intangible assets under IAS 38 unless they are 'held for sale in the ordinary course of a business', according to the IFRIC; in the case of the latter, IAS 2 Inventories, applies.

The IFRIC Agenda Paper cites IAS 38, paragraphs 8 and 12 and maintains,

> The Committee observed that a holding of cryptocurrency meets the definition of an intangible asset in IAS 38 because (a) it is capable of being separated from the holder and sold or transferred individually, and (b) it does not give the holder a right to receive a fixed or determinable number of units of currency.[244]

IAS 38: *Intangible Assets* defines an intangible asset as 'an identifiable non-monetary asset without physical substance'. Do those definitional criteria cumulatively apply?

[i] Identifiable

Bitcoins do not have unique identities. However, Bitcoin balances are stored in uniquely identifiable 'transaction outputs' that can only be spent by the owner of the recipient address.[245]

---

242. China Daily, China's digital Yuan can leverage the Road Initiative. https://www.chinadaily.com.cn/a/202208/12/WS62f9a7d1a310fd2b29e722e9.html, accessed 16 February 2023.
243. IFRIC Update March 2019, Holding of Cryptocurrencies, Agenda Paper 4, https://www.ifrs.org/news-and-events/updates/ifric/2019/ifric-update-march-2019/#1, accessed 6 March 2023.
244. *Ibid.*
245. Ivy Wigmore, Bitcoin Address, https://www.techtarget.com/whatis/definition/Bitcoin-address, accessed 1 March 2023. *Compare also* Southern and Weidmann (2023), 83.

According to the definition of IAS 38, an asset is identifiable if it is either:

(a) separable, i.e., is capable of being separated or divided from the entity and sold, transferred, licensed, rented or exchanged, either individually or together with a related contract, identifiable asset or liability, regardless of whether the entity intends to do so; or
(b) arises from contractual or other legal rights, regardless of whether those rights are transferable or separable from the entity or from other rights and obligations.[246]

One may argue that because they are capable of being separated from the holder and sold or transferred individually, cryptocurrencies are also identifiable.[247]

For example, Bitcoins are easily transferrable in peer-to-peer transactions or at decentralised Bitcoin exchanges.[248] At those exchanges, Bitcoin holders can convert their Bitcoin into cash, similar to traditional currencies, provided there are buyers and sellers. Hence, as cryptocurrencies can be traded at an exchange, cryptocurrencies should be considered identifiable.[249]

[ii] Non-monetary Asset?

However, the IFRS Interpretations Committee regards cryptocurrencies neither as cash nor cash equivalent in their tentative agenda decision, see above.[250] Because IAS 21 defines monetary items as 'units of currency held and assets and liabilities to be received or paid in a fixed or determinable number of units of currency',[251] it has been argued by *Grant Thornton* that the value of a cryptocurrency 'is not fixed or determinable but subject to major variations that arise from supply and demand and cannot be predicted. Therefore, it is not monetary but non-monetary in nature'.[252]

The value of cryptocurrency fluctuates like other currencies as well, just at a higher volatility. Cryptocurrencies can be exchanged into a precisely determinable amount of traditional currency through cryptocurrency exchanges. Cryptocurrencies, like every other traditional currency, depend on the market of buyers and sellers, even if they are not backed by the economic growth of an economy and even if it is not legal

246. IAS 38, para. 12.
247. *Compare* Southern and Weidmann (2023), 84.
248. Crowe, Accounting for cryptocurrencies in financial statements, https://www.crowe.com/my/insights/how-should-cryptocurrencies--be-accounted--for-in-the--financial-statements, accessed 1 March 2023; ACCA, Accounting for Cryptocurrencies, https://www.accaglobal.com/in/en/student/exam-support-resources/professional-exams-study-resources/strategic-business-reporting/technical-articles/cryptocurrencies.html, accessed 1 March 2023.
249. *Compare* Southern and Weidmann (2023), 84.
250. IFRIC Update March 2019, Holding of Cryptocurrencies, Agenda Paper 4.
251. IAS 21, para 8.
252. Grant Thornton, IFRS Viewpoint, Accounting for Cryptocurrencies – the basics (May 2018), https://www.grantthornton.global/globalassets/1.-member-firms/global/insights/article-pdfs/ifrs/ifrs-viewpoint-9---accounting-for-cryptocurrencies--the-basics.pdf, accessed 28 February 2023.

tender.[253] Thus, in the author's opinion, the argument that cryptocurrencies are non-monetary assets is weak.

[iii] Without Physical Substance?

Cryptocurrencies are digital values and, therefore, do not have a physical presence.

To sum up the arguments, the majority of UK accounting firms regard the classification of cryptocurrencies as intangible assets under IAS 38 as an appropriate classification based on the arguments outlined above. The author, however, maintains that there are strong arguments for the alternative position, which regards cryptocurrencies as digital cash and not as intangible assets.[254]

[2] Measurement of Cryptoassets under IFRS

In the following, the measurement of cryptocurrencies is based on the majority view in the accounting firms which classify cryptoassets as intangible assets.

The author proposes that the consequences of accounting for cryptocurrencies as intangible assets are as follows:

For companies, there are the following possibilities to measure intangible assets following their classification: cost model, revaluation model or fair value model.

The fair value model is applied if cryptocurrencies are held in the context of trading activity.

For companies holding cryptocurrencies as an investment, the cost or revaluation model applies. If the cost model is used, intangible assets are measured at cost upon initial recognition and subsequently measured at cost, less accumulated amortisation and impairment losses, if any.

If the revaluation model is applied, intangible assets can be accounted for at a revalued amount if there is an active market for them. Thus, if a business holds different cryptocurrencies for investment purposes and there is not an active market for all cryptocurrencies held, those assets should be measured using the cost model upon initial recognition and 'subsequently measured at cost'.[255]

Under IAS 38, it has to be determined if the cryptocurrency has a finite or indefinite useful life. IAS 38 states in this respect that '[a]n intangible asset shall be regarded by the entity as having an indefinite useful life when, based on an analysis of all of the relevant factors, there is no foreseeable limit to the period over which the asset is expected to generate net cash inflows for the entity'.[256]

If IAS 38 is applied to cryptocurrencies, many accountancy firms regard cryptocurrencies as having an indefinite useful life as cryptocurrencies have no maturity.

253. NDTV, Can cryptocurrency Be converted into Cash? 31 October 2021, https://www.ndtv.com/business/can-cryptocurrency-be-converted-into-cash-read-on-to-find-out-2594499, accessed 17 March 2023. *Compare* Southern and Weidmann (2023), 84.
254. *Compare* Southern and Weidmann (2023), 79-81.
255. Southern and Weidmann (2023), 85.
256. IAS 38, para 88.

For example, *Grant Thornton* maintains, '[g]iven that cryptocurrencies are designed to act as a store of value over time, our view is that they would be considered to have an indefinite life for the purposes of IAS 38.[257] Similarly, *PWC* states that 'in most cases, no amortisation is expected for cryptocurrencies'.[258]

If under IAS 38, cryptocurrencies can be considered to have an indefinite useful life, the consequence is that no amortisation takes place but only a regular testing for impairment.[259] That means that if a company applies the cost model, any movements above cost are not recognised in the accounts, whereas any movements below cost are recognised as impairment.[260]

One can see the benefit of this accounting treatment under IAS 38 for taxpayers: as no upside movements are recognised but any downside movements through impairments, taxpayers can use cryptocurrency positions to offset profits from other businesses, thereby deferring their tax liability until they sell the cryptocurrencies.[261]

[B] Accounting of Cryptoassets under UK GAAP

[1] Classification of Cryptoassets under FRS 102, Section 18

FRS 102, Section 18 applies to intangible assets other than goodwill. It is similar to the definition in IFRS 38. Under FRS 102, paragraph 18, an intangible asset is defined as:

> An identifiable non-monetary asset without physical substance. Such an asset is identifiable when:
>
> - it is separable, i.e., capable of being separated or divided from the entity and sold, transferred, licensed, rented or exchanged, either individually or together with a related contract, asset or liability; or
> - it arises from contractual or other legal rights, regardless of whether those rights are transferable or separable from the entity or from other rights and obligations.[262]

257. Grant Thornton, 'IFRS Viewpoint, Accounting for Cryptocurrencies – the basics' (May 2018), 8, https://www.grantthornton.global/globalassets/1.-member-firms/global/insights/article-pdf s/ifrs/ifrs-viewpoint-9---accounting-for-cryptocurrencies--the-basics.pdf, accessed 2 October 2023.
258. *PWC*, 'Cryptographic assets and related transactions: accounting considerations under IFRS', *In depth: A look at current financial reporting issues* (December 2019), No. 2019-05, 6, para. 2.2.2, https://www.pwc.com/gx/en/audit-services/ifrs/publications/ifrs-16/cryptographic-assets-related-transactions-accounting-considerations-ifrs-pwc-in-depth.pdf, accessed 23 October 2023.
259. IAS 38, para 108(b).
260. Southern and Weidmann (2023), 84-85.
261. *Ibid.*, 89-96.
262. FRS Glossary: Intangible Asset; *compare* ACCA, Technical factsheet, Accounting for cryptocurrencies (September 2022) https://www.accaglobal.com/uk/en/technical-activities/technical-resources-search/2022/september/tf-accounting-for-cryptocurrencies.html, accessed 1 March 2023.

Thus, FRS 102, paragraph 18.2 suggests that – in parallel to IFRS 38 – an intangible asset is:

- identifiable
- non-monetary asset
- without physical presence.

Identifiable means it must be separable and arise from contractual or other legal rights.[263]

The Association of Chartered Accountants (ACCA), in parallel to the IFRS Interpretations Committee, maintains that cryptoassets are neither cash nor cash equivalent under UK GAAP but instead should be classified as intangible assets.[264] The arguments brought forward by *ACCA* are similar to the arguments suggested by the IFRS Interpretations Committee on why cryptoassets, and in particular cryptocurrencies, should not be regarded as cash or cash equivalent:[265]

> IAS 21, *The Effects of Changes in Foreign Exchange Rates*, explains that an essential feature of a non-monetary item is the absence of a right to receive (or an obligation to deliver) a fixed or determinable number of units of currency. Hence, *ACCA* would agree that cryptocurrency meets the definition of an intangible asset per FRS 102 as it is capable of being separated from the holder and sold or transferred individually. In addition, when judged against the requirements of IAS 21, it does not give the holder a right to receive a fixed or determinable number of units of currency. Cryptocurrencies do not have a physical substance, and hence, the most appropriate classification is that of an intangible asset.[266]

However, '[a]n entity can only recognise an intangible asset on the balance sheet (statement of financial position) when:

(a) it is probable (i.e., more likely than not) that the expected future economic benefits that are attributable to the asset will flow to the entity, and
(b) the cost or value of the asset can be measured reliably'.[267]

ACCA argues that because cryptocurrencies 'can be traded on an exchange, there is an expectation that the entity will receive an inflow of economic benefits. However, as is well known, the value of cryptocurrencies can be significantly volatile and hence they are regarded as non-monetary for the purposes of financial reporting'.[268]

The author believes that those arguments mix up the questions (1) whether the asset can be recognised as an intangible asset on the balance sheet at all, and (2) whether cryptocurrencies should be regarded as (non-monetary) intangible assets.

263. Des O'Neill, OMNIPRO, FRS 102 Summary – Section 18 – Intangible Assets other than goodwill (18 December 2015), https://frs102.com/blog/2015/12/18/frs-102-summary-section-18-intangible-assets-other-than-goodwill/, accessed 23 February 2023.
264. ACCA, Technical factsheet (2022), 2-4.
265. *Ibid.*, 2-3.
266. *Ibid.*, 4.
267. *Ibid.*
268. *Ibid.*

If one follows the proposition of the *ACCA* that cryptocurrencies are non-monetary intangible assets, that still does not mean that they should be recognised specifically as intangible assets on the balance sheet. As the volatility of cryptoassets is very high, for example, with a 70% decline in value of Bitcoin between December 2021 and December 2022, one may indeed argue that it does not seem probable (more likely than not) that the future economic benefits that are attributable to the cryptoasset will flow to the entity.

One might indeed suggest that cryptocurrencies are rather an elaborate gambling activity rather than a solid economic investment activity, particularly since cryptocurrencies do not contain any inherent value other than the 'game of supply and demand' (or greed and fear) that is played between the participants because of the perceived scarcity of cryptocurrencies like Bitcoin.[269]

[2] Measurement of Cryptoassets under FRS 102, Section 18

There are some differences in the accounting rules under IFRS and FRS 102 applying to intangible assets. Those differences have been outlined in the 2022 *LunaNet (UK) Limited* White paper.[270]

Similar to IAS 38, '[a]fter initial recognition at cost, FRS 102, Section 18 allows an intangible asset to be subsequently measured under the cost model or revaluation model'.[271]

ACCA maintains that if a company applies the cost model, intangible assets are measured at cost.[272] Those include all directly attributable costs, such as brokerage fees and exchange fees, as well as the acquisition price, less subsequent amortisation and any impairment losses. If a company applies the revaluation model, intangible assets, and thus cryptocurrencies, 'are measured at the revalued amount, provided that there is an active market for them (which may not be the case for all cryptocurrencies)'.[273] In the FRS 102 Glossary, an *active market* is defined as '[a] market in which all the following conditions exist:

(a) the items traded in the market are homogeneous;
(b) willing buyers and sellers can normally be found at any time; and
(c) prices are available to the public'.[274]

ACCA suggests that 'where no active market exists for the cryptocurrency, they must be measured under the cost model'.[275]

269. Southern and Weidmann (2023), 70-71.
270. LunaNet, White paper, 'Key differences between IFRS and UK GAAP' (2022) https://www.icaew.com/-/media/corporate/files/insights/sponsored-content/key-differences-between-uk-gaap-and-ifrs-uk.ashx?la=en, accessed 1 March 2023.
271. ACCA, Technical factsheet (2022), 4.
272. *Ibid.*
273. *Ibid.*
274. FRS 102, Glossary: *active market.*
275. ACCA, Technical factsheet (2022), 4.

Cryptocurrencies have an active market if they can be traded at decentralised exchanges. Thus, for certain cryptocurrencies, companies can apply the revaluation model, with any 'revaluation increases recognised in other comprehensive income and accumulated in equity'.[276]

The problem, however, occurs if companies hold more than one cryptocurrency and one of them does not have an active market. 'Where an active market does exist for the cryptocurrency and the entity's accounting policy is to measure them under the revaluation model, then that model must be applied to all cryptocurrencies in that asset class.'[277]

Thus, if companies want to justify the use of the cost model, they can simply buy one unit of cryptocurrency which does not have an active market, and they immediately *must* apply the cost model.

The author suggests that those strategies can – in particular – be applied if the company regards applying the cost model for accounting purposes as beneficial for the tax treatment of cryptocurrencies.

The different accounting treatment of intangible assets under IAS 38 and FRS 102, Section 18 also has significance for the measurement of cryptoassets, particularly cryptocurrencies.

The accounting differences between IFRS and FRS 102 in respect of the useful life of intangible assets have been highlighted in the 2022 *LunaNet (UK) Limited* White paper as follows:[278]

> Under FRS 102, paragraph 18.19, all intangible assets are considered to have a finite useful life. If an entity *is unable to make a reliable estimate* of the useful life, *the life shall not exceed 10 years.*

The *LucaNet* White paper states in this respect:

> According to IAS 38.88, an entity has to determine whether the useful life of an intangible asset is finite or indefinite. If the useful life is finite, the intangible asset is amortized over its useful life. In case of an indefinite useful life, i.e., there is no foreseeable limit to the period over which the asset is expected to generate net cash flows, the intangible asset shall not be amortized. In accordance with IAS 36 *Impairment of Assets*, an entity must test intangible assets with indefinite useful life for impairment in each period.[279]

For the accounting of cryptoassets, and in particular cryptocurrencies, under FRS 102, Section 18, it may mean that cryptocurrencies cannot be regarded as having an indefinite useful life simply because no intangible asset can have an indefinite useful

276. *Ibid.*, 5.
277. *Ibid.*
278. LunaNet, 'Key differences between IFRS and UK GAAP' (2022) https://www.icaew.com/-/media/corporate/files/insights/sponsored-content/key-differences-between-uk-gaap-and-ifrs-uk.ashx?la=en, accessed 1 March 2023.
279. *Ibid.*, 5.

life under FRS 102, Section 18.[280] That is in stark contrast to IAS 38, where an entity is allowed to assign an indefinite useful life to an intangible asset.[281]

Under FRS 102, Section 18, intangible assets 'must be amortised on a systematic basis over the useful economic life. If management are unable to assign a reliable useful economic life to a cryptocurrency, the maximum amortisation is ten years. It can be shorter, but not longer'.[282]

ACCA reminds preparers that the ten-year 'cap' on amortisation applies only in situations where management cannot reliably estimate the useful economic life. Where a longer life can be justified with supporting documentation, then that period should be used.[283]

The last sentence of this statement, however, leaves the door open for taxpayers that seek an optimisation of their tax position. If the taxpayers can, for example, argue that cryptocurrencies have – in contrast to other intangible items – an indefinite life – or at least a life until 2140 when the last Bitcoins are minted – because of its character as a digital currency, taxpayers may also be able to circumvent any amortisation of cryptocurrencies under FRS 102, Section 18. Thus, the author suggests that despite the differences in the measurement of cryptocurrencies under IAS 38 and FRS 102, Section 18, those differences may, in practice, disappear if the taxpayer provides suitable documentation.

[C] Accounting of Cryptoassets under German GAAP

Cryptoassets have not been comprehensively dealt with by the German accounting standard setter.

The German *IDW*[284] issued a 'Knowledge paper' in 2022 that outlines the functionality of cryptoassets without extensively discussing their accounting treatment.[285]

In this paper, it is, however, stated that cryptoassets neither generate payment streams nor have underlyings based on which prices can be determined, and thus it is not possible to base their valuation on any valuation model; instead, their value is based on supply and demand.[286]

In the accounting literature, *Stobbe* distinguishes between cryptocurrencies, which are held for investment purposes, and those which are held as a means of alternative payment.[287]

---

280. *Ibid.*
281. IAS 38, para 88.
282. ACCA, Technical factsheet (2022), 5; *compare* FRS 102, para 18.20.
283. ACCA, Technical factsheet (2022), 5.
284. Institut deutscher Wirtschaftspruefer – Institute of German Public Accountants.
285. IDW, Kryptowaehrungen (May 2022), *https://www.idw.de/IDW/Medien/Knowledge-Paper/Down-KP-Kryptowaehrungen-web.pdf, accessed 1 October 2022.*
286. *Ibid*, para 4.4.
287. Susanne Stobbe, Bitcoin & Co, Kryptowährungen im externen Rechnungswesen, Westermann (2021), https://www.westermann.de/landing/schmolke-deitermann/bitcoin#p394643, accessed 6 August 2023.

In a letter ruling of 2022 concerning the income taxation of cryptoassets, the *Federal Ministry of Finance*[288] states in relation to the accounting treatment of cryptoassets:

> Units of virtual currency are non-depreciable assets that are categorised under tangible assets and classified as fixed or current assets in accordance with general tax law accounting principles. If classified as fixed assets, they are presented under long-term financial assets within the meaning of section 266 (2) A. III. of the Commercial Code (*Handelsgesetzbuch*); if classified as current assets, they are presented under other assets within the meaning of section 266 (2) B. II. 4 of the Commercial Code.

In the German accounting literature, there is a tendency to regard cryptocurrencies as *intangible assets* in parallel to the classification under IFRS if they are held as long-term investments (*Anlagevermögen*).[289]

If cryptocurrencies are held short-term for payment purposes, they are attributed to the inventory as short-term assets (*Umlaufvermögen*) under the category of 'other assets' according to section 266(2) B. II. 4. German Commercial Code (*HGB*).[290]

If cryptoassets are acquired, the acquisition cost:

> is the market price at the time of acquisition of the units of virtual currency or other tokens (by inference from section 6 (6) sentence 1 of the Income Tax Act). If a quoted price on an exchange is available, this is to be taken as the market price. If there is no quoted price on an exchange, the price can be taken from a trading platform (such as Kraken, Coinbase or Bitpanda) or from a web-based listing (such as https://coinmarketcap.com/).[291]

Independently, if the cryptocurrencies are held for long-term purposes (*Anlagevermögen*) or short-term purposes (*Umlaufvermögen*), they are initially measured at cost.[292]

'The *First In First Out (FIFO) accounting method* is appropriate for determining cryptocurrency's cost basis',[293] meaning that the first cryptocurrency coins purchased

288. BMR, Schreiben of 10 May 22, Einzelfragen zur ertragsteuerrechtlichen Behandlung von virtuellen Währungen und von sonstigen Token (IV C 1 – S 2256/19/ 10003:001, DOK 2022/0493899), para 41. *See* Courtesy translation of the Federal Ministry of Finance's circular 'Einzelfragen zur ertragsteuerrechtlichen Behandlung von virtuellen Währungen und von sonstigen Token' of 10 May 2022, Federal Tax Gazette I, 668, para. 41, https://www.bundesfinanzministerium.de/Content/DE/Downloads/BMF_Schreiben/Steuerarten/Einkommensteuer/2022-05-09-einzelfragen-zur-ertragsteuerrechtlichen-behandlung-von-virtuellen-waehrungen-und-von-sonstigen-token-englische-version.pdf?__blob = publicationFile&v = 4, accessed 1 October 2023.
289. NWB Experten Blog, Bilanzierung von Kryptowaehrungen nach HGB, https://www.nwb-experten-blog.de/bilanzierung-von-kryptowaehrungen-nach-hgb/, accessed 6 August 2023; Stobbe (2021); Falko Tappen and Simon Wehe, Bilanzierung von Kryptoassets, IWW Institute (1 July 2022), https://www.iww.de/pstr/schwerpunktthema/kryptowaehrungen-bilanzierung-von-kryptoassets-f146883, accessed 1 October 2023.
290. BMR, Schreiben of 10 May 22, IV C 1 – S 2256/19/ 10003:001, para 41.
291. *Ibid.*, para 43.
292. *Ibid.*, para 44.
293. Arthur Teller, CoinTax, 'The Essential Guide to Crypto Tax in Germany' (23 February 2023), https://tokentax.co/blog/crypto-taxes-in-germany, accessed 21 April 2023.

are the first sold for calculating the tax liability on cryptocurrencies.[294] Amortisation for cryptocurrencies does not take place, and they are regarded as having an infinite life.[295]

In case of cryptocurrencies held for long-term purposes, a depreciation can only take place in the case of permanent depreciations in value – which are usually only given if a cryptocurrency goes to zero in value (and defaults) according to section 253 (3) sentence 5 German Commercial Code. It means that impairment losses for cryptoassets which are held as investments cannot be recognised in the financial accounts. However, in the case of short-term inventory, a depreciation for temporary depreciation in value must be recognised in the accounts,[296] meaning impairment losses are recognised in the financial accounts if cryptoassets are held short-term. However, in case the cryptocurrency appreciates in value, a write-up until the initial acquisition costs must be recognised in the accounts.[297]

In the first court decision on cryptocurrencies in 2019, the Lower Tax Court of Berlin and Brandenburg (*Finanzgericht Berlin and Brandenburg*) confirmed that cryptocurrencies should be regarded as 'assets' (*Wirtschaftsgüter*).[298] In 2023, the Federal Fiscal Court decided that the cryptocurrencies Bitcoin, Ethereum and Monero should be regarded as 'virtual currencies'.[299]

[D] Accounting of Cryptoassets in Other Jurisdictions

The author has chosen two jurisdictions where cryptoassets are traded at a high volume and where the accounting bodies have very different positions compared to the *IFRS Interpretations Committee* or those under UK or German GAAP.

[1] US GAAP

The accounting treatment and measurement of cryptoassets in the US is worth investigating in more detail. The author could not determine for certain what caused the change in the accounting policy with respect to the measurement of cryptocurrencies in the US. Still, it is worth understanding the previous and current position of the US *FASB* in respect of the accounting treatment of cryptoassets.

---

294. Teller (2023).
295. BMR, Schreiben of 10 May 22, IV C 1 – S 2256/19/ 10003:001, para 41; Stobbe (2021).
296. *Ibid.*
297. *Ibid.*
298. FG Berlin-Brandenburg, 20 June 2019 – 13 V 13100/19, openJur 2020, 42838, https://openjur.de/u/2257934.html, accessed 1 October 2023. *Compare* Reedsmith Client Alerts, First German Tax Court decision on the qualification of Bitcoins (2020), https://www.reedsmith.com/en/perspectives/2020/02/first-german-tax-court-decision-on-qualification-of-bitcoins, accessed 1 September 2023.
299. BFH decision of 14 February 2023, IX R 3/22, ECLI:DE:BFH:2023:U.140223.IXR3.22.0, https://www.bundesfinanzhof.de/de/entscheidung/entscheidungen-online/detail/STRE202310057/, accessed 1 October 2023; *also* Christopher Arndt, Bitcoin & Co: BFH rules crypto profits are taxable! What do crypto investors need to know now?, Acconisis (2023), https://www.acconsis.de/en/bitcoin-co-bfh-rules-crypto-profits-are-taxable-what-do-crypto-investors-need-to-know-now/, accessed 1 October 2023.

US companies that had heavily invested in cryptocurrencies as part of their overall strategy, like MicroStrategy, Block et al., reported significant impairment losses in Q2 of 2022,[300] while their cryptocurrency holdings often still stood at an overall gain on a fair value basis.[301]

For example, MicroStrategy reported a total of USD 918 million in impairment losses in Q2 2022, which they described as 'digital impairment charges' or 'non-cash charges', and a total of USD 425 million in Q1 2022.[302] 'As of December 31, 2022, the carrying value of MicroStrategy's digital assets (comprised of approximately 132,500 Bitcoins) was USD 1.840 billion, which reflects cumulative impairment losses of USD 2.153 billion since acquisition.'[303] According to their financial reports, they only paid minimal corporate taxes, perhaps because they were able to use accumulated impairment losses to set off against their profits.[304]

In a June 2022 Forbes article, *Shehan Chandrasekera* explained the US GAAP treatment of cryptocurrencies with the following words:

> Currently, digital assets like Bitcoins are classified as 'intangible assets with indefinite lives' under GAAP. In simple terms, this accounting treatment requires companies to report a loss when digital asset prices fall below the cost; however, it prohibits marking up digital assets to its true value if prices later recover.[305]

Shortly before the appearance of the Forbes article, the *FASB* decided to 'add a project to its technical agenda to improve the accounting for and disclosure of certain digital assets'.[306] From October 2022 onwards, the *FASB* Board released several *Tentative Board Decisions* which deal with the scope, presentation, classification, disclosure and measurement of cryptoassets.

The *FASB Tentative Board Decision* of 12 October 2022 is a milestone in relation to the measurement of cryptoassets as the *FASB* Board digressed in its tentative

300. MicroStrategy, Q2 Financial Results, 17, https://assets.contentstack.io/v3/assets/bltb564490bc5201f31/blt877d68364545d726/6541023a20567d001b090c87/Q2-2022_microstrategy-earnings-presentation_(1).pdf, accessed 28 February 2024.
301. Oluwapelumi Adejumo, Public companies holding Bitcoin face impairment losses amid market crash, https://cryptoslate.com/public-companies-holding-bitcoin-face-impairment-losses-amid-market-crash/, accessed February 2023.
302. The problem of accounting and taxation treatment of impairment losses is discussed in more detail in: Southern and Weidmann (2023), 89-90.
303. MicroStrategy, Press release, MicroStrategy Announces Fourth Quarter 2022 Financial Results (2 February 2023), https://assets.contentstack.io/v3/assets/bltb564490bc5201f31/bltb01b5df34532ba81/654a3b67e965d6040a3dd779/Q4-2022_microstrategy-earnings-presentation_(2).pdf, accessed 21 February 2024.
304. Francine McKenna, Taxes are a wild card for public companies holding crypto, https://finance.yahoo.com/news/taxes-wild-card-public-companies-145853836.html, accessed 28 February 2023.
305. Shehan Chandrasekera, Bitcoin's Accounting Treatment Is Depressing MicroStrategy's Bottom Line, June 2022, https://www.forbes.com/sites/shehanchandrasekera/2022/06/01/bitcoins-accounting-treatment-is-artificially-degrading-microstrategys-bottom-line/?sh=d9dd55233e11, accessed 28 February 2023.
306. *FASB*, Minutes of May 11, 2022 Board Meeting on Exchange Traded Digital Assets, https://www.fasb.org/Page/ShowPdf?path=CRYPTO-bmin-20220511.pdf&title=May%2011,%202022%20Board%20Meeting%20Minutes—Accounting%20for%20Exchange-Traded%20Digital%20Assets%20and%20Commodities, accessed 1 October 2023.

decision from its previous position, which allowed the measurement of cryptoassets at cost less impairments. Instead, they proposed that businesses should be required to 'measure cryptoassets at fair value, using the guidance in Topic 820, Fair Value Measurement [and] *recognize increases and decreases* in *fair value in comprehensive income* each reporting period'.[307]

In the Technical Agenda, the *FASB* outlines a timetable regarding recognition and measurement of cryptoassets, their presentation and disclosure, as well as the conceptual framework.[308]

The *FASB Tentative Board Decision* of 14 December 2022 concerned the disclosure, presentation and measurement of cryptoassets in the financial statements.[309] Based on these statements, it seems that the *FASB* requested to continue to classify cryptocurrencies and other digital assets as intangible assets for accounting purposes. In relation to the presentation of cryptoassets, the *FASB* did not apply a more differentiated approach as was originally suggested by International Swaps and Derivatives Association (ISDA), which stated:

> The terms of asset-referencing digital assets can vary widely, and therefore, the accounting framework to be applied under US GAAP needs to be considered on a case-by-case basis. For example [...] stablecoins differ from native digital assets in that they include mechanisms designed to minimize price volatility by linking their values to the value of a more traditional asset, such as a fiat currency, a commodity, or with an ownership interest in the issuing company. In the case where the stablecoin represents an ownership interest, it should be evaluated under relevant GAAP (for example, ASC 321, Investments – Equity Securities; ASC 323, Investments – Equity Method and Joint Ventures; or ASC 810, Consolidation). Other types of stablecoins may be financial assets or financial instruments containing an embedded feature that should be evaluated under ASC 815, Derivatives and Hedging.[310]

The author agrees that the approach proposed by ISDA to classify certain cryptoassets, such as stablecoins, as financial assets, may provide a more coherent solution that mirrors the nature of stablecoins. ISDA, in this respect, outlines that '[t]he initial recognition and measurement of the digital asset will depend on whether it is classified as an intangible asset such as Bitcoin or a financial asset such as a stablecoin, and whether the entity applies the industry specific guidance in ASC 940 or ASC 946'.[311]

---

307. *FASB*, Tentative Board Decisions, 12 October 2022, https://fasb.org/Page/ShowPdf?path=CRYPTO-MIN-20221012.pdf&title=October%2012,%202022%20Board%20Meeting%20Minutes:%20Accounting%20for%20and%20Disclosure%20of%20Crypto%20Assets, accessed 1 December 2023
308. *FASB*, Tentative Board Decisions, 14 December 2022, *FASB* Board Meeting, https://fasb.org/page/PageContent?pageId=/news_and_meetings/past-meetings/12-14-22.html, accessed 6 October 2023.
309. *Ibid.*
310. ISDA, Accounting for Digital Assets, Key considerations (May 2022) https://www.isda.org/a/88VgE/Accounting-for-Digital-Assets-Key-Considerations.pdf, accessed 20 August 2023, 13.
311. ISDA, Accounting for Digital Assets, Key considerations (May 2022), 14.

In March 2023, the *FASB* issued an Exposure Draft called *Proposed Accounting Standards Update* concerning Intangibles - Goodwill and Other - Crypto Assets,[312] where it defines the criteria for cryptoassets to fall within the proposed standard. It reiterates its decision from October 2022 and maintains that if cryptoassets meet those criteria, the entity holding the cryptoassets would be required to 'subsequently measure cryptoassets that meet those criteria at fair value with changes recognized in net income each reporting period'.[313]

In the *FASB* decision reached in a meeting on 6 September 2023, the *FASB* affirmed most previous proposals by the Board in relation to scope, presentation, disclosure and measurement, and confirms:

> the *scope* of the proposed Accounting Standards Update, which would apply to holdings of cryptoassets that meet all of the following criteria:
>
> (a) meet the definition of intangible assets as defined in the Codification Master Glossary;
> (b) do not provide the asset holder with enforceable rights to, or claims on, underlying goods, services, or other assets;
> (c) are created or reside on a distributed ledger based on blockchain technology;
> (d) are secured through cryptography;
> (e) are fungible;
> (f) are not created or issued by the reporting entity or its related parties.[314]

The Board decided to modify criterion (c) to include assets that are created or reside on a distributed ledger based on technology that is similar to blockchain technology.[315]

In relation to the *presentation* of cryptoassets, the *FASB* Board affirmed the previously proposed requirements.[316] In relation to the *disclosure* of cryptoassets, the Board affirmed:

> the proposed requirements, which would require that an entity disclose:
>
> 1. At both annual and interim periods, the following information about each significant crypto asset holding (as determined by the fair value of that holding): the name of the crypto asset, fair value, units held, and cost basis. Additionally, an entity would disclose the fair value and cost basis of other crypto asset holdings, which may be aggregated into a single line item.

312. *FASB*, Exposure Draft, Goodwill and Other - Crypto Assets, Accounting for and Disclosure of Crypto Assets (23 March 2023), https://www.fasb.org/page/ShowPdf?path=Prop%20ASU—Intangibles—Goodwill%20and%20Other—Crypto%20Assets%20(Subtopic%20350-60)—Accounting%20for%20and%20Disclosure%20of%20Crypto%20Assets.pdf&title=Proposed%20Accounting%20Standards%20Update—Intangibles—Goodwill%20and%20Other—Crypto%20Assets%20(Subtopic%20350-60), accessed 29 August 2023.
313. *Ibid.*
314. FASB, Minutes of the September, 6, 2023 Board Meeting on Accounting for and Disclosure of Crypto Assets, 14 September 2023, https://www.fasb.org/Page/ShowPdf?path=CRYPTO-MIN-20230906.pdf&title=September%206,%202023%20Board%20Meeting%20Minutes-Accounting%20for%20and%20Disclosure%20of%20Crypto%20Assets, accessed 1 November 2023.
315. *Ibid.*
316. *Ibid.*

2. At both interim and annual periods, the fair value of the crypto assets that are restricted from sale, the nature and remaining duration of the restriction, and circumstances that could cause a lapse in the restriction(s). The Board affirmed the proposed requirement that would require that an entity discloses at annual periods a reconciliation, as described in paragraphs 350-60-50-3 through 50-4 of the proposed Update. However, the Board decided that an entity need not include activity related to crypto assets received as noncash consideration in the ordinary course of business and converted nearly immediately into cash in that disclosure.[317]

In the same meeting, the *FASB* Board also affirmed 'the proposed requirements that an entity subsequently measure cryptoassets within the proposed scope at fair value in accordance with Topic 820, Fair Value Measurement'.[318] The final standard on cryptoassets will be issued by the *FASB* in Q4, 2023.[319] It has also been confirmed by the *FASB* that the new accounting standard for cryptoassets will be 'effective for fiscal years beginning after December 15, 2024, including interim periods within those fiscal years, for all entities'.[320]

The author is not certain if the change of the guidelines followed the *FASB's* recognition that impairment losses were used as a means of reducing some companies' tax liabilities or if the new position that requires cryptocurrencies to be measured on a fair value basis was solely based on accounting considerations. It is, however, notable that those changes in the measurement of cryptocurrencies only occurred after the reporting of substantial impairment losses on Bitcoin holdings by some US companies.

Further, the ISDA repeatedly warned in respect of a mismatch between the cost accounting less impairment losses versus the market value of Bitcoin holdings in a letter of 7 June 2021 to the *FASB* in response to their public request on how investors should account for cryptoassets, stating:

> U.S. businesses and American entrepreneurs are investing billions of dollars in this important innovation. Business intelligence software provider MicroStrategy Incorporated, for example, had acquired and was holding a total of 70,469 bitcoins as of December 31, 2020, which had an approximate market value of $2.0 billion at the time, yet the bitcoin were reflected on its year-end balance sheet as having a carrying value of only $1.1 billion due to the accounting treatment under GAAP currently in effect.[321]

The ISDA highlights the consequences of the measurement of cryptoassets at cost less impairments: significant impairment write-downs with no subsequent recognition of any increases in value reflected in the accounts.

317. *Ibid.*
318. *Ibid.*
319. *Ibid.*
320. *Ibid.*
321. ISDA, Letter to the *FASB*, Agenda Request: Investors accounting for crypto assets (7 June 2021), 3, https://www.isda.org/a/3SEgE/Agenda-Request-Investors-accounting-for-crypto-assets.pdf, accessed 6 August 2023.

The ISDA, in this respect, proposed that:

> Under the current model, companies will only have the ability to write down the value of cryptoassets and will not have the ability to recognize any gains until the assets are transferred to another party. *This is misleading and not a faithful representation of these assets to users of financial statements. as the balance sheet will not reflect the true liquid nature and value of these assets.* For example, companies who have been invested in Bitcoin over the past year would have had to have impaired their assets to a price of $4,000 per Bitcoin. At points in 2021, these companies would now reflect the current market value in excess of $50,000. The inability for companies to reflect this change in value of a liquid asset that is held for trading could be misleading to users of the financial statements.[322]

The ISDA later confirmed their critique in another White paper of May 2022.[323] There, the ISDA suggests that 'the existing accounting model under ASC 350 is not aligned with the economics of digital assets, and therefore current accounting will not reflect the true nature and value of these assets'.[324]

To reiterate, the ISDA's critique relates to the accounting treatment of cryptoassets under US GAAP before the October 2022 *FASB* letter and criticises the measurement of cryptocurrencies at cost less impairment losses with the inability to account for any subsequent gains in the value of the cryptocurrency.

In the author's view, this observation applies in a similar way to the accounting treatment under IFRS. That is concerning as the *IFRS Interpretations Committee* still advises measuring cryptoassets at cost less impairments (without any amortisation).

Although the warnings by the ISDA may have contributed to the *FASB*'s revision of its position on the measurement of cryptoassets from cost accounting less impairments towards a fair value measurement, one needs to understand the differences between the ISDA recommendations and the outcome of the fair value measurement requirement as proposed by the *FASB*.

The ISDA concluded that they believe that 'a framework should be developed that will *allow* all entities, and not just investment companies and broker dealers, to account for cryptoassets at fair value. Accounting for cryptoassets at fair value would better reflect the economics and intent for why companies are transacting and investing in these products'.[325]

It should be noted that the ISDA is primarily advocating for the *Fair Value Option* (FVO), whereas the *FASB* introduced a *fair value requirement*.

The ISDA proposed the FVO for cryptoassets with the following reasoning:

> [A]n accounting model should be designed to properly reflect the nature, liquidity and value of the cryptoassets and is consistent with the economic reality that entities and individuals are trading and investing in these products for their inherent value. A more appropriate accounting model for highly liquid cryptoassets that would meet the definition of readily convertible to cash, similar to the derivative definition would be to allow the *fair value option*. Since derivatives, an

322. *Ibid.*, emphasis added.
323. ISDA, Accounting for Digital Assets, Key considerations (May 2022).
324. *Ibid.*, 17.
325. *Ibid.*, 20.

instrument that is readily convertible to cash and tied to an underlying, is accounted for at fair value, we believe similar instruments such as cryptoassets should be permitted as well.[326]

It is interesting to note that ISDA compares in this respect cryptoassets with derivatives in terms of their ability to be readily convertible to cash.

The May 2022 ISDA paper further clarifies ISDA's position on why it proposes the FVO:

> An *accounting model that could be considered for digital assets would be to allow the fair value option (FVO) resulting in similar treatment as derivatives instruments.* From the Basis for Conclusions from the Statement of Financial Accounting Standards No. 159, the board decided to permit entities to elect the FVO for financial assets and liabilities for the following reasons:
>
> a. A FVO would enable entities to mitigate the volatility in earnings that results from different measuring attributes in reporting related to financial assets and liabilities;
> b. A FVO would enable entities to achieve consistent accounting and, potentially, an offsetting effect for the changes in the fair value of related assets and liabilities;
> c. The board believes fair value for financial assets and financial liabilities provides more relevant and understandable information than cost or cost-based measures. The board considers fair value measurement of financial instruments to be more relevant to financial statement users than cost-based measurements because fair value reflects the current cash equivalent of the entity's financial instruments rather than the price of a past transaction. The board also believes that, with the passage of time, historical prices become irrelevant in assessing an entity's current financial position.[327]

The ISDA continues to suggest:

> Digital assets should have the option to be measured at fair value for the same reasons the board permitted the FVO for financial assets and liabilities. The FVO would enable entities to mitigate volatility in earnings from different measuring attributes in assets and liabilities. The FVO for digital assets would also provide more consistent accounting for the offsetting changes between digital assets and digital liabilities. Finally, accounting for digital assets at fair value would provide users of financial statements with more relevant and understandable information as to the value of the digital assets and liabilities at the time of the financial statements, as opposed to historical data based on a cost less impairment model.[328]

The ISDA further proposes an alternative to the FVO, stipulating that:

> An alternative model would be to account for all digital assets *at fair value unless the assets do not have a readily determinable fair value,* in which case they could apply an alternate model. [...] For assets without a readily determinable fair value, entities have an option to apply the cost less impairment model [...].[329]

326. ISDA, Letter to the FASB (2021).
327. *Ibid.*, 18.
328. *Ibid.*
329. *Ibid.*, 19.

The alternative ISDA proposal is somewhat closer to the *FASB* fair value requirement compared to the FVO proposal by the ISDA. Compared to the *FASB* Tentative Agenda Decision, the ISDA alternative proposal allows cryptoassets which do not have a readily determinable fair value to be subsequently measured at cost less impairment.[330]

The *FASB*, however, explicitly excluded those options, stating: 'The Board also considered [...] [v]arious *measurement alternatives for crypto assets with inactive markets* and *decided not to pursue those alternatives*'[331] [...] and further decided 'that the measurement and recognition requirements should be the same for all entities'.[332]

In the author's view, the above statement confirms that *FASB* takes a rigorous stance on the measurement of cryptoassets – possibly to avoid any accounting and tax structuring in relation to cryptoasset impairment losses.

[2] Australian Accounting Standards Board

The *Australian Accounting Standards Board* (AASB) proposed in a 2016 policy paper that neither the cost model nor the revaluation model in IAS 38 provides relevant information on cryptocurrencies.[333]

The *AASB*'s reasons are as follows:

> *We do not believe that IAS 38's measurement guidance provides relevant information*, because:
>
> - IAS 38 is written from the perspective of assets (without physical substance) used in the production of cash flows. It is not designed to deal with items held for speculative or investment purposes or for items with cash-like features used for the payment of goods or services;
>
> *Cost approach*:
>
> - Cost is a historical measurement and does not provide current information;
> - Amortisation reflects the pattern of consumption which is irrelevant for items held for investment purposes;
> - Impairments would only recognise decreases in value;
>
> *Revaluation approach*:
>
> - IAS 38 only allows a revaluation approach when active markets exist for an intangible asset. Under IAS 38, if a market becomes inactive, the entity will not be permitted to continue the use of the revaluation and records only subsequent amortisation and impairment from the point when the market became inactive. On the other hand, IFRS 13 Fair Value Measurement guidance adequately and robustly considers fair value measurements in scenarios where markets become inactive;

330. *Ibid.*, 20.
331. *FASB*, Tentative Board Decisions, 12 October 2022.
332. *Ibid.*
333. ASSB, Digital Currency – A case for standard setting activity, https://www.aasb.gov.au/admin/file/content102/c3/AASB_ASAF_DigitalCurrency.pdf, page 12, accessed 28 August 2023.

- Revaluation changes are not always reflected in profit or loss. Consequently, profit and loss is not appropriately reflecting the performance of an asset held for speculative purposes or for items with cash-like features.[334]

So far, the *AASB* also departs from the view of the *IFRS Interpretations Committee* and seems to tend to a fair value accounting in the same way as the US *FASB*.

§5.06 ACCOUNTING OF CRYPTO DERIVATIVES

Only a few papers and letters on crypto derivatives accounting have been published so far. The author will discuss the material and then consider the general accounting definitions for derivatives and investigate how crypto derivatives should be accounted for.

In 2021, ISDA responded to the *FASB's* 'Invitation to comment'.[335] In their response letter, ISDA states:

> [B]anks are also setting up trading desks to provide customers with exposure to crypto assets. This includes buying and selling crypto assets, as well as derivatives, structured notes and other transactions that reference crypto assets [...] Not only have new derivatives products and financial arrangements linked to cryptocurrency been introduced to the market, but consumer products are also being made available.[336]

The letter did not provide further guidance on the position of the ISDA on how to account for crypto derivatives under US GAAP. However, in the May 2022 paper, the ISDA provides a quick overview of what problems may arise in the accounting treatment of crypto derivatives under US GAAP[337] if cryptoassets are measured at cost less impairments. Those considerations are also highly relevant in respect of IFRS as the IFRS Interpretations Committee is still mirroring *FASB's* previous opinion regarding the measurement of cryptoassets.

The May 2022 ISDA paper mentions in particular three aspects, namely:

(1) problems in the context of hedging of crypto derivatives
(2) differences between accounting treatment of underlying assets (cryptocurrencies) and crypto derivatives
(3) problems in the context of embedded derivatives.

334. *Ibid.*, 16-17, emphasis added.
335. *FASB*, Invitation to comment, 24 June 2021, https://www.fasb.org/Page/ShowPdf?path=PCC%20-%20Topic%203%20AgendaConsultationHO%20web%202021%2012%2017.pdf, accessed 1 October 2023.
336. ISDA, Letter to the *FASB* (2021).
337. ISDA, Accounting for Digital Assets: Key Considerations (May 2022), 17, emphasis added.

With regards to hedging of crypto derivatives, the ISDA paper states:

> Under US GAAP, ASC 815, derivatives must be accounted for at fair value, with changes in fair value reported through earnings, while the underlying digital asset is measured at cost less impairment. Companies that enter into derivatives for hedging purposes will be exposed to earnings volatility when marking the derivative to fair value without any offsetting mark-to-market on the digital asset.[338]

The ISDA paper also highlights the problems that may occur if companies subsequently measure crypto derivatives at fair value whereas they measure cryptoasset underlyings or hedge crypto derivatives at cost less impairments, suggesting that:

> [...] companies that enter into digital asset derivatives to gain exposure to that digital asset will have different accounting and financial reporting results to companies that own the underlying digital assets. As the digital asset derivatives market continues to grow, companies will face challenges in the subsequent measurement model for digital assets as compared to derivatives. Companies are more commonly using derivatives to hedge the risk associated with the significant price volatility of digital assets, or speculatively to take advantage of that volatility.[339]

The problems of the accounting of embedded derivatives are summarised by the ISDA as such:

> Another complexity in the existing accounting model exists where companies may be required to recognize a digital asset on the balance sheet and bifurcate an embedded derivative liability to return the digital asset. As discussed above, this issue will commonly occur in digital asset lending transactions or in custodial relationships where the custodian retains control of the digital asset.[340]

Since the *FASB* will require businesses to subsequently measure cryptoassets at fair value in the near future based on their proposed effective date for the new standard,[341] the accounting mismatches between cryptoassets and crypto derivatives will no longer be relevant for businesses following US GAAP from that point onwards as both instruments have to be measured at fair value.

[A] Accounting of Crypto Derivatives in the UK

In the following subsection, the classification and measurements of crypto derivatives under IFRS and UK FRS are discussed. It should be noted that so far, no guidance in

338. *Ibid.*, 18.
339. *Ibid.*
340. *Ibid.*
341. FASB, Minutes of the September 6, 2023 Board Meeting on Accounting for and Disclosure of Crypto Assets, 14 September 2023,https://www.fasb.org/Page/ShowPdf?path=CRYPTO-MIN-20230906.pdf&title=September%206,%202023%20Board%20Meeting%20Minutes—Accounting%20for%20and%20Disclosure%20of%20Crypto%20Assets, accessed 1 November 2023.
    The *FASB* Board proposed in this meeting the effective date for the updated standard as: 'effective for fiscal years beginning after December 15, 2024'.

respect of this topic has been published. Hence, the classification and measurement of crypto derivatives reflect largely the author's view of a possible accounting treatment of those instruments. The author will discuss in detail cash-settled and physically settled crypto derivatives and ask whether the derivatives accounting definition will apply to those derivative contracts.

[1] Accounting under FRS 102

From an economic point of view, a derivative is a derivative if it can be *stochastically replicated by using combinations of other financial instruments, cash and/or derivatives.*[342] The author outlined in Chapter 4 that this is the case for crypto derivatives and also confirmed that they should fall under the tax definition of derivatives as long as there is another asset which is fungible and liquid that can be used to hedge the crypto derivative. In the case of Bitcoin and Ethereum futures and options, this would be the underlying asset, i.e., Bitcoin or Ethereum.

FRS 102, Glossary, defines derivatives as 'a financial instrument or other contract with all three of the following characteristics:

(a) its value changes in response to the change in a specified interest rate, financial instrument price, commodity price, foreign exchange rate, index of prices or rates, credit rating or credit index, or other variable (sometimes called the 'underlying'), provided in the case of a non-financial variable that the variable is not specific to a party to the contract;
(b) it requires no initial net investment or an initial net investment that is smaller than would be required for other types of contracts that would be expected to have a similar response to changes in market factors; and
(c) it is settled at a future date'.

There are de facto *four elements to the definition*, meaning the derivatives must be:

(a) a financial instrument or other contract, which
(b) value changes in response dot the change of an underlying, provided in the case of a non-financial variable that the variable is not specific to a party to the contract,
(c) it requires no or little net investment, and
(d) it is settled at a future date.

342. *See* Ch. 2 §2.02[A], referring to Rubinstein (1999a) Mark Rubinstein, *Rubinstein on Derivatives* (1st edn, Risk Books 1999) 71-72 and 179-192.

[a] A Derivative Is a Financial Instrument or 'Other Contract'

[i] Is a Crypto Derivative a Financial Instrument?

A financial instrument is defined by FRS 102, Glossary as 'a *contract* that gives rise to a financial asset of one entity and a financial liability or equity instrument of another entity'.[343]

What is needed for a crypto derivative to qualify as a *financial instrument* is the following:

(1) a contract which
(2) gives rise to a financial asset of one party, and a financial liability (or equity instrument) of another party.

The author proposes that we have to carefully distinguish between cash and physically settled crypto derivatives to determine if the definition of a financial instrument is fulfilled. As we have seen in Chapter 4, listed crypto derivatives in the US include:

(1) *cash-settled* CME Bitcoin Futures,[344]
(2) CME options on Bitcoin Futures,[345] and
(3) Bitnomial Bitcoin US Dollar Futures,[346] which are physically settled only.

In contrast to crypto futures, crypto options (cash or physically settled) provide the holder with the right but not the obligation to buy or sell an asset at a predefined price and date.[347]

The author refers to the *EY* paper on crypto derivatives, which outlined that:

> Crypto futures contracts represent the value of a specific cryptocurrency at a specified time. These are agreements between traders to buy or sell a particular asset at a predetermined price on a specified date in the future. In a traditional

343. FRS 102, Glossary.
344. For the contract specifications of the Bitcoin futures, *see* CME Group, Bitcoin Futures, https://www.cmegroup.com/markets/cryptocurrencies/bitcoin/bitcoin.contractSpecs.html, accessed 11 August 2023.
345. CME Group, Get to know options on Bitcoin futures, https://www.cmegroup.com/education/courses/introduction-to-bitcoin/get-to-know-options-on-bitcoin-futures.html, accessed 11 January 2023.
346. Bitnomial, Bitcoin US Dollar Futures, https://bitnomial.com/products/bitcoin-us-dollar-futures, accessed 11 January 2023; *Compare Bitcoin Magazine, Bitnomial launches margined, physically settled bitcoin futures*, https://bitcoinmagazine.com/markets/bitnomial-launches-margined-physically-settled-bitcoin-futures, accessed 25 April 2023; *business wire, A Berkshire Hathaway Company, Bitnomial Launches Margined, Physically Settled Bitcoin futures in the US* (15 November 2021) https://www.businesswire.com/news/home/20211115005890/en/Bitnomial-Launches-Margined-Physically-Settled-Bitcoin-Futures-in-the-US, accessed 23 April 2023.
347. *Ibid.*

futures contract, the holder of the position is under an obligation to buy or sell the underlying asset at the contract price at expiry.[348]

This description in the *EY* paper, therefore, seems to refer to physically settled crypto futures.

Non-deliverable forwards (NDFs) are another category of crypto derivatives.[349] The *EY* paper describes them as being like traditional forward contracts dependent on the price of an underlying – in this case, a cryptoasset. NDFs can be *cash settled only.*[350] *EY* mentions in its report that Goldman Sachs is offering Bitcoin-based NDFs to their clients.[351] To hedge themselves from the risk exposure, Goldman Sachs buys and sells Bitcoin futures in block trades on the CME Group Inc. exchange.[352]

Cash-settled crypto derivatives fulfil all definitional criteria as follows:

(1) a contract

'Contract' and 'contractual' are an important part of the definitions in the realm of financial instruments. They refer to an agreement between two or more parties that has clear economic consequences that the parties have little, if any, discretion to avoid, usually because the agreement is enforceable by law. Contracts, and therefore financial instruments, may take a variety of forms and need not be in writing (IAS 32.13). Consequently, assets or liabilities that are not contractual are not financial instruments. For example, taxes and levies imposed by governments are not financial liabilities because they are not contractual.[353]

Crypto derivatives are binding contracts between two or more parties and thus fall under the definition of a contract.

(2) gives rise to a financial asset of one party and a financial liability (or equity instrument) of another party

A *financial asset* is defined as any asset that is:

(a) cash;
(b) an equity instrument of another entity;
(c) a *contractual right:*
    (i) to *receive cash or another financial asset from another entity*, or
    (ii) to exchange financial assets or financial liabilities with another entity under conditions that are potentially favourable to the entity; or

348. Binance, Crypto Futures and Options: What Are the Similarities and Differences? (4 January 2023), https://www.binance.com/en/blog/futures/crypto-futures-and-options-what-are-the-similarities-and-differences-421499824684902074, accessed 12 January 2023.
349. Shanny Basar, Marketsmedia, NDFs could boost institutional crypto use, 11 March 2021, https://www.marketsmedia.com/ndfs-could-boost-institutional-crypto-use/, accessed 25 April 2023.
350. *EY*, Crypto derivatives (2022), 9.
351. *Ibid.*
352. *Ibid.*, referring to an article in Bloomberg Law, (6 May 2021), Goldman Offers New Bitcoin Derivatives to Wall Street Investors, https://news.bloomberglaw.com/banking-law/goldman-offers-new-bitcoin-derivatives-to-wall-street-investors, accessed 11 January 2023.
353. IFRSCommunity.com, Financial Instruments, definition (IAS 32), updated 7 January 2023, https://ifrscommunity.com/knowledge-base/financial-instruments-definitions/, accessed 25 April 2023.

(d) a contract that will or may be settled in the entity's own equity instruments and is:
   (i) a non-derivative for which the entity is or may be obliged to receive a variable number of the entity's own equity instruments; or
   (ii) a *derivative* that will or may be settled other than by the exchange of a fixed amount of cash or another financial asset for a fixed number of the entity's own equity instruments. For this purpose, the entity's own equity instruments do not include instruments that are themselves contracts for the future receipt or delivery of the entity's own equity instruments.[354]

Vice versa, a *financial liability* is:

(a) a contractual obligation:
   (i) to deliver cash or another financial asset to another entity; or
   (ii) to exchange financial assets or financial liabilities with another entity under conditions that are potentially unfavourable to the entity; or
(b) a contract that will or may be settled in the entity's own equity instruments and is:
   (i) a non-derivative for which the entity is or may be obliged to deliver a variable number of the entity's own equity instruments; or
   (ii) a *derivative* that will or may be settled other than by the exchange of a fixed amount of cash or another financial asset for a fixed number of the entity's own equity instruments. For this purpose, the entity's own equity instruments do not include instruments that are themselves contracts for the future receipt or delivery of the entity's own equity instruments.[355]

If a crypto derivative, for example, a crypto future, is cash settled, then if the value of the underlying cryptoasset is above the strike price, the crypto future short party will have to pay to the long party of the future the difference between the market value of the cryptoasset and the strike price. This cash settlement amount is a financial asset for the long position holder.

Vice versa, if the market value of the cryptoasset is below the strike price, the short party to the futures contract will receive the difference between the market value of the cryptoasset and the strike price from the long position crypto derivative holder.

The cash settlement amount is a financial liability for the long party (long position holder) to the crypto derivative.

(3) Is a physically settled crypto derivative also a derivative within the definition?

As seen above, the majority view regards cryptocurrencies – or cryptoassets in general – neither as cash, cash equivalent, nor as satisfying any other definition outlined in the financial asset or financial liability definitions.

However, the question in the context of this subchapter is if a derivative over the underlying cryptocurrency could be regarded as a financial asset – even if the underlying is not.

354. FRS 102, Glossary.
355. FRS 102, Glossary.

If a crypto derivative is physically settled, the long position holder will not receive a financial asset if the cryptoasset is delivered at the settlement date against payment of the strike price. The reason is that the cryptoasset is regarded as an intangible asset, but not as a financial asset, as determined by the majority view in the accounting literature, see above Chapter 5 §5.05.

Although physically settled crypto derivatives may not be regarded as financial assets, they may still qualify as 'other contract' within the definition of a derivative under FRS 102, Glossary.

It is not defined in FRS 102 what constitutes 'other contract' in the context of the derivative definition. The term 'other contract' is also not defined in the glossary of FRS 102.

In contrast to IAS 39 or IFRS 9, FRS 102 does not refer to 'other contract' 'within this standard'.[356] The author, therefore, believes that the term should have a wide meaning, which is derived from the general meaning of the words.

A physically settled derivative over cryptoassets is a bilateral contract. Further, the term 'other contract only' refers to the fact that the contract is something other than a financial instrument and that those contracts which cannot be regarded as financial instruments can qualify as derivatives, nonetheless. The author, therefore, believes that physically settled crypto derivatives would, in principle, fall within the scope of 'other contract' even if they were not regarded as financial instruments.

[b] The Value Changes in Response to the Change of an Underlying, Provided in the Case of a Non-financial Variable That the Variable Is Not Specific to a Party to the Contract

For both cash and physically settled crypto derivatives, the value changes in response to the value of the underlying cryptoasset, like all traditional derivatives.

However, the phrase 'provided in the case of a non-financial variable that the variable is not specific to a party to the contract' has to be analysed.

The underlying asset, the cryptoasset, is, in any case, a non-financial variable, i.e., by the majority view in the accounting literature, an *intangible asset*. Thus, it needs to be determined what the wording 'that the variable is not specific to a party to the contract' means.

The author puts forward that this meaning is similar to the description in IFRS 9, BA5. Thus, the value of a specific cryptocurrency, like Bitcoin, is not specific to the party to the contract, and thus, crypto derivatives would fall within the scope of [b].

Whether, for example, derivatives over cryptoassets that are created by the issuer of a cryptocurrency would qualify as 'specific' is open to debate. Such a crypto derivative may indeed fall outside the definition as the creator of a cryptocurrency is the one who initially attributed value to it.

356. *Compare* HMRC, CFM50230 – Derivative contracts: accounting conditions: meaning of derivative, CTA09/S579.

[c] It Requires No or Little Net Investment

As with every derivative, a crypto derivative should require a net investment that is smaller than the value of the underlying cryptoassets. Again, this may change in the event of a sharp crypto decline where sellers of the crypto derivatives would require the purchaser of a crypto derivative to supply 100% of the purchase price of the underlying cryptoasset or fully collateralise because of the swift and unexpected change in value of some cryptocurrencies.

[d] It Is Settled at a Future Date

Crypto derivatives, such as futures over Bitcoin or Bitcoin options, are settled at a future date, and thus, the criteria are also fulfilled.

Hence, crypto derivatives should, in principle, fulfil the definition of a derivative within the meaning of FRS 102, Glossary.

[e] Explicit Exception of FRS 102, Paragraph 12.5

FRS 102, Section 12 provides that:

> this section applies to contracts to buy or sell non-financial items *if the contract can be settled net in cash or another financial instrument*, or by exchanging financial instruments as if the contracts were financial instruments, with the following exception: contracts that were entered into and continue to be held for the purpose of the *receipt or delivery of a non-financial item in accordance with the entity's expected purchase, sale or usage requirements are not financial instruments for the purposes of this section.*[357]

That means that only cash-settled crypto derivatives would fall within the definition of FRS 102 - derivatives. Physically settled crypto derivatives, where the cryptoasset - an intangible asset, and thus a non-financial item - is delivered, would fall outside the scope of FRS 102, Section 12.

[2] Accounting under IAS 39 and IFRS 9

Under IFRS 9/IAS 39, 'a financial instrument or *other contract within the scope of this Standard* with all three of the following characteristics.

> (a) its value changes in response to the change in a specified interest rate, financial instrument price, commodity price, foreign exchange rate, index of prices or rates, credit rating or credit index, or other variable, provided in the case of a non-financial variable that the variable is not specific to a party to the contract (sometimes called the 'underlying').

357. FRS 102, para. 12.5.

(b) it requires no initial net investment or an initial net investment that is smaller than would be required for other types of contracts that would be expected to have a similar response to changes in market factors.
(c) it is settled at a future date'.[358]

Again, there is 'an exception relating to non-financial variable specific to a party to the contract'.[359]

The definition of a derivative in IFRS 9/IAS 39 is similar to the derivatives' definition in FRS 102, Glossary, apart from the reference that it applies only 'to financial instruments and other contracts within the scope of IFRS 9'.

So far, the definition of a derivative is somewhat narrower than that of FRS 102, Section 12. One could indeed question whether crypto derivatives are contracts within the scope of IFRS 9/IAS 39 since IAS 38 applies to the underlying cryptoassets.

Hence, one could argue that although a cash-settled crypto derivative qualifies as a financial instrument, a physically settled crypto derivative may not as it is not an 'other contract within the scope of this standard'. The author believes that further discussions are needed.

HMRC maintains in the Corporate Finance Manual CFM50230 that:

> The definition of a derivative is essentially the same in each of IAS 39, IFRS 9, FRS 26 and FRS 102.
>
> The only difference between FRS 25 and the definitions in IAS 39/IFRS 9 is that the words "within the scope of this Standard (see paragraphs 2–7)" are replaced by an analogous reference to the relevant paragraphs of IAS 39/IFRS 9.
>
> FRS 102 contains no wording equivalent to "within this standard". However, the requirement for tax, in S579(1)(a), is that the contracts should be "treated for accounting purposes as a derivative". Under FRS 102, a relevant contract is only treated for as a derivative if either its falls to be a derivative under Section 12 for non-basic financial instruments, or the company chooses to apply IAS 39/IFRS 9 instead and the instrument falls to be treated as a derivative under those standards[...].[360]

It follows that any difference between FRS 102 and FRS 26/IAS 39/IFRS 9 is one of nuance and unlikely to be of practical significance.[361]

In respect of physically settled derivative contracts over other non-financial items, CFM50230 states:

> Section 12 contains a list of exclusions from the scope of the section which is broadly equivalent to the exclusions from FRS 26. In particular, there are exclusions for [...] contracts to buy or sell a non-financial item that (i) do not impose risks that are not typical for such contracts and (ii) were entered into and continue

358. IFRS 9, Appendix 1.
359. IFRScommunity.com, Blog, Derivatives and Embedded Derivatives: Definitions and Characteristics (IFRS 9).
360. HMRC, CFM50230 – Derivative contracts: accounting conditions: meaning of derivative, CTA09/S579.
361. *Ibid.*

> to be held for the purpose of the receipt or delivery of a non-financial item in accordance with the entity's expected purchase, sale or usage requirements.[362]

The Blog, *IFRS.Community.com*, in this respect, suggests:

> Contracts to buy or sell non-financial items, such as commodities like oil or copper, typically do not meet the definition of a financial instrument as they do not lead to a financial asset for either party. In such contracts, the party paying cash is entitled to receive a physical asset, which is not a financial asset. However, exceptions exist when:
>
> - Such contracts can be settled net or by exchanging financial instruments, typically seen in contracts related to commodities, or
> - Entity regularly takes delivery of the underlying assets and sells them shortly thereafter to profit from price fluctuations or dealer's margin.

In these cases, such contracts are treated as though they were financial instruments (i.e., derivatives).[363]

Thus, if one applied this view to physically settled crypto derivatives, it would mean that if the crypto derivative contract also allows for cash settlement (and not only physical settlement) or if the entity (the long position holder of the crypto derivatives) takes delivery of the cryptoasset but sells the cryptoasset within a short time after delivery to generate a profit, those contracts would likely be accounted for as if they were financial instruments. Thus, there may indeed be a slight nuance between FRS 102, section 12 and IAS 39/IFRS 9 in the context of crypto derivatives. The definition of IAS 39, paragraph 9, is similar to that of IFRS 9, Appendix 1, and thus the same considerations apply.

[B] Accounting of Crypto Derivatives in Germany

There is absolutely no guidance for the accounting of crypto derivatives in Germany. The author believes that the rules applying to derivatives accounting are also likely to apply to the accounting treatment of crypto derivatives. The author refers in this respect to Chapter 5 §5.03.

[C] Policy Outlook

The accounting standard setters should consider guidance on how to account for crypto derivatives.

---

362. *Ibid.*
363. IFRSCommunity.com, Financial Instruments, definition (IAS 32), updated 7 January 2023, https://ifrscommunity.com/knowledge-base/financial-instruments-definitions/, accessed 25 August 2023.

In principle, there are three routes to account for crypto derivatives; namely, they are accounted for:

(1) in the same way as any other derivatives, and it is irrelevant if the underlying is a cryptocurrency or any other non-financial assets;
(2) in the same way as the underlying assets, i.e., as the cryptoassets themselves; or
(3) cryptoassets and crypto derivatives are accounted for at fair value through profit or loss.

If the standard setter applies the first solution, taxpayers still have the possibility to set up an arbitrage between a crypto derivative and the underlying asset and also benefit from the difference in tax treatment of cash-settled crypto derivatives (within the definition) and physically settled derivatives - provided that the tax rules follow the accounting treatment.

If the taxpayer applies the second solution and treats both crypto derivatives and cryptoassets as intangible assets, the problem of the recognition of impairment losses, as discussed above, still exists. Hence, also, in terms of protection of the tax base, the second solution should be avoided by tax legislators.

The author proposes to follow solution number three and account for crypto derivatives and cryptoassets at fair value through profit or loss. Only this solution will prevent tax arbitrage strategies using cryptoassets or their derivatives unless the legislator chooses to divert from the accounts and disallow impairment losses when taxing cryptoassets and their derivatives.

§5.07 ACCOUNTING OF ESG DERIVATIVES

ESG derivatives and ESG-linked structured products raise several issues. ESG derivatives are discussed in this chapter, and ESG-linked structured products in Chapter 8. The default position should always be to apply the general rules as most ESG derivatives fall within the traditional types of derivatives and often contain - unlike cryptoassets - traditional underlying with some ESG features added.

In a recent paper, *PWC* states that:

> Climate-related risks could have a significant impact on an entity's operations and financial performance and users of the financial statements are increasingly looking for evidence that the entity has incorporated climate risk factors when making estimates and judgements in the preparation of financial statements. The accounting standards have an overarching requirement to disclose information that users need to understand the impact of particular transactions, other events and conditions on the entity's financial position and financial performance. Therefore, in light of the current focus on, and impact of, climate change, entities should ensure that they have undertaken a rigorous assessment to provide all the material and relevant information affecting the financial statements.[364]

364. *PWC*, UK GAAP Illustrative financial statements, For 2021 Year ends, January 2022, https://viewpoint.pwc.com/dt/uk/en/pwc/ilustrative_financia/assets/UK_illustrative_accounts_year_ended_31_December_2021_FRS_102_0222.pdf, accessed 6 May 2023.

The *International Sustainability Standards Board* (ISSB) issued the first two ESG Accounting standards in June 2023, called IFRS S1 *General Requirements for Disclosure of Sustainability-related Financial Information*[365] and IFRS S2 *Climate-related Disclosures*.[366] IFRS S1 and IFRS S2 are effective for accounting periods starting on or after 1 January 2024, with earlier application allowed as long as the other standard (of the two) is applied at the same time.[367]

IFRS S1 states that '[t]he objective of IFRS S1 is to require an entity to disclose information about its sustainability-related risks and opportunities that is useful to users of general purpose financial reports in making decisions relating to providing resources to the entity'.[368] IFRS S2's objective 'is to require an entity to disclose information about its climate-related risks and opportunities that is useful to users of general purpose financial reports in making decisions relating to providing resources to the entity'.[369]

The IASB has issued educational material where it discussed the impact of climate change on the accounting standards.[370] The material has been updated and republished in July 2023 'to reflect an agenda decision published by the IFRS Interpretations Committee in July 2022 and minor editorial changes'.[371] In the educational material, accounting questions (both in terms of classification and measurement) are discussed not only in relation to ESG derivatives but also in the context of ESG-linked structured products. In relation to IFRS 9, it confirms that any climate-related matters 'may affect the accounting for financial statements in a number of ways'.[372]

The IASB paper gives the example of loan contracts that may 'include terms linking contractual cash flows to a company's achievement of climate-related targets'.[373] It outlines that the classification and the measurement of those loans may be affected.[374] This can, for example, be decisive in the context of ESG-related structured products, which are discussed further in Chapter 8.

In those scenarios, the lender 'would need to consider those terms in assessing whether the contractual terms of the financial asset give rise to cash flows that are

365. ISSB, IFRS S1 *General Requirements for Disclosure of Sustainability-related Financial Information*, June 2023, https://www.ifrs.org/issued-standards/ifrs-sustainability-standards-navigator/ifrs-s1-general-requirements/#standard, accessed 25 July 2023.
366. ISSB IFRS S2, Climate-related Disclosures, June 2023, https://www.ifrs.org/issued-standards/ifrs-sustainability-standards-navigator/ifrs-s1-general-requirements/#standard, accessed 25 July 2023.
367. ISSB, IFRS S1; ISSB IFRS S2.
368. ISSB, IFRS S1.
369. ISSB IFRS S2.
370. IASB, Effects of climate related matters on financial statements (November 2020), https://www.ifrs.org/content/dam/ifrs/supporting-implementation/documents/effects-of-climate-related-matters-on-financial-statements.pdf, accessed 1 June 2023.
371. IASB, Effects of climate related matters on financial statements (Republished July 2023), https://www.ifrs.org/content/dam/ifrs/supporting-implementation/documents/effects-of-climate-related-matters-on-financial-statements.pdf, accessed 25 August 2023.
372. *Ibid.*, 5.
373. *Ibid.*
374. *Ibid.*

solely payments of principal and interest on the principal amount outstanding. For the borrower, those targets may affect whether there are embedded derivatives that need to be separated from the host contract'.[375]

In relation to credit risk, the IASB states that 'climate-related matters may also affect a lender's exposure to credit losses'.[376] The IASB gives examples of 'wildfires, floods or policy and regulatory changes'[377] which:

> could negatively affect a borrower's ability to meet its debt obligations to the lender. Further, assets could become inaccessible or uninsurable, affecting the value of collateral for lenders. In recognising and measuring expected credit losses, IFRS 9 requires use of all reasonable and supportable information that is available without undue cost or effort. Climate-related matters may therefore be relevant – for example, they could affect the range of potential future economic scenarios, the lender's assessment of significant increases in credit risk, whether a financial asset is credit impaired and/or the measurement of expected credit losses.[378]

§5.08 SOLUTIONS ON THE ALIGNMENT OF ACCOUNTING AND TAXATION RULES AND THE APPLICATION OF FAIR VALUE ACCOUNTING FOR TAX PURPOSES

In the following subchapter the author discusses whether an alignment of financial accounting and taxation rules is desirable in the context of derivatives, and second, whether the recognition of income, gains and losses on a fair value basis should also be used as a method to determine when to tax those income, gains and losses from derivatives.

The following considerations regarding the alignment of accounting standards also apply to some extent to those instruments but should be primarily viewed as a suggestion for traditional derivatives.

In relation to cryptoassets and crypto derivatives, the author proposed fair value accounting for those instruments in Chapter 5 §5.05 and §5.06.

[A] Aligning Financial Accounting Rules with Taxation Rules?

Thuronyi suggests that the taxation of derivatives poses less of a problem if those rules are based on financial accounting rules.[379] He proposes that there are good arguments for such an alignment. 'In countries that formulate their tax rules independently of accounting principles, it may be necessary to provide detailed rules for the taxation of financial instruments so that taxpayers cannot use them to avoid taxation.'[380]

375. *Ibid.*
376. *Ibid.*
377. *Ibid.*
378. *Ibid.*
379. Thuronyi (2001a) 263; Thuronyi (2001b) 2; similar: Neighbour (1997) 935.
380. Thuronyi (2001a) 263-264.

He further argues that accounting rules are more flexible and provide a basis for taxing derivatives in such a way that it does not lead to the erosion of the tax base.[381] Likewise, the OECD has suggested that an alignment of tax legislation with accounting standards would help tax systems cope more easily with financial product innovation.[382]

There has been a general trend within the last twenty years to align financial accounts with the taxation rules.

However, if tax rules follow – without deep analysis – the financial accounts, this might not be the best answer. A balance is often hard to find between the concerns of tax policymakers and those of accounting standards setters, even if a unified set of tax and accounting rules may simplify compliance for taxpayers.

The aims of accounting standard setters and tax legislators can be considerably different depending on whether the respective accounting standards focus on the protection of creditors and apply an overarching prudence principle (such as German GAAP) or whether the accounts are designed for the information purposes of a variety of users, such as the company's shareholders, potential investors, lenders and other creditors.[383]

IFRS accounts are focused on the provision of information for the capital markets, and hence, data is used, which allows shareholders and future investors to take a view of the future performance and the potential risk and reward profile when investing in the company.[384] Hence, the criterion of 'relevance' is of importance.[385]

Taxation is, however, based on principles of objectivity, proportionality, and certainty. Thus, data that is used as a basis for taxation should not be based on an assessment of probabilities of future performance.

For example, *Freedman* argues that 'the different objectives of tax and financial accounts make it desirable that the rules for each one are not unduly influenced by the rules for the other'.[386] However, accounting standards and tax law do not only have different objectives. Their nature is also entirely different.

Or, as *Southern* puts it: 'Accounting is judgmental. Law is prescriptive. Tax is a matter of law, not of accounting. There cannot be a straight read-through from the accounting result to the tax result, because there can be more than one possible accounting treatment, but only one tax outcome.'[387]

Whereas accounting standards can provide more than one possible right outcome because of the application of different accounting methods, tax law requires only one correct outcome[388] because the notion of 'certainty' in tax law is absolute as it is a

381. *Ibid.*, 263; Thuronyi (2001c) 6.
382. OECD (2001) para. 99.
383. IFRS Foundation, *The Conceptual Framework for Financial Reporting 2011*, DOI: 10.1002/978 1119207917.ch1, accessed 1 December 2023, Ch. 1, OB2-OB10.
384. *IFRS* Foundation, Conceptual Framework, Ch. 1, OB2-OB3.
385. Herzig (2006) 560.
386. Freedman (2004a) 76.
387. David Southern, 'Accounting, Certainty and Tax' Tax Journal (2011), Issue No 1076, 8.
388. OECD (2001) para. 10; *also* Freedman (2004a) 75.

'component of the rule of law, [which] embodies the fundamental principle of legality, to which the tax system should conform'.[389]

The alignment of accounting standards and tax rules, therefore, may not always be the right answer to the question of how tax systems should deal with the problems posed by derivatives.

'Accounting principles do not necessarily reduce the risk that similar instruments would be given different tax treatments on the basis of disparate interpretations of accounting rules.'[390]

Particularly, if accounting rules are designed by a private standard setter, such as the IASB, specific issues and needs of domestic tax systems are likely not to have been taken into account.[391]

In the author's opinion, tax experts have so far underestimated the substantial risk that the alignment of accounting standards and tax rules may, on the contrary, provide taxpayers with an opportunity for tax arbitrage as accounting rules are not designed with the view of avoiding the erosion of the tax base.[392] For example, opportunities for tax arbitrage, partly caused by the alignment of applicable accounting standards for cryptoassets and their taxation rules, can be observed for this new asset class.

As previously explained in Chapter 5 §5.05, the majority of the accounting firms and the Tentative Decisions of the *IFRS Interpretations Committee* regard cryptoassets as intangible assets with an infinite lifetime and allow for an accounting of those assets at cost (without amortisation) but with provisions for impairments. As shown above, this allows a company to write down any impairment losses on cryptoassets but does not allow for a write-up in the accounts, with the result that if the cost method is followed, those cryptoasset positions will indefinitely stand at a loss, although they economically may stand at a gain, until their disposal.

As tax follows the accounts in this respect, those cryptoasset transactions and impairment losses allow taxpayers to indefinitely defer their tax liabilities by offsetting those impairment losses (which may not exist at the end of the tax year anymore economically) against any gains from other business ventures. To avoid an erosion of the country's tax base, the US *FASB* has already reacted and is about to close that tax loophole by requiring businesses to measure cryptoassets at fair value instead of cost less impairments. So far, the *IFRS Interpretations Committee* has not reacted and still maintains that cryptoassets should be accounted for at cost less impairments.

Similar considerations apply to crypto derivatives. Crypto derivatives could be used to create a completely economically hedged position of cryptoassets without selecting a hedge accounting treatment. Again, that means that companies can generate an economically hedged position with cryptoassets and derivatives and, at the same time, profit from impairment losses on their positions without the need to recognise any gains above cost if the cost model is applied.

389. Southern (2011) col 2.
390. OECD (2001) para. 100.
391. Christopher Nobes, A Conceptual Framework for the Taxable Income of Businesses, and How to Apply it under IFRS (2004) 23; *also* Freedman (2004b) 9.
392. In the UK, HMRC has started to recognise that the alignment of accounting standards and tax rules may in certain cases lead to tax arbitrage opportunities for taxpayers. *See* HMRC, *Consultation on corporate debt and derivative contracts taxation* (2013) paras 4.3-4.24.

Also, in the context of withholding taxes, it is the legal form rather than the economic substance that is decisive.[393] Hence, the complete alignment of accounting and tax rules may not provide a solution for cross-border taxation issues arising in the context of derivatives, as withholding tax rules are specifically designed and laid down in the tax legislation to serve the purpose of withholding at source.[394] The author believes that this issue also applies to cryptoassets and crypto derivatives. Also, here, either the accounting rules would need to be changed to require fair value accounting for those instruments, or the tax legislator would have to intervene and disallow any impairment losses to be used for tax purposes if cryptoassets or crypto derivatives are held.

Although a complete alignment of accounting and taxation rules might simplify taxing derivatives and cryptoassets, the better solution for tax systems might be the introduction of a completely different set of taxation rules for derivatives and cryptoassets. Indeed, a taxation of derivatives and cryptoassets based on separate taxation rules, including the timing of when to tax these instruments, may be better tailored to the needs of the tax system than taxation rules that purely rely on accounting standards.

[B] Application of Fair Value Accounting of Derivatives for Tax Purposes?

The question of whether tax legislation should be aligned with accounting standards in the context of taxing derivatives is closely interlinked with the question of which accounting approaches should be adopted for the valuation of derivatives.

The introduction of fair value accounting for derivatives is likely to change the picture for the taxation of corporate taxpayers if governments decide to use IFRS as a basis for taxation. That is, for example, the case in the UK, where corporate taxpayers apply fair value accounting to account for derivatives and where that treatment is also a basis for taxation, with exceptions applying only for some derivatives.

Before the obligatory introduction of IFRS/IAS in the consolidated group accounts of listed companies in the EU, countries like Germany used fair value accounting for derivatives only for banks and other financial institutions and relied on historical cost accounting in their group accounts for all other investors.

Whether fair value accounting of derivatives offers the best solution in the context of the taxation of derivatives is not without doubt.

Under IAS 39/IFRS 9, derivatives, except those designated to hedge other financial instruments, are deemed to be 'held for trading'.[395] They are accounted for at fair value, with all changes in those fair values being recognised in the P&L account at each balance sheet date, except in the case of hedge accounting.[396]

393. Thuronyi (2001b) 2.
394. *Ibid.*
395. For a brief summary, *see* Ch. 6 §6.02[C].
396. Compare Ch. 7 §7.03[A][1]. A further exception applied to equity derivatives over unquoted equity instruments. These are accounted for at amortised cost. *See* Ch. 6 §6.02[C].

Gains and losses on derivatives should be shown in the commercial accounts to give the shareholders and creditors the full picture of which risks the company has assumed and whether there is a risk of credit default. Hence, derivatives should be on the balance sheet for both shareholder and creditor information purposes.

An alignment of commercial accounts with the tax rules combined with an application of fair value accounting for derivatives may, however, mean that any *unrealised gains* from unmatured derivative contracts that exist on the balance sheet date would have to be *recognised* for tax purposes, although it cannot be predicted whether these derivatives will stand at a gain or loss at maturity.

As a taxation of unrealised gains, however, contradicts the *ability-to-pay principle* (which should, in the author's view, guide taxation in general),[397] the fair value method may not constitute -in the author's view - an appropriate method to tax derivatives. By taxing unrealised gains, the corporate taxpayer may be forced to either finance the tax bill on the unrealised gains with a bank loan, thus reducing the economic gain on the derivative, or in extreme scenarios, *sell the derivative* before they actually intended because they have to pay taxes on those instruments but may not have the funds to do so.[398]

For gains and losses in trading books of banks and financial services companies, both the realisation argument and the ability-to-pay argument will not be relevant as banks can finance, realise and buy back any assets or derivatives contained in the trading book easily in the financial market as they have privileged, cheap access to the financial markets as well as to the lending markets.

Hence, a taxation of profits and losses arising in the trading books of banks and similar market participants based on a fair value accounting method constitutes an appropriate solution for domestic tax legislators. In respect of the banking book and the long-term assets, it may be beneficial for banks to tax their profits and losses according to an accruals method to avoid taxation of unrealised gains from strategic derivatives positions.

The opinion of *Cullinane* regarding the introduction of international accounting standards for accounting purposes is, in the author's view, also valid when applying the fair value accounting method as a basis for the taxation of derivatives held by companies: 'We may have had the falling of the Bastille, but the terror may be yet to come.'[399]

Thus, one could argue that an *amortised cost basis of accounting* might be the more appropriate method to determine the value and point of time at which derivatives should be recognised for corporate tax purposes. Alternatively, tax legislators may want to introduce a new tax realisation principle, as *Freedman* has suggested.[400]

397. Discussing the pros and cons of the ability-to-pay principle in taxation: Schön (2004) 14-19. For a critical discussion of Schön's view: Sheppard (2004) 1377-1379.
398. Schön (2004) 20.
399. John Cullinane, 'IAS - What's It All About (Part 2)' (2005) Tax Adviser 10, 11.
400. Freedman (2004a) 85. *See also* Ch. 5 §5.04.

CHAPTER 6

The Special Regime Approach Versus the Integrative Approach, the Distinction of Income and Capital, and Equity and Debt

You really don't need leverage in this world much. If you're smart, you're going to make a lot of money without borrowing.

— Warren Buffett, *1991 speech at the University of Notre Dame*

This chapter contains several taxation questions concerning derivatives and cryptoassets.

In relation to derivatives, the following problems are analysed:

(1) Tax systems may either apply their general taxation rules to derivatives[1] or establish a special taxation regime exclusively for derivatives.[2] Both approaches are investigated, and the advantages and disadvantages are highlighted.
(2) Problems in the taxation of derivatives may occur if the tax rules distinguish according to the character of income, either by applying a more favourable tax regime or lower tax rates to capital gains compared to other income.
(3) Issues can arise if the tax legislator taxes returns from equity differently compared to those from debt, for example, privileges equity capital gains over debt capital gains or dividends over interest.
(4) The question of whether the application of different taxation rules applying to options and futures over cryptocurrencies and CFDs over cryptocurrencies is appropriate to tax those instruments.

1. The author will call this the *integrative approach*.
2. The author will call this the *special regime approach*.

In Chapters 6 §6.01 to §6.03, the different approaches to taxing derivatives adopted in the UK and German corporate tax legislation will be highlighted, and the general principles will be explained. The taxation of crypto derivatives will be discussed.

Chapters 6 §6.02 and §6.04 contain an analysis of how far the UK and German tax legislation rely on the dichotomy of income versus capital and equity versus debt in order to tax derivatives for corporate law purposes.[3] After a high-level analysis of those approaches, Chapters 6 §6.05 to §6.06 discuss the specific taxation rules applying to derivatives entered into by companies in the UK[4] and Germany.[5] In relation to crypto derivatives, the taxation of options and futures on cryptocurrencies is compared with the taxation of CFDs over cryptocurrencies in Chapters 6 §6.05.

In Chapter 6 §6.07, the author compares the rules of both countries and evaluates the merits and disadvantages of both approaches.

Chapter 6 §6.08 deals with the taxation of cryptoassets, particularly with the tax treatment of impairment losses based on their accounting treatment.

Chapter 6 §6.09 discusses possible solutions to achieve a coherent taxation of derivatives and cryptoassets in a domestic tax system.

§6.01 A SPECIAL TAXATION REGIME APPLYING TO DERIVATIVES HELD BY COMPANIES IN THE UK

In the UK, *a special taxation regime* applies to derivative contracts entered into by companies. The derivative contracts regime is a comprehensive regime that subjects almost all derivatives to the rules established in CTA 2009, Part 7.

It has been broadly designed as follows:

Rule number one: income regime

As a general rule, 'all profits arising to a company from its derivative contracts are chargeable to corporation tax as income'[6] in accordance with CTA 2009, Part 7.

---

3. A discussion of the rules applying to individuals and non-corporate businesses would go beyond the scope of this work and thus is not part of it.
4. For the UK, *see* Ch. 6 §6.05.
   A comprehensive analysis of the taxation of derivatives can be found in: Ghosh, Johnson and Miller (2022), Part E (issue 28) and Southern (2017) Chs 13 to 16.
5. For Germany, a summary of the tax law principles applying to derivatives can be found in Ch. 6 §6.06 of this book. The taxation of derivatives in relation to private individuals has been dealt with in several letter rulings by the Ministry of Finance, such as BMF, Schreiben vom 18 Januar 2016. *Einzelfragen zur Abgeltungssteuer*, GZ IV C 1 – S 2252/08/10004 DOK 2015/0468306, https://www.bzst.de/SharedDocs/BMF/DE/Downloads/bmf_Schreiben_20160118_Einzelfrage n_Abgeltungsteuer.html, accessed 15 July 2023, and BMF, Schreiben vom 3 Juni 2021, IV C 1 – S 2252/19/10003:002 BStBl 2021 I S. 723, *Einzelfragen zur Abgeltungsteuer; Ergänzung des BMF-Schreibens vom 18. Januar 2016* (BStBl 2016 I S. 85), https://datenbank.nwb.de/Dokument /857870/, accessed 15 July 2023.
6. CTA 2009, s. 571(1).

Rule number two: trading versus non-trading income

Different taxation results follow, depending on whether the derivative contract is entered by the company for the purpose of a trade or not.[7]

CTA 2009, section 573(1) provides that all credits and debits under a derivative contract for the purpose of the company's trade will be brought into account as trading profits and losses under CTA 2009, Part 3.[8]

Trading credits are taxable as trading receipts,[9] whereas any debits will be deductible as expenses of the trade,[10] even if they would normally not be deductible under the general corporation tax regime because they are of a capital nature.[11] Special loss relief rules are not necessary because any debits can be offset against trading income in the same way as any other trading losses under CTA 2009, Part 3.[12] In contrast, any credits or debits on derivative contracts that are not entered for the purpose of a trade are treated as if they were non-trading credits or non-trading debits of a loan relationship within the meaning of CTA 2009, Part 5.[13]

Rule number three: chargeable gains regime

Certain derivative contracts are chargeable to corporation tax as *chargeable gains* if they fall under *Chapter 7 or 8* of CTA 2009, Part 7.[14] The *trading and non-trading distinction* is also important for derivative contracts, which fall within Chapter 7 of CTA 2009, Part 7.[15]

If those contracts are held for the purpose of the trade, any credits or debits will normally be brought into account under CTA 2009, Part 3 as trading credits or debits unless the exceptions of CTA 2009, section 651 apply.[16]

If certain embedded or non-embedded derivative contracts that fall under CTA 2009, sections 643, 645, 648 and 650 are entered for non-trading purposes, the special rules of Chapter 7 will apply,[17] and any credits or debits may be subject to corporation tax as chargeable gains and any debits may be relieved as allowable losses.[18]

7. *See* Ch. 6 §6.05[B][2][a][i].
8. Ghosh, Johnson and Miller (2022) [E3.2]-[E3.10] (issue 28).
9. CTA 2009, s. 573(2).
10. CTA 2009, s. 573(3).
11. CTA 2009, s. 573 takes precedence over the general rules of CTA 2009, ss 53, 54; *see* CTA 2009, s. 573(4)(a), (b). *Compare* Bramwell et al. (2023), H1.4.18; *Simon's Taxes*, vol 5, D1.875 (issue 171).
12. Ghosh, Johnson and Miller (2022) [E3.13] (issue 28).
13. CTA 2009, s. 574(2). *Compare* Ch. 6 §6.05[B][2][a][i].

    See also Bramwell et al. (2023), H1.4.18; Haworth and Hollis (2010) 26.

    Regarding losses, any non-trading losses can be offset against other income and profits of the same accounting period, carried back against non-trading income up to 12 months and carried forward against non-trading profits. *Compare* Ghosh, Johnson and Miller (2022) [E3.14] (issue 28).
14. CTA 2009, s. 571(2) and ss 639(1), (2). Note that CTA 2009, s. 571(2) only refers to Ch. 7, not to Ch. 8.
15. Ghosh, Johnson and Miller (2022) [E3.16]-[E3.20] (issue 28).
16. CTA 2009, s. 651(1), (2)(a), (b).
17. CTA 2009, s. 640(1).
18. CTA 2009, ss 640, 641; Ghosh, Johnson and Miller (2022) [E3.16]-[E3.20] (issue 28).

> *Example 34:*
>
> Company A purchases an equity-linked note over the EURO STOXX 50 index for non-trading purposes. If the company applies IAS 39 in their accounts based on the accounting choice made under FRS 102, the note will be bifurcated into a debt instrument and an embedded equity derivative. In this case, tax law will follow this bifurcation. The loan relationship rules would apply with respect to the debt instrument. Profit or losses on the embedded derivative would be subject to a capital gains treatment under Chapter 7 of CTA 2009, Part 7.[19]

Rule number four: excluded contracts

Derivative contracts with an *excluded subject matter* under CTA 2009, section 589 will fall completely outside the derivative contracts regime of CTA 2009, Part 7. '[C]orporation tax is charged on chargeable gains accruing to a company on the disposal of assets charged on chargeable gains accruing to a company on the disposal of assets.'[20] The capital gains tax regime of TCGA 1992, sections 143, 144 applies to those excluded contracts,[21] meaning that any capital gains arising to a company out of derivatives contracts with excluded subject matters are chargeable to capital gains tax and treated in accordance with TCGA 1992, sections 143 and 144.[22]

The excluded contracts rules of CTA 2009, sections 589-593 are complex and contain several cases of derivatives being excluded from CTA 2009, Part 7. They will be discussed further in Chapter 6 § 6.02 and § 6.05 below.

§6.02 THE DISTINCTION BETWEEN INCOME AND CAPITAL, AND BETWEEN EQUITY AND DEBT IN THE UK

In the UK, the distinction between income and capital is an overarching principle, both for individuals and for corporate taxpayers.[23] Even though UK companies are taxed on all profits, including both income and chargeable gains[24] at the same corporation tax

19. CTA 2009, ss 641(1), (2)(c), (3), 648, 649(2)(b).
20. TCGA 1992, s. 2(1) as amended by FA 2019 Sch. 1, referring to s. 2(1) and (2) of CTA 2009. TCGA 1992, s. 2(2) stipulates that '[t]he charge to corporation tax on chargeable gains has effect in accordance with this Act and all other relevant provisions of the Corporation Tax Acts'.
21. Ghosh, Johnson and Miller (2022) [E2.471] and [E2.522] (issue 28).
22. *Ibid.*, [E2.471].
    Any gains a company makes on financial futures, traded options or financial options are not taxed as miscellaneous income. *Compare* CTA 2009, s. 981(1); HMRC, CFM50070.
23. For a general discussion of the distinction between capital and income: *Glenboig Union Fireclay Co Ltd v. IRC* (1922) 12 TC 427 (HL); *IRC v. John Lewis Properties plc* [2003] STC 117 (CA).
24. CTA 2009, s. 2(2).
    CTA 2009, s. 4 explicitly provides: 'Capital gains tax is not charged on gains accruing to a company in respect of which the company is chargeable to corporation tax or would be so chargeable but for an exemption.' With the provision of TCGA 1992, s. 2(1), mirroring the provision in CTA 2009, s. 4: 'Corporation tax is charged on chargeable gains accruing to a company on the disposal of assets.'

rate[25] under the Corporation Tax Acts,[26] one needs to distinguish between profits qualifying as *income* and those qualifying as *capital gains*.

If the profits qualify as capital gains, any chargeable gain and allowable loss will be calculated broadly in accordance with the capital gains tax principles.[27] Hence, allowable capital losses can only be deducted from other capital gains in the same accounting period[28] or carried forward and offset against any future gains.[29]

Any revenues on financial assets, such as distributions on shares[30] and interest on bonds, will - as a basic rule - qualify as normal income and hence be taxed in accordance with income tax principles. The taxation of any revenues on financial assets in accordance with income tax principles is coherent because dividends and interest income are *fruits of the tree*.

In addition to the dividing line between income and capital, the legislator distinguishes between equity and debt as a further means of distinction in the context of financial instruments.

The fundamental divide between equity and debt is as follows:

Capital gains from equity and equity-based financial instruments[31] will generally be taxed under the *capital gains regime*[32] on a *realisation basis*.[33] Gains from debt, debt-based financial instruments and derivative contracts will principally fall under the income regime and be taxed on an *accounts basis*.[34]

A reason for this classification and respective tax consequences is the intention of the legislator to privilege equity risk over debt risk. As *Southern* explains it:

> [Debt] financial instruments [...] are regarded as imposing obligations to transfer benefits to third parties. These liabilities give rise to expenses of the business, and so are deductible in computing profits. Hence, debt obligations are untaxed in the paying company, and profits and gains are taxed on an accounts basis in the hands of the recipient.[35]

25. *Simon's Taxes*, vol 5, D1.1201 (issue 171); Laukkanen (2007) 165.
26. CTA 2009, CTA 2010, TIOPA 2010.
27. *Simon's Taxes*, vol 5, D1.901 (issue 171).
28. TCGA 1992, s. 8(1).
29. *Simon's Taxes*, vol 5, D1.903 (issue 171).
30. CTA 2010, s. 1000(1). *Compare* HMRC, Company Taxation Manual CTM15200 - Distributions: general: dividends and tax law: CTA10/S1000 (1) A, (16 April 2016, updated 14 July 2023).
31. Southern (2017) para. 1.5.
32. Southern (2017) para. 1.19.
33. The realisation basis or principle (for accounting and taxation purposes) means that the gain on the asset will only be taxed when the asset is disposed of or matures, thus a realisation event occurs. *See* Ch. 6 §6.01 below; also: Laukkanen (2007) 100.
34. Southern (2017) paras 1.19 and 1.20.

    Haworth and Hollis (2010) 23 identify three accounts driven regimes for non-traders under CTA 2009: the loan relationship rules, the derivative contracts rules and the intangible fixed assets rules. Accounts basis of taxation means that the income for tax purposes will be disclosed in the accounts of the company in each accounting period. An accounts basis can either be an accruals accounting or a fair value accounting basis. For a definition of these terms, *see* Ch. 6 §6.01 below.
35. Southern (2017) paras 1.5 and 1.6.

In contrast, an equity participation only provides a right of participation in the profits or gains if all debtors have been paid off beforehand.[36] Consequently, dividends paid to shareholders are non-deductible for the company '[a]s there is no assurance that any benefits will be obtained. Therefore, gains from disposals of equity interests are taxed on a *realisation basis* because such instruments carry equity risk'.[37]

The distinction between income and capital and equity and debt is still somewhat mirrored in the derivative contracts regime of CTA 2009, Part 7.

CTA 2009, Part 7 entails two regimes:

(1) As a general rule, profits from derivative contracts – whether income streams or gains from the disposal of derivatives – are treated as income for tax purposes,[38] and
(2) As an exception, capital gains from certain derivatives are subject to a capital gains regime within CTA 2009, Part 7.[39]

Despite the fact that most *equity derivatives* fall within the income regime and are taxed as derivative contracts under CTA 2009, Part 7,[40] certain explicit carve-outs still apply, namely:[41]

- Shares may qualify as excluded subject matter under CTA 2009, sections 598 and 591, or the equity derivative may already fail the accounting test of CTA 2009, section 579(1).[42]
- Certain equity derivatives held by a life insurance company, CTA 2009, s. 591(2).[43]
- An important carve-out applies to equity derivatives, where a hedging relationship between the equity derivative and the underlying equities exists, CTA 2009, s. 591(3).[44]
- Further, although embedded equity derivatives will generally fall under CTA 2009, Part 7, they will be taxed in most cases on a chargeable gains basis under CTA 2009, Part 7 Chapter 7.[45]

36. *Ibid.*, paras 1.25, 1.27 and 1.33.
37. *See* an older version of: David Southern, *Taxation of Loan Relationships and Derivative Contracts* (9th edn, Bloomsbury Professional 2012) para. 1.69.
38. An all-income regime for certain but not all derivative contracts was first established by FA 1994 and extended by FA 2002, Sch. 26; *see* Ghosh, Johnson and Miller (2022) [E2.15]-[E2.20] (issue 28).
39. Southern (2017) para. 13.5.
40. CTA 2009, s. 574.
41. *See* for an extensive discussion in relation to equity derivatives: Ghosh, Johnson and Miller (2022) [E2.432]-[E2.471] (issue 28).
42. Ghosh, Johnson and Miller (2022) [E2.432] (issue 28).
43. HMRC, Corporate Finance Manual, CFM50750). *Compare* Ghosh, Johnson and Miller (2022), [E2.437]-[E2.440] (issue 28).
44. CTA 2009, s. 591(3). *Compare* Ghosh, Johnson and Miller (2022), [E2.441]-[E2.446] (issue 28).
45. CTA 2009, ss 640, 641, 645, 648.

- Derivative contracts, which are hedging embedded derivatives that are bifurcated from loan relationships, will not be subject to the income regime, but the capital gains tax regime will apply.[46]

To reiterate, the following main taxation rules apply to relevant derivative contracts that satisfy the accounting test of CTA 2009, section 579:

Rule number one: income regime

An income regime within CTA 2009, Part 7 applies to derivative contracts

(a) whose underlying subject matter is not a chargeable asset under Chapter 7 or 8,
(b) if they are not held for the purpose of a trade, and
(c) where the underlying subject matter is not excluded under CTA 2009, section 589.[47]

Profits and losses will be assimilated to income as non-trading credits and debits[48] and will normally be brought into account on a fair value basis[49] in accordance with FRS 102 or IFRS 9.[50]

Rule number two: trading income

An income regime applies,

(a) if the derivative contract is held for trading purposes, and
(b) the underlying subject matter is not excluded under CTA 2009, section 589.[51]

Any profits and losses under the derivative contract will be assimilated to trading income.[52]

Rule number three: chargeable gains regime

A capital gains regime applies to those derivative contracts whose underlying subject matter constitutes a chargeable asset within CTA 2009, Part 7 Chapter 7 or 8,[53]

(a) if the contract is not held for the purpose of a trade,[54] and
(b) is not excluded under CTA 2009, section 589.[55]

---

46. CTA 2009, s. 591(6).
47. CTA 2009, s. 571(1).
48. CTA 2009, s. 574(1) and (2).
49. Ghosh, Johnson and Miller (2022) [E2.471] (issue 28).
50. Bramwell et al. (2023), H1.4.1.
51. *See* CTA 2009, s. 573.
52. CTA 2009, s. 573(2) and (3). *See also* Ghosh, Johnson and Miller (2022) [E2.471] (issue 28).
53. They include primarily bifurcated embedded derivative contracts from convertibles and physically settled equity derivatives, for example equity warrants.
54. This is usually the case if the contract is not held by a bank, financial trader, or collective investment scheme. *See* Southern (2017) para. 13.4.
55. CTA 2009, s. 571(2). *See* Ghosh, Johnson and Miller (2022) [E2.471] (issue 28).

The amount charged to capital gains would be the accounting profit, as determined under FRS 102.11 or IFRS 9.

Rule number four: excluded contracts

A capital gains tax regime applies to those derivative contracts which fall entirely outside of Part 7 because the underlying subject matter is excluded under CTA 2009, section 589.[56] CTA 2009, section 981(1) stipulates that those gains from financial futures, traded options and financial options are not taxed as miscellaneous income.

Derivatives related to 'excluded property'[57] are, for example:

(a) options and futures over intangible fixed assets,[58] which are chargeable to corporation tax under CTA 2009, Part 8;[59]
(b) certain relevant contracts over shares,[60] which will be subject to the rules of TCGA 1992, sections 143, 144, by virtue of TCGA 1992, s. 2(1) as amended by FA 2019 Schedule 1, referring to sections 2(1) and (2) of CTA 2009;[61]
(c) derivatives over units in a unit trust, subject to certain carve-outs for shares.[62]

The following example illustrates the remainder of the income and capital divide in the UK derivative contracts regime in the example of equity options.

Example 35:

If a company enters into a plain vanilla equity option, it will be taxed on its profits and losses in accordance with its accounts.[63] If the taxpayer applies 'fair value accounting' under FRS 102.11 or IFRS 9, any gains and losses on the option will be recognised in the accounts on a fair value basis and taxable at business year-end, irrespective of whether the option has matured. This treatment will apply regardless of whether the taxpayer is the option buyer or the option seller. If the taxpayer, however, uses the option to hedge underlying shares, the grant of an equity option will be a taxable disposal for the purposes of the capital gains tax computation[64] for corporation tax purposes and will not fall under CTA 2009, Part 7.

56. CTA 2009, [E2.471].
Any traded option over own shares within the meaning given by TCGA 1992, s. 144(8)(b) would, for example, fall under a capital gains tax regime because the underlying subject matter is excluded under CTA 2009, s. 589.
57. CTA 2009, s. 589 (2).
58. CTA 2009, s. 589 (2)(a) and (4). *Compare* Southern (2017), para. 13.3.
59. CTA 2009, s. 589 (2)(a). *Compare* Southern (2017) Ch. 13, paras 13.31 and 13.36.
60. Ghosh, Johnson and Miller (2022) [E2.432]-[E2.471] (issue 28).
61. Bramwell et al. (2023), H4.1.1-H4.2.1; Ghosh, Johnson and Miller (2022) [E2.471] (issue 28).
62. Ghosh, Johnson and Miller (2022) [E2.425] (issue 28).
63. CTA 2009, s. 595(2).
64. TCGA 1992, s. 144.

In summary, although the legislator, in principle, aimed to abolish the distinction between income and capital and equity and debt for derivative contracts and subject in principle all contracts entered into by companies to an income regime, some exceptions still apply to certain derivative contracts. They are either chargeable to corporation tax as chargeable gains within CTA 2009, Part 7,[65] or fall completely outside the taxation regime of CTA 2009, Part 7 because they entail an excluded subject matter under CTA 2009, section 589.[66]

§6.03 THE INTEGRATIVE APPROACH APPLYING TO DERIVATIVES HELD BY COMPANIES IN GERMANY

In contrast to the UK, the German tax legislator applies an integrative approach to the taxation of derivatives entered into by companies. No special taxation regime has been implemented for derivatives. Instead, the general corporate taxation rules of the Corporation Tax Act (CTA)[67] are applied.[68] As the German CTA refers to the German Income Tax Act (ITA)[69] for the purpose of determining taxable income, the provisions of the ITA will also apply to companies unless the CTA provides for more specific provisions that override the provisions of the ITA.[70]

At maturity, gains and losses from derivatives are taxed as ordinary corporate income.[71] Losses from derivatives[72] may, however, be subject to the loss ring-fencing provision of section 15(4) sentence 3 to 5 ITA.[73] This section is the only provision in the ITA that applies specifically to derivative contracts. It applies not only to non-corporate businesses but also to companies by way of reference.[74]

Under this provision, derivatives losses cannot be offset against other business income of the company but only against other derivatives gains.[75] The losses cannot be carried back or forward to set off against other business income (loss ring-fencing).[76] A loss carry back or forward is only possible against derivatives gains.[77] For a discussion of the exceptions to the derivatives loss ring-fencing rule,[78] *see* Chapter 6 §6.06 below.

65. CTA 2009, Part 7 Chs 7 and 8.
66. In those cases, TCGA 1992, ss 143, 144 will apply by virtue of TCGA 1992, s. 2(1) as amended by FA 2019 Sch. 1, referring to s. 2(1) and (2) of CTA 2009.
67. 'Körperschaftsteuergesetz' - KStG.
68. *See* Ch. 6 §6.06 for an outline of the taxation rules applying to derivatives held by companies.
69. 'Einkommensteuergesetz' - EStG.
70. Sections 7(2) and 8(1) CTA.
71. Section 8(1) CTA in conjunction with s. 15(1) ITA.
72. *See* for the discussion whether the section applies only to cash-settled derivatives or also to physically settled derivatives: Ch. 4 §4.03[C][1] and §4.03[C][2].
73. Conlon & Aquilino: Derivatives, D2.03[6].
74. Section 8(1) CTA.
75. Section 15(4) sent. 1 and 3 ITA.
76. Sections 15(4) sent. 1 2nd part, sent. 3 and s. 10d(1) ITA.
77. Section 15(4) sent. 2 and 3 ITA.
78. Section 15(4) sent. 4 and 5 ITA.

§6.04 THE DISTINCTION BETWEEN INCOME AND CAPITAL, AND BETWEEN EQUITY AND DEBT IN GERMANY

For corporate tax purposes, both ordinary business income and capital gains on bonds are subject to the same tax rate.[79] Interest received is fully taxable, and interest paid is, in principle, deductible subject to certain exceptions under the debt cap provisions.[80]

Equity investments made by corporate taxpayers are subject to a favourable tax regime. Section 8b(2) CTA provides a 95% corporate tax exemption for equity capital gains from the disposal of shares.[81] Section 8b(1) provides a 95% exemption for non-portfolio dividends. For trade tax purposes, non-portfolio dividends are only exempt if the company receiving the dividends holds 15% or more of the share capital, section 9 No. 2a Trade Tax Act (TTA). In contrast, equity capital gains from the disposal of shares are 95% tax-exempt for trade tax purposes.[82]

A total of 5% of the dividends and capital gains are deemed as non-deductible expenses for corporation tax purposes.[83] Correspondingly, any losses from the disposal of shares or expenses in the context of write-downs in the shareholding are disallowed.[84]

The legislator has exempted equity capital gains from the disposal of shares from corporation tax because the gains have already been subject to corporation tax at the level of the shareholding held by the corporate taxpayer.

Portfolio dividends were initially 95% tax-exempt for corporation tax purposes.[85] In 2009, a decision of the Court of Justice of the European Union (CJEU) forced Germany to either introduce a complete exemption of dividends for both domestic and foreign corporate shareholders or, alternatively, to also tax portfolio dividends in the hands of domestic corporate shareholders.[86]

The German tax legislator then opted for the taxation of portfolio dividends where the shareholding consists of less than 10% of the share capital.[87] Dividends will be, in principle, subject to economic double taxation due to taxation at the company level and again at the level of the corporate shareholder. Dividends remain 95% tax-free for corporate tax purposes if the shareholding is 10% or more of the share capital at the beginning of the calendar year.[88]

79. Section 8(2) CTA. Exceptions only apply in cases of certain unincorporated associations, foundations and other societies within the meaning of s. 1(1) No. 4 to No. 6 CTA.
80. Ch. 6 §6.06[A].
81. Section 8b(1), (2) and (4) CTA.
82. Section 7 TTA.
83. Sections 8b(3) sent. 1 CTA (equity capital gains) and 8b(5) sent. 1 CTA (dividends).
84. Section 8b(3) sent. 3 CTA.
85. Portfolio dividends were and are still subject to German trade tax (s. 8 No. 5 TTA).
86. C-284/09 *Commission v. Germany* [2011] ECR I-09879.
87. Section 8b(4) sent. 1 CTA.
88. A shareholding of at least 10% that is acquired during the calendar year is deemed to be acquired at the beginning of the calendar year and thus falls under the dividend exemption of s. 8b(1) CTA.

Regarding derivatives, gains from the disposal of shares received or delivered in the context of physically settled derivatives are 95% tax-free,[89] whereas cash-settled derivatives are taxed as ordinary business income.[90]

The distinction between equity and debt also has relevance in relation to the loss ring-fencing provision of section 15(4) sentence 3 ITA. The loss ring-fencing provision does not apply if the taxpayer is a bank, credit institution, financial service company or financial company[91] and if the derivative belongs to the regular course of business of those taxpayers.[92]

In addition, the loss ring-fencing provision does not apply to other taxpayers if the derivative is used to hedge business activities that are 'part of the regular course of the taxpayer's business'.[93]

Both carve-outs do not apply, and the derivatives losses are ring-fenced if the derivative is used to hedge *equity positions* that would qualify as *tax-exempt* for the taxpayer.[94]

Thus, for banks, other financial services institutions and financial companies, derivatives losses are not ring-fenced if they hedge equity positions that are attributed to the trading book of a bank or a financial services institution[95] or if they hedge equity positions that had been acquired with the aim of making a short-term trading profit (in case of financial companies).[96]

However, if the equities are attributed to the banking book of a bank[97] or to the fixed assets (*Anlagevermögen*)[98] of a financial company, any derivatives losses in conjunction with the hedge of the equities will be ring-fenced.[99]

89. The 95% tax exemption for equity capital gains under s. 8b(2) CTA also applies to the subsequent disposal of shares that were delivered under a physically settled equity derivative. The physical settlement of the derivative is treated as a tax neutral acquisition of the underlying shares.
90. Conlon & Aquilino: Derivatives, D2.03[6] (issue December 2022).
91. Financial companies are those within the meaning of s. 1(3) *Kreditwesengesetz* (German Banking Act).
92. Section 15(4) sent. 4 1st alt ITA. *See* Conlon & Aquilino: Derivatives D2.03[6]; Haisch and Helios (2011) 269.
93. Sections 8(1) CTA, 15(4) sent. 4 2nd alt ITA. *See also* Conlon & Aquilino: Derivatives D2.03[6]; also: Haisch and Helios (2011) 270-274.
94. Section 15(4) sent. 5 ITA. *See also* Conlon & Aquilino: Derivatives D2.03[6].
95. Sections 8b(7) sent. 1 CTA, 15(4) sent. 5 ITA.
96. If financial companies attribute the equities to the current assets, it will be assumed that they were acquired with the aim to make short-term trading profits. *Compare* sections 8b(7) sent. 2 CTA, 15(4) sent. 5 ITA. *See* Haisch and Helios (2011) 276.
97. If a bank attributes the equities to the banking book, they will be normally be accounted for as fixed assets (s. 340e(1) sent. 1 CLA). *Compare* Paul Scharpf and Mathias Schaber, *Handbuch Bankbilanz* (3rd edn, IDW Verlag 2009) 183-184.
98. The term *Anlagevermögen* (fixed assets or permanent assets) is used in German GAAP for those assets which are designated for long-term use in the company. This term includes fixed tangible assets, fixed intangible assets as well as financial assets. In contrast, *Umlaufvermögen* (current assets) under German GAAP are those assets of a company which are designated for short-term, non-permanent use in the company.
99. Häuselmann (2005) 47; Conlon & Aquilino: Derivatives, D2.03[6].

§6.05 THE UK TAXATION RULES ON DERIVATIVE CONTRACTS ENTERED INTO BY COMPANIES

This section analyses key aspects of the taxation of derivatives entered into by corporate taxpayers in the UK. Anti-avoidance rules in relation to derivatives and the approach to risk transfer schemes in the UK have been discussed in Chapters 7 and 10.

The UK legislator has developed a comprehensive taxation regime for derivatives held only by companies because derivatives are not widely used by private investors, except in the cases of structured retail products,[100] certain listed derivatives,[101] and employee share option schemes.[102]

[A] The General Taxation Principles for Companies

UK resident companies are chargeable to corporation tax on all profits wherever they arise, i.e., all their worldwide income.[103] For corporation tax purposes, any body corporate or unincorporated association[104] qualifies as a company, but partnerships and local authority associations are excluded.[105] Trustees of an authorised unit trust are treated as a company.[106]

A non-UK resident company is only liable to corporation tax in the UK if:

(a) it carries on a trade of dealing in or developing UK land,[107]
(b) it carries on a trade in the United Kingdom (other than a trade of dealing in or developing UK land) through a permanent establishment in the United Kingdom,
(c) it carries on a UK property business, or
(d) it has other UK property income.[108]

Whereas individuals and non-corporate business investors are subject to income tax under the income tax rules and subject to capital gains tax under the TCGA 1992, a company is not subject to capital gains tax.[109] Instead, all income *and* capital gains are chargeable under the Corporation Tax Acts.[110]

100. Ghosh, Johnson and Miller (2022) [E1.52]-[E1.60] (issue 28).
101. These were taxed under TCGA 1992, ss 143, 144.
102. Now taxed under ITEPA 2003, ss 417ff.
103. CTA 2009, s. 5(1).
104. An unincorporated association is not defined in the law. They include trade associations and member clubs. *See* Simon's Taxes, vol 5, D1.104 (issue 171).
105. CTA 2009, s. 1121(1).
106. CTA 2009, s. 617(1)(a). The unit holders of the trust are treated as if they were holding shares in that company, *see* CTA 2009, s. 617(1)(b).
107. CTA 2009, s. 5B.
108. CTA 2009, ss 5(2), 9.
109. CTA 2009, s. 4. *See* Simon's Taxes, vol 5, D.1.901 (issue 171).
110. *See* CTA 2009, s. 2(2).

Before 2009, the UK operated a credit system for dividends. Since 1 July 2009, dividends and other distributions[111] both from domestic and non-domestic sources are – in principle – subject to corporation tax unless they are exempt under certain threshold conditions.[112] The dividend tax exemption applies if:

(1) the distribution falls within five exempt classes,[113]
(2) it is not excluded from these classes by anti-avoidance provisions,[114] and
(3) the distribution is not deductible in a foreign jurisdiction.[115]

[B] Taxation of Derivatives Income

The following section entails an analysis of the tax treatment of derivative contracts held by companies in the UK.

The definition of a derivative contract under CTA 2009, Part 7 has been discussed in detail in Chapter 4. In the context of this chapter, the author discusses the taxation of certain types of derivatives, such as futures, options and swaps, as well as derivatives over specific underlying variables, such as equity derivatives, crypto derivatives and ESG derivatives.

More general issues, such as the alignment of accounting standards and tax law in the context of derivatives,[116] the accounting and tax treatment of derivative contracts that are used for hedging purposes,[117] and accounting and taxation rules in relation to embedded derivatives,[118] have been discussed in the respective chapters of this work.

Specific anti-avoidance rules in relation to domestic[119] and cross-border derivatives transactions[120] have been discussed in Chapter 10.[121] The UK approach to risk transfer schemes[122] has been outlined in Chapter 7 §7.04[B].

The Corporation Tax Acts dealing with the taxation of income and chargeable gains as well as company distributions are the Corporation Tax Act 2009, Corporation Tax Act 2010 and Taxation (International and Other Provisions) Act 2010, which were enacted in the course of the Tax Law Re-write project.

111. That applies regardless of whether the dividends or distributions are of an income or capital nature. *See* Finance (No. 3) Act 2010, Sch. 3 para. 3(2); CTA 2010, s. 1000(1); *also* Freshfields (2012) 46.
112. CTA 2009, s. 931A.
113. CTA 2009, ss. 931D(a), 931E–931I.
114. CTA 2009, ss 931J-Q.
115. CTA 2009, s. 931D(c).
116. Ch. 6 §6.02[D].
117. Ch. 7 §7.03[A].
118. Ch. 8 §8.05.
119. CTA 2009, ss 606A-H, 629, 690, 695, 698.
120. CTA 2009, ss 696 and 697.
121. Ch. 10 §10.01.
122. CTA 2010, Part 21A.

[1] *Analysis of Historical Change of Rules and Policy Background*

Due to various tax policy reasons, such as:

(1) providing a more simplified but coherent regime for the taxation of derivatives,[123]
(2) the need to provide comprehensive and reliable rules for companies using derivative contracts in the UK,
(3) overcoming difficulties in the context of the income and capital distinction,[124] and
(4) aligning tax legislation to accounting standards,[125]

the UK tax legislator has changed the rules regarding corporate taxation of derivatives substantially since 1993.[126]

A look at the historical development of the derivative contracts legislation will help to understand the initial principles and policy behind the derivative contracts rules.

Before the introduction of the financial instrument rules in FA 1994,[127] which were accompanied by the foreign exchange rules[128] and the loan relationship rules,[129] no comprehensive rules for the taxation of derivatives income existed.[130] Instead, all income and capital gains from derivative contracts held by companies not on trading accounts[131] were either taxed under Sch D Case VI[132] or under the chargeable gains rules.[133]

Because of tax disparities in the treatment of derivative contracts and the tax arbitrage opportunities arising due to the distinction between income and capital when taxing derivative contracts, the legislator abolished this distinction[134] and opted for an

123. HM Treasury, Corporation tax reform – A consultation document (LNB News 13 August 2003) 1.5.
124. Ghosh, Johnson and Miller (2022) [E 2.4] (issue 28).
125. Southern (2017) para. 2.1.
126. Foreign exchange rules were introduced by FA 1993, and financial instrument rules by FA 1994.
For a detailed description of the historical changes in the taxation of derivative contracts, *see* Ghosh, Johnson and Miller (2022) [E2.1]-[E2.30B] (issue 28); *see also* HMRC, CFM83010-CFM83050.
127. FA 1994, ss 147-177 and Sch. 18 and SI 1994/3233.
128. FA 1993, ss 60, 92-96, 125-170, Sch. 15-18; SI 1994/3226-3232.
129. FA 1996, ss 80-105 and Sch. 8-15.
130. Ghosh, Johnson and Miller (2022) [E2.1] (issue 28).
131. Companies, which held derivative contracts for trading purposes, such as banks and securities dealers, were able to tax all profits and losses from derivative contracts based on their accounts also under the pre-FA 1994 rules. *Compare* Ghosh, Johnson and Miller (2022) [E2.2]
132. This was mainly the case for profits from financial or commodity futures before 6 April 1985. Later, both exchange-traded financial futures (from 6 April 1985) and OTC forwards and traded and financial options (from 29 April 1988) were brought into the capital gains regime.
133. Ghosh, Johnson and Miller (2022) [E2.3] (issue 28).
134. Inland Revenue, Technical Note on tax legislation for exchange gains and losses, derivative financial instruments, and corporate and government debt (8 November 2000).

all-income regime in the FA 1993 FX rules, the FA 1994 financial instrument rules, and the FA 1996 loan relationship rules. Thus, all income and expenditure, as well as all capital gains and losses, which fell within the rules, were treated as arising on revenue and not on capital account,[135] with the consequence that capital was recognised and measured on an accounts basis[136] and not on a realisation basis.[137]

The financial instruments regime of FA 1994 was, however, not comprehensive enough as it only applied to a restricted set of 'qualified contracts' and 'qualifying payments'[138] and did not cover newly emerging derivatives, such as credit derivatives, which fell outside the regime. Because of a combination of a 'following the accounts' approach and an approach that subjected only certain derivatives to the taxation regime, tax arbitrage opportunities were created, especially in the area of FX derivatives.[139]

To overcome the shortcomings of the financial instruments regime in FA 1994, the rules were replaced by the derivative contracts regime of FA 2002, Schedule 26.[140] Under FA 2002, Schedule 26, several steps were taken towards a regime that permitted more comprehensive taxation of derivative contracts.

First, derivatives relating to foreign exchange were brought within the derivative contracts regime.[141]

Second, the FA 2002, Schedule 26 rules aligned the tax treatment of derivative contracts more closely to the accounting treatment.[142] As the relevant accounting standard FRS 13 at the time of introduction of FA 2002, Schedule 26 did not provide detailed accounting treatment of all derivative contracts covered by Schedule 26, 'there was some concern about whether the accounting treatment was sufficiently clear or robust'[143] as a basis for taxing derivative contracts.

To provide certainty for tax purposes, profits and losses recognised in the accounts were only a basis for taxation if an 'authorised accounting basis', being either

135. Southern (2017) paras 1.105ff.
136. Ghosh, Johnson and Miller (2022) [E2.13] (issue 28).
137. Shares were outside the regime as they are not regarded as falling under the rules but are non-monetary assets for which the capital gains treatment and hence the realisation principle still applied.
138. The FA 1994 rules did not look at the P&L of the derivative contract as a whole but instead only taxed and relieved single 'qualifying payments'. *Compare* Ghosh, Johnson and Miller (2022) [E2.13] (issue 28).
139. *See Prudential plc v. HMRC* [2009] EWCA Civ 622 for a foreign exchange related derivatives transaction that tried to generate a tax arbitrage opportunity for the taxpayer. In the case, upfront payments were made in the context of foreign currency swaps to hedge foreign currency exposure in respect of two loans. The taxpayer sought a deduction for corporation tax purposes with respect to those upfront payments. The Special Commissioners (*Prudential plc v. HMRC* [2007] UKSPC SPC00636), the High Court and then the Court of Appeal held that those payments did not qualify as 'qualifying payments' and therefore dismissed the case. *Compare* Ghosh, Johnson and Miller (2022) [E2.14] (issue 28).
140. *Ibid.*, [E2.15]; Southern (2012) para. 1.108.
141. FA 2002, Sch. 26, para. 16(1). *See* Ghosh, Johnson and Miller (2022) [E2.16] (issue 28); Simon's Taxes, vol 5 D1.801 (issue 171).
142. Ghosh, Johnson and Miller (2022) [E2.15] (issue 28).
143. *Ibid.*, [E2.15]; Southern (2004) para. 17.73.

the accruals or the mark-to-market method,[144] was used.[145] The introduction of the accounting standards IAS 39 and FRS 26 as a basis for taxation solved the problem of comprehensiveness of the accounting standards for derivatives, but at the same time, required extensive changes to the existing legislation,[146] thus leading to a new complexity of the derivative contracts regime.

The third major difference of FA 2002, Schedule 26 in comparison to the financial instrument rules of FA 1994 was that Schedule 26 covered a wide range of derivative contracts as 'relevant contracts',[147] including both stand-alone derivatives as well as embedded derivatives.[148] In addition, the Treasury had the power to extend or narrow the scope of the regime, thereby enabling the Treasury to react more swiftly to newly emerging derivative contracts and product innovation.[149]

The definition of derivative contracts in FA 2002, Schedule 26, was, however, criticised as being too unclear to determine what fell within the Schedule and what outside, as it was one of 'inclusions and exclusions that no overall concept of a "derivative contract" as such emerges'.[150]

The intention of the derivative contracts regime of FA 2002, Schedule 26 was to bring all derivatives into an income regime,[151] except for certain contracts where the underlying subject matter was shares or chargeable assets.[152]

Those derivatives were in a first step included within Schedule 26[153] but not taxed under the income regime rules as all other derivatives.[154] Instead, a capital gains regime applied to those derivative contracts with gains and losses treated as chargeable gains and losses for corporation tax purposes,[155] provided they were not held by a bank, financial trader or collective investment scheme.[156]

The original rules in FA 2002, Schedule 26 were subject to several amendments by FA 2004, FA 2005 and various Statutory Instruments[157] in order 'to ensure that companies could expect broadly the same after-tax result for equivalent transactions accounted for under old UK GAAP, new UK GAAP or IFRS'.[158]

144. Former FA 2002, Sch. 26, para. 17(1).
145. David Southern, Tolley's Taxation of Corporate Debt, Foreign Exchange and Derivative Contracts (6th edn, Tolley LexisNexis 2002) para. 18.1.
146. Ghosh, Johnson and Miller (2022) [E2.17] (issue 28); Southern (2012) para. 16.13.
147. FA 2002, Sch. 26, para. 2(2). *See* Simon's Taxes, vol 5, D1.801 (issue 171).
148. Southern (2012) para. 16.1.
149. FA 2002, Sch. 26, para. 13.
The provision was amended by FA 2004, Sch. 9, para. 2, and is now contained in CTA 2009, s. 701.
150. Southern (2004) para. 17.73.
151. *Simon's Taxes*, vol 5, D1.801 (issue 171).
152. Derivative contracts falling under this exception were mainly equity and property derivatives, *see* FA 2002, Sch. 26, para. 45.
153. FA 2002, Sch. 26, paras 45-45M; Southern (2007) para. 16.30.
154. Southern (2007) para. 16.30.
155. FA 2002, Sch. 26, para. 45A.
156. Southern (2007) para. 16.2.
157. For example, SI 2004/2201, SI 2004/3256, SI 2005/646, SI 2005/2012 and SI 2005/3256.
158. *Ibid.*, para. 15.51.

Certain derivatives, previously excluded, were included in the derivative contracts regime,[159] such as property derivatives (including derivatives on land and tangible movable property) and embedded derivatives whose underlying subject matter is shares[160] or tracking contracts whose subject matter is land or listed ordinary shares.[161] Those contracts were brought into a special regime within the derivative contracts regime but nevertheless granted capital gains tax treatment for credits and debits on derivative contracts having those underlying subject matters or in case of loan relationships with embedded derivatives.[162]

In addition, FA 2002, Schedule 26 was redrafted to bring most equity derivatives within the income regime, except for those equity derivatives used for non-trading purposes to hedge shares (Schedule 26 paragraph 4).[163] In those cases, FA 2002, Schedule 26 did not apply. Profits and losses on those derivatives were treated as chargeable gains and allowable losses under the capital gains tax regime.[164]

Amending the derivative contracts regime to include almost all derivatives has been successful insofar as Schedule 26 provided a framework to deal with the taxation of derivatives comprehensively. Those amendments, however, led to very complex corporate tax legislation on derivatives that spanned three Schedules (FA 2002, Schedule 26 to Schedule 28) and more than fifty paragraphs. Furthermore, the rules effectively maintained the distinction between income and capital as two different regimes applied to derivatives within FA 2002, Schedule 26.[165]

In addition, equity derivatives held for non-hedging purposes were subject to tax as chargeable gains. The application of different sets of rules and the distinction between an income and capital gains tax regime within FA 2002, Schedule 26 and equity and debt also caused problems of legal qualification in the context of cross-border transactions.[166]

In the author's view, the intense effort of HMRC to establish a comprehensive regime for derivative contracts was partly driven by the importance of such a regime for the growth of the UK financial sector, and partly to counteract tax avoidance schemes.

As London has established itself globally as one of the most important markets for complex and/or OTC derivatives, a robust and reliable regime for the taxation of

159. The Finance Act 2002, Schedule 26, Part 2 and 9 (Amendment) No. 2 Order 2004, SI 2004/3270.
160. FA 2002, Sch. 26, para. 2(3).
161. FA 2002, para. 45F.
162. FA 2002, para. 45A(1); FA 1996, s. 94A. For a detailed analysis of the amended legislation: John Lindsay, 'Derivative Contracts' in Antony Brown (ed), *CCH British Tax Reporter, Taxation of Companies*, vol 7 (Wolters Kluwer (UK) 2005); *see also* Ghosh, Johnson and Miller (2022) [E2.20] (issue 28)
163. Explanatory Memorandum, The Finance Act 2002, Schedule 26, Part 2 and 9 (Amendment) Order 2005 (SI 2005 No. 646).
164. TCGA 1992, s. 143.
165. Those regimes are the income regime for all derivatives whose underlying subject matters were not chargeable assets and the chargeable gains regime for those derivatives, whose underlying subject matters were chargeable assets.
166. Conlon & Aquilino: Derivatives, D1.03[4] (issue December 2022).

derivative contracts was necessary to foster economic growth. However, in addition to the development of the derivatives market, banks and securities firms also used the instruments as a means for tax arbitrage strategies.[167] HMRC counteracted those schemes not only by enacting comprehensive legislation concerning the taxation of loan relationships and derivatives[168] but also by introducing specific anti-avoidance rules within these taxation regimes.[169]

[2] Taxation of Derivative Contracts under CTA 2009, Part 7

As a rule, 'all profits arising to a company from its derivative contracts are chargeable to corporation tax as income in accordance with' CTA 2009, Part 7.[170] As a result of CTA 2009, section 571(1), the distinction between derivative contracts entered into on trading account or on capital account has been largely eliminated.[171] However, certain derivative contracts are chargeable to corporation tax as chargeable gains if they fall under Chapter 7 or 8[172] of CTA 2009, Part 7.[173] Other derivatives with an excluded subject matter under CTA 2009, section 589 will fall completely outside the taxation regime of CTA 2009, Part 7, but TCGA 1992, sections 143, 144 will apply by way of referral of CTA 2009, section 2(2) and TCGA 1992, section 2(1).[174]

How profits or losses are brought into account for the purposes of the derivative contracts regime has been part of the accounting discussion in Chapter 5.[175] As a general rule, the amounts to be brought into account as credits or debits from a derivatives transaction by a company 'are those which are recognised in determining the company's profit or loss for the period in accordance with the generally accepted accounting practice'.[176]

Before discussing the taxation of various forms of derivatives, such as options, futures and swaps, as well as the tax treatment of derivatives on various underlyings, the author briefly outlines the difference between contracts entered for trading and non-trading purposes as well as the treatment of expenses.

167. Tax arbitrage strategies by banks were mostly designed to use loopholes provided by the law and were backed by legal opinions of law firms as banks wanted to avoid entering into illegal tax-evasion schemes. *See* House of Commons and House of Lords *Parliamentary Commission on Banking Standards*, 5 February 2013, Q3649 to Q 3660, discussing the market activities of the Structured Capital Markets division at Barclays.
168. Ghosh, Johnson and Miller (2022) [E2.4] (issue 28) provides an example of how the anomalies under the pre-FA 1994 regime created tax arbitrage opportunities for taxpayers.
169. FA 1996, Sch. 9 and FA 2002, Sch. 26, paras 23 and 24.
170. CTA 2009, s. 571(1). *See* Southern (2017) para. 13.3.
171. Ghosh, Johnson and Miller (2022) [E3.11] (issue 28).
172. Chapter 8 contains ss 660-673.
173. CTA 2009, s. 571(2) and ss 639(1), (2). Note that CTA 2009, s. 571(2) only refers to Ch. 7, not to Ch. 8.
174. Ghosh, Johnson and Miller (2022) [E3.471] (issue 28).
175. Ch. 5 §5.02[A], §5.02[B] and §5.02[D].
176. CTA 2009, s. 595(2).

[a] Derivative Contracts Entered into for Trading and Non-trading Purposes

Companies can conclude derivative contracts either for trading[177] or non-trading purposes.[178] As CTA 2009, section 573(1) does not define 'for the purpose of a trade', one has to rely on the ordinary commercial meaning of the term.[179]

Under CTA 2010, section 1119, which applies to the income of a company for corporation tax purposes, the term 'trade' 'includes any venture in the nature of trade'.[180] As this statutory provision is not precise enough to determine what a trade actually is, the meaning of 'trade' must be sought from case law[181] in connection with the badges of trade.[182] Banks and other financial traders that deal in derivative contracts will normally enter those contracts for the purpose of a trade.[183]

For companies which are not banks or financial traders, it depends on the intention of the parties whether the contract was entered for the purpose of the trade.[184] A derivative contract may also be acquired for trading purposes, even if the company uses the derivative contract for purposes that are ancillary to trading operations carried out.[185]

Vice versa, '[a] company will have a non-trading derivative contract if it is not a party to a derivative contract for the purposes of its trade. For example, if [...] as a trading company, it holds derivative contracts for investment or speculative purposes, or to hedge a non-trading asset or liability, such as a loan taken out to acquire shares in a subsidiary'.[186]

There are also cases where derivative contracts are acquired for the purpose of the trade by a company and which are entered into for the purpose of hedging exposure to risk in a commercial financial transaction.

177. CTA 2009, s. 573(1).
178. CTA 2009, s. 574(2).
179. Ghosh, Johnson and Miller (2022) [E3.11] (issue 28); *Simon's Taxes*, vol 5, D1.875 (issue 171).
180. Former ICTA 1988, s. 832(1) defined a trade as including 'every trade, manufacture, adventure, or concern in the nature of a trade'.
181. In *CIR v. Livingston* [1926] 11 TC 538, 542 Lord Clyde defined the term 'in the nature of trade', as 'whether the operations involved in it are of the same kind, and carried on in the same way, as those which are characteristic of ordinary trading in the line of business in which the venture was made'. In *Ransom v. Higgs* [1974] 50 TC 1, 78I Lord Reid defined a trade as 'operations of a commercial character by which the trader provides to the customers for reward some kind of goods or services'. For distinguishing investment from trading regarding the subject matter of realisation, *see Rutledge v. IRC* [1929] 14 TC 490 and *Trustees of the British Telecom Pension Schemes v. Clark (Inspector of Taxes)* [2000] STC 222.
182. Royal Commission, Final Report on the Taxation of Profits and Income (Cmd 9474, 1955) and *Marson v. Morton and Others* [1986] 59 TC 381, 391-392.
183. HMRC, CFM51030.
184. If the contract was entered into for speculative purposes, it will not be entered for the purposes of the trade. If the derivative was entered into for hedging or investment purposes, the contract would be entered for the purpose of the trade. In *Morgan Grenfell Ltd v. Welwyn Hatfield District Council* [1995] 1 All ER 1, it was discussed whether interest-rate swaps entered by local authorities were gaming and wagering contracts, or not.
185. HMRC, CFM51030.
186. *Ibid.*

Example 36:

A textile manufacturing company wants to protect itself against the rising prices of cotton to secure its profit margins on the garments it sells. The company enters into cotton futures or call options on cotton to hedge its exposure against rising cotton prices in the future. The cotton futures or options will be entered for the purpose of the trade to hedge the raw material prices.

Hedging for the purpose of the trade may involve broader activities than the typical hedging against rising commodity prices by a manufacturing company.

Example 37:

A textile manufacturing company wants to purchase cotton for its production. It borrows money from a bank to purchase this cotton at a floating interest rate. To hedge its interest rate exposure, it concludes a floating-for-fixed interest-rate swap with another bank, under which it pays a fixed interest rate and receives a floating interest rate. The interest rate it receives under the swap is used to hedge its exposure under its outstanding floating interest rate loan. From a tax perspective, the company has entered into the interest-rate swap for the purpose of its trade.

In other cases, it may, however, be more difficult to determine whether the derivatives transaction entered into is for the purpose of the trade or not, even if hedging is involved.

Example 38:

Company A is a property developing company. The company concludes derivative contracts in order to hedge against falling prices of commercial property. The profits or losses of the property business will be subject to tax under CTA 2009, Part 4, not under Part 3 as trading income.[187] Consequently, the derivative contracts used to hedge the property business will be taxed under the non-trading rules of CTA 2009, section 574(2).

Different taxation results follow depending on whether the derivative contract is entered by the company for the purpose of a trade or not.[188] CTA 2009, section 573(1)

187. The profits of the company will be taxed as property income under CTA 2009, Part 4, ss 202-291, not as trading income under CTA 2009, Part 3.
188. Ch. 6 §6.02.

provides that all trading credits and debits under a derivative contract for the purpose of the company's trade will be brought into account under CTA 2009, Part 3, the credits being taxable as trading receipts.[189] Any debits will be deductible as expenses of the trade,[190] even if they would normally not be deductible under the general corporation tax regime because they are of a capital nature.[191] Special loss relief rules are not applicable because any debits can be offset against trading income in the same way as any other trading losses under CTA 2009, Part 3.[192]

In contrast, any credits or debits, where the derivative contract is not entered for the purpose of a trade, are treated as if they were non-trading credits or debits under the loan relationship rules of CTA 2009, Part 5.[193] Thus, they are taxed and relieved the same way as non-trading loan relationship credits and debits. Regarding losses, any non-trading losses can be offset against other income and profits of the same accounting period, carried back against non-trading income for up to twelve months and carried forward against non-trading profits.[194]

The trading and non-trading distinction is also important for derivative contracts, which fall within Chapter 7 of CTA 2009, Part 7. If those contracts are held for the purpose of the trade, any credits or debits will be brought into account under CTA 2009, Part 3 as trading credits or debits. If the derivative contract is entered for non-trading purposes, the special rules of Chapter 7 will apply, and any credits or debits may be subject to corporation tax as chargeable gains, and any debits may be relieved as allowable losses.[195] However, with regard to non-embedded equity derivatives, this capital treatment will not apply. Instead, any profits or losses on those derivatives will be charged as income.[196]

[b] Profits and Losses of Derivative Contracts under CTA 2009, Section 595(3)(a)

Whether the credits or debits will be taxed is subject to the provision of CTA 2009, section 595(3). CTA 2009, section 595(3)(a) requires that the 'credits and debits must be the amounts which, taken together, *fairly represent* the profits and losses arising to the company for the period from its derivative contracts and *related transactions* (excluding expenses)'.[197]

Profits and losses are insofar distinguished from expenses, which are relievable only under the conditions of CTA 2009, section 595(3)(b).[198] They include both capital

189. CTA 2009, s. 573(2).
190. CTA 2009, s. 573(3).
191. CTA 2009, s. 573 takes precedence over the general rules of CTA 2009, ss 53, 54. *See* Bramwell et al. (2023), H1.4.18; *Simon's Taxes*, vol 5, D1.875 (issue 171).
192. Ghosh, Johnson and Miller (2022) [E3.13] (issue 28).
193. CTA 2009, s. 574(2).
194. Ghosh, Johnson and Miller (2022) [E3.14] (issue 28).
195. *Ibid.*, [E3.16]-[E3.20].
196. CTA 2009, s. 572.
197. HMRC, CFM51040.
198. Ghosh, Johnson and Miller (2022) [E3.51] (issue 28).

profits and losses as well as any income amounts.[199] CTA 2009, section 53, which deals with capital expenditure, is disapplied for trading credits and debits in respect of derivative contracts of a company[200] with the result that no distinction between capital and income is made.[201] The profits or losses in CTA 2009, section 595(3) are calculated based on the gross credits and debits, which, taken together, constitute the profit or the loss.[202]

What is meant by the terms 'fairly represent' and 'related transactions' has been discussed in two cases.

In *DCC Holdings v. HMRC*,[203] the Court of Appeal suggested that the term 'fairly represent' in the context of the pre-2007 repo rules meant a 'sensible, realistic and just result' and that adjustments can be made to the correct accounting treatment if it reflects this result.[204]

In the derivative contracts legislation, a 'related transaction' is defined in section 596(1) as 'any disposal or acquisition (in whole or in part) of rights or liabilities under the contract'.[205]

The case *HBOS Treasury Services plc v. HMRC*[206] concerned a failed tax avoidance scheme, where it was intended to novate a derivatives transaction for creditworthiness reasons of the counterparty without triggering a latent tax liability.

The case discussed whether an amendment agreement to a derivative contract could constitute a 'related transaction' within the meaning of FA 2002, Schedule 26 paragraph 28, now CTA 2009, section 625.[207] Although it was held that the novation of a swap was a 'related transaction' within the meaning of FA 2002, Schedule 26, paragraph 28, it was decided that the new swaps were not 'equivalent' to the old swaps, although their terms were nearly identical because of an additional termination event added to the new swaps, however unlikely the termination event was to be exercised.[208] Although the judge maintained that he decided purely on technical grounds,[209] it seems that the strict interpretation of the term 'equivalence condition' was applied because the case concerned a tax avoidance scheme.[210]

---

199. *Ibid.*
200. CTA 2009, s. 573(4)(a).
201. Ghosh, Johnson and Miller (2022) [E3.52] (issue 28).
202. *See Gallagher v. Jones* [1993] STC 537 for the definition of the term 'profit'.
203. *DCC Holdings v. HMRC* [2010] STC 80 (CA). The decision was upheld by the UK Supreme Court: *HMRC v. DCC Holdings (UK) Limited*, paras 25-26 and 41-44. For an extensive discussion of the case, Ghosh, Johnson and Miller (2022) [E3.54]-[E3.61D] (issue 28).
204. *DCC Holdings v. HMRC*, para. 108. The former repo legislation was effectively subject to a purposive interpretation of the law as the Court of Appeal used the term 'fairly represents' as a means to alter the tax treatment which was based on a correct accounting treatment.
205. CTA 2009, s. 596(1).
206. *HBOS Treasury Services plc v. HMRC* [2009] UKFTT 261 (TC), [2010] SFTD 134.
207. The intention of the taxpayer was that the novation of the swap should be tax neutral under FA 2002, Sch. 26 para. 28, now CTA 2009, s. 625.
208. Ghosh, Johnson and Miller (2022) [E3.63K]-[E3.63N] (issue 28).
209. *HBOS Treasury Services v. HMRC*, para. 86.
210. Ghosh, Johnson and Miller (2022) [E3.63P] (issue 28) suggest that HMRC is more likely to raise these technical issues in tax avoidance schemes than in purely commercial cases. The

[c] *Expenses Incurred in Relation to Derivative Contracts*

CTA 2009, sections 595(3)(b) and (4) provide that only direct expenses incurred by the company in relation to derivative contracts are deductible, namely expenses:

> incurred directly –
>
> (a) in bringing any of the derivative contracts to existence,
> (b) in entering into or giving effect to any of the related transactions,
> (c) in making payments under any of those contracts or as a result of any of those transactions, or
> (d) in taking steps to ensure the receipt of payments under any of those contracts or in accordance with any of those transactions.[211]

The courts have already dealt with expenses in relation to derivative contracts under the old FA 2002, Schedule 26 paragraph 15(1)(b) rules. In *HBOS Treasury Services plc v. HMRC*, the court held that a fee in relation to an amendment of swap contracts could be regarded as an expense with respect to related transactions of a derivative contract under FA 2002, Schedule 26 paragraph 15(1)(b), now CTA 2009, section 595(3)(b), (4)(b).[212]

Other common expenses are those costs incurred in bringing derivative contracts into existence, such as arrangement fees, commissions, option premiums or costs of checking the creditworthiness of the counterparty of the derivative.[213]

Example 39:

Company A needs to protect against rising Aluminium prices for its manufacturing business. Hence, Company A buys Aluminium futures. The commission Company A pays the broker to purchase Aluminium futures is a direct expense in relation to the futures and, hence, deductible according to CTA 2009, section 595(4)(a).[214]

Although HMRC tends to favour a wider interpretation of what direct expenses are in relation to loan relationship rules,[215] it is yet uncertain what exactly the types of expenses are which are regarded as relievable.

---

interpretation of the 'equivalence condition' by the judge seems to me too narrow because the only difference was an extra termination right, which was highly unlikely to make a difference in economic terms.

211. CTA 2009, s. 595(4)(a) to (d) mentions only four cases, in which expenses incurred are deductible. Those expenses must be incurred directly on one of the activities specified in the legislation.
212. *HBOS Treasury Services v. HMRC*, para. 116.
213. HMRC, CFM51090; Ghosh, Johnson and Miller (2022) [E3.64] (issue 28).
214. For other examples of direct expenses: HMRC, CFM51090.
215. Ghosh, Johnson and Miller (2022) [E3.65] (issue 28).

Example 40:

Company A considers buying a credit protection from Bank C in relation to a credit exposure Company A has against Company B because it purchased a corporate bond that was issued by Company B. Before entering into a credit default swap with Bank C in relation to the corporate bond issued by Company B, Company A incurs additional costs in determining the likelihood of a credit default of Company B. Those costs may not be regarded as direct expenses in relation to the CDS because these are costs for the company incurred in deciding whether it should enter into the CDS at all. It could be argued that those costs do not directly relate to bringing the derivative contract into existence but are pre-contract expenses in determining the necessity of such a contract for the company and thus will not be relieved under CTA 2009, section 595(4).[216]

However, pre-contract expenses and expenses incurred in relation to abortive transactions will be relievable under CTA 2009, section 607 if they are regarded as directly linked expenses with the derivative contract as under CTA 2009, section 595(3)(b).[217]

In *Example 40*, the costs may be regarded as pre-contract expenses directly relating to the derivative contract, independently of whether the CDS will be concluded or not.

[d] FX Gains and Losses in Relation to Derivative Contracts

FX gains or losses are those gains or losses which arise by comparing the valuation of one currency used by the company for accounting purposes with the valuation of another currency regarding an asset or liability of the company on at least two different points of time.[218]

FX gains or losses in relation to derivative contracts can occur in two different forms.

They can occur in the context of currency derivatives, such as currency swaps, currency options or futures, where the underlying subject matter of the derivative is wholly or partly a currency.[219]

Example 41:

Under a plain vanilla currency swap, a specified amount in one currency, say USD 100, will be exchanged for another currency, say GBP, at a specified date in

216. It should however be noted that this example has not been mentioned by HMRC nor been discussed so far in the academic literature.
217. CTA 2009, s. 607(1)(c).
218. CTA 2009, s. 705(1).
219. Bramwell et al. (2023), H1.4.15.

the future at a given rate of exchange, say 1:0.6. The future rate of exchange is called the 'forward rate', and its calculation includes the interest rates of both currencies.[220]

A company which concludes the above currency swap contract has to fulfil its obligation at the pre-agreed forward rate irrespective of the prevailing market exchange rate at maturity (the 'spot rate'). If an exchange of USD 100 at the spot rate would be more profitable (i.e., at a prevailing exchange rate of 1:0.7), the company would have made a currency loss, and vice versa.

Or, FX gains or losses resulting from a translation from one currency to another of the profit or loss of the company's business, for example, FX profits or losses in relation to non-currency derivative contracts of an overseas branch translated into the local or functional currency of the company.

Example 42:

UK resident company A (headquarters) purchases an equity option in USD in its US branch for an option premium of USD 100. At the time of the purchase, the USD exchange rate is USD 1.60 per GBP. Due to market movement in the underlying equity, the option gains USD 10 to a value of USD 110. At the same time, the GBP devalues against the USD by 20%, hence resulting in an exchange rate of USD 1.92 per GBP.

Even though the US branch made a profit of USD 10, the option value has changed from an original value of GBP 62.5 (USD 100/1.6) to an actual value of GBP 57.3 (USD 110/1.92), resulting in a loss of GBP 5.2 for the headquarter (company A) as it is accounting its profits and losses in a different currency than the branch.

FX gains or losses can be accounted for either in the P&L account, in the *statement of recognised gains and losses* (STRGL) account, or in the changes in equity account in the case of IFRS.

For tax purposes, CTA 2009, section 606(1) determines that all exchange gains or losses in the context of derivative contracts include any exchange gains or losses so arising. Thus, any FX gains or losses relating to derivative contracts – either arising in the context of currency derivatives or otherwise – are, in principle, treated as normal

220. *Compare* Southern (2017) para. 14.50, Example 14.12, which explains the calculation of the forward rate in a currency swap.

credits or debits under the derivative contract regime and taxed accordingly (subject to the exceptions below).[221]

> *Example 43:*
>
> *See example 41 above – plain vanilla currency swap.*
> Any changes in the value of the USD against the GBP over the term of the contract will give rise to an exchange gain or loss, depending on whether the liability under the contract decreases or increases, which will – if the profits or losses are accounted for in the P&L account – be taxed as an exchange gain or loss under CTA 2009, sections 595(3), 606(1).[222]

In order to prevent adverse tax consequences, both CTA 2009, section 606(3) and CTA 2009, section 606(4), in connection with the Disregard Regulations SI 2004/3256,[223] provide mandatory matching rules for currency contracts if the conditions are fulfilled.[224] When CTA 2009, section 606(3) applies, FX gains and losses are not taxed at the balance sheet date because they are taken to reserves.[225] That means they are accounted for through STRGL or the statement of changes in equity rather than the P&L account.[226]

In the case of 'translated' FX gains or losses in relation to an overseas branch, FX gains or losses are also ignored for tax purposes if they are attributed accounting-wise to STRGL, the statement of recognised income and expense, the statement of changes in equity or the statement of income and retained earnings, and not to the P&L account.[227]

These mandatory matching rules generally apply in the context of hedging the underlying currency risks of an asset or liability through currency derivatives or hedging currency risks of a foreign branch.[228] The hedge accounting rules under UK GAAP and IFRS and their interaction with the taxation rules are discussed in detail in Chapter 7 §7.03[A].

When the FX gains or losses are brought into account under the derivative contracts rules depends on their recognition in the accounts based on the applied accounting method.[229]

221. CTA 2009, s. 606(1) refers in this respect to s. 595(3) and expressly maintains that FX gains or losses are part of the derivative contracts profits or losses within the meaning of CTA 2009, s. 595(3). *See* Ghosh, Johnson and Miller (2022) [E3.82] (issue 28); *Simon's Taxes,* vol 5, D1.851 (issue 171).
222. Ghosh, Johnson and Miller (2022) (2010) [E3.84] (issue 28).
223. Loan Relationship and Derivative Contracts (Disregard and Bringing into Account of Profits and Losses) Regulations 2004, SI 2004/3256.
224. Ghosh, Johnson and Miller (2022) [E3.82] (issue 28).
225. *Simon's Taxes,* vol 5, D1.851 (issue 171).
226. CTA 2009, s. 606(3)(a) and (b).
227. CTA 2009, s. 606(3)(a) and (b).
228. *Simon's Taxes,* vol 5, D1.851 (issue 171).
229. Ghosh, Johnson and Miller (2022) [E3.121] (issue 28).

If derivative contracts are accounted for at a fair value basis, any FX gains or losses from currency fluctuation will be part of the fair value calculation at the balance sheet date.[230] If derivative contracts are accounted for at an amortised cost basis, such as certain equity derivatives, any unrealised FX gains or losses will not be recognised until the realisation of the derivative contract.

[e] Taxation of Specific Derivative Contracts over Land

If the underlying of a derivative consists of land or tangible movable property, CTA 2009, sections 641(1), (2)(a), 643 and 644 treat any gains or losses on the contract as chargeable gains or allowable losses for corporation tax purposes,[231] provided that the contract is not entered for the purpose of a trade and the company is not an excluded body.[232]

> *Example 44:*
>
> Company A purchases a cash-settled call option over a selected portfolio of commercial properties for non-trading purposes. The term of the option is two years. The value of the portfolio at the inception of the option is GBP 100 million. Company A pays an option premium of, say, GBP 5 million. The strike of the option is set at 100% of the value of the portfolio.
>
> If the price of the commercial property were to rise 10% over the two years, company A would make a gain of GBP 5 million (GBP 110 million – strike price – option premium paid). If the price of the property portfolio does not rise over the term of the option, company A will make a loss of GBP 5 million, which equals the option premium paid.[233] For tax purposes, the cash-settled call option is treated as a CFD, and the profits or losses will be subject to tax as chargeable gains or allowable losses under CTA 2009, section 641.

The capital gains tax treatment may also apply to gains or losses on property-based total return swaps, which are brought into account under CTA 2009, section 641.[234] Under CTA 2009, sections 641(2)(d) 650, gains or losses on a swap over a property index may be subject to a capital gains treatment within the derivative contracts rules if they belong to the property element of the contract.[235] The aim of CTA

230. *Ibid.*, [E3.122].
231. *Simon's Taxes*, vol 5, D1.884 (issue 171).
232. CTA 2009, s. 643(3) and (4). An excluded body is defined in CTA 2009, s. 706. They are, for example, open-ended investment companies or venture capital trusts.
233. Note that the loss company A can make will never be more than GBP 5 million because company A has purchased an option, not a swap or future.
234. For an example of segregation of property-related amount and interest-related amount: HMRC, CFM55120.
235. Ghosh, Johnson and Miller (2022) [E9.78] (issue 28).

2009, section 650, is to segregate property-related amounts from interest-related amounts.[236]

In order to avoid the conversion of capital losses into income losses between connected parties,[237] CTA 2009, section 650 (as amended by FA 2013) does not apply among connected persons.[238] In addition, a tax avoidance 'mini-clause' was added, which ensures that CTA 2009, section 650 only applies if 'the securing of a tax advantage is neither the main purpose, nor one of the main purposes, for which the company is a party to the derivative contract'.[239] 'If section 650 does not apply, it merely means that the debits and credits are brought into account as income rather than capital.'[240]

[f] Equity Derivatives

Generally, derivative contracts are subject to an income regime under the derivative contracts rules of CTA 2009, Part 7.[241] With regard to certain equity derivatives and embedded derivatives over shares,[242] a regime was introduced by FA 2002, Schedule 26, paragraph 45A-45KA, which can now be found in CTA 2009, Part 7, Chapters 7 and 8,[243] which subjects those derivative contracts to chargeable gains or allowable losses instead of taxing them as income profits or losses.[244] The following subchapter discusses the treatment of those contracts.

[i] Taxation of Plain Vanilla Equity Options or Futures

Physically settled plain vanilla equity options or futures, which are not embedded into another financial instrument,[245] fall under the normal provisions of CTA 2009, Part 7 and are not subject to the capital gains treatment of CTA 2009, Part 7 Chapter 7 or 8.[246] Instead, any profits or losses are taxed as derivatives income under CTA 2009, section 574.

236. HMRC, CFM55110.
237. Ghosh, Johnson and Miller (2022) [U1.39] (issue 28).
238. CTA 2009, s. 650(8), as introduced by FA 2013, s. 41 (3)(b).
239. CTA 2009, s. 650(9), as introduced by FA 2013, s. 41 (3)(b).
240. Ghosh, Johnson and Miller (2022) [U1.41] (Issue 28).
241. CTA 2009, s. 571 brings credits and debits into charge as income.
242. Although embedded derivatives over shares are covered by this special regime of CTA 2009, Part 7, Ch. 7 and 8, they will be discussed separately in Ch. 8 of this work in the context of bifurcation.
243. *See* SI2004/2001, SI2004/3270, SI2005/646, SI2005/2082, SI2005/3440 and SI2006/3270, on which the introduction of the chargeable gains regime for equity derivatives and derivatives over land was based.
244. Ghosh, Johnson and Miller (2022) [E9.21] (issue 28).
245. CTA 2009, s. 708 defines a plain vanilla derivative contract as a contract, which is not embedded into another contract. In the case of embedded derivatives, most derivatives will be embedded into loan relationship contracts. There are however cases where a derivative contract is embedded into a non-loan-relationship contract, such as sale and repurchase agreements. *See* Bramwell et al. (2023) H1.4.36; Ghosh, Johnson and Miller (2022) [E9.133] (issue 28).
246. Share-based derivative contracts were previously excluded from the derivative contracts regime but were included into Sch. 26 from 16 March 2005 onwards, unless certain conditions

Any subsequent sales of the shares received due to the exercise of the options or the futures will, however, be subject to capital gains treatment under TCGA 1992.[247]

One should note that the base cost of the shares[248] has to be adjusted in case of an acquisition of shares through an option exercise or through a futures contract in order to reflect any gain or loss on the option or future, which has already been taxed under the derivative contracts rules.[249] In order to avoid the double-counting of gains or losses for tax purposes, the non-double counting rules of CTA 2009, sections 667 and 668 will apply to plain vanilla equity options or futures if the option was exercised or the future has led to delivery of shares.[250]

[ii] Taxation of Equity Swaps

Under an equity swap, the party which wants to take the (synthetic) share position pays its counterparty a fixed or floating interest payment and a payment for any downside movement of a certain share, share basket or equity index. It receives any dividends of this share, share basket or equity index and a payment relating to any upside movement of the shares.[251]

Many equity swaps are settled in cash, but the market also recognises equity swaps, which are settled physically by delivering the underlying equities.[252] The taxation of equity swaps is less clear than the taxation of equity options or futures. If the equity swap is cash settled, the swap would qualify as a CFD under CTA 2009, section 577(1), and any gain or loss would be taxable as income under CTA 2009, Part 7, provided all other definition criteria are fulfilled.

If the equity swap is physically settled, it would, in the author's opinion, qualify as a future under CTA 2009, 581.[253] Any gains or losses from a physically settled equity swap would be subject to tax as income under the derivative contracts rules, provided that the equity swap was accounted for as a derivative[254] and the carve-outs set out in CTA 2009, sections 589(2), (5) and 591[255] would not apply.[256]

---

as set out in CTA 2009, s. 591 were satisfied. The rules were further redrafted in 2008 to include also equity derivative contracts that produce an interest-like return into the derivative contracts regime. *See* HMRC, CFM13108, CFM50730 and CFM50740; Ghosh, Johnson and Miller (2022) [E9.111] (issue 28).

247. TCGA 1992 will only apply if the shares are not held on trading account. *See* Ghosh, Johnson and Miller (2022) [E9.111] (issue 28).
248. For the purposes of calculating the base cost in accordance with TCGA 1992, s. 38.
249. Bramwell et al. (2023), H3.4.2.
250. Ghosh, Johnson and Miller (2022) [E9.112] (issue 28).
251. Hull (2006) 174. For an example of a cash-settled total return equity swap, *see* Bramwell et al. (2023), H5.1.17.
252. In case of equity swaps on single equities or equity baskets, such a delivery of shares is possible. In case of equity swaps on equity indices, such a delivery is normally not possible. Hence, equity index swaps are settled in cash only.
253. For the argument to include also physical settled equity swaps into the definition of a future: *see* Ch. 4 §4.03[A][2][a][i].
254. It should be noted that an equity swap entered by a corporate entity is generally unlikely to satisfy the accounting test of CTA 2009, s. 579(1) and (2), where the equity swap relates to a subsidiary, joint venture, or partnership of that company. In this case, it would not be subject

If the equity swap is physically settled at maturity and the shares are delivered, the double-counting provisions of CTA 2009, sections 667 and 668 would apply because the equity swap will qualify as a future. Hence, in the case of physically settled equity swaps, double counting can only be avoided through the application of CTA 2009, sections 667 and 668, as these rules take priority over the more general rules of TCGA 1992, sections 37 and 39.[257]

[3] Taxation of Derivative Contracts That Are Excluded by Virtue of Their Underlying Subject Matter

Certain derivatives are excluded from the derivative contracts regime of CTA 2009, Part 7 by virtue of their underlying subject matter according to CTA 2009, section 589.[258] Those derivatives are:

(a) futures and options over intangible fixed assets,[259]
(b) certain equity derivatives, and
(c) rights of a holder in a unit trust that fulfil the conditions set out in CTA 2009, section 591.

[a] Options and Futures over Intangible Fixed Assets: Cryptocurrencies

Options and futures over intangible fixed assets – as mentioned in CTA 2009, section 589(2), (4) – will be subject to tax under the intangible fixed assets legislation.[260]

CTA 2009, section 712 defines intangible assets as having 'the meaning it has for accounting purposes'.[261]

CTA 2009, section 713(1) defines intangible fixed assets in relation to a company as 'an intangible asset acquired or created by the company for use on a continuing basis in the course of the company's activities',[262] and CTA 2009, section 713(2) confirms that this:

> includes an option or other right –
>
> (a) to acquire an intangible asset that would be a fixed asset if it were acquired, or
> (b) to dispose of an intangible fixed asset.[263]

---

to tax under the derivative contracts rules of CTA 2009, Part 7 but rather the general capital gains tax principles would apply, TCGA 1992, s. 8.

255. The most common carve-out is the hedging provision of CTA 2009, s. 591(3).
256. For carve-outs: HMRC, CFM50730.
257. As applied by TCGA 1992, s. 8(4) for corporation tax purposes.
258. Ch. 4 §4.03[A][2][c].
259. CTA 2009, s. 589(2)(a) and (4).
260. CTA 2009, s. 713(2).
261. CTA 2009, s. 712(1).
262. CTA 2009, s. 713(1).
263. CTA 2009, s. 713(2).

CTA 2009, section 589(2)(a), (4) only mentions *options and futures over intangible fixed assets* as containing excluded subject matter.

Contracts for differences (CFDs) *over intangible fixed assets* are not mentioned in those sections. Thus, CFDs over intangible fixed assets are not derivative contracts over excluded property as defined in CTA 2009, section 589(2)(a), (4), and consequently, the taxation regime of CTA 2009, Part 8 will not apply to those contracts.

Instead, CFDs over intangible fixed assets will fall within the derivative contracts regime of CTA 2009, Part 7. CTA 2009, section 579(2) applies to those derivative contracts so that CFDs over intangible fixed assets do not need to fulfil the accounting definition of CTA 2009, section 579(1).[264]

In the UK, cryptocurrencies are widely seen as intangible fixed assets within the meaning of the accounting definition of IAS 38.[265] In the June 2019 Agenda Paper, the *IFRS Interpretations Committee* proposes in a tentative decision that cryptocurrencies should be regarded as intangible assets.[266]

The IFRS Interpretations Committee refers to paragraphs 8 and 12 of IAS 38 and maintains:

> The Committee observed that a holding of cryptocurrency meets the definition of an intangible asset in IAS 38 on the grounds that (a) it is capable of being separated from the holder and sold or transferred individually; and (b) it does not give the holder a right to receive a fixed or determinable number of units of currency.[267]

Similarly, PwC stated:

> Holding a unit of a cryptocurrency typically does not give the holder a contractual right to receive cash or another financial asset, nor does the cryptocurrency come into existence as a result of a contractual relationship. Moreover, cryptocurrencies do not provide the holder with a residual interest in the assets of an entity after deducting all of its liabilities. Therefore, cryptocurrencies that we have seen so far (November 2019) do not meet the definition of a financial asset.[268]

HMRC maintains that:

> [c]ompanies that account for exchange tokens as "intangible assets" may be taxed under Corporation Tax rules for intangible fixed assets if the token is both:
>
> - an 'intangible asset' for accounting purposes
> - an 'intangible fixed asset' (this means it has been created or acquired by a company for use on a continuing basis. Exchange tokens which are simply held by the company, even when held in the course of its activities, will not meet this definition)'.[269]

264. Ghosh, Johnson and Miller (2022) [E3.243] (issue 28).
265. *Compare* Southern and Weidmann (2023), 68, 84.
266. IFRS, *IFRIC Update June 2019*, Holding of Cryptocurrencies – Agenda Paper 12.
267. *Ibid.*
268. PwC, 'Cryptographic assets and related transactions: accounting considerations under IFRS', *In depth: A look at current financial reporting issues* (December 2019), No. 2019-05, 5, 2.2.1.
269. HMRC, Cryptoassets Manual (updated 2 May 2023), CRYPTO41150.

Thus, the author proposes that *options and futures over cryptocurrencies* are 'Excluded property' within the meaning of CTA 2009, section 589(2), (4). Instead, options and futures over cryptocurrencies should fall under the intangible fixed asset legislation of CTA 2009, Part 8. The author believes that this means that those options and futures over cryptocurrencies would be accounted for at cost less impairments in the same way as the underlying cryptocurrencies.

In contrast, CFDs over cryptocurrencies do not fall within the intangible fixed asset legislation of CTA 2009, Part 8, because 'intangible fixed assets are not excluded subject matter in respect of contracts for differences'.[270]

Consequently, CFDs over cryptocurrencies would qualify as derivative contracts within CTA 2009, Part 7, and be taxed under those rules. The author has explained in Chapter 5 what the conditions are under which a crypto derivative is seen as a derivative for accounting purposes under the derivatives definition of FRS 102, Section 12, IFRS 9, Appendix A or IAS 39, Glossary.

As there is no specific legislative provision regarding which subjects those CFDs over cryptocurrencies to the capital gains regime, the author is of the opinion that those contracts are treated under the income regime of CTA 2009, Part 7.

The result of this disparity is, however, quite odd. Cryptocurrency options and futures would be measured at cost less impairment losses (if any) for accounting purposes and taxed according to CTA 2009, Part 8 because they fall under the excluded subject matter provisions.

However, CFDs over cryptocurrencies would be treated differently. The cryptocurrency itself is treated as an intangible asset under IAS 38, according to the majority view for IFRS accounting purposes.[271] CFDs over cryptocurrencies should be regarded as *derivative contracts for accounting purposes* and thus should be subject to a fair value accounting treatment.

For tax purposes, those CFDs over cryptocurrencies would be taxed as derivative contracts under CTA 2009, Part 7 and be taxed under the income regime of Part 7, provided they do not qualify as gambling.[272]

The question as to whether CFDs over cryptocurrencies should be considered as gambling is, however, not clear cut.

A derivative is a derivative if it can be *stochastically replicated by using combinations of other financial instruments, cash and/or derivatives*.[273]According to *Hull*, a derivative is defined as 'a financial instrument whose value depends on the value of other, more basic, underlying variables'.[274]

From the perspective of the tax legislation, the inclusion of a replication criterion in the definition of derivatives ensures that derivatives can be distinguished from betting.

270. Ghosh, Johnson Miller (2022) [E2.423] (issue 28).
271. *See* Ch. 5 §5.05[A][1].
272. *See* Ch. 2 §2.02[A].
273. *See* Ch. 2 §2.02[A], referring to Rubinstein (1999a) Mark Rubinstein, *Rubinstein on Derivatives* (1st edn, Risk Books 1999) 71-72 and 179-192.
274. Hull (2018) 1.

According to the author's view, a derivative can be distinguished from betting because a derivative can be replicated and hedged.[275] Derivative traders partly or fully hedge the risks of their portfolios, whereas a gambler takes the full risk. Hence, derivatives and betting can also be distinguished by the existence of a *final risk taker*. In a betting transaction, both parties take some, not necessarily the corresponding risk of losing.

In a derivatives transaction, both counterparties can have a trading position at maturity, with neither of them having lost on their position as both parties can hedge themselves.[276] If both counterparties can hedge the final payoff, no final risk taker is needed.

In terms of cryptoassets, 'HMRC does not consider the buying and selling of cryptoassets as gambling.'[277] Thus, only if a cryptoasset transaction falls into the definition of gambling or if that transaction is identified as a highly speculative activity, the transaction may not be taxable.

HMRC suggests that all the facts of a transaction involving cryptoassets need to be considered to conclude that the transaction classifies as gambling. In practice, HMRC taxes cryptoassets in the hands of individuals, businesses and companies but also allows a deduction of capital losses from cryptoassets with certain recording and time limitations,[278] including the tax deduction for impairment losses.

The qualification of crypto derivatives, therefore, narrows down to two questions:

(1) Can cryptoassets (which include NFTs and in-game digital items) be sufficiently hedged?
(2) Can crypto derivatives be hedged using fungible, liquid and tradable cryptocurrencies, other cryptocurrency derivatives and/or cash?

Only if those conditions are satisfied should crypto derivatives qualify as derivatives for tax purposes according to the definition outlined above.

Thus, cryptoassets and their respective derivatives, which cannot be sufficiently hedged (so that a final risk taker is needed), would qualify as gambling activity and should be outside the scope of (direct) taxation, according to the definition developed in Chapter 4.

In contrast, those crypto derivatives which can be sufficiently hedged should be inside the taxation scope and should qualify as derivatives for tax purposes.

Parallel to the discussions of credit derivatives and particularly *Credit Linked Notes*, which can be found in Chapter 4 §4.06[C], crypto derivatives should only qualify as derivatives for tax purposes if the underlying reference assets are tradable,

275. Ch. 2 §2.02[A].
276. Ch. 2 §2.02[B].
277. HMRC, CRYPTO10450.
278. *Ibid.*

fungible, and liquid assets, or if other tradable, fungible, and liquid crypto derivatives exist that allow to hedge the assumed cryptocurrency risks.[279]

That means that the underlying reference asset – here, the specific cryptocurrency – needs to be (i) tradable, (ii) fungible, and (iii) liquid for the crypto derivative over that cryptocurrency to qualify as a derivative for tax purposes.

There are crypto futures in existence on the largest cryptocurrencies, such as Bitcoin and Ethereum.[280]

One can argue that as long as the markets for underlying cryptocurrencies (or other crypto derivatives over that cryptocurrency) provide sufficient liquidity, a crypto derivative on those cryptocurrencies should qualify as a derivative for tax purposes because such a crypto derivative could be hedged with a liquid, fungible and tradable cryptocurrency (or alternatively another crypto derivative over the same cryptocurrency) – or used as a hedge for the underlying cryptocurrency.

In a recent White paper, ISDA argues in a similar way with the hedge effectiveness of crypto derivatives. It distinguishes between highly liquid 'Group 2a crypto assets' such as Bitcoin and Ethereum,[281] 'for which there is a liquid two-way market[282] and all other cryptoassets which are referred to as Group B. The distinction goes back to a Consultative Document of *the Basel Committee on Banking Supervision* (BCBS) that has made proposals for the 'Prudential treatment of banks' crypto-asset exposures'.[283]

ISDA argues that hedging Group 2a cryptoassets, such as Bitcoin and Ethereum,

> with their respective futures or exchange-traded funds (ETFs) is effective. Hence, the capital treatment should therefore allow for offsetting a given Group 2a crypto asset with its futures or ETFs. The paper also demonstrates that the basis risk profile of Group 2a crypto-asset futures is comparable with that of existing financial assets.[284]

The author agrees, but if, however – at some point in time – those crypto exchanges became dysfunctional, or if the cryptocurrency itself ceases to become tradable, fungible and liquid, there are good arguments to maintain that crypto derivatives would at that point in time not qualify as derivatives for tax purposes according to the proposed definition but merely as gambling, with the result that any gains or losses would *not* be subject to taxation.

The author understands that this view may leave crypto derivatives investors with the risk that crypto derivatives losses may not be tax deductible, although cryptocurrency gains were previously taxable. The author believes that tax legislators,

279. Ch. 4 §4.06[C].
280. Binance, Ether Futures, https://www.binance.com/en/e/ether_futures, accessed 12 February 2023.
281. ISDA, Crypto-asset Risk and Hedging Analysis (2022), 3, https://www.isda.org/a/pMWgE/Crypto-asset-Risks-and-Hedging-Analysis.pdf, accessed 18 April 2023.
282. ISDA, Crypto-asset Risk and Hedging Analysis (2022), 3.
283. Basel Committee on Banking Supervision, Consultative Document, 'Prudential treatment of banks' crypto-asset exposures' (June 2021), https://www.bis.org/bcbs/publ/d519.pdf, accessed 18 April 2023.
284. ISDA, Crypto-asset Risk and Hedging Analysis (2022), 3.

including HMRC, should consider the topic of cryptoassets and crypto derivatives carefully in the near future.

If things are left uncertain, countries may face an erosion of their tax base if crypto (derivatives) losses are made deductible (without any restrictions). Thus, the author proposes that the interaction of the accounting and taxation treatment of cryptoassets in relation to crypto derivatives should be considered by tax legislators carefully and in every detail.

In the author's view, a different tax treatment of options and futures over cryptocurrencies and cryptocurrency CFDs does not make much sense and, again, may open the door for tax arbitrage, for example, by buying options and futures over cryptoassets that completely hedge the underlying cryptoasset position, thereby generating an economically neutral position, while obtaining a tax deduction for impairment losses that may arise.

[b] Certain Equity Derivatives

The provision regarded excluded subject matters concerning shares as an underlying issue that has been subject to a number of changes.[285] *Ghosh, Johnson and Miller* highlight that not all relevant contracts over shares will satisfy the accounting test.[286] For example, the following contracts do not fall within the definition of derivatives within FRS 102, IAS 39 or IFRS 9, namely those:

> (a) derivatives over an interest in a subsidiary, quasi-subsidiary, associated undertaxing, joint venture or partnership if the derivative meets the definition of an equity instrument of the entity in [IAS 32];[287] or
> (b) financial instruments issued by the entity that meet the definition of an equity instrument in IAS 32 [...].[288]

Those contracts neither fulfil the accounting test of CTA 2009, section 579(1) nor section 579(2), and thus do not constitute derivative contracts.[289] There is an exclusion for certain equity derivatives mentioned in CTA 2009, sections 589(2)(b) and (c), (5)(a) and 591(1)-(6), such as:

- quoted options to subscribe for shares;
- derivatives that hedge shareholdings, CTA 2009, section 591(3);
- derivatives to acquire substantial shareholdings, CTA 2009, section 591(5); and
- derivatives entered by a life insurance company.[290]

285. Ghosh, Johnson and Miller (2022) [E2.432] (issue 28).
286. *Ibid.*
287. *Ibid.*
288. *Ibid.*
289. *Ibid.*
290. Southern (2017) para. 13.32.

Those contracts are excluded contracts, and they fall under the capital gains regime of TCGA 1992.[291] However, in certain cases, excluded contracts may be taxed as trading income if the company has entered the contract for the purpose of its trade.[292]

[i] Quoted Options to Subscribe for Shares[293]

CTA 2009, s. 589 (5) provides that *only those equity derivatives are excluded* from the derivatives contract regime which meet (a) any of the conditions A to E in section 591, and (b) are not a disguised debt instrument, i.e., they are a relevant contract that 'is not designed to produce a return which equates in substance to the return on an investment of money at a commercial rate of interest'.[294]

As *Ghosh, Johnson and Miller* put it: 'Clearly, HMRC do not want those contracts within the capital gains regime and thus subject to a realisation basis. Rather, they would prefer them within Part 7.'[295]

CTA 2009, s. 591 (4) then mentions the quoted options over shares, requiring that the contract is *not* acquired for trading purposes and that the equity derivative is 'an option which is listed on a recognised stock exchange to subscribe for shares in a company'.

If those conditions are fulfilled, the exchange-listed options to subscribe for shares will fall outside the scope of the derivatives contract regime.

[ii] Derivatives That Hedge Shareholdings, CTA 2009, Section 591(3)

CTA 2009, section 591(3) applies to relevant derivative contracts that are used to hedge the risks of the holding of shares. It is important that a hedge which is entered into is also effective from a post-tax perspective, i.e., that no tax disparity between the hedged instrument and the hedging instrument destroys the effectiveness of the hedging position from a post-tax perspective.

CTA 2009, section 591(3) – Condition B – stipulates that it applies to situations where:

> (a) the relevant contract is entered into or acquired by a company otherwise than for the purposes of a trade carried on by it;
> (b) there is a *hedging relationship* between the [derivative][296] *contract* and—
>   (i) an asset of the company which consists of *shares or rights of a unit holder under a unit trust scheme, or*

291. Bramwell et al. (2023), H4.1.2.
292. For example, excluded derivative contracts entered into by a life insurance company.
293. Shares are defined within this section by CTA 2009, s. 589(3) as: '(a)shares to which section 524 or 526 (shares subject to outstanding third-party obligations and shares which are non-qualifying shares) applies, and (b)shares in an open-ended investment company in relation to which section 490 has effect'.
294. CTA 2009, s. 589 (5)(b).
295. Ghosh, Johnson and Miller (2022) [E2.435] (issue 28).
296. Word added.

   (ii) any *share capital of the company* or any liability related to share capital of the company, and
 (c) the relevant contract is not one to which the company is treated as a party under section 585(2) (loan relationships with embedded derivatives).[297]

That means it is a derivative contract (a) that is not entered for the purposes of a trade, (b) which is in a hedging relationship with the underlying shares, and (c) it is not treated as a loan relationship with an embedded derivative.

The company must have designated the derivative contract as 'a hedging instrument under the relevant accounting standard (CTA 2009, s. 710)'.[298]

Moreover, to form a hedging relationship, both the hedging instrument and the hedged instrument have to be designated as a hedge.

[iii] Derivatives to Acquire Substantial Shareholdings, CTA 2009, s. 591(5)

An option or future to acquire more than 10% of the share capital of a company is outside the scope of the derivative contracts legislation of CTA 2009, Part 7.

CTA 2009, s. 591(5) - named as Condition D, stipulates that:

 (a) the relevant contract is entered into or acquired by a company otherwise than in the course of activities forming an integral part of a trade carried on by it,
 (b) the relevant contract is—
   (i) an option to acquire shares in a company, or
   (ii) a future requiring delivery of shares in a company,
 (c) the relevant contract is not one to which the company is treated as a party under section 585(2), and
 (d) the shares to be acquired or delivered—
   (i) constitute a substantial shareholding within the meaning of paragraph 8 of Schedule 7AC to TCGA 1992 (meaning of "substantial shareholding"), or
   (ii) would do so if acquired or delivered.[299]

CTA 2009, section 591(5)(d)(i) refers to the substantial shareholding definition of TCGA 1992, Schedule 7AC, paragraph 8, which requires a shareholding of 10% - the reference is made to the nominal share capital, entitlement to dividends and distributions on a notional winding up.[300] This exception means that any option over 10% of the shares in a company will fall outside the derivatives contract legislation of CTA 2009, Part 7. No distinction is made as to what kind of company it is - trading or not-trading - so any option over a 10% shareholding of any type of company will qualify as being outside of the derivatives contract regime. There is also no requirement that the shares are 'actually ever held' but the right to acquire a substantial shareholding suffices.[301]

297. CTA 2009, s. 591(3), emphasis added.
298. Ghosh, Johnson and Miller (2022) [E2.435] (issue 28).
299. CTA 2009, s. 591(5).
300. Ghosh, Johnson and Miller (2022) [E2.450] (issue 28).
301. *Ibid.*

[iv] Derivatives Entered by a Life Insurance Company

This condition only applies to life insurance companies and thus will not be discussed any further here.

[c] Units of a Unit Trust Scheme

Units of a unit trust scheme generally constitute excluded subject matter.[302] There are, however, a number of carve-outs.

Ghosh, Johnson and Miller explain:

> First, if CTA 2009, section 490 applies, then that holding will be treated for Part 6 purposes as a loan relationship. Such a holding will not constitute excluded subject matter (section 589(2)(c)). Second, the exclusions at section 591(2)-(6) need to be considered, though not all will apply to units in a unit trust (e.g., section 591(5) will not apply as it can only apply to contracts over shares). Also, the relevant contracts will not be excluded if they are 'designated to produce a return which equates, in substance, to the return on an investment of money at a commercial rate of interest'.[303]

§6.06 GERMAN TAXATION RULES APPLYING TO DERIVATIVES ENTERED INTO BY COMPANIES

This section outlines the *key aspects* of the German taxation of derivatives held by companies. It does not claim to be conclusive, but is rather a comprehensive summary of the key rules.

[A] General Taxation Principles for Companies

Any income received or expenses incurred and any gains or losses made by a company are only subject to corporation tax in Germany if (1) the company is generally subject to tax in Germany, and (2) the income is regarded as income under the German Corporation Tax Act (CTA).[304]

Companies resident in Germany are chargeable to corporation tax on their worldwide income[305] if they have their place of management or their seat in Germany (so-called unlimited taxation or residence principle of taxation).[306]

Companies with no place of management or seat in Germany are subject to 'limited taxation' with certain sources of German income (source taxation of income).[307] For example, non-resident companies can be liable to corporation tax in

302. Southern (2017) para. 13.33.
303. Ghosh, Johnson and Miller (2022) [E2.475]-[E2.490] (issue 28).
304. *Körperschaftsteuergesetz.*
305. Section 1(2) CTA.
306. Section 1(1) CTA.
307. Sections 2 No. 1, 8(1) CTA and s. 49(1) ITA.

Germany if they carry on a trade in Germany through a German permanent establishment.[308] In other cases of source taxation of companies, the tax will normally be levied by imposing a German withholding tax.[309]

A German corporate taxpayer is charged an effective rate of approximately 30% of total German corporate tax, consisting of corporate income tax,[310] trade tax[311] and solidarity surcharge,[312] both for distributed and retained profits.[313] The trade tax liability cannot be credited against the corporate income tax.[314]

As the German CTA refers to the German Income Tax Act (ITA)[315] for the purpose of determining taxable income, the provisions of the ITA will also apply to companies unless the CTA provides for more specific provisions that override the provisions of the ITA.[316] Income received or expenses incurred, as well as capital gains or losses, with the exception of equity capital gains or losses of a company, will be subject to the same tax rate.[317]

Interest received is fully taxable, and interest paid in principle is deductible subject to section 8a CTA in conjunction with section 4h ITA, which provides a limitation for the deduction of interest expenses if the expenses are in excess of the interest income (debt cap provisions).[318] The provisions, however, do not apply if the company is a single company and does not belong to a group of companies.[319]

With respect to equity investments, the German corporate tax legislation provides a favourable treatment for certain dividends and capital gains. Domestic and foreign dividends and capital gains from disposals of shares are, in principle, tax-exempt from corporation tax.[320] A total of 5% of the dividends and capital gains are deemed as non-deductible expenses.[321] Correspondingly, losses from the disposal of

308. Section 49(1) No. 2a ITA.
309. Section 32(1) No. 2 CTA. *See* Ewald Dötsch et al., *Körperschaftsteuer* (15 edn, Schäfer-Poeschel Verlag 2009) 34-35; Gosch (2009) § 32, paras 1-2; Conlon & Aquilino: Derivatives D2.03[1].
310. Corporate income tax is levied at a rate of 15%, s. 23(1) CTA.
311. The rate is approximately 14% based on an assumed trade tax multiplier of 400%, *see* s. 11(1) and (2) Trade Tax Act.
312. Section 4 sent. 1 Solidarity Surcharge Tax Act levies solidarity surcharge at 5.5% of the corporate tax liability, which amounts to approximately 0.83%. BFH v. 17.01.2023, Az. IX R 15/20 confirmed that the leverage of the Solidarity Surcharge Tax Act is still constitutional.
313. Dötsch et al. (2009) 346.
314. Conlon & Aquilino: Derivatives, D2.03[7] (issue December 2022).
315. *Einkommensteuergesetz*.
316. Sections 7(2) and 8(1) CTA.
317. For example, interest and capital gains on bonds are both treated as taxable income subject to the same tax rate.
318. The debt cap provisions only apply if the interest expenses after the deduction of the interest income are in excess of EUR 3,000,000 (s. 4h(2) ITA). In excess cases, only 30% of the offsettable EBITDA are deductible (s. 4h(1) ITA).
319. If the company belongs to a group, the prohibition of interest expense deduction does not apply if the equity quota of the single company equals or exceeds the equity quota of the group of companies, *see* s. 4 h(2) b) and c) ITA. The legislative aim of the provision was to avoid interest deduction in thin capitalisation cases.
320. Section 8b(1), (2) and (4) CTA. Portfolio dividends are fully subject to trade tax (s. 8 No. 5 TTA). 'Non-portfolio dividends' are only tax-exempt if the company receiving the dividends holds at least 15% of the share capital (s. 9 No. 2a TTA). Equity capital gains from the disposal of shares are 95% tax-exempt for trade tax purposes (s. 7 TTA).
321. Sections 8b(3) sent. 1 CTA (equity capital gains) and 8b(5) sent. 1 CTA (dividends).

shares or expenses from write-downs in a shareholding are non-deductible.[322] There are, however, two important exceptions to these rules.

First, legislation was introduced that subjects portfolio dividends to corporation tax[323] if the shareholding consists of less than 10% of the share capital at the beginning of the calendar year.[324] Second, both dividends and capital gains from the disposal of shares are fully taxable, and losses and expenses are fully tax deductible if the shares are attributed to a trading book of a bank or other financial institution or are held by a life insurance company.[325]

[B] General Accounting Principles as a Basis for German Business Taxation

The general principles of orderly accounting laid down in the Commercial Law Act (CLA) are the basis for the calculation of commercial profits.

For a summary of the general accounting principles and their interaction with the tax rules, *see* Chapter 5 §5.03[A].

[C] Taxation of Derivatives Held by Companies

In the following sections, the author will analyse the general tax treatment of derivative contracts held by companies. The author will also briefly discuss the taxation of derivatives entered into by financial institutions where necessary.

In Germany, the tax authorities have dealt more comprehensively with the taxation of derivatives held by private investors than with those held by business investors.[326]

As the taxation of derivatives held by (non-corporate and corporate) business investors is based on the treatment of derivatives in the financial accounts, the German legislator has simply not bothered to draft special rules for derivatives taxation, with the exception of introducing a provision that limits the offset of derivatives losses against other business gains by way of ring-fencing these derivatives losses.[327]

Attempts by German companies or financial institutions to use derivative contracts as a means of tax planning have been dealt with by introducing new anti-avoidance rules or by means of 'letter rulings' (or 'circular letters')[328] issued by the German Revenue that have attempted to clarify the application of the general taxation rules in the context of derivatives.

---

322. Section 8b(3) sent. 3 CTA.
323. *Gesetz zur Umsetzung des EuGH-Urteils vom 20. Oktober 2011 in der Rechtssache C-284/09 (EuGHDivUmsG) of 21 March 2013* (legislation implementing the ECJ decision of 20 October 2011, C-284/09).
324. Section 8b(4) sent. 1 CTA.
325. Sections 8b(7) and (8) CTA.
326. Conlon & Aquilino: Derivatives D2.01.
327. Section 15(4) sent. 3 to 5 ITA.
328. *BMF – Schreiben.*

The tax treatment of derivatives concerns two different stages: the treatment of derivatives during the term of the transaction and the taxation of their respective gains and losses at maturity.

[1] Tax Treatment of a Derivative Contract During Its Term

The tax treatment of derivatives in the financial accounts is, in principle, decisive for determining their treatment in the tax accounts.[329] Details of the treatment of derivatives during the term of the transactions and the general accounting principles applying to the taxation of derivatives can be found in Chapter 5 §5.03[B].

If a derivative hedges an existing asset, hedge accounting may apply with the consequence that the general accounting principles are disapplied, and no depreciation of the underlying asset or the derivative has to take place at the balance sheet date.[330]

[2] Taxation of Derivatives Held by Corporate Investors at Maturity

[a] Taxation of Futures, Forwards and Swaps

At maturity, gains and losses from cash-settled futures, forwards and swaps are taxed as ordinary corporate income.[331]

For the derivatives counterparty delivering the underlying asset, physically settled derivatives are taxed upon settlement. The delivery will be regarded as a disposal of the underlying.

For the party of the derivative that receives the underlying asset, no immediate taxation takes place upon delivery of the underlying.[332] Instead, the underlying asset received is recorded with its acquisition costs in the accounts. The subsequent disposal of the underlying may lead to taxable gains or tax-deductible losses.

The equity exemption for capital gains of section 8b(2) CTA also applies to physically settled derivatives entered into by companies. Hence, gains from the disposal of the shares received under a physically settled derivative contract are 95%

329. *See* Conlon & Aquilino: Derivatives D2.03[2]. Section 5(1) sent. 1 ITA applies as a general accounting rule also in respect to the accounting of derivative contracts.
330. *See* Ch. 7 §7.03[B][2]. *See also* Häuselmann and Wagner (2002b) 2171; Conlon & Aquilino: Derivatives D2.06[3][b].
331. *Ibid.*
332. In case of unrealised losses on the delivered underlying, it will only be possible to recognise these losses at the next balance sheet date. In the commercial accounts, a recognition of the losses at the next balance sheet date has to take place in case of permanent depreciation of the underlying asset, s. 253(3) sent. 3 CLA; it may also take place in case of a non-permanent depreciation if the underlyings delivered are regarded as financial assets, s. 253(3) sent. 4 CLA. For tax purposes, a recognition of unrealised losses will only be possible in case of an expected permanent depreciation of the underlying asset (ss 6(1) No. 1 sent. 2 or 6(1) No. 2 sent. 2 ITA may apply depending on the type of underlying). The Federal Fiscal Court has defined the term 'expected permanent depreciation' in relation to shares, *see* BFH, decision of 26 September 2007 - I R 58/06, BStBl II 2009, 294.

tax-free upon disposal of the equities. Losses from the disposal of the equities are non-deductible.[333]

Regarding derivatives losses, the loss ring-fencing provision that is contained in ITA also applies to companies.[334] Under section 15(4) sentence 3 ITA, losses can principally not be offset against other income of the company but only against derivatives gains.[335]

The loss ring-fencing provision, however, does not apply if the taxpayer is a bank, credit institution, financial service company or financial company.[336]

In addition, the loss ring-fencing provision does not apply to other taxpayers if the derivative is used to hedge business activities that are 'part of the regular course of the taxpayer's business'.[337] However, when considering the meaning of that phrase, it is uncertain under which circumstances derivatives are seen as a hedge to an underlying 'in the regular course of the business' because no definition can be found in the legislation.[338] No guidance is available from the German Revenue either.

Wendt suggests that the term 'regular course of the taxpayer's business' means that those transactions have to be the subject matter of the business, i.e., the transactions have to be attributed to the ordinary income in the P&L account and have to be executed regularly.[339]

Others suggest that this view is too narrow.[340] Some authors maintain that it is sufficient if this kind of business occurs in the specific sector in which the company is doing business.[341]

Brandis/Heuermann suggests that in addition to the objective connection of use and function, there must also be a subjective intention of compensating the risks of the hedged transaction by entering into the hedging transaction(s).[342]

Conlon & Aquilino propose that a functional nexus between the hedged transaction and the investor's core business should suffice.[343] They suggest that 'where transactions similar to the hedged transaction are carried out regularly and on a large scale and constitute a separate business line, they could also form part of a regular course of the taxpayer's business'.[344]

The view of *Wendt*[345] is too narrow as the intention of the legislator (when introducing the ring-fencing provision) was to avoid losses incurred in speculative

333. Section 8b(3) sent. 3 CTA.
334. Sections 8(1) CTA, 15(4) sent. 3 ITA.
335. For the discussion whether the ring-fencing rule applies only to cash-settled derivatives or also to physically settled derivatives, *see* Ch. 4 §4.03[C][2].
336. Section 15(4) sent. 4 1st alt ITA. *See* Conlon & Aquilino: Derivatives D2.03[6]; Haisch and Helios (2011) 269.
337. Section 15(4) sent. 4 2nd alt ITA. *See* Conlon & Aquilino: Derivatives D2.03[6].
338. Hans-Jürgen Feyerabend, '§ 15 EStG' in Bernd Erle and Thomas Sauter (eds), *Heidelberger Kommentar zum Körperschaftsteuergesetz* (3 edn, C.F. Müller 2010) 1994.
339. Wendt in Herrmann/Heuer/Raupach, Steuerreform I (2001) § 15 para. R17.
340. Feyerabend *in Erle/Sauter, § 15 EStG*, 1994; Conlon & Aquilino: Derivatives, D 2.03[6].
341. Haisch and Helios (2011) 271.
342. Brandis/Heuermann (2022), para. 718.
343. Conlon & Aquilino: Derivatives, D 2.03[6].
344. *Ibid.*
345. Wendt in Herrmann/Heuer/Raupach, Steuerreform I (2001) § 15 para. R17.

transactions being offset against regular business income.[346] This, however, does not mean that only those derivatives losses can be offset which were incurred in the course of hedging transactions that belong to the ordinary income in the commercial accounts.

Also, those transactions are 'typical' or 'common' and are not connected with the day-to-day business, such as acquisitions of other businesses,[347] even if they do not occur on a regular basis. Hence, a loss-offset against regular business income should be permissible in those cases.

In the author's opinion, the view expressed in *Conlon & Aquilino*, which proposes a possible offset against losses for all hedged transactions which are carried out regularly and on a large scale and constitute a separate business line, is too wide. It does not sufficiently consider the intention of the legislator to de-incentivise a loss-offset for derivatives that are used in the context of speculation.[348]

Example 45:

Company A produces textiles. If Company A buys commodity futures on cotton to hedge its costs and fix a certain wholesale price, the commodity futures hedge its regular business, and thus, any loss is tax deductible and not ring-fenced. If Company A starts buying commodity futures on wheat, any losses should be ring-fenced as the wheat futures do not hedge the regular business of the taxpayer.

But what if the manufacturer decides that more money is to be made in buying and selling wheat and soya and regularly enters into transactions in this field?

Applying the opinion expressed in *Conlon & Aquilino*, these transactions could lead to a new business line, and hence, derivatives hedging this purchase and selling activity could be offset against ordinary business income. However, such a solution would, in the author's opinion, not be in line with the legislative intention behind section 15(4) sentence 4 ITA. The legislator wants producers to manufacture and produce, not to speculate on the prices of commodities, equities or bonds.

In addition, the term 'hedging' of the regular business is not defined in section 15(4) sentence 4 ITA. From a business perspective, the term 'hedging' should not only be restricted to hedges, which fully hedge all underlying risks of the business transaction, but also allow for hedges which partially hedge the risks of the transaction.[349]

First, it should be at the discretion of the company to decide which parts of the transaction will be hedged and which will not.

Second, the provision would be too narrow if only 'perfect hedges' of all risks were allowed to qualify for a hedge under section 15(4) sentence 4 ITA, as, in practice,

346. BT-Drucksache 14/443, 28.
347. Feyerabend in *Erle/Sauter*, § 15 EStG, 1994.
348. BT-Drucksache 14/443, 28.
349. Feyerabend *in Erle/Sauter*, § 15 EStG, 1995; Haisch and Helios (2011) 271.

almost all transactions have residual risks of some sort, whether credit, interest or currency risks that are left unhedged because they are either remote, too expensive to hedge or no liquid market exists for the hedge.[350]

On the other hand, in case of overhedging using derivatives, a loss-offset should be denied as the reason for this behaviour would again be of a speculative nature.[351]

The jurisprudence in recent years has brought some clarity to the discussion as to what constitutes a perfect hedge, which means a complete hedge is not necessary to qualify for the provision of section 15 paragraph 4 sentence 4 ITA.[352]

In terms of crypto derivatives hedging cryptoassets, if the company holds the cryptoassets as investments, the crypto derivatives may not be regarded as 'hedging of the regular business of the taxpayer'. In those cases, any cryptoasset gains which could be offset by losses of crypto derivatives in a hedging relationship may not be able to be used in this context, thus leading to a hedge ineffectiveness between the cryptoasset and the crypto derivative for tax purposes.

[b] Taxation of Options

[i] Taxation of Long Positions and Short Positions

With regard to the taxation of options, one has to distinguish between long and short option positions.

(1) Long Positions (Long Call and Put Options)

(A) Option Premiums

Option premiums paid in the case of long call and put options are not regarded as an expense at the inception of the transaction.[353] Instead, the option acquired is

350. In many cases, the 'perfect hedge' is only to sell the same underlying, with the same maturity and same size, etc.
351. *Other opinion* Feyerabend *in Erle/Sauter*, § 15 EStG, 1995 who suggests that the wording of s. 15(4) sent. 3 and 4 ITA permits a loss-offset if the derivative serves the subjective purpose of hedging. Hence the extent of the hedge would be irrelevant. This view is inconsistent, as overhedging – at the inception of the trade – involves taking a market risk to benefit from price movements. Hence, it is of speculative nature, and therefore should be ring-fenced applying the legislator's intention of the law. Peter Schmittmann and Axel Welper, 'Voraussetzungen der Verlustausgleichsbeschränkung bei Termingeschäften im Betriebsvermögen' DStR 2001 1783, 1787 suggest that an unrestricted loss offsetting should only be permitted for the part that matches the underlying positions that is hedged.
352. Finanzgericht Koeln, decision of 18 December 2018, 8K 3086/16: an objective business connection may exist if the risk from a business loan with variable interest is to be compensated by a combination of an interest rate and currency swap (cross currency swap); Finanzgericht Baden Wuertemberg (FG BaWue), decision of 22 July 2019, 10K 1157/17 held that a small currency risk does not mean that the cross currency swap is not suitable for hedging the underlying transaction.
353. Conlon & Aquilino: Derivatives D2.06[3][a]; also: Häuselmann (2005) 99.

capitalised at acquisition cost, with the premium paid in both the commercial[354] and the tax accounts.[355] At the balance sheet date, the option premium is recorded at cost or the relevant lower market value.[356]

(B) Termination of Long Positions

Option positions can be terminated in three ways:

- expiry without exercise of the option, usually if the option is worthless and lapses;
- exercise, either physical or cash settlement;
- close-out of the position.

(aa) Expiry or Exercise of Long Call Options

1. Cash-Settled Long Call Options

If a long call option is cash settled, any gain is taxable, being the settlement payment minus the option premium paid.[357] The option will be derecognised, and the option premium reduces the taxable gain. A de-recognition and write-off of the option premium in the financial and tax accounts also have to take place if the option lapses worthless.[358]

The 9th Senate of the Federal Fiscal Court has, however, decided in the case of a lapsed call option held by a private investor that any loss from a lapsed call option

354. IDW, BFA 2/1995, Bilanzierung von Optionsgeschäften (1995) *WPg 1995, 421* and IDW, RS BFA 6, Handelsrechtliche Bilanzierung von Optionsgeschäften bei Instituten (18 August 2011) WPg Supplement 4/2011, 50ff, FN-IDW 10/2011, 656ff., para. 12 (statements of the Institute of Public Auditors).

Although the above statements by the Institute were issued with regard to the accounting of derivatives by financial institutions, it has been suggested that they can also be applied by approximation in other sectors for the accounting of those instruments. *See* Maulshagen, Trepte and Walterscheidt (2008) 150; Nguyen (2007) 67.

355. Conlon & Aquilino: Derivatives D2.06[3][a].

356. For accounting purposes, the option has to be written down at balance sheet date if it belongs to the fixed assets of the company in case of a permanent depreciation in the value of the option (s. 253(3) sent. 3 CLA); it can be written down at balance sheet date even if no permanent depreciation in the value of the option exists (s. 253(3) sent. 4 CLA). If the option has been attributed to the current assets, a write down has to take place, even if no permanent depreciation of the option occurred (s. 253(4) CLA). For tax purposes, a write down to the lower market value *can* (but does not have to) take place in the case of a permanent depreciation in the value of the option at balance sheet date (both in the case of attribution of the option to the fixed or the current assets, ss 6(1) No. 1 sent. 2 ITA or 6(1) No. 2 sent. 2 ITA). In cases where no permanent depreciation in the value of the option has occurred at balance sheet date, a write down to the lower market value is not permitted (both in the case of the attribution of the option to the fixed or the current assets, ss 6(1) No. 1 sent. 2 and 4 ITA or 6(1) No. 2 sent. 2 ITA). *See* Haisch and Helios (2011) 188.

357. IDW (2011b) para. 12ff; similar: Conlon & Aquilino: Derivatives, D2.06[3][a].

358. Conlon & Aquilino: Derivatives D2.06[3][a]; Häuselmann (2005) 100; Haisch and Helios (2011) 267; Nguyen (2007) 70.

cannot be regarded as losses from cash-settled derivatives within section 23(1) No. 4 ITA (2008) because no actual cash settlement had taken place.[359]

This decision has been widely criticised in the expert literature.[360] Before the decision of the Federal Fiscal Court, the lower tax courts took the view that lapsed option premiums should be deductible for private individuals.[361]

In the author's opinion, the Federal Fiscal Court decision on lapsed option premiums contradicts the tax principles of equity, legal certainty and tax neutrality. Independently of the form of termination, the option premium would have been expensed and, therefore, should be tax deductible (but possibly ring-fenced; *see* below).[362]

359. BFH, decision of 19 December 2007 - IX R 11/06 DStR 2008, 968 and BFH, decision of 9.10.2008 - IX R 69/07, BFH/NV 2009, 152. The decisions concerned the deductibility of a call option premium if a long call option lapsed that was purchased by a private individual. The court denied the deductibility of the option premium in case of a lapse of the call option and suggested that the facts of s. 23(1) No. 4 ITA (2008) are only fulfilled if the holder of the option receives a cash settlement by exercising the option because s. 23(1) No. 4 ITA (2008) would only apply to income which is received through the exercise of the option. If no exercise would take place, the income as well as any losses would not fall under s. 23(1) No. 4 ITA (2008).

In BFH, decision of 17 April 2007 - IX R 40/06, BStBl II 2007, 608, DStR 2007, 1075 the court held that option premiums received would fall in 'other income' under s. 22 No. 3 ITA (2008) and are not treated as income or gains from derivatives transactions under 23(1) No. 4 ITA (2008). The argument that the court used in BFH, decision of 19 December 2007 - IX R 11/06 DStR 2008, 968 (based on its previous decision of 17 April 2007) is as follows: The option premium received does not qualify as income or gains under s. 23(1) No. 4 ITA (2008). Hence, any losses with regard to the option premium generated do also not qualify as losses under s. 23(1) No. 4 ITA (2008) if the option is not exercised. This has also been the view of the German Revenue in context of lapsed option premiums within s. 23(1) No. 4 ITA (2008), i.e., derivatives held by private investors. *See* BMF, *Schreiben vom 27. November 2001, Einkommensteuerliche Behandlung von Termingeschäften im Bereich der privaten Vermögensverwaltung* (IV C 3 - S 2256 - 265/01 BStBl I 2001, 986) para. 23.

360. *Legal commentaries*: Heinrich Glenk, '§ 23 EStG' in Bernd Heuermann (ed), *Blümich, EStG, KStG, GewStG* (108 edn, Verlag Franz Vahlen München 2010) para. 74; Jutta Jacobs-Soyka, '§ 23' in Eberhard Littmann, Horst Bitz and Hartmut Pust (eds), *EStG – Das Einkommensteuerrecht* (82 edn, 2009) para. 59; Weber-Grellet *Schmidt, EStG* (2012), § 20, para. 133.

The view that lapsed option premiums should be deductible for private individuals is also shared by the following publications in *law journals*: Udo Delp, 'Erste Anwendungs- und Zweifelsfragen bei der Besteuerung von Termingeschäften privater Personen nach dem SEG 1999/2000/2002' INF 1999 584, 586; Matthias Geurts, 'Besteuerung von Finanzderivaten im Privatvermögen' DB 2002 110, 113; Rüdiger Philipowski, 'Verfall wertlos gewordener Kauf- und Verkaufsoptionen' DStR 2004 978, 979; Rüdiger Philipowski, 'Werbungskosten bei fehlgeschlagenen Termingeschäften' DStR 2007 1615, 1615; Andre Reislhuber and Friedrich Bacmeister, 'Weitere ausgewählte Aspekte des neuen BMF - Anwendungsschreibens zur Abgeltungsteuer' DStR 2010 684, 685.

361. FG Baden-Württemberg, decision of 5 June 2003 - 14 K 190/02, EFG 2004, 907; FG Rheinland-Pfalz, decision of 19 May 2005 - 4 K 1678/02, DStRE 2005, 1326; FG Münster, decision of 7 December 2005 - 10 K 5715/04, EFG 2006, 669; Niedersächsisches FG, decision of 12 September 2007 - 2 K 252/05, DStRE 2008, 473 (reversed by: BFH decision of 9 October 2008 - IX R 69/07, BFH/NV 2009, 152).

362. The German tax literature also criticises the decision because it contradicts the German tax principle that expenses which are in direct relationship with the income should be tax deductible (*'objektives Nettoprinzip'*). *See* Reislhuber and Bacmeister (2010), DStR 2010, 684, 685.

A new section 20 paragraph 2 sentence 1 No 3a ITA now determines that the taxation of the profit from the derivatives transaction no longer depends on the termination of the right, which is contrary to the previous applicable legislation.[363] As a consequence of the new wording and considering the aim of the new legislation, the Federal Fiscal Court ruled in a new decision that the lapse of an option (meaning the right to sell lapses in case of a put option or the right to acquire the shares lapses in case of a call option) leads to a tax-deductible loss, i.e., any profit or loss is recognised for tax purposes from an option lapse.[364] This decision confirms the view of the author that the lapsed option premiums should be tax deductible.

2. Physically Settled Long Call Options

If a long call option is physically settled, there will be no immediate recognition of the gain for accounting and tax purposes. Instead, the underlying acquired will be capitalised at acquisition cost,[365] being the strike price plus the option premium paid.[366] Thus, the option premium will be derecognised in the financial and tax accounts and will reduce the potential taxable gain from a later disposal.[367]

If the physically settled long call option lapses worthless, the loss, being the option premium paid, should be tax deductible.[368]

According to the majority view in the literature, which does not apply the loss ring-fencing rule of section 15(4) sentence 3 ITA to physically settled derivatives, option premiums from lapsed options would be treated as fully tax deductible (as any other losses from physically settled derivatives).[369] This is confirmed by various recent decisions of the Federal Fiscal Court. In three decisions of 2016,[370] 2017[371] and 2018,[372] the Federal Fiscal Court held that derivatives that are intended for physical delivery of the underlying at maturity are not subject to the loss ring-fencing rule. The wording of the rule states that the taxpayer receives a cash settlement or a benefit, which must be

363. Section 20 para. 2 No. 3 a reads: 'der Gewinn bei Termingeschäften, durch die der Steuerpflichtige einen Differenzausgleich oder einen durch den Wert einer veränderlichen Bezugsgröße bestimmten Geldbetrag oder Vorteil erlangt'.
364. BFH decision of 12 January 2016, IX R 48/14, BStBl 2016 II, 456.
365. Conlon & Aquilino: Derivatives D2.06[3][a].
366. IDW (2011b) para. 12ff; IDW (1995) para. 22; also: Häuselmann (2005) 100; Conlon & Aquilino: Derivatives D2.06[3][a].
367. *Similar* Conlon & Aquilino: Derivatives D2.06[3][a]. *Other opinion* Hubert Schmid and Georg Renner, 'Bilanzielle und steuerliche Behandlung einer Kaufoption (long call)' DStR 2005 815, 817 who suggest that the option premium paid should be treated as tax deductible expense upon exercise of the physically settled call option. The option premium paid should not be added to the strike price, thus leading to higher capital gains (which are potentially virtually tax-free in case of equity options).
368. Ch. 4 §4.03[C][2]; also: BFH decision of 12 January 2016, IX R 48/14, BStBl 2016 II, 456.
369. Conlon & Aquilino: Derivatives D2.06[3][a]; *similar* Häuselmann (2005) 100. For the discussion, *see* Ch. 4 §4.03[C][2].
370. BFH decision of 6 July 2016 – I R 25/14, BStBl II, 124.
371. BFH decision of 24 October 2017 – VIII R 35/15, BStBl II 2018, 189.
372. BFH decision of 20 November 2018- VIII R 37/15, BStBl. II 2019, 507.

determined by the value of a variable reference value.[373] The question is if one could regard a physical settlement as such a benefit, which must be determined by reference to a variable reference value.

There is no dependence on a variable reference value if the underlying asset is delivered at the due date. An exception, however, applies for those derivatives which are not intended for physical delivery but for cash settlement if an offsetting transaction has been concluded before the maturity of the initial opening transaction.[374]

Gains from a later disposal of the underlying assets are taxable unless the 95% capital gains tax exemption applies in cases where the underlying asset is qualified as equity.[375]

(bb) Expiry or Exercise of Long Put Options

If the long put position is cash settled, any gain or loss is calculated as the settlement payment minus the book value of the put option premium paid,[376] which means the put option premium will be derecognised and reduces the taxable gain. If the option lapses worthless, any loss will be ring-fenced.[377]

If the long put position is physically settled, the capital gain is the strike price received minus the book value of the underlying delivered (minus the put option premium paid).[378] The book value of the put option premium paid will be rolled into the sale proceeds and will reduce any capital gain.[379] If the physically settled put option lapses worthless, the author proposes that any loss should be ring-fenced.[380]

Gains from the disposal of the underlying being delivered under the put option are taxable unless the 95% capital gains tax exemption applies if the underlying is equity.[381]

(cc) Close-Out of Long Call and Put Positions

With regard to close-outs of option positions, one has to distinguish between exchange-traded transactions and OTC derivatives.

Exchange-traded derivatives, such as exchange-traded options or futures, are closed out by entering into an opposite trade to the original one.[382] The close-out of the

373. Section 15 para. 4 sent. 3 states: 'Verluste aus Termingeschäften, durch die der Steuerpflichtige einen Differenzausgleich oder einen durch den Wert einer veränderlichen Bezugsgröße bestimmten Geldbetrag oder Vorteil erlangt.'
374. Herrmann/Heuer/Raupach, *EStG, KStG* (2022), paras 643ff.
375. *See* above Ch. 6 §6.02[A].
376. IDW (2011b) para. 22; Nguyen (2007) 71.
377. *See* above Ch. 6 §6.06[C][2][b][i][A][2][aa] 1. Cash-Settled Long Call Options. *Other opinion* Conlon & Aquilino: Derivatives D2.06[3][b].
378. *Ibid.*, D2.06[3][b].
379. Nguyen (2007) 71 (for financial accounts); Conlon & Aquilino: Derivatives D2.06[3][b] (for tax accounts).
380. *See* above Ch. 6 §6.06[C][2][b][i][A][2][aa] 1. Cash-Settled Long Call Options. *Other opinion* Conlon & Aquilino: Derivatives D2.06[3][b].
381. *See* above Ch. 6 §6.02[A].
382. Hull (1997b) 17.
The parties have to enter into an opposite trade because the 'other side' of the transaction is not known due to the anonymity of the exchange. Both parties have only

transaction by way of an opposite trade at an exchange is regarded as a settlement for legal and tax purposes.[383] Thus, if an exchange-traded call or put option is closed out by entering into an offsetting option position, the difference between the value of both options will constitute a taxable gain[384] or a deductible but ring-fenced loss.[385]

OTC derivatives can be 'economically' closed out in two ways: between the parties or with a third party. If they want to close-out the position, usually, both parties of the OTC contract will agree to cancel all rights and duties under the derivative contract.[386]

Thereby, the contract ceases to exist. Hence, if an OTC call or put option is closed out (by cancellation of the contract), the option ceases to exist. The difference between the option premium paid and any close-out payment received or paid will be booked as a profit or loss in the financial accounts[387] and correspondingly be reflected in the tax accounts.

If both parties do not close-out with each other but enter into an opposite trade to the original one with a third party, this also qualifies as an economic close-out as the positions offset each other. Legally, this close-out can, however, only be qualified as a hedge and has to follow the rules for hedge accounting,[388] rather than for a close-out, as all contracts remain legally intact.[389]

(2) Short Positions (Short Call and Put Options)

(A) Option Premiums Received

According to a decision of the Federal Fiscal Court, option premiums received by the writer of the option are not taxable at inception but only at maturity.[390] The option contract has to be shown as a 'liability' in the financial[391] and tax accounts.[392]

The German Ministry of Finance shares this view but maintains that a reserve for expected losses has to be established in the financial accounts at the balance sheet date

contracted with the exchange, not with each other.

383. BFH decision of 18 December 2002 - I R 17/02, BStBl II 2004, 126, BB 2003, 1006, 1007. *See* Häuselmann (2005) 101.
384. Häuselmann (2005) 101.
385. In case of a loss, the loss ring-fencing provision of s. 15(4) sent. 3 ITA applies. As the close-out is similar to a cash settlement, ring-fencing should apply independently from the form of settlement at which the option is aimed at (cash or physical).
386. Scharpf and Schaber (2009) 563.
387. Nguyen (2007) 71.
388. *See* Ch. 7 §7.03[B][2].
389. Häuselmann (2005) 101.
390. BFH, decision of 18 December 2002 - I R 17/02, BStBl II 2004, 126, BB 2003, 1006; confirmed by BFH, decision of 11 October 2007 - IV R 52/04, BStBl II 2009, 705, WPg 2008, 216.
391. Scharpf and Luz (2000) 414; Scharpf and Schaber (2009) 579; IDW (2011b) para. 17.
392. Conlon & Aquilino: Derivatives D2.06[3][c] referring to the predominant opinion in the literature and the decision of the Federal Fiscal Court. *Other opinion* Häuselmann (2005) 104 suggests that the option premium should be treated as (transitionary) deferred income and the option contract be accounted for as 'other liability'. He maintains that the alternative accounting treatment as 'liability' would lead to an accounting of a reserve for expected losses which would not be the appropriate accounting method.

if the option value is higher than the option premium received, i.e., when the option writer is in a loss position.[393]

The German Institute of Certified Accountants also shares this view for financial accounts.[394] Such a reserve can, however, not be shown in the tax accounts.[395]

(B) Termination of Short Positions (Call and Put Options)

(aa) Exercise or Expiry of Short Call Positions

If a short call option is cash settled, gains or losses are computed as the premium received minus any settlement payment made.[396] Gains are fully taxable, whereas losses are only offsettable against gains from other derivatives transactions.[397]

If the short call option is physically settled, the capital gain or loss is computed as the sales proceeds of the underlying (strike price) received minus the book value of the underlying delivered and the costs of the sale.[398] If the book value of the shares is lower than the market value of the shares delivered, any gain will be calculated as the strike price received minus the book value of the shares delivered.

If the book value equals the market value of the shares delivered, any loss being the strike price received minus the market value of the shares should be subject to the loss ring-fencing rule of section 15(4) sentence 3 ITA.[399]

It is not entirely certain whether the call option premium received is treated as separate, fully taxable business income,[400] or whether it is rolled into the capital gain or loss from the sale of the underlying.[401] According to the latter view, the call option premium received could be added to the strike price received[402] and would reduce any capital loss (or increase any capital gain) on the sale of the underlying. In case of a

393. BMF, *Schreiben betr. steuerbilanzielle Behandlung von Optionsprämien beim Stillhalter* (IV A 6 – S 2133 – 17/03, BStBl I 2004, 192, 12 January 2004).
394. IDW (2011b) para. 18.
395. Section 5(4a) sent. 1 ITA.
396. Häuselmann and Wagner (2002b) 2173; Häuselmann (2005) 113.
397. Section 15(4) sent. 3 ITA. *See* Häuselmann (2005) 113. *Other opinion* Conlon & Aquilino: Derivatives D2.06[3][c] who suggest that the application of the decision of the Federal Fiscal Court regarding the lapsed option premiums paid for private investors (BFH, decision of 17 April 2007 – IX R 40/06, BStBl II 2007, 608, DStR 2007, 1075) would lead to the result that loss ring-fencing would not apply with regard to losses generated from the option contract, both in case of physical and cash-settled derivatives. The wording of the law and the intention of the legislator do however not support such a view.
398. Häuselmann (2005) 112-113.
399. *Other opinion* Conlon & Aquilino: Derivatives, D2.06[3][c] (issue December 2022): no loss ring-fencing rule applies.
    In case of the underlying being equities, any loss would be non-deductible for corporate investors, s. 8b(3) CTA, if the shares delivered would fall under the capital gains tax exemption of s. 8b(2) CTA.
400. Häuselmann (2005) 112 suggests that the option premium should be treated as fully taxable business income (only discussed in relation to equity options).
401. Nguyen (2007) 70 (accounting treatment); Conlon & Aquilino: Derivatives D2.06[3][c] (tax treatment).
402. Conlon & Aquilino: Derivatives D2.06[3][c] (issue December 2022) propose that the option premium received should be rolled into the sales price of the underlying unless the underlying assets are shares.

worthless expiry of the call option, the 'liability' being the short call option position should be derecognised in the accounts, and the option premium received should qualify as normal business income.[403]

(bb) Exercise or Expiry of Short Put Positions

If the short put option is cash settled, gains are taxable, and any losses are tax deductible (calculated as the option premium received minus the settlement payment made) with the losses being ring-fenced.[404]

If the short put option is physically settled, the option writer does not immediately recognise any loss upon acquisition of the underlying but capitalises the asset at acquisition cost.[405] The acquisition cost of the underlying is the strike price paid for the acquisition of the underlying minus the option premium received.[406]

At a later disposal of the underlying, the option premium remains rolled into the acquisition cost base. In case of a worthless expiry of the put option, the 'liability' being the short put option position should be derecognised in the accounts. The option premium received would qualify as normal business income.[407]

(cc) Close-Out of Short Option Positions

The close-out of short call or put option positions is treated in the same way as the cash settlement of a short call or put option, i.e., any gain would be taxable, and any loss would be deductible but ring-fenced.[408]

[ii] Taxation of Equity Options

As CTA section 8b(1) and (2) provide a tax exemption for equity capital gains and non-portfolio dividends, those provisions will result in a different tax treatment of cash- and physically settled equity derivatives, including cash and physically settled equity options.[409]

If the underlying shares are physically delivered under the equity option (at maturity), the delivery is treated as a sale of these shares for the party delivering the shares, i.e., the short call and the long put party. It is treated as a tax-exempt equity capital gain[410] and as a non-deductible equity capital loss – in case of a loss.[411]

403. Häuselmann (2005) 113 (in relation to equity options).
404. Section 15(4) sent. 3 ITA. *Other opinion* Conlon & Aquilino: Derivatives D2.06.[3][d], again citing the decision of the Federal Fiscal Court on lapsed option premiums.
405. Häuselmann (2005) 114.
406. IDW (2011b) para. 24. Also: Häuselmann (2005) 114; Conlon & Aquilino: Derivatives D2.06.[3][d] (issue December 2022); Nguyen (2007) 71.
407. Häuselmann (2005) 114.
408. Section 15(4) sent. 3 ITA.
409. The tax exemption will not apply to equities held in the trading book of a bank (s. 8b(7) CTA) or to shares held by life insurance companies (s. 8b(8) CTA).
410. Section 8b(2) CTA.
411. Section 8b(3) CTA.

This does not apply to cash-settled derivatives, however. Gains from cash-settled equity options are taxable, and losses are tax deductible but ring-fenced.[412]

The option premium paid at inception of the transaction by the long call or long put party is not regarded as an expense. Instead, the option purchased is capitalised at acquisition cost, with the premium paid rolled into it.[413] Any option premiums received under a short equity option will be subject to tax as normal income and will not qualify for the equity capital gains exemption, even if the equity option is physically settled.[414]

[c] *Taxation of Equity Swaps*

Under an equity swap, the total return (being any dividends and any appreciation in the share price) of an underlying equity or equity index will be exchanged against a fixed or floating rate of interest and any depreciation in the share price.[415]

For a corporate taxpayer who is not a bank or financial services institution, a swap is regarded as a *'pending transaction'* for legal and accounting purposes.[416] Thus, entering into a swap agreement will not show in the financial[417] or tax accounts.[418] At the balance sheet date, a reserve must be shown in the financial accounts for any unrealised losses, whereas a reserve is not permitted to be set up in the tax accounts.[419]

[i] Taxation of the Equity Performance Seller (Protection Buyer)

Under an equity swap, the equity performance seller (and protection buyer) will pay manufactured dividends[420] and receive manufactured interest payments.[421]

(1) Cash-Settled Equity Swaps

If the equity swap is cash settled, the equity performance seller (protection buyer) receives the difference of the price of the underlying shares between inception and

412. Section 15(4) sent. 3 ITA.
413. Conlon & Aquilino: Derivatives D2.06[3][a] (issue December 2022).
414. BFH, decision of 6 March 2013, I R 18/12, DB 2013, 1274 confirmed that received option premium will not fall under the equity capital gains exemption.
415. Anand Bhattacharya and Frank Fabozzi, 'Interest-rate swaps' in Frank Fabozzi (ed), *Handbook of fixed income securities* (5 edn, Irwin Professional Publishing 1997) 1264; Hull (2006) 747; Scharpf and Luz (2000) 506. Equity swaps are commonly used to convert returns from equity investments into fixed or floating rate investment returns or vice versa. *See* Hull (2006) 175.
416. Häuselmann and Wagner (2002b) 2174; Almut Maulshagen and Olaf Maulshagen, 'Rechtliche und bilanzielle Behandlung von Swapgeschäften' BB 2000 243, 248.
417. Paul Scharpf and Günther Luz, *Risikomanagement, Bilanzierung und Aufsicht von Finanzderivaten* (1 edn, Schäffer-Poeschel Verlag 1999) 419.
418. Conlon & Aquilino: Derivatives D2.06[4][a]; also: Häuselmann and Wagner (2002b) 2175.
419. Section 5(4a) ITA. *See* Häuselmann and Wagner (2002b) 2175; Conlon & Aquilino: Derivatives D2.06[4][a].
420. The manufactured dividends represent the real dividends received by the protection buyer with regard to the equities to which the swap is referenced.
421. IDW (2001b) 196; Matthias Geurts, 'Steuerliche Behandlung von Kreditderivaten' DB 2001 1163 (with regard to Total Return Swaps); Häuselmann and Wagner (2002b) 2175.

maturity if the share price goes down and pays the difference between the two if the share price goes up during the term of the transaction.[422]

Any losses under the equity swap will be ring-fenced under the loss ring-fencing provision.[423] Any payments made with respect to the price fluctuations of the underlying shares are not recognised in the P&L account until maturity of the transaction.[424]

Manufactured dividend payments made during the term of the swap are recognised upon payment, and interest income received is recognised on an accrual basis, according to one view in the expert literature with regard to total return swaps.[425]

Another view in the tax literature, however, suggests that any payment made or received during the term of the transaction, i.e., interest and manufactured dividends, should only be taxed at maturity, not during the term of the transaction, to avoid a timing mismatch between the manufactured dividend expensed and the interest received.[426] They argue that 'this accounts for the nature of the "interim payments" as prepayments on the final obligations due at maturity of the equity swap'.[427] Further, they suggest that only the interest payments could be referenced to a certain period within the term of the swap, whereas manufactured dividends could not be referenced to a certain period but could only be attributed to the transaction.[428]

The author does not agree with this view that regards all payments under the swap during the term of the transaction as 'interim payments'. In the author's view, manufactured dividends paid and interest income received should be seen separately from the payments with respect to any price fluctuations of the underlying shares.

The following arguments support the author's view: The manufactured dividend payments made under the swap are in lieu of the actual dividends received. They do not constitute part of the payments in respect of the price fluctuations of the underlying shares but are related to a completely separate payment stream. Whereas manufactured dividends mirror the recurring income on the underlying, the balance payment mirrors any capital gains or losses arising from a change of the price in the underlying shares at maturity compared to the price at inception. Hence, they are distinct payments and should, therefore, be accounted for and taxed separately.

The argument that manufactured dividend payments cannot be attributed to a certain period of the term of the swap is flawed. Equity swaps are a means to invest synthetically into equities. Hence, they mirror the performance and the dividend payments of equities. Dividends are periodic payments, and each dividend can be attributed to a specific period. As manufactured dividends mirror real dividends, manufactured dividends can also be attributed to a specific period.

422. Geurts (2001) 1163; Häuselmann and Wagner (2002b) 2174.
423. Section 8(1) CTA in conjunction with s. 15(4) sent. 3 ITA.
424. Conlon & Aquilino: Derivatives D2.06[4][a]; also: Geurts (2001) 1165; Häuselmann and Wagner (2002b) 2175.
425. This view has been established with regard to Total Return Swaps, where the underlying assets are usually bonds. It can be in the same way applied to equity swaps. *See* IDW (2001b) para. 21; also: Geurts (2001) 1165.
426. Häuselmann and Wagner (2002b) 2175; Häuselmann (2005) 140; Conlon & Aquilino: Derivatives D2.06[4][a] (issue December 2022).
427. Conlon & Aquilino: Derivatives D2.06[4][a]; similar: Häuselmann (2005) 139-140.
428. Häuselmann and Wagner (2002b) 2175.

Example 46:

Under the equity swap (four-year term) concluded between two parties, the upside performance of RBS shares and any dividend payments are exchanged in return for receiving a protection on the downside performance of the RBS share price and a payment of interest based on the three-month EURIBOR rate. RBS pays quarterly dividends. The manufactured dividends can be attributed to a specific period of the swap in the same way as the real dividends can be attributed to an earnings period of the RBS shares.

(2) Physically Settled Equity Swaps

If the equity swap is settled physically, the equity performance seller (protection buyer) will deliver the underlying equity at maturity and will receive the pre-agreed strike price. Because of the application of the tax exemption for the disposal of equities,[429] any gains from the physical delivery of the shares under the equity swap will be 95 %[430] tax-exempt for companies, and any losses will be non-deductible because the underlying equities are delivered under the swap.[431]

Manufactured dividends paid by the protection buyer should be tax deductible, whereas the interest payments received should be fully taxable income.[432] As manufactured dividends are only made in lieu of the actual dividends, they are not treated as real dividends and are, therefore, fully taxable for corporate investors. The manufactured dividends paid may, however, be treated as ring-fenced losses as these payments are part of the derivative payments/expenses.[433] The leading view in the literature would treat those manufactured dividend payments as fully deductible losses without any limitation (no ring-fencing).[434]

[ii] Taxation of the Equity Performance Buyer (Protection Seller)

The protection seller bears the price risk and dividend risk of the underlying shares during the term of the contract (protection seller).

The equity performance buyer (protection seller) will receive manufactured dividends over the term of the swap (sometimes called dividend equalisation payments) and pay interest.

429. Section 8b(2) CTA.
430. A total of 5% of the gains are deemed as non-deductible business expenses according to s. 8b(3) sent. 1 CTA.
431. Section 8b(3) sent. 3 CTA.
432. Some authors argue that the payments made or received over the life of the equity swap should be rolled into the sales proceeds of the shares because they regard the manufactured dividends and interest as 'interim payments', *see* above Ch. 6 §6.06[C][2][c][i][aa] Cash-Settled Equity Swap. *Compare* Conlon & Aquilino: Derivatives D2.06[4][a] (issue December 2022).
433. Section 15(4) sent. 3 ITA.
434. *See* Ch. 4 §4.03[C][2].

Manufactured dividends received are fully taxable when received (no accruals accounting takes place with regard to the manufactured dividends), and the interest paid is deductible as a business expense when made.[435]

As manufactured dividends are only made in lieu of the actual dividends, they are not treated as real dividends and are, therefore, not tax-exempt but fully taxable for corporate investors.[436]

If the equity swap is cash settled, the equity performance buyer (protection seller) will receive the difference between the share price at maturity and the share price at inception if the share price goes up and will pay to the equity performance seller (protection buyer) the difference between both prices if the share price goes down in value. Any gain from this difference payment under the equity swap is fully taxable, and any loss is tax deductible but ring-fenced.[437]

If the swap is physically settled, the protection seller will receive the underlying shares at maturity and pay the pre-agreed sales price. The sales price paid will constitute the acquisition cost of the shares.[438] Any gain from the subsequent disposal of the shares would be 95% tax-exempt, whereas any losses would be non-deductible.[439]

§6.07 COMPARISON OF THE UK AND GERMAN CORPORATE TAXATION RULES APPLYING TO DERIVATIVES

[A] Comparison of the Special Regime Approach Applied in the UK with the Integrative Approach Applied in German Corporate Tax Law

As outlined in Chapter 6 §6.01, the UK tax legislator has adopted a special regime approach in taxing derivatives and applies an exclusive set of rules to 'derivative contracts' entered into by companies. The benefit of this approach is that those rules were specifically tailored to apply only to derivatives and thus can potentially, in the author's view, deal more successfully with the issues that arise in the context of the taxation of these instruments.

In contrast, the German tax legislator has decided on an integrative approach and applies the general taxation rules to derivatives held by companies. Only one taxation provision applies specifically to derivatives, requiring the ring-fencing of derivatives losses.[440]

---

435. Conlon & Aquilino: Derivatives D2.06[4][b] (issue December 2022).
436. Häuselmann (2005) 140; Conlon & Aquilino: Derivatives D2.06[4][b] (issue December 2022).
437. Section 15(4) sent. 3 ITA. *See* Häuselmann (2005) 140; Häuselmann and Wagner (2002b) 2175; Conlon & Aquilino: Derivatives D 2.06[4][b] (issue December 2022).
438. *Other opinion* Conlon & Aquilino: Derivatives (issue December 2022) who suggest that also manufactured dividends received and interest paid should be part of the calculation of the total gain or loss under the equity swap for tax purposes.
439. Sections 8b(3) sent. 3 CTA.
440. Only one specific derivatives taxation provision exists that requires the ring-fencing of losses specifically for derivatives, *see* Ch. 4 §4.03[C][2] and Ch. 6 §6.03.

As the general corporate tax rules are not tailored specifically to derivatives, the integrative approach applied in the German corporate tax legislation leads, in the author's view, to a less coherent taxation regime for derivatives compared to the special regime approach adopted in the UK, partly also due to the fact that the German tax legislator still very much privileges equity over debt.

For example, different general rules are applicable to cash and physically settled equity derivatives. Thus, applying the general corporate taxation rules to derivatives can, in certain cases, lead to different taxation results for economically similar derivatives.[441]

[B] Abolition of the Income and Capital Divide in the UK and German Corporate Taxation Rules

The distinction between income and capital has been largely abolished in the UK, with both ordinary business income and capital gains being subject to corporation tax. Also, regarding derivatives, the UK legislator has largely abolished the income and capital divide for derivative contracts held by corporate taxpayers with the introduction and further amendments of the FA 2002, Schedule 26 rules, now CTA 2009, Part 7.

Similarly, the income and capital divide does not play a role in German corporate taxation as income and capital gains are, in principle, subject to the same tax rules as ordinary business income.[442]

[C] The Equity and Debt Divide in the UK and German Corporate Tax Legislation

The attribution to equity or debt still makes a difference in both the UK and German corporate taxation. In the context of derivatives held by corporates, the UK legislator applies a divide between equity and debt and privileges certain equity derivatives over other derivative contracts.[443] With regard to timing when the income is recognised, and also whether capital allowances can be claimed and losses offset, the application of the capital gains tax rules can, therefore, still lead to different results for taxpayers.

Also, German corporate taxation rules still very much privilege equity income and capital gains over debt income and capital gains because non-portfolio dividends and capital gains from shares are 95% exempt from corporate tax.[444] The 95% tax exemption for equity capital gains also applies to physically settled equity derivatives, whereas gains from cash-settled equity derivatives are treated as normal income.[445]

Depending on the form of settlement, the taxation of these equity derivatives may either result in fully taxable gains and tax deductible but possibly ring-fenced losses

441. *See* Ch. 6 §6.05[C].
442. Section 8(2) CTA.
443. Southern (2017) para. 1.9; For example, in the case of equity derivatives that hedge shares, *see* Ch. 6 §6.02;
444. Ch. 6 §6.04.
445. *Ibid.*

(cash-settled derivatives) or in virtually tax-free gains and non-deductible losses (physically settled contracts upon disposal of the shares).[446] By applying the equity privilege to physically settled derivatives but not to cash-settled contracts, taxpayers may use these instruments for tax planning purposes.[447]

§6.08 TAXATION OF CRYPTOASSETS

In the author's view, tax authorities and taxpayers face significant challenges in relation to the location of cryptoassets, the alignment of accounting standards and tax law, and the tax treatment of impairment losses. In Chapter 5 of this work, the author has extensively discussed the accounting treatment of cryptoassets and crypto derivatives and outlined the advantages and disadvantages of the alignment of accounting standards and tax law in the context of cryptoassets. With respect to the location of cryptoassets, the author refers for details to the article written by her and *Southern*. The problem of the location of cryptoassets is particularly relevant for individual taxpayers who are taxed according to the remittance basis.[448] Thus, it is not further discussed in this book.

In the context of corporate taxpayers, the author will focus on the tax treatment of impairment losses for tax purposes. Those losses can be generated without selling the cryptoassets and thus may lead to tax avoidance schemes being employed by taxpayers. Thus, the recognition of impairment losses for tax purposes should be closely monitored by the domestic tax authorities.

[A] Taxation of Cryptoassets in the UK

The current UK rules tax cryptoassets under the intangible fixed assets regime of CTA 2009, Part 8. For direct tax purposes, HMRC regards cryptoassets neither as a currency, cash or cash equivalent.[449] Companies who hold cryptoassets for investment purposes account for them as intangible assets under IAS 38; *see* Chapter 5 §5.05[A][1].[450] Because the cryptoassets are classified as intangible assets, companies applying cost accounting may recognise impairment losses for any downside movement below cost. In contrast, any write-up is not recognised in the financial accounts until the disposal of the cryptoassets.[451]

---

446. Section 8b (2) and (3) sent. 3 CTA. *See* Ch. 6 §6.04.
447. Preferential tax outcomes may be achieved by converting interest income into equity capital gains, *see* Ch. 10 §10.01[A]). Likewise, tax arbitrage schemes may be set up that generate virtually tax-free capital gains on one leg of the transaction, and tax-deductible losses on the other leg of the transaction, thereby effectively creating tax capacity that can be used by the taxpayer to offset against ordinary business income, *see* Ch. 10 §10.01[B].
448. Southern and Weidmann (2023), 68, 88-89.
449. *Ibid.*, 89.
450. *Ibid.*
451. *Ibid.*

HMRC states that companies holding cryptocurrencies as an investment 'are liable to pay Corporation Tax on any gains they realise when they dispose of it'.[452] In cases where a company 'disposes of cryptocurrencies for less than the allowable costs, it realises a capital loss upon disposal'.[453]

In the Cryptoassets Manual CRYPTO41300, HMRC suggests that:

> Section 38 of the Taxation of Chargeable Gains Act (TCGA) 1992 provides for the types of costs which can be deducted. HMRC's view is that these include:
>
> - the consideration (in pound sterling) originally paid for the asset,
> - transaction fees paid for having the transaction included on the distributed ledger,
> - advertising for a purchaser or a vendor,
> - professional costs to draw up a contract for the acquisition or disposal of the tokens, and
> - costs of making a valuation or apportionment to be able to calculate gains or losses.[454]

Cryptoassets are either accounted for as inventory according to IAS 2 or FRS 102, Section 13 or as intangible property under IAS 38 or FRS 102, Section 18.[455] This classification 'depends upon whether they are acquired with the intention of selling them within twelve months (stock) or with the intention of holding them for a longer period (intangible property)'.[456]

In cases where cryptoassets are 'held as inventory, cryptoassets will be valued at the year-end at the lower of cost or net realisable value. That means that there will be the usual stock adjustment at the year-end. Unsold stock is an add-back to profit because it represents a cost of the next year's sales, not of this year's sales'.[457]

If a company applies the cost model to account for cryptocurrencies which are held as investments under IAS 38, any movements above cost are not recognised in the accounts, whereas any movements below cost are recognised as impairment losses.[458]

Southern and the author state with respect to impairment losses that '[t]he accounting issue arises from the tension between balance sheet recognition (historical cost) and upward or downward revaluation/impairment. The tax treatment will follow the accounting treatment; hence if an impairment loss is recognised in the financial accounts, it will also show in the tax accounts'.[459]

Southern and the author maintain that '[i]t should be noted that the same measurement model should be used for all assets in an asset class. Hence, if a business is holding different cryptocurrencies for investment purposes and there is not an active

452. HMRC, CRYPTO 41200.
453. Southern and Weidmann (2023) BTR, 68, 90.
454. HMRC, CRYPTO41300.
455. *Ibid.*
456. *Ibid.*
457. *Ibid.*
458. Southern and Weidmann (2023), 68, 84-85.
459. *Ibid*, 91.

market for all cryptocurrencies held, those assets should be measured using the cost model'.[460]

As no amortisation takes place due to the infinite life of cryptocurrencies,[461] only regular testing for impairment takes place, which can also happen during the accounting year, i.e., in case the cryptocurrency has depreciated in value.[462]

Thus, entities can recognise impairment losses whenever the cryptocurrency depreciates in value. Then, impairment is tested, and those impairment losses are recognised in the financial accounts. However, if the cryptocurrency subsequently appreciates in value, the cost accounting method prohibits a 'write-up' to the higher value. That means that the cryptocurrency position is left at a lower value for accounting purposes, although its market value appreciated. The increased value of the cryptoasset position will not show when applying cost accounting whereas, if fair value measurement is applied, it will (which is currently not the case for cryptoassets).

[B] Taxation of Cryptoassets in Germany

Germany taxes cryptoassets under the general corporate taxation rules. No specific taxation regime exists that deals with the taxation of cryptoassets. However, the German Ministry of Finance issued a letter ruling in 2022 where it discussed in detail the taxation of cryptoassets for private individuals. This letter ruling also contains some paragraphs that deal with the taxation of businesses.

In the 2022 letter ruling, the Federal Ministry of Finance regards cryptocurrencies as non-depreciable assets that are categorised under the tangible assets rules and 'classified as fixed or current assets in accordance with general tax law accounting principles'.[463] The accounting literature regards cryptoassets as intangible assets under German GAAP if they are held as long-term assets.[464]

Cryptoassets are initially measured at cost under German GAAP; they have an infinite lifetime, and no amortisation takes place.[465]

If cryptoassets are held as investments, no impairment losses are recognised under German GAAP unless the cryptoasset defaults,[466] according to section 253 (3) sentence 5 German Commercial Code.

In the context of short-term crypto holdings, recognition of impairment losses is possible in the financial accounts.[467] But even in that case, any increase in the value of the cryptoassets up to the initial acquisition costs has to be recognised in the financial

460. *Ibid.*, 85.
461. Ch. 5 §5.05[A][2].
462. IAS 38, para 108(b).
463. BMR, Schreiben of 10 May 22, IV C 1 – S 2256/19/ 10003:001, DOK 2022/0493899, para 41. *See* Courtesy translation of the Federal Ministry of Finance's circular 'Einzelfragen zur ertragsteuerrechtlichen Behandlung von virtuellen Währungen und von sonstigen Token' of 10 May 2022, Federal Tax Gazette I, 668, para. 41.
464. *See* Ch. 5 §5.05[C].
465. *Ibid.*, *compare* BMR, Schreiben of 10 May 22, IV C 1 – S 2256/19/ 10003:001, para 41.
466. *See* Ch. 5 §5.05[C].
467. *Ibid.*, *see also* Stobbe (2021).

accounts.[468] Hence, under German GAAP, the use of impairment losses for tax avoidance purposes is limited as any impairment losses have to be again written-up in cases of subsequent cryptoasset gains up to the initial acquisition costs of the cryptoassets. In the author's opinion, as no specific ring-fencing rules apply to cryptoassets in the German tax legislation, the German tax administration should remain vigilant with regard to impairment losses in the crypto realm.

The Lower Tax Court of Berlin and Brandenburg (Finanzgericht Berlin and Brandenburg) confirmed in 2019 that cryptocurrencies should be regarded as 'assets' (Wirtschaftsgüter).[469] Further, in 2023, the Federal Fiscal Court decided that the cryptocurrencies Bitcoin, Ethereum and Monero should be regarded as 'virtual currencies'.[470] The court, in this context, confirmed for private individuals that cryptoassets are regarded as 'other assets' under section 23(1) No. 2 ITA.[471] 'Other assets' according to this provision are, for example, precious metals, such as gold, foreign currencies, art, other mobile assets and intangible assets.[472] Although the decision was made in the context of private sales transactions, this categorisation may also be relevant in the context of business and corporate investors. It is not certain if the Federal Fiscal Court refers to cryptocurrencies as foreign currencies or as intangible assets as it uses the term 'virtual currency'. Thus, further clarification in relation to business and corporate taxation is needed.

[C] Outlook

A further discussion of the taxation regime applying to cryptoassets is not part of this chapter, as neither the UK nor Germany has established specific taxation rules applying to cryptoassets.

The author believes that a special taxation regime for cryptoassets is desirable to tax those instruments as such a regime would allow the tax administration to shape taxation rules that align with the unique digital nature of cryptoassets. The author proposes that tax reporting of cryptoassets alone, as envisaged under the *Council Directive amending Directive 2011/16/EU on administrative cooperation in the field of taxation* (DAC8), will not solve the issues connected with the taxation of cryptoassets.

---

468. *See* Ch. 5 §5.05[C].
469. FG Berlin-Brandenburg, 20 June 2019 – 13 V 13100/19, openJur 2020, 42838, https://openjur.de/u/2257934.html, accessed 1 October 2023.
470. BFH decision of 14 February 2023, IX R 3/22, ECLI:DE:BFH:2023:U.140223.IXR3.22.0, https://www.bundesfinanzhof.de/de/entscheidung/entscheidungen-online/detail/STRE202310057/, accessed 1 October 2023; *see also* Christopher Arndt, Bitcoin & Co: BFH rules crypto profits are taxable! What do crypto investors need to know now?, Acconisis (2023), https://www.acconsis.de/en/bitcoin-co-bfh-rules-crypto-profits-are-taxable-what-do-crypto-investors-need-to-know-now/, accessed 1 October 2023.
471. BFH decision of 14 February 2023, IX R 3/22, ECLI:DE:BFH:2023:U.140223.IXR3.22.0, https://www.bundesfinanzhof.de/de/entscheidung/entscheidungen-online/detail/STRE202310057/, accessed 1 October 2023; *see also* Arndt, (2023).
472. Michael Hoheisel in: Littmann/Bitz/Pust, Das Einkommensteuerrecht, EStG § 23 Abs 1 Nr 2 EStG, 2. Andere Wirtschaftgueter, para 82, (issue 142, April 2020).

In summary, the taxation of cryptoassets is very much a work in progress. Beyond the discussion in Chapter 6 §6.08, the problems arising in the context of cryptoassets are analysed in various sections in Chapters 4, 5, 7, 8 and 10, where the author deals with the specific issues. For example, Chapter 10 §10.04 discusses in detail how the accounting treatment of cryptoasset impairment losses in the UK may be used by taxpayers to achieve tax deferrals for gains other than those of a crypto nature.

§6.09 SOLUTION TO PROBLEM 3: COHERENCE IN DOMESTIC TAX RULES

A coherence of domestic tax rules is important when dealing with the taxation of derivatives and cryptoassets. There are mainly two ways a domestic tax system can decide how to deal with the taxation of derivatives: the *integrative approach* that applies the general tax rules to derivatives and cryptoassets and the *special regime approach* that applies a separate set of rules when taxing those instruments.

[A] The Integrative Approach

With respect to derivatives, if the tax legislator decides on an integrative approach, it should ensure that income and capital gains from derivatives are treated in the same way.[473] Furthermore, a revision of the traditional distinction between equity and debt should be considered.

Countries, in principle, have good reasons to privilege equity over debt as they may want to avoid economic double taxation issues and cascade effects when taxing dividends and equity capital gains in the hands of corporate investors.

Additionally, they may want to encourage risk-taking and foster economic growth and thus privilege investments into companies compared to debt investments that are generally seen as less risky alternatives to equity.

However, tax systems that apply the general taxation rules to derivatives and at the same time distinguish between equity, debt and other instruments are likely to have more problems with arbitrage strategies than those countries which apply the same tax rates to equity and debt instruments and derivatives.[474]

In relation to cryptoassets, the author proposes that an integrative regime will not be appropriate to tax this newly emerged asset class as those instruments are unique in their digital nature, and hence, tax rules should take those specific features into account.

473. OECD (2001) paras 49-51 and 98; Thuronyi (2001a) 263.

474. *See* Thuronyi (2001a) 263 more generally on the problems of the distinction between income and capital gains; similar: Neighbour (1997) 933; also: Ch. 6 §6.05[C], Ch. 10 §10.01[A] and [B].

[B] The Special Regime Approach

To avoid an application of the traditional tax rules that often distinguish between equity and debt and/or income and capital gains, domestic tax systems may opt for a specific taxation regime concerning derivatives that includes both physically and cash-settled derivatives.

If such a tax system allows taxing derivatives independently from the traditional categories of income and capital, it needs to be able to manage the taxation of specific derivatives categories properly, such as equity derivatives. This is possible with the help of targeted anti-avoidance legislation applying to avoidance schemes utilising derivatives.

The UK has, in principle, achieved such coherence due to the introduction of the derivative contracts regime in 2002 and its various amendments, although it did not abolish the distinction between equity derivatives and other derivatives in its entirety.

Countries which apply an equity privilege and at the same time classify derivatives as a third category beyond equity and debt may also face tax arbitrage if they subject derivatives to a different taxation regime or tax rate than equity and debt, as income and gains or losses from one category may be converted to the other category by means of economic replication.[475]

In relation to cryptoassets, the author proposes that the special regime approach is more appropriate to tax those instruments than an integrative approach, as cryptoassets are a novel asset class with specific features stemming from their existence in the virtual realm.

[C] Coherent Solutions: Integrative Versus Special Regime Approach

Both the integrative approach and the special regime approach require slightly different prerequisites to achieve coherent solutions for taxing derivatives.

[1] Achieving Coherence in Applying an Integrative Approach?

An integrative tax system faces the following challenges:

(1) If the tax legislator decides to apply the general taxation rules to derivatives, it has to ensure that both income from derivatives, as well as capital gains from disposal, assignment or close-out of derivatives, are taxed similarly. This can normally only be achieved if the general tax system subjects income to the same taxation rules as capital gains, including the time of realisation and the tax rate.

(2) If the integrative tax system privileges equity over debt,[476] gains from physically settled equity derivatives may fall under the equity privilege,

475. Ch. 2 §2.02[A][1].
476. *See* Ch. 6 §6.04.

whereas gains from cash-settled equity derivatives will be subject to normal taxation rules. In such a system, tax arbitrage schemes that exploit the difference in taxation between cash and physically settled derivatives are more likely than in a tax system where all derivatives are taxed in the same way.

(3) If the general tax rules apply to hybrid instruments as well as to structured products, the legislator must decide whether these instruments will be bifurcated or not for tax purposes. Furthermore, a legislative decision or a decision by the courts has to be made with regard to the circumstances under which hybrid instruments will fall into the category of equity or debt.

(4) Gains or income from derivatives may fall into the domestic categories of 'interest'[477] or 'dividends'[478] if no special tax rules exist that attribute income or gains from derivatives to a separate category of income, thus potentially leading to qualification conflicts in cross-border transactions. In a cross-border context, the legislator might also negotiate with other countries to include income from certain derivatives within the categories of interest[479] or dividends[480] instead of qualifying it as business profits,[481] capital gains[482] or other income[483] in their double tax treaties.

(5) In a system where the general rules are applied to derivatives, extensive anti-avoidance rules will be mandatory to prevent tax arbitrage.

[2] Achieving Coherence in Applying a Special Regime Approach?

If a legislator decides on a special regime for derivatives, the focus should be slightly different:

(1) It should be ensured that all derivatives are included in the regime and that the regime caters for both cash and physically settled derivatives.

(2) The special regime should include equity derivatives. If the general tax system applying to traditional instruments taxes equity differently to debt, it also has to be explicitly decided whether equity derivatives are treated any differently from other derivatives.

(3) The special rules should also deal with structured products and hybrid instruments and determine whether a bifurcation or integration approach is applied.

477. For example, gains from interest-rate swaps may be categorised as interest.
478. Manufactured dividends paid under dividend swaps may be categorised as real dividends.
479. Article 11 OECD Model.
480. Article 10 OECD Model.
481. Article 7 OECD Model.
482. Article 13 OECD Model.
483. Article 21 OECD Model.

(4) At a cross-border level, the tax legislator has to decide whether derivatives will be subject to any withholding taxes and, if so, how those taxes are applied in comparison to interest withholding taxes and dividend withholding taxes.
(5) The special regime should include targeted anti-avoidance rules that deal with the issue of derivatives tax arbitrage.

[3] Special Regime Approach as the More Appropriate Solution

In the author's view, in practice, it will be very difficult to tax derivatives coherently within a general tax system based on an integrative approach. The tax legislator would have to carefully revise the general tax system and consider all the issues outlined in Chapter 6 §6.06[C][1] in order to avoid problems of tax arbitrage that are made possible by incongruent taxation of gains and losses of instruments with similar payoffs.

Most domestic tax systems will, however, be structured in a way that still includes elements of privileging capital gains over income and equity over debt in their general rules, even if this privilege only occurs in the form of a timing benefit.

Considering the practicability of both approaches, the special regime approach is likely to achieve more coherent taxation results than the integrative approach,[484] provided that the special regime fulfils the criteria outlined in Chapter 6 §6.06[C][2].

In a special regime applying to derivatives, tax arbitrage may, however, still be an issue as replication possibilities based on the put-call parity will enable taxpayers to convert non-privileged derivatives gains into privileged equity capital gains. Thus, tax legislators that implement a special tax regime for derivatives will have the following options in order to minimise tax arbitrage opportunities:

They implement anti-avoidance rules that prevent the tax-motivated conversion of non-privileged derivatives gains into privileged equity capital gains if they want to maintain the equity privilege for tax policy reasons.

Or, they abolish or minimise the preferential taxation (or at least the preferential tax rates) of equity capital gains as far as possible.

Whether tax systems need to abolish a privileged taxation of dividends is more difficult to answer, as tax legislators have good reasons to avoid an economic double taxation of dividends.

If comprehensive anti-avoidance rules, including CFC rules, exist, which target tax avoidance schemes that generate derivatives gains in low-tax jurisdictions and distribute them as tax-free dividends, it should be possible for tax systems to maintain a preferential tax rate for dividends that are distributed to corporate shareholders.

The author believes that tax administrations should develop a special taxation regime which is designed to cater for the specific challenges and tax avoidance

484. *Other opinion* OECD (2001) paras 95-96, suggesting that it is more difficult to achieve the tax policy goals of neutrality and equity, simplicity, certainty and robustness in a tax system that applies the special regime approach compared to a tax system that adopts the integrative approach, based on the assumption that the integrative approach would entail a more flexible tax system compared to a special regime approach. The author does not agree based on my arguments above.

opportunities that cryptoassets provide due to the tax treatment of impairment losses if the corporate taxpayer accounts for cryptoassets at cost and recognises impairment losses which can potentially be offset with other capital gains also for tax purposes. For example, the UK's current rules, which tax cryptoassets under the intangible fixed assets regime of CTA 2009, Part 8, may not be appropriate to tax those instruments due to the disparate tax treatment of cryptoasset gains and (impairment) losses.

CHAPTER 7
The Taxation of Derivatives and Cryptoassets in the Context of Hedging Transactions

People far too often associate derivatives markets with mere speculation, but there are very legitimate businesses that need derivatives to protect themselves against risk.

— Fred Ehrsam, *Founder of Coinbase*

In this chapter, the author analyses how hedging transactions, particularly those that use or hedge derivatives or cryptoassets, are treated for accounting and tax purposes in the UK and Germany.

In relation to derivatives, the author compares and evaluates the different approaches in both countries and discusses the UK's and Germany's position towards tax-neutral matching of gains and losses of a hedged item and the hedge on a post-tax basis. In this context, the author analyses possible anti-avoidance approaches that both countries take against transactions that exploit loopholes in the domestic tax legislation through overhedging or underhedging market risks.

Hedging and hedge effectiveness in the context of cryptoassets and crypto derivatives are topics which have only received limited attention so far. In Chapter 7 §7.06, the author will investigate how hedge relationships between cryptoassets and crypto derivatives are treated for accounting and tax purposes.

§7.01 THE ECONOMIC BACKGROUND OF HEDGING APPROACHES

A hedging transaction may be defined as any transaction undertaken to reduce or eliminate specific risk components of a derivative, any other financial instrument or underlying variable.[1] Hedging can take any form as long as there is a risk involved and tradable financial instruments exist in a liquid market which can be used to hedge those risks.[2] If, when and how companies hedge their various risks is decided by a range of risk takers in banks and insurance companies, such as individual traders, the treasury and risk departments, and the Asset and Liability Management (ALM).[3]

One can principally distinguish between three approaches to hedging risk: micro hedging, portfolio hedging and macro hedging.

In a *micro hedge*, a 'derivative fully or partly balances risks pertaining to an individual balance sheet item'.[4] The hedging of a particular risk of a balance sheet item is typically achieved by entering into an offsetting risk position,[5] which in many cases is achieved by the purchase or sale of one or more derivatives that provide a partially or fully offsetting risk profile with regard to the specific risk that the company wants to hedge.[6]

Portfolio hedging means that risks of several similar balance sheet items are hedged by one or more hedging transactions.[7]

Example 47:

Trader A holds a portfolio of 100 equity options with various strike prices and maturities over the DAX. Trader A wants to hedge this portfolio of DAX options. Equity options can be – in theory – perfectly hedged by applying the Black-Scholes formula.[8]

Each risk class of the equity options (e.g., delta (Δ), gamma (Γ), vega (υ), theta (Θ) and rho (ρ)[9]) has to be hedged separately. It is, however, possible to add all deltas of the 100 equity options and hedge the overall delta, for example, with additional DAX futures.

The overall gamma of the equity options portfolio is dynamically hedged with DAX options; the same applies to the vega position of the portfolio. Rho can be hedged with interest rate swaps.

1. OECD (2001) para. 115.
2. *See* Ch. 2 §2.02[B].
3. IASB, *Financial Instruments* (Replacement of IAS 39) – Hedge Accounting, Macro hedge accounting – the economic objective (Staff paper, 2010) para. 7.
4. Conlon & Aquilino: Derivatives D2.03[5][a].
5. OECD (2013a) 13.
6. For the definition of hedging, how it is achieved, its relationship to replication and the distinction between static and dynamic hedging, *see* Ch. 2 §2.02[B].
7. BR-Drucksache 344/08 (23 May 2008), Gesetzentwurf der Bundesregierung, Entwurf eines Gesetzes zur Modernisierung des Bilanzrechts (Bilanzrechtsmodernisierungsgesetz – BilMoG) 126; IDW, RS HFA 35, *Handelsrechtliche Bilanzierung von Bewertungseinheiten* (10 June 2011) WPg Supplement 3/2011, 59 ff., FN-IDW 7/2011, 445 ff., para. 17.
8. *See* Ch. 2 §2.02[A][2] and §2.02[C].
9. *See* Hull (2006) 344-363 for the explanation of hedging using the 'Greeks'.

Macro hedging considers the risk-compensating effect of whole groups of similar balance sheet items.[10] Risk compensation is achieved by hedging those groups of balance sheet items together based on the net exposure of the risk.[11] In contrast to micro and portfolio hedging, macro hedging does not seek a full hedge of the risk position. Instead, it aims to hedge a range of risk classes that risk managers consider similar.[12]

Furthermore, many companies do not aim to fully hedge their risk position but instead opt for underhedging of the risk position to achieve an overall risk for the group of balance sheet items that is acceptable to bear for the company.[13] Thus, macro hedging usually only achieves an approximate hedge of the risk.

Typical risks that banks and large companies consider macro hedging are interest rate, commodity and FX risks.[14] Likewise, risk departments or trading units sometimes seek to macro hedge a portfolio of different equity positions, bonds or credit instruments.

Example 48:

In 2008, Company A intended to hedge its portfolio of various European government bonds (including Greek bonds). The internal risk model assumed that all Euro-denominated bonds belong to the same risk category.

Hence, Company A's risk committee decided that the Euro-denominated bonds are hedged via a macro hedge and that Bund futures are used to macro hedge this portfolio of European government bonds.

---

10. Macro hedging is also a topic discussed by the IASB as banks and big companies often rely on macro hedging to manage their interest rate risks, commodity risks or FX risks at the level of the company in addition to or instead of the risk management of single portfolios.

    See IASB, *Macro hedging* (2010); Deloitte, 'Financial Instruments – Macro Hedge accounting' http://www.iasplus.com/en/projects/major/macro-hedge-accounting, accessed 16 October 2023.

    In 2013-2014, the IASB discussed whether the risk management approach of macro hedging groups of asset or liability portfolios on a continuous basis and at a portfolio level should also be mirrored in some way in the accounts by way of revaluations of the hedging portfolios.

    See IASB, *Financial instruments: Accounting for macro hedging* (2013), https://www.ifrs.org/content/dam/ifrs/meetings/2013/may/iasb/accounting-for-macro-hedging/ap4b-what-the-model-should-apply-to.pdf, accessed 16 October 2023.

    A discussion paper was issued in April 2014; see IASB, Discussion Paper DP/2014/1, *Accounting for Dynamic Risk Management: a Portfolio Revaluation Approach to Macro Hedging*, https://www.ifrs.org/content/dam/ifrs/project/dynamic-risk-management/discussion-paper/published-documents/dp-accounting-for-dynamic-risk-management.pdf, accessed 13 May 2023.

    As of October 2023, the development of a Dynamic Risk Management (DRM) model by the IASB is still ongoing, and the IASB is working towards an Exposure Draft.

    See IASB, Dynamic Risk Management (2023), https://www.ifrs.org/projects/work-plan/dynamic-risk-management/#current-stage, accessed 1 December 2023.
11. IDW (2011a) para. 19.
12. IASB, *Macro hedging* (2010) paras 24-26.
13. *Ibid.*, para. 27.
14. IASB, *Accounting for Macro Hedging, Risks other than interest rate* (Staff Paper, December 2012, 2012).

Due to decreasing confidence levels in Greece's ability to repay debt in 2009/2010, the value of Greek government bonds dropped approximately 60%, and Company A lost 60% of the value of the Greek government bonds. At the same time, Company A also made a loss on short Bund futures of, say, 30%, as the demand for German Government bonds due to a large-scale 'flight to quality' significantly increased.

Thus, Company A lost on both the hedged item and the hedge as it had assumed a macro hedge based on the assumption that a portfolio of European government bonds would have the same risk propositions.

§7.02 THE ACCOUNTING AND TAX TREATMENT OF HEDGING RELATIONSHIPS INVOLVING DERIVATIVES

One must distinguish the accounting and tax treatment of hedging relationships from the economic proposition of hedging.

Hedging raises two main issues concerning derivatives, which should be distinguished from each other:

(1) hedge accounting and its tax treatment during the term of a hedging relationship; and
(2) the treatment of hedging relationships from a post-tax perspective.

[A] Hedge Accounting and Its Tax Treatment During the Term of the Transaction

The purpose of hedge accounting is to reduce earnings volatility caused by accounting mismatches between the hedged item and the hedging instrument during the term of the hedging relationship.[15] These mismatches may arise if both instruments are accounted for on a different accounting basis, leading to the recognition of profits or losses in different accounting periods.

Hedge accounting of derivatives can follow two different approaches:

(1) The hedge and the hedged item may be treated as a single 'synthetic' off-balance sheet transaction[16] or valuation unit.[17]

15. Southern (2017) paras 16.4-16.5; OECD (2001) para. 121.
16. Under old UK GAAP, the hedge and the hedged item were accounted off-balance sheet. *See* HMRC, CFM57010; Haworth and Hollis (2010) 28.
17. German accounting rules treat a hedging relationship for accounting purposes as a 'valuation unit' (*Bewertungseinheit*). *See* IDW (2011a) para. 11.

(2) The impact of the hedged item may be matched with the hedging instrument in the income statement by recognising profits and losses on both items in the same accounting period.[18]

From a tax perspective, the issue of hedge accounting is primarily one of timing, as profits and losses from the hedge and the hedged item should be matched and taxed in the same accounting period.

A tax system needs to provide appropriate (tax) hedging provisions for taxpayers in order to allow tax-neutral and cost-efficient hedging of risks arising in assets and liabilities and other balance sheet items during the term of the transaction.[19] However, tax hedging provisions typically do not provide an answer as to how the hedge and the hedged item are treated for tax purposes at maturity, as they only concern the treatment during the term.

[B] Treatment of Hedging Relationships from a Post-tax Perspective

The second question concerns the tax treatment of the hedged item and the hedge on a post-tax basis, i.e., whether gains or losses of the hedge and the hedged item are taxed differently, thus leading to a mismatch in taxation of both items and an incomplete hedge on a post-tax basis.[20]

Example 49:

Company A holds shares in Company B. Gains on these shares are tax-exempt, and losses are non-deductible. Company A hedges its equity position with the purchase of a reverse equity note that provides an exposure opposite to the performance in the shares of Company B. Gains on this note are treated as taxable, and losses are treated as tax deductible.

If Company A makes a gain on the shares, this gain will be tax-exempt. At the same time, Company A will make a loss on the note, which is tax deductible, leading to a favourable tax position for Company A on a post-tax basis.

If the shares stand at a loss, the loss will be non-deductible, whereas the corresponding gain on the note will be fully taxable. Thus, Company A will have an incomplete hedge on a post-tax basis.[21]

The question of tax-efficient post-tax hedging is primarily one of tax law as it concerns the question of whether gains or losses of the hedged item and the hedge are

18. Southern (2017) para. 16.20.
19. *See* Ch. 3 §3.04. *Compare* Neighbour (2001) para. 14; OECD (2001) paras 80, 118 and 121.
20. OECD (2013a) 15.
21. *Ibid.*, 15-17, Table 2a and 2b.

subject to the same tax treatment or whether they are treated differently for tax purposes, thus leading to disparities and incomplete hedges on a post-tax basis.[22]

§7.03 TREATMENT OF HEDGING TRANSACTIONS UNTIL MATURITY IN THE UK AND GERMANY

[A] Derivatives Hedging Transactions in the UK

[1] Treatment Hedging Transactions for Accounting Purposes

Companies can account for derivatives under FRS 102, Sections 11 and 12, IAS 39 or IFRS 9, applying the accounting choice they have under FRS 102. Alternatively, they can account under IFRS 9 directly.[23]

The International Accounting Standards Board (IASB) states that in cases of hedge accounting, companies still have the choice of whether to continue to apply the 'old' hedge accounting provisions under IAS 39 or switch to IFRS 9.[24] The following outlines the hedge accounting provisions of FRS 102, IAS 39 and IFRS 9.

'Hedging is an accruals/historical cost concept',[25] not a fair value concept. Under old UK GAAP, in cases where FRS 26 was not adopted, 'some hedging contracts were left off-balance sheet: the company simply reflected the result of the overall transaction'.[26]

In contrast, under former FRS 26, now codified in FRS 102, Schedule 12, 'all derivatives are measured on the balance sheet at their fair value even if they are accounted for as a hedge. Hedge accounting is only possible where certain conditions, such as the nature of the hedging instrument and the documentation of the hedge, are met'.[27]

[a] Hedge Accounting under FRS 102, Section 12

Hedge accounting is optional under FRS 102, Section 12, which means '[p]rovided the qualifying conditions in paragraph 12.18 are met, an entity may apply hedge accounting'.[28]

A hedging relationship consists of a hedged item and a hedging item.[29]

22. This question is closely interlinked with the question of the different tax treatment of equity and debt for tax purposes.
23. *See* Ch. 6 §6.02[B].
24. IFRS, IAS 39, Recognition and Measurement, Standard 2022 Issued, About, https://www.ifrs.org/projects/completed-projects/2010/disclosures-transfers-of-financial-assets-amendments-to-ifrs-7/, accessed 9 August 2023.
25. Southern (2017) para. 16.3.
26. Haworth and Hollis (2010) 28; *also* HMRC, CFM57010.
27. HMRC, CFM57010.
28. FRS 102, para. 12.15 sent. 2.
29. FRS 102, para. 12.15 sent. 1; *see* Southern (2017) para. 16.17.

[i] Hedged Item

FRS 102 defines that a hedged item can be:

(1) a recognised asset or liability;
(2) an unrecognised firm commitment;
(3) a highly probable forecast transaction;
(4) a net investment in a foreign operation; or
(5) a component of any such item, provided the item is reliably measurable.[30]

Thus, all of the above items must be reliably measurable to qualify as a hedged item.[31]

[ii] Hedging Instrument

FRS 102, paragraph 12.17 confirms that an instrument may be a *hedging instrument* if all of the following criteria are met:

(a) it is a financial instrument measured at fair value through profit or loss;
(b) it is a contract with a party external to the reporting entity (i.e., external to the group or individual entity that is being reported on); and
(c) it is not a written option, except as described in paragraph 12.17C.[32]

FRS 102, paragraph 12.17C confirms that written options are not hedging instruments 'unless the written option is an offset to or is combined with a purchased option and the effect of the offset or combination is not a net written option. An example of a combination of a written and a purchased option that is not a net written option is a zero-cost interest rate collar'.[33]

The reason is evident: a written option only generates a premium, and the option writer assumes a one-sided risk. Hence, they cannot be regarded as a hedging instrument.

FRS 102, paragraph 12.17A further limits the eligibility as a hedging instrument, meaning that a financial instrument can only be a hedging instrument:

(a) in its entirety;
(b) by designating a proportion of such an instrument or a proportion of a combination of such instruments, e.g., 50% of the nominal amount of the instrument; or
(c) by separating the spot risk element of a foreign currency contract and excluding the forward element or by separating the *intrinsic value* of an option and excluding the change in time value.[34]

30. FRS 102, para. 12.16.
31. Ghosh, Johnson and Miller (2022), [B5.78] (issue 28).
32. FRS 102, para. 12.17.
33. FRS 102, para. 12.17C.
34. FRS 102, para. 12.17A.

[iii] Hedge Accounting Conditions

FRS 102, paragraph 12.18 sets out the hedge accounting conditions as follows:

(a) the hedging relationship consists only of a hedging instrument and a hedged item;
(b) the hedging relationship is consistent with the management objectives for undertaking hedges;
(c) there is an economic relationship between the hedged item and the hedging instrument;
(d) there must be a documentation of the hedging relationship, the hedged item and the hedging instrument; and
(e) the entity has determined and documented causes of hedge ineffectiveness.[35]

FRS 102, paragraph 12.18 further states that hedging treatment is permitted from the date when all those above conditions are satisfied.[36] The economic relationship is further described in FRS 102, paragraph 12.18A:

> An economic relationship between a hedged item and a hedging instrument exists when the entity expects that the values of the hedged item and the hedging instrument will typically move in opposite directions in response to movements in the same risk, which is the hedged risk.[37]

[iv] Types of Hedges Permitted

FRS 102 defines three types of hedges (in analogy with IAS 39/IFRS 9), namely:

(a) fair value hedge;
(b) cash flow hedge; and
(c) hedge of the net investment in a foreign corporation.

(1) Fair value hedge

FRS 102, paragraph 12.19(a) defines a fair value hedge as 'a hedge of the exposure to changes in fair value of a recognised asset or liability or an unrecognised firm commitment, or a component of any such item, that are attributable to a particular risk and could affect profit or loss'.

Southern confirms that if a company uses a derivative as a hedging instrument, it must record a fair value hedge as follows:

- The derivative, i.e., the hedging instrument, must be measured at fair value.[38]

35. FRS 102, para. 12.18.
36. Ghosh, Johnson and Miller (2022), [B5.77] (issue 28).
37. FRS 102, para. 12.18A.
38. FRS 102, para 12.20(a) confirms that 'the gain or loss on the hedging instrument shall be recognised in profit or loss'.

- 'The carrying value of the hedged item is adjusted for the hedged risk only, i.e., if it is normally carried at amortised cost, the hedged item is not adjusted to its full fair value but adjusted in respect to the risk that is being hedged.'[39]
- 'Gains and losses on both the hedging instrument and the hedged item are taken to the income statement so that there is little, if any, net profit and loss effect other than any hedge ineffectiveness.'[40]

(2) Cash flow hedge

FRS 102, paragraph 12.19 (b) defines a cash flow hedge as 'a hedge of the exposure to variability in cash flows that is attributable to a particular risk associated with all, or a component of, a recognised asset or liability (such as all or some future interest payments on variable rate debt) or a highly probable forecast transaction and could affect profit or loss'.[41]

If the 'hedging instrument comprises a derivative contract [it must be measured at fair value] to the extent that it is effective'.[42] The ineffective portion of the gain or loss on the derivative is recognised in P&L.[43] The effective portion is recognised in 'other comprehensive income'.[44]

(3) Net investment hedge

FRS 102, paragraph 12.24 states:

> Hedges of a net investment in a foreign operation, including a hedge of a monetary item that is accounted for as part of the net investment [...] shall be accounted for similarly to cash flow hedges from the date the conditions of paragraph 12.18 are met:
>
> (a) the portion of the gain or loss on the hedging instrument that is determined to be an effective hedge shall be recognised in other comprehensive income [...]; and
> (b) the ineffective portion shall be recognised in profit or loss.[45]

As net investment hedging cannot be used in the solus accounts but only in the consolidated accounts, it is rarely relevant for tax computations.[46]

39. Southern (2017) para. 16.29; *see* FRS 102, para. 12.20(b).
40. Southern (2017) para. 16.29.
41. FRS 102, para. 12.19 (b).
42. Southern (2017) para. 16.31.
43. FRS 102, para. 12.23(c); *compare* Ghosh, Johnson and Miller (2022), [B5.79] issue 28.
44. FRS 102, para. 12.23(b).
45. FRS 102, para. 12.24.
46. Ghosh, Johnson and Miller (2022), [B5.81] (issue 28).

[b] Hedge Accounting under IAS 39

Hedge accounting under IAS 39 is defined as 'recognis[ing] the offsetting effects on profit or loss of changes in the fair value of the hedging instrument and the hedged item'.[47]

Under IAS 39, the hedging instrument and the hedged item are not regarded as one synthetic transaction but are left on the balance sheet and accounted for separately.[48]

It is possible to use derivatives and non-derivative instruments as hedging instruments under IAS 39. However, in practice, the most common instruments used for hedging are derivatives.

In principle, IAS 39 requires all derivatives to be reported at fair value, with all fair value changes being reported in the P&L account as they would be classified as held for trading.[49]

A company, however, can get relief from the P&L volatility resulting from applying fair value accounting on its derivatives if it applies the hedge accounting provisions of IAS 39.

Under IAS 39, a hedging relationship only qualifies for hedge accounting if all conditions, narrowly defined within IAS 39, paragraph 88 (a)-(e) are met, including the designation and documentation as a hedge,[50] the prediction that the hedge is expected to be 'highly effective',[51] and the ongoing effectiveness testing,[52] which includes reliable means of the company to measure the hedge effectiveness.[53]

'Highly effective' in achieving the offsetting changes in fair value or cash flows attributable to the hedged risk means that both at inception and during the transaction, the hedge is within the range of 80% to 125% based on actual results.[54]

IAS 39 only allows for cash flow hedges, fair value hedges and hedges of a net investment in a foreign operation.[55]

A cash flow hedge is 'a hedge of exposure to variability in cash flows that (i) is attributable to a particular risk associated with a recognised asset or liability [...] or a highly probable forecast transaction and (ii) could affect profit or loss'.[56]

An example of a cash flow hedge is a floating-to-fixed interest rate swap, which fixes the cash flows of a floating-rate loan until maturity.

47. IAS 39, para. 85.
48. Southern (2017) para. 16.20.
49. IAS 39 (2009), para. 9(a)(iii).
50. IAS 39, para. 88(a).
51. IAS 39, para. 88(b).
52. IAS 39, para. 88(e); Southern (2017) para. 16.17.
53. IAS 39, para. 88(d); Haworth and Hollis (2010) 28.
54. IAS 39, AG 105; Southern (2017) para. 16.21.
55. IAS 39, para. 86.
56. IAS 39, para. 86(b).

Example 50:

Company A buys a floating-to-fixed interest rate swap from Bank B with a term of two years, which fixes the cash flows of a floating-rate loan until maturity.

Fair value hedges are 'hedge[s] of the exposure to changes in fair value of a recognised asset or liability or an unrecognised firm commitment [...], that is attributable to a particular risk and could affect profit or loss'.[57]

Example 51:

Company A holds a fixed-rate bond with a remaining maturity of two years. It purchases a two-year fixed-to-floating interest rate swap, which converts the interest rate of the fixed-rate bond into a floating rate, thereby effectively eliminating changes in the fair value of the underlying bond until maturity.

Thus, fair value hedging effectively allows for the set-off and netting of profits and losses of the hedged item and the hedge.

Example 52:

Company A hedges with a fixed-to-floating interest rate swap, as above. The gains or losses from the swap would have to be measured at fair value under IAS 39, paragraph 89(a). Gains and losses from the bond attributable to the specific risk hedged under the swap could be used to adjust the carrying value of the bond under IAS 39, paragraph 89(b).

The gains and losses of both the hedging swap and the hedged bonds would then be taken to the Income Statement, leading to no net profit or loss other than due to hedge ineffectiveness.[58] If the hedge is partially ineffective, any fair value movements of the ineffective portion of the swap would be taken to the Income Statement. The carrying value of the bond cannot be adjusted as the hedging swap is not an effective hedge with regard to that portion of the bond. This leads to the result that 'the fair value movements of the ineffective portion of the hedge will not be matched by equal and opposite movements in the value of the hedged item'.

57. IAS 39, para. 86(a).
58. Southern (2017) para. 16.25.

Under IAS 39, fair value hedge accounting for portfolio hedges of interest rate risk is also possible.[59]

[c] Hedge Accounting under IFRS 9

Hedge accounting under IFRS 9 is optional. There are significant similarities between IFRS 9, IAS 39 and FRS 102, Section 12, namely:

(1) They all recognise the same three types of hedges: fair value hedge, cash flow hedge and hedge of net investment in a foreign operation.[60]
(2) All derivatives must be recognised at fair value (on-balance sheet).[61]

In addition, IFRS 9 contains further requirements in respect of:

- designation;
- documentation; and
- the testing of the hedge effectiveness.[62]

The test of the hedge effectiveness is a prospective test, which means it needs to be assessed if one expects the hedge to be effective in the future.

A company that applies hedge accounting under IFRS 9 must designate and document the following items:

(a) the hedging relationship;
(b) the entity's risk management objective and strategy for undertaking the hedge;
(c) the identification of the hedged item and the hedging instrument; and
(d) how the hedge effectiveness will be measured.[63]

Further, the following hedge effectiveness requirements need to be met:

(a) existence of an economic relationship between the hedged item and the hedging instrument;[64]
(b) any counterparty credit risk must not dominate changes in fair value of the derivative;[65] and
(c) 'the hedge ratio (the relative weighting of the hedged item and the hedging instrument) used for hedging purposes should generally be the same as that used for risk management.'[66]

---

59. IAS 39, AG 114-AG 132.
60. Ghosh, Johnson and Miller (2022), [B5.70 and B5.76].
61. *Ibid.*, [B5.70].
62. Southern (2017) para. 16.42.
63. Ghosh, Johnson and Miller (2022), [B5.71] (issue 28).
64. IFRS 9, para 6.4.1 (c) (i).
65. 'This could be the case where the collateral is not provided by the counterparty in respect of a derivative contract which has become "out of the money" as regards that counterparty.' *See* Ghosh, Johnson and Miller (2022), [B5.71] (issue 28).
66. *Ibid.*

[i] Hedged Items

Hedged items can be single items, a group of items, or a component of such items or groups of items.[67] IFRS 9, paragraph 6.3.1. states that a hedged item can be a recognised asset or liability, an unrecognised *firm commitm*ent – in contrast, a firm commitment arises where there is a contract in place, a forecast transaction, i.e., that means it is an uncommitted but anticipated future transaction or a net investment in a foreign operation.[68]

[ii] Hedging Instruments

IFRS 9, paragraph 6.2.1. provides that '[a] derivative measured at fair value through profit or loss may be designated as a hedging instrument, except for some written options [...]'.[69]

IFRS 9, paragraph 6.2.2, sentence 1 further states:

> A non-derivative financial asset or a non-derivative financial liability measured at fair value through profit or loss may be designated as a *hedging instrument* unless it is a financial liability designated as at fair value through profit or loss for which the amount of its change in fair value that is attributable to changes in the credit risk of that liability is presented in other comprehensive income [...].[70]

Also, a foreign currency component of a non-derivative financial instrument can be designated as a hedge of foreign exchange risk.[71]

IFRS 9, paragraph 6.2.2. sentence 2 stipulates:

> [f]or a hedge of foreign currency risk, the foreign currency risk component of a non-derivative financial asset or a non-derivative financial liability may be designated as a hedging instrument provided that it is not an investment in an equity instrument for which an entity has elected to present changes in fair value in other comprehensive income.[72]

IFRS 9, paragraph 6.2.3. provides that '[f]or hedge accounting purposes, only contracts with a party external to the reporting entity (i.e., external to the group or individual entity that is being reported on) can be designated as hedging instruments'.[73]

Although the rule of default is that hedging instruments are designated in their entirety, there are notable exceptions which allow for a proportion of the hedging

67. IFRS 9, para. 6.3.1.
68. Ghosh, Johnson and Miller (2022), [B5.72] (issue 28); *see* IFRS 9, para. 6.3.1.
69. IFRS 9, para. 6.2.1.
70. IFRS 9, para. 6.2.2. sent. 1; emphasis added.
71. IFRS 9, para. 6.2.2. sent. 2.
72. IFRS 9, para. 6.2.2. sent. 2.
73. IFRS 9, para. 6.2.3.

instrument to be designated only.[74] Those exceptions are permitted in the following cases:

(a) separating the intrinsic value and time value of an option contract and designating as the hedging instrument only the change in the intrinsic value of an option and not the change in its time value;
(b) separating the forward element and the spot element of a forward contract and designating as the hedging instrument only the change in the value of the spot element of a forward contract and not the forward element; similarly, the foreign currency basis spread may be separated and excluded from the designation of a financial instrument as the hedging instrument; and
(c) a proportion of the entire hedging instrument, such as 50 per cent of the nominal amount, may be designated as the hedging instrument in a hedging relationship. However, a hedging instrument may not be designated for a part of its change in fair value that results from only a portion of the time period during which the hedging instrument remains outstanding.[75]

IFRS 9, B6.2.4 states that a written option 'does not qualify as a hedging instrument unless it is designated as an offset to a purchased option, including one that is embedded in another financial instrument (e.g., a written call option used to hedge a callable liability)'.[76]

[iii] Types of Hedges under IFRS 9

(1) Fair value hedge

A fair value hedge is defined as 'a hedge of the exposure to changes in fair value of a recognised asset or liability or an unrecognised firm commitment, or a component of any such item, that is attributable to a particular risk and could affect profit or loss'.[77]

IFRS 9, paragraph 6.5.8 stipulates:

> As long as a *fair value hedge meets the qualifying criteria* in paragraph 6.4.1, the hedging relationship shall be accounted for as follows:
>
> (a) the *gain or loss on the hedging instrument* shall be recognised in *profit or loss* (or *other comprehensive income if the hedging instrument hedges an equity instrument* for which an entity has elected to present changes in fair value in other comprehensive income in accordance with paragraph 5.7.5).
> (b) the hedging *gain or loss* on the *hedged item* shall *adjust the carrying amount of the hedged item (if applicable) and be recognised in profit or loss.* If the hedged item is a financial asset (or a component thereof) that is measured at fair value through other comprehensive income in accordance with paragraph 4.1.2A, the hedging gain or loss on the hedged item shall be recognised in profit or loss. However, if the *hedged item* is an *equity instrument* for which an entity

74. Deloitte, IFRS 9 – Financial Instruments, Hedge Accounting, https://www.iasplus.com/en-gb/standards/ifrs-en-gb/ifrs9, accessed 1 October 2023. *Compare* IFRS 9, para 6.2.4.
75. IFRS 9, para. 6.2.4.
76. IFRS 9, para. B6.2.4.
77. IFRS 9, para. 6.5.2.(a).

> has elected to present changes in fair value in other comprehensive income in accordance with paragraph 5.7.5, those amounts shall remain in other comprehensive income. When a hedged item is an unrecognised firm commitment (or a component thereof), the cumulative change in the fair value of the hedged item subsequent to its designation is recognised as an asset or a liability with a corresponding gain or loss recognised in profit or loss.[78]

Ghosh, Johnson and Miller sum up the treatment of a derivative designated as a fair value hedge as follows:

> Where a derivative contract is designated as a fair value hedge, to the extent that the hedge is an effective hedge, the hedged item may be revalued for movements in the value of the risk that is being hedged and such fair value movements are recognised in profit and loss, even where fair value movements arising on the financial asset or liability would otherwise be recognised in other comprehensive income.[79]

This is stipulated in IFRS 9, paragraph 6.5.8(a) and (b). There is, however, an exception, which is outlined in paragraph 6.5.8(a): if the hedged item is an equity instrument, and the company holding this instrument has elected fair value movements to be recognised in other comprehensive income. Then, for this equity instrument, which is the hedged item under the fair value hedge, IFRS 9, paragraph 6.5.8(b) says that 'those amounts shall remain in other comprehensive income'.[80]

Ghosh, Johnson and Miller discuss the example of a fair value hedge 'where a company has "swapped" the fixed interest payable on a fixed-rate borrowing for a floating rate using a fixed-for-floating interest rate swap. In such cases, the loan could be revalued for movements in interest rate risk'.[81]

(2) Cash flow hedge

IFRS 9 defines a cash flow hedge as 'a hedge of the exposure to variability in cash flows that is attributable to a particular risk associated with all, or a component of, a recognised asset or liability (such as all or some future interest payments on variable-rate debt) or a highly probable forecast transaction and could affect profit or loss'.[82]

Ghosh, Johnson and Miller outline the example of a floating-to-fixed interest rate swap where the floating-rate interest payable on a loan is exchanged for a fixed rate[83] and state that under such a swap, the company entering into the swap would receive 'fixed rate payments determined by reference to the swap notional amount [from the swap counterparty] and would be obliged to make floating rate payments on the swap notional principal amount'.[84]

78. IFRS 9, para. 6.5.8.
79. Ghosh, Johnson and Miller (2022), [B5.73] (issue 28).
80. IFRS 9, para. 6.5.8.(b).
81. Ghosh, Johnson and Miller (2022), [B5.73] (issue 28).
82. IFRS 9, para. 6.5.2.(b).
83. Ghosh, Johnson and Miller (2022), [B5.74] (issue 28).
84. *Ibid.*

IFRS 9, paragraph 6.5.11. states that where the hedge is an effective hedge, gains or losses relating to the hedging relationship 'shall be recognised in other comprehensive income'.[85] They are 'released to profit or loss in the same period or periods during which the hedged expected future cash flow affect profit or loss'.[86]

Using the example of an interest rate swap, *Ghosh, Johnson and Miller* confirm that if the 'hedge income or expense' is recognised in the company's accounts, '[any] gains or losses arising on the portion of the contract that is determined to be ineffective continue to be recognised in profit or loss',[87] citing IFRS 9, paragraph 6.5.11(c).

(3) Net investment hedge in a foreign corporation

A net investment hedge in a foreign corporation is defined in IAS 21. It is 'designed to reduce exposure to foreign exchange differences on translation of a foreign operation on consolidation'.[88] Those hedges are, in principle, accounted for in the same way as a cash flow hedge.[89] They are usually only recognised in the consolidated accounts.[90]

If a currency risk is hedged (not a currency risk in a foreign operation), it can be accounted for as either a fair value hedge or a cash flow hedge.[91]

[2] Treatment of Derivatives Hedging Transactions for Tax Purposes

In principle, UK tax law follows the treatment of derivatives in the financial accounts. However, for derivatives used for hedging purposes, 'following the accounts' would raise serious problems in the taxation of these instruments because of the application of mandatory fair value accounting under FRS 102, Section 12, IAS 39 and IFRS 9.[92]

For example, if one applied the narrow hedge accounting provisions of IAS 39 also for tax purposes, hedge accounting would only be effective tax-wise if the hedge effectiveness lay between 80% and 125%.[93] In contrast to IAS 39, and to some extent also to IFRS 9, FRS 102, Section 12 'does not contain prescriptive effectiveness tests'.[94] But even if the taxpayer qualified for hedge accounting under the narrow hedge accounting conditions, it would, in many cases, not be possible to achieve effective hedging for tax purposes.

First, regarding the 'ineffective portion' both in the case of fair value and cash flow hedges, it would not be possible to achieve a hedge for tax purposes, as any gains

85. IFRS 9, para. 6.5.11.(b).
86. Ghosh, Johnson and Miller (2022), [B5.74] (issue 28).
87. *Ibid.*
88. Southern (2017) para. 16.26.
89. Ghosh, Johnson and Miller (2022), [B5.75] (issue 28).
90. Southern (2017) para. 16.26.
91. *Ibid.*, para. 16.27.
92. HMRC, CFM57030; *Compare* Ghosh, Johnson and Miller (2022), [B5.41] (issue 28); Haworth and Hollis (2010) 28.
93. Bramwell et al. (2023), H2.4.3.
94. *Ibid.*

or losses from that portion would be recognised on a fair value basis in the P&L account.[95]

Second, with regard to cash flow hedges of exchange rate risk, amounts would have been taken to either reserves or to equity and be 'included in computing a company's profits for the purposes of the derivative contracts legislation',[96] even if the hedge was 'highly effective'.

To avoid these adverse consequences of applying restrictive hedge accounting provisions to hedging transactions for tax purposes, current UK tax law has found a solution. Finance (No. 2) Act 2015 amended the derivative contracts regime and 'now only brings amounts into account where they are recognised in profit or loss'.[97]

There is still a problem with undesignated hedges, however. HMRC's Corporate Finance Manual states in this respect in CFM57030:

> There can still be an issue where a company is economically hedged but is unable to use hedge accounting (perhaps because the hedge is not sufficiently effective) or chooses not to designate a hedge, the derivative must be accounted for at fair value through profit and loss. This may create a mismatch between the accounting treatment of the hedging derivative and that of the hedged item. Such a mismatch (the 'undesignated hedge problem') would – in the absence of any special tax rules – follow through to the tax treatment.[98]

To solve the issue, the UK tax legislator introduced the 'Disregard Regulations',[99] which mirror the rules of old UK GAAP (excluding FRS 26), even where a company accounts under FRS 102, Section 12, IAS 39 or IFRS 9.[100] The Disregard Regulations came into effect on/after 1 January 2005.[101]

The purpose of the introduction of those special tax provisions (the 'Disregard Regulations') was to 'reduce tax volatility by disregarding fair value movements on particular derivative contracts for tax purposes'[102] and instead enable a company to apply accruals treatment for tax purposes with regard to derivatives used for hedging purposes.[103] Thus, for hedging transactions that include derivatives, UK tax law, in essence, does not follow the financial accounts.[104]

The Disregard Regulations only apply to certain 'derivative contracts' used in hedging transactions, such as currency, commodity and debt contracts, used to hedge a forecast transaction or firm commitment,[105] interest rate contracts used to hedge

---

95. IAS 39, AG105 and FRS 26, AG105. *See also* Bramwell et al. (2023), H2.4.2-H2.4.3.
96. *Ibid.*; Ghosh, Johnson and Miller (2022), [B5.77]; HMRC, CFM57020 and CFM57030.
97. HMRC, CFM57030.
98. *Ibid.*
99. Loan Relationships and Derivative Contracts (Disregard and Bringing into Account of Profit and Losses) Regulations 2004 No. 3256, as amended by SI 2005/2012, 2005/3374, 2007/3431 and 2011/698, introduced pursuant to CTA 2009, s. 606(4).
100. Haworth and Hollis (2010) 28; HMRC, CFM57010; Southern (2017) para. 16.37.
101. Southern (2017) para. 16.50.
102. HMRC, CFM57360.
103. Haworth and Hollis (2010) 28.
104. There is however an exception if the taxpayer applies 'old UK GAAP' without FRS 102, para. 12 (former FRS 26). In those circumstances, the tax rules follow in essence the accounts.
105. SI 2004/3256, regulations 7 and 8. *See also* HMRC, CFM57040.

certain balance sheet items[106] and currency contracts, used to hedge a net investment in a foreign operation (shares, ships or aircraft).[107]

As a result of the Disregard Regulations, all amounts arising from the hedging transactions are disregarded or deferred until the maturity of the hedge or disposal of the hedged asset,[108] which would otherwise be brought into account under FRS 102 Section 12/IAS 39 /IFRS 9 if a fair value – through profits or loss – measurement was adopted for these hedging transactions.[109]

In summary, the Disregard Regulations allow for matching of the hedging (derivative) contract and the hedged asset for tax purposes in a broader range of circumstances than FRS 102, Section 12, IFRS 9 or IAS 39, independently of whether hedge accounting would be permitted in the financial accounts or not.[110]

Although HMRC launched a consultation on 'Modernising the taxation of corporate debt and derivative contracts',[111] they confirmed that they would not make 'fundamental changes to the operation of the "Disregard Regulations" concerned with foreign exchange and hedging arrangements'[112] as 'there was [...] widespread opposition to any move significantly to change or do away with the functions of these Regulations, particularly at a time when the accounting rules are changing'.[113] Limited changes were, however, envisaged.[114]

HMRC outlines those changes:

> As a result of the consultation, changes were made to the derivative contracts regime in CTA09/PT 7 by F(No.2)A 2015. SI 2015/1961 was laid in December 2015 to make the necessary consequential amendments. In particular, this repealed regulation 9A as this became redundant as a result of following the income statement. Effectively, the regulation 9A approach has been embedded in the core provisions for dealing with derivative contracts. The changes apply to accounting periods beginning on or after 1 January 2016.[115]

Regulation 8 concerns both commodity and debt contracts but excludes interest rate contracts. *See* Haworth and Hollis (2010) 28.

106. SI 2004/3256, regulation 9.
 See HMRC, CFM57040; Haworth and Hollis (2010) 28.
107. SI 2004/3256, regulations 3 and 4.
 See Ghosh, Johnson and Miller (2022), [F2.65]; Haworth and Hollis (2010) 28.
108. SI 2002/1970 (the Bringing into Account Gains or Losses Regulations).
109. Ghosh, Johnson and Miller (2022), [E3.131B] (issue 28).
110. Haworth and Hollis (2010) 28; Southern (2017) para. 16.39.
111. The consultation was published on 6 June 2013. The main changes to UK derivative contracts rules arising from the consultation are envisaged to be included in the Finance Bill 2015.
112. HMRC, *Modernising the Taxation of Corporate Debt and Derivative Contracts, Technical Note* (8 April 2014) at Ch. 2 para. 2.18, http://www.hmrc.gov.uk/news/tech-note-corp-debt.pdf, accessed 24 July 2023.
113. *Ibid.*, at Ch. 4 para. 4.5.
114. For accounting periods starting on or after 1 January 2015, companies must elect into regulations 7, 8 and 9, rather than electing out. *See* HMRC, *Corporation Tax: Disregard Regulations for derivative contracts*, Business tax – guidance (27 March 2015) https://www.gov.uk/corporation-tax-disregard-regulations-for-derivative-contracts, accessed 1 March 2023.
115. HMRC, CFM57030.

The Corporate Finance Manual CFM57060 outlines how election into the Disregard Regulations works.[116] To reiterate, companies that want to disregard the fair value movement as prescribed by the accounting rules can opt into regulations 7, 8, and 9 of the Disregard Regulations.[117]

[a] *Summary of the Current UK Disregard Regulations Applying to Hedging Transactions*

[i] Purpose and Background

HMRC explains in detail the motivation and the background of the Disregard Regulations as follows:

> Under old UK Generally Accepted Accounting Practice (GAAP) (except where Financial Reporting Standard (FRS) 26 was applied) it was common for derivatives that were hedging one or more risks to be off balance sheet. The asset, liability or transaction being hedged by the derivative, and the derivative itself may have been accounted for as a single item. For tax purposes, this equated to accounting for the derivative contract on an authorised accruals basis.
>
> In contrast, under International Financial Reporting Standard (IFRS), FRS 101, FRS 102 and FRS 26 all derivatives are on the balance sheet at their fair value even if they are accounted for as a hedge. Companies could therefore (absent special rules) be subject to considerable volatility in their taxable profits because of fair value changes in derivatives. The Disregard Regulations (Statutory Instruments 2004/3256) were introduced in 2004 to address this issue.[118]

HMRC explains that the purpose of the Disregard Regulations is:

> to largely restore the old UK GAAP position (except where FRS 26 was applied) where a derivative is part of a hedging relationship. The operation of the tax rules will depend on the type of hedge, whether it is designated as such for accounting purposes and whether the company has elected in to the particular regulation that applies to that type of hedge. There are 3 main regulations dealing with fair value accounting for derivatives:
>
> - regulation 7: currency contracts
> - regulation 8: debt and commodity contracts
> - regulation 9: interest rate contracts
>
> The criteria for all 3 regulations are broadly the same:
>
> - there must be a designated or intended hedging relationship
> - the hedged item must not be taxed on a fair value basis

116. HMRC, CFM57060.
117. HMRC, CFM57041.
118. HMRC, Overview of Disregard Regulations (27 March 2015), https://www.gov.uk/government/publications/corporation-tax-hedging-derivative-contracts-and-disregard-regulations/overview-of-disregard-regulations, accessed 18 August 2023.

> The broad effect of these regulations is to disregard the fair value movements on the derivative and instead to bring profits and losses into account for Corporation Tax purposes in line with the hedged risk.[119]

[ii] Mechanism of the Disregard Regulations

Regulation 2(5) defines what is meant by a hedging relationship.[120] The Disregard Regulations apply to both designated and non-designated hedges.[121] HMRC explains the mechanism as follows:

> If the derivative and the hedged item are accounted for by the company as a hedge in accordance with IFRS, New UK GAAP or FRS 26 of Old UK GAAP, there is automatically a 'hedging relationship' for the purposes of the Disregard Regulations. Where a hedging relationship has been accounted for as a hedge under the relevant accounting standard, the company will have documented its hedging strategy, and the nature and purpose of the particular hedge under consideration [...].
>
> There may, however, be a 'hedging relationship' for tax purposes even where the criteria in IFRS, New UK GAAP, or FRS 26 of Old UK GAAP for hedge accounting are not satisfied. The test is whether the hedging instrument is intended to act as a hedge of:
>
> - the exposure to changes in fair value of an asset or liability, or an unrecognised firm commitment, which is attributable to a particular risk and could affect the company's profit or loss;
> - the exposure to variability in cash flows associated with an asset, liability or forecast transaction, which is attributable to a particular risk and could affect profit or loss; or
> - a net investment in a foreign operation of the company.[122]

Southern explains that '[t]he Disregard Regulations are in essence a solution to the problem of the undesignated hedge'[123] because, under IFRS, hedges have to meet strict criteria of (i) designation, (ii) documentation, (iii) and the testing of hedge effectiveness.[124]

Regulation 4 includes situations where profits and losses arising in respect of *currency derivative contracts* are *designated fair value hedges of FX risk* or where a

119. *Ibid.*
120. HMRC, CFM57050.
121. Southern (2017) para. 16.54, referring to regulation 2(5).
122. HMRC, CFM57050.
123. Southern (2017) para. 16.55.
124. *Ibid.*, para. 16.42.

'hedging relationship'[125] exists to reduce the economic risk in relation to FX fluctuations in respect of shares, ships or aircraft.[126]

> *Example 53:*
>
> UK Company A purchases USD-denominated shares at the New York Stock Exchange (NYSE). To hedge the FX risk with regard to the shares, it enters into a three-year currency swap, under which it swaps its USD exposure of the shares into GBP. Any gains and losses under the swap would fall under regulation 4 of the Disregard Regulations as the company intends to hedge its FX exposure on the shares with the swap.

As stated above, for accounting periods on or after 1 January 2015, it is necessary to *opt-in* to *regulations 7, 8 and 9*,[127] whereas no election is required for regulation 4.[128]

Regulation 7, which applies if 'the company has elected for regulation 7 to apply',[129] deals with fair value profits or losses on currency derivative contracts that hedge FX risk in cases of a 'hedging relationship' between the derivative and any 'forecast transaction or firm commitment' (so-called anticipatory hedges),[130] provided that the hedged item would itself not give rise to any FX gains or losses in the company's P&L account.[131] HMRC confirms that '[t]he regulation does not apply if the currency contract hedges foreign exchange risk on an existing asset or liability - for example, it will not apply to a forward currency contract hedging an existing loan'.[132] Regulation 7 can apply to cash flow hedges or fair value hedges.

Regulation 8 applies to commodity contracts and debt contracts. Regulations 8 and 10 apply to hedges *of commodity price risk* on forecast transactions or *firm transactions by commodity contracts or debt contracts.*[133] Regulation 8 only applies to

125. A hedging relationship does not require a designation as a hedge, rather it is sufficient that the company intends, and can reasonably expect to eliminate or reduce the FX risks in relation to these particular hedged assets. *See* SI 2004/3256, regulation 4(3) Condition 3; *also* HMRC, CFM57060.

CFM57060 further states that:

> A company's intention in undertaking a financial transaction is expressed through the intentions of its directors, although in many cases decisions will be delegated to a lower level of management. Particularly in large companies, the board of directors (or the group board) is likely to have set out a detailed policy on risk management. A company that has adopted IFRS, New UK GAAP, or FRS 26 under Old UK GAAP and wishes to use hedge accounting must have such documentation.

126. HMRC, CFM57040; Haworth and Hollis (2010) 28.
127. HMRC, CFM57041.
128. Southern (2017), para. 16.58.
129. HMRC, CFM57080.
130. SI 2004/3256, regulation 7(2); HMRC, CFM57090.
131. SI 2004/3256, regulation 7(2)(b). *See* Haworth and Hollis (2010) 28.
132. HMRC, CFM57090.
133. Southern (2017) para. 16.61.

commodity contacts, whereas deferred gains and losses will be brought into charge under Regulation 10.[134]

Regulation 9 applies to *interest rate derivatives,* which hedge balance sheet items, such as assets, liabilities, receipts and expenses, if the profits and losses on the hedged item are accounted for at amortised cost.[135] The regulation requires the derivative contract to be treated on an 'appropriate accruals basis and effectively requires that all fair value P&L during the term of the hedging relationship is disregarded'.[136] Instead of two balance sheet items, being the hedging item and the hedged item, only the P&L of the overall transaction is reflected in the accounts, effectively showing the P&L of only one synthetic instrument instead of two balance sheet items.[137]

Companies holding many derivative contracts may want to decrease the tax compliance burden of the Disregard Regulations and instead accept some degree of tax volatility by applying fair value accounting under FRS 102, Section 12, IAS 39 or IFRS 9 instead of applying additional accruals accounting only for tax purposes.[138]

Regulation 6A provides the choice for companies to elect alternative tax treatments.[139] HMRC states in relation to regulation 6A that:

> Many companies may wish for all of regulations 7,8 and 9 to apply to their hedging derivative contracts. However, it is permissible to make the election in respect of any combination of these three regulations as long as this is clear from the election.
>
> A company cannot choose different treatments for the same type of contract. If a company held various currency contracts, for example, it could either not make an election (and bring into account amounts recognised in profit or loss) or elect into regulation 7 (and disregard fair value movements on all currency contracts held which meet the relevant conditions). It cannot elect into regulation 7 for only some of the contracts.[140]

Southern summarises that the Disregard Regulations apply in the following situations to derivatives:

(1) net investment hedging, i.e., an FX hedging relationship between a derivative contract of a company and an investment in shares, ships or aircraft (regulations 3 and 4);[141]
(2) hedging of prospective transactions using currency contracts, i.e., a company has a derivative contract which hedges FX risk in respect of a forecast transaction, firm commitment or future share issue (regulation 7);[142]

134. HMRC, CFM57210; Southern (2017) para. 16.61.
135. HMRC, CFM57310; Haworth and Hollis (2010) 28. *Compare* Southern (2017) para. 16.61.
136. HMRC, CFM57320; Haworth and Hollis (2010) 28; Southern (2017) para. 16.64.
137. Southern (2017) para. 16.64.
138. HMRC, CFM57360; Haworth and Hollis (2010) 28.
139. HMRC, CFM57360.
140. *Ibid.*
141. Southern (2017) para. 16.60.
142. *Ibid.*

(3) hedging of prospective transactions using commodity contracts and debt contracts, that means where a company has an economic relationship between a commodity or debt contract and a forecast transaction or firm commitment (regulation 8);[143]
(4) hedging of creditor and debtor relationships using interest rate contracts, i.e., where there is an economic hedging relationship between a loan and an interest rate derivative (regulation 9).[144]

[B] Derivatives Hedging Transactions in Germany

[1] Treatment of Hedges for Accounting Purposes

As international accounting standards can only be applied on a group accounts basis in Germany,[145] IAS 39 and IFRS 9 in the context of hedging transactions are only relevant in the context of these group accounts, not at the level of single company accounts.

Applying German GAAP in the context of derivatives which hedge other balance sheet items would prima facie require the application of the realisation and imparity principle[146] with the consequence that 'unrealized profits (e.g., under the hedging transaction) [would have] to be ignored, [whereas] unrealized losses (e.g., under the hedged transaction) [would have] to be shown on the balance sheet'.[147]

To avoid these accounting mismatches, section 254 sentence 1 Commercial Law Act (CLA) explicitly *permits* hedge accounting if certain conditions are met.[148] When hedge accounting is applied, the principle of unit valuation, the realisation and imparity principles,[149] the acquisition cost principle[150] and the requirement of setting up provisions[151] are misapplied.[152]

The law, laid down in section 254 CLA in this respect, states:

> If assets, debts, pending transactions or highly probable transactions to hedge interest rate, currency and default risks or similar risks are combined with financial instruments (valuation unit), sections 249 paragraph 1, 252 paragraph 1 Nos. 3 and 4, 253 paragraph 1 sentence 1 and 256a [of CLA] are not applicable if the hedging relationship [between the hedged item and the hedging item] makes it impossible for the hedged risks to materialise.[153]

143. *Ibid.*
144. *Ibid.*
145. *See* Ch. 5 §5.03[A].
146. Section 252(1) Nos 3 and 4 Commercial Law Act (CLA).
147. Conlon & Aquilino: Derivatives D2.03[5].
148. Section 254 CLA, as introduced by *Gesetz zur Modernisierung des Bilanzrechts* (BilMoG) of 25 May 2009 (BStBl I 2009, 650ff.). Suggesting a voluntary application of hedge accounting: IDW (2011a) para. 4; Conlon & Aquilino: Derivatives D2.03[5][a]. *Other opinion:* Scharpf and Schaber (2009) 308 and 312, suggesting a mandatory application of hedge accounting.
149. Section 252(1) Nos 3 and 4 CLA.
150. Section 253(1) sent. 1 CLA.
151. Section 249(1) CLA.
152. Section 254(1) sent. 1 CLA. *See* Scharpf and Schaber (2009) 309.
153. Unofficial translation of s. 254(1) CLA which reads in the original as follows: 'Werden Vermögensgegenstände, Schulden, schwebende Geschäfte oder mit hoher Wahrscheinlichkeit

The reason for the application of hedge accounting and the deviation from general GAAP is to avoid write-downs of non-realised losses insofar as they were compensated by unrealised gains from the hedging transaction.[154]

As the criteria for hedge accounting are not defined in the law, one has to resort to the guidelines of the German Institute of Certified Auditors (*'Institut der Wirtschaftsprüfer'* (*IDW*)), which - although not part of German GAAP - can assist in the interpretation of GAAP.[155] The guidelines allow for hedge accounting if, cumulatively:

(1) the hedge is suitable for hedging the specific risk of the balance sheet item;[156]
(2) the hedge effectiveness with regard to the risk that needs to be hedged can be proved;[157] and
(3) the intention to hedge the balance sheet item has been documented.[158]

It should be noted that any financial instruments, not only derivatives, can be used to form a hedging relationship for accounting purposes.[159] This is particularly important in relation to hedge accounting positions that involve cryptoassets and crypto derivatives. This will be discussed below.

Section 254 CLA allows for full or partial compensation of risks[160] without requiring strict 'hedge effectiveness margins' as used in IAS 39.[161] The hedge accounting provision of section 254 CLA is only applicable with regard to the effective part of the hedge, whereas the ineffective part has to be accounted for outside the hedging relationship, applying the basic provisions of German GAAP, like the imparity principle.[162]

Section 254 CLA allows all kinds of hedges, including micro hedges, macro hedges and portfolio hedges,[163] insofar as a definite attribution of the hedged items and the hedging transactions has been documented.[164] Hedge accounting in the case of portfolio hedging and macro hedging is, however, only permissible if an appropriate, documented and functional risk management system for these transactions has been

vorgesehene Transaktionen zur Absicherung von Zins-, Währungs- und Ausfallrisiken oder gleichartiger Risiken mit Finanzinstrumenten zusammengefasst (Bewertungseinheit), sind § 249 Abs. 1, § 252 Abs. 1 Nr. 3 und 4, § 253 Abs. 1 Satz 1 und § 256a nicht anzuwenden, soweit der Eintritt der abgesicherten Risiken ausgeschlossen ist.'

154. BR-Drucksache 344/08, 125. *See also* Conlon & Aquilino: Derivatives D2.03[5][a]; Scharpf and Schaber (2009) 309.
155. Conlon & Aquilino: Derivatives D2.03[2].
156. IDW (2011a) para. 3; Scharpf and Schaber (2009) 313.
According to Häuselmann (2005) 50, the hedged item and the hedge must be non-ambiguously identifiable, i.e., a functional nexus between the hedged asset and the hedging derivative contract must be recognisable.
157. BR-Drucksache 344/08, 126; IDW (2011a) para. 3; Scharpf and Schaber (2009) 317.
158. IDW (2011a) paras 3 and 14.
159. BR-Drucksache 344/08, 125.
160. *Ibid.*, 127. *See also* Conlon & Aquilino: Derivatives D2.03[5][a].
161. Scharpf and Schaber (2009) 318.
162. IDW (2011a) paras 6ff.
163. Conlon & Aquilino: Derivatives D2.03[5][a].
164. BR-Drucksache 344/08, 126; IDW (2011a) para. 16.

implemented by the company.[165] Section 254 CLA also allows for anticipatory hedges of future transactions if the expected transaction is highly likely, meaning that there is a high probability that the transaction will actually be executed.[166] Similar to IAS 39, section 254 CLA allows both fair value hedges to hedge the risk of a change in the fair value[167] and cash flow hedges[168] to hedge the risk of a change in the cash flow.[169]

[2] Treatment of Hedging Transactions for Tax Purposes

German GAAP hedge accounting rules are also decisive for the tax accounts[170] because 'whenever hedge accounting is applied in the financial accounts, it must also be applied in the tax accounts'.[171] Hedge accounting for tax purposes has the same wide scope as the hedge accounting rules under German GAAP and allows micro hedging, portfolio hedging and macro hedging.[172] As it is sufficient under German GAAP that the hedge is only partially effective, transactions are also more likely to qualify for hedge accounting treatment in the single company accounts than in 'consolidated company accounts' that are drawn in accordance with IFRS.

From a tax perspective, gains and losses of the hedge and the hedged item are offset and not recognised for tax purposes until maturity or if the hedge is dissolved, thereby ensuring that no P&L volatility occurs during the term of the transaction.

[C] Comparison of Tax Hedge Accounting Approaches in the UK and Germany

Both the UK and the German tax systems have generous provisions for allowing hedging transactions to be effective for tax purposes, which also include the permission of anticipatory hedges for tax purposes. The way effective hedging for tax purposes is achieved is, however, quite different.

In the UK, the tax legislator has decided to allow a deviation from the financial accounts for the tax treatment of derivative contracts used in hedging transactions when a company accounts under FRS 102, Section 12/IAS 39/IFRS 9 in order to mitigate for tax purposes 'some of the more wide-reaching effects of mandatory fair

165. IDW (2011a) paras 3 and 20.
166. *Ibid.*, para. 32; *also* Scharpf and Schaber (2009) 308.
167. As defined in the guideline of the IDW, a risk of change in the fair value is given if the fair value of a balance sheet asset, liability or pending transaction can adversely change over time for the company accounting the asset/liability. *See* IDW (2011a) para. 21; Scharpf and Schaber (2009) 310.
168. A risk of change in the cash flows is given if there is a risk that the actual amount of future payments from the asset/liability adversely differs from the expected amount for the company accounting the asset/liability.
    See IDW (2011a) para. 21; Scharpf and Schaber (2009) 310.
169. *BR-Drucksache* 344/08, 126; IDW (2011a) paras 10 and 21.
170. Section 5(1a) sent. 2 ITA.
171. Conlon & Aquilino: Derivatives D2.03[5][b].
172. BMF, *Schreiben vom 25. August 2010, betr. steuerliche Gewinnermittlung bei der Bildung von Bewertungseinheiten* (IVC 6 – S 2133/07/10001, Der Betrieb 2010, 2024).

value accounting'.[173] Matching of the hedged item and the hedge is permitted for tax purposes regardless of whether it is permitted or not for accounting purposes under FRS 102, Section 12/IAS 39/IFRS 9,[174] leading to more generous tax rules permitting hedging compared to the narrow hedge accounting conditions under IAS 39 or FRS 102, Section 12/ IFRS 9.[175]

In addition, regulation 9 of the Disregard Regulations provides for an alternative approach to IAS/IFRS and new GAAP by treating the hedged item and the hedge as a single 'synthetic' balance sheet item instead of only recognising the P&L of both items in the same accounting period.[176] By introducing the Disregard Regulations, the UK has aimed to tackle the taxation problems of derivatives in relation to the tax treatment of hedges by opting to depart from FRS 102, Section 12/IAS 39/IFRS 9 in the context of hedging transactions.

For example, if companies elect in the Disregard Regulations, they can avoid recognising gains or losses for tax purposes in cases where derivatives fall out of the narrow IAS 39 'hedge effectiveness range' due to highly volatile capital markets.

In Germany, IFRS is only accepted as an accounting standard for group company accounts but not for single company accounts, which have to be drawn in accordance with German GAAP.

The German tax legislation follows the financial accounts with respect to hedge accounting. As the hedging provisions under German GAAP are generous, taxpayers can easily achieve hedge accounting in the German tax accounts during the term of the transactions.[177]

§7.04 PRE- AND POST-TAX HEDGING APPROACHES

[A] The Policy Aim of Tax Neutral Post-tax Hedges

For the effectiveness of an economic hedge, one cannot only consider whether the hedging transaction hedges the risk of the hedged item on a pre-tax basis, but one must also determine whether the hedge still has the same effectiveness after taking into account the taxation of the hedged item and the hedging instrument.[178]

Example 54:

Company A wishes to dynamically hedge options over the shares in Company B. Dynamic hedging entails the buying and selling of the underlying shares when the delta of the option[179] changes due to a change in the underlying market price

173. Haworth and Hollis (2010) 28.
174. *See* Ch. 7 §7.03[A][2].
175. Haworth and Hollis (2010) 28.
176. *See* Ch. 7 §7.03[A][2][a].
177. *See* Ch. 7 §7.03[B][2].
178. Neighbour (2001) para. 14.
179. *See* for a description of the term 'delta of an option', Ch. 2 §2.02[A][2].

of the shares. For a perfect dynamic hedge on a post-tax basis, the company must consider at which tax rates the dividends are taxed. Accordingly, the delta of the option will depend on the tax rate of the dividends and thus will be different on a pre- and post-tax basis.

Tax legislators should aim for tax-neutral hedging rules with regard to commercial hedging transactions that ensure that the hedge is as effective on an after-tax basis as it is on a pre-tax basis.[180]

When taxing hedging transactions, tax authorities should aim for tax rules that, in principle, fully tax any gains from the hedged item and allow for a full offset against losses from the hedging transaction and vice versa. For example, effective post-tax hedging rules would allow for an offset of a gain on a currency derivative against the loss on a loan denoted in a different currency, and vice versa, as they would aim for 'symmetrical positions treatment'.[181]

If the hedged asset or liability is subject to a different tax regime[182] or a different tax rate, or if the hedge cannot be offset against the hedged item for any other reason, the hedge will not be fully effective on a post-tax basis[183] with the result that the taxpayer has to overhedge on a pre-tax basis in order to achieve a tax-neutral post-tax hedge.

If the hedge is not neutral on a pre- and post-tax basis because of the different taxation of the hedged item and the hedge, taxpayers may be tempted to exploit the difference by deliberately overhedging or underhedging and thereby generating economic benefits by shifting the commercial loss-risk of the hedge towards the Revenue via an increased tax deduction.[184]

[B] Approach Towards Pre- and Post-tax Hedging in the UK

HMRC acknowledges that it is important for commercial hedging transactions to be treated on a tax-neutral basis by symmetrically taxing the hedged item and the hedge.[185]

Example 55:

Company A accounts in GBP. It wishes to hedge the currency risk of a one-year Euro loan of EUR 10 million and wants to protect against the Euro rising against

180. HMRC, *Technical Note on overhedging and underhedging* (2009); Neighbour (2001) para. 16.
181. HMRC, *Overhedging and underhedging*.
182. For example, if the gain on the hedged item is treated as income, and the loss on the hedging instrument is treated as capital, provided the tax system only allows a loss-offset of capital losses against capital gains, not against income.
183. OECD (2001) para. 118.
184. OECD (2013a) 20ff.; HMRC, CFM63310; HMRC, *Overhedging and underhedging*.
185. OECD (2013a) 3; HMRC, *Overhedging and underhedging*.

the British Pound. If unhedged, Company A must convert more GBP into Euro when repaying the Euro loan after one year in case of an appreciation of the Euro. As Company A wants to avoid any profit or loss due to currency fluctuations between the Euro and GBP, it concludes a one-year currency forward with Bank B that perfectly hedges the currency risk on the Euro loan. The Euro to GBP conversion rate on that day 1 is, say, EUR 1.25 to GBP 1.00.

If the exchange rate were the same rate after one year, Company A would have to convert GBP 8 million into EUR 10 million to pay back the Euro loan. It would make no loss on the loan. Correspondingly, it would make no gain on the currency forward.

If, after one year, the Euro had appreciated against the GBP, say, at a conversion rate of EUR 1,00 to GBP 1,00, Company A would have to convert GBP 10 million into EUR 10 million, thus effectively converting GBP 2 million more into Euro because of the Euro appreciation. Company A would, therefore, make a loss of GBP 2 million on the Euro loan due to a change in the exchange rate.[186] Correspondingly, Company A would generate a gain of GBP 2 million on the currency forward.[187] Under the UK tax rules, Company A would be able to offset the currency loss on the loan against the currency gain on the forward.[188]

Taxpayers have, however, exploited hedging techniques for arbitrage purposes by overhedging or underhedging a balance sheet item. They entered into so-called risk transfer schemes that allowed them to 'obtain a higher return or lower borrowing costs without actually bearing the risk that is priced into that financial outcome'.[189] Under these schemes, the values of assets and liabilities were subject to opposite price movements in relation to a reference index.

Although the positive exposure in the index by investing in one asset or liability was only partly hedged on a pre-tax basis, a second transaction provided an inverse exposure to the same index, thereby achieving a full hedge on a post-tax basis due to the different tax treatment of the hedged asset or liability and the hedging transaction.

As a result, the taxpayer (at least as a group) did not bear any economic exposure because the taxpayer shifted the exposure to the Revenue due to a mismatch in taxation of the hedged item and the hedge.[190] Although many schemes were based on overhedging or underhedging of currency risks,[191] other risk transfer schemes obtained the same tax benefit in a more disguised manner by reference to non-FX indices.

186. Vice versa, if the Euro further depreciated against the GBP to, say, EUR 1.60 for GBP 1.00, Company A would have to convert only GBP 6.25 million to receive EUR 10 million to pay back the Euro loan. It would make a profit of GBP 1.75 million due to the change in the exchange rate. The profit on the loan would however be compensated by a loss of GBP 1.75 million on the currency forward.
187. Interest payments are not taken into account here in order to simplify the calculation.
188. SI 2004/3256, Regulation 7; HMRC, *Overhedging and underhedging*.
189. HMRC, *Overhedging and underhedging*; HMRC, CFM63310.
190. HMRC, CFM63310.
191. A detailed description of these currency risk transfer schemes can be found in CFM63310.

Example 56:

Facts:
A UK tax resident parent company ('Parent') holds 100% of the equity of an existing UK tax resident subsidiary ('Sub'). Sub is equity financed by Parent.[192] Sub enters into an (economic) total return swap (the 'Derivative') with a UK bank ('Bank'). The Derivative is documented as a forward contract or as options. Under the terms of the Derivative, Sub receives the long performance in relation to GBP 100 million notional of a reference index or asset ('Index')[193] plus a subsidy[194] calculated by reference to the past performance of the Index in return for paying SONIA-based financing to Bank on GBP 100 million.[195] The Index has been chosen to have high volatility/expected return based on past performance of the Index.[196]

The Derivative has a one-year term, is documented under ISDA and is gross cash settled at maturity. It is unfunded. Parent hedges its exposure to the Sub by entering into a corresponding derivative (the 'Hedging Derivative') with Bank over *100% of the shares* in Sub.[197]

According to the terms of the hedge, Parent passes the long performance of the shares in Sub, which equals GBP 100 million notional plus the post-tax value of the Index performance plus the subsidy to Bank in return for a SONIA-based financing spread.[198] The Hedging Derivative has the same term as the Derivative except that it is physically settled only.

At maturity, the Derivative is cash settled, and the Hedging Derivative is physically settled only. Both Parent and Sub are assumed to account under IFRS. Parent elects to fair value its interest in Sub. They are UK tax resident and

192. The amount of equity financing is assumed to be GBP 75 million, the amount of debt finance by Bank is GBP 25 million. It can also be GBP 100 million equity financed by Parent in cases where taxpayers further disguise the risk transfer transactions.
193. This can be a currency index or any other type of index or asset.
194. The payment of the subsidy is based on the historical average Index performance over a pre-determined number of years. The cash amount of past performance of the Index is taken out at outset of the transaction to finance the 'subsidy' which is passed on from Bank to Sub under the Derivative, and under the Hedging Derivative, again passed on from Parent to Bank. In theory, after taking out this subsidy, the future performance of the Index will now be zero as it is assumed that the future performance of the Index would approximate to the average past return over the term of the transaction.
See also OECD (2013a) 25-26.
195. The 'subsidy' is paid in the form of an increased payment (compared to a normal total return swap) under the Derivative and the Hedging Derivative to Sub and to Parent. For simplicity purposes (and to show that the group is fully hedged on a post-tax basis), the subsidy has been left out of the explanation in *Example 56.*
196. In efficient markets, past performance is no indicator for future performance.
See 'Efficient-market hypothesis' of Eugine Fama, 'Efficient Capital Markets: A Review of Theory and Empirical Work' (1970) The Journal of Finance 383, DOI: 10.2307/2325486, accessed 1 December 2024.
197. Thereby, Parent effectively leaves the economic exposure to the index directly within Sub.
198. Thus, by being long the shares in Sub, which means also being long the reference index, and by passing on the performance of Sub to Bank, Parent is economically flat.

members of the same group relief group.[199] Parent is assumed to have excess capital losses of GBP 25 million.[200]

Tax analysis:
Any changes in the fair value of the Derivative flow through the P&L account and are taxed as non-trading debit or credit. Non-trading debits can be carried back, group relieved to Parent or within the group relief group in return for payment, or they are carried forward. The Hedging Derivative falls outside the derivative contracts regime as excluded property as it is an equity derivative. Any capital gains or losses are offset with existing capital losses or are carried forward.

Scenario analysis:
Scenario 1: Index increases in value by 10%
Ignoring the subsidy in the scenario analysis, Sub would earn GBP 10 million (10% × GBP 100 million notional on the Derivative) pre-tax and GBP 7.5 million on a post-tax basis (GBP 10 million minus 25% corporate tax).[201] Sub B's share capital plus reserves now equal GBP 82.5 million, assuming GBP 75 million of equity. Under the Hedging Derivative with Bank over the performance of the shares in Sub, Parent must pay the difference between the initial value of Sub (GBP 75 million) and its final value (GBP 82.5 million) to Bank, thus GBP 7.5 million. On a combined basis, the group would be fully hedged on a post-tax basis.
Scenario 2: Index decreases in value by 10%
Again, ignoring the subsidy, Sub would make a loss of GBP 10 million (-10% × GBP 100 million notional on the Derivative) pre-tax and on a post-tax basis only GBP 7.5 million (after deducting tax). The non-trading debit of GBP 7.5 million can be offset against non-trading credits or group relieved at a corporate tax rate of 25%. Sub B's share capital minus losses now equals GBP 67.5 million, assuming GBP 75 million of equity. Under the Hedging Derivative with Bank over the performance of the shares in Sub, Parent will receive the difference between the initial value of Sub (GBP 75 million) and its final value (GBP 67.5 million) from Bank, thus GBP 7.5 million. On a combined basis, the group would be fully hedged on a post-tax basis.

When considering the above scenarios, one can note that the complete post-tax hedge was achieved due to a mismatch in the accounting treatment of the Derivative and the Hedging Derivative, which was also applied for tax purposes. Any changes in the value of the Derivative were taxed and relieved as income, whereas the changes in

199. Non-trading debits can be surrendered to a 75% owned subsidiary or a 75% sister company of a common holding company. *See* HMRC, *Company Taxation Manual* (2012) CTM80155.
200. For other examples of these transactions: HMRC, CFM63320.
201. *Example 56* is based on the main corporate tax rate of 25% and is only provided for illustrative purposes.

value on the other side (Hedging Derivative) were treated as chargeable gains or allowable losses, which could be offset against existing capital losses.[202]

Because the Disregard Regulations were deliberately not applied in the above example, a tax-neutral hedging result could be circumvented, and instead, the taxpayer could achieve an offset against existing capital losses, which were effectively recycled into deductible income losses.

To avoid a higher-than-normal yield of return on these transactions by shifting the downside risk of the transaction to the UK Revenue, the tax authorities have introduced legislation under CTA 2010, Part 21A,[203] which tackles risk transfer schemes.[204] The provisions are laid down in CTA 2010, sections 937A to 970.[205] HMRC states that '[t]he effect of the legislation is that where a company is a party to a risk transfer scheme, certain losses are "ring-fenced" for tax purposes and can only be relieved to the extent that there are profits from the same risk transfer scheme'.[206]

The anti-avoidance rules on risk transfer schemes do not only include schemes that transfer the risk of exchange rates,[207] but 'relevant risks' also include 'any price or other value'.[208]

In addition, HMRC introduced rules tackling group mismatch schemes. Those are briefly highlighted in Chapter 10.

[C] Approach Towards Pre- and Post-tax Hedging in Germany

The tax rules will follow the hedge accounting rules of German GAAP to deal with derivatives that hedge other balance sheet items.[209] Upon disposal of the derivative that hedges other balance sheet items, specific loss ring-fencing provisions of section 15(4) ITA can, however, apply.[210] As a result, the loss ring-fencing provisions can lead to tax inefficiencies in the post-tax hedging position compared to the pre-tax position.

Example 57:

Facts:
German resident Company A enters into a Japanese Yen (JPY) 100 million loan in order to obtain cheap financing. Financing in JPY is not part of the regular business activity of Company A. To hedge against the JPY exposure, Company A

202. HMRC, *Overhedging and underhedging.*
203. HMRC, CFM63310.
204. In addition, CTA 2010, Part 21B introduced legislation to prevent 'Group Mismatch Schemes' that take advantage of intra-group tax mismatches. For details: Ghosh, Johnson and Miller (2022), [H9.15]-[H9.45].
205. HMRC, CFM63330.
206. *Ibid.*
207. CTA 2010, s. 937C(3)(a); HMRC, CFM63320 provides an example of a common risk transfer scheme that provides for overhedging in order to benefit from differences in exchange rates.
208. CTA 2010, s. 937C(3)(c).
209. Ch. 7 §7.03[B][2].
210. *See* Ch. 6 §6.03 and §6.04 for a detailed discussion of the loss ring-fencing rules.

enters into a currency swap with Bank B. If the JPY were to fall in value, Company A would have to convert less Euros into JPY in order to pay back the loan. It would make a gain on the loan. On the other hand, Company A would make a loss on the currency swap.

Tax treatment:
If one assumed that JPY Financing was not part of the *regular business activity* of Company A, it could not offset the loss on the swap contract against the gain on the loan but only against other gains from derivatives.[211] Hence, Company A would have had a perfect hedge on a pre-tax basis but would not have been effectively hedged on a post-tax basis because of the denial of loss offset.

German tax rules do not provide any specific anti-avoidance approaches which counteract overhedging or underhedging transactions that exploit the mismatch between the taxation of equity and debt.

In mid-2021, the legislator introduced the so-called legislation transposing the EU's Anti-Tax-Avoidance Directive (ATAD) measures into German tax law. Those measures also concern hybrid mismatches, which are 'based on differences in the legal characterisation of payments (financial instruments) or companies or permanent establishments between two countries. This may result in tax deductions in both countries (so-called double deduction) or a deduction in one country without inclusion in the tax base of the other country ("deduction/non-inclusion")'.[212] Those hybrid mismatches, however, may not be able to tackle overhedging or underhedging schemes.

Hence, taxpayers may be able to transfer the economic risk of the transaction to the German Revenue and achieve an increased tax deduction, entering into transactions similar to the one described in Chapter 7 §7.04[B] by underhedging fully taxable and tax deductible 'risky' debt instruments with tax-free equity instruments that are inversely linked to the performance of the debt instruments, thereby creating high-interest investments with a fully hedged position on a post-tax basis. The effect of those hedging strategies would result in the German fisc's participation in the losses by way of granting a tax deduction in case of a decrease in the value of the debt instrument.

[D] Comparison of Approaches Towards Pre- and Post-tax Hedging in the UK and Germany

When comparing the approaches towards pre- and post-tax hedging in the UK and Germany, one can conclude that the German tax rules do not always provide a tax-neutral hedging regime for transactions using derivatives.[213]

211. Section 15(4) sent. 4 ITA.
212. KPMG, Germany: Legislation transposing ATAD measures (exit taxation, CFC rules, hybrid mismatches) (30 June 2021) https://kpmg.com/us/en/home/insights/2021/06/tnf-germany-legislation-transposing-atad-measures-exit-taxation-cfc-rules-hybrid-mismatches.html, accessed 24 August 2023.
213. *See* Ch. 7 §7.04[C], *Example 57*.

Hence, German taxpayers will often experience hedges that are ineffective on a post-tax basis, and they are sometimes forced to overhedge to achieve an efficient hedge on a post-tax basis.

On the other hand, German tax authorities have not yet introduced specific tax avoidance rules that target post-tax hedging schemes based on deliberate overhedging or underhedging.

In contrast, UK tax rules also permit effective hedging on a post-tax basis. Furthermore, the UK Revenue has enacted sufficient anti-avoidance measures[214] that allow them to counteract schemes that exploit the one-sided risk transfer towards the Revenue.

§7.05 PROBLEM 4: SOLUTIONS ON HOW TO TAX HEDGED POSITIONS AND POST-TAX HEDGING SCHEMES

In the following, the author will discuss which solutions the tax legislator could adopt that allow taxpayers to tax-efficiently match the hedged item and the hedge in the same accounting period. Second, the author will outline solutions that can achieve tax-efficient post-tax hedging results at the maturity of a transaction. The author will also discuss which measures could be adopted to prevent risk transfer schemes.

[A] Solutions in the Context of General Hedge Accounting Provisions

In response to tax discrepancies in the context of hedging transactions, tax policymakers should seek to match the timing and character of the gain or loss on the hedged transaction with that of the hedging instrument.[215] This could be achieved by a deferral of gains or losses on the hedging instrument from the time they occur to the time when the gains or losses on the hedged transaction are actually realised. In addition, tax systems may adopt the approach to change the character of a financial instrument if it serves as a hedge to avoid tax disparities and provide a match between the hedged item and the hedge.

Second, tax systems must find an answer to the question of whether they should allow only 'micro hedging' for tax purposes or also 'portfolio hedging' and 'macro hedging'. Tax systems are, in practice, more likely to apply a micro hedging approach where one can simply match specific tax attributes among selected instruments rather than permitting an amalgamation of cash flows of the hedged instruments into one synthetic risk portfolio for tax purposes, as in the case of portfolio or macro hedges.

In the author's view, tax systems should not only allow micro hedging but also permit portfolio hedging (in the narrow sense) in the tax accounts, as this allows banks and companies to avoid earnings volatility in their positions.

As seen in *Example 47* on portfolio hedging, traders and risk managers will be able to fully hedge trading positions in derivatives over the same underlyings by

214. CTA 2010, Part 21A and Part 21B.
215. OECD (2001) para. 80.

hedging the different risk classes. Tax law should mirror these common hedging approaches for tax purposes and allow a hedging relationship between the portfolio (containing the same risks) and the hedge, thereby minimising earnings volatility for tax purposes. The attribution of a single equity option in a portfolio to the hedging transaction for tax purposes would be artificial and would put an unduly heavy compliance burden on banks and companies.

In contrast, although the permission of macro hedging for tax purposes may be preferable for pure efficiency, the author proposes that tax law should *not* follow macro hedging approaches that may be adopted for economic and accounting purposes. Disallowing macro hedging for tax purposes is likely to prevent the extensive use of favourable hedging provisions in the tax law. As macro hedging is inexact and as almost all balance sheet positions could be attributed to the macro hedge, allowing macro hedging for tax purposes would open up various tax arbitrage possibilities for deferring otherwise taxable income.

Third, tax systems have to decide whether to apply the hedging provisions of IFRS 9, the provisions used in local accounting rules, or whether they design a separate set of hedging rules for tax purposes. The application of the hedge accounting provisions of IFRS 9 in single company accounts leads to significant challenges that the tax legislator has to deal with. When applying IFRS 9 to single company accounts for tax purposes, the tax legislator can follow IFRS 9 with the consequence of restrictive hedging provisions, which may lead to significant P&L volatility tax-wise.

Alternatively, a deviation from the hedging provisions of IFRS 9 has to be implemented for tax purposes with the consequence of separate tax rules that deal in detail with the criteria that allow hedge accounting for tax purposes.[216]

In the author's view, tax systems should rather seek to incorporate a different set of hedging rules into their tax laws that provide tax-neutral hedge accounting for micro and portfolio hedging positions instead of applying IFRS 9 indiscriminately in the tax legislation as tax rules can be better tailored to serve the purpose of reducing earnings volatility during the term of the transaction for tax purposes.

Problems may also occur if the local legislator permits all hedging approaches both in the financial and tax accounts, as macro hedging may be used as a means of deferring income by allowing the assets and derivatives to be part of a macro hedging relationship.

Fourth, anti-avoidance provisions may have to be introduced that tackle transactions that use the hedging rules as a means to defer income to the future for tax purposes.

As a solution to manage tax arbitrage risks, tax authorities may limit hedging provisions to apply only to certain types of transactions and only allow certain hedging approaches, such as micro hedging and portfolio hedging.

Additionally, tax legislators may also introduce specific tests to determine whether the hedge is, in fact, used for risk reduction purposes. In this respect, the

216. *See* Ch. 7 §7.03[A][2].

criteria of 'hedge effectiveness' may be used as a quasi-anti-avoidance measure for tax purposes to determine whether hedging tax provisions can be applied or not.[217]

[B] Solutions in Respect of the Tax Treatment of Hedges on a Post-tax Basis

The question arises whether tax systems should only recognise pre-tax hedges or whether they should also permit post-tax hedging for tax purposes if hedging strategies are not fully effective on a post-tax basis.[218]

For example, a pre-tax hedge may not provide a full hedge on a post-tax basis if the hedged item and the hedge are treated differently for tax purposes.[219] Hedging rules that only consider the pre-tax position of the taxpayer may lead to taxation results where the taxpayer is left with an incomplete hedge on a post-tax basis.[220] Or, the taxpayer earns tax-free gains on an asset, which are overcompensated by tax-deductible losses from the hedge.[221]

On the other hand, in the absence of specific anti-avoidance rules, tax arbitrage strategies could be implemented, which allow taxpayers to profit from different taxation treatment of the hedged item and the respective hedge. Nonetheless, the existence of hedges that are partly ineffective on a post-tax basis highlight the weakness of a policy approach that allows the hedge to be efficient on a pre-tax basis but does not provide hedge neutrality on a post-tax basis.[222]

In the author's view, tax legislators have to consider several factors in order to draft the (tax) hedging rules carefully in a way that neither deters businesses from hedging their risk positions due to ineffective post-tax hedges nor increases hedging costs because of the need to overhedge, nor provides too much room for unwanted risk shifting schemes that move certain market risks of transactions from the taxpayer to the fisc.

First, a tax legislator should consider general mismatches in the taxation of different items of income, financial assets and liabilities and abolish these mismatches as far as possible.

217. Alternatively, the legislator may limit the possibility of hedge accounting by an acceptable range in order to avoid tax arbitrage of hedging provisions. In the context of accounting, this approach is favoured by IAS 39, AG 105, which provides that a hedge is only effective for accounting purposes if it remains during the whole time of the hedging relationship in the range between 80% and 125%. The same applies in the context of IFRS 9.
218. OECD (2013a) 15.
219. Neighbour (2001) 5, explains the negative outcome of a pre-tax hedge at the example of a currency forward, where the tax authorities may tax an FX gain although the taxpayer has incurred a net FX loss.
220. This is the case if arising losses from the hedged asset are non-deductible (e.g., equity losses), whereas corresponding gains on the hedge are fully taxable.
221. The outcome will depend on the price movements in the underlying asset and correspondingly the price movements in the hedging instrument.
222. *Similar* Neighbour (2001) 8.

Second, the tax legislator should investigate whether the tax legislation applying to hedging relationships is potentially prone to unwanted tax arbitrage in the form of overhedging or underhedging schemes.

Third, if a potential for tax avoidance (either due to taxing mismatches or the hedging rules) has been identified, tax systems should consider how they want to deal with tax avoidance schemes that utilise the differences in taxation between the hedged items and the hedge. To counter those schemes, tax legislators may want to introduce targeted anti-avoidance rules.

Fourth, if the legislator wants to design a competitive tax system that aims to lower hedging costs for taxpayers and abolish any obstacles that hinder efficient post-tax hedging, the tax rules should determine under which conditions post-tax hedging approaches are permissible.

Lastly, if post-tax hedging is permitted in certain cases, the tax legislator should also determine in the legislation the circumstances under which post-tax hedging results will be disallowed and an increased tax deduction denied based on anti-avoidance considerations in respect of risk transfer schemes. Targeted anti-avoidance rules combined with a disclosure regime may be an effective means to tackle risk transfer schemes.[223]

§7.06 HEDGING RELATIONSHIPS WITH CRYPTOASSETS AND CRYPTO DERIVATIVES

The following subchapter deals with the issue of how cryptoassets and crypto derivatives should be treated for accounting and tax purposes when those assets are part of a hedging relationship.

The literature on this issue is sparse. Hedge accounting in the context of cryptoassets and crypto derivatives has been discussed in some detail in a 2022 ISDA White paper called *Crypto-asset Risk and Hedging Analysis*.[224] In this paper, ISDA observes that the cryptoasset market has:

> a growing number of new entrants [...], including hedge funds, banks, insurance companies, sovereign wealth funds, pension funds and endowment funds.
>
> This rapid growth has been accompanied by strong interest in *crypto derivatives*, as market participants increasingly look for *ways to take synthetic exposure to crypto assets* or to *protect their crypto-asset holdings from adverse market risk*. As in any market, derivatives play a vital role in enabling participants to manage risks, deepen liquidity and broaden market access.[225]

As no guidance exists from the *IFRS Interpretations Committee* or domestic accounting standard setters on how to hedge account cryptoassets and their derivatives, the author will resort to publications concerning the regulation of bank capital as

223. *See* Ch. 10 §10.05[B][1] and §10.05[B][2].
224. ISDA, Crypto-asset Risk and Hedging Analysis (May 2022), https://www.isda.org/a/pMWgE/Crypto-asset-Risks-and-Hedging-Analysis.pdf, accessed 18 August 2023.
225. *Ibid.*, 3.

a tool to develop viable solutions for the hedge accounting of cryptoasset – crypto derivatives positions. The author believes that those new regulatory bank capital standards concerning cryptoassets may also indicate how to hedge account crypto positions of non-banking companies.

[A] General Considerations: Hedge Accounting of Cryptoassets in the Banking Sector

In 2021, the Basel Committee on Banking Supervision (BCBS), which deals with banking supervision and the regulation of bank capital, published a *Consultative Document*[226] where it discussed the regulatory bank capital treatment of cryptoassets exposures held by financial institutions. For banks, it is necessary to determine if they can apply hedge accounting to cryptoasset positions for bank capital purposes or if the cryptoasset and the hedging instrument have to be accounted for on a stand-alone basis in order to obtain an accurate picture of their minimum capital requirements under the Basel accords.[227]

The *2021 BCBS Consultative Document* classifies cryptoassets into two groups, namely 'Group 1 cryptoassets', which are those 'that meet all the classification conditions set out in the document and which will be subject to the at least equivalent risk-based capital requirements based on the risk weights of underlying exposures'.[228] 'Group 1 cryptoassets include tokenised traditional assets (Group 1a) and 'cryptoassets with effective stabilisation mechanisms (Group 1b)', which includes certain stable-coins. Condition 1, however, restricted Group 1b as only encompassing those stable-coins 'that have a stabilisation mechanism that is effective at all times'.[229]

Group 2 cryptoassets are those which fail to meet any of the conditions which define Group 1 cryptoassets.[230] In a *2021 Comment Letter*, ISDA and other trade organisations criticised the *2021 BCBS Consultative Document* and argued that the classifications of cryptoassets, in particular those assets falling under Group 1, are too restrictive.[231]

The *2021 Comment Letter* urged the BCBS to 'recognize hedging in the prudential framework; otherwise, underlying exposures would be significantly overstated'.[232] The

226. BCBS, Consultative Document 'Prudential treatment of cryptoasset exposures' (10 September 2021), https://www.bis.org/bcbs/publ/d519.pdf, accessed 20 August 2023.
227. The Basel Committee on Banking Supervision (BCBS) developed international capital regulatory standards through a number of accords, known as Basel I, II and III. Those Basel accords are soft law but member states of the BCBS implement them into national law and prescribe the bank capital and liquidity requirements for their domestic banks which are then supervised by their national banking regulators.
228. BCBS, *2021 BCBS Consultative Document*, 3.
229. *Ibid.*, 4.
230. *2021 BCBS Consultative Document*, 3-5.
231. ISDA et al., *Joint Trade Associations Comment Letter*, Re Comments in Response to the Consultative Document on Prudential Treatment of Cryptoasset Exposures, September 20, 2021, https://www.isda.org/a/OBggE/Joint-Trades-Comment-Letter-Prudential-Treatment-of-Cryptoasset-Exposures.pdf, accessed 21 December 2023.
232. *Ibid.*

2021 Comment Letter also observed that 'if a prudential framework for cryptoassets is too punitive for bank involvement in this market, competition may be stifled'.[233]

In the *2022 ISDA White paper*, ISDA reiterates its critique concerning the *2021 BCBS Consultative Document* and states that if the proposals made by the BCBS were implemented, they 'would lead to particularly punitive capital requirements for banks holding some types of crypto assets and disincentivize traditional financial intermediaries from playing an active role in crypto markets'.[234]

As a response to the criticism put forward by ISDA and other trade organisations in the *2021 Comment Letter*, the BCBS issued a *Second consultation* document in June 2022,[235] where it included a set of hedging recognition criteria for certain 'Group 2 cryptoassets', which they called in line with ISDA's *2021 Comment Letter* 'Group 2a cryptoassets'.[236]

For those cryptoassets, the BCBS permits 'a limited degree of hedge recognition in the calculation of the bank's net exposure'.[237]

The following diagram, developed by the BCBS, explains the risk-based capital requirements which were discussed in the second consultation:

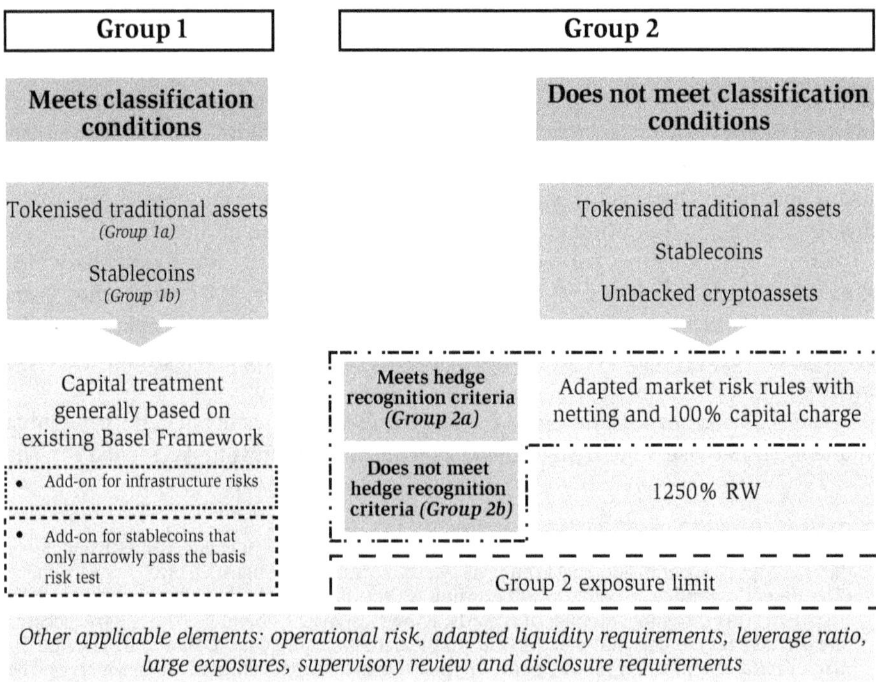

Source: BCBS, Second consultation on the prudential treatment of cryptoasset exposures' (2022), 2

233. *Ibid.*
234. ISDA, Crypto-asset Risk and Hedging Analysis (2022), 3.
235. BCBS, 'Second consultation on the prudential treatment of cryptoasset exposures' (June 2022), 3, https://www.bis.org/bcbs/publ/d533.pdf, accessed 20 August 2023.
236. *Ibid.*
237. *Ibid*, 2.

The BCBS consultation was concluded in December 2022 and led to *SCO60 Cryptoasset exposures*,[238] a 'capital requirement standard' which deals with 'the prudential treatment of banks' exposures to cryptoassets'.[239] The new *SCO60 Cryptoasset Standard* is set to be implemented by national banking regulators by 1 January 2025.[240] It, however, triggered further discussions and resulted in the *2023 Consultative Document*, issued by the BCBS in December 2023, which concerns proposed amendments to the *SCO60 Cryptoasset Standard* and deals with the attribution criteria of certain stablecoins to the Group 1b instead of the Group 2 category.[241]

[B] Accounting and Tax Considerations: United Kingdom

The following subchapter outlines the author's preliminary proposals in relation to hedge accounting of cryptoassets and crypto derivatives under IFRS and UK GAAP based on the author's view on how a hedged position of cryptoassets and crypto derivatives should be accounted for and taxed.

As no authoritative guidance on this topic has been published by the IFRS Interpretations Committee, the FRC or HMRC, the author will develop her views with the help of two ISDA papers, the BCBS consultation documents, the *SCO60 Cryptoasset Standard* and more general publications applying to either cryptoassets or crypto derivatives.

For example, in a 2022 paper, which deals with key considerations on the accounting of cryptoassets, ISDA observed that 'the institutional adoption of digital assets is leading more companies to seek ways to hedge the risk associated with the volatility in digital asset prices'.[242] ISDA states in relation to US GAAP that:

> derivatives must be accounted for at fair value, with changes in fair value reported through earnings, while the underlying digital asset is measured at cost less impairment. Companies that enter into derivatives for hedging purposes will be exposed to earnings volatility when marking the derivative to fair value without any offsetting mark-to-market on the digital asset.[243]

A similar accounting mismatch may occur for certain cryptoassets that are hedged with crypto derivatives under IFRS.

Since CME Group has launched the exchange trading of Bitcoin and Ether futures, the BCBS position on hedging cryptoassets added further complexity in terms of hedge accounting of crypto derivatives for banks as they must also consider the bank capital

238. BCBS, SCO60 – Cryptoasset exposures, 16 December 2022, https://www.bis.org/basel_framework/chapter/SCO/60.htm?tldate=20230521&inforce=20250101&published=20221216, accessed 26 December 2023.
239. BCBS, Prudential Treatment of Cryptoasset Exposures (December 2022), https://www.bis.org/bcbs/publ/d545.pdf, accessed 26 December 2023.
240. BCBS, Consultative Document, Cryptoassets standards amendments (14 December 2023), https://www.bis.org/bcbs/publ/d567.pdf, accessed 26 December 2023.
241. *Ibid.*
242. ISDA, Accounting for Digital Assets, Key considerations (2022), 17.
243. *Ibid.*

requirements put forward by the BCBS. Further, as the above-mentioned exchange-traded futures are physically settled only, careful consideration has to be given to how those instruments have to be treated under the existing accounting standards.

[1] Accounting Considerations

In the UK, hedge accounting will follow the rules in FRS 102, Section 12, IAS 39 or IFRS 9. In Chapter 5, the author has outlined that the accounting of cryptoassets and crypto derivatives is rather complex and that in terms of crypto derivatives, a distinction between cash and physically settled derivatives is made.

Hedge accounting adds another layer to the complexity of the accounting of cryptoassets and crypto derivatives as it introduces the concept of hedge effectiveness. Hence, careful consideration of the existing hedge accounting rules and their application to cryptoassets and crypto derivatives is needed, in addition to the awareness that the area of cryptoassets and crypto derivatives may provide particular challenges due to their novelty and the fact that they cannot be easily compared to other asset classes and derivatives.

The following investigation concerns situations where *cryptoassets*, for example, Bitcoin or Ethereum, which are fungible and liquid cryptocurrencies, are *hedged with crypto derivatives*, such as Bitcoin futures or options.

There are also examples where cryptoassets hedge crypto derivatives, but those cases are not discussed below. In the case of the latter, a careful analysis of the accounting treatment on a case-by-case basis is needed. The author's ideas outlined below may also prove helpful in those constellations.

[a] FRS 102, Section 12

Under FRS 102, Section 12, hedge accounting is optional, which means '[p]rovided the qualifying conditions in paragraph 12.18 are met, an entity may apply hedge accounting'.[244]

[i] Hedge Accounting Conditions

A hedging relationship consists of a *hedged item* and a *hedging instrument*.[245]

(1) Hedged items

FRS 102 defines that a *hedged item* may be:

(a) a *recognised asset or liability*;
(b) an *unrecognised firm commitment*;

244. FRS 102, para. 12.15 sent. 2.
245. FRS 102, para. 12.15 sent. 1; *also* Southern (2017) para. 16.17.

(c) a *highly probable forecast transaction*;
(d) a *net investment in a foreign operation*; or
(e) *a component of any such item*, provided the item is reliably measurable.[246]

That means that all of the above items have to be reliably measurable in order to qualify as hedged items.[247]

In the context of cryptoassets, cryptocurrencies like Bitcoin and Ethereum can be reliably measured because a liquid market exists for them. Thus, they would fall under the definition of a hedged item. Hence, cryptocurrencies qualify as a recognised asset in this context.

(2) Hedging instruments

Crypto derivatives, such as Bitcoin and Ethereum futures and options, must fall under the definition of a *hedging instrument* under FRS 102, para 12.17:

> An instrument may be treated as a *hedging instrument* provided all of the following conditions are met:
>
> (a) it is *a financial instrument measured at fair value through* profit or loss;
> (b) it is a contract with a party external to the reporting entity (i.e., external to the group or individual entity that is being reported on); and
> (c) it is not a written option, except as described in paragraph 12.17C.[248]

FRS 102, para 12.17C provides an exception to para 12.17 and states that:

> A written option is not a hedging instrument unless the written option is an offset to or is combined with a purchased option and the effect of the offset or combination is not a net written option. An example of a combination of a written and a purchased option that is not a net written option is a zero-cost interest rate collar.[249]

(A) Cash-settled crypto derivatives

As outlined in Chapter 5 §5.06, cash-settled crypto derivatives fall within the definition of derivatives of FRS 102, Glossary.

They are financial instruments that are measured at fair value through profit or loss, and thus, they fulfil condition (a) outlined above for a hedging instrument.

Further, if those crypto derivatives would be concluded with a party external to the reporting entity and are not written options (short call or put options),[250] they

246. FRS 102, para. 12.16.
247. Ghosh, Johnson and Miller (2022), [B5.78] (issue 28).
248. FRS 102, para. 12.17.
249. FRS 102, para. 12.17C.
250. It should be noted that option combinations, such as collars, do not fall under the exception.

would also fulfil criteria (b) and (c) of the definition of FRS 102, para 12.17, and, thus, qualify as *hedging instruments*.

(B) Physically settled crypto derivatives

Crypto derivatives, which are *physically settled only*, such as Bitnomial Bitcoin US dollar futures,[251] may not qualify as hedging instruments.

First, they do not qualify as derivatives for accounting purposes under FRS 102, Section 12. This may be the case because the exception of FRS 102, paragraph 12.5 applies, which states that 'contracts that were entered into and continue to be held for the purpose of the receipt or delivery of a non-financial item in accordance with the entity's expected purchase, sale or usage requirements are not financial instruments for the purposes of this section'.[252]

The underlying cryptoasset (Bitcoin or Ethereum) qualifies as a non-financial item, namely an intangible asset, according to the majority view in the accounting literature, as seen in Chapter 5 of this work. Thus, they are not financial instruments for the purposes of FRS 102, Section 12.[253]

Hence, physically settled crypto derivatives, which are held for the purpose of receiving those underlying cryptoassets, therefore may not qualify as hedging instruments within the scope of FRS 102, paragraph 12.17, although they may technically fulfil the criteria of the definition of a derivative in FRS 102, Glossary.

(C) Further criteria

It should also be noted that in relation to crypto derivatives, FRS 102, paragraph 12.17A limits the eligibility as a hedging instrument as such that an instrument may only be a hedging instrument:

(a) in its entirety;
(b) by designating a proportion of such an instrument or a proportion of a combination of such instruments, e.g., 50% of the nominal amount of the instrument; or
(c) by separating the spot risk element of a foreign currency contract and excluding the forward element or by separating the intrinsic value of an option and excluding the change in time value.[254]

251. Bitnomial, Bitcoin US Dollar Futures, https://bitnomial.com/products/bitcoin-us-dollar-futures, accessed 1 January 2024; *compare Bitcoin Magazine, Bitnomial launches margined, physically settled bitcoin futures*, https://bitcoinmagazine.com/markets/bitnomial-launches-margined-physically-settled-bitcoin-futures, accessed 25 April 2023; Business Wire, A Berkshire Hathaway Company, Bitnomial Launches Margined, Physically Settled Bitcoin futures in the US (15 November 2021), https://www.businesswire.com/news/home/20211115005890/en/Bitnomial-Launches-Margined-Physically-Settled-Bitcoin-Futures-in-the-US, accessed 23 April 2023.
252. FRS 102, para. 12.5.
253. *Ibid.*
254. FRS 102, para. 12.17A.

FRS 102, paragraph 12.18 sets out the hedge accounting conditions as follows:

(a) the hedging relationship consists only of a hedging instrument and a hedged item [...];
(b) the hedging relationship is consistent with the entity's risk management objectives for undertaking hedges;
(c) there is an economic relationship between the hedged item and the hedging instrument;
(d) the entity has documented the hedging relationship so that the risk being hedged, the hedged item and the hedging instrument are clearly identified; and
(e) the entity has determined and documented causes of hedge ineffectiveness.[255]

The economic relationship is further described in FRS 102, paragraph 12.18A, which states that 'an economic relationship between a hedged item and hedging instrument exists when the entity expects that the values of the hedged item and hedging instrument will typically move in opposite directions in response to movements in the same risk, which is the hedged risk'.[256] Thus, FRS 102, paragraph 12.18A addresses the question of risk correlation between the hedged item and the hedging instrument.

With respect to hedge effectiveness, the *2022 ISDA White paper* is again relevant. A sufficiently *effective hedging relationship* that permits hedge accounting between a cryptoasset and a crypto derivative can only be assumed if there is a *high enough correlation* in the price movement of the cryptoasset and the crypto derivative used as an instrument to hedge the cryptoasset. The *2022 ISDA White paper* explains this correlation criterion concerning Group 2a cryptoassets, such as Ethereum and Bitcoin and their respective futures:

> Correlation between Group 2a spot (Bitcoin and Ethereum) and their futures is sufficiently high to support effective hedging. The basis between spot Bitcoin and Ethereum and their respective futures has historically been relatively muted, which would enable effective hedging. The basis is within the same magnitude as the basis between large equity indices and their futures.[257]

(D) Proposed Outcome

In summary, provided that those conditions outlined above are met between the cryptoasset and the crypto derivative hedging it, hedge accounting is permitted under FRS 102, Schedule 12 for cash-settled crypto derivatives.

However, hedge accounting may only be allowed if cash-settled crypto derivatives are used, as physically settled crypto derivatives likely do not qualify as *hedging instruments* under the current accounting rules, based on the considerations mentioned above.

The author believes that such a distinction is arbitrary and should be addressed by the UK accounting standard setter. Companies may be able to work around those

255. FRS 102, para. 12.18.
256. FRS 102, para. 12.18A.
257. ISDA, Crypto-asset Risk and Hedging Analysis (May 2022), 4.

accounting anomalies by including a cash-settlement option into the terms of the documentation of physically settled, non-exchange traded crypto derivatives.[258]

The author proposes that it would be beneficial to create a new section within FRS 102 that specifically addresses the various questions relating to the accounting of cryptoassets, crypto derivatives and hedge accounting of those instruments. Such a new schedule would need to address – among many other issues – the accounting treatment of physically settled, exchange-traded crypto derivatives, such as Bitnomial's Bitcoin US Dollar futures, which have highly standardised terms and provide for physical settlement only.[259]

[ii] Types of Hedges Permitted

FRS 102, Schedule 12 defines in analogy with IAS 39/IFRS 9 three types of hedges:

(a) fair value hedge;
(b) cash flow hedge; and
(c) hedge of the net investment in a foreign corporation.

The author believes that all three types of hedges may be applicable to cryptoassets that are hedged by crypto derivatives.

(1) Fair value hedge

FRS 102, paragraph 12.19(a) defines a fair value hedge as 'a hedge of the exposure to changes in fair value of a recognised asset or liability or an unrecognised firm commitment, or a component of any such item, that are attributable to a particular risk and could affect profit or loss'.

If a company uses a crypto derivative as a hedging instrument, the company must record a fair value hedge as follows:

- The crypto derivative, i.e., the hedging instrument, must be measured at fair value.[260]
- 'The carrying value of the hedged item [the cryptoasset] is adjusted for the hedged risk only, i.e., if it is normally carried at amortised cost, the hedged

258. Crypto derivatives would normally be documented under the standard ISDA documentation architecture, containing termsheets, confirmations and master agreements, using the ISDA Digital Assets Derivatives Definitions that 'are designed for use by participants in privately negotiated transactions to document non-deliverable digital asset forwards and options referencing Bitcoin (BTC) or Ether (ETH)', *compare* ISDA, ISDA Digital Asset Definitions (2023).
See also ISDA, Bringing Legal Certainty to Digital Asset Derivatives, derivatiViews, informal comments by ISDA CEO Scott O'Malia, 30 January 2023, https://www.isda.org/2023/01/30/bringing-legal-certainty-to-digital-asset-derivatives/, accessed 25 December 2023.
259. Bitnomial, Bitcoin US Dollar Futures.
260. FRS 102, para. 12.20(a).

item is not adjusted to its full fair value but simply adjusted in respect to the risk that is being hedged'.[261]
- 'Gains and losses on both the hedging instrument [the crypto derivative] and the hedged item [the cryptoasset] are taken to the income statement so that there is little, if any, net profit and loss effect other than any hedging ineffectiveness'.[262]

(2) Cash flow hedge

FRS 102, paragraph 12.19 (b) defines a cash flow hedge as 'a hedge of the exposure to variability in cash flows that is attributable to a particular risk associated with all, or a component of, a recognised asset or liability (such as all or some future interest payments on variable rate debt) or a highly probable forecast transaction and could affect profit or loss'.

The hedging instrument, which is, in this case, the crypto derivative, must be measured at fair value.[263] The ineffective portion of the gain or loss on the derivative is recognised in the profit or loss statement.[264] The effective portion is recognised in 'other comprehensive income'.[265]

[b] IAS 39

For cash-settled crypto derivatives, the same conditions as under FRS 102, Section 12 should apply. Thus, cash-settled crypto derivatives should also be eligible hedging instruments for IAS 39 accounting purposes as they should qualify as financial instruments. In terms of hedge effectiveness, the *2022 ISDA White paper* outlines that:

> IAS 39 deems a hedge highly effective if two conditions are met:
> 1. The offset is in the range of 80-125%, meaning the slope parameter (Beta) of the regression of the returns of the hedging instrument against the hedged item's return is within the range of 0.80-1.25;
> 2. The coefficient of determination of the regression (the R-squared parameter) is equal to or greater than 0.80. R-squared is a statistical measure that, in this case, represents the proportion of variance of the hedging instrument's returns that is explained by the variance of the hedged item's returns.

In summary, a hedge is considered highly effective under IAS 39 if the following conditions are met:

(1) $0.80 \leq |ß| \leq 1.25$
(2) $R^2 \geq 0.80$ [266]

261. Southern (2017) para. 16.29; *compare also* FRS 102, para. 12.20(b).
262. Southern (2017) para. 16.29.
263. *Ibid.*
264. FRS 102, para. 12.23(c); *compare* Ghosh, Johnson and Miller (2022), [B5.62] issue 28.
265. FRS 102, para. 12.23(b).
266. ISDA, Crypto-asset Risk and Hedging Analysis (2022), 9.

The *2022 ISDA White paper* confirms that 'while the International Accounting Standards Board has recently replaced the IAS 39 quantitative criterion with a principles-based approach [under IFRS 9], the quantitative hedge effectiveness test remains widely used by financial institutions to determine the effectiveness of a hedging relationship'.[267]

In terms of the effectiveness of the hedging relationship, the *2022 ISDA White paper* summarises that:

> [The] analysis using the hedge accounting quantitative test under International Accounting Standard 39 (IAS 39) demonstrates that hedging Group 2a spot using their futures and ETFs is highly effective. The IAS 39 hedge accounting quantitative test was used to assess the hedge effectiveness of Bitcoin and Ethereum and their respective futures and ETFs. This supports the industry position that offsetting a Group 2a spot crypto assets against its futures or ETFs should be allowed.[268]

The *2022 ISDA White paper* concludes that those circumstances 'show an opportunity to establish a crypto-asset hedging framework by using the strong relationship and relatively small basis between Group 2a crypto assets and their futures and ETFs'.[269]

In relation to physically settled crypto derivatives, the author proposes that they may qualify as hedging instruments under IAS 39 under certain circumstances. To reiterate, in Chapter 5 §5.06, the author agreed with the view concerning physically settled derivative contracts over other non-financial items, such as futures and options to purchase physical commodities, that those 'contracts to buy or sell non-financial items [...] do not meet the definition of a financial instrument, as they do not give rise to a financial asset to neither of the parties'.[270]

Nonetheless, under IAS 39, crypto derivatives that provide for cash or physical settlement in their documentation may be accounted for as if they were financial instruments and, thus, should be eligible as a hedging instrument to hedge cryptoassets of a similar risk profile. Similarly, in those cases where the company 'has a practice of taking delivery of the underlying assets and selling them within a short period after delivery for the purpose of generating a profit from short-term fluctuations in price or dealer's margin',[271] crypto derivatives may be eligible hedging instruments.

To conclude, certain physically settled crypto derivatives may form a hedging relationship with a cryptoasset of a similar nature (i.e., Bitcoin futures with Bitcoin) if either:

- the crypto derivative *also* allowed for cash settlement (and not only physical settlement); or

267. *Ibid.*
268. *Ibid.*, 4.
269. *Ibid.*
270. IFRSCommunity.com, Financial Instruments, definition (IAS 32), updated 7 January 2023, https://ifrscommunity.com/knowledge-base/financial-instruments-definitions/, accessed 25 April 2023.
271. *Ibid.*

- the entity (the long position holder of the crypto derivatives) takes delivery of the cryptoassets and sells them within a short time after delivery to generate a profit.

In those two cases, physically settled crypto derivatives may also be accounted for as if they were financial instruments. Thus, there might indeed be a slight nuance between FRS 102, Section 12 and IAS 39 in the context of crypto derivatives, and the author regards it as desirable if the FRC addressed those questions in FRS 102.

[c] IFRS 9

As outlined above, although IFRS 9 became mandatory from 1 January 2018 for IFRS users as the new international accounting standard, companies have the choice between two standards in terms of hedge accounting. They can continue to apply the requirements of IAS 39, or they can apply the new requirements of IFRS 9.[272]

The definition of IAS 39, paragraph 9 is similar to that of IFRS 9, Appendix 1; thus, the same considerations in relation to the definition apply. However, there are differences in the way that hedge effectiveness is determined, which may lead to different results in relation to the hedge accounting of crypto derivatives. 'Under IAS 39, hedge effectiveness had to be proven using a retrospective test [the statistical calculation outlined above, also branded as a quantitative test by ISDA], which was onerous to implement, and prevented some fundamentally effective hedges from qualifying.'[273]

In terms of the hedging relationship, IFRS 9, paragraph 6.4.1. states that a hedging relationship only qualifies for hedge accounting if all of the following criteria are met:

(a) the hedging relationship consists only of *eligible hedging instruments*[274] *and eligible hedged items*,[275]

272. Pierre Vidal, Refinitiv, 'IFRS 9 hedge accounting: a financial opportunity for corporate treasuries' (24 May 2018) – on file with the author.
273. *Ibid.*
274. IFRS 9, paras 6.2.1. and 6.2.2. outline that only the following instruments are qualifying hedging instruments within IFRS 9.6.4.1, i.e., they can be designated as hedging instruments, namely:

 - derivatives measured at fair value through profit or loss (FVTPL), with an exception for most written options, *see* IFRS 9, B6.2.4; or
 - non-derivative financial instruments or liabilities measured at FVTPL. Financial liabilities designated at FVTPL or assets measured at fair value though other comprehensive income (FVOCI) are excluded, *see* IFRSCommunity.com, Hedge accounting, IFRS 9, https://ifrscommunity.com/knowledge-base/ifrs-9-hedge-accounting/#link-hedging-instruments, updated 10 May 2022, accessed 25 April 2023.

275. IFRS 9, paras 6.3.1. and 6.3.2. outline what hedged items are, namely:

 - a recognised asset;
 - a recognised liability;
 - an unrecognised firm commitment;

(b) at the inception of the hedging relationship, there is a *formal designation and documentation* of the hedging relationship and the entity's risk management objective and strategy for undertaking the hedge [...].[276]

(c) the hedging relationship meets all of the following *hedge effectiveness requirements:*

   (i) there is an economic relationship between the hedged item and the hedging instrument);

   (ii) the effect of credit risk does not dominate the value changes that result from that economic relationship; and

   (iii) the hedge ratio of the hedging relationship is the same as that resulting from the quantity of the hedged item that the entity actually hedges and the quantity of the hedging instrument that the entity actually uses to hedge that quantity of hedged item. However, that designation shall not reflect an imbalance between the weightings of the hedged item and the hedging instrument that would create hedge ineffectiveness (irrespective of whether recognised or not) that could result in an accounting outcome that would be inconsistent with the purpose of hedge accounting.[277]

That means that under IFRS 9, the strict hedge effectiveness test, i.e., the 80% to 125% rule, is removed,[278] although 'hedge effectiveness is still a requirement in order to apply hedge accounting, but is established based on a prospective and qualitative assessment',[279] namely the following hedge effectiveness requirements have to be met:

(1) There is an economic relationship between the hedged item and the hedging instrument that gives rise to [an] offset.

(2) The effect of credit risk does not dominate the value changes that result from that economic relationship.

(3) The hedge ratio is the one the entity actually uses under its risk management strategy unless it would create ineffectiveness inconsistent with the purpose of hedge accounting.[280]

- a highly probable forecast transaction (IFRS 9.6.3.3);
- aggregated exposures; and
- a net investment in a foreign operation.

The definition of a hedged item is similar to that of IAS 39. *Compare* IFRSCommunity.com, Hedge accounting, IFRS 9, https://ifrscommunity.com/knowledge-base/ifrs-9-hedge-accounting/#link-hedging-instruments, updated 10 May 2022, accessed 25 April 2023.

276. IFRS 9, para 6.4.1. states that: 'That documentation shall include identification of the hedging instrument, the hedged item, the nature of the risk being hedged and how the entity will assess whether the hedging relationship meets the hedge effectiveness requirements (including its analysis of the sources of hedge ineffectiveness and how it determines the *hedge ratio*).'

277. IFRS 9, para 6.4.1. That means that '[t]he hedge ratio is the one the entity actually uses under its risk management strategy unless it would create ineffectiveness inconsistent with the purpose of hedge accounting'; *see* IFRSCommunity.com, Hedge accounting, IFRS 9, https://ifrscommunity.com/knowledge-base/ifrs-9-hedge-accounting/#link-hedging-instruments, updated 10 May 2022, accessed 25 April 2023.

278. Vidal (2018).

279. *Ibid.*

280. *Ibid.*; *compare also* IFRSCommunity.com, Hedge accounting, IFRS 9, 23.

In terms of crypto derivatives, there is indeed an economic relationship between the hedged item and the hedging instrument that gives rise to an offset. As outlined in the *2022 ISDA White paper*, the correlation between Group 2a cryptoassets, such as Bitcoin and Ethereum, and their respective crypto derivatives is high enough to support effective hedging,[281] which means that there is an economic relationship between the hedged cryptoasset and the hedging crypto derivative.

If the cryptoasset and the crypto derivative are traded on the same exchange, no effect of credit risk should dominate the value changes. Also, in cases where crypto derivatives are traded on liquid exchanges, the credit risk should not dominate the value changes, except in cases of bankruptcy of the exchange, as was the case of FTX Trading Ltd. However, unlike IAS 39, the hedge effectiveness is not tested retroactively but prospectively.[282]

IFRS 9 requires measurement and recognition of ineffectiveness in a hedging relationship even though the hedge meets the effectiveness criteria.[283]

If the third criterion is also fulfilled, i.e., the hedge ratio is the one the entity actually uses under its risk management strategy, crypto derivatives, which have an underlying cryptoasset of Group 2a, should normally qualify for hedge accounting under IFRS 9 as the hedge can be regarded as effective.

Furthermore, as the strict 80% to 125% criteria is not applied, other, less liquid cryptocurrencies that are hedged with OTC crypto derivatives may form an effective hedging relationship.

The *2022 ISDA White paper*, however, does not go that far and only proposes hedge effectiveness for Group 2a cryptoassets, such as Bitcoin and Ethereum.

The author believes that those constellations which contain less liquid cryptoassets as hedged items need to be addressed by the *IFRS Interpretations Committee* to clarify the hedge accounting treatment not only of the most liquid cryptoassets, such as Bitcoin and Ethereum, but also that of lesser-known cryptocurrencies.

[2] Taxation

In terms of taxation, one needs to distinguish between Group 1a, 1b and Group 2a cryptoassets and those falling in Group 2b.

[a] Group 1a, 1b and Group 2a Cryptoassets and Their Derivatives

If one applied the hedge accounting provisions of IAS 39 also for tax purposes, hedge accounting would only be effective tax-wise if the hedge effectiveness lay between 80% and 125%.[284] As explained above, the cryptoassets of Group 1a and 1b, as well as

281. ISDA, Crypto-asset Risk and Hedging Analysis (2022), 6.
282. Vidal (2018).
283. PWC, Hedge effectiveness criterion, 13 October 2019, https://viewpoint.pwc.com/dt/us/en/pwc/accounting_guides/ifrs_and_us_gaap_sim/ifrs_and_us_gaap_sim_US/chapter_11_derivativ_US/118hedge_effectivene_US.html, accessed 25 April 2023.
284. Bramwell et al. (2023), H2.4.3.

Group 2a, such as Bitcoin and Ethereum, would fulfil that criterion as the hedge effectiveness is generally between 80% and 125%.

Also, under FRS 102, Schedule 12 and IFRS 9, 'hedge effectiveness is still a requirement in order to apply hedge accounting but is established based on a prospective and qualitative assessment'.[285] Hence, for cryptoassets like Bitcoin and Ethereum, their respective derivatives, and certain stablecoins, which fall under Group 1b, the hedges would generally be effective under FRS 102, Section 12 or IFRS 9 as the hedge effectiveness is likely to lay between 80% and 125% in most cases.

[b] *Application of the Disregard Regulations?*

In the following subsection, the author determines if the Disregard Regulations, particularly regulations 4, 7, 8, or 9, could be applied to hedging relationships between cryptoassets and crypto derivatives.

To recap, in the UK, the tax legislator has decided to allow a deviation from the financial accounts for the tax treatment of derivative contracts used in hedging transactions when a company accounts under FRS 102, Section 12, IAS 39 or IFRS 9 to mitigate for tax purposes 'some of the more wide-reaching effects of mandatory fair value accounting'.[286] Under the Disregard Regulations, matching of the hedged item and the hedging instrument is permitted for tax purposes *regardless of whether it is permitted or not for accounting* purposes,[287] leading to more generous tax rules permitting hedging compared to the narrow hedge accounting conditions under FRS 102, Section 12, IAS 39 or IFRS 9.[288]

The Disregard Regulations apply to both designated and non-designated hedges.[289]

If companies that hold cryptoassets and use crypto derivatives as a hedge could elect into the Disregard Regulations, they could avoid recognising gains or losses for tax purposes in cases where derivatives fall out of the IAS 39 'hedge effectiveness range' due to highly volatile markets in cryptoassets and their derivatives. In particular, for companies that hold 'non-Group 1a, 1b or 2a'-cryptoassets and hedge them with crypto derivatives, an application of the *Disregard Regulation* could be beneficial as it would allow them to maintain tax-effective hedging positions on a post-tax basis, i.e., disregard earnings volatility in those positions during the term of the hedge.

For example, regulation 4 applies to situations where profits and losses arising in respect of *currency derivative contracts* are designated fair value hedges of FX risk or where a 'hedging relationship'[290] exists to reduce the economic risk in relation to FX fluctuations in respect of shares, ships or aircraft.[291]

285. Vidal (2018).
286. Haworth and Hollis (2010) 28.
287. *See* Ch. 7 §7.03[A][2].
288. Haworth and Hollis (2010) 28.
289. Southern (2017) para. 16.54, referring to regulation 2(5).
290. A hedging relationship does not require a designation as a hedge, rather it is sufficient that the company intends, and can reasonably expect to eliminate or reduce the FX risks in relation to these particular hedged assets. *See* SI 2004/3256, regulation 4(3) Condition 3; *also* HMRC, CFM57060.

Regulation 7 applies to *fair value profits or losses on currency derivatives contracts that hedge FX risk* in cases of a 'hedging relationship' between the derivative and any 'forecast transaction or firm commitment' (so-called anticipatory hedges).[292]

Regulation 8 applies to commodity contracts and debt contracts, whereas deferred gains and losses will be brought into charge under regulation 10.[293] Specifically, regulations 8 and 10 apply to hedges *of commodity price risk* on forecast transactions or firm transactions by commodity contracts or debt contracts.[294]

The question arises if a crypto derivative that hedges a crypto asset could be seen as a hedge of commodity price risk. A commodity is a basic good used in commerce that is interchangeable with other goods of the same type. They are most often used as inputs in the production of other goods or services. The term 'commodity' usually refers to a raw material used to manufacture finished goods.[295]

Crypto derivatives do not qualify as commodity derivative contracts as the underlying cryptoassets do not meet the characteristics of a commodity. Similarly, crypto derivatives are also not debt or interest derivative contracts.

Instead, cryptoassets, which serve as an underlying for crypto derivatives, are regarded as intangible assets for accounting purposes. Consequently, none of the regulations of the Disregard Regulations, as they stand today, apply.

Thus, only those cryptoasset – crypto derivative hedging combinations which are designated as a hedge for accounting purposes and fulfil all criteria outlined above, particularly the hedge effectiveness criterion, will be eligible for a tax deferral on the hedged transactions.

In summary, insofar as the hedge is effective for accounting purposes under FRS 102, Section 12, IAS 39 or IFRS 9, it will also be allowed as a hedge for tax purposes. The ineffective portion of the gain or loss on the hedging instrument, i.e., the crypto derivative, is recognised in the profit or loss statement for accounting purposes[296] and thus would also be recognised for tax purposes.

For crypto derivatives which are unlikely to fulfil the criteria of hedge effectiveness, such as derivatives on Group 2b cryptoassets, P&L volatility of the single positions cannot be avoided for tax purposes.

CFM57060 further states that:

> A company's intention in undertaking a financial transaction is expressed through the intentions of its directors, although in many cases decisions will be delegated to a lower level of management. Particularly in large companies, the board of directors (or the group board) is likely to have set out a detailed policy on risk management. A company that has adopted IFRS, New UK GAAP, or FRS 26 under Old UK GAAP and wishes to use hedge accounting must have such documentation.

291. HMRC, CFM57040; Haworth and Hollis (2010) 28.
292. SI 2004/3256, Regulation 7(2); HMRC, CFM57090.
293. HMRC, CFM57210; Southern (2017) para. 16.61.
294. Southern (2017) para. 16.61.
295. Investopedia, commodity contract, https://www.investopedia.com/terms/c/commodity.asp, accessed 26 April 2023.
296. FRS 102, para. 12.23(c); *compare* Ghosh, Johnson and Miller (2022), [B5.62] issue 28.

The following two examples contain scenarios where a company generates a gain on the cryptoassets and a loss on the crypto derivatives, and vice versa.

Example 58:

Company A holds Dogecoin tokens as investments. After a change of strategy, Company A decides that the Dogecoin market risk is (temporarily) too high in 2022 and fully hedges the Dogecoin token holdings with OTC crypto derivatives, which it enters into with a Crypto broker B. The Dogecoin tokens will fall *outside* of Group 2a as defined in the *Cryptoassets Standard* but are instead Group 2b tokens. Thus, no effective hedge for accounting purposes is possible if the standard is applied.

Company A buys the token initially for 10 and buys the crypto derivatives hedge position when the token has a value of 50. At the end of the year, the value of the token is 100. The (unrealised) profit on the cryptoasset is 90 (current price of 100 minus acquisition costs of 10). The unrealised loss on the crypto derivative hedge is 50 (short position, difference between 100 and 50 (initial strike price)).

If Company A accounts for the Dogecoin tokens at (historical) cost, no amortisation of the intangible asset takes place, and the 90 in profits are not shown in the accounts until the cryptoasset is disposed of (no revaluation).

The short crypto derivative has generated a loss of 50 (which is the market price of 100 minus the strike price of 50) as the hedge took place when the price of the crypto asset was already at 50.

As the crypto derivative is accounted for at fair value through profit or loss, the loss of 50 is recognised both in the financial accounts and tax accounts. The result is that the company does not have to tax the gains on the cryptoasset token until realisation, whereas it can recognise the losses, as a hedging relationship is neither recognised for accounting nor tax purposes.

Vice versa, if losses are generated on the cryptoassets, whereas gains are generated on the crypto derivatives, the position may also create an offset both for accounting and tax purposes.

Example 59:

Company A buys a portfolio of Dogecoins (Doge) at an initial cost of 30. After a change of strategy, the board of Company A decides to fully hedge the Dogecoin position with OTC Dogecoin futures. The price of Dogecoin at the time of the hedge is 20, and the company has already recognised an impairment loss of 10 on the Dogecoin (30 minus 20). After buying the Dogecoin futures at 20, the market in Dogecoin completely declines. Dogecoin now has a value of 5. The corresponding gain on the Dogecoin future is 15. At this point in time, the company recognises a further impairment loss of 15 (without selling the Dogecoin), which it offsets against the gain of 15 generated on the Dogecoin future. Thus, the profit is zero for accounting and tax purposes. However, Company A can use the impairment loss of 10 on the Dogecoin position and offset it against other non-crypto profits.

The two examples show that the company can realise a gain in the overall position if the Dogecoins go up in value. For tax purposes, it does not need to show that gain until the disposal of the Dogecoin, whereas it can use the losses from the Dogecoin derivative to offset against other profits. In case the Dogecoin goes down in value, the Dogecoin position can realise an impairment loss for accounting and tax purposes, which can be offset with the derivative gain for tax purposes.

The examples show that the hedged position created an opportunity to generate tax-deductible losses (in case Dogecoin goes up in value) without taking any market risks (as the position is a hedged position).

[C] Accounting and Tax Considerations: Germany

[1] Accounting Treatment in Germany

Section 254 sentence 1 CLA explicitly *permits* hedge accounting if certain conditions are met.[297] The reason for the application of hedge accounting and the deviation from general German GAAP is to avoid write-downs of non-realised losses insofar as they were compensated by unrealised gains from the hedging transaction.[298] Hedge accounting is permissible if, cumulatively:

(1) the hedge is suitable for hedging the specific risk of the balance sheet item;[299]
(2) the hedge effectiveness with regard to the risk that needs to be hedged can be proved;[300] and
(3) the intention to hedge the balance sheet item has been documented.[301]

It should be noted that any financial instruments, not only derivatives, can be used to form a hedging relationship for accounting purposes.[302] This is particularly

297. Section 254 CLA, as introduced by *Gesetz zur Modernisierung des Bilanzrechts* (BilMoG) of 25 May 2009 (BStBl I 2009, 650ff.). Suggesting a voluntary application of hedge accounting: IDW (2011a) para. 4; Conlon & Aquilino: Derivatives D2.03[5][a].
Other opinion Scharpf and Schaber (2009) 308 and 312, suggesting a mandatory application of hedge accounting.
298. BR-Drucksache 344/08, 125. *See also* Conlon & Aquilino: Derivatives D2.03[5][a]; Scharpf and Schaber (2009) 309.
299. IDW (2011a) para. 3; Scharpf and Schaber (2009) 313. According to Häuselmann (2005) 50, the hedged item and the hedge must be non-ambiguously identifiable, i.e., a functional nexus between the hedged asset and the hedging derivative contract must be recognisable.
300. BR-Drucksache 344/08, 126; IDW (2011a) para. 3; Scharpf and Schaber (2009) 317.
301. IDW (2011a) paras 3 and 14.
302. BR-Drucksache 344/08, 125.

important in relation to hedge accounting positions that involve cryptoassets and crypto derivatives.

Section 254 CLA allows for full as well as partial compensation of risks[303] without requiring strict 'hedge effectiveness margins' as used, for example, under IAS 39.[304] The hedge accounting provision of section 254 CLA is only applicable with regard to the effective part of the hedge, whereas the ineffective part has to be accounted for outside the hedging relationship, applying the basic provisions of German GAAP, like the imparity principle.[305]

Section 254 CLA allows all kinds of hedges, including micro hedges, macro hedges and portfolio hedges,[306] insofar as a definite attribution of the hedged items and the hedging transactions has been documented.[307] Hedge accounting in the case of portfolio hedging and macro hedging is, however, only permissible if an appropriate, documented and functional risk management system for this transaction has been implemented by the company.[308] Section 254 CLA also allows for anticipatory hedges of future transactions if the expected transaction is highly likely, meaning that there is a high probability that the transaction will actually be executed.[309] Similar to IAS 39, section 254 CLA allows both fair value hedges to hedge the risk of a change in the fair value[310] and cash flow hedges[311] to hedge the risk of a change in the cash flow.[312] Thus, the author believes that cryptoassets and crypto derivatives can form hedging relationships under German GAAP independent of the categorisation of the underlying cryptoasset as proposed by the BCBS consultation papers or strict hedge effectiveness criteria.

[2] Treatment of Crypto Hedging Transactions for Tax Purposes

German GAAP hedge accounting rules are also decisive for tax accounts.[313] 'Whenever hedge accounting is applied in the financial accounts, it must also be applied in the tax accounts.'[314] Hedge accounting for tax purposes has the same wide scope as the hedge

303. *Ibid.*, 127. *See also* Conlon & Aquilino: Derivatives D2.03[5][a].
304. Scharpf and Schaber (2009) 318.
305. IDW (2011a) paras 6ff.
306. Conlon & Aquilino: Derivatives D2.03[5][a].
307. BR-Drucksache 344/08, 126; IDW (2011a) para. 16.
308. IDW (2011a) paras 3 and 20.
309. *Ibid.*, para. 32; *also* Scharpf and Schaber (2009) 308.
310. As defined in the guideline of the IDW, a risk of change in the fair value is given if the fair value of a balance sheet asset, liability or pending transaction can adversely change over time for the company accounting the asset/liability. *See* IDW (2011a) para. 21; Scharpf and Schaber (2009) 310.
311. A risk of change in the cash flows is given if there is a risk that the actual amount of future payments from the asset/liability adversely differs from the expected amount for the company accounting the asset/liability.
 See IDW (2011a) para. 21; Scharpf and Schaber (2009) 310.
312. BR-Drucksache 344/08, 126; IDW (2011a) paras 10 and 21.
313. Section 5(1a) sent. 2 ITA.
314. Conlon & Aquilino: Derivatives D2.03[5][b].

accounting rules under German GAAP and allows micro hedging, portfolio hedging and macro hedging.[315]

As previously explained, it is sufficient under German GAAP that the hedge is only partially effective; transactions are also more likely to qualify for hedge accounting treatment in the single company accounts than in 'consolidated company accounts' that are drawn in accordance with IFRS.

From a tax perspective, gains and losses of the hedge and the hedged item are offset and not recognised for tax purposes until maturity or if the hedge is dissolved, thereby ensuring that no P&L volatility occurs during the term of the transaction.

In terms of cryptoassets that are hedged by crypto derivatives, one can observe the effectiveness of hedging positions for accounting and tax purposes in the following example:

Example 60:

Company A holds Dogecoin tokens as investments, which it initially purchased at 10. After a change of strategy, Company A decides that the Dogecoin token market risk is (temporarily) too high in 2022 and fully hedges the Dogecoin token holdings with OTC crypto derivatives, which it enters into with a Crypto broker B. The Dogecoin tokens fall outside Group 2a but are instead Group 2b tokens.

Under German GAAP, Company A determines that Dogecoin and the Dogecoin future are in a hedging relationship (*Bewertungseinheit*).

Company A documents that:

(1) the hedge is suitable for hedging the specific risk of the balance sheet item;[316]

(2) the hedge effectiveness with regard to the risk that needs to be hedged can be proved;[317] and

(3) the intention to hedge the balance sheet item has been documented.[318]

It is assumed that the hedge effectiveness has been proven to be 75% between the Dogecoin and the Dogecoin futures contract.

Company A will have the following results in its financial and tax accounts:

- The hedge is recognised for accounting purposes.
- The hedge is recognised in terms of the effective part also for tax purposes, and the cryptoassets and the crypto derivatives form an accounting unit in this respect.

315. BMF, *Schreiben vom 25. August 2010, betr. steuerliche Gewinnermittlung bei der Bildung von Bewertungseinheiten* (IVC 6 – S 2133/07/10001, Der Betrieb 2010, 2024).

316. IDW (2011a) para. 3; Scharpf and Schaber (2009) 313. According to Häuselmann (2005) 50, the hedged item and the hedge must be non-ambiguously identifiable, i.e., a functional nexus between the hedged asset and the hedging derivative contract must be recognisable.

317. BR-Drucksache 344/08, 126; IDW (2011a) para. 3; Scharpf and Schaber (2009) 317.

318. IDW (2011a) paras 3 and 14.

As German GAAP recognises cryptoassets as intangible assets (in the same way as the accounting treatment of cryptoassets under IAS/IFRS), any cryptoasset gain would only be shown if the gain is realised, whereas any impairment loss is recognised on impairment.

However, this volatility is normally avoided for tax purposes (insofar as the hedge is effective) so that any Dogecoin gains are offset with crypto derivatives losses, and vice versa, any Dogecoin losses could be offset against derivatives gains.

The loss ring-fencing rules of section 15 paragraph 4 ITA may, however, make the hedge ineffective for tax purposes. First, the hedge accounting provisions may only apply to the extent that the hedging relationship is effective. Second, the hedging instrument needs to serve as an instrument to hedge the ordinary business operations of the company. If that is not the case, any crypto derivatives losses would be ring-fenced and not offsetable against any gains in the cryptoasset position.

CHAPTER 8
Taxation of Structured Products and Hybrid Instruments

Every statement about complexes can be analysed into a statement about their constituent parts and into those propositions which completely describe the complexes.

— Ludwig Wittgenstein, *Tractatus Logico Philosophicus*

In this chapter, the author provides a definition of structured products for tax purposes and distinguishes them from non-structured products and hybrid instruments.

Second, the author analyses the possibility of bifurcation for certain structured products based on financial mathematics and investigates whether hybrid instruments could be bifurcated in the same way.

Third, the author discusses the bifurcation and integration approaches in relation to structured products and hybrid instruments in the UK and German tax legislation. In this context, the author also outlines the approach towards bifurcation and integration under FRS 102, Sections 11 and 12, IFRS 9, IAS 39 and German GAAP and analyses how the accounting treatment of those financial instruments influences their taxation.

Fourth, the author evaluates the various approaches adopted by the UK and Germany to tax structured products and hybrid instruments and proposes solutions to the question of whether to bifurcate or integrate them based on their respective characteristics.

Lastly, the author discusses exotic structured products and hybrid instruments with particular underlyings or special features, such as crypto structured and ESG-linked structured products, in subchapters §8.09 and §8.10 and analyses their accounting and tax treatment.

§8.01 DEFINING STRUCTURED PRODUCTS

[A] Development of a Definition of Structured Products for Tax Purposes

One can define a structured product as a *legally inseparable linear combination* of at least *two non-structured financial instruments*, which consists of:

(1) at least one non-derivative, 'traditional' financial instrument; and
(2) one or more derivatives.[1]

Non-structured financial instruments are all instruments that cannot be further bifurcated into other financial instruments. They may, however, be statically replicated by using the 'basic building blocks' of the put-call parity formula.[2]

The term 'non-structured financial instruments' has to be differentiated from the term 'basic building block'.

Basic building blocks are only those instruments contained in the put-call parity formula, i.e., call options (C), put options (P), underlying assets (S)[3] and zero-coupon bonds that equal the present value of the strike price K, expressed as PV(K). In addition, PV(D) refers to the present value of income from the underlying, i.e., dividends or interest, representing cash amounts only and, therefore, cannot be regarded as a separate basic building block.

Non-structured financial instruments (traditional financial instruments as well as derivatives) entail the basic building blocks but go beyond them and include all cash instruments traded at a spot market and every derivative that cannot be further bifurcated.

The graphic below shows the relationship between non-structured financial instruments and basic building blocks, the latter being only a part of the broader category of non-structured financial instruments.

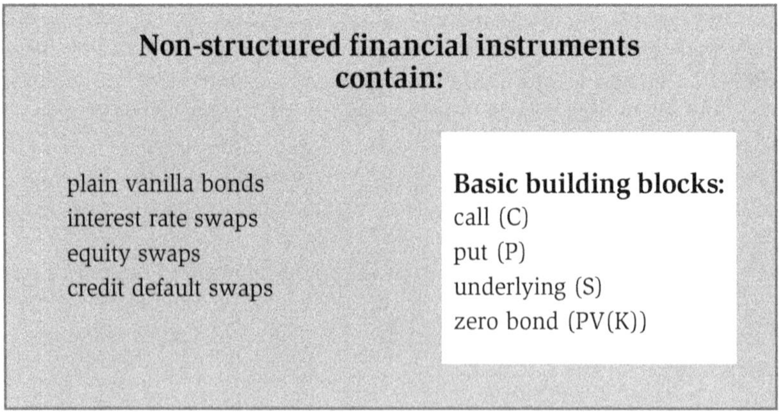

1. Compare similar definitions: Fabozzi et al. (2002) 389; Conlon & Aquilino: Derivatives, A1.06[1].
2. *See* Ch. 2 §2.02[A][1].
3. The underlying (S) can be shares but also any other financial instrument.

[B] Application of the Definition to Structured Products

By applying the above definition, one can distinguish genuine structured products from 'false friends', as one may call them.

Those false friends may have the 'look' of a structured product at first sight, but they do not qualify as structured products under the above definition as they lack one or more definitional criteria.

[1] False Friends I: Put-Call Parity Combinations

From genuine *structured products*, one has to distinguish artificial combinations of instruments that consist of three of the four basic building blocks used in the put-call parity formula if those combinations can be mathematically described as a *single* basic building block by applying the put-call parity formula.

> *Example 61:*
>
> $P = C - S + PV(K) + PV(D)$
>
> The above formula means that the purchase of an equity put option can also be mathematically replicated using the put-call parity. Thus, instead of buying a put option, one achieves the same payout with a combination of instruments: a purchase of an equity call option, a disposal of the underlying shares and a purchase of a zero-coupon bond, and then add the present value of the dividends until maturity of the put option, if there are any.

The combination of the basic building blocks, expressed as $C - S + PV(K)$ of the above-mentioned put-call parity formula, does not qualify as a genuine structured product under the above definition as it is economically simply a purchase of a put option, even if all instruments on the other side of the formula were combined in one contract.[4]

In contrast, a linear combination of a long call option and a long zero-coupon bond would qualify as a structured product because the combination of the call and the bond could not be mathematically expressed as a single basic building block with the help of the put-call parity.

4. It is necessary to distinguish genuine structured products from other combinations in order to prevent tax arbitrage strategies that achieve a more favourable tax treatment by combining basic building blocks using the put-call parity formula instead of using the simple derivative in a transaction.

Example 62:

C + PV(K) = S + P – PV(D)

The purchase of a call option and a zero-coupon bond equals the purchase of the underlying asset and a put option less discounted income. Here, a combination of a traditional financial instrument and derivative is on both sides of the formula.

The above formula expresses the payoff of a structured capital guarantee product. The combination of a long call option and a long zero-coupon bond allows the investor to participate in the performance of the underlying via the purchased call option. At the same time, it protects the investor against losses of the capital at maturity due to the purchase of a zero-coupon bond.

[2] False Friends II: Legally Separable Combinations

As stated above, structured products are *legally inseparable combinations* of at least one traditional financial instrument and one or more derivatives that are 'wrapped up in one legal contract'.[5]

A legally inseparable combination can be assumed if either the instrument is securitised as a structured product or if both elements of the structured products are contained in a single legal confirmation in such a way that one part of the product cannot be sold, assigned or re-hypothecated without the other part. Whether the structured product is in securitised or un-securitised form is irrelevant as long as the combination is legally inseparable.

Structured products must be distinguished from combinations of a traditional financial instrument and one or more derivatives that can be divided into two or more separate legal contracts.

Financial instruments that can be legally divided, such as bond cum warrants or stripped bonds, will not fall within the definition of structured products[6] as the warrants or coupons can be traded separately from the bond and thus are not part of a legally inseparable unit.[7]

In contrast, a combination of a bond and an option that is contained in one legal confirmation will qualify as a structured product, provided both parts cannot be divided and sold or assigned separately.

5. Paul Scharpf and Günther Luz, *Risikomanagement, Bilanzierung und Aufsicht von Finanzderivaten* (2nd edn, Schäffer-Pöschel Verlag 2000) 723 define structured products for accounting purposes as legally inseparable combinations of a non-derivative host contract and one or more embedded derivative contracts.
6. Häuselmann (2005) 144 describes these instruments as 'artificial compound instruments' (*unechte Compound Instruments*).
7. Scharpf and Luz (2000) 653 and 723; *also* Häuselmann (2005) 144.

[3] False Friends III: Combinations of Two or More Derivative Contracts

Combinations of two or more *derivatives* will not qualify as structured products under the above definition, even if they are contained in one legally inseparable contract, as they do not consist of a traditional financial instrument and one or more derivatives.[8]

Thus, any combination of options, such as call spreads, put spreads, collars, or other combinations of derivatives,[9] will not qualify as structured products for tax purposes under the above definition.[10]

> *Example 63:*
>
> Company A purchases a call option with a strike price of 100 and sells another call option with a strike price of 115. Both options have the same maturity. The combined portfolio has a payoff that is zero below 100, 15 above 115 and linear in between.
>
> This so-called bull spread would not qualify as a structured product even if it were documented in one legal confirmation, as it does not consist of a traditional financial instrument and a derivative but only of two derivatives.

Sometimes, it is not easy to distinguish these derivative combinations from genuine structured products. Strictly applying the definitional criteria for structured products will provide a non-ambiguous answer.

> *Example 64:*
>
> Company A purchases a discount certificate. The payoff of a discount certificate equals the payoff of a purchased zero-strike call and a written call option.[11]
>
> The instrument in *Example 64* does not qualify as a structured product, even if it is securitised as one financial instrument, as it consists of two derivatives and not a traditional financial instrument and a derivative.

---

8. Scharpf and Luz (2000) 723 rightfully leave out of their definition combinations of two derivatives that are 'wrapped up' in one legal contract.
9. Consequently, a combination of a purchased call option and a sold put options which equals the payoff of a forward if taken together would not qualify as a structured product under the above definition. This combination consists of two derivatives and not of a traditional financial instrument and a derivative.
10. BMF, *Schreiben vom 27. November 2001, Einkommensteuerliche Behandlung von Termingeschäften im Bereich der privaten Vermögensverwaltung* (IVC3 - S2256 - 265/01 BStBl I 2001, 986) describes a combination of options as two separate legal instruments, which are entailed in a single term sheet.
11. This specific combination of options is called a bull spread because it benefits from a rising market.

[4] *Reverse Convertible Bonds as an Example of Structured Products*

A reverse convertible bond is a corporate bond where the *issuer* has the right to deliver a pre-determined number of shares[12] to the holder of the bond instead of paying back the notional amount of the bond at maturity.[13]

The reverse convertible bond pays a higher coupon compared to a normal corporate bond.[14] The additional coupon amount equals the premium received under a short put option over the shares, which is spread over the term of the reverse convertible bond.

Reverse convertible bonds[15] will qualify as structured products under the above definition for tax purposes as they are legally inseparable linear combinations of a straight bond and a short put option for the holder of the bond.[16] Correspondingly, from the issuer's position, the reverse convertible is a linear combination of a short bond plus a long put option to sell a pre-determined number of shares to the investor at a pre-determined value (the sum of which usually equals the notional value of the bond).[17]

§8.02 BIFURCATION OF STRUCTURED PRODUCTS

One can best describe the bifurcation of structured products by comparing it to the LEGO® principle: one puts together two or more LEGO® bricks and builds a small structure. The small structure can always be taken apart, leaving us with the same bricks. Hence, the small structure consists of nothing more than single LEGO® bricks,[18] and bifurcation is the process of separating the small structure into its bricks.

Ghosh, Johnson and Miller state that 'bifurcation is the term used to describe the splitting of an instrument into two separate components for accounting purposes'.[19]

For example, as a reverse convertible bond is a legally inseparable linear combination of a traditional financial instrument and a call option, it should be

12. The issuer can either deliver own equity or equity of another company as defined in the terms, depending on whether the company itself issues the reverse convertible or a bank.
13. Inmoo Lee and Eduardo Repetto, *Structured Products* (Dimensional Fund Advisors, 2010) 2; *also* Laukkanen (2007) 47; Scharpf and Schaber (2009) 527; Andreas Schumacher, 'Die Besteuerung von Compound Instruments beim Privatanleger am Beispiel von Reverse Convertibles' DStR 2000 416, 417; Eberhard Schwark, 'Ist die Aktienanleihe ein Börsentermingeschäft?' WM 2000 1973, 1973.
14. Andreas Schumacher, 'Nochmals: Besteuerung von Hochzins- und Umtauschanleihen' DStR 2001 1021, 1021.
15. The term 'reverse convertible bond' is quite misleading because the position in a reverse convertible bond is not the opposite position as holding a convertible bond.
16. Scharpf and Schaber (2009) 538; Schumacher (2000) 417; Schumacher (2001) 1021.
17. Lee and Repetto (2010) 2.
18. One needs to distinguish between the (static) replication of derivatives, using the put-call parity formula, and the bifurcation of structured products in order to exclude 'false friends' (that cannot be bifurcated but only replicated) from the definition of genuine structured products (that can be bifurcated); see Ch. 8 §8.01[B][1]. For a definition of the term static replication, see Ch. 2 §2.02[A][1].
19. Ghosh, Johnson and Miller (2022) [G1.11] (issue 28).

bifurcated into a bond and a put option for tax purposes. In the following example, the economic mechanism of the purchase of a reverse convertible bond will be compared with its components, being the purchase of a straight bond and the sale of a put option.

Example 65:

Company A purchases a reverse convertible bond issued by Company B. The term of the reverse convertible is one year, the yield is 8%, and the bond has a notional value of GBP 1,000.

Under the reverse convertible bond, Company B has the right to put a pre-determined number of its shares to Company A at maturity for a pre-determined strike price of GBP 100 instead of paying back the notional amount of the bond to Company A. Assuming the value of each share is equal to the strike price (i.e., GBP 100) at inception, the issuer would deliver 10 shares for each bond.

Alternatively, Company B could have issued a comparable straight bond with a coupon of 5% p.a. and a term of one year. The difference in the coupon of 3% can be attributed to the value of the put option, which is contained in the reverse convertible bond.

Company A would have to write a comparable put option over the shares of Company B with the same strike price in order to have the same yield pick-up of 3% at maturity. The option premium would, in this case, however, be received by Company A at the inception of the option, not at maturity. Thus, the yield pick-up would have to be discounted accordingly,[20] leading to an option premium of GBP 28.57 received at inception, which would equal a 3% coupon on GBP 1,000 received after one year (assuming a riskless interest rate of 5%).[21] Thus, an additional coupon of 3% at maturity would be paid by Company B in order to have the right to put shares to Company A at maturity of the bond.

Company B will normally only exercise its right to deliver its shares instead of the notional amount of the bond if the market value of its shares lies below the strike price at maturity of the bond, meaning that the shares would have a lower market price at maturity than the notional amount to be paid back to Company A. Only in such a case, would the incorporated put option be in the money for Company B.

20. Put option price = 3% × GBP 1,000/(1 + riskless interest rate of the straight bond) = GBP 30/(1 + 0.05) = GBP 28.57.
21. As a 'riskless interest rate', one would have to consider the rate paid under the straight bond, leaving out any credit risk considerations.

The possibility of bifurcation of a reverse convertible bond is also confirmed by two facts:

(1) The total gains or losses under the reverse convertible bond equal the total gains or losses under a corporate bond and a short put option.[22]
(2) A reverse convertible bond can be priced and valued by subtracting the value of a put option (using a simple Black-Scholes pricing model for valuing the put option) from the theoretical value of the corporate bond.[23]

§8.03 DEFINING HYBRID INSTRUMENTS

Hybrid instruments are another form of non-linear derivative instruments. Their legal and economic character is in between debt and equity as they have features of both debt and equity.[24] Hybrid instruments do not qualify as structured products under the above definition as they are not linear combinations of a non-derivative traditional financial instrument and one or more derivatives.

Examples of hybrid instruments for which the term will be used in this work are *convertible bonds* and *exchangeable bonds*.

A convertible bond is a corporate bond 'that *can* be converted by the holder of the bond into a pre-determined number of shares of the issuer of the bond'.[25]

Similarly, exchangeable bonds are corporate bonds that can be converted into a pre-determined number of shares in a company other than the issuer's company at certain times during its life.[26] Thus, in the case of exchangeable bonds, the issuer of the bond does not deliver its own equity but the equity of another company.

§8.04 NO BIFURCATION OF HYBRID INSTRUMENTS

In contrast to structured products, hybrid instruments *cannot* be economically bifurcated, as they are not linear combinations of two other financial instruments. The LEGO® principle, as explained in Chapter 8 §8.02, cannot be applied as the hybrid instrument cannot be taken apart as a structure.

Consequently, a convertible bond cannot be bifurcated from a financial perspective, nor can it be replicated using *static* replication, as it cannot be mathematically deconstructed by applying the put-call parity. Only a dynamic replication of the value of the convertible bond and thus dynamic hedging is possible by constantly trading in

22. When taking into account the value of the option premium received and comparing it with the present value of the coupon payments received under the reverse convertible bond.
23. The theoretical value of the bonds is calculated by adding the present value of the coupons until maturity and the present value of the notional.
24. Thuronyi (2001a) 271; Southern (2017) para. 4.52; Ghosh, Johnson and Miller (2022) [G1.1.] (issue 28).
25. Hull (2006) 745; Wilmott (2000) 463.
26. Fabozzi (1997) 12.

a portfolio of underlying bonds and underlying equities.[27] Such a dynamic replication, however, does not allow bifurcation.[28]

Some authors in the academic tax literature assume that hybrid instruments are built of a traditional (debt) financial instrument and one or more derivatives.[29] The assumption that a convertible or exchangeable bond can be mathematically deconstructed into basic building blocks is a common misconception, leading to the result that these authors propose that a convertible or exchangeable bond can be economically bifurcated into a bond plus a call option.[30]

The author disagrees with this proposition because neither a bifurcation nor a static replication is possible when applying mathematical standards to such a bifurcation.[31] The reason for the author's proposition is quite simple. The holder of a convertible bond only ever holds one financial instrument, not two, because, at maturity, the convertible bond holder will either receive the notional back (in case the convertible bond is not exercised) or the holder will hold shares due to exercise of the convertible, but never both, cash and shares.[32]

27. A convertible bond can be dynamically replicated by constant buying or selling of the underlying bond and the underlying equity. How many bonds, and how many equities must be purchased in the replicating portfolio at a time, depends on whether the character of the convertible bond is more bond or more equity at any point in time during the lifetime of the convertible bond.
28. As a dynamic replication is possible and all other criteria for a derivative are fulfilled, one would consequently classify a convertible bond as a stand-alone derivative, as it would fulfil the criteria for a derivative as outlined in Ch. 4 §4.06[B][5] of this work.
29. Conlon & Aquilino: Derivatives D2.06.[1; Laukkanen (2007) 314.
30. Conlon & Aquilino: Derivatives D2.06.[1] regard a convertible bond as 'consisting of a bond and an embedded (call) option right (compound instrument)' from a commercial perspective. The authors however suggest the accounting and taxation of the convertible bond as a single asset, because 'there is only one legal relationship between the issuer and the investor'.

    Laukkanen (2007) 314 maintains that a 'convertible bond, consists of a bond, an option and a right, but not the obligation, to convert the bonds at a certain time and by defined conditions into the shares of the issuing company'.

    In contrast, Southern (2017) para. 1.58 acknowledges that 'convertibles are contingent equity'.

    In the same way, Holger Häuselmann, 'Wandelanleihen in der Handels- und Steuerbilanz des Emittenten' BB 2000 139, 145 and Häuselmann (2005) 160 acknowledge the status of convertible bonds as hybrid instruments between equity and debt. The above-mentioned articles explain by way of comparison between a bond cum warrant and a convertible bond that the warrant constitutes a separate element from the bond because it gives the holder a right to receive shares, whereas a convertible only contains a legally dependent and not separable right to convert the bond into shares.
31. They might have derived the view that convertible bonds could be bifurcated from IAS 32, para. 29, which proposes that 'the economic effect of issuing such an instrument is *substantially* the same as issuing simultaneously a debt instrument with early settlement provision and warrants to purchase ordinary shares'.

    In Ch. 8 §8.08, the author explains the reasons why accounting standards have previously followed a bifurcation approach and explains that national tax legislation should not.
32. *See* OECD (2001) para. 110. This paragraph of the OECD document suggests that 'bifurcating a convertible security and taxing the discount on an accruals basis assumes that there will be redemption, i.e., no conversion'. However, as one cannot predict before maturity of the convertible, whether the convertible bond is converted into equity or not, the assumption that there will be no conversion is wrong, and therefore cannot – in the author's view – justify a bifurcation approach in relation to convertibles.

If the right to convert into shares is exercised, the holder of the convertible bond will not get the invested capital back but will get shares. Hence, no bond exists upon conversion but only the shares. The bond element ceases to exist upon exercise of the right to receive shares and upon conversion into shares. Convertible bonds economically behave either more like a bond or like equity, depending on the change of price in the underlying equity during the term of the convertible.[33]

Example 66:

C approaches the car dealer D of Audi and BMW and leases an Audi (A). At the end of the three-year leasing contract, C may purchase the Audi for the pre-determined amount X.[34] C also receives the right from D to alternatively acquire a three-year BMW (B) with equal mileage (compared to the Audi) at maturity of the leasing contract for a price of X.

C pays a little more than the standard leasing rate for an Audi in order to acquire the right to swap the car after three years into a BMW. Looking at pure economics, C may decide to acquire the BMW instead of the Audi under the leasing contract after three years if the price of a used BMW is higher than the price of the used Audi at that time.

The example of the car-leasing contract with a conversion option illustrates the following: the conversion right is a right to convert A into B, but it is not a separate option to acquire B. The conversion right has a certain value, which is the amount paid in excess of the standard car-leasing contract, but it also shows that this conversion right cannot be separated from the standard car-leasing contract to lease and acquire A.

The owner of the leasing contract with the conversion option will either acquire an Audi and pay the purchase price or acquire a BMW instead. He will, however, never own an Audi *and* a BMW for the agreed purchase price. The conversion right only turns one asset into another asset but does not enable the holder to hold both assets.

The same principle, as described in *Example 66*, applies to convertible bonds: they do not consist of a bond plus an option to acquire shares, but the convertible bond only contains the conversion right to convert the bond into equities.[35] This conversion right has a separate value, but it cannot be regarded as a separate equity option and thus cannot be bifurcated from the bond.[36]

The approach to the pricing of convertible bonds also supports the author's proposition that a convertible or exchangeable bond cannot be bifurcated into a bond and an equity option. Instead, it has to be treated as one hybrid instrument that simply

33. Wilmott (2000) 473.
34. The example assumes that C pays the leasing rates and the additional purchase price, which present value equals the value of the Audi at inception of the contract plus an appropriate profit margin for the car dealer D due to entering into a leasing contract with C.
35. Häuselmann (2000) 145.
36. Häuselmann (2005) 160.

possesses a conversion option to convert the bond into equity, which can be valued separately, but is itself no separate call option to acquire shares. One can value a convertible bond by considering that it depends on both:

- its conversion value, which is the conversion value of the shares received if the bond is converted immediately,[37] and
- its value as a corporate bond, including the notional value of the bond or the final principal and the coupons paid during the life of the bond.[38]

A valuation formula would take into account the probability under which the convertible would end up as a bond, with no conversion taking place, as well as the probability the convertible would be converted into equity, considering the number of shares, that the holder of the convertible would get if they converted the bond into equity.[39]

If a convertible bond was bifurcated in – or statically replicated by – a corporate bond and an equity option, one could price the convertible bond as a combination of a corporate bond plus an equity option and, thus, simply determine the fair value of the corporate bond, the price of the equity option and add the two together. However, one would get the wrong price for the convertible bond if one used such a pricing methodology, as the price of the combined bond plus option will always be higher than the price of a convertible bond.

Or, as *Derman*[40] puts it: 'A convertible bond is a *centaur*, half risky bond, half stock. Convertible bond models take you from the liquid stock price and the liquid risky bond price to the value of the *centaur*, the hybrid itself.'[41] The same applies to exchangeable bonds because they are constructed in the same way as convertible bonds, albeit with a different issuer.

For convertible bonds, a simple valuation formula could look as follows:

$$CB_t = S_t \times n_S \times Prob_S + (PV(B_T) + PV(r_{t..T})) \times Prob_B$$

whereas

CB_t = convertible bond price at t

S_t = share price at t

n_S = number of shares (conversion ratio)

$Prob_S$ = probability of conversion of the bond into shares

B_T = redemption value of the Bond at maturity

$r_{t...T}$ = compounded interest (coupons) until maturity

$Prob_B$ = probability that bond is not converted into shares

37. The conversion value equals the market price of the stock multiplied by the conversion ratio.
38. Wilmott (2000) 463.
39. For a more detailed discussion of the valuation formula of convertible bonds, *see* Annex §A8.01.
40. *Emanuel Derman* is a former Goldman Sachs quantitative analyst.
41. Interview with Emanuel Derman in: Espen Gaarder Haug, *Derivatives, Models on Models* (John Wiley & Sons Ltd 2007) 105.

One can see from the formula that the value of a convertible bond will always be smaller than the value of a bond plus the value of an equity call option because it has to be taken into account that the holder of the convertible bond will either end up with a bond or the equities, but not with both, which is translated in the formula with the probabilities of conversion and non-conversion.

The pricing complexity of a convertible bond as a hybrid instrument also shows in the pricing model. Convertible bonds are priced using an advanced binominal tree model, for example, the *Espen Gaarder Haug model*,[42] which does not assume that the price of a convertible is a combined price of a straight bond plus an equity option but uses a calculation based on probabilities of conversion.[43]

In summary, because one cannot deconstruct the convertible bond into a bond plus an equity option, the convertible bond will not qualify as a structured product but as a *hybrid instrument*. This is also proven by the fact that static replication, using the put-call parity formula, is not possible in the case of a convertible bond.

If one wanted to further classify convertible and exchangeable bonds beyond the description that they are something between equity and debt, one would have to acknowledge that a dynamic replication is possible and all other definitional criteria for a derivative, as described in Chapter 4 §4.06[B][5], are fulfilled.

Consequently, one would have to classify convertible and exchangeable bonds as stand-alone derivatives for tax purposes under the abstract derivatives definition suggested in Chapter 4 §4.06[B][5].

§8.05 BIFURCATION VERSUS INTEGRATION APPROACHES IN THE UK

The UK taxation of structured products and hybrid instruments is, in principle, based on the accounting treatment of these instruments under FRS 102, Sections 11 and 12, IAS 39 or IFRS 9. In the following, the author briefly compares the accounting treatment of these instruments under (1) old UK GAAP, (2) IAS 32 and IAS 39, (3) IFRS 9 and (4) FRS 102, Section 11 or 12.

The historical outline discussed in Chapter 8 §8.05[A] shows the transformation from old GAAP to IFRS 9 and highlights how the changes in accounting treatment led to changes in the tax treatment of structured products and hybrid instruments.

The author reiterates that FRS 102, paragraph 11.2 allows companies to apply the accounting standards of FRS 102, Sections 11 and 12, IAS 39 or IFRS 9 to recognise and measure financial instruments.[44] Thus, not only can FRS 102, Schedule 11 or 12 or IFRS 9 be applied, but also, alternatively, as a policy option, UK companies can still

42. The calculation of the model is described by: Abukar M Ali, 'Convertible Bond Pricing Model' http://www.yieldcurve.com/Mktsoftware/excelCB.htm, accessed 12 February 2023.
43. Wilmott (2000) 473 notes that from a pricing and hedging perspective, convertible bonds are highly complex instruments.
44. *Compare* Ch. 5 §5.02[B], and FRS 102, The Financial Reporting Standards applicable in the UK and the Republic of Ireland (January 2022), para. 11.2, https://www.frc.org.uk/getattachment/c66c1d97-5943-413c-b354-f122e07f144d/Redacted-FRS-102-(January-2022).pdf, accessed 10 May 2023.

apply IAS 39. That means, although IFRS 9 superseded IAS 39,[45] under FRS 102, UK companies basically still have three options to recognise and measure financial instruments:[46]

(1) FRS 102, Sections 11 and 12;
(2) IAS 39 *Financial Instruments: Recognition and Measurement*;[47] or
(3) IFRS 9 *Financial Instruments*.[48]

The Financial Reporting Council (FRC) states that:

> [t]he choice to apply IAS 39 or IFRS 9 might be relevant to entities that previously applied FRS 26 (IAS 39) Financial Instruments: Recognition and Measurement or when the simplified accounting in FRS 102 means that certain options within IAS 39 or IFRS 9 are not available. [...] the option to apply IAS 39 through FRS 102 continues to be available after IAS 39 has been superseded by IFRS 9 for IFRS reporters.[49]

[A] Historical Accounting Treatment of Hybrid Instruments under Old UK GAAP

FRS 4 dealt with the accounting of convertible and exchangeable bonds and was withdrawn following the implementation of FRS 25 and FRS 26.[50] 'Under FRS 4, the issuer of convertible debt measured such debt at cost (less issue costs) as a single liability. On conversion, equity was issued and measured at the value of the liability on the date of conversion.'[51] Old UK GAAP followed the legal approach and treated convertible and exchangeable bonds as a single instrument.

45. Deloitte, IAS 39 – Financial Instruments: Recognition and Measurement, https://www.iasplus.com/en/standards/ias/ias39, accessed 27 April 2023.
46. LucaNet, White paper, 'Key differences between IFRS and UK GAAP', 16.
47. It is stated in the footnote 47 of s. 11.2 of FRS 102 that: Until IAS 39 Financial Instruments: Recognition and Measurement is fully superseded by IFRS 9 Financial Instruments (i.e., for all entities, including insurers), an entity shall apply the version of IAS 39 that is in effect at the entity's reporting date. When IAS 39 is fully superseded by IFRS 9, an entity shall apply the version of IAS 39 that applied immediately prior to IFRS 9 fully superseding IAS 39. A copy of that version will be retained for reference on the FRC website. Entities shall apply the so-called EU carve-out of IAS 39, which amended para. 81A and related Application Guidance in IAS 39.
48. *Compare also* Ghosh, Johnson and Miller (2022) [B2.3A] (issue 28); FRS 102, Factsheet 4, Financial Instruments (December 2018), 1, https://www.frc.org.uk/getattachment/f790644d-4802-459a-816a-b57df46c92b6/FS-04-FRS-102-Financial-Instruments-(Dec-2018).pdf, accessed 16 March 2023; LucaNet, White paper, 'Key differences between IFRS and UK GAAP', 9.
49. FRS 102, Factsheet 4, Financial Instruments (December 2018), 2.
50. FRS 4: Capital Instruments.
51. HMRC, CFM 25020.

[B] Accounting Treatment of Structured Products and Hybrid Instruments under IAS 32 and IAS 39

[1] The Basic Rules

IAS 39 describes the accounting treatment of structured products and hybrid instruments from the perspective of the holder of the instrument,[52] whereas the accounting treatment of hybrid instruments from the issuer's perspective is dealt with in IAS 32.[53]

IAS 39, paragraph 10, provides a definition of an *embedded derivative*. It is defined as 'a component of a hybrid (combined) instrument that also includes a non-derivative host contract – with the effect that some or all of the cash flows of the combined instrument vary in a way similar to a stand-alone derivative'.[54]

If the embedded derivative is bifurcated from the host contract for accounting purposes, it must be accounted for on the balance sheet at fair value with the changes going through the income statement, whereas the host contract will be accounted for under IAS 39 if it is a financial instrument,[55] or under another appropriate standard, if it is not a financial instrument.[56]

IAS 39 does not explicitly distinguish between structured products[57] and hybrid instruments[58] from an accounting perspective of the holder of the instrument.

Both instruments are dealt with under IAS 39, paragraphs 10-13 as 'Embedded Derivatives' – as one can also see from the mixed-up term 'hybrid (combined) instruments' in the definition of an embedded derivative.

IAS 39, paragraphs 10-11, are based on the assumption that structured products and hybrid instruments are linear combinations of a non-derivative host contract and embedded derivative(s).[59]

Because no distinction between structured products and hybrid instruments has been made at the level of classification under IAS 39, additional criteria had to be established in order to determine whether a structured product or hybrid instrument should be bifurcated or not for accounting purposes.

Under IAS 39, paragraph 11, bifurcation of the *embedded derivative* from the host contract is only permitted if:

52. IAS 39 (2009), paras 10-13 (Embedded Derivatives). This was in line with former FRS 26.
53. IAS 32, Financial Instruments: Disclosure and Presentation, paras 28-32 (Compound financial instruments). IAS 32, paras 28-32 does not explicitly deal with the issuer's accounting treatment of genuine structured products as defined in Ch. 8 §8.01 but only with the issuer's treatment of convertible bonds. *See* IAS 32, IE34 – IE50, Examples 9-12.
54. IAS 39 (2009), para. 10 sent. 1.
55. IAS 32, para. 11; Southern (2017) para. 15.6.
56. Host contracts do not only include debt contracts, but also equity contracts (financial instruments) – and insurance contracts, lease contracts and contracts for goods and services (non-financial instruments).
57. *See* for a definition of structured products: Ch. 8 §8.01.
58. *See* for a definition of hybrid instruments: Ch. 8 §8.03.
59. Southern (2017) para. 15.2.

(1) the economic characteristics and risk of the embedded derivative and the host contract are not closely related;
(2) the embedded derivative, if it were a stand-alone derivative, would meet the definition of a derivative in IAS 39, paragraph 9; and
(3) the combined instrument is *not already itself measured at fair value* with any changes in the fair value recognised in the income statement.[60]

These additional definitional criteria, however, added further uncertainty to the classification of structured products and hybrid instruments because they are not defined comprehensively in IAS 39.[61]

From the perspective of a holder of a convertible bond, IAS 39 does not suggest explicitly that a convertible bond can be bifurcated into a debt host contract and an equity option.

The decision for a bifurcation approach, which the holder of convertible bonds has to apply, can be derived from a statement in the Application Guidance to IAS 39. It proposes a bifurcation of convertible bonds because the equity conversion *feature* is 'not closely related' to the host contract.[62]

From the perspective of the *issuer*, IAS 32, paragraphs 28-32 suggest explicitly that a convertible bond must be bifurcated into a financial liability and an equity instrument,[63] resulting in the equity component normally being allocated to equity.[64]

Even the authors of IAS 32 seem a little uneasy with their proposition that convertible bonds can be bifurcated into a financial liability and an equity component. In their economic analysis of these instruments, they suggest that:

> [t]he economic effect of issuing such an instrument is *substantially* the same as issuing simultaneously a debt instrument with early settlement provision and warrants to purchase ordinary shares or issuing a debt instrument with detachable share purchase warrants.[65]

In the author's view, this statement acknowledges that the economic effect, meaning the pricing, is *not exactly the same* as the issuance of a straight debt instrument and warrants to purchase shares of this company.[66]

60. Bramwell et al. (2023) H1.2.3.
61. Southern (2017) para. 15.9.
62. IAS 39 (2009) AG30(f).
63. IAS 32, para. 29 sent. 3.
64. *See* Southern (2017) para. 15.17.
Only in cases, where the issuer has the option to cash settle, the equity component will not be accounted for as equity but as an embedded derivative accounted for at fair value in the issuer's accounts with any changes in the fair value recognised in the income statement. *Compare* John Lindsay, 'Convertibles and Exchangeables, Part 1: The Position for Issuers' (2006) Tax Journal 11, 12.
65. IAS 32, para. 29 sent. 4.
66. The combined price for a straight bond plus and equity option will always be higher than the price for a convertible bond, *see* Ch. 8 §8.04.
Compare Jeff Strnad, 'Taxing Convertible Debt' (2003) 56 SMU Law Review 399, 404. Strnad acknowledges that at least in cases where early conversion is a possibility, 'the bond plus warrant package and the convertible bond differ because the holder of the package will retain the

If the purpose of accounting was to mirror exactly the economic and pricing reality of the accounted instruments, it should be considered from an accounting perspective whether the bifurcation of convertible bonds into a debt host contract and equity (issuer's perspective) or an embedded derivative (holder's perspective) is a suitable approach or not.

[2] Definitional Criteria under IAS 39, Paragraph 11 as an Indicator for Bifurcation

Under IAS 39, paragraph 11, bifurcation of the embedded derivative from the host contract is only permitted if:

(a) the economic *characteristics and risks of the embedded derivative are not closely related* to the economic characteristics and risks of the host contract [...]
(b) a *separate instrument* with the same terms as the embedded derivative would meet the *definition of a derivative*;
(c) the hybrid (combined) contract is *not measured at fair value with changes in fair value recognised in profit or loss* (i.e., a derivative that is embedded in a financial liability at fair value through profit or loss is not separated); and
(d) the host is outside the scope of IFRS 9.[67]

The term 'not closely related' is not defined in IAS 39.[68] Instead, only examples are given by the standard that show what closely related means.[69]

Example 67:

Equity-linked or commodity-linked interest or principal payments are never closely related to a debt host contract. Thus, separation would be required in cases where interest or principal payments are dependent on equity or commodity prices.[70]

Whereas some examples (as the one above) are easy to put into the category 'not closely related', others are more difficult to categorise.

Example 68:

When the payments of the contract are related to the credit risk of the issuer of the debt instrument itself, the feature will be regarded as closely related, and no

bond upon early exercise of the warrant, while exercising the convertible bond means surrendering the straight bond returns inherent in the convertible bond'.

67. IAS 39, para. 11; *compare also* Southern (2017) para. 15.7.
68. Southern (2017) para. 15.9.
69. IAS 39 (2009), AG30 and AG33. *See* Southern (2017) para. 15.9.
70. IAS 39 (2009), AG30 (d) and (e). *Compare* Southern (2017) para. 15.9 and para. 15.2, Example 15.1.

separation of the credit feature is allowed. In contrast, where the payments depend on the credit risk of a reference asset other than the debt instrument itself, a separation will be required.[71]

Again, other examples of bifurcation of an embedded derivatives component from a host contract do not mirror the economic reality of these instruments.

Example 69:

In the case of inflation-linked bonds, both the coupon and the notional are indexed to an inflation index. The holder of the bond not only receives less interest but also protection against rising inflation by way of indexation of the coupons and the notional to an inflation index.

IAS 39, AG33(f) seems to suggest that no separation is required if the inflation index is one that is commonly used for this purpose in the economic environment in which the debt is denominated and that separation would be required if the inflation index relates to a different economic environment, or the index is not one that is commonly used for this purpose.[72]

Under IAS 39, paragraph 11, if the embedded derivative was a stand-alone derivative with the same terms as the embedded derivative, it would be considered as meeting the definition of a derivative in IAS 39.[73] In the author's view, the second criterion in IAS 39, paragraph 11, must be analysed more rigorously.[74]

In the above example, the indexation component would not fulfil the criteria of IAS 39, paragraph 11(b) because the indexation is not achieved by any embedded derivative contract.[75] Thus, the example in IAS 39, AG33(f) cannot be considered a proper example of an embedded derivative contract as the indexation feature would not meet the definition of a derivative under IAS 39, paragraph 9, if it were a similar stand-alone instrument.

Furthermore, because the definition in IAS 39 is at the same time very wide and too narrow, it (1) *includes* financial instruments that would not qualify as derivatives

71. IAS 39 (2009), AG30 (h). *See* KPMG, *Financial Instruments Accounting* (2004) 25, Table 3.2 (on file with the author).
72. KPMG (2004) 25, Table 3.2.
73. Southern (2017) para. 15.6.
74. In this context, an embedded derivative can be regarded as 'one or more implicit or explicit terms in a contract that affect the cash flows of the contract in a manner similar to a stand-alone derivative instrument', *see* HMRC, *International Accounting Standards, Comparison Document,* para. 397, http://webarchive.nationalarchives.gov.uk/20130129110402/http://www.hm-treasury.gov.uk/d/comparison_document.pdf, accessed 15 February 2023; *also* KPMG (2004), 20, Table 3.1.
75. In the above example of the inflation index, the embedded feature would likely not qualify as a stand-alone derivative contract under IAS 39 (2009) para. 9 because a pure indexation is no financial instrument or other contract.

from an economic perspective and (2) *excludes* certain derivatives that would qualify as derivatives from an economic perspective. As a consequence, some instruments would be bifurcated in the accounts, although a bifurcation may not be possible from an economic point of view.

Also, compared to the definition of derivative contracts developed in Chapter 4 of this work,[76] some instruments would be included in the definition of derivatives under IAS 39 as the IAS 39 definition does not contain the criterion of 'replication'.

[C] Accounting Treatment of Structured Products and Hybrid Instruments under IFRS 9

[1] Summary of the Rules

The following subchapter discusses the bifurcation versus an integration approach from the perspective of IFRS 9.

The IASB became increasingly aware of the problems that users faced when applying the bifurcation approach towards hybrid instruments and structured products and reacted with the issuance of IFRS 9.

IFRS 9 provides significant changes in relation to structured products and hybrid instruments by moving away from a bifurcation approach towards an integration approach for those instruments. IFRS 9 eliminated the requirement to bifurcate embedded derivatives from financial assets.[77]

Hybrid instruments and structured products are not defined in IFRS 9, but it provides a definition of an *embedded derivative*, stating that:

> It is a component of a hybrid contract that also includes a non-derivative host – with the effect that some of the cash flows of the combined instrument vary in a way similar to a stand-alone derivative. [...] A derivative that is attached to a financial instrument but is contractually transferable independently of that instrument, or has a different counterparty, is not an embedded derivative, but a separate financial instrument.[78]

Under the accounting rules of IFRS 9,[79] hybrid instruments and structured products which contain a host contract that is a *financial asset* within the scope of IFRS 9 are no longer bifurcated but are instead accounted for as a single instrument, according to IFRS 9, paragraph 4.3.2.[80]

---

76. *See* Ch. 4 §4.06[B][5].
77. Ghosh, Johnson and Miller (2022) [G1.5A].
78. IFRS 9, para. 4.3.1.
79. IFRS 9 has become mandatorily effective for accounting periods beginning on or after 1 January 2018. *See* Ch. 4 §4.05 and Ch. 6 § 6.02[C]; *also* IASB, IFRS 9 Project Summary (2014) 3.
80. IFRS 9 (2014) para. 4.3.2; *also* Deloitte, Embedded derivatives: Key differences between US GAAP and IFRSs (2014) http://www.iasplus.com/en-us/standards/ifrs-usgaap/embedded-derivatives accessed 13 May 2023.

With regard to hybrid instruments or structured products which contain a *financial liability* or a *non-financial asset*,[81] the accounting approach has not changed significantly.[82] The requirement to bifurcate embedded derivatives still applies to financial liabilities that fall within IFRS 9.[83] That is confirmed by IFRS 9, paragraph 4.3.3.

The issuance of a convertible bond is the classic example where a hybrid instrument creates a financial asset in one entity for accounting purposes, whereas it creates a financial liability and an equity instrument in another entity under IFRS 9.[84] Under IFRS 9, the debt and equity instruments are *split and accounted for separately*:[85]

> On initial recognition, the debt element will be measured at fair value – i.e., the present value of the future cash flow, with the equity element representing the balancing figure. Transaction costs have been ignored but would have to be split proportionately between the debt and equity elements. The value ascribed to the equity element is the balancing figure.[86]

It should be noted that split accounting is slightly different from bifurcation as the value of the equity element is never revalued under split accounting, whereas, for example, under an IAS 39 bifurcation, the embedded derivative 'is revalued at fair value' for each accounting period.[87]

If hybrid instruments contain a *host contract that is not an asset within the scope of IFRS 9*, i.e., a non-financial asset, the embedded derivative shall be bifurcated from the host contract under the conditions of IFRS 9, paragraph 4.3.3, that are:

> (a) the economic characteristics and risks of the embedded derivative are not closely related to the economic characteristics and risks of the host [...];
> (b) a separate instrument with the same terms as the embedded derivative would meet the definition of a derivative; and
> (c) the hybrid contract is not measured at fair value with changes in fair value recognised in profit or loss (i.e., a derivative that is embedded in a financial liability at fair value through profit or loss is not separated).[88]

The conditions set out in IFRS 9, paragraph 4.3.3, are similar to the conditions set out in IAS 39, paragraph 11.

IFRS 9, paragraph 4.3.5 also provides an option to designate the whole hybrid instrument or structured product as measured at fair value through profit or loss, even

81. Non-financial assets are, for example, leasing contracts, insurance contracts or contracts on the purchase of non-financial assets.
82. IASB, *IFRS 9: Financial Instruments; Phase I: Classification and measurement* (2010) – on file with the author.
83. Ghosh, Johnson and Miller (2022) [G1.5A].
84. ACCA, What is a financial instrument? – part 2, https://www.accaglobal.com/gb/en/student/exam-support-resources/fundamentals-exams-study-resources/f7/technical-articles/financial-instrument-part2.html, accessed 2 May 2023.
85. Ghosh, Johnson and Miller (2022) [G1.57].
86. ACCA, Financial instrument.
87. Ghosh, Johnson and Miller (2022) [G1.58].
88. Deloitte, 'IFRS 9 – Financial Instruments', *Embedded derivatives*, http://www.iasplus.com/en/standards/ifrs/ifrs9, accessed 11 May 2023.

if it was to be separated under IFRS 9, paragraphs 4.3.3 and 4.3.4, if certain conditions set out in paragraph 4.3.5(a) or (b) are met.[89]

[2] The Reasons for Moving from Bifurcation to Integration: From IAS 39 Towards IFRS 9

One must ask why the accounting standard setter may have originally preferred the bifurcation approach but has now *reconsidered* the approach to bifurcate convertible and exchangeable bonds notwithstanding their economic construction and features, and now – under IFRS 9 – applies an *integrative approach* instead of bifurcation for financial assets.

The author suggests that the following factors may have played a role:

First, the reason for an economically incorrect bifurcation of convertible bonds under IAS 39 may not per se lie in a misunderstanding of their valuation but rather a *simplification for accounting purposes*,[90] leading to an artificial bifurcation of those instruments for initial classification purposes into a 'virtual' straight bond, and the attribution of the remaining value of the convertible bond to equity.[91]

Second, by assuming a bifurcation of the convertible bond into a 'virtual' straight bond and 'something else' under IAS 39, the remaining value of the convertible is classified as an equity instrument or an equity option. This artificial bifurcation allows accountants to use *different accounting methods for both components*, accounting for the virtual straight bond at an amortised cost basis and the equity option as a derivative at fair value.[92] This approach may allow accountants an easier handling of these instruments in the accounts. In practice, many holders will, however, not bifurcate a convertible bond. Instead, they either classify the whole instrument as held for trading or account it at fair value through profit or loss due to designation.[93]

Third, the wording in IAS 32 indirectly acknowledges that the artificial bifurcation for accounting purposes does not mirror the economic reality by stating that 'the equity component is assigned the residual amount after deducting from the fair value of the instrument as a whole the amount separately determined for the liability component'.[94] Also, the wording in IAS 32, paragraph 32, sentence 2 seems to support this view when stating that '[t]he carrying amount of the equity instrument represented by the option to convert the instrument into ordinary shares is then determined by deducting the fair value of the financial liability from the fair value of the compound financial instrument as a whole'.

Fourth, in the context of the measurement of convertible bonds, IAS 32, paragraph 30 confirms that a change in the value of the convertible bond would not

89. *Ibid.*, 'Fair value option'.
90. Ghosh, Johnson and Miller (2022) suggest in an old issue (Issue 4) [B1.109]-[B1.120] that the main driver for the introduction of IFRS 9 'has been to reduce complexity of accounting for financial instruments'.
91. IAS 32, para. 29, sent. 2.
92. HMRC, CFM37630.
93. *Ibid.*
94. IAS 32, para. 31, sent. 2 part 2.

lead to a revision of the classification of the virtual liability and the equity component for accounting purposes by stating that the 'classification of the liability and equity components of a convertible instrument is not revised as a result of a change in the likelihood that a conversion option will be exercised, even when exercise of the option may appear to have become economically advantageous to some holders'.[95] IAS 32, paragraph 30, acknowledges that the accounting treatment does not mirror the change in the economic value of a convertible bond during the term of the convertible by explicitly ignoring the likelihood of conversion of the equity option.[96] By doing so, the accounting standards assume a static value of the intrinsic call option feature, whereas based on economic reality, call option values change dynamically.[97]

In the author's view, one reason why the accounting standard setter wanted to deviate from the correct mathematical treatment of convertible bonds and instead wanted to bifurcate convertible bonds for accounting purposes could be found in the *difficulty of valuation of convertible bonds* during the term of the bond.

Hence, in order to provide different holders and issuers and their accountants an easy-to-apply handling of convertible bonds, the standard setter had chosen the *simplified approach of bifurcation* for accounting purposes by attributing a certain value to a virtual straight bond and equity for classification purposes at inception, and a measurement of both components at the initial value during the term notwithstanding a change in value of the equity element due to a change in the likelihood of the conversion.

Fifth, the standard setter also suggests another reason why the initial value of the equity element is not changed despite a change in the likelihood of the conversion, i.e., when an increase in the value of the equity leads to an in-the-moneyness of the convertible bond and thus an increase in the likelihood of the conversion from a pure economic and trading perspective. In IAS 32, it is stated that '[h]olders may not always act in the way that might be expected because, for example, the tax consequences

---

95. In practice, when to exercise an in-the-money convertible bond is predominantly a trading decision of the holder. Many holders would want to exercise a convertible bond after the share price of the underlying equity has increased substantially. Thus, a holder would want to exercise the bond early if they have made a profit on the convertible bond because of the increase in the underlying share price and if they expect that the share price will not further increase substantially until the end of the early exercise period.

    Commonly, a trader will want to lock in profits when they occur. Holders may also have other reasons for exercising a convertible bond early apart from a pure trading decision. If the convertible bond holder wants to hold the shares physically before a shareholder meeting in order to vote for or against a certain decision, they will have to exercise the convertible bond in order to receive the shares.

    See Edward Kleinbard, 'Taxing Convertible Debt: A Layman's Perspective' (2003) 56 SMU Law Review 453, 464, at fn. 42.

    Strnad (2003) 404 suggests that investors may seek to convert early if the expected dividend yield on the underlying stock exceeds the potential interest return of the investor on the bond. Other reasons for early conversion may be simply trading needs, such as that the buyer of the bond needs to obtain the shares to close out a short position that became too expensive to hold, which he had built up for arbitrage purposes.
96. *See* Ch. 8 §8.04, explaining the need of continuous dynamic hedging of convertible bond positions for hedging purposes.
97. *See* for a detailed explanation of dynamic replication of options, Ch. 2 §2.02[A][2].

resulting from conversion may differ among holders'.[98] This means that a conversion of an in-the-money convertible may not only depend on the economic value of the conversion option during the term of the convertible but also on other factors, such as tax.

In the author's view, *tax consequences* will, however, only be a valid decision criterion if the conversion decision, which includes the tax paid or saved, compares the net outcome of a conversion with the net outcome of a non-conversion into equity on an overall post-tax basis.

The statement in IAS 32, paragraph 30 sentence 2, is rather unspecific, as it does not specify in what kind of tax environment a holder may choose not to convert into equity, although it would be preferable from a pre-tax perspective. Not converting into equity either means that the holder sells the convertible bond before expiry or keeps the convertible bond until expiry and receives back only the redemption amount.

In both scenarios, it is, in the author's view, highly unlikely that bondholders will choose to sell the convertible bond or let the bond expire instead of converting the bonds into equity because of tax consequences.

In an efficient market, it can be assumed that the trader will make the same profit by selling an in-the-money convertible bond at a certain date (x) to a third party in the market *or* by exercising the bond at the same date, receiving the shares and selling these shares in the market. Hence, there should be no preference to sell an in-the-money convertible bond or exercise the bond at that date (x) from a pure (pre-tax) trading perspective.

From a *post-tax perspective*, the holder may prefer the exercise of the convertible and the sale of shares instead of the sale of the convertible bond in tax systems which privilege equity capital gains over normal corporation tax income. A scenario where the holder prefers to sell the convertible bond instead of exercising the bond and selling the equity is only thinkable in tax systems that would privilege the sale of the convertible bond over the sale of the equity.[99]

The statement in IAS 32, paragraph 30 sentence 2 could also mean that holders may not convert a convertible bond into equity during the conversion period (nor sell the convertible bond before expiry), even if the price of the equity is above the conversion level and thus a conversion would be per se attractive from a pre-tax perspective, because the conversion may not be economically attractive on a post-tax basis due to adverse tax treatment of the equity upon conversion.

Example 70:

Facts:
The convertible bond has a redemption amount of 100. The price of the underlying equity has increased from 100 to 102. The conversion period ends the next day (day one).

98. IAS 32, para. 30, sent. 2.
99. However, such a scenario seems highly unlikely as tax systems rather privilege equity over debt but not debt over equity.

On day two, the convertible bond will pay a coupon of 1.75. On day three, the convertible bond will expire. The outcomes would be as follows on a pre-tax basis:

(1) The holder converts into equity on day one and immediately sells the shares in the market. He will not receive the coupon on day two, but he will have made a gain of 2 (102-100).
Pre-tax gain: 2.

(2) The holder does not convert into equity on day one and receives the coupon of 1.75 on day two. He will receive the redemption amount of 100 when the convertible expires.
Pre-tax income: 1.75.

Tax analysis:
From a pre-tax basis, the holder will always choose scenario 1 over scenario 2 if no other non-economic decision criteria come into play. From a post-tax basis, the holder will only choose scenario 2 instead of scenario 1 if the post-tax outcome in scenario 2 is higher than the post-tax result in scenario 1, i.e., if the holder has to pay significantly more tax on the equity gain of 2 in scenario 1 than on the interest income from the convertible of 1.75 in scenario 2.

The example shows that such an outcome would be highly unlikely as many tax systems privilege equity capital gains over normal income or interest income, but most tax systems do not privilege interest income over equity capital gains. In the author's view, such a scenario is highly unlikely, and thus, the suggestion that holders may not convert into equity because of tax consequences seems not to be a valid one.

[D] Integration Versus Bifurcation of Structured Products and Hybrid Instruments under FRS 102, Sections 11 and 12

FRS 102, Section 12, the UK accounting standard applying to financial instruments, is very similar to IFRS 9. The FRC states that '[t]he requirements in FRS 102 are based on the IASB's International Financial Reporting Standard for Small and Medium-sized Entities ('the *IFRS for SMEs* Accounting Standard'), with some significant amendments made for application in the UK and Republic of Ireland'.[100] The changes mainly concern some differences in the hedge accounting provisions of IFRS 9 and FRS, Section 12.[101]

100. FRC, FRS 102, The Financial Reporting Standards Applicable in the United Kingdom and the Republic of Ireland, https://www.frc.org.uk/accountants/accounting-and-reporting-policy/uk-accounting-standards/standards-in-issue/frs-102-the-financial-reporting-standard-applicabl, accessed 1 August 2023.

101. FRC, Significant Differences between FRS 102 and IFRS for SMEs Standard, https://www.frc.org.uk/accountants/accounting-and-reporting-policy/uk-accounting-standards/significant-differences-between-frs-102-and-the-if#section-12, accessed 1 May 2023.

However, one first needs to carefully analyse if a hybrid instrument or structured product qualifies as a basic financial instrument under FRS 102, Section 11 or if it qualifies as 'other instrument' under FRS 102, Section 12.

The following subsection analyses both FRS 102, Section 11 and Section 12 in relation to hybrid instruments and structured products separately, discusses both the position of the holder and the issuer and determines if the instrument needs to be bifurcated or integrated.

[1] Holder of Plain Vanilla Convertible Bonds (Hybrid Instruments)

FRS 102, Section 11 applies to basic financial instruments, which must be accounted for on an amortised cost basis with the option to treat certain debt instruments on a fair value through profit or loss basis (FVTPL).[102] FRS 102, Section 12 applies to other financial instruments which are accounted for at FVTPL, with certain exceptions.[103] Hence, one needs to determine if holding a convertible bond is regarded as holding a basic financial instrument (with the consequences of FRS 102, Section 11) or if it qualifies as 'other financial instrument' within FRS 102, Section 12.

FRS 102, paragraph 11.8 states:

> An entity shall account for the following financial instruments as basic financial instruments in accordance with this section:
>
> (a) cash;
> (b) a debt instrument (such as an account, note, or loan receivable or payable) that meets the conditions in paragraph 11.9 and is not a derivative financial instrument;
> (bA) a debt instrument that, whilst not meeting the conditions in paragraph 11.9, nevertheless is consistent with the description in paragraph 11.9A, and is not a derivative financial instrument;
> (c) commitments to receive or make a loan to another entity that:
>   (i) cannot be settled net in cash; and
>   (ii) when the commitment is executed, are expected to meet the conditions in paragraph 11.9 or be consistent with the description in paragraph 11.9A; and
> (d) an investment in a non-derivative financial instrument that is equity of the issuer (e.g., most ordinary shares and certain preference shares).[104]

FRS 102, paragraph 11.9 outlines the conditions under which a financial instrument qualifies as basic, and if one of those conditions is not met, 'the financial instrument is not basic, unless it meets the principle-based description in paragraph 11.9A'.[105]

---

102. Ghosh, Johnson and Miller (2022) [B2.3a] (issued 28).
103. *Ibid.*
104. FRS 102, para. 11.8.
105. FRC, FRS 102, Factsheet 4, Financial Instruments, https://www.frc.org.uk/getattachment/f790644d-4802-459a-816a-b57df46c92b6/FS-04-FRS-102-Financial-Instruments-(Dec-2018).pdf, accessed 1 August 2023.

FRS 102, paragraph 11.11 (d) explicitly states that 'investments in convertible debt, because the return to the holder can vary with the price of the issuer's equity shares rather than just with market interest rates',[106] do not qualify under FRS 102, paragraph 11A, and thus, 'are therefore within the scope of Section 12'.[107]

Consequently, 'the holder of a convertible loan note will not have to bifurcate it, and, since it will not be a "basic financial instrument" will have to account for it as FVTPL'.[108] Thus, to sum it up, because a convertible bond is not a basic financial instrument under FRS 102, Section 11 for the holder, it falls under FRS 102, Section 12, and FRS 102, Section 12 eliminates 'the requirement to bifurcate embedded derivatives from financial assets. Instead, the entity is required to assess the hybrid contract as a whole for classification'.[109]

Ghosh, Johnson and Miller remind their readers that 'it is still possible under FRS 102 to elect to use the recognition and measurement rules under IAS 39 (FRS 102,112(b) and 102.12.2(b)). In such a case, the IAS 39 rules [...] will apply to determine whether bifurcation is required'.[110]

[2] Issuer of Plain Vanilla Convertible Bonds (Hybrid Instruments)

Again, one needs to determine if the issuance of a convertible bond qualifies as a basic financial instrument within FRS 102, Section 11, or if it is an 'other instrument' within the meaning of FRS 102, Section 12. If the conversion feature of the bond results in a variable return, it will not be basic but qualify as 'other instrument' within FRS 102, Section 12.[111]

Deloitte confirms in respect of the distinction between basic and non-basic financial instruments under FRS 102:

> All terms of a debt instrument must be considered before concluding on its classification as basic or non-basic. This is because a single non-basic feature will cause the *instrument as a whole to be classified as non-basic.* A single contractual term may also impact more than one of the conditions. Therefore, all contractual features should be assessed against all the conditions.[112]

FRS 102, paragraph 11.9 states:

> A debt instrument that satisfies the following conditions shall be considered a basic financial instrument:
>
> (a) The *contractual return to the holder* (the lender), assessed in the currency in which the debt instrument is denominated, is:

106. FRS 102, para. 11.11.(d).
107. FRS 102, para. 11.11.
108. Ghosh, Johnson and Miller (2022) [B2.3A] (issue 28).
109. *Ibid.*; *also* Deloitte, A closer look - 'Basic/non-basic' classification of debt instruments under FRS 102 (June 2015), 6, https://www.iasplus.com/en-gb/publications/uk/closer-look/2015/a-closerlook-basic-non-basic-frs-102, accessed 3 August 2023.
110. Ghosh, Johnson and Miller (2022) [G1.5A] (issue 28).
111. Deloitte (2015) 7.
112. *Ibid.*, 4.

(i) a fixed amount;
(ii) a *positive fixed rate or a positive variable rate*; *or*
(aA) The contract may provide for repayments of the principal or the return to the holder (but not both) to be linked to a single relevant observable index of general price inflation of the currency in which the debt instrument is denominated, provided such links are not leveraged.
(aB) The contract may provide for a determinable variation of the return to the holder during the life of the instrument, provided that:
(i) the new rate satisfies condition (a) and the variation is not contingent on future events other than:
(1) a change of a contractual variable rate;
(2) to protect the holder against credit deterioration of the issuer; or
(3) changes in levies applied by a central bank or arising from changes in relevant taxation or law; or
(ii) the new rate is a market rate of interest and satisfies condition (a).

Contractual terms that give the lender the unilateral option to change the terms of the contract are not determinable for this purpose.

(b) There is no contractual provision that could, by its terms, result in the holder losing the principal amount or any interest attributable to the current period or prior periods. The fact that a debt instrument is subordinated to other debt instruments is not an example of such a contractual provision.
(c) Contractual provisions that permit the issuer (the borrower) to prepay a debt instrument or permit the holder (the lender) to put it back to the issuer before maturity are not contingent on future events other than to protect:
(i) the holder against the credit deterioration of the issuer (eg defaults, credit downgrades or loan covenant violations), or a change in control of the issuer; or
(ii) the holder or issuer against changes in levies applied by a central bank or arising from changes in relevant taxation or law.

The inclusion of contractual terms that, as a result of the early termination, require reasonable compensation for the early termination to be paid by either the holder or the issuer does not, in itself, constitute a breach of the conditions in paragraph 11.9.

(d) [Deleted]
(e) Contractual provisions may permit the extension of the term of the debt instrument, provided that the return to the holder and any other contractual provisions applicable during the extended term satisfy the conditions of paragraphs (a) to (c).[113]

Deloitte states that 'in order to be classified as basic, the returns of a debt instrument must meet the conditions in FRS 102.11.9(a) (the 'Condition for Returns')'[114] and explains with the help of the following example when those conditions in FRS 102, paragraph 11.9(a) are met:

113. FRS 102, para. 11.9.
114. Deloitte (2015) 4.

Example 71:

taken from the Deloitte paper

Entity F issues a bond for £9.5 million that pays no interest before maturity. At maturity, Entity F is required to deliver as many of its own equity instruments as are equivalent in value to £10 million. Although the *bond is convertible into equity*, it is not a compound instrument because it has *no equity component*. [from the issuer's perspective]

Entity F has issued a bond that provides a return that is a *fixed amount to the holder*. The *linkage to the equity of the issuer does not cause the return to vary*. The *return is the difference between the proceeds from the bond issue and the amount due from Entity F at maturity* (£10 million - £9.5 million = £0.5 million). Therefore, the bond meets the Condition Returns.[115]

The example provided by *Deloitte* shows that convertible bonds can be regarded as basic from an issuer's perspective if certain conditions are met with the consequence that those instruments are accounted for at amortised cost because they are basic financial instruments.

In other cases, the answer is not that simple. If the issuer of a convertible bond *pays interest* on the bond and if the holder of the bond has the right to receive either shares (equity) or the return of the initial loan (debt), from the perspective of the issuer, the position is as follows:

There is a *loan element*, and if the holder of the bond decides on the delivery of the shares (normally, if the price of the shares is above the value of the debt element), the holder will exercise the convertible bond and receive the shares.

In accounting terms, FRS 102, paragraph 12.3 explicitly states:

> This paragraph applies to all financial instruments except for:
>
> [...]
>
> (e) Financial instruments that meet the definition of an entity's own equity and the equity component of compound financial instruments issued by the reporting entity that contain both a liability and an equity component (see 22 Liabilities and Equity).[116]

Hence, if a convertible bond was to be considered a compound financial instrument from the issuer's perspective because it contains both a liability and equity component, FRS 102, Section 12 would still not apply because of the exception of FRS 102, paragraph 12.3 with the consequence that the instrument would not - as the entire instrument - be accounted for at fair value through profit and loss. Instead, FRS 102, Section 22 *Liabilities and Equity* applies.

115. *Ibid*., 7, emphasis added.
116. FRS 102, para. 12.3.

FRS 102, paragraph 22.13 states:

> On issuing convertible debt or similar compound financial instruments that contain both a liability and an equity component, an entity *shall allocate the proceeds between the liability component and the equity component.* To make the allocation, the entity shall first determine the *amount of the liability component as the fair value of a similar liability* that does not have a conversion feature or similar associated equity component. The entity *shall allocate the residual amount as the equity component.* Transaction costs shall be allocated between the debt component and the equity component on the basis of their relative fair values.[117]

That means that the issuer of a convertible bond would have to apply *split accounting* to the convertible bond under FRS 102, Section 22 and account separately for a *loan element* and an *equity element* (which is the conversion obligation to deliver equity at the option of the holder of the convertible and depending on the market price of the equity at maturity).[118]

Ghosh, Johnson and Miller state that '[s]plit accounting requires that the fair value of the liability to make payments under the loan element is first valued and the initial carrying value of the equity component is then taken to be the residual value'.[119]

This is confirmed by FRS 102, paragraph 22.13, which states: '[t]o make the allocation, the entity shall first determine the amount of the *liability component as the fair value of a similar liability* that does not have a conversion feature or similar associated equity component. The entity shall allocate the *residual amount* as the *equity component*'.[120]

The differences between *split accounting* under FRS 102, Section 22 (and IFRS 9) and *bifurcation* under IAS 39 for the issuer of a convertible bond should be noted:

[a] FRS 102, Section 22/IFRS 9: Split Accounting

'Split accounting' accounts separately for the loan element and the equity element, with the loan element valued first and – *initially* at its fair value – and the rest attributed to the equity element.[121] The equity element is not revalued under split accounting. FRS 102, paragraph 22.14 explicitly states that 'entity shall not revise the allocation in a subsequent period',[122] which confirms that the equity element is static.[123]

FRS 102, paragraph 22.15 states that 'in periods after the instruments were issued, the entity shall account for the liability component as a financial instrument in accordance with Section 11 *Basic Financial Instruments* or Section 12 *Other Financial Instruments Issues* as appropriate'.[124]

117. FRS 102, para. 22.13, emphasis added.
118. Ghosh, Johnson and Miller (2022) [G1.53]-[G1.58] (issue 28).
119. *Ibid.*, [G1.56] (issue 28).
120. FRS 102, para. 22.13, sent. 2 and 3, emphasis added.
121. Ghosh, Johnson and Miller (2022) [G1.56] (issue 28).
122. FRS 102, para. 22.14.
123. Ghosh, Johnson and Miller (2022) [G1.58] (issue 28).
124. FRS 102, para. 22.15.

One sees the possible outcomes under FRS 102:

Under narrow circumstances, the entire convertible bond may qualify as basic (*Example 71* above) under FRS 102, Section 11.[125]

In most circumstances, a plain vanilla interest-bearing convertible bond would be split into a loan element and an equity element under FRS 102, Section 22, with the loan element (as a stand-alone) either qualifying as a basic financial instrument (FRS 102, Section 11) or 'other financial instrument' (FRS 102, Section 12). While the equity element is not revalued (carried at the initial attributed value),[126] the initially fair-valued loan element will either be subsequently accounted for at amortised cost (Section 11) or fair value (Section 12), depending on its categorisation.

[b] IAS 39: Bifurcation

The convertible bond must be bifurcated into a derivative element (embedded derivative) and a non-derivative contract element (loan element) if the conditions of IAS 39, paragraph 11 apply.[127] The same test applies to the issuer and the holder of a convertible bond.[128]

In the first step, the fair value of the embedded derivative is calculated, and 'the initial carrying value of the loan relationship will then be taken to be the residual amount'.[129]

For each accounting period, the embedded derivative 'is revalued at fair value'.[130] That means that:

> an increase in the share price of the company will increase the liability under the embedded option, thus depressing profits (but not generally taxable profits – *see* CTA 2009 s 651). If a company using [...] IAS 39 wants to ensure equity instrument treatment, the terms are critical. In particular, the issuer will need to ensure that it has no obligation to cash-settle the conversion obligation since this would be a

125. Deloitte (2015) 7.
126. Ghosh, Johnson and Miller (2022) [G1.58] (issue 28).
127. IAS 39, para. 11 states:

> An embedded derivative shall be separated from the host contract and accounted for as a derivative under this Standard if, and only if:
>
> (a) the economic characteristics and risks of the embedded derivative are not closely related to the economic characteristics and risks of the host contract (*see* Appendix A paragraphs AG30 and AG33);
> (b) a separate instrument with the same terms as the embedded derivative would meet the definition of a derivative;
> (c) the hybrid (combined) contract is not measured at fair value with changes in fair value recognised in profit or loss (i.e., a derivative that is embedded in a financial liability at fair value through profit or loss is not separated); and
> (d) the host is outside the scope of IFRS 9.

128. Ghosh, Johnson and Miller (2022) [G1.58] (issue 28).
129. *Ibid.*, [G1.56].
130. *Ibid.*

contractual obligation to provide cash and would cause the derivative to fall outside the definition of an equity instrument.[131]

[3] Issuance of Other Instruments

The issuance of an exchangeable bond where the company has the obligation to deliver shares in another company is still a hybrid instrument as its character is between equity and debt. Still, for accounting purposes, the 'obligation to deliver shares in another company will not constitute an equity instrument for the issuer for accounting purposes'.[132]

Suppose a company applies IAS 39, it would likely apply the IAS 39 test for embedded derivatives and bifurcate the exchangeable bond into a debt instrument and embedded derivative, provided the test for qualifying as an embedded derivative is fulfilled).

In contrast, the accounting treatment under FRS 102, Section 11 or 12 would mean that the company would likely not bifurcate the exchangeable bond because the option of the holder of the exchangeable to receive delivery of the underlying shares is not treated as an equity instrument for the issuer.[133]

In case of 'a convertible where the shares to be delivered are themselves not an equity instrument (for example redeemable preference shares)', the company would apply the IAS 39 test, if applicable, and either bifurcate or not depending on whether there is an embedded option. Under FRS 12, paragraph 22.3A, those redeemable preference shares are likely to not be split-accounted.[134]

Southern states that '[w]hen a financial instrument requires mandatory redemption by the issuer for a fixed or determinate amount, a contractual obligation to deliver cash at redemption exists. The instrument must, therefore, be classified as a liability: IAS 32, para 16; FRS 102, paragraph 22.3A'.[135]

[4] Holder of Structured Products (Reverse Convertible Bonds)

The question arises if certain structured products (bond plus embedded derivative(s)) may qualify as basic instruments under FRS 102, Schedule 11.

Although zero-coupon bonds are mentioned as an example in FRS 102, paragraph 11.9A, there are no structured products within the above definition. Although one may replicate a zero-coupon bond with a long call option and a short put option minus the present value of the expected dividends, this does not constitute a true bifurcation but is only a combination of 'false friends' in the context of the put-call parity.

131. *Ibid.*
132. *Ibid.*, [G1.59].
133. *Ibid.*; *compare* FRS 102, Sections 11 and 22.
134. Ghosh, Johnson and Miller (2022) [G1.59] (issue 28).
135. David Southern, The Taxation of Redeemable Preference Shares, FCTC Digest, 14th ed, 2023, 66, https://www.fieldtax.com/wp-content/uploads/2023/09/FCTC-Digest-14th-Edition-March-2023.pdf, accessed 1 November 2023.

Hence, structured products would fall commonly under the definition of FRS 102, Section 12 as 'other financial instruments' and would – in parallel to a convertible bond – not be bifurcated by the holder of the structured product under FRS 102, Section 12.

[5] Issuer of Structured Products (Reverse Convertible Bonds)

FRS 102, Section 12 describes when a financial liability falls into the 'other instrument category', namely if 'it contains contractual terms that introduce exposure to unrelated risks of volatility (e.g., changes in equity prices or commodity prices (FRS 102, paragraph 11.9A) or it carries rights to acquire shares and the embedded option is not eligible to be treated as an equity instrument'.[136]

Ghosh, Johnson and Miller explain that:

> the sole circumstance in which a financial liability may be bifurcated is where a financial liability included an embedded option to acquire shares in the issuer and the embedded option meets the requirements to be treated as an equity instrument (these are broadly the same conditions as apply for IAS 32). In such cases, the financial liability will be bifurcated into a host contract and an embedded equity instrument in broadly the same way as applies where a company prepares its accounts in accordance with IFRS 9 (FRS 102, ss 22.13-22.15 and Appendix to s 22).[137]

[E] Evaluation of the Bifurcation Approach for Structured Products and Hybrid Instruments under IAS 39, IFRS 9 and FRS 102, Schedules 11 or 12

In the author's opinion, the bifurcation of structured products for accounting purposes – as it was previously envisaged by IAS 39 – was a legitimate approach as it followed the mathematically possible decomposition of these instruments into a traditional financial instrument and at least one derivative.[138] In contrast, the bifurcation of hybrid instruments for accounting purposes raises substantial concerns, as it is not possible to deconstruct them mathematically into two or more basic instruments by means of static replication.[139]

Nevertheless, the accounting standard setter decided on a bifurcation approach of hybrid instruments in IAS 32 and 39 because of the aim of simplifying the accounting treatment of these instruments and also finding a standard accounting treatment for all different kinds of users, although such an accounting treatment may not have been correct from a purely economic and risk management perspective.

Although the argument of simplification is, in essence, a valid one when designing accounting standards, it is not a strong one to justify a bifurcation of

136. Ghosh, Johnson and Miller (2022) [B3.43C].
137. *Ibid.*
138. *See* §8.02.
139. *See* §8.04.

convertible bonds for accounting purposes as such an accounting treatment simply does not mirror reality from an economic and risk management perspective.[140] In the author's view, the additional argument of different tax consequences among holders of convertibles does not hold true in reality.

Moving away from a bifurcation approach under IAS 39 towards an integration approach under IFRS 9 and FRS 102, Schedules 11 and 12 for financial assets that contain some form of equity feature allows the recognition of convertible and exchangeable bonds as one unit for economic and accounting purposes instead of bifurcating them which is mathematically incorrect in all cases.[141]

The author believes that IFRS 9 may, however, not have gone far enough. For hybrid instruments, a similar approach of moving away from bifurcation towards integration approach should also be considered in the context of financial liabilities and non-financial assets because of their economic reality. As previously explained, convertible bonds are hybrids between equity and debt; they are not structured products that can be financially decomposed into separate economic parts.

[F] Treatment of Structured Products and Hybrid Instruments under UK Tax Law

The following part only deals with the tax treatment of structured products and hybrid instruments issued or held by UK corporate entities. The taxation rules applying to banks and financial institutions issuing these instruments and holders of these instruments that are connected to the issuer may differ from these general rules in the case of regulatory capital instruments, i.e., those financial instruments which are not shares and which comprise additional Tier 1 or Tier 2 capital of a credit institution.[142] These specific taxation rules applying to regulatory capital instruments will not be discussed in this work.[143]

[1] Summary of the Rules

The taxation of structured products and hybrid instruments broadly follows the basic principles:

[a] Cases of Non-bifurcation

If a structured product or hybrid instrument[144] is not bifurcated for accounting purposes under UK GAAP or IFRS, it will be taxed under the loan relationship rules of

140. In IFRS 9 (2010) para. BC 4.86, the IASB explicitly acknowledged that the bifurcation approach did not contribute to a simplification, or an increased understanding of the information provided by the financial statements.
141. *See* §8.05[C].
142. The Taxation of Regulatory Capital Securities Regulations 2013 (SI 2013/3209).
143. A good summary can be found in: Ghosh, Johnson and Miller (2022) [U.1.24]-[U1.50].
144. The term 'hybrid instruments' is used for convertible and exchangeable bonds in this context; *see* Ch. 8 §8.03.

CTA 2009, Part 5. 'The fact that the instrument [may contain] a conversion right will not, of itself, prevent it qualifying as a loan relationship.'[145] That means that the derivative contract rules will not apply to the structured product or hybrid instrument or a part of it (i.e., the embedded derivative) because there is no bifurcation for accounting purposes. CTA 2009, sections 415 and 585 'will not require bifurcation for tax purposes'.[146]

[b] Cases of bifurcation: CTA 2009, sections 584-586

If a structured product or hybrid instrument is bifurcated for accounting purposes, the rules of CTA 2009, sections 584-586, determine in which cases an embedded derivative contract will be bifurcated from the host contract for tax purposes and if the company holding (or issuing) the structured product or hybrid instrument will be treated as a party to a separate relevant contract under CTA 2009, Part 7 in relation to the embedded derivative(s).[147]

A split accounting treatment or bifurcation for tax purposes – as the case may be – under CTA 2009, sections 584-586 will apply to the following structured products and hybrid instruments in the circumstances outlined below.

[i] Hybrid Derivatives with Embedded Derivatives

CTA 2009, section 584, applies to cases where the hybrid derivative is split 'into one and more derivatives'[148] and not treated as one instrument for accounting purposes.[149]

[ii] Loan Relationships with Embedded Derivatives

CTA 2009, section 585 applies if the company bifurcates the structured product or hybrid instrument for accounting purposes under UK GAAP or IFRS.[150] The host contract will be separately taxed under the loan relationship rules of CTA 2009, Part 5.[151] The bifurcated embedded derivative will be taxed separately under CTA 2009, Part 7.[152]

[iii] Other Contracts with Embedded Derivatives

CTA 2009, section 586, applies to other contracts where the host contract is neither a loan relationship nor are the contracts hybrid derivatives. If the company treats these

145. Ghosh, Johnson and Miller (2022) [G2.21] (issue 28).
146. *Ibid.*
147. Haworth and Hollis (2010) 25.
148. Ghosh, Johnson and Miller (2022) [E9.142] (issue 280.
149. *Ibid.*
150. *Ibid.*, [G2.3].
151. CTA 2009, s. 415; confirmed by CTA 2009, ss 584 and 585.
152. Southern (2017) para. 15.30.

contracts as bifurcated for accounting purposes, and the company has elected back into the taxation in accordance with the accounts under CTA 2009, section 617(1),[153] the general rule is that the bifurcation is reversed for tax purposes. Thus, in this case, the company is treated for tax purposes as though the *combined other contract with an embedded derivative* had not been bifurcated.[154]

[iv] Tax Treatment of the Embedded Derivative Contract as Capital Gains

If bifurcation occurs, *gains or losses of the bifurcated embedded derivative* will, in principle, be realised on a *fair value basis*. In the case of convertible and exchangeable bonds (which are bifurcated as loan relationships and embedded derivatives for the holder for accounting purposes, for example, under IAS 39), the holder of the bifurcated debt element will, however, treat these gains and losses that are attributed to the embedded equity derivative contract as capital gains for tax purposes under the derivative contracts regime of CTA 2009, Part 7 Chapters 7 and 8.[155]

[v] Issuer of Structured Products and Hybrid Instruments

CTA 2009, sections 584-586, also apply to issuers of structured products and hybrid instruments, as these sections determine in which cases these financial instruments are bifurcated for tax purposes. From an issuer's perspective, the part bifurcated from the host contract will either be treated as equity or as an embedded derivative contract.[156] If the residual embedded element is treated as an equity instrument, no revaluations will take place;[157] if it is treated as an embedded derivative, it will be accounted for on a fair value basis, but 'the annual fair value movements are ignored for tax purposes'.[158] However, if the issuer treats the entire convertible or exchangeable bond as one, does not bifurcate (nor split-account), and accounts for the entire instrument as fair value through profit and loss, the loan relationships rules of CTA 2009, Part 5 apply.[159]

---

153. CTA 2009, s. 586(2), but subject to the exception of CTA 2009, ss 586(4), 616.
154. CTA 2009, ss 616(4) and (5). *See* Ghosh, Johnson and Miller (2022) [E9.145]; Southern (2017) para. 15.29.
155. CTA 2009, ss 640, 641 and 645; Haworth and Hollis (2010) 29; Southern (2017) para. 15.30(3).
156. Southern (2017) para. 15.30(4).
157. HMRC, CFM55510 suggests that 'the embedded obligation to convert debt into its own shares will generally be a "tax nothing", giving rise to no taxable debits or credits under either an income or chargeable gains code'.
    See also Southern (2017) para. 15.30.
158. *Compare* CTA 2009, Part 7, Ch. 8, ss 651-655.
    Southern (2017) para. 15.30; Haworth and Hollis (2010) 29.
159. Southern (2017) para. 15.31.

[2] *The UK Tax Treatment of Structured Products and Hybrid Instruments in Detail*

The following subsection discusses the taxation of structured products and hybrid instruments and the tax treatment of embedded derivatives and the host contracts under CTA 2009, sections 584 to 586, in more detail.

[a] *Embedded Derivatives under CTA 2009, Sections 584-586*

[i] Hybrid Derivatives with Embedded Derivatives

CTA 2009, section 584 applies to a *'hybrid derivative'*:[160]

(a) where the contract as a whole is a 'relevant contract'; it is as a whole not treated as a derivative contract for accounting purposes under CTA 2009, section 579(1)(a), but it meets the condition in CTA 2009, section 579(1)(b) or (c);[161]
(b) which is bifurcated under GAAP into:
   (i) 'rights and liabilities under one or more derivatives ('embedded derivatives'); and
   (ii) the remaining rights and liabilities'[162] (the host contract).
(c) where the host contract - consisting of only those remaining rights and liabilities - would be a relevant contract within CTA 2009, section 577.[163]

First, one needs to understand what exactly a 'hybrid derivative' within CTA 2009, section 584 is. HMRC states in CFM50410: '[o]ccasionally a contract - when viewed as a whole - may be a relevant contract but may also contain features that are themselves embedded derivatives. Such an embedded derivative is referred to in this guidance as a *nested derivative*, but this is not a term used in the legislation'.[164]

HMRC gives an example of:

> contracts for the supply of commodities, such as oil or gas, where the value of the contract as a whole is dependent on the price of the underlying commodity. Such a contract may not fall to be accounted for as a derivative under IAS 39, IFRS 9 or FRS 102 (or formerly FRS 26), perhaps because it is always intended to proceed to delivery, but it may nonetheless be a future' and thus a relevant contract which is deemed to satisfy the accounting condition (commodities).[165]

160. HMRC, CFM50410 defines hybrid derivatives as contracts that 'when viewed as a whole - resemble a derivative, but also contain features that are themselves embedded derivatives'.
161. This means, the hybrid derivative - as a whole - fails the accounting test of CTA 2009, s. 579(1)(a).
162. CTA 2009, s. 584(1)(b).
163. CTA 2009, s. 584(1)(c). *See also* HMRC, CFM52550 and CFM50410.
164. HMRC, CFM50410.
165. *Ibid.*

HMRC explains that those contracts may contain clauses that constitute embedded derivatives, 'which are not closely related to the host contract'.[166] This is, for example, the case of an option to settle in a different currency.

Two different tax treatments of the embedded derivative are possible under CTA 2009, section 584, according to HMRC:

> If the combined embedded derivative and the remaining rights and liabilities qualify as one derivative contract by fulfilling the accounting condition of CTA 2009, section 579(1)(a) as the whole,[167] they will also be treated for tax purposes as one derivative contract and will not be bifurcated.[168] If the whole contract is treated as a derivative for accounting purposes under IAS 39, IFRS 9 (old FRS 26) or FRS 102, the whole contract is accounted for at fair value through profit and loss, and any credits or debits will be taxed based on the accounts.[169]
>
> If the hybrid derivative is not accounted for as a derivative but fulfils alternative accounting conditions and is bifurcated for accounting purposes into two or more parts, CTA 2009, section 584(2) and (5) will apply.[170] According to CTA 2009, section 584(2), the company will be treated as a party to the embedded derivative and separately also as a party to the host 'rump' contract, meaning both the 'embedded derivative(s)' and the remaining rights and liabilities will be treated as relevant contracts within CTA 2009, Part 7.[171] That means that the tax treatment follows, in this case, the accounting treatment.

To reiterate, according to HMRC, the conditions for CTA 2009, section 584 to apply are as follows:

- the contract as a whole is a relevant contract (a future, option or CFD), which is not treated for accounting purposes as a derivative but satisfies the condition in CTA 09/S579(1)(b) or (c);
- in accordance with GAAP, the company splits the contract into a host contract plus one or more embedded derivatives; and
- the host contract, looked at by itself, would be a relevant contract.[172]

CTA 2009, sections 584(5)(b), 616(3) then determine that although a hybrid derivative is bifurcated for accounting purposes, it will be 'taxed on the basis of "old" UK GAAP',[173] meaning that the embedded derivative contract will not be bifurcated for tax purposes.

As a result, the hybrid derivative will be taxed as one instrument on an amortised cost basis of accounting.[174]

---

166. *Ibid.*
167. *Ibid.*
168. Haworth and Hollis (2010) 26; Southern (2017) para. 15.46.
169. HMRC, CFM50410.
170. *Ibid.*; *see also* Haworth and Hollis (2010) 26.
171. CTA 2009, s. 584(2) and (3). That means that each of the embedded derivative contracts and also the host contract will be either an option, future or CFD. *See* HMRC, CFM52550 and CFM50410; Haworth and Hollis (2010) 26.
172. HMRC, CFM50410.
173. HMRC, CFM52550.
174. CTA 2009, ss 584(3), 616(3)(a)(b). *See* Haworth and Hollis (2010) 26.

[ii] Loan Relationships with Embedded Derivatives

If under FRS 102, IAS 39 or IFRS 9, either the holder or the issuer bifurcates the instrument, the tax rules of CTA 2009, sections 415 and 585 follow that bifurcation approach. Those structured products or hybrid instruments are bifurcated into a loan relationship host contract and embedded derivative(s) or an equity instrument for accounting purposes.[175] Thus, mainly (1) convertible and exchangeable bonds, (2) structured products accounted for under IAS 39 for the holder of the structured product, and (3) hybrid instruments and structured products for the issuer will be bifurcated for tax purposes.[176]

(1) Tax Position of the Holder

Where the investor bifurcates the convertible or exchangeable bond for accounting purposes, the tax law will follow that approach. Thus, the loan relationship host contract will be subject to tax under CTA 2009, Part 5.[177] That means it will be recognised initially at fair value, but gains or losses on the debt host contract will be measured and taxed at each balance sheet date on an amortised cost basis, applying the effective interest method of IAS 39, paragraph 9 or Appendix A to IFRS 9, and FRS 102, Section 11.[178] The embedded derivative that is bifurcated for accounting purposes will be subject to tax under CTA 2009, Part 7.[179]

Thus, with regard to the embedded derivative contract, it has to be determined whether:

(1) it is a derivative contract under CTA 2009, Part 7; and
(2) how it is treated for tax purposes.[180]

Depending on the character of the deemed separate contract, the embedded derivative is treated as a relevant contract, which can be an option, future or contract for differences.[181]

To qualify as a derivative contract under CTA 2009, Part 7, the embedded derivative also has to fulfil the accounting test of CTA 2009, section 579,[182] and it should not be excluded because of its underlying subject matter.[183]

---

175. CTA 2009, ss 415 and 585(1). *See* Haworth and Hollis (2010) 26; Southern (2017) para. 15.22. CTA 2009, s. 415 determines that the host contract is treated as a loan relationship. *See* HMRC, CFM50420.
176. CTA 2009, s. 415.
177. *Compare* CTA 2009, s. 415(1), (2).
178. Southern (2012) para. 5.31.
179. CTA 2009, s. 585(2). *See* HMRC, CFM50420; Southern (2017) para. 15.27.
180. HMRC, CFM52510.
181. CTA 2009, s. 585(3).
182. HMRC, CFM50420.
183. CTA 2009, ss 589, 590.

In principle, any gains or losses from the embedded derivative are realised on a fair value basis for accounting purposes, but for tax purposes, they are treated on a chargeable gains basis as capital gains or allowable losses[184] and taxed on an annual basis subject to certain conditions.[185] Depending on the character of the embedded derivative, specific tax sections apply to different derivatives embedded in loan relationships.

CTA 2009, sections 641(2)(b), (3) and 645 subject embedded options within convertible and exchangeable bonds to a capital gains tax treatment, provided that the conditions A to E of CTA 2009, section 645(2)-(6) are fulfilled.[186] CTA 2009, sections 641, 648, 649 apply to embedded equity derivatives, which are exactly tracking contracts for differences and subject these embedded CFDs also to a capital gains tax treatment[187] if certain conditions apply.[188]

Debits or credits that are taxed as chargeable gains under CTA 2009, section 641 are not exempt capital gains as 'the asset representing the creditor relationship is not a QCB for chargeable gains purposes'.[189]

In addition, CTA 2009, sections 585(5), 415, 416 allows a company 'to be treated for tax purposes as bifurcating the asset, even though it does not actually do so for accounting purposes'.[190]

This tax treatment can also be elected by a company that continued to account under old UK GAAP.[191] If the election was made, the company will be treated for tax purposes as if it were bifurcating the instrument, provided that it could bifurcate this instrument if it had adopted IFRS or 'new UK GAAP'.[192] As the election had to be made by December 2005, most instruments will, however, not be subject to this treatment anymore.

Convertible and *exchangeable bonds*, as well as asset-linked securities, are accounted for as a single instrument at fair value through profit or loss in the accounts of the holder of the instrument under IFRS 9 or FRS 102. Where a company accounts under IAS 39, *share-linked securities* will have to be bifurcated into debt host contracts and embedded swaps for accounting purposes.[193] HMRC defines them as follows: 'Share-linked securities are those where the final redemption amount depends in some way on the value of a specific share or basket of shares, or a share index.'[194]

The tax treatment under CTA 2009, sections 415 and 585 follows the respective accounting treatment.

184. CTA 2009, s. 641(1), (2)(b) and (c), (3), (4) and (5).
185. HMRC, CFM55210. *See also* John Lindsay, 'Convertibles and Exchangeables, Part 2: The position for investors' [2006] Tax Journal 13, 14; Southern (2012) para. 15.27.
186. CTA 2009, s. 645(1). *See* HMRC, CFM55220.
187. CTA 2009, s. 641(2)(c), (3). *See* HMRC, CFM55290.
188. CTA 2009, s. 648(2) to (7) define Conditions A to F.
189. HMRC, CFM55290. *Compare* CTA 2009, ss 645(7) and 648(8).
190. HMRC, CFM50420 and CFM37660; Southern (2017) para. 15.25.
191. The election could be made by 31 December 2005. *See* Lindsay (2006b) 16.
192. HMRC, CFM37720. *See also* Haworth and Hollis (2010) 26; Southern (2017) para. 15.25.
193. IAS 39, AG28. *Compare also* HMRC, CFM55410.
194. HMRC, CFM55290.

(2) *Tax Position of the Issuer*

The accounting and tax treatment of the 'structured debt instrument' in the accounts of the issuer will depend on whether the instrument is a standard convertible bond, an exchangeable bond, a convertible bond with a cash settlement option or a share-linked security.[195]

If the company applies IAS 32/39, *standard convertible bonds* with no cash settlement option will be bifurcated for accounting purposes into a debt host contract and equity instrument under IAS 32.[196] The debt host contract will initially be recognised at fair value and measured at fair value through profit or loss or at amortised cost.[197] The value of the equity component will be determined by deducting the value of the host contract from the value of the structured product as a whole.[198]

Non-standard convertible bonds, i.e., convertible bonds with a cash settlement option, or *exchangeable bonds*[199] will be bifurcated into a host debt contract and an embedded derivative under IAS 39.[200]

The issuer of the structured debt instrument can opt not to bifurcate the security in its accounts in cases where the embedded option is treated as an embedded derivative and where the security, i.e., the rump host contract, is designated as at fair value through profit or loss in the issuer's accounts.[201]

If the structured debt instrument is bifurcated in the financial accounts, the issuer will also adopt the bifurcation approach for tax purposes.[202] The bifurcated debt host contract[203] is subject to tax under CTA 2009, Part 5 and will be treated as a discounted bond with the result that the actual financing costs recognised in the accounts (interest amount paid to the holder of the convertible plus discount) can in principle be deducted for tax purposes.[204]

The issuer will deduct these financing costs on an amortised cost basis, relieving the effective rate of interest as income under CTA 2009, Part 5.[205]

195. HMRC, CFM55410. HMRC includes in the term 'structured debt instrument' both hybrid instruments (convertible and exchangeable bonds) and structured products (share-linked securities).
196. IAS 32, para. 29.
197. IAS 39, paras 43 and 47.
198. IAS 32, para. 31. *Compare also* HMRC, CFM21260.
199. These are bonds where the holder has the option to convert the bond into shares other than those in the issuing company.
200. HMRC, CFM55410.
201. IAS 39, paras 9 and 11(c).
202. CTA 2009, ss 415, 585. *Compare also* Ghosh, Johnson and Miller (2022) [G2.3] (issue 28); Southern (2017) para. 15.27.
203. *Compare* Ghosh, Johnson and Miller (2022) [G3.22] and [G3.23] (issue 28); Southern (2017) para. 15.27.

     In case of convertible bonds, exceptions may apply and a re-characterisation of excess interest into a distribution may take place under CTA 2010, ss 1000, 1001F, 1015 if the convertible bond is held by a company that is not subject to UK corporation tax. For companies that are subject to UK corporation tax, CTA 2010, s. 1032 will apply and no re-characterisation of interest will take place.
204. Southern (2017) para. 15.30.
205. *Ibid.*, para. 15.31.

The tax treatment of the embedded option will depend on whether the issuer treats it as an equity instrument (IAS 32) or as a derivative for accounting purposes (IAS 39). If the embedded derivative is accounted for as an 'equity instrument' (this is the case for a standard convertible bond), no revaluations of the 'equity instrument' will take place.[206]

Although the equity instrument is treated as a relevant contract under CTA 2009, section 585, it will not qualify as a 'derivative contract' as it will fail the accounting test of CTA 2009, section 579(1)(a).[207] Consequently, '(i)t is a "tax nothing". The issue of shares in satisfaction of the company's obligations under the security has no tax consequences'[208] unless all or part of the obligation is settled in cash.[209]

If the embedded derivative is accounted for as an embedded option (e.g., in the case of a non-standard convertible bond with cash settlement option), gains or losses from the embedded derivative will not be subject to tax on a fair value basis, but they are treated as capital gains or losses for tax purposes.[210] Hence, no annual tax charge is imposed upon a change in the fair value of the embedded option.[211] Upon exercise of the 'deemed option', any gain or loss will be taxed as chargeable gains or allowable losses.[212]

A share-linked bond will be bifurcated into a debt host contract and an embedded derivative (which qualifies as a CFD) for tax purposes.[213] Under CTA 2009, section 658, any gains or losses from the CFD are treated as capital gains or allowable losses for the issuer of the share-linked bond upon conversion if the CFD exactly tracks the underlying shares.[214]

For issuers accounting under IFRS 9 or FRS 102, Schedule 12, the tax treatment should be the same for those instruments as the hybrid instruments and structured products are bifurcated for accounting purposes. Thus, taxation follows the accounting approach.

206. IAS 32.16 confirm that no revaluations will take place for accounting purposes. This treatment is also followed for tax purposes. *Compare* Ghosh, Johnson and Miller (2022) [G3.23], Example (issue 28); Southern (2017) para. 15.30.
207. HMRC, CFM55410 and CFM50420; Ghosh, Johnson and Miller (2022) [G3.24] and [G3.48] (issue 28); Lindsay (2006a), 14.
208. HMRC, CFM55410, referencing to: TCGA 1992, s. 116(8B). *See also* Lindsay (2006a) 14.
209. In this case, CTA 2009, ss 665, 666 may apply. For details, *see* Ghosh, Johnson and Miller (2022) [G3.24] and [G3.49]-[G3.54].
210. CTA 2009, ss 573 and 574 are disapplied, *see* CTA 2009, s. 651(1).
211. Southern (2017) para. 15.30; Lindsay (2006a) 15.
212. CTA 2009, s. 653, TCGA 1992, s. 144(2) apply in case of an exercise of the 'deemed option' that leads to an issue or transfer of shares (physical settlement). CTA 2009, s. 654 deals with the taxation in case of a cash settlement of the 'deemed option', i.e., no delivery of shares takes place, but a cash amount is paid in fulfilment of the obligation.

    Details of the taxation of the embedded option upon assignment, conversion or exchange, cash settlement or redemption can be found in: Ghosh, Johnson and Miller (2022) [G3.64]-[G3.82] (issue 28) and Southern (2017) para. 15.30.
213. HMRC, CFM55410.
214. *Ibid.*

    Compare also CTA 2009, ss 656(1) to (7), 657.

[iii] Other Contracts with Embedded Derivatives

Other structured products that are neither hybrid derivatives nor loan relationships[215] and which are bifurcated into any other host contract[216] and one or more embedded derivative contracts for accounting purposes[217] will be subject to tax under the rules in CTA 2009, section 586 in conjunction with CTA 2009, section 616.[218]

Applying these rules, the derivative(s) embedded in a 'contract that is not a loan relationship' will be treated as relevant contract(s) under CTA 2009, Part 7.[219] However, for tax purposes, those embedded derivative(s) are then treated as if they were closely related to the host contract.[220] Consequently, fair value accounting of these embedded derivatives is disapplied[221] by virtue of CTA 2009, sections 586(4), 616(2), (4) and (5), with the result that the original contract as a whole is treated as if old UK GAAP still applied.[222] Those tax rules follow a 'deemed' or fictitious accounting under old UK GAAP[223] and treat both the host contract and the embedded derivative as an integrated instrument[224] that is accounted for and taxed as one instrument on an amortised cost basis.[225]

These rules can, however, be disapplied and a bifurcation approach that follows the accounting treatment under FRS 102 or IFRS can be elected by the taxpayer,[226] unless the contract is a contract of long-term insurance or if the underlying subject matter of the embedded derivative includes commodities, CTA 2009, section 617.[227]

§8.06 BIFURCATION VERSUS INTEGRATION APPROACHES IN GERMANY

[A] Accounting of Structured Products and Hybrid Instruments under German GAAP

German GAAP[228] does not contain specific rules regarding the accounting of structured products.[229] The only exception is the rule stated in section 272(2) No. 2 Commercial

215. CTA 2009, s. 586(1)(a).
216. The host contract can be, for example, a lease or a purchase contract, *compare* HMRC, CFM52520.
217. CTA 2009, s. 586(1)(b).
218. HMRC, CFM52520.
219. CTA 2009, s. 586(2) and (3); HMRC, CFM52530.
220. HMRC, CFM52530.
221. Southern (2017) para. 15.53.
222. HMRC, CFM52520.
223. *Ibid.*
224. *Ibid.*
225. Haworth and Hollis (2010) 27; Southern (2017) para. 15.52.
226. CTA 2009, s. 617(1). For an example of an embedded derivative in a purchase contract, *see* HMRC, CFM52540.
227. CTA 2009, s. 617(2). *See also* Southern (2017) para. 15.52.
228. *See* Ch. 5 §5.03[A].
229. Scharpf and Schaber (2009) 236. *See also* Olaf Maulshagen, Folker Trepte and Sven Walterscheidt, *Derivative Finanzinstrumente in Industrieunternehmen* (4th edn, Fachverlag Moderne

Law Act (CLA), which requires the bifurcation of convertible bonds and bonds cum warrants from the perspective of the issuer of the bond.[230] The general accounting principles, including the principles of orderly accounting, will also apply for structured products and hybrid instruments, including that every asset or liability has to be accounted for by observing the item-per-item valuation principle both in the financial and tax accounts.[231] Thus, in principle, every asset or liability should be accounted for and valued in its entirety.[232]

[1] Bifurcation Versus Integration for Structured Products under German GAAP (IDW View)

With regard to the accounting of structured products, the *Institut der Wirtschaftsprue-fer* (IDW), translated as 'Institute of Public Auditors', issued a statement in 2008.[233] IDW statements are not part of German GAAP, but public auditors have to verify in their audits whether those statements are applicable and give reasons in each case where they want to deviate from the accounting approach laid down in the IDW statements.[234] Hence, those statements are widely used as guidance when interpreting German GAAP.[235]

As a general principle, the IDW statement confirms that a structured product has to be treated as one financial asset or liability in the accounts because of the item-per-item valuation principle[236] and because it is designed as one legal contract.[237] To value structured products correctly, the IDW statement, however, requests that all circumstances influencing the valuation must be taken into account. As a consequence, the IDW suggests mandatory bifurcation for many structured products for the purposes of valuation and measurement in financial accounts.[238]

Wirtschaft 2008) 244; Tristian Nguyen, *Bilanzielle Abbildung von Finanzderivaten und Sicherungsgeschäften* (1st edn, Herbert Utz Verlag 2007) 76.

230. Conlon & Aquilino: Derivatives D2.03[4]; Nguyen (2007) 76; Scharpf and Schaber (2009) 243; Schmitz and Huthmann (2012) 132.
231. Sections 246(1), 252(1) No. 3 CLA.
 See Conlon & Aquilino: Derivatives D2.03[4]; Scharpf and Schaber (2009) 236; Schmitz and Huthmann (2012) 132.
232. Scharpf and Schaber (2009) 236.
233. IDW, RS HFA 22, *Zur einheitlichen und getrennten handelsrechtlichen Bilanzierung strukturierter Finanzinstrumente* (2 September 2008) WPg Supplement 4/2008, 41ff, FN-IDW 10/2008, 455ff. The new statement substitutes the old statement of IDW, *RH BFA 1.003, Rechnungslegungshinweis: Zur Bilanzierung strukturierter Produkte* (2001) WPg 2001 916 which was authoritative only for audits of financial institutions. The new statement by the IDW is applicable to all audits of persons, partnerships and corporate entities that engage in a trade and account under s. 4(1), 5(1) CLA, independently of their legal form and the industry sector of their trade activities. *See* IDW (2008) para. 1.
234. IDW, *WP-Handbuch 2012, Anhang 3, Die fachlichen Verlautbarungen des IDW* (2012) 3009.
235. In contrast, International Standards of Auditing (ISA) will be directly applicable and binding on auditors when they will be adopted by the respective Member State of the EU.
236. Sections 246(1) and 252(1) No. 3 CLA.
237. IDW (2008) paras 6 and 9.
238. *Ibid.*, paras 7-8 and 10; *also* Schmitz and Huthmann (2012) 133.

It has been advanced in favour of applying a bifurcation approach (notwithstanding the general accounting principle of item-per-item valuation) that structured products have a specific risk and reward profile due to the combination of a host contract with an embedded derivative compared to other (accounts) receivables or liabilities.[239] In addition, it has been argued in the accounting literature that an integration approach, which applies the general accounting principle of item-per-item valuation and respects the structured product as one legal contract, would lead to economically wrong results in the financial accounts.[240] These authors maintain that the specific risks and rewards of the embedded derivative would be misrepresented in the accounts if the structured product were accounted for as a single instrument.[241]

The IDW statement proposes a mandatory bifurcation for structured products in cases where these instruments contain significantly increased or different risks and rewards compared to non-structured financial instruments because they contain embedded derivative(s).[242] Thus, the approach adopted by the IDW broadly mirrors the approach towards bifurcation stipulated in IAS 32 and 39.[243] The IDW statement was updated in 2015 but does not contain any material changes.[244] Although companies applying IFRS 9 in their accounts will follow the IASB approach towards bifurcation and integration of structured products and hybrid instruments, those applying German GAAP will have to rely on the current IDW statement of 2015.

A more detailed discussion on the bifurcation and integration approach applying to various structured products in the accounts of the holders and the issuers can be found below.

[a] Accounting Treatment of the Holder of Structured Products

According to the IDW statement concerning the accounting of structured products, bifurcation of structured products is mandatory for the holder of the instrument if the embedded derivative increases an existing market risk or generates additional market risks in comparison to the basic financial instrument.[245] These risks can be, for example, equity or FX risks.[246]

239. Scharpf and Luz (2000) 683; Scharpf and Schaber (2009) 236; *also* IDW (2008) para. 10.
240. Nguyen (2007) 77; *also* Andreas Barckow, *Die Bilanzierung von derivaten Finanzinstrumenten und Sicherungsgeschäften* (1st edn, IDW Verlag 2004) 87; Scharpf and Schaber (2009) 236; Schmitz and Huthmann (2012) 133.
241. Scharpf and Schaber (2009) 236.
242. IDW (2008) paras 8, 10 and 15; *also* Schaber et al. (2010) 16.
243. Conlon & Aquilino: Derivatives D2.03[4].
244. IDW RS HFA 22, Zur einheitlichen oder getrennten handelsrechtlichen Bilanzierung strukturierter Finanzinstrumente, WPg Supplement 4/2015, 30 ff.
245. IDW (2008) para. 15.
246. *Ibid.*, para. 16; Conlon & Aquilino: Derivatives D2.03[4]; Scharpf and Schaber (2009) 239; Schmitz and Huthmann (2012) 136.

Example 72:

Company A purchases a reverse convertible bond from issuer B. Under the terms of the bond, the issuer has the right to deliver a pre-determined number of shares instead of paying back the notional amount of the bond.[247] The reverse convertible bond is a linear combination of a straight bond and a short put option from the perspective of the holder.[248] Because the embedded put option contains equity risk that increases the risk and reward profile of the bond, the bond has to be bifurcated according to the IDW.

In addition, bifurcation is proposed if the capital invested is subject not only to the credit risk of the issuer but also to other credit risks or events[249] or non-market risks like insurance risks or weather events.[250] Furthermore, bifurcation is requested by the IDW in cases where the embedded derivative may lead to a negative yield of the investment.[251]

Bifurcation of structured products is also suggested in various other cases, where it is assumed that the risk and reward profile of the host contract has been significantly changed due to the embedded derivative.

In the following cases, a bifurcation of structured products has been suggested by the IDW:

(1) The embedded derivative leads to further commitments to purchase financial instruments under conditions fixed at inception of the structured product.[252]
(2) The embedded derivative contains provisions for the prolongation of the term of the structured product without adjustment to the current market interest rate at the moment of prolongation.[253]
(3) The embedded interest rate derivative can at least double the interest rate of the underlying variable (which can be either an interest rate or an interest rate index) and may lead to an overall interest yield which is at least double the market yield of interest compared to a contract with the same conditions as the underlying variable.[254]

247. *See* for a detailed description of a reverse convertible bond: Ch. 8 §8.01[B][4].
248. The holder receives a put option premium in the form of an increased interest rate under the bond.
249. Other credit risks are, for example, credit risks of third parties. This is the case for Credit-Linked Notes, where a Credit Default Swap is embedded in the debt host contract. *See* Conlon & Aquilino: Derivatives D2.03[4]; Scharpf and Schaber (2009) 239.
250. IDW (2008) para. 16b); Schaber et al. (2010) 22.
251. IDW (2008) para. 16c). *See also* Conlon & Aquilino: Derivatives D2.03[4]; Scharpf and Schaber (2009) 239; Schaber et al. (2010) 28; Schmitz and Huthmann (2012) 136.
252. IDW (2008) para. 16e).
253. *Ibid.*, para. 16f).
254. *Ibid.*, para. 16d). *See*, for further examples, Scharpf and Schaber (2009) 239ff and Schaber et al. (2010) 18ff.

In principle, accounting of a structured product as a single item is only possible where the risks and rewards are not significantly increased by an embedded derivative or where they are not different compared to non-structured financial instruments.[255]

In some cases, where the accounting as a single asset would lead to a correct representation of the financial, earnings and assets position, the IDW statement proposes a deviation from the bifurcation approach, even if the risks and rewards are significantly increased or different because of the embedded derivative (the exception).[256]

This is, for example, the case where either the structured products are purchased on the trading account of credit institutions, banks or financial services firms,[257] or where these instruments are attributed to the current assets[258] and valued at the lower of amortised cost or fair value, provided that the valuation is based on prices in an active market.[259]

In addition, structured products can be accounted for as one instrument if the issuer provides a capital guarantee and if the holder has attributed the instrument to permanent assets with the intention and capability to hold the instrument until maturity.[260]

[b] Accounting Treatment of the Issuer of Structured Products

Under the rules proposed by the IDW statement, structured products will, in principle, be integrated or bifurcated according to the same rules for the investor and for the issuer of the instrument.[261] Thus, according to the IDW, many structured products will also be bifurcated in the accounts of the issuer.

In cases where the exception of IDW RS HFA 22, paragraph 14 applies, the integration approach and not the bifurcation approach would have to apply, and the structured products would have to be shown in the accounts of the issuer as a single instrument notwithstanding the increase of risks and rewards.[262]

In the accounting literature, it has been doubted whether the exceptions of IDW RS HFA 22, paragraph 14 could also apply to liabilities.[263] Rather, it has been proposed that it should be decided on a case-by-case basis whether an integration or bifurcation approach is justified in the accounts of the issuer.[264] According to this view, an integration approach should only be applied in the accounts of the issuer if the

255. Schaber et al. (2010) 11.
256. IDW (2008) paras 13 and 14. *See* Scharpf and Schaber (2009) 238; Schaber et al. (2010) 45.
257. IDW (2008) para. 14b). *See* Schaber et al. (2010) 49; Schmitz and Huthmann (2012) 135.
258. Now s. 253(4) CLA.
259. IDW (2008) para. 14a). *See* Scharpf and Schaber (2009) 238; Schaber et al. (2010) 46; Schmitz and Huthmann (2012) 134.
260. IDW (2008) para. 14c). *See* Schaber et al. (2010) 50; Schmitz and Huthmann (2012) 135.
261. IDW (2008) paras 13, 22. *See also* Scharpf and Schaber (2009) 241; Schaber et al. (2010) 55.
262. IDW (2008) para. 22.
263. Schaber et al. (2010) 55.
264. *Ibid.*

accounting as a single instrument reflects the true financial, assets and earnings situation of the issuer.[265]

[2] *Bifurcation Versus Integration for Hybrid Instruments under German GAAP*

[a] *Accounting Treatment of the Holder of Hybrid Instruments*

The position of the IDW regarding the bifurcation of hybrid instruments remains uncertain, as the IDW statement does not contain an explicit confirmation of whether convertible and exchangeable bonds have to be bifurcated or integrated by the holder.[266] In the accounting literature, it has been suggested that convertible and exchangeable bonds have to be bifurcated into a bond and a call option.[267] They argue that the 'embedded call option' would change the risk and reward profile of the bond.[268]

[b] *Accounting Treatment of the Issuer of Hybrid Instruments*

In the case of convertible bonds, the issuer has to apply the specific provision of section 272(2) No. 2 CLA in its accounts.[269]

The convertible bond is taken into the accounts with the redemption amount,[270] but, at the same time, the issuer has to book an item into capital reserves, which equals the amount that the issuer receives for the provision of the conversion right,[271] i.e., the present value of the difference of the coupon payments of a straight bond and the coupon payments of a convertible bond.

In the case of exchangeable bonds, the accounting literature suggests that exchangeable bonds have to be bifurcated or integrated according to the same principles that the IDW statement has laid down for the holder of those instruments.[272]

265. *Ibid.*
266. IDW (2008) para. 22 at fn 16 only states that convertible bonds in the hands of the *issuer* always have to be bifurcated because of s. 272(2) No. 1 CLA.
267. Schaber et al. (2010) 20.
268. *Ibid.*
269. IDW (2008) para. 22 at fn 16; Schaber et al. (2010) 55.
270. Section 253(1) sent. 2 CLA.
271. Section 272(2) No. 2 CLA. *See* Häuselmann (2005) 159; Holger Häuselmann and Siegfried Wagner, 'Steuerbilanzielle Erfassung aktienbezogener Anleihen: Options-, Wandel, Umtausch- und Aktienanleihen' BB 2002, 2431, 2432.
272. Schaber et al. (2010) 55, referring to IDW (2008) para. 22. However, no explicit reference exists in the IDW statement that prescribes the bifurcation of exchangeable bonds in the accounts of the holder of such instruments.

[B] Taxation of Structured Products and Hybrid Instruments in Germany

[1] Taxation of Structured Products: Holders and Issuers

In sharp contrast to the bifurcation approach adopted by the IDW and the accounting literature,[273] the tax literature has mainly taken the view that structured products will have to be accounted for as a single item following the integration approach both in the financial and the tax accounts.[274]

Their arguments are as follows:

(1) The general accounting principles of orderly accounting, especially the principle of item-per-item valuation, also apply to structured products in the absence of more specific accounting rules for these instruments.
(2) Legal form has priority over the economic content. Structured products are normally wrapped up in one legal contract and thus can only be disposed of as a single asset or liability.[275]
(3) German GAAP is not pursuing 'a generally binding concept of bifurcation [as] [s]ection 272(2) No. 2 Commercial Code is the only provision demanding a bifurcation of legally unseparated assets and addresses exclusively the accounting of convertible bonds (*Wandelanleihen*) and bonds with detachable warrants (*Optionsanleihen*) at the level of the issuer'.[276]

The author does not agree with the purely economic view of the IDW and the accounting literature which argues in favour of a bifurcation approach, as no explicit legal basis in the current German GAAP exists. Furthermore, the bifurcation approach for structured products directly contradicts the item-per-item valuation principle of German GAAP.[277]

---

273. Scharpf and Luz (2000) 683; Schaber et al. (2010) 10ff; Scharpf and Schaber (2009) 236.
274. Gerhard Dreyer and Harald Herrmann, 'Die Besteuerung von Aktien-, Wandel- und Umtauschanleihen' Betriebs-Berater 2001, 705, 708; Häuselmann (2005) 143; Häuselmann and Wagner (2002a) 2432-2434; Conlon & Aquilino: Derivatives D2.03[4].
   Differentiating Götz Wiese and Thomas Dammer, 'Zusammengesetzte Finanzinstrumente der AG' DStR 1999 867, 869 suggest an integration approach for 'genuine' hybrid instruments like convertible bonds, but bifurcation for 'non-genuine hybrid instruments', like bonds cum warrants.
   Other opinion Stephan Rau, 'Zur steuerbilanziellen Behandlung von Aktienanleihen' DStR 2006 627, 628-630.
275. Häuselmann (2005) 142 proposes an accounting as a single instrument also for bond cum warrants and stripped bonds. They however would not fall under the definition of structured products used in this work, as they are not legally inseparable units but can be disposed of separately.
   See also Ch. 8 §8.01[B][2].
276. Conlon & Aquilino: Derivatives D2.03[4].
277. Nguyen (2007) 76; *also* Walther Busse von Colbe and Thomas Seeberg, *Vereinbarkeit internationaler Konzernrechnungslegung mit handelsrechtlichen Grundsätzen* (Empfehlungen des Arbeitskreises 'Externe Unternehmensrechnung' der Schmalenbach-Gesellschaft – Deutsche Gesellschaft für Betriebswirtschaft e.v. 1999) 118.

In the author's view, if a bifurcation approach for structured products was to be applied under German GAAP, an explicit legal basis would be necessary, and specific bifurcation rules for structured products would have to be introduced in the legislation, which stipulated an exception from the general accounting principles.

A statement by the IDW that presupposes bifurcation for many of these instruments is not sufficient as this statement does not have legal character and thus cannot be legally binding for the purposes of German GAAP.

Based on the current German accounting law, the author agrees with the majority view of the tax literature that an integration approach has to be followed for structured products in the financial accounts.

By applying this view, structured products would have to be accounted for on an integration basis as single instruments in the financial accounts and, thus, also in the tax accounts.[278]

In real-life cases, where many companies and their auditors follow the view of the IDW and bifurcate structured products in their financial accounts, it is, however, not certain whether an integration or bifurcation approach has to be followed in the tax accounts.

At first sight, one might argue that the tax accounts will have to follow the financial accounts, and thus, the bifurcation approach will be authoritative in the financial accounts. The authoritative principle, however, only prescribes a 'follow the accounts' approach for tax purposes with regard to the 'general principles of orderly accounting'.[279]

The majority of the tax literature suggests that these principles of orderly accounting only entail the general principles applying to all businesses, not specific principles that apply only to corporate businesses.[280] *Others* suggest that general principles of orderly accounting are also those which only apply to a specific group of businesses and thus are also authoritative for tax accounts of these businesses.[281]

The accounting literature cites as a reason for the bifurcation of structured products that the financial, assets and earnings position has to be mirrored in the accounts correctly according to section 264(2) CLA.[282]

As section 264(2) CLA applies only to companies and limited partnerships, this section will, in the author's view, not constitute a 'general principle of orderly accounting' on which the argument of bifurcation could be based.

Hence, as section 264(2) CLA would not be authoritative for the tax accounts, a bifurcation approach in the tax accounts should not be applied, even if the taxpayer bifurcated the structured products of the financial accounts.

278. Whether this approach should generally be followed or not will be discussed in Ch. 8 §8.08.
279. Section 5(1) sent. 1 1st part CLA.
280. Häuselmann (2005) 160; Weber-Grellet *Schmidt, EStG* (2012) § 5, para. 58; Thomas Stobbe, '§ 5' in Carl Herrmann, Gerhard Heuer and Arndt Raupach (eds), *Einkommensteuer – und Körperschaftsteuergesetz Kommentar* (Verlag Dr Otto Schmidt KG 2013) para. 200.
281. Klaus Buciek, '§ 5 EStG' in Bernd Heuermann and Peter Brandis (eds), *Blümich, EStG, KStG GewStG Kommentar* (120th edn, 2013) § 5, para. 207.
282. Scharpf and Schaber (2009) 236.

[2] *Taxation of Hybrid Instruments*

[a] *Taxation of the Holder of Hybrid Instruments*

The predominant view in the tax literature also applies an integration approach to hybrid instruments, such as convertible or exchangeable bonds in the accounts of the investor.[283] Thus, the holder (investor) has to account for the hybrid instrument as one instrument with its acquisition costs[284] in the financial accounts and tax accounts.[285] Convertible bonds and exchangeable bonds will be treated differently for accounting and tax purposes upon conversion of the bond into the underlying equities.

If the investor converts a *convertible bond* into shares, no realisation event takes place,[286] as the contractual relationship has already existed before and was not terminated or amended.[287] Instead, the shares received are accounted for at the former book value of the convertible bond.[288] Additional payments by the investor upon conversion will be treated as additional acquisition costs that increase the initial costs.[289]

Capital gains from a later disposal of the equities, including any appreciation in the value of the convertible bond before conversion into shares, will be treated as 95% tax-exempt equity capital gains under section 8b(2) CTA for the investor.[290]

If the investor disposes of the convertible bond before conversion, any capital gains will not be treated as privileged equity capital gains but will instead be fully taxable.[291] If the investor converts an exchangeable bond into shares, this is regarded as a neutral exchange against shares in the commercial accounts.[292]

For tax purposes, the conversion into third-party shares in case of an *exchangeable bond* leads to a realisation event with the capital gains being calculated as the difference between the book value of the exchangeable bond and the market value of

283. Dreyer and Herrmann (2001) 708; Häuselmann (2005) 161; Häuselmann and Wagner (2002a) 2432 and 2434; Conlon & Aquilino: Derivatives D2.06[1].
284. Sections 253(1) sent. 1 and 255(1) CLA.
285. Conlon & Aquilino: Derivatives D2.06[1] and [2]; *also* Häuselmann and Wagner (2002a) 2432.
In the financial accounts, the holder may write down the instrument to the lower market value if the value of the hybrid at the balance sheet date is below the initial acquisition costs. A write-down has to take place in case of an expected permanent depreciation of the convertible bond. *See* s. 253(3) sents 3 and 4 CLA (For the qualification under s. 253(3) sents 3 and 4 CLA, it has been assumed that the convertible bond will be attributed to the fixed assets in the accounts of the holder). In the tax accounts, a write-down will only be possible in case of an expected permanent depreciation of the convertible bond; *see* s. 6(1) No. 1 sent. 2 CLA (assumed attribution of the convertible bond to the fixed assets in the accounts of the holder).
286. Häuselmann (2005) 162; Conlon & Aquilino: Derivatives D2.06[1]. *Other opinion* Thomas Hahn, 'Bilanzierung und Besteuerung von Wandelanleihen' (Master Thesis (Diplomarbeit), 2007) 42ff.
287. Häuselmann (2005) 162 describes this convertible contract legally as a '*facultas alternativa*', which existed with the same terms from the beginning of the contract.
288. Conlon & Aquilino: Derivatives D2.06[1].
289. Section 255(1) sent. 2 CLA. *See also* Häuselmann (2005) 162.
290. Conlon & Aquilino: Derivatives D2.06[1]; Häuselmann (2005) 162.
291. Häuselmann (2005) 162; *also* Jutta Rengers, '§ 8b KStG' in Bernd Heuermann and Peter Brandis (eds), *Blümich, EStG, KStG GewStG Kommentar* (120th edn, 2013) § 8b, para. 212.
292. Häuselmann (2005) 166.

the shares at the time of exchange.[293] The acquisition costs of the shares will equal the fair value of the exchangeable bonds at the time of exchange.[294]

Capital gains from a later disposal of the equities, calculated as the difference between the acquisition costs of the shares and the market value at the time of disposal,[295] will be 95% tax-exempt under section 8b(2) CTA for the investor and any losses will be non-deductible (section 8b(3) sentence 3 CTA).[296]

If the investor disposes of the exchangeable bond before conversion, any capital gains will be fully taxable.

[b] Taxation of the Issuer of Hybrid Instruments

For the issuer of a *convertible bond*, the specific provision of section 272(2) No. 2 CLA that applies in the financial accounts requires the value of the conversion right to be recognised in the capital reserves at inception.[297]

Whether that treatment of the conversion right under section 272(2) No. 2 CLA has to be followed for tax purposes depends on whether that provision is authoritative for tax purposes or not.[298]

In a specific decision concerning *Optionsanleihen*,[299] the Federal Fiscal Court (*BFH*) has presupposed that the tax accounts of companies have to follow the financial accounts also with respect to the principles of orderly accounting that only apply to companies.[300] Thus, the BFH applied the provision of section 272(2) No. 2 CLA in the tax accounts of a company and accepted the set-up of a capital reserve for the provision of the option right for tax purposes.

The decision of the BFH, however, explicitly acknowledges that it would not override a previous decision of the BFH, which stipulated that convertible bonds have to be attributed to debt and not to equity as a whole until the conversion right is exercised.[301] Thus, despite the BFH decision regarding *Optionsanleihen* in the context

293. Conlon & Aquilino: Derivatives D2.06[2]; similar: Häuselmann (2005) 166.
294. Section 6(6) sent. 1 ITA. *See* Häuselmann (2005) 166.
295. This tax treatment of the exchangeable is in sharp contrast to the tax treatment of a convertible bond, where any value appreciations until conversion into the shares are included in the tax-exempt capital gains upon disposal of the shares as no realisation event takes place upon conversion of the convertible bond into shares.
296. Conlon & Aquilino: Derivatives D2.06[2].
297. *See* Ch. 8 §8.06[A][2][b].
298. Häuselmann (2000) 145.
299. It is difficult to translate the term 'Optionsanleihe' precisely. The specific decision did not concern bonds with detachable warrants, as prescribed in the law, but a structured product, which consisted of a straight bond and an option right for the holder to convert into a specific number of shares at a specific price in addition to the payment of the redemption amount at maturity. The bond and the embedded option were contained in one legal contract and could not be separated legally nor traded separately. The issuer paid a lower coupon to the holder of the structured bond because of the provision of the option right.
300. BFH, decision of 30 November 2005, I R 26/04, DStRE 2006, 385, 386. According to that decision, the issuer of a '*Optionsanleihe*' has to bifurcate this particular structured product also for tax purposes into a liability and an equity element for which a capital reserve has to be set up.
301. BFH, decision of 21 February 1973, I R 106/71, BFHE 109, 22, BStBl II 1973, 460.

of section 272(2) No. 2 CLA, *Häuselmann* suggests that there are still good arguments not to bifurcate a convertible bond into a liability and an equity element in the tax accounts of the issuer.[302] The *majority view* in the tax literature, however, bifurcates convertible bonds both in the financial *and* tax accounts based on the application of section 272(2) No. 2 CLA and the 'authoritative principle' under German GAAP.[303]

With regard to *exchangeable bonds*, a capital reserve for the right to exchange into equity would not be permissible in tax accounts as section 272(2) No. 2 CLA only applies to convertible bonds and bonds cum warrants but not to exchangeable bonds.

In the author's view, even if the exchangeable bond were to be bifurcated in the accounts by following the view of the accounting literature, such bifurcation should not be followed in the tax accounts as an explicit provision requesting a bifurcation exists neither in the specific accounting rules applying to companies nor in the general accounting principles of German GAAP.

§8.07 COMPARISON OF THE TAXATION RULES FOR STRUCTURED PRODUCTS AND HYBRID INSTRUMENTS IN THE UK AND GERMANY

The UK tax law, in principle, applies a 'follow the accounts' approach. Although hybrid instruments and structured products under FRS 102, Sections 11 and 12 and IFRS 9 are integrated for the holder of the instrument and bifurcated for the issuer of the instruments under IFRS 9 and FRS 102, Sections 11 and 12, tax law deviates in many cases from this approach in the tax legislation.

For example, hybrid instruments, such as exchangeable bonds and convertible bonds, are bifurcated for tax purposes as 'loan relationships with embedded derivatives' under CTA 2009, section 585.[304] On the other hand, structured products that fall under the categories 'hybrid derivatives with embedded derivatives'[305] and 'other contracts with embedded derivatives'[306] will not be bifurcated for tax purposes but taxed as one instrument, as the tax law deems old UK GAAP to apply, and thus prescribes the integration approach.[307]

302. *See* Häuselmann (2000) 145; Häuselmann (2005) 160. By following the *minority view* of Häuselmann, the specific rule of s. 272(2) No. 2 CLA that requires the set up of a capital reserve for the conversion right, would not be authoritative for tax purposes with the consequence that a convertible bond would have to be accounted as a single instrument for the issuer in their tax accounts, although it would have to be bifurcated in the financial accounts. According to that view, no capital reserve would be permissible in the tax accounts and the issuer would book a liability with the notional value of the convertible bond in its accounts. Any interest received by the issuer would be taxed when due. If the holder converted into shares, the liability would have to be deleted from the tax accounts, and instead the amount would have to be assigned to equity.

303. Haisch and Helios (2011) 185-186 with further references at fn. 117; Conlon & Aquilino: Derivatives D2.03[4]; Wiese and Dammer (1999) 869.

304. CTA 2009, s. 585.

305. CTA 2009, s. 586.

306. CTA 2009, s. 586.

307. Ch. 8 §8.05[E].

Although the UK approach towards bifurcation in the tax accounts is codified properly and in detail, it is, in the author's view, quite arbitrary as it depends on the characterisation of the host contract as a loan relationship or a 'non-loan relationship'.

However, although the UK approach is often complicated and sometimes inconsistent, it is still more advanced than the German approach.

The German approach towards bifurcation in the tax accounts is entirely uncertain as no codified rules exist in German accounting or tax law dealing specifically with the bifurcation or integration approach towards structured products and hybrid instruments apart from section 272(2) No. 2 CLA.[308] Thus, there is a substantial debate between accounting and tax academics and practitioners on whether to bifurcate these instruments in the accounts or not.[309]

As the majority of the tax accounting literature suggests that German GAAP explicitly prescribes an integration approach, they will follow an integration approach also for tax purposes.[310] In cases where taxpayers bifurcate structured products and hybrid instruments in their financial accounts following the view of the IDW, there is additional uncertainty about whether the tax accounts have to follow a bifurcation approach in the financial accounts. No consensus opinion has been reached by the courts or in the literature so far.[311]

§8.08 SOLUTION TO PROBLEM 5: BIFURCATION FOR STRUCTURED PRODUCTS AND INTEGRATION FOR HYBRID INSTRUMENTS?

For *accounting purposes*, bifurcation approaches are often adopted for structured products[312] as well as for hybrid instruments.[313]

Based on more general accounting considerations, an integration approach might be appropriate for structured products and hybrid instruments[314] based on the following arguments:

- Specific risks and rewards cannot only be found in embedded derivatives but also in a similar fashion in receivables or liabilities that entail a guarantee, some form of insurance contract or capital protection. Nevertheless, these receivables or liabilities will, in most cases, not be bifurcated for accounting purposes.
- Risks and rewards of an embedded derivative can also be mirrored when the whole instrument is accounted for at fair value without the necessity to resort to bifurcation.[315]

308. Ch. 8 §8.06[B][2][b].
309. Ch. 8 §8.06[A][1] and §8.06[B][1].
310. *For all* Häuselmann (2005) 142-144.
311. Ch. 8 §8.06[B][1].
312. Ch. 8 §8.02.
313. *See* Ch. 8 §8.05[B] and §8.06[A].
314. For further arguments in respect of hybrid instruments, *see* Ch. 8 §8.04.
315. This is also mirrored by IFRS 9 which proposes an integration approach for structured products and hybrid instruments that are financial assets.

For *tax purposes*, legislators also have to consider whether to follow a bifurcation approach by separating each of the components and subject those units to separate tax rules or whether to tax structured products and hybrid instruments as a single instrument, thereby following an integration approach for tax purposes.

Tax policymakers might decide on a *bifurcation approach* for structured products and hybrid instruments based on the following considerations:

- Tax policymakers do not want to subject similar instruments to a different tax treatment merely because they are wrapped up in a host contract, as a treatment of a single instrument may provide taxpayers with tax arbitrage opportunities. By breaking up the transaction into its components, 'bifurcation can reveal the time value of money elements of transactions that are not being accrued'.[316]
- The combination of different financial instruments into one composite instrument may blur the essential features of the separate instrument. Thus, tax systems may require bifurcation for tax purposes and tax each of the components separately.[317] By doing so, they try to achieve consistency in the taxation, especially if the separate components are subject to different taxation rules based on their qualification as equity, debt or derivatives compared to the non-bifurcated structured product.

Although bifurcation approaches might, in theory, provide an appropriate solution to deal with the problems in the context of structured products and hybrid instruments, a bifurcation approach will also have disadvantages and does not always provide the right solution for taxing those instruments.

One commonly finds the following arguments *against a bifurcation approach* of structured products and hybrid instruments for tax purposes:

- Bifurcation approaches may not offer an acceptable solution because payoffs of financial instruments can be replicated using other instruments and derivatives.[318]
- Bifurcation may lead to wrong taxation results if the tax legislator applies bifurcation indiscriminately, notwithstanding the economic composition of the financial instruments. This is, for example, the case if hybrid instruments are bifurcated for tax purposes, although, economically, a correct bifurcation of these instruments would not be possible.[319]

Because of the difficulties in applying the bifurcation approach for tax purposes, a separation and taxation of the single components will, in some cases, not constitute an appropriate solution when taxing structured products and hybrid instruments.

316. OECD (2001) para. 105.
317. *Ibid.*, para. 106.
318. *Ibid.*, para. 108.
319. *See* Ch. 8 §8.04.

A carefully balanced solution has to be found that decides on an integration or bifurcation approach depending on (1) the category of the structured product, and (2) the taxation rules applying to the single components.

[A] Hybrid Instruments

Only financial instruments that can be bifurcated economically should also be bifurcated for tax purposes in order to achieve taxation results that mirror the economic reality as closely as possible. Hence, hybrid instruments should not be bifurcated for tax purposes as they do not constitute combinations of two financial instruments but are economically inseparable.[320] Integration of hybrid instruments for tax purposes should be considered independently from whether these instruments are bifurcated for accounting purposes.[321] In the author's view, based on economic considerations, an integration approach seems to be an appropriate solution to recognise hybrid instruments in tax accounts.

[B] Structured Products

Regarding structured products, tax legislators have to decide whether they adopt a more differentiated approach or opt for less differentiation. The solutions proposed in the following will also depend on tax policy considerations that the tax legislator has already chosen to apply for the categories of equity, debt and derivatives.

[1] Solution 1 for Structured Products: Bifurcation

If the tax legislator has decided to reward risk-taking by taxpayers and thus already preferentially taxes equity and equity derivatives[322] compared to debt, it would be consequent to apply this approach also to the taxation of structured products.

If such a tax policy is applied, the legislator may want to bifurcate structured products that consist of the different constituents of debt, equity and/or derivatives and tax the single components of the structured product according to the rules of the single instruments in order to allow taxation according to the different risk categories.

[2] Solution 2 for Structured Products: Integration

If the tax legislator focuses on minimising tax arbitrage opportunities and thus taxes equity, debt and derivatives according to the same rules, an integration approach for taxing genuine structured products may be applied.

If all separate elements of the structured product are taxed according to the same rules, the tax legislator will have, in the author's view, no justification nor an incentive to tax structured products any differently from their components and thus can easily

320. *See* Ch. 8 §8.03 and §8.04.
321. *See* arguments in Ch. 8 §8.04.
322. Tax systems may also privilege the taxation of land and other intangible assets.

opt for an integration approach of all structured products for tax purposes - both for holders and issuers of those instruments.
In the context of both solutions [1] and [2], the following rules should apply to structured products and 'false friends'[323] to prevent tax arbitrage opportunities:

(1) Any legally separable combinations,[324] such as bonds cum warrants, should be taxed separately according to their single constituents. A decision on whether an integration or bifurcation approach has to be applied is not necessary in such cases.
(2) A tax system should adopt an integration approach for those instruments which cannot be defined as genuine structured products but are 'false friend put-call parity combinations' because these combinations have been created by arbitrating out the put-call parity.[325] The reason is that a bifurcation of those artificially created combinations could lead to distorted taxation results if the bifurcated elements of the 'false friends' are taxed more favourably for the taxpayer than the integrated 'false friends'. Thus, an integration approach is necessary to avoid tax arbitrage opportunities.
(3) Combinations of derivatives will also fall under the 'false friends' category.[326] As a tax system normally taxes the single derivatives in the same way as the combination of derivatives, an integration approach should create no problems for these derivatives combinations. If, however, the combination of derivatives is taxed differently compared to the single derivatives entailed in the combination, the tax legislator should either consider changing the rules regarding the taxation of single derivatives (or the tax rules dealing with the combinations) or apply a mandatory bifurcation approach for these combinations of derivatives in order to avoid tax arbitrage opportunities.

In summary, a tax system would have to develop a special taxation regime for structured products and hybrid instruments that applies a differentiated integration and bifurcation approach to the various instruments according to the above-outlined criteria.

Such a differentiated approach would not necessarily follow the accounting rules for those instruments as accounting rules are not formulated to prevent the erosion of the tax base, and thus, the accounting rules may legitimately bifurcate or integrate structured products and hybrid instruments according to different criteria.

323. *See* Ch. 8 §8.01[B][1] to §8.01[B][3].
324. *See* Ch. 8 §8.01[B][2].
325. *See* Ch. 8 §8.01[B][1].
326. *See* Ch. 8 §8.01[B][3].

§8.09 CRYPTO STRUCTURED PRODUCTS AND CRYPTOASSETS WITH EMBEDDED DERIVATIVES

Structured products have been used for many years in traditional finance to sell investors complex payoff profiles, where they usually give up some of the upside of an underlying asset against partial or full downside protection of the price movements of an asset or index.

Crypto structured products are no exception to that. They have developed on the back of the introduction of exchange-traded crypto derivatives only recently, with the first crypto structured product being launched in 2021.[327] The following part discusses crypto structured products as a new subcategory of structured products. Some of the considerations will also apply to ESG-linked structured products, while others will not.

[A] The Economic Properties of Crypto Structured Products

Bybit defines crypto structured products as 'packaged investments linked to digital assets to enhance risk-return metrics for investors'.[328] Further, the blog *Yield App* outlines that:

> Crypto structured products work in much the same way as structured products based on traditional financial market instruments, utilizing derivatives to achieve specific financial outcomes. While derivative products in traditional financial markets are a mature asset class in their own right, they have only relatively recently become available for crypto markets.[329]

Trofi Group defines crypto structured products as:

> packaged financial instruments that use a combination of fixed-income assets and derivatives for achieving a risk-return objective, such as principal protection, enhancing yields, or betting on volatility. The performance or value of these financial instruments, or structured products, is linked to that of an underlying asset, product, or index. These could be cryptocurrencies, crypto indices, or a combination of these.[330]

The author believes that this definition comes closest to traditional definitions of structured products as containing a host – usually debt – instrument and one or more embedded derivatives.

327. Yield App, An introduction to crypto structured products: Variable risk return profiles, blog, https://yield.app/blog/intro-crypto-structured-products#: ~ :text = Structured%20products%20are%20investment%20products,the%20return%20profile%20in%20the, accessed 30 August 2023.
328. Bybit, Crypto Structured Products: Maximising Yields During Choppy Markets (27 July 2022) https://learn.bybit.com/bybit-shark-fin/crypto-structured-products/, accessed 29 May 2023.
329. Yield App, An introduction to crypto structured products: Variable risk return profiles.
330. Trofi Group, What are crypto structured products, blog (4 May 2022), https://blog.trofi.group/what-are-crypto-structured-products-1c3f648f163f, accessed 29 May 2023.

Trofi Group observes that most crypto structured products incorporate options.[331] The blog *Yield App* explains with respect to those embedded options and crypto structured products that:

> Crypto structured products can take many forms depending on the payoff objectives. With over seven times the volatility of equity markets, crypto options typically offer larger premiums and therefore more customization options. For example, crypto structured products allow an investor to express a view on the future performance of an underlying digital asset, such as Bitcoin. They can be used to earn yield from the extreme price movements of cryptocurrencies – Bitcoin has moved between roughly $51,000 and $16,000 during 2022 – powering volatility-driven yields as a result.[332]

That all sounds very much like traditional structured products, where some of the products give investors returns in falling equity markets, whereas others provide returns on rising markets, and again, others profit from equity volatility via volatility swaps incorporated in the structured product.

There are a couple of other players around in the market of crypto structured products, with the first products launched in 2021.

For example, *Trofi Group* offers 'Buffered Return Enhanced Note linked to the performance of Ethereum'.[333] *Trofi Group* states that the strategy of this note 'provides leveraged returns along with partial protection on the downside risk. This Note is suitable for stablecoin holders who look to participate in market rallies but are also concerned about downside risk. It is constructed through a combination of fixed-income products, selling put options, and buying call spread options'.[334]

Trofi Group provides example terms and a payout profile, which are shown below:

Example 73:

The following example shows *illustrative terms* of the *Trofi Group Buffered Return Enhanced Note.* It is directly cited and taken from the Trophy Group website.

Buffered Return Enhanced Note

Investment Asset: USD Tether (USDT)Tenor: 6 months
Initial Ethereum (ETH) price: USD 3,000
Put Strike Price: 80% of initial ETH price (i.e., USD 2400)
Participation Rate (PR): 180%
Cap: 40%[335]

331. *Ibid.*
332. Yield App, An introduction to crypto structured products: Variable risk return profiles.
333. Trofi Group, What are crypto structured products, (4 May 2022).
334. *Ibid.*
335. *Ibid.*

Trofi Group provides the following explanation for this simplified term sheet: 'The put option sold has an out-of-the-money strike, which provides a 20% buffer to the downside price movement of Ethereum (ETH).'[336] The holders of the Buffered Return Enhanced Note ('Noteholders') 'may only be exposed to any ETH downside below the Put Strike. The call spread options allow Noteholders to participate on the upside performance, capped at 40%, which is magnified by the Participation Rate of 180%'.[337]

The following graphic (taken from the *Trofi Group* website) shows the payoff profile (P&L diagram) of a Buffered Return Enhanced Note at maturity:

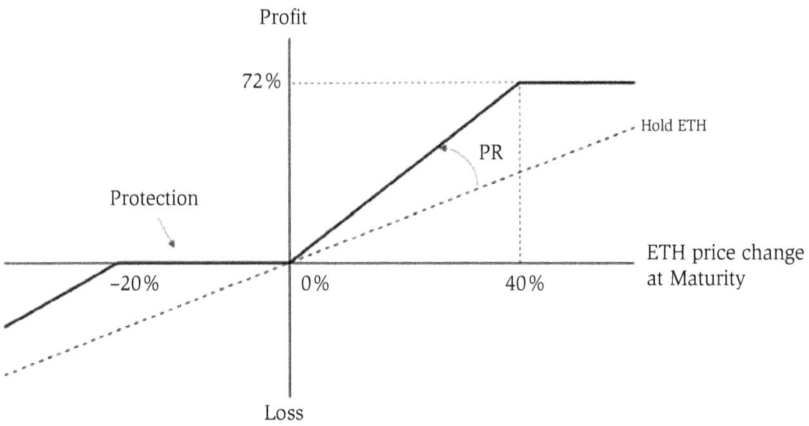

Source: Picture: *Trofi Group*.

The following scenarios may apply at maturity of the note:

Scenario 1:
'If ETH price is below USD 2400, [for example] USD 1800, the Noteholders receive back 75% of notional in USDT (i.e., 100% principal – the 25% downside performance of ETH from the Put Strike).'[338]

Scenario 2:
'If ETH price is above USD 2400 but below USD 3000, Noteholders receive back 100% of notional in USDT.'[339]

Scenario 3:
'If ETH price is equal to or above USD 3000, let's say USD 3900; Noteholders receive back 154% of notional in USDT (i.e., 100% principal + the 30% upside performance of ETH, multiplied by the Participation Rate of 1.8x)'.

336. *Ibid.*
337. *Ibid.*
338. *Ibid.*
339. *Ibid.*

> *Scenario 4:*
> 'If the ETH price is above USD 4200, the maximum redemption is capped at 172% of notional (i.e., 40% Cap × PR 1.8x)'.[340]

InvestDEFI does not only offer various cryptocurrency option strategies but also structured products that track the *investDEFI* volatility index or the *DEFI Blockchain Project Index tracker.*[341]

The demand for structured products is there because many institutional investors cannot or do not want to invest in cryptoassets directly.[342] Those products do not only include tailor-made structured products for large institutional clients, but some of them are even exchange-traded, such as *Exchange-Traded Notes* (ETNs).[343]

Another structured product is called 'Sharkfin', which is named after the graph of the payoff profile of the product and provides investors returns if the market goes moderately up in Bitcoin.[344] An example of this structured product is discussed in the below example, which is taken from the blog *Yield App.*

> *Example 74:*
>
> The 'Sharkfin' structured product achieves the highest returns 'when the price of the underlying asset appreciates but does not exceed a predetermined upper level. [...] if the price falls below the current level or rises above the predetermined upper level, the product still pays a guaranteed minimum coupon (i.e., annual interest)'.[345]
>
> However, 'if the price rises above the predetermined level, the investor receives the principal investment back in' USD Coin (USDC), and additionally the minimum coupon.[346]
>
> *YieldApp* states that '[i]f the price falls below the buy level, the investment and the guaranteed coupon get converted to the underlying asset (e.g., Bitcoin) at the

340. *Ibid.*
341. 'InvestDEFY Equal Weight DeFi Index seeks to replicate the top 10 smart contract enabled proof-of-stake (PoS) blockchains which power DeFi and the top 10 DeFi Projects built with blockchain technology. The index constituents are equal weighted, determined through a scoring methodology that factors in market cap and liquidity to arrive at 50% DEFI blockchains and 50% DeFi projects. The index will be rebalanced monthly', *see* investDEFI, Driving the Evolution of Crypto investing, https://www.investdefy.com, accessed 29 August 2023; Jugita Lapienyte, InvestDEFY launches Equal Weighted Metaverse + Web 3.0 NFT index for investors, cybernews, https://cybernews.com/news/investdefy-launches-equal-weighted-metaverse-web-3-0-nft-index-for-investors/, accessed 1 October 2023.
342. Cryptoresearch, Structured Products for Digital Assets (3 March 2021) https://cryptoresearch.report/crypto-research/structured-products-for-digital-assets/, accessed 29 August 2029.
343. *Ibid.*
344. Yield App, An introduction to crypto structured products: Variable risk return profiles.
345. *Ibid.*
346. *Ibid.*

buy level. As such, the downside of this product is that if prices fall, the investor is obliged to buy the underlying asset at a higher-than-market price'.[347]

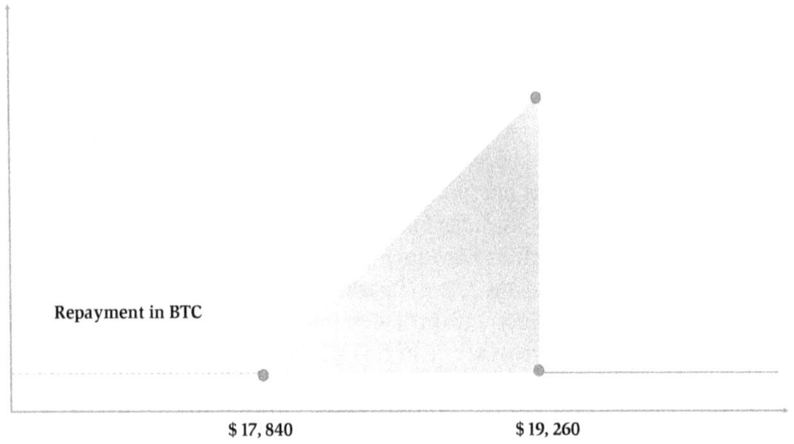

Source: Picture: Yield App.

The market of exchange-traded crypto structured products is, in particular, flourishing in Germany. For example, *Boerse Stuttgart* offers those *ETN*s which mirror the price movements of Bitcoin and Ethereum.[348] *Eurex* has even issued futures on ETNs backed by Bitcoins.[349] *Boerse Frankfurt* has listed an *ETC Group* Physical Bitcoin, which is an exchange-traded fund (ETF) with more than EUR 500 million assets under management.[350] Although it is not a structured product but an ETF, it proves that the demand for cryptoasset investment products is there.

Risk.net explains that:

> The original crypto structured products were housed in so-called DeFi options vaults (DOVs). Users deposit crypto anonymously into the DOVs – whether that be stablecoins like tether or USDC or assets such as Ethereum (ETH) or Bitcoin – and

347. *Ibid.*
348. Boerse Stuttgart, Using ETNs to invest in Bitcoin, dollars, etc. https://www.boerse-stuttgart.de/en/products/etps/etns/, accessed 29 May 2023; Boerse Stuttgart, BTCetc Bitcoin Exchange Traded Crypto (BTCE), https://www.boerse-stuttgart.de/de-de/produkte/etps/etns/stuttgart/a27z30-btcetc-bitcoin-exchange-traded-crypto-btce, accessed 29 May 2023.
349. Deutsche Boerse Group, Eurex announces launch of Bitcoin ETN futures (20 August 2021) https://deutsche-boerse.com/dbg-en/media/press-releases/Eurex-announces-launch-of-Bitcoin-ETN-futures-2713576, accessed 30 May 2023.
350. Boerse Frankfurt, ETC Group Physical Bitcoin, https://www.boerse-frankfurt.de/en/etf/de000a27z304-etc-issuance-gmbh-0-000, accessed 29 May 2023.

> the DOVs go out and run an investment strategy on behalf of the investors. The original DOVs ran simple covered call or put selling strategies.[351]
>
> But since then, more sophisticated structured products have been issued. For example, *Ribbon Finance* launched a principal-protected product in August [2022], which earns yield from lending USDC deposits to market-makers such as Folkvang and Wintermute and uses a portion of the interest payments to buy weekly out-of-the-money barrier options at around 8% on the top and downside. It offers a base yield of 4% with the potential for yields of up to 13%, depending on whether the options finish in the money.[352]

Also, *Zerocap* launched its credit-rated crypto structured product, which is a *Principal Protected Note* (PPN), which 'gives predefined exposure to an underlying asset while protecting against negative performance'.[353] The structured product is a Bitcoin-linked PPN 'which allows investors to participate in the potential upside performance of BTC with 90% protection of their capital. The investor will participate in 60% of BTC's upside price appreciation above the Strike Level. The maximum loss for this investment is 10% of capital invested'.[354] *Zerocap* also offers *Autocallable Barrier Reverse Convertible Notes,* which 'earn monthly income on the back of BTC's price movements. The notes are autocallable because they will be redeemed early if BTC closes above autocall-level on an observation date'.[355]

Those product descriptions show that the crypto structured product market is using the classical structuring methods for structured products by combining a debt instrument with sophisticated crypto options strategies.

[B] Accounting of Crypto Structured Products

The accounting treatment of crypto structured products is far from settled. ISDA observes that 'another complexity in the existing accounting model exists where companies may be required to recognize a digital asset on the balance sheet and bifurcate an embedded derivative liability to return the digital asset'.[356] For example, with respect to crypto lending transactions, *PwC* states in relation to US GAAP:

> The borrower in a crypto lending arrangement may determine that it has obtained control of the asset and would accordingly recognize the crypto asset on its balance sheet. It would also recognize an obligation to return the crypto asset to the lender. While the asset may be accounted for under ASC 350 as an intangible, the obligation to return the asset could be viewed as a hybrid instrument with a

351. Lukas Becker, Risk.net, Crypto structured products come of age, (8 November 2022), https://www.risk.net/our-take/7955057/crypto-structured-products-come-of-age, accessed 29 May 2023.
352. *Ibid.*
353. Berkeley Cox, Zerocap, Introducing Crypto Structured Products with Investment Grade Credit Ratings (17 March 2023) https://zerocap.com/insights/articles/zerocap-partners-with-marex/, accessed 29 May 2023.
354. *Ibid.*
355. *Ibid.*
356. ISDA, Accounting for Digital Assets, Key considerations (May 2022) https://www.isda.org/a/88VgE/Accounting-for-Digital-Assets-Key-Considerations.pdf, accessed 20 May 2023, 13.

debt host contract and payments linked to the fair value of the crypto assets. Accordingly, the borrower may need to assess whether *bifurcation of the embedded feature* is required under ASC 815, *Derivatives and hedging*, with specific consideration given to whether the crypto assets could be net settled.[357]

The author believes that the IASB needs to refine the existing accounting standards for them to apply to crypto structured products in order to reflect the complexity of those products and the derivatives embedded in them.

Crypto structured products seem, by and large, to consist of a debt instrument and one or more embedded derivatives over cryptoassets. Thus, those crypto structured products will meet the definition of a structured product proposed in Chapter 8 §8.01, as they are legally inseparable linear combinations of at least two non-structured products, which consist of:

(1) at least one non-derivative, traditional financial instrument; and
(2) one or more derivatives.

For example, the 'Sharkfin', *Zerocap*'s 'Autocallable Barrier Reverse Convertible Notes' and *Trophy Group*'s 'Buffered Return Enhanced Note' all fall under the above definition of structured products.

Hence, the author proposes to apply the same accounting rules for bifurcation and integration as for traditional structured products. For example, under IFRS 9 or FRS 102, Section 12, crypto structured products should be integrated for accounting purposes and measured as one instrument at fair value through profit and loss instead of bifurcating them into a loan element. Under the current IFRS 9 accounting rules, issuers of those crypto structured products would have to bifurcate them into the loan element and the embedded derivatives. As the author has suggested in relation to traditional structured products, an integration for the issuer may be the answer to ensure that profits or losses of those structured products would be reflected in the accounts at the appropriate time.[358]

[C] Taxation of Crypto Structured Products

The author believes that crypto structured products should be taxed as one instrument for tax purposes in the hands of the holders of those instruments. If the accounting treatment applied an integrated approach for tax purposes, the tax treatment would simply follow the accounts to reflect a fair value accounting through profit or loss of the whole instrument.

357. PWC, Crypto assets, August 2021, 3-5, https://viewpoint.pwc.com/dt/us/en/pwc/accounting_guides/crypto-assets-guide/assets/crypto9202021.pdf, accessed 29 May 2023.
358. Ch. 8 §8.08[B][2].

[1] UK Taxation of Crypto Structured Products

From a UK tax perspective, the author believes that the rules of CTA 2009, ss 584 to 586, would not apply as any embedded derivatives would not have to be bifurcated for accounting purposes in the first place due to their crypto nature.

For issuers of those crypto structured products, it is likely that tax accounts would follow the financial accounts and bifurcate the instruments into the loan relationship, which is taxed under CTA 2009, Part 5, and into the embedded derivatives. It is, however, not certain how those embedded derivatives would be taxed as they would likely fall outside of the derivative contract regime of CTA 2009, Part 7. Rather, they may be taxed as intangible assets, in the same way as the underlying cryptoassets, under CTA 2009, Part 8, or under the loan relationship rules of CTA 2009, Part 5, although this seems more unlikely.

The author, therefore, proposes that it would be beneficial to amend the current taxation rules and ensure they also apply to crypto structured products. That could be achieved by either (1) integrating crypto derivatives in the existing derivative contracts regime, (2) amending CTA 2009, ss 584 to 586, or (3) prescribing that those crypto structured products are integrated and taxed as one financial instrument also for the issuer of those instruments.

From a tax policy perspective, the author believes that tax legislators have to decide (1) if they develop specific rules to deal with crypto structured products and preferably tax them as one financial instrument based on an accounting measurement at fair value through profit or loss for the holder, or (2) if those crypto structured products are taxed under existing loan relationship rules.

The author further proposes that tax treatment of crypto structured products as one instrument may de-incentivise taxpayers to use those instruments for tax structuring or arbitrage purposes, given the incongruent treatment of impairment losses relating to cryptoassets in the financial accounts.

[2] German Tax Treatment of Crypto Structured Products

Although crypto structured products are actively sold to investors in Germany, neither their accounting nor their tax treatment is settled.

The author believes that tax authorities would follow their accounting treatment, and if the company bifurcated those instruments in their accounts, the tax law would follow this treatment. If crypto structured products are bifurcated in the German GAAP accounts for the holder and the issuer, the loan would be taxed separately, and any losses arising on the embedded derivative instrument may be ring-fenced for tax purposes.

§8.10 ESG-LINKED STRUCTURED PRODUCTS

ESG-linked structured products are a relatively new phenomenon. They have seen exceptional growth in recent years as investors seek to invest in companies which are deemed to be ethical, using environmental, social and governance criteria to manage their business. In the United States, the first ESG-linked structured product was issued in 2018 by the Bank of America Merrill Lynch, the arranging bank for the so-called *Providus Collateralised Debt Obligation I*, managed by Permira Debt Managers.[359]

The first European Residential Mortgage Back Security was issued in 2016 under the name *Green Storm 2016*.[360] *Bloomberg* confirms that ESG-linked structured products issuance 'has surged in recent years, going from zero to around $10-15 billion, partly driven by investors looking to customize their exposure to ESG factors. This sharp increase reflects a wider trend: there were over $35 trillion ESG assets under administration in 2020, a number estimated by Bloomberg Intelligence to exceed $50 trillion by 2025'.[361]

As explained in Chapter 2 §2.01[D], ESG criteria are not free of doubt. Nonetheless, institutional investors are increasingly inclined to invest in companies with high ESG scores due to pressure from their shareholders but also other stakeholders, like, for example, non-governmental organisations (NGOs). In the same way, private investors who traditionally invest in ETFs but also in structured products increasingly ask banks and other financial institutions to provide financial products that not only provide a high investment return but also make the investor feel good by 'investing green'.

For example, *Bloomberg* discussed the trend towards ESG-linked structured products in a recent article, maintaining that:

> [w]hile the European Union's pledge to issue 225 billion euros in green bonds [...] the global race to net-zero emissions may accelerate the market share of the debt as an asset class. [...] BlackRock was the top holder of green bonds with $12.5 billion in assets as of June (doubling its position within the past six months), increasing its market share by 2.5% to 7.3%, followed by Vanguard (4.65%), Allianz (4.47%), Credit Agricole and Japan Pension Fund (both at 2.6%).[362]

[A] What Are ESG-Linked Structured Products?

As outlined in Chapter 8 §8.01, the author proposes to define structured products as:

> legally inseparable linear combinations of at least two non-structured products, which consist of
>
> (1) at least one non-derivative, traditional financial instrument; and
> (2) one or more derivatives.

359. PRI – Principles for Responsible Investments, ESG incorporation in securitised products: challenges ahead (May 2021) https://www.unpri.org/download?ac=13412, accessed 25 May 2023, 10.
360. *Ibid.*, 11.
361. Nitin Ananda, Bloomberg Professional Services, How to analyze, create, and risk-manage ESG-linked structured products (May 2022), https://www.bloomberg.com/professional/blog/how-to-analyze-create-and-risk-manage-esg-linked-structured-products/, accessed 1 October 2023.
362. Bloomberg Intelligence, Game on! ESG debt issuance passes $ 3 trillion with record speed, 21 June 2021, https://www.bloomberg.com/professional/blog/game-on-esg-debt-issuance-passes-3-trillion-with-record-speed/, accessed 26 August 2023.

Incorporating ESG elements in securitised products is, however, still in its infancy, the reason being their complex nature.[363] *Bloomberg* suggests that 'the market is showing demand for structured products that allow buyers to build specific exposure to ESG sectors while maintaining bespoke risk characteristics'.[364]

For example, European *ESG Collateralised Loan Obligations* 'have proliferated, while the green, social and sustainability-labelled issuance of other products is also developing. Investors are looking at how to build frameworks to assess ESG factors across all securitised products and to determine whether ESG-labelled securitised products are genuine'.[365]

There can be various assets underlying those ESG-linked structured products, such as residential and commercial mortgages or pools of corporate loans. Underlying assets of those *ESG-linked asset-backed securities* (ABS) can also be consumer products, such as car loans or credit card receivables.[366] 'Among popular ESG investments are notes that offer high coupons on condition that an underlying equity index breaks a certain level.'[367] Those products seem, however, more traditional 'barrier structured products', as can be seen in the example below.

Example 75:

based on Wappenschmidt in Bloomberg[368]

A standard autocallable note is linked to the MSCI World ESG Leaders Index. It pays a coupon if the underlying index passes an upside barrier, at which point it automatically matures, and the investor's principal is returned.

If the ESG index goes up by 10% in its first year, the note is redeemed early, and the investor can accrue a coupon of around 21%, while the investor is protected against any decline in the ESG index of less than 20% on a structured note priced at 100.

[B] Regulation

ESG-linked structured products face various challenges. ESG investments 'are only as sound as the data that feeds them. Without reliable and comparable data sets, investors

363. PRI – Principles for Responsible Investments, ESG incorporation in securitised products: challenges ahead (May 2021) https://www.unpri.org/fixed-income/esg-incorporation-in-securitised-products-the-challenges-ahead/7462.article, accessed 25 May 2023.
364. Luca Wappenschmidt, Bloomberg Professional Services, ESG structured products rise to meet investor demands, (29 May 2022), https://www.bloomberg.com/professional/blog/esg-structured-products-rise-to-meet-investor-demand/?bbgsum-page=DG-WS-PROF-BLOG-POST-137418&tactic-page=630365, accessed 25 May 2023.
365. PRI – Principles for Responsible Investments (2021).
366. *Ibid.*
367. Wappenschmidt (2022).
368. *Ibid.*

are sailing blind, vulnerable to greenwashing and dependent on divergent standards and anecdotal evidence to orientate their investments',[369] states *Bloomberg*.

On the other hand, fund managers may have difficulty explaining why they have made some investment decisions in light of increasing ESG awareness, which can easily lead to investor scrutiny.[370]

There is progress, however. 'More ESG-linked investment products are being released as the European Union supports sustainable investment activities, including a taxonomy of activities regulators will promote or punish.'[371]

The EU has issued various regulations and a Directive in the ESG space, namely the *Sustainable Finance Disclosures Regulation* (SFDR),[372] the *Corporate Sustainability Reporting Directive* (CSRD)[373] and the *Taxonomy Regulation*.[374] Those regulations and the CSRD 'tighten disclosure requirements and help standardize definitions of what constitutes green'.[375]

The EU also proposed the *Green Bond Standard*. That standard lays 'the foundation for a common framework of rules for issuers to use the designated *European Green Bond* for bonds where the use of proceeds is aligned with the EU Taxonomy Regulation'.[376] The Green Bond Standard was expected to reach a political agreement during the first half of 2023.[377]

In October 2023, the European Parliament and the Council adopted the new regulation.[378] In the UK, the Financial Conduct Authority (FCA) confirmed in 2022 that it is not currently proposing to develop a UK version of a green bond standard and expressed support for existing industry standards.[379]

Also, other areas of the globe, like, for example, the Asia Pacific, are working on their own taxonomies for ESG and climate-related investments. Until there is more clarity on what constitutes green finance, ESG-focused investors will still have to deal with greenwashing issues, however.

---

369. Ananda (2022).
370. *Ibid.*
371. Wappenschmidt (2022).
372. Regulation (EU) 2019/2088 of the European Parliament and of the Council of 27 November 2019 on sustainability-related disclosures in the financial services sector.
373. Directive 2022/2464/EU on corporate sustainability reporting; *compare also* Ananda (2022).
374. Regulation (EU) 2020/852 of the European Parliament and of the Council of 18 June 2020 on the establishment of a framework to facilitate sustainable investment and amending Regulation (EU) 2019/2088.
375. Ananda (2022)
376. Linklaters, ESG Legal Outlook 2023, 8.
377. *Ibid.*
378. Council of the EU, *European Green Bonds: Council adopts new regulation to promote sustainable finance, Press release,* 24 October 2023, https://www.consilium.europa.eu/en/press/press-releases/2023/10/24/european-green-bonds-council-adopts-new-regulation-to-promote-sustainable-finance/, accessed 1 December 2023. The Regulation is named: Regulation of the European Parliament and of the Council on European Green Bonds and optional disclosures for bonds marketed as environmentally sustainable and for sustainability-linked bonds, https://data.consilium.europa.eu/doc/document/PE-27-2023-INIT/en/pdf, accessed 31 December 2023.
379. Linklaters, ESG Legal Outlook 2023, 7.

[C] Categories of ESG-Linked Structured Products

There is a kaleidoscope of ESG-linked structured products, such as green asset-backed securities (ABS) bonds, green bonds, social bonds, sustainability-linked loans, green loans and sustainability-linked bonds.[380]

In the realm of ESG-linked structured products, there are ESG Collateralised Loan Obligations (CLOs), ESG-linked securitised products, such as residential or commercial mortgage back securities, other ESG-linked asset-backed securities, bonds with some ESG factor, and structured products that package carbon credits.

One can put those instruments broadly into three buckets: (i) products which are securities to pass on some ESG and other risks; (ii) dedicated structured products which include, among other components, some ESG element; and (iii) carbon-credit structured products.

Within the third subcategory, one can expect increasing investor demand due to the introduction of the 2022 ISDA Verified Carbon Credit Transaction Definitions (2022 ISDA VCC Definitions).[381] The 2022 ISDA VCC Definitions 'are in the form of a standard definitional booklet for physically settled secondary market Verified Carbon Credit (VCC) transactions and are accompanied by template confirmations for VCC spot, forward and option transactions'.[382]

The world of carbon credits, carbon allowances and carbon offsets has fast become a world of its own. Whereas a carbon allowance is the amount of greenhouse gas emissions 'a company has the legal right to emit'[383], a carbon credit is 'a unit of measurement for those emissions'.[384]

Carbon credits are, in this respect, 'a financial market-based instrument which is used to put a price tag on a specific amount of carbon emissions (usually one metric ton of carbon dioxide emissions or its equivalent (tCO2e)) and trade it at a secondary market'.[385]

Carbon credits could be potentially viewed as some form of commodity, and investors and manufacturers may not only use ESG derivatives but also specifically tailored carbon credit-linked structured products to hedge their exposure to rising costs of their carbon allowances, mirrored by an increase in the price of carbon credits. How stable the carbon credit market is remains to be seen. Similar to cryptoassets, the author predicts a certain volatility of the VCC market if large carbon offset projects collapse. This can be demonstrated by the recent difficulties faced by one of the world's

380. Bloomberg Intelligence (2021).
381. ISDA, 2022 ISDA Verified Carbon Credit Transaction Definitions, https://www.isda.org/book/2022-isda-verified-carbon-credit-transaction-definitions/, accessed 28 May 2023.
382. Leanne Banfield, Linklaters, Derivatives and Structured Products Legal Outlook 2023, https://www.linklaters.com/en/insights/publications/legal-outlook/2023/derivatives-and-structured-products, accessed 28 December 2023.
383. EcoCart, What are Carbon Credits? Carbon Credits v Carbon Offsets, 29 December 2022, https://ecocart.io/what-are-carbon-credits-carbon-credits-vs-carbon-offsets/, accessed 5 September 2023.
384. *Ibid.*
385. EcoCart, What are Carbon Credits? Carbon Credits v Carbon Offsets.

biggest carbon offset projects in Africa, which 'raises new doubt about carbon market's ability to backstop failures'.[386]

Hence, due to the volatility of carbon credits, the accounting treatment of impairment losses on carbon credits may soon become a topic of importance. For accounting purposes, carbon credits are likely to be seen as intangible assets; see below.

In the context of other ESG-linked structured products, '[s]ustainable notes and repackagings remain a key mechanism for providing investors with sustainable investments in a familiar format. As well as green or blue bonds being repackaged and sustainable payouts being included, sustainable commodities can be used to create a green product'.[387]

Banfield suggests that also in 2023, 'green regulatory capital transactions/ synthetic securitisations'[388] and ESG CLOs will enjoy popularity, 'with the market focusing on how ESG can be integrated into these products ahead of the development of a specific sustainable securitisation framework, and investors in them seeking assistance from arrangers in meeting their regulatory disclosure obligations'.[389] *Banfield* regards green structured products firmly established in the market with an increased focus on the social factor, for example, 'significant interest in social financing structures designed to facilitate financing into a developing country',[390] which can be in note or loan form, 'often backed by insurance or a guarantee given by a World Bank entity'.[391]

The ESG market keeps growing, although there has been some slowing during the global pandemic, as *Banfield* observed.[392] *Linklaters* see a trend to more sophistication and diversity in the product categories, stating that 'overall issuance levels of green, social and sustainable bonds and other labelled bonds such as blue bonds, transition bonds and sustainability-linked bonds were more muted in 2022 as compared to previous years, those that did proceed demonstrated an increasingly sophisticated and nuanced product'.[393] For example, in 2022, the World Bank issued the first of its kind 'conservation bond', called the 'Rhino Bond'.[394]

386. Ben Elgin and Natasha White, Carbon Offset Market Faces Chaos as African Mega Project Collapses, Bloomberg, 27 October 2023, https://www.bloomberg.com/news/articles/2023-10-27/shaky-zimbabwe-project-puts-whole-carbon-market-at-risk?leadSource=uverify%20wall, accessed 28 October 2023.
387. Banfield (2023).
388. *Ibid.*
389. *Ibid.*
390. *Ibid.*
391. *Ibid.*
392. *Ibid.*
393. Linklaters, ESG Legal Outlook 2023, 7, https://lpscdn.linklaters.com/-/media/digital-marketing-image-library/files/01_insights/publications/legal-outlook/2023/linklaters_esg-legal-outlook-2023.ashx?rev=bbb9e054-d57b-4cc7-aaf1-565cf9a2b9cc&extension=pdf&hash=B0956C799EF9661F42F6463E880EA5F9, accessed 28 August 2023.
394. Linklaters, ESG Legal Outlook 2023, 8.

[D] Accounting of ESG-Linked Structured Products

[1] IFRS S1 and S2

In 2021, the 'IFRS Foundation formally announced the creation of the International Sustainability Standards Board (ISSB) which acts in parallel to the IASB under the IFRS Foundation.'[395]

IFRS S1 concerns the 'General Requirements for Disclosure of Sustainability-related Financial Information',[396] and IFRS S2 deals with 'Climate-related Disclosures'.[397]

Although the ISSB tentatively decided the effective date for IFRS S1 and S2 to be 1 January 2024,[398] the individual jurisdictions will decide if they want to apply them.[399] Earlier application is allowed, but only if both standards are applied.[400]

Some companies may choose to adopt those standards voluntarily, thereby responding to investor and/or societal pressure.[401] The introduction will not take full effect immediately as the ISSB will 'provide various reliefs in the first year of adopting IFRS Sustainability Disclosure Standards – for example [...] allowing entities to not disclose Scope 3 GHG[402] emissions'.[403]

Eccles and Mirchandani outline that:

> the ISSB will provide a 'global baseline' for high-quality sustainability reporting that will support the work being done in the US by the Securities and Exchange Commission (SEC) and the European Union (EU)'s Corporate Sustainability Reporting Directive ('CSRD'). The ISSB is focused on 'single materiality' or the ESG information that drives valuation and matters to investors. This is also the focus of the SEC, so the mandates are consistent. In contrast, the CSRD has a broader 'double materiality' mandate, which means it will cover information of interest to stakeholders even if it is not of interest to investors. Linking the two is the concept of 'dynamic materiality' – ESG issues that investors don't care about today can

395. KPMG, IFRS announce new ESG reporting standard, 2021 https://kpmg.com/dp/en/home/insights/2021/10/ifrs-announce-new-esg-reporting-standard.html, accessed 27 May 2023.
396. ISSB, IFRS S1 *General Requirements for Disclosure of Sustainability-related Financial Information*.
397. ISSB, IFRS S2, *Climate-related Disclosures*. For more details, *see* Ch. 5 §5.07.
398. PWC, Latest News from the Standardsetters and Regulators.
399. KPMG, Get ready for global sustainability standards.
400. PWC, Latest News from the Standardsetters and Regulators.
401. KPMG, Get ready for global sustainability standards.
402. 'The Corporate Value Chain (Scope 3) Accounting and Reporting Standard allows companies to assess their entire value chain emissions impact and identify where to focus reduction activities.' *See* Greenhouse Gas Protocol, Corporate Value Chain (Scope 3) https://ghgprotocol.org/corporate-value-chain-scope-3-standard, accessed 27 May 2023. The Corporate Value Chain Accounting and Reporting Standard can be found at: Greenhouse Gas Protocol, Corporate Value Chain (Scope 3) Accounting and Reporting Standard, https://ghgprotocol.org/sites/default/files/standards/Corporate-Value-Chain-Accounting-Reporing-Standard_041613_2.pdf, accessed 27 May 2023.
403. PWC, Latest News from the Standard setters and Regulators.

> become ones they care about in the future. The most striking current example is climate change.[404]

Eccles and Mirchandani state that the ideal outcome would be standards that are focused on investor needs.[405] *KPMG* suggests that IFRS S1 and S2 'aim to create a global baseline for investor-focused sustainability reporting that local jurisdictions can adopt or build into their own local requirements'.[406]

Some domestic accounting standard setters have started developing accounting standards for ESG-related investments. For example, the Australian Accounting Standards Board released a consultation paper in December 2022 'that seeks initial views on proposals to introduce standardised, internationally aligned legislative requirements for disclosure of climate-related financial risks and opportunities from financial years 2024-25 in Australia'.[407]

[2] Accounting Treatment of ESG-Linked CLOs and ABS and Other ESG-Linked Securitised Products

The author proposes that the accounting treatment of those ESG-linked structured products will follow the accounting treatment of the main instrument. For example, if there is an ESG-linked CLO, those CLOs will be accounted for as normal CLOs. The same applies to ESG-linked ABS or similar products.

Deloitte states in relation to sustainability-linked debt instruments with cash flows linked to environmental factors that the main question is:

> if the arrangement contains an embedded derivative that must be accounted for separately on the basis of the applicable accounting guidance. In many instances, this assessment depends on whether the variability linked to the environmental factors includes economic risks that are not clearly and closely related to the debt instrument itself.

If a company determines that a sustainability-linked debt instrument includes an embedded derivative, such a derivative must be accounted for separately at fair value both at the inception of the arrangement and for the life of the arrangement. The determination of the fair value of environmental-factor-related embedded derivatives involves complexity and often requires the involvement of valuation specialists.[408]

Thus, with respect to many ESG-linked structured products, it means that their accounting mainly follows the accounting treatment of other, more common structured products, although the fair value determination of the ESG element bears some difficulties.

---

404. Robert G. Eccles and Bhakti Mirchandani, We Need Universal ESG Accounting Standards, Harvard Business Review.
405. *Ibid.*
406. KPMG, Get ready for global sustainability standards.
407. *Ibid.*
408. Deloitte, Accounting and financial implications of ESG initiatives, https://www2.deloitte.com/us/en/pages/audit/articles/hu-accounting-reporting-esg.html, accessed 27 May 2023.

[3] Accounting of Structured Products Based on Carbon Credits

The following subsection focuses on the purchase of *exchange-traded carbon credits* only. It outlines the challenges that are likely to arise if companies need to account for carbon credits, which are embedded in a structured product.

There is no IFRS guidance in relation to the accounting treatment of purchased carbon credits.[409] If carbon credits are purchased with the intention of selling them in the ordinary course of the business, it is likely that the carbon credit is treated as *Inventory* under IFRS 2. If a carbon credit is held for use, i.e., to offset a company's own emissions, *KPMG* suggests that carbon credits may be accounted for as intangible assets under IAS 38.[410] In this case, they can have, according to their type, a finite or an infinite lifetime.[411]

If companies choose to account for carbon credits classified as intangible assets at historical cost instead of using the revaluation method, this potentially allows the recognition of impairment losses under IFRS if the carbon credits are subject to impairment due to falling prices, while any subsequent price increase may not be recorded in the financial accounts. Thus, the accounting treatment of carbon credits is similar to that of cryptoassets under IFRS.

If those carbon credits are embedded in structured products, one needs to consider if those structured products would have to be bifurcated in a loan element and the embedded carbon credit or an embedded derivative.

For the holder of those structured products with embedded carbon credits or embedded derivatives replicating carbon credits, the author believes that they should be accounted for as one instrument and measured at fair value through profit or loss. That allows one to mirror fluctuations in the value of the embedded carbon credit in a timely manner and avoids an accounting distortion due to potential disparity in writing down the carbon credits in case of an impairment loss without a corresponding write-up in case of a value increase of those carbon credits.

For the issuer of the structured product, the situation is more complex. If IFRS 9 or FRS 102, Section 12 is applied, those instruments are likely to be bifurcated for the issuer of the structured product. That means if the embedded instrument is a *derivative replicating carbon credits* (i.e., with carbon credits as underlyings), those structured products are likely to be bifurcated into a debt instrument and the embedded derivative under IFRS 9 or FRS 102, Section 12 in the financial accounts of the issuer.

---

409. KPMG, What might a company that purchases carbon credits voluntarily need to consider? (12 July 2023), https://kpmg.com/xx/en/home/insights/2023/07/climatechange-ias2-voluntary-carbon-credits.html, accessed 1 October 2023.
410. *Ibid.*; *also* KPMG, Carbon offsets and credits under IFRS® Accounting Standards (March 2023) https://kpmg.com/us/en/articles/2023/carbon-offsets-credits-ifrs-accounting-standards.html, accessed 2 October 2023.
411. Deloitte, Accounting and Reporting Considerations for Environmental Credits (updated May 2023), https://dart.deloitte.com/USDART/home/publications/deloitte/accounting-spotlight/2022/environmental-credits, accessed 1 October 2023.

In cases where the carbon credits are embedded, the author believes that a bifurcation in the accounts of the issuer is also indicated in the same way as in the case of embedded carbon credit derivatives.

Again, standard setters may consider overhauling their existing rules and allowing for an integration of structured products with embedded carbon credits or carbon credit derivatives for the issuer.

[4] Outlook

The author believes that the accounting of ESG-linked structured products will rapidly develop and that standard setters, like the ISSB, will further define accounting standards for those products within the next few years due to the need for investors to disclose, classify and measure ESG risks entailed in ESG-linked structured products as well as ESG derivatives.

[E] Taxation of ESG-Linked Structured Products

In relation to ESG-linked structured products, tax authorities urgently need to determine how those instruments are taxed. The author believes that one needs to distinguish between ESG-linked structured products which contain some abstract ESG element or goal and those which have embedded carbon credits or derivatives over carbon credits.

[1] UK Tax Treatment of ESG-Linked Structured Products

[a] Tax Treatment of ESG-Linked CLOs and ABSs and Related Structured Products

The author proposes that for this category of ESG-linked structured products, the existing taxation of CTA 2009, ss 584-586, is sufficient to tax those instruments. The reason is that those structured products simply contain a factor in the pricing formula or marketing that relates to ESG. That means the underlying products are traditional products and should be taxed accordingly. The ESG factor may have been separately valued and measured and, in those cases, may be taxed separately.

The author proposes that the approach for those ESG-linked CLOs and ABS should be as follows:

(1) Determine the economic properties of the ESG-structured product. Is it an ABS, a CLO, a structured certificate or something else?
(2) Determine what accounting standard the company holding or issuing the structured products uses (FRS 102, Section 11 or Section 12, IFRS 9 or IAS 39).
(3) According to the used accounting standard, determine if the structured product is bifurcated or integrated for accounting purposes according to the

applicable traditional rules. In particular, determine if the ESG element constitutes some embedded derivative or not.

(4) The taxation rules of CTA 2009, sections 585 or 586, are applied depending on whether the host contract is an underlying loan relationship or another contract - neither being loan relationships nor hybrid derivatives with an embedded derivative according to CTA 2009, section 586.

[b] Tax Treatment of Structured Products with Embedded Carbon Credits or Carbon Credit Derivatives

Challenges are likely to arise if structured products are taxed following their accounting treatment under IFRS 9 or FRS 102, Section 12 without consideration of the tax consequences. As explained above, there is no IFRS guidance as to how to account for carbon credits. It is likely that for accounting purposes, carbon credits are treated as either qualifying as inventory under IFRS 2 (if purchased with the intention of reselling them) or as intangible assets under IFRS 38 (if purchased as long-term investments to offset the entity's own carbon footprint obligations).

If, for example, carbon credits are seen as intangible assets which are accounted for and subsequently measured at cost with no amortisation as they are regarded as having an infinite lifetime, taxpayers may be inclined to recognise impairment losses if the carbon credit prices drop while maintaining the intangible assets at the lower historical cost value when carbon credit prices rise. In a way, the tax treatment would be very similar to the tax treatment of impairment losses on cryptoassets.

Such disparate taxation treatment may lead to opportunities for tax deferral and tax arbitrage in the context of structured products with embedded carbon credits.

If the ESG element of the structured product is bifurcated from the debt element for accounting purposes, this may indeed allow taxpayers to use impairment losses recognised on the embedded carbon credits to offset against profits from other income sources until the structured product either matures or is sold.

The same would apply if a carbon credit structured product consists of a loan relationship and embedded carbon credit derivatives. While the loan relationship would be taxed under CTA 2009, Part 4, the embedded derivative would likely fall under the intangible assets rules of CTA 2009, Part 8 and not under the derivative contracts rules of Part 7. Thus, CTA 2009, ss. 584-586 would not apply.

Again, for accounting purposes, the author proposes to account for ESG-linked structured products that have some form of carbon credit embedded as a single instrument - both for the holder and for the issuer. That would also allow for the taxing of those instruments in a timely manner under the existing loan relationship rules of CTA 2009, Part 5. That would, however, require the accounting standard setters to prescribe the accounting for those instruments in that way. Meanwhile, the author proposes that the UK tax legislator introduce rules that prescribe structured products with embedded carbon credits to be treated as one instrument for accounting purposes - both for the holder and the issuer of those instruments.

By doing so, neither holders nor issuers of structured products with embedded carbon credits can utilise carbon credits or associated derivatives to create favourable post-tax outcomes by utilising impairment losses.

[2] German Tax Treatment of ESG-Linked Structured Products

The author believes that tax authorities would apply the same approach to ESG-linked structured products and crypto structured products. Thus, under German GAAP, those instruments may be bifurcated if they contain embedded carbon credit derivatives or carbon credits. If that is the case, tax law would follow this accounting treatment. Any losses relating to embedded carbon credit derivatives may be ring-fenced, whereas losses from embedded carbon credits should be taxed without any ring-fencing restriction.

[3] Outlook

As a preliminary conclusion based on the above, the author proposes that it is decisive to determine for taxation purposes the exact economic properties and nature of the specific structured product and then tax the ESG-linked structured products according to the rules of the respective instrument category. Tax legislators should incorporate detailed tax legislation swiftly to deal not only with the underlying carbon credits but also with related structured products.

CHAPTER 9

Derivatives in a Cross-Border Context: Beneficial Ownership and Withholding Taxes

A lack of transparency results in distrust and a deep sense of insecurity.

— Dalai Lama

In the following chapter, the author will expand on the specific problems of derivatives in a cross-border context. For that purpose, the author will analyse the UK and German tax legislation on withholding taxes in relation to derivatives. Further, the author will discuss how the term 'beneficial owner' has been interpreted at an international level. In particular, the author will highlight the problems in interpreting the term in the context of derivatives transactions and discuss examples of recent court decisions in Spain and a series of cases in Switzerland.

In the 'solutions' section of Chapter 9, the author will analyse how legislators could deal with withholding taxes on derivatives and the problem of transfer of beneficial ownership in the cases where derivatives are used to transfer the risks and rewards of assets or income streams to a party that is not the legal owner of the assets or the beneficiary of the income.

Cryptoassets challenge the traditional concept of beneficial ownership due to their intangible nature and the instant peer-to-peer transfer between owners within the virtual world.[1] An analysis of the jurisdictional and ownership problems would be a work in its own right and, thus, cannot be discussed in the context of this publication.

The topic of cross-border problems arising in the context of hybrid instruments will be analysed in Chapter 10.[2]

1. Gemma Lardner et al., Demystifying jurisdiction and ownership of crypto assets, IFLR 2023, https://www.iflr.com/article/2c5v0ti3bg7v249x1yneo/demystifying-jurisdiction-and-ownership-of-crypto-assets, accessed 18 October 2023.
2. *See* Ch. 10 §10.01[E].

§9.01 WITHHOLDING TAXES ON DERIVATIVES IN THE UK AND GERMANY

In the following section, the author will outline and evaluate the application of withholding taxes on derivatives income received by companies in the UK and Germany.

[A] Withholding Taxes on Derivatives in the UK

A company is not required to withhold tax on payments made by it under any derivative contract if that contract falls within the derivative contracts regime of CTA 2009, Part 7.[3]

> *Example 76:*
>
> Company A enters into a single stock future over UK shares, which is traded on a UK stock exchange. As the future is a relevant contract that satisfies the accounting tests and its underlying is not an excluded subject matter, it will qualify as a derivative contract under CTA 2009, Part 7. Thus, it will be explicitly excluded from the withholding tax regimes under ITA 2007, section 980(1).

Payments on derivatives that fall outside the regime of Part 7 might be caught by other withholding tax provisions.[4] ITA 2007, Part 15 applies to both individuals and companies[5] and provides rules for withholding taxes on annual interest,[6] annual payments,[7] manufactured payments and payments to non-resident landlords.[8] However, in many cases, withholding taxes will not be levied, as the payments under these contracts may not fit under the definitions of ITA 2007, Part 15.

> *Example 77:*
>
> Company A enters into an interest rate swap with Company B. The contract falls outside CTA 2009, Part 7, for example, because the accounting tests under CTA

3. ITA 2007, s. 980(1) and (2). *See* Ghosh, Johnson and Miller (2022), [E2.541] (issue 28); HMRC, CFM13608.
4. Ghosh, Johnson and Miller (2022), [E.2.543].
5. HMRC, *Proposed changes to tax rules on manufactured payments, Consultation document* (27 March 2012), https://assets.publishing.service.gov.uk/government/uploads/system/uploads/attachment_data/file/179263/manufactured_payments.pdf.pdf, accessed 29 May 2023, stating that: 'The new rules will apply to manufactured payments that are representative of dividends or interest paid on or after 1 January 2014.' HMRC, CFM50080 states that 'the principles also apply where – exceptionally – a swap held by a company is not within Part 7 CTA09'.
6. ITA 2007, s. 874.
7. Types of payments are, for example, life annuity payments and royalties (ITA 2009, s. 899); *see* ITA 2007, Part 15, Ch. 6.
8. ITA 2007, Part 15, Ch. 9.

2009, section 579 are not satisfied. The swap would not be subject to the withholding tax rules on interest, as these payments would not qualify as yearly interest within the meaning of ITA 2007, section 874(1). Payments under interest rate swaps are reciprocal obligations under swap contracts.[9] Thus, they would generally not constitute 'income received by the recipient', which would be an implicit condition for the qualification as annual payments.[10]

[B] Withholding Taxes on Derivatives in Germany

In the context of withholding taxes on investment income, German tax rules distinguish between resident companies and foreign corporate investors. Domestic companies, in principle, pay withholding taxes on investment income.[11] This withholding tax payment can, however, be credited against the corporate tax liability.[12] Any excess tax will be refunded.[13] With regard to certain investment income, such as income from foreign dividends,[14] received option premiums,[15] derivatives income,[16] and income from most structured products,[17] no withholding tax will be levied if the income is received by a domestic company.[18] No withholding tax is levied on capital gains received by companies from the sale of shares.[19]

Withholding tax is due, however, on income from convertible bonds[20] as well as on domestic dividends.[21]

Non-resident corporate investors are only liable to withholding tax on investment income if:

(1) the investor falls under the source taxation rules (limited tax liability) under section 49(1) ITA; and
(2) the payments are subject to the withholding tax regime under section 43ff ITA.[22]

9. Ghosh, Johnson and Miller (2022), [E.2.545]; *see* HMRC, CFM50080.
10. HMRC, CFM50080.
11. Sections 43(1), (4) and (5) sent. 2 ITA, 8(1) CTA.
12. Sections 36(2) No. 2 ITA. *See* Conlon & Aquilino: Derivatives D2.04[2][b]; Klaus Lindberg, '§ 43 EStG' in Bernd Heuermann and Peter Brandis (eds), *Blümich, EStG, KStG, GewStG, Kommentar* (120 edn, 2013) § 43, para. 127.
13. Section 36(4) sent. 2 ITA. *See* Conlon & Aquilino: Derivatives D2.04[2][b]; Ronald Ettlich, '§ 36 EStG' in Bernd Heuermann and Peter Brandis (eds), *Blümich, EStG, KStG GewStG Kommentar* (120 edn, 2013) § 36, para. 246.
14. Sections 43(2) sent. 3 No. 1, 43(1) No. 6 ITA.
15. Section 43(1) No. 8, 20(1) No. 11 ITA.
16. Section 43(1) No 11 ITA.
17. Section 43(1) No. 10 ITA.
18. Section 43(2) sent. 3 No. 1 ITA.
19. Sections 43(2) sent. 3 No. 1, 43(1) No. 9 ITA.
20. Section 43(1) No. 2 ITA.
21. Section 43(1) No. 1 ITA.
22. Conlon & Aquilino: Derivatives D2.04[2][c].

Derivatives, like options, swaps, forwards and futures entered into by foreign investors with German counterparties, as well as received option premiums, will typically not be subject to withholding taxes as they generally do not fall under the catalogue provided in the source taxation rules of section 49(1) ITA.[23]

Although payments would principally be subject to withholding taxes if the derivative contract is entered into by a permanent establishment (PE) of a company and held in the PE's business assets,[24] section 43(2) sentence 3 No. 2 ITA provides for an exemption from withholding taxes on derivatives payments and certain other investment income if the PE confirms that this income is attributed to the PE's business and applies on an official form for an exemption from withholding tax.

With regard to derivatives income and income from option premiums received by foreign companies, which is not attributed to a PE, no withholding tax is levied as the income does not fall within the catalogue of the source taxation rules of section 49(1) ITA.[25]

Income from convertible bonds that are issued by a German resident debtor will, however, be subject to withholding tax for foreign corporate investors.[26] Likewise, income from certain structured debt products, which entail a partial or full capital guarantee, is subject to withholding tax for foreign investors if certain narrow conditions are met.[27] For these instruments, the deduction of withholding tax entirely satisfies the limited tax liability of the foreign investor.[28]

Although no full tax credit on this kind of investment income received by non-resident companies is granted,[29] Germany provides a partial refund of two-fifths of the paid withholding tax,[30] leaving the foreign company with a total tax liability of 15% (which equals the corporate tax liability of a domestic company).[31] Furthermore, a full or partial tax credit may be granted at the level of the tax treaty if the treaty excludes or limits Germany's right to tax that income.[32]

[C] Withholding Tax Rules in the UK and Germany Applying to Dividend Swaps and Equity Swaps

[1] The UK Dividend Withholding Tax Regime

In the UK, no withholding taxes apply to derivative contracts within the derivative contracts regime of CTA 2009, Part 7.

23. Thomas Wiesenbart, 'Internationale Steuerfragen bei derivativen Finanzinstrumenten' Recht der Finanzinstrumente (2011) 106, 112-114; *also* Conlon & Aquilino: Derivatives D2.04[2][c].
24. Section 49(1) No. 2a) ITA.
25. Wiesenbart (2011), 113-114.
26. Sections 49(1) No. 5 a), 43(1) No. 2 ITA. *See* Conlon & Aquilino: Derivatives D2.04[2][c].
27. *Ibid.*, D2.04[2][c]. *See* sections 49(1) No. 5d), 43(10), 20(2) sent. 1 No. 7, 20(1) No. 7 ITA.
28. Section 32(1) No. 2 CTA. *Compare* Dietmar Gosch (ed) *Körperschaftsteuergesetz* (2 edn, 2009) § 32, paras 12 and 20-21.
29. Conlon & Aquilino: Derivatives D2.04[2][c].
30. Sections 44a(9) sent. 1, 36(4) sent. 2 ITA.
31. Otto Jacobs, Dieter Endres and Christoph Spengel (eds), *Internationale Unternehmensbesteuerung* (7th edn, 2011) 271.
32. Conlon & Aquilino: Derivatives D2.04[2][c].

With regard to manufactured overseas dividends (MODs),[33] which may have arisen in the context of dividend swaps, equity swaps or total return swaps, the *old rules* were complex, and UK payers of MODs were subject to withholding tax,[34] subject to various exceptions. In the case of MODs paid by a foreign payer to a UK resident, the UK resident recipient was subject to a 'reverse charge', again subject to various exceptions.[35]

New legislation was introduced by the Finance Act 2013, Schedule 29, in order to simplify the taxation of manufactured payments.[36] The manufactured payment rules of CTA 2010, Part 17A, apply to manufactured dividends as well as to manufactured overseas dividends.[37]

The taxation of the manufactured payments is based on the following principles:

(1) In principle, no withholding tax is levied on dividends paid by UK companies unless the distribution is made by a real estate investment trust (REIT) out of tax-exempt rental profits.[38]
(2) Manufactured dividends in respect of UK shares are treated the same way as real dividends, and thus, they are generally not subject to withholding taxes.[39]
(3) In respect of manufactured overseas dividends, the amended legislation denies any entitlement to double taxation relief,[40] as MOD payments will generally not be subject to withholding tax and thus do not provide entitlement to a tax credit.[41]

In the author's view, by abolishing all tax credits for MODs while at the same time simplifying the manufactured dividend rules, the UK government has adopted a pragmatic approach towards dividend withholding taxes, which is based on the understanding that only a complete abolition of tax credits for dividends and MODs will significantly reduce tax avoidance schemes in that area.[42]

---

33. *Compare* former ITA 2007, s. 581(1), omitted by FA 2013, Sch. 29, Part 3, s. 18(a): A MOD is a manufactured dividend, which is paid by a UK resident or foreign payer, and which is an amount 'representative of overseas dividends on overseas securities'.
34. Former CTA 2010, ss 792 and 793 referred to ITA 2007, s. 922 – now omitted by FA 2013, Sch. 29, Part 3, ss 43 and 25.
35. Former CTA 2010, s. 794 referring to ITA 2007, s. 923 – now omitted by FA 2013, Sch. 29, Part 3, ss 43 and 25.
36. FA 2013, Sch. 29. *See also* HMRC, *Corporation tax and income tax: changes to rules for manufactured payments* (2012) https://www.gov.uk/government/uploads/system/uploads/attachment_data/file/179263/manufactured_payments.pdf.pdf, accessed 13 January 2023.
37. HMRC, CFM74430.
38. In the case of distribution by REITs, a 20% withholding tax applies subject to relief under a tax treaty. *Compare* Deloitte, International Tax, United Kingdom Highlights (2012) 2.
39. CTA 2010, Part 17A, s. 814D(2) with exceptions in s. 814D(4)-(8). As an important exception, manufactured dividends received by a financial trader will be taxable as trade receipts, and when paid by a financial trader, tax deductible. *Compare also* HMRC, CFM74440, 'Manufactured Dividends'.
40. HMRC, *Corporation tax and income tax: changes to rules for manufactured payments* (2012).
41. CTA 2010, s. 814D(5) and (7); HMRC, CFM74450.
42. *See* solutions, Ch. 9 §9.03[B].

[2] *The German Dividend Withholding Tax Regime*

Germany de facto exempts domestic business and corporate investors from withholding taxes as the withholding tax only constitutes a 'pre-payment' on the business or corporate income tax liability. It, however, applies withholding taxes on certain investment income received by foreign businesses and corporate investors.[43] In relation to dividends, this disparity between domestic and foreign investors led to a discrimination of the foreign investors under EU law.[44]

Dividends were 95% tax-exempt for corporate tax purposes for domestic investors, leading to a full refund of withholding taxes on dividends.[45] In contrast, foreign corporate investors did not receive a full refund but had to pay the reduced treaty rate of 15% in most cases.[46]

To abolish this discrimination, portfolio dividends received by domestic corporate investors are now subject to 15% corporate income tax. Any withholding tax paid can be offset against the corporate tax liability.[47] The same withholding tax applies to foreign corporate investors under the two-step approach described above.[48] The non-application of the source taxation rules to derivatives under German domestic and tax treaty law also includes dividend swaps, equity swaps, price swaps and total return swaps, no matter whether dividends or manufactured dividends are paid under these derivatives or are rolled up in the pricing.[49] This position led to tax avoidance schemes with gaps closed later with anti-avoidance legislation.[50]

§9.02 BENEFICIAL OWNERSHIP AND THE USE OF DERIVATIVES

Beneficial ownership has become a difficult concept when derivatives are part of more complex transactions that shift the economic 'essence' of assets, liabilities or income streams without a change of legal ownership in the asset, the liability or the income stream.[51] It is, in many cases, far from certain whether income should be attributed to the legal owner of the assets or the income or to the beneficial owner.

Thus, both in a domestic and a cross-border context, it is essential to establish ownership for tax purposes in order to determine who is taxable in relation to income, gains and losses.

---

43. *See* Ch. 9 §9.01[B].
44. C-284/09 *Commission v. Germany*.
45. Sections 31(1) CTA and 36(2) No. 2 and (4) sent. 2 ITA.
46. Most German double tax treaties apply the 15% reduced treaty rate to 'portfolio dividends' as proposed under Art. 10(2) sent. 1, 2nd part, lit b) OECD Model. *See* Vogel and Lehner (2008) Art. 10 OECD-MA, para. 67.
47. For an evaluation of the dividend withholding tax paid by foreign investors and the same rate of corporate tax paid by domestic investors, *see* Ch. 9 §9.03 below.
48. *See* Ch. 9 §9.01[B].
49. In relation to dividend swaps: Vogel and Lehner (2008) Art. 10 OECD-MA, para. 188. In relation to equity swaps under the US/Germany treaty: Uwe Woywode, 'Die abkommensrechtliche Einordnung von Einkünften aus Swapverträgen' IStR 2006 368, 368-371.
50. Those schemes will not be discussed as they would go beyond the scope of this work.
51. *See* Ch. 3 §3.06[C].

[A] The Domestic Beneficial Ownership Concept in Relation to Derivatives

Common law countries and civil law countries have different concepts of beneficial ownership.[52] Common law countries would normally regard a person as the 'beneficial owner' if that person enjoys the economic benefits and at the same time bears the economic burden of the asset.[53] In a very technical sense, the term 'beneficial owner' would exclude, among others, a legal owner who is a trustee for another person.[54]

In contrast, civil law countries tend to have a more legalistic concept of ownership and look at the legal form rather than the economic substance.[55] The following section outlines and compares the domestic concepts of beneficial ownership in the UK and Germany.

[B] The UK Domestic Concept of Beneficial Ownership

HMRC defines beneficial ownership as 'the sole and unfettered right to use, enjoy or dispose of the asset or income in question'.[56] In *J Sainsbury plc v. O'Connor*,[57] the question arose whether equity options could deprive the owner of the beneficial ownership in the shares.

> *Example 78:*
>
> Sainsbury held 75% of the shares in a joint venture with a Belgian company that owned 25% of the shares. At the same time, the Belgium company entered into a collateral agreement under which the Belgium company had an option to purchase a further 5% of shares from Sainsbury, which was, however, not exercisable for an initial period of five years. The options were never exercised. Sainsbury wanted to claim group relief for losses of the joint venture company under ICTA 1970, section 258, which required a 75% (beneficial) ownership of

52. Baker (2012) 10B-13; Christoph Busin and Matthias Erik Vock, 'Abkommensberechtigung von ausländischen Holdingesellschaften' [2002] Der Schweizer Treuhänder 6-7/02 624, 627ff.; Kilius, 'The Concept of "Beneficial Ownership" of Items of Income under German Tax Treaties' (1989) Intertax 340ff. DOI: 10.54648/taxi1989068; Vogel and Lehner (2008), Vor Art. 10 bis 12, paras 13-18.
53. The distinction between legal ownership and beneficial ownership under UK law draws upon a distinction between legal and equitable ownership in English law. *See* HMRC, *Inheritance Tax Manual*, IHTM04441.
54. Baker (2012) 10B-13.
55. For the civil law concept of beneficial ownership, for example: Hoge Raad (Dutch Supreme Court), No. 28 638 of 4 April 1994, BNB 1994/217, cited in Du Toit, Beneficial Ownership of Royalties in Bilateral Treaties, 151ff.
56. HMRC, *International Manual*, INTM332010.
57. *J Sainsbury plc v. O'Connor (Inspector of Taxes)* [1991] STC 318.

shares in order to qualify for group relief of losses. As Sainsbury retained nearly all rights of ownership until a possible exercise of the option, the Court of Appeal held that Sainsbury was the beneficial owner of the shares until a possible exercise of the options. Consequently, the court granted group relief.[58]

In the author's view, the Sainsbury case shows that the grant of options should not shift ownership of the underlying assets as it is uncertain whether the options will ever be exercised or not. For the question of beneficial ownership in tax law, options are different from an unconditional contract for sale.[59]

However, in cases where it is economically certain that the option would be exercised, for example, in the case of very deep in-the-money options, one would have to consider whether these options would de facto deprive the holder of the shares of all ownership rights or not.

[C] The German Domestic Concept of Economic Ownership

As a general principle, *economic ownership*[60] follows the legal ownership of the asset according to section 39(1) General Tax Act (GTA). As an exception to the general rule, section 39(2) No. 1 GTA determines that the asset is, in certain circumstances, attributed to the *economic owner* instead of the legal owner.

The economic owner is defined as the person who can exercise factual control over the asset in such a way that they can exclude the legal owner from any economic influence over the asset for the expected useful life of the asset.[61] That is usually the case if the right of repossession of the legal owner has no economic content or the right of repossession does not exist by law.[62]

Example 79:

Economic ownership can be assumed if an asset is leased to a leaseholder and the lessor is excluded from any influence on the asset during the lease. In contrast, a rental agreement will not lead to the assumption of economic ownership under domestic law.[63]

58. *Ibid.*
59. HMRC, CTM06030.
60. In German domestic tax law, the concept of 'wirtschaftliches Eigentum' is best translated by the term 'economic ownership'.
61. Section 39(2) No. 1 sent. 1 GTA.
62. BFH, decision of 12 September 1991, III R 233/90, BStBl II 1992, 182.
63. Michael Bartsch, 'Gabler Wirtschaftslexikon, Stichwort: wirtschaftlichen Eigentum' (Gabler Verlag) http://wirtschaftslexikon.gabler.de/Archiv/8693/wirtschaftliches-eigentum-v9.html, accessed 5 August 2023.

With regard to certain derivatives and repo transactions, the IDW has issued a draft statement that discusses questions of the transfer of economic ownership and profit realisation under German GAAP.[64]

As the views on economic ownership in the draft guideline may lead to adverse tax consequences in the form of profit realisation due to the 'authoritative principle'[65] of German GAAP, the IDW has simply decided not to finalise the guidelines but to keep them as a draft.[66] In these draft guidelines, the term 'economic ownership' is described for accounting purposes as including the risks and rewards of the asset, the right to use and the right to dispose of the asset.[67]

With regard to total return swaps (TRS), the draft guidelines suggest that the mere disposal of an asset while keeping the economic risks and rewards and the income of the asset by entering into a TRS will not lead to a transfer of economic ownership of the asset upon disposal of the asset but only upon maturity of the TRS.[68]

In contrast, if the seller of the asset not only sells it but also enters into a short put option with the buyer (the buyer having a long put option and the right to sell back the asset for a certain price), economic ownership will in principle not remain with the seller of the asset but will be transferred to the buyer of the asset.[69]

Correspondingly, a plain vanilla long call option of the seller of the asset will not hinder the transfer of legal and economic ownership to the buyer.[70] However, if the seller holds a long call option and the buyer a long put option, economic ownership will not be transferred to the buyer of the asset if it is highly likely that either the call option or the put option will be exercised due to their terms.[71]

The IDW draft may serve as a guideline for accountants when drawing up financial accounts, but it will not be authoritative for tax purposes.[72] The concept of economic ownership under section 39(2) No. 1 GTA is somewhat narrower than the concept of beneficial ownership. According to the decisions of the Federal Fiscal Court, a beneficial owner ('Nutzungsberechtigter'), whether the right is conferred by the law of obligations or in rem, does not necessarily have economic ownership of the asset as defined in section 39(2) No. 1 GTA.[73]

In the author's view, the term 'economic owner' in German tax law cannot be used interchangeably with the term 'beneficial owner' but has to be distinguished even if the differences in practice are only relevant in very few cases.

---

64. IDW, Entwurf einer Neufassung der IDW Stellungnahmen zur Rechnungslegung: Einzelfragen zum Übergang von wirtschaftlichem Eigentum und zur Gewinnrealisierung nach HGB, IDW ERS HFA 13 n.F. (29 November 2006), WPg Supplement 1/2007, 69ff.
65. *See* Ch. 6 §6.03[A].
66. IDW, Comment on IDW ERS HFA 13 n.F. (26/27 November 2009).
67. IDW (2006) paras 7-9.
68. *Ibid.*, paras 52-54.
69. *Ibid.*, paras 22-26. Exceptions will, however, apply, and economic ownership will not be transferred if the seller has agreed to buy back the assets at the same price as he has disposed of the asset because the seller then bears the risk of a decline of the asset price.
70. *Ibid.*, para. 27.
71. *Ibid.*, para. 30.
72. *Ibid.*, Introduction.
73. BFH, decision of 1 October 1997, X R 91/94, BStBl II 1998, 203; *also* BFH, decision of 19 December 2006, IX R 33/04, BFH/NV 2007, 1097.

[D] Interpretation of the Term 'Beneficial Owner' at the Tax Treaty Level

The following subsections will discuss how the concept of beneficial ownership is used in Articles 10, 11 and 12 of the OECD Model. It focuses on the recent amendments of the OECD Model Tax Convention as well as important Swiss cases that influenced the 2014 Update of the OECD Model.

[1] Interpretation of the Treaty Term 'Beneficial Owner' in UK Tax Law

The UK Court of Appeal in *Indofood v. JPMorgan Chase Bank N.A.* has moved from a purely domestic understanding of beneficial ownership[74] to the term having an 'international fiscal meaning' when interpreting double tax treaties.[75] The court's view is in line with *Baker*'s position 'that the term should be accorded an "international fiscal meaning" not derived from the laws of the Contracting States'.[76] Consequently, the Court of Appeal held that '[t]he concept of beneficial ownership is incompatible with that of the formal owner who does not have "the full privilege to directly benefit from the income"'.[77]

Based on the recent *Indofood* case, HMRC suggests:

> [W]here there is treaty abuse [...], interpreting 'beneficial ownership' in [...] its 'narrow technical' UK domestic law meaning would not give effect to the purpose and object of the DTC of preventing fiscal evasion, indeed it would be contrary to the object of the DTC to allow such treaty abuse. On the other hand, interpreting 'beneficial ownership' in what the Court of Appeal called its 'international fiscal meaning' clearly gives effect to the purpose and object of the DTC by excluding abusive cases such as 'treaty shopping' from the benefits of a DTC.[78]

As a result, beneficial ownership issues in cases involving UK double tax treaties will have to be interpreted not in light of UK domestic law, but the 'international meaning' of beneficial ownership has to be considered. The *Indofood* case shows that the UK courts increasingly rely on an international interpretation of terms used in the OECD Model and its Commentary rather than on domestic definitions.

---

74. Article 3(2) OECD Model allows applying the domestic meaning of terms in the interpretation of a double tax treaty if those terms are not defined in the OECD Model. *See* Baker (2012) Art. 3, 3C.13.1.
75. *Indofood v. JPMorgan Chase Bank N.A.* [2006] EWCA Civ 158, para. 42.
76. Baker (2012) Art. 10, 10B-14. In *Indofood*, the court has directly adopted the position of *Baker* in para. 42 of its decision.
77. *Indofood*, para. 42.
78. HMRC, INTM332050; Disagreeing with HMRC that the term 'beneficial owner' results in an anti-conduit rule: Ross Fraser and J.D.B. Oliver, 'Beneficial Ownership: HMRC's Draft Guidance on Interpretation of the Indofood Decision' (2007) BTR 39.

[2] *Interpretation of the Treaty Term 'Beneficial Owner' in German Tax Law*

The German term used in the OECD Model and in the German treaties for the term 'beneficial owner' is 'Nutzungsberechtigter', which could be translated literally with 'holder of rights of use' or 'entitled to use'.

Although it has been acknowledged by leading German legal commentaries that the term has a treaty meaning,[79] it has been suggested by *Wassermeyer*[80] in relation to dividends that the term 'beneficial owner' in the OECD Model has to be interpreted in the same way as the term 'shareholder' used in domestic law in section 20(5) ITA.[81] Thus, the German interpretation of the term 'beneficial owner' used in the German tax treaties still very much relies on comparable domestic definitions.[82]

Wassermeyer proposes that it is not decisive for the attribution of the dividend to the beneficial owner whether he is entitled to use the dividend, but whether he is entitled to use the shares, in particular, whether he has been attributed the membership rights, including the voting rights at the time of the resolution of appropriation of profits at the annual shareholders' meeting.[83] Hence, according to that interpretation, the beneficial owner is the person who holds the shareholder rights, who is not necessarily the person who receives the dividends or who is legally entitled to the dividends.

In contrast, *Vogel and Lehner* suggest that the beneficial owner is the person who is entitled to decide who uses either the asset *or* the fruits, i.e., the dividends. They explicitly maintain that the beneficial owner of the dividends does not have to be the same as the beneficial owner of the asset.[84]

[3] *Interpretation of the Treaty Term 'Beneficial Owner' by the OECD*

In the OECD Model, the term 'beneficial owner' is mentioned in relation to dividends, interest and royalties.[85] The OECD proposes that beneficial ownership has to be understood in the light of the OECD Model and, therefore, has not a domestic but an

79. Vogel and Lehner (2008) Vor Art. 10 bis 12, para. 15; Wassermeyer (2013) Art. 10 OECD-MA, para. 68.
80. The work by *Wassermeyer* is one of the two leading commentaries on double tax treaties in Germany. The editor and a couple of authors of the commentary are former or current judges of the Federal Fiscal Court or the lower tax courts. Thus, it particularly mirrors the predominant views of the German fiscal courts as well as the view taken by the German tax administration.
81. Wassermeyer (2013) Art. 10 OECD-MA, para. 68.
82. When interpreting the treaty, the domestic meaning of terms that are used in the OECD Model may only be used if the term has not been defined within the Model, *see* Art. 3(2) OECD Model. *See* Baker (2012) Art. 3, 3C.13.1.
83. Wassermeyer (2013) Art. 10 OECD-MA, paras 68-69.
84. Vogel and Lehner (2008) Vor Art. 10 bis 12, paras 16-18.
85. Articles 10(2), 11(4) and 12(3) OECD Model.

'international fiscal meaning'.[86] However, the term 'beneficial owner' is not comprehensively defined in the OECD Model.[87]

The Commentary to Article 10 OECD Model excludes intermediaries, such as 'nominees or agents, who are not treated as owners of income in their country of residence',[88] and any other conduit, which holds formal ownership but has very narrow powers in relation to the income concerned, thus being 'a mere fiduciary or administrator acting on account of the interested parties'.[89]

The OECD suggests that in determining beneficial ownership, it may be decisive who has the right to dispose or on-lend the asset and who has the risks and rewards with respect to the asset.[90] How exactly the term 'beneficial owner' is to be interpreted in a treaty context has been left unclear.[91]

The OECD issued a public discussion draft in 2011 ('2011 OECD Discussion Draft') in order to clarify the term 'beneficial owner' used in Articles 10, 11 and 12 of the OECD Model.[92] In the context of Article 10, the *2011 OECD Discussion Draft* suggested that:

> [t]he recipient of a dividend is the 'beneficial owner' of that dividend where he has the full right to use and enjoy the dividend unconstrained by a contractual or legal obligation to pass the payment received to another person. Such an obligation will normally derive from relevant legal documents but may also be found to exist on the basis of facts and circumstances showing that, in substance, the recipient clearly does not have the full right to use and enjoy the dividend.[93]

The term 'beneficial owner' is further opened up by this discussion draft by stating that '[t]he fact that the recipient of a dividend is considered to be the beneficial owner of that dividend does not mean, however, that the limitation of tax provided for by paragraph 2 must automatically be granted. The limitation of tax should not be granted in cases of abuse of this provision'.[94]

In the author's view, the *2011 OECD Discussion Draft* has not clarified the term but rather introduced a wide meaning of the term 'beneficial owner'. The wide meaning of the term may also catch many common derivatives transactions of banks, such as equity swaps, bond swaps and total return swaps.

86. Baker (2012) Art. 10, 10B-14. Also compare the wordings in: OECD Model (2010), Commentary on Art. 10, para. 12. and OECD Model (2014), Commentary on Art. 10, para. 12.1.
87. Neither, Art. 10 OECD Model, nor the Commentary on Art. 10 OECD Model defines this term comprehensively. Although the 2014 Update of the OECD Model has clarified that the term has a wide meaning, no exact definition of the term can be found in the Model or the Commentary.
88. Baker (2012) Art. 10, 10B-10.4 describes in plain English the rather crude wording in OECD Model (2010), Commentary on Art. 10, para. 12.2, now to be found in OECD Model (2014), Commentary on Art. 10, para. 12.7.
89. OECD Model (2010) Commentary on Art. 10, para. 12.1 (last paragraph).
90. OECD (2001) para. 76.
91. Richard Collier, 'Clarity, Opacity and Beneficial Ownership' (2011) BTR 684, 685.
92. OECD, Clarification of the meaning of 'beneficial owner' in the OECD model tax convention, discussion draft (2011).
93. *Ibid.*, 4, amendment of para. 12.4 of the OECD Commentary.
94. *Ibid.*, amendment of para. 12.5.

Example 80:

Company A hedges its economic exposure against a portfolio of bonds with cash-settled total return swaps (TRSs) entered into with Bank B. Under the TRSs, Company A pays Bank B any increase in the value of the bonds and any interest received, and Company A receives from Bank B any decrease in the value of the bonds and LIBOR[95]-based interest payments.[96] By applying the description of the term 'beneficial owner' used in the *2011 OECD Discussion Draft*, Company A could be regarded as passing on the beneficial ownership of the bonds to Bank B under the TRSs, although the obligations under the swaps are independent of the ownership of the bonds.[97]

Because of the wide interpretation of the term 'beneficial owner', taxpayers and their advisers sharply criticised the *2011 OECD Discussion Draft*.[98] It was suggested that the OECD had established the beneficial ownership criterion as a 'tax-avoidance fall-back clause' for tax authorities to tackle cross-border transactions in cases where general tax-avoidance clauses would not apply.[99]

In light of the arguments of the banking industry and other stakeholders, the OECD issued revised proposals in 2012 ('2012 Revised Proposals'), which confirmed that the mere obligation to pass on the dividend received to another person would not deny beneficial ownership.[100] In the *2012 Revised Proposals*, the Commentary on Article 10, paragraph 12.4. reads as follows:

> In these various examples, [...] the recipient of the dividend is not the 'beneficial owner' because that recipient's right to use and enjoy the dividend is constrained by a contractual or legal obligation to pass on the payment received to another person. Such an obligation [...] may also be found to exist on the basis of facts and circumstances showing that, in substance, the recipient does not have the right to use and enjoy the dividend *unconstrained by a contractual or legal obligation to pass on the payment received to another person*. This type of obligation must be related to the payment received; it would therefore not include contractual or legal obligations unrelated to the payment received even if those obligations could effectively result in the recipient using the payment received to satisfy those

95. LIBOR has been replaced by the overnight rates SONIA and SFOR.
96. Hull (2006) 515.
97. Mark Herbert, 'HSBC: Comments on Discussion Draft – Clarification of the Meaning of "Beneficial Ownership" in the OECD Model Tax Convention' (2011), http://www.oecd.org/tax/treaties/47643872.pdf, accessed 30 January 2013.
98. Gavin Helmer, 'Beneficial Ownership: A Looming Disaster?' pwc, http://www.pwc.com/sg/en/tax/tax-issue20120730.jhtml, accessed 31 January 2023; Herbert (2011); Collier (2011) 701-702.
99. Helmer (2012). *More differentiated:* Collier (2011) 701, who suggested that the tax authorities may cite the proposed wording selectively in support of substance-based interpretation of the term 'beneficial owner'.
100. OECD, *OECD Model Tax Convention: Revised Proposals concerning the meaning of 'beneficial owner' in Articles 10, 11 and 12* (2012) http://www.oecd.org/ctp/treaties/Beneficialownership.pdf, paras 11-19, accessed 30 July 2023.

> obligations. Examples of such unrelated obligations are those unrelated obligations that the recipient may have as a debtor or as a party to financial transactions [...].[101]

Under the *2012 Revised Proposals*, paragraph 12.4, one would be able to argue that beneficial ownership is not passed in cases where a derivatives transaction was a hedge of an exposure arising out of a share purchase as the derivative contract would constitute a legal obligation that is unrelated to the dividends received, even if the dividends were passed on to the party of the derivative.

In the *2012 Revised Proposals*, the OECD dismissed the further argument of stakeholders that the criterion of beneficial ownership could be 'misused' by the tax authorities as an additional anti-abuse clause and confirmed that '[t]he Working Party, however, strongly disagreed with the view that a beneficial owner should be immune from the application of other anti-abuse rules, a view that would be inconsistent with the guidance already included in paragraphs 7 to 26.1 of the Commentary in Article 1'.[102]

Hence, it was concluded in the *2012 Revised Proposals* that the new paragraph 12.5. should not be modified apart from two clarifying changes.[103] In 2013, the stakeholder comments on the *2012 Revised Proposals* were considered by the OECD Committee on Fiscal Affairs, Working Party 1.[104]

The 2014 Update to the OECD Model Tax Convention contains further clarifications of the term 'beneficial owner' in the new Commentary to Article 10, paragraphs 12.1 and 12.4. to 12.6. It is not entirely clear whether the clarifications in the wording of paragraph 12.4. were intended to change the meaning of the paragraph or not.

Compared to the 2012 *Revised Proposals*, there have been particular changes in the 2014 Update relating to the Commentary to Article 10, paragraph 12.4. sentence 3, namely:

> This type of obligation would *not include* contractual or legal *obligations that are not dependent on the receipt of the payment by the direct recipient*, such as an obligation that is not dependent on the receipt of the payment and which the direct recipient has as [...] a party to financial transactions.[105]

In the author's view, the meaning of paragraph 12.4, sentence 3 may have changed significantly compared to the version in the *2012 Revised Proposals* as 'not dependent on the receipt' has a much narrower meaning than 'unrelated to the payment'. Hence, derivatives transactions, where dividends are received by one party and passed on under a swap agreement to the counterparty – like in the *Swiss Swaps* case[106] – would be caught under the new wording of paragraph 12.4, sentence 3.

---

101. *Ibid.*, E, para. 12.4. of the Commentary on Art. 10 (2012 Revised proposals). Emphasis added.
102. *Ibid.*, F, para. 20.
103. *Ibid.*, F, para. 23.
104. *See* OECD, *2014 Update to the OECD Model Tax Convention* (OECD Publishing), Executive Summary, 2.
105. *Ibid.*, 13.
106. *See* Ch. 9 §9.02[B][2][a] below.

Under a standard TRS documented under ISDA, not the expected dividends are passed on but the dividend amounts that were actually paid out to the shareholders after the dividends were declared.[107] If the dividends that are paid out are different from what were the reasonable expectations of both parties when entering into the TRS, the short party of the TRS will have to pay the realised, not the expected dividends. Thus, for a TRS documented under standard ISDA terms, the obligations of the short party of the TRS (holder of the shares who passes on the dividend) will be dependent on the receipt of the actual dividend.

Under the version of sentence 3 in the *2012 Revised Proposals*, one could still argue that the swaps were unrelated to the shareholding and receiving the dividends if the transaction was considered a hedge.

In contrast, under the 2014 Update to Article 10, paragraph 12.4, sentence 3, the conclusion of a TRS agreement, under which the exposure of a shareholding and the dividends are passed to a swap counterparty, may lead to a transfer of beneficial ownership of the dividends as the *obligations* of the short party under a standard TRS *are dependent* on the receipt of the dividends by the direct recipient. Hence, in the author's view, the OECD has de facto introduced an 'economic ownership test' by changing the wording of sentence 3.[108]

Before the 2014 Update of the OECD Model, domestic tax authorities were concerned that a narrow interpretation of the term 'beneficial owner' may foster tax arbitrage schemes as derivatives can be easily used to transfer the economic risks and rewards of an asset or liability.

> *Example 81:*
>
> Company A wants to pass legal ownership of bonds to Bank B but wants to retain economic exposure to the bonds. Thus, it sells the bonds to Bank B and, at the same time, enters into a TRS over the bonds with Bank B. Company A may have entered into the transaction because Bank B does not have to suffer withholding tax on the coupons as Bank B is resident in the country where the bonds were issued. In contrast, Company A is non-resident in that country and would have suffered withholding tax on the coupons. As a result of the transaction, Bank B will receive the bond coupons free of withholding tax and will pass on this benefit partly to Company A. At the same time, the TRS enables Company A to retain the economic risks and rewards of the bonds.

The 2014 Update of the OECD Model and its Commentary provides tax authorities with a justification to apply a wide definition of the term 'beneficial owner' and use the wide interpretation of the term as a means to counter tax arbitrage transactions that are designed to avoid withholding taxes on interest or dividends.

107. *See* Ch. 9 §9.03[A] below.
108. *See also* the stakeholder comments on the 'economic ownership test' contained in: OECD (2012a), Revised Proposals, para. 16.

[E] Broad Versus Narrow Interpretation of the Treaty Term 'Beneficial Owner' by the Courts

In the UK, the courts have not decided cases on dividend withholding tax transactions in a tax treaty context that use derivatives to transfer or maintain beneficial ownership of the shares.[109] Only in the context of so-called broken repo transactions that were entered by UK companies or banks and US counterparties with the aim to achieve a UK tax credit for manufactured dividends, the topic of beneficial ownership of the shares and the dividends under the US/UK tax treaty arose.[110] The explanation is simple. The UK does not levy withholding tax on dividends paid by UK companies unless the distribution is made by a real estate investment trust (REIT) out of tax-exempt rental profits.[111]

There is also no specific German case law dealing with the transfer of beneficial ownership to a third party in the context of cross-border hedged derivatives transactions.

In Spain and Switzerland, the courts have decided on cross-border transactions that concern the question of whether beneficial ownership is transferred in hedged derivatives transactions or not. In those cases, derivatives were used to hedge market risk in the shares and to pass the economic exposure in the shares and the dividends to the derivatives counterparty.

In both countries, the courts interpreted the term 'beneficial owner' differently. These cases will be discussed below in detail as they were landmark cases for the interpretation of beneficial ownership in the context of hedged derivatives transactions where the parties aimed to transfer some dividend withholding tax benefit from one derivative party to the other. The author, therefore, solely focuses on the decisions below, which all concern the question of beneficial ownership in relation to dividends in the context of derivative transactions.

[1] The Spanish Cases

In two Spanish cases,[112] a Spanish resident company bought from Goldman Sachs 'special dividend shares' that were issued by Royal Bank of Scotland (RBS):

> The RBS shares granted the shareholder the right to receive a predetermined flow of dividends between the date of subscription – July 2002 – and December 2003. After one British Pound per share had been paid to the shareholder in December 2003, the shares would be withdrawn from the stock exchange and cancelled. At

109. *HMRC v. DCC Holdings (UK) Limited* [2010] UKSC 58, [2011] STC 326 deals with manufactured dividends in the context of repo transactions, but concerns domestic law, not tax treaty law.
110. Yaron Reich, 'International Arbitrage Transactions Involving Creditable Taxes' (2007) Taxes – The Tax Magazine 53, 60; Lee Sheppard, 'New Analysis: Banks' Foreign Tax Credit Arbitrage' (2006) Tax Notes International 193, 194ff.
111. In the case of distribution by REITs, a 20% withholding tax applies subject to relief under a tax treaty. *Compare* Deloitte, International Tax, United Kingdom Highlights (2012) 2.
112. *Goldman Sachs case I* Audiencia Nacional of 25 November 2010, rec no. 389/2007; *Goldman Sachs case II* Audiencia Nacional of 23 February 2012, rec no. 182/2009.

> the date of the purchase of the shares, the Spanish resident company entered into a set of swap and forward transactions with Goldman Sachs under which Goldman Sachs would repurchase the shares before November 2003 and although the dividends were paid to the Spanish resident company, this company had the contractual obligation to repay the amounts received to Goldman Sachs.[113]

As a result of the envisaged transaction, the Spanish company would have received dividends that were subject to 35% Spanish tax but would claim a 17.5% tax credit on the dividends received, thus reducing the corporate tax liability on the dividends to 17.5%.

Further, the Spanish company would receive a corporate tax reduction for the gross dividend paid to Goldman Sachs under the swap that it could offset against other corporate income, thus allowing the Spanish company to receive 50% tax-free income on one side but have a full tax deduction on the other side.

In this case, the court decided that the Spanish resident company was not the beneficial owner of the dividends, as the dividends were transferred to Goldman Sachs under the swap a day after they were received by the Spanish resident company.[114]

The Spanish court denied the Spanish company the 50% reduction in Spanish tax for holding EU shares under domestic law because it did not regard the Spanish company as 'the real and effective owner of the dividends received'[115] as it had to pass the dividends on to Goldman Sachs under the swap.

The Spanish court interpreted the term 'beneficial owner' very broadly. Hence, it could deny the Spanish 50% tax credit on the dividends. It regarded the swap transaction as a contract that stripped the holder of the shares and the receiver of the dividends of its ownership rights with respect to the dividends and transferred beneficial ownership to Goldman Sachs, although the swap was a separate contract from (1) the purchase contract of the shares, and (2) the forward contract which allowed the Spanish company to sell the shares back to Goldman Sachs after the dividend was received.

[2] The Swiss Cases

In 2012 two cases, the Swiss Federal Administrative Court decided on the treaty interpretation of the term 'beneficial owner' in the case of dividends received from Swiss shares by a Danish bank or a Danish company, where the shares were hedged

113. Adolfo Martin Jimenez, Beneficial Ownership as an Attribution-of-Income Rule in Spain: Source and Residence Country Perspectives in: Beneficial Ownership: Recent Trends (IBFD 2013) Ch. 14, 199, 202. The author of this work thanks *Adolfo Martin Jimenez* for providing his written commentary of the *Goldman Sachs cases* before publication. The summary of the case provided above is an almost literal citation of the text that was written by Adolfo Martin Jimenez.
114. Jimenez (2013) 203.
115. *Ibid.*, 203.

with total return swaps[116] or with SMI futures.[117] Those decisions were later overturned by the Swiss Federal Supreme Court.

The Swiss beneficial ownership cases are discussed in detail below as they had an influence on the development of the beneficial ownership concept of the OECD in the 2014 Update of the OECD Model and its Commentary.[118]

[a] *The Swiss Swaps Case*[119]

[i] The Decision of the Lower Swiss Federal Administrative Court

In the *Swiss Swaps* case,[120] a Danish bank ('Danish Bank')[121] entered into total return swaps (TRSs) over Swiss equities with various counterparty banks from the UK, the US, France and Germany.[122] At the same time, the Danish Bank purchased Swiss shares traded on the Swiss stock exchange to hedge the swaps.[123]

Under the swaps, the Danish Bank (being the short TRS party)[124] would pay any appreciation in the value of the shares to its counterparties and receive any depreciation in the value of the shares.[125] In addition, it would pay any dividends[126] that arise during the term of the swaps with respect to certain Swiss equities to the various counterparty banks (the long TRS parties).[127] The Danish Bank would receive a market interest rate, in this case, the London Interbank Offered Rate (LIBOR),[128] plus a margin.[129] The swaps had a minimum holding period of three months (average six

116. Swiss Federal Administrative Court (*Bundesverwaltungsgericht*) decision of 7 March 2012, A-6537/2010, reported in: Re Swiss Swaps Case, A-6537/2010, 14 ITLR 638ff.
117. Swiss Federal Administrative Court *(Bundesverwaltungsgericht)* decision of 23 July 2012, A-1246/2011 (*SMI Futures* case).
118. *Compare also* Editor's Note in: *A. SÀRL v. Federal Tax Administration* (beneficial ownership) Case 2C_209/2017, 22 ITLR 435, 436-437.
119. The following discussion – in the form of a more in-depth analysis of the case – was previously published in the journal *Intertax*: Oktavia Weidmann, 'Beneficial Ownership and Derivatives: An Analysis of the Decision of the Swiss Federal Supreme Court Concerning Total Return Swaps' (2016) 44(8&9) Intertax 620-641.
120. Re *Swiss Swaps* Case, *A-6537/2010 (2012) 14 ITLR 638*, 672ff.
121. *Ibid.*, paras H. and 6.2.4. and 7.2, referring to banking clients of the Danish Bank. *See also* Marcus Desax and Martin Busenhart, 'Swiss Tribunal Rules on Ownership and Treaty Abuse Issues Regarding Total Return Swaps' (2012) Tax Notes International 557.
122. Re *Swiss Swaps* Case, *A-6537/2010 (2012) 14 ITLR 638*, 672ff, para. K.
123. *Ibid.*, para. 5.1. *See also* Desax & Busenhart (2012) 557.
124. The Danish Bank is the short party to the TRS, as it has to pay the dividends and upside in the share price and it is protected against any downside movements. Thus, it has assumed de facto a cash position by holding the shares and shorting the TRS.
125. *A-6537/2010 (2012) 14 ITLR 638*, 672ff, para. 6.1.
126. *Ibid.*, paras 6.1. and 6.2.1.
127. The counterparty banks were synthetically 'long' the shares under the TRSs.
128. The LIBOR rate paid to the short party represents the amount of interest that the short party will pay to a third-party lender for the cash it needs to purchase the underlying shares physically in order to be fully hedged. It is assumed here, that Danish Bank will be able to finance itself at LIBOR flat.
129. *A-6537/2010 (2012) 14 ITLR 638*, 693, para. 6.1.

months). Each swap was concluded over different equities traded on the Swiss stock exchange (the 'equity baskets').[130]

The Swiss shares hedging the swaps provided the Danish Bank with the dividends, which it then paid to the counterparty banks under the swaps. The purchase and sale of the shares were conducted in OTC transactions with an international broker, with the bank confirming that the parties of the swaps were not the same parties as the seller of the shares.[131]

Under Swiss law, a 35% withholding tax is levied at source on the dividends received from Swiss equities. The Danish Bank claimed a refund of the 35% withholding tax levied on the dividends under Article 26(2) of the Switzerland/Denmark Double Taxation Convention[132] as the treaty reduced the withholding tax rate to zero and allowed a reclaim of these withholding taxes.[133] No withholding tax was due on the payments under the swaps.[134]

The Swiss tax authorities denied the tax refund,[135] claiming that the shares were purchased systematically shortly before the dividend date and were sold after the dividend due dates with the aim of passing on the dividends under the swaps to unknown counterparties free of Swiss withholding tax.[136] They concluded that the Danish Bank was not the beneficial owner of the dividends because it had passed on the market risk to the counterparties of the swaps. The Swiss tax authorities also argued that the transactions should be regarded as treaty abuse[137] on the basis that the combined transactions were highly unusual in size and structure and only motivated by purely fiscal considerations.[138]

In their decision, the Swiss Federal Administrative Court applied a narrow interpretation of the term 'beneficial owner' and decided that the Danish Bank was the beneficial owner of the dividends because:

> [r]egardless of whether it received the dividends, the complainant was obliged to pay the counterparty the amounts equivalent to the dividends. At the same time,

130. *Ibid.*, para. 6.1.
It can be assumed that such a total return swap contract would encompass synthetic dividend payments in respect of most or all dividend-paying SMI shares over the annual dividend season which lasts from beginning of March to Mid-September (6 ½ months).
131. *A-6537/2010 (2012) 14 ITLR 638*, 677, para. K.
132. Abkommen der Schweizerischen Eidgenossenschaft und dem Königreich Dänemark zur Vermeidung der Doppelbesteuerung auf dem Gebiete der Steuern vom Einkommen und vom Vermögen (1973).
133. Article 26(2) in conjunction with Art. 10(1) Switzerland/Denmark Double Taxation Convention (1973).
Compare also A-6537/2010 (2012) 14 ITLR 638, 685, para. 3.1.
134. Desax & Busenhart (2012) at 557.
135. *A-6537/2010 (2012) 14 ITLR 638*, 693, paras F. and I.
136. *Ibid.*, para. I.
The Federal Administrative Court rejected this argument and regarded the time between the purchase and the disposal of the shares and the fiscal motive as irrelevant for determining who is the beneficial owner of the shares as the concept of beneficial ownership would not contain any subjective elements. *See A-6537/2010 (2012) 14 ITLR 638*, 693, paras 6.2.3. and 3.4.2.
137. No general anti-abuse clause was contained in the Switzerland /Denmark Double Taxation Convention of 1973.
138. *A-6537/2010 (2012) 14 ITLR 638*, 674, para. I.

> the complainant was free to decide, independently of the swap contracts, whether to buy the shares in question and to receive the corresponding dividends.[139]

On the second ground, the court decided that there was no treaty abuse.[140] With regard to this question, the court only questioned whether the Danish Bank had a seat in Denmark and engaged in genuine commercial activity. As this was the case, it did not investigate further the question of abuse as it deemed a general commercial activity of the Danish Bank sufficient to deny treaty abuse.[141] The court further considered whether there was a link between the purchase and the sale of the shares and the swap agreements. The court denied that link and assumed no interdependence of both transactions.[142]

In the author's view, the Federal Administrative Court's decision shows the general difficulties in applying the concept of beneficial ownership in transactions where derivatives are used to transfer all (or some) economic risks and rewards of the underlying asset to the derivatives counterparty.

From a legal perspective, the concept of beneficial ownership can be interpreted widely to encompass an anti-abuse element or narrowly by regarding the concept as distinct from any question of abuse of legal rights.[143] The Federal Administrative Court applied a narrow interpretation of the term 'beneficial owner' and decided not to interpret the term widely as a quasi-anti-avoidance measure, stating:

> Seen in its proper perspective, however, the concept of beneficial ownership is merely a condition of entitlement like, say, the concept of residence, rather than a singular abuse clause [...] Only once all the conditions of entitlement under a DTC are met (including beneficial ownership) does the question of potential abuse of the convention arise. This outcome accords with Federal Supreme Court practice, which draws a clear distinction between the concept of beneficial ownership and abuse of legal rights.[144]

[ii] The Decision of the Swiss Federal Supreme Court

In 2015, the Federal Supreme Court overturned the decision of the Federal Administrative Court and denied the Danish Bank the claim for a refund for withholding taxes paid in 2007 and 2008,[145] and referred the case back to the Federal Administrative Court in respect of the repayments of already refunded withholding taxes by the Danish Bank in relation to dividends received in 2006.[146]

---

139. *Ibid.*, para. 6.2.1.
140. *Ibid.*, para. 7.2.
141. *Ibid.*
142. *Ibid.*, paras 3.4.2 and 6.2.1.
143. *See* Klaus Vogel and Moris Lehner, *Doppelbesteuerungsabkommen, Kommentar* (6th ed. 2015) Vor Art. 10 bis 12, paras 17-19.
144. *A-6537/2010 (2012) 14 ITLR 638*, 690, para. 3.4.3.
145. *Swiss Federal Supreme Court (Bundesgericht)*, decision of 5 May 2015, 2C_364/2012 and 2C_377/2012, reported in: Re *Swiss Swaps* Case I/A, Case 2C_364/2012, 18 ITLR, 138ff:
146. Swiss Federal Supreme Court, 2C_364/2012 and 2C_377/2012, paras 8-8.7.

It is worth analysing in more detail the following questions, which were explicitly (or implicitly) dealt with in the *Swiss Swaps* case:

(1) Is the Beneficial Ownership Criterion Implicitly Contained in the Switzerland/Denmark Double Taxation Convention (1973)?

The 'beneficial ownership' criterion is not explicitly mentioned in the Switzerland/Denmark Double Taxation Convention (1973).[147] The Federal Supreme Court, however, maintains that the criterion of beneficial ownership applies to all double taxation conventions concluded by Switzerland, even if the specific treaty only refers to a '"payment" to a "person resident" in another state'.[148] It notes that the majority of Swiss legal writings support the argument of an implicit 'beneficial ownership' criterion in cases where the treaty does not explicitly contain such a condition. Thus, it concludes that the criterion is also implicitly contained in the Switzerland/Denmark Double Taxation Convention (1973).

The Federal Supreme Court suggests that the introduction of the 'beneficial ownership' criterion by the Protocol in 2009 confirms the understanding of Switzerland[149] to the Switzerland/Denmark Double Taxation Convention (1973)[150] that the fulfilment of the 'beneficial ownership' criterion was a prerequisite for the withholding tax repayment and assumes that the treaty was always based on this understanding and that the Protocol – by introducing the 'beneficial ownership' criterion – contains a mere 'clarification' to the treaty, following the 'concretisation' of the OECD Model in relation to the 'beneficial ownership' criterion.[151]

The Federal Supreme Court further concludes that the common understanding between Switzerland and Denmark is in line with what can be regarded as the (smallest) common denominator in the 'international sphere' in relation to the criterion of beneficial ownership, namely that it was accepted by the various states that it cannot be the purpose of a double tax treaty to allow those persons or companies to benefit from the treaty who have, for example, only a formal relationship to the country of residence.[152]

It concludes that a purely formalistic 'beneficial ownership' requirement would not be sufficient (as in the sense of a common law interpretation of beneficial ownership to exclude cases of nominees, trustees and agents). It suggests that it is also an international understanding that the 'beneficial ownership' criterion should be used to exclude those transactions from the benefit of the double tax treaty, which employ 'complex financial transactions' to obtain benefits under a certain double tax treaty.[153]

147. Switzerland/Denmark Double Taxation Convention (1973), Art. 10. *See also* Swiss Federal Supreme Court, 2C_364/2012 and 2C_377/2012, para. 4.1.
148. Swiss Federal Supreme Court, 2C_364/2012 and 2C_377/2012, para. 4.2, 2nd para.
149. Referring to a note of the Swiss 'Bundesrat' to the Protocol.
150. *Ibid.*, paras 4.1-4.4.
151. Swiss Federal Supreme Court, 2C_364/2012 and 2C_377/2012, para. 4.4.1.
152. *Ibid.*, para. 4.4.3.
153. *Ibid.*

It should be noted that the Switzerland/Denmark Double Taxation Convention (1973), which was concluded before the introduction of the 'beneficial ownership' criterion in the 1977 OECD Model, did not contain a reference to the 'beneficial owner' of the dividends. Only in August 2009, the Protocol to the Switzerland/Denmark Double Taxation Convention introduced the 'beneficial ownership' criterion explicitly. The reclaims for withholding taxes in the case only concern the years 2006, 2007 and 2008, which means they took place before the conclusion of the Protocol.[154] The court argues that the introduction of the 'beneficial ownership' criterion was a 'mere clarification' of the treaty but not a change or addition of a new criterion.[155]

If the term 'beneficial owner' has the important function of preventing treaty shopping, then one might regard the term 'beneficial owner' rather as an additional limitation of Article 10, not as a 'mere clarification' of the OECD Model.

Baker suggests that the 'beneficial ownership' criterion was introduced as a *limitation* of Article 10 of the OECD Model and is intended to *exclude*:

> (a) mere *nominees or agents*, who are not treated as owners of the income in their country of residence;
> (b) any other *conduit* which, though the formal owner of the income, has very narrow powers over the income, which renders the conduit as a mere fiduciary or administration of the income on behalf of the beneficial owner.[156]

The Swiss Federal Supreme Court rightfully suggests that it does not have to decide the academic debate whether the term 'beneficial owner' constitutes a 'mere clarification' or an additional limiting criterion only in relation to the Switzerland/Denmark Double Taxation Convention. It maintains that the relevant authorities in Switzerland and Denmark agreed that the implicit 'beneficial ownership' criterion constitutes a prerequisite for the reduction of dividend withholding taxes to zero in the source state.[157]

(2) Does the Court Follow a Narrow or Wide Beneficial Ownership Concept?

The Federal Supreme Court suggests that it would be unnecessary to investigate:

(a) in which relationship the criterion of beneficial ownership and the criterion of treaty abuse stand as instruments for the interpretation of a double tax treaty; and
(b) if and to what extent the criterion of beneficial ownership is designed to prevent treaty abuse.[158]

---

154. *Ibid.*, para. A.
155. *Ibid.*, paras 4.2-4.4.1.
156. Baker (2012), Art. 10, 10B-14.
The exclusion of nominees, agents and conduits is now explicitly mentioned in the Commentary to OECD Model (2014), *see* OECD Model (2014), Commentary on Art. 10, para. 12.4. 1st sent.
157. Swiss Federal Supreme Court, 2C_364/2012 and 2C_377/2012, para. 4.4 in conjunction with paras 4.4.1. and 4.4.2.
158. Swiss Federal Supreme Court, 2C_364/2012 and 2C_377/2012, para. 4.5.

The Supreme Court missed the opportunity to explicitly decide whether these cases should be interpreted applying a 'narrow beneficial ownership concept' or a 'wide beneficial ownership concept' that contains an anti-abuse element.[159] In the decision of the Swiss Federal Administrative Court, it was suggested that the domestic law contained a provision for domestic cases that denied the refund of dividend withholding taxes in cases of abuse of law.[160] The domestic abuse provision can, however, not be applied in treaty cases.[161]

(3) Does the Treaty Concept of Beneficial Ownership Involve Properties of Ownership and of Economic Control or of the Actually Exercised Powers?

The Swiss Federal Supreme Court suggests that the key element of beneficial ownership is the *power of disposition*.[162] It maintains that the German equivalent of the term 'beneficial owner'[163] is the term 'Nutzungsberechtigter',[164] and it contains both 'properties of ownership and control or of the actually exercised powers. [...] The German term emphasises that beneficial ownership is not to be understood in a narrow technical or legalistic sense but rather by taking into account also the economic circumstances'.[165]

The Swiss Federal Supreme Court follows this substance-over-form concept[166] and suggests that the term 'beneficial owner' should not be understood in a technical or legalistic sense but that the economic circumstances have to be taken into account.[167] This particularly concerns all restrictions of the entitlement [to the dividend].[168] Although an obligation limiting the full use [of the dividend] generally results from legal documents, it may also be based on facts or circumstances from which it appears that the recipient does not fully enjoy the full power of disposition and (full) beneficial ownership.[169]

The Swiss Federal Supreme Court maintains that a limitation of the entitlement can normally be derived from the legal documents, but the *restrictions of the entitlement can also result from the actual facts and circumstances* that show that the recipient of the dividend is not the beneficial owner.[170] This suggests that the Swiss Federal

159. *Ibid.*; a brief overview of the academic discussion can be found in: Vogel and Lehner (2015), 145, Vor Art. 10 bis 12, paras 17-18.
160. *A-6537/2010 (2012) 14 ITLR 638*, para. 2.2.
161. *Ibid.*, para. 2.3.
162. Swiss Federal Supreme Court, 2C_364/2012 and 2C_377/2012, para. 5.2.
163. *See* Weidmann (2016), at 173-174 and 322-324. The article also discusses the distinction between the German treaty term *Nutzungsberechtigter* (beneficial owner) and the German domestic law term *wirtschaftlicher Eigentümer* (economic owner).
164. *Nutzungsberechtigter* is the term used in the OECD Model and in all German-language treaties (Germany, Austria, Switzerland) for the English term 'beneficial owner'. This term could be literally translated as: 'holder of rights of use' or 'entitled to use'.
165. Swiss Federal Supreme Court, 2C_364/2012 and 2C_377/2012, para. 5.2.1, 2nd para.
166. Explicitly: Swiss Federal Supreme Court, 2C_364/2012 and 2C_377/2012, paras 5.2.2, 2nd paragraph and 5.2.5.
167. *Ibid.*, para. 5.2.1. 2nd paragraph.
168. *Ibid.*, 3rd paragraph.
169. *Ibid.*
170. Swiss Federal Supreme Court, 2C_364/2012 and 2C_377/2012, para. 5.2.1, 3rd para.

Supreme Court follows the interpretation that it is not necessary that a legal obligation exists that restricts the right to enjoy the dividend but that it may suffice that a restricting obligation is based on facts or circumstances which make it clear that the recipient has not the full power of disposition and beneficial ownership.[171]

(4) Is There an Interdependence between the Receipt of the Dividends (by the Danish Bank) and Passing on the Dividends to the Swap Counterparties under the Total Return Swaps?

The argument that there is an 'interdependence' between the receipt of the dividends and the passing on of the dividends under the TRSs is the core argument that leads to the Federal Supreme Court's decision that the Danish Bank is not the beneficial owner of the dividends.

The Federal Supreme Court refers to a definition of beneficial ownership that was presented by *Baumgartner*,[172] which assumes beneficial ownership:

> if the recipient of the relevant income is able not only to make very limited decisions but [...] is able to make at least certain decisions independently. This power of decision must be denied to a person if the person must pass on the earnings on the basis of contractual obligations entered into before the payment date or because of actual restrictions. The existence of an actual restriction can be assumed if both of the following characteristics have been cumulatively fulfilled: On the one hand, obtaining the income must depend on the obligation to pass on this income; on the other hand, the obligation to pass on the income must depend on this income being obtained.[173]

According to this view, an actual restriction can be assumed if there is an 'interdependence' between receiving the dividends and the obligation to pass on the dividends, namely:

(a) obtaining the income depends on the obligation to pass on the income; and
(b) the obligation to pass on the income depends on this income being obtained.[174]

The Federal Supreme Court further elaborates that the Federal Administrative Court does not only assume that an 'interdependence' is given if a (direct) legal

171. For a summary of this opinion, *see* Vogel and Lehner (2015), Vor Art. 10 bis 12, paras 17-19 who discuss this (opposing) view and refer to the decision of the Swiss Federal Administrative Court in the *Swiss Swaps* case as an example of this opinion. Vogel and Lehner give examples of factual restrictions of the power of disposition.
172. *Ibid.*, para. 5.2.2.
See Beat Baumgartner, *Das Konzept des beneficial owner im internationalen Steuerrecht der Schweiz: Unter besonderer Berücksichtigung der Weiterleitung von abkommensbegünstigten Dividenden- und Zinseinkünften*, PhD dissertation, Schriften zum Steuerrecht, vol. 21 (Schulthess Verlag 2010), 130ff.
173. Swiss Federal Supreme Court, 2C_364/2012 and 2C_377/2012, para. 5.2.2. 1st para.
174. *Ibid.*, citing *Baumgartner* at 130ff. and 150.

obligation to pass on the dividends exists but also in the case of a 'de facto obligation' to pass on the dividends.[175]

The court suggests that the recipient of the dividend was not entitled to claim the reduced treaty rate (as the beneficial owner of the dividends) if the distributed amount is not retained by the recipient of the dividend because the recipient is legally or economically obliged to pass on the dividends.[176] That was the case if the recipient in the resident state did not retain the income themselves but passed on the income to the party that is the real 'economic owner' resident outside of the resident state because of a contractual, company law or economic structure of the transactions.[177]

The court elaborates on two common examples where beneficial ownership is passed from the recipient of the dividend to the 'real beneficial owner', namely in cases of direct conduit companies passing on the income and in the case of the 'stepping stone (conduit)' structure'.[178] It suggests that the following rule has to be applied: the greater the (inter)dependence between the income and the obligation to pass it on, the weaker the beneficial ownership.[179]

Furthermore, the court reiterates the second dependence, according to which the passing on of the received dividend amounts must depend on these amounts actually being obtained.[180] The court suggests that this second dependence addresses the question of who has to bear the risks associated with the share transactions, in particular, the risk that the company resident in the source state does not distribute any dividends.[181]

According to the court, all other risk factors (specifically the credit risk and the share price risk) have to be examined to determine whether payments have to be made [under the swaps] even if no payments have been received.[182]

It is interesting to note that the Federal Supreme Court acknowledges that the Danish Bank 'was neither legally nor de facto obliged to hedge the swap agreements entered into by the acquisition of the respective shares'.[183] Nevertheless, the absence of such an obligation was immaterial for several reasons:[184]

First, it was important that the Danish Bank purchased the shares as a hedge simultaneously with the swaps and that they provided a hedge to the full extent.[185] The court suggests that the full, simultaneous and exceptionless hedge of the swaps with the underlying shares occurred in the immediate interest of the Danish Bank as it needed to ensure that it received the dividends and the share performance in order to pass it on to the swap counterparties.[186]

175. *Ibid.*, para. 5.2.2. 1st paragraph.
176. *Ibid.*, 2nd paragraph.
177. *Ibid.*
178. *Ibid.*, para. 5.2.3.
179. *Ibid.*, para. 5.2.4.
180. *Ibid.*, para. 5.3.
181. *Ibid.*
182. *Ibid.*
183. *Ibid.*, para. 6.3.
184. *Ibid.*
185. *Ibid.*, para. 6.3.1.
186. *Ibid.*, para. 6.3.2.

Second, the swap agreements not only required the purchase of the underlying shares by the Danish Bank, but they facilitated the share purchase as the *interest* and the margin paid under the swap allowed the Danish Bank to debt-finance the purchase of the shares.[187]

Although the court concluded that there was no legal or de facto obligation of the Danish Bank to purchase the shares, the debt-financed purchase of the shares was enabled by the contractual clauses and drafting of the swap agreements.[188] Considering the 'economic processes', the court concluded that a 'significant interdependence' existed between the financing of the shares (made possible due to the interest payments under the swaps) and the purchase of the shares.[189]

Third, the court concluded that the purchase of the shares (as a hedge) did not result in any significant risks for the Danish Bank due to the specific conditions of the swaps, meaning that the Danish Bank did not obtain any share price or dividend risk as those risks were transferred to the swap counterparties.[190] In particular, the court highlights that the swap counterparties bear the risk that the dividends are not paid at all.[191]

With respect to an 'obligation' to conclude the purchase of the shares as a hedge for the swaps, the court suggests that the swap contracts provided several compelling reasons for the Danish Bank to hedge itself comprehensively, simultaneously and without exception. The court concludes that without the interest payments under the swaps as a basis for the purchase of the shares and the transfer of the various risks to the swap counterparties, it was unlikely that the Danish Bank would have entered into the hedging transaction in the same manner.[192] Hence, the court assumes a 'dependence' of the purchase of the shares (respectively, the receipt of the payments obtained as a result thereof) on the swap agreements.[193]

If applying a narrow legal view of the transactions, one would have to acknowledge that the swap contracts did not oblige the Danish Bank to pass on the dividends from the Swiss shares to the swap counterparties but only those amounts that equalled these dividends in full.[194]

187. *Ibid.*, para. 6.3.3.
188. *Ibid.*
189. *Ibid.*
190. *Ibid.*, para. 6.3.4. 1st and 2nd paragraphs.
191. *Ibid.*, 2nd paragraph.
Under a standard TRS documented under ISDA, not the expected dividends are passed on, but the dividend amounts that were actually paid out to the shareholders after the dividends were declared. Hence, if the dividends that are paid out are different from what were the reasonable expectations of both parties when entering into the TRS, the short party of the TRS will have to pay the realised, not the expected dividends. Thus, for a TRS documented under standard ISDA terms, the obligations of the short party of the TRS (i.e., the holder of the shares that passes on the dividends) will be dependent on the receipt of the actual dividends.
192. *Ibid.*, para. 6.3.5.
193. *Ibid.*
194. Swiss Federal Supreme Court, 2C_364/2012 and 2C_377/2012, para. 6.4.

The Federal Supreme Court rejects this narrow view and proposes a wider (economic) view. It suggests that the receipt of the dividends by the Danish Bank and the contractual obligation under the TRSs entered with the swap counterparties were linked in such a way that a de facto obligation to transfer the dividends could be assumed.[195] The court concluded that interdependence between the receipt of the dividends and the passing on of the dividends to the swap counterparties existed for the following reasons:

(i) The interest and margin payments under the swaps not only allowed the purchase of the shares as a hedge but also permitted the receipt of the dividends.[196]
(ii) The distribution of risks under the swaps meant that the dividend amounts passed on to the swap counterparties always corresponded with the actual dividends received by the Danish Bank, even if there was no dividend payment at all.[197]
(iii) The purchase of the shares was concluded systematically before the dividend due date with the purpose of passing on the dividend as a (manufactured) dividend to the swap counterparties free of Swiss dividend withholding tax.[198]

In conclusion, the court suggests – in direct application of the 'stepping stone conduit' model – that the distributed dividends were fully passed on to the swap counterparties as an expense and that this passing on to non-resident counterparties was planned before the dividend due date.[199] Thus, the court denied the Danish Bank the 'beneficial owner' status in relation to the dividends received.[200]
The court further suggests that the criterion of 'interdependence' asks whether the obligation to pass on the income must depend on this income being obtained (called 'second dependence').[201] The court suggests that this criterion also asks the question of who has to bear the risks associated with the purchase of the shares used as a hedge.[202] That includes the dividend risk, meaning the risk that the distributing company in the source state does not distribute a dividend at all, but would also include all other risk factors, such as the credit risk and the share price risk.[203] The court concludes that all major risks with respect to the shares were borne by the swap counterparties and not by the Danish Bank.[204]

It should be noted that the Swiss Federal Administrative Court followed this view, *see A-6537/2010 (2012) 14 ITLR 638*, para. 3.4.2.
195. Swiss Federal Supreme Court, 2C_364/2012 and 2C_377/2012, para. 6.4.2.
196. *Ibid.*, para. 6.4.1.
197. *Ibid.*, paras 5.3, 6.3.4. and 6.4.1.
198. *Ibid.*, paras 5.2.5. and 6.4.2.
199. *Ibid.*, paras 5.2.3. and 6.4.2.
200. *Ibid.*, para. 6.5.
201. Swiss Federal Supreme Court, 2C_364/2012 and 2C_377/2012, para. 5.3.
202. *Ibid.*, para. 5.3.
203. *Ibid.*
204. *Ibid.*, para. 6.3.4.

[iii] The *Swiss Swaps* Case in Light of the OECD Model Commentary on Article 10, Paragraph 12.4

Concerning the question of whether 'obtaining the income depends on the obligation to pass on the income', the argument of the Swiss Federal Supreme Court was based on the notion that obtaining the income depends on the obligation to pass on the income under the swaps (1st dependence). This notion of 'interdependence' or 'dependence' seems to be similar to the term used in the OECD Model (2017), Commentary on Article 10, paragraph 12.4, which was added to the OECD Model (2014) in July 2014.

Thus, the author will investigate if the wording in the Commentary introduced to the OECD Model (2014) and maintained in the OECD Model (2017) may have the same meaning as the notion of 'interdependence' used by the Swiss Federal Supreme Court and will determine whether the court went beyond the notion of 'dependence' supported by the OECD Commentary.

The OECD proposes that the term 'beneficial owner' has to be understood in light of the OECD Model and therefore has not a domestic but an 'international fiscal meaning'.[205] How exactly the term 'beneficial ownership' is to be interpreted in a treaty context has been left unclear.[206]

The OECD issued a public discussion draft in 2011 ('2011 OECD Discussion Draft') in order to clarify the term 'beneficial owner' used in Articles 10, 11 and 12 of the OECD Model.[207] In the context of the Commentary on Article 10, the *2011 OECD Discussion Draft* suggested that:

> [t]he recipient of a dividend is the 'beneficial owner' of that dividend where he has the full right to use and enjoy the dividend unconstrained by a contractual or legal obligation to pass the payment received to another person. Such an obligation will normally derive from relevant legal documents but may also be found to exist on the basis of facts and circumstances showing that, in substance, the recipient clearly does not have the full right to use and enjoy the dividend.[208]

The *2011 OECD Discussion Draft*, however, maintained that:

> [t]he fact that the recipient of a dividend is considered to be the beneficial owner of that dividend does not mean, however, that the limitation of tax provided for by paragraph 2 must automatically be granted. The limitation of tax should not be granted in cases of abuse of this provision.[209]

The *2011 OECD Discussion Draft*, therefore, introduced a *wide meaning* of 'beneficial owner'. This wide understanding of the term 'beneficial owner' might, however, also apply to many common derivatives transactions of banks and hedge funds, which are used for non-tax reasons to allow these market participants to enter

205. OECD Model (2014), Commentary on Art. 10, para. 12.1. *See also* Baker (2012), Art. 10, 10B-14.
206. Richard Collier (2011) 684, 685.
207. OECD, *Clarification of the meaning of 'beneficial owner' in the OECD model tax convention, discussion draft* (2011).
208. *Ibid.*, amendment of para. 12.4 of the OECD Commentary.
209. *Ibid.*, amendment of para. 12.5. of the OECD Commentary.

into leveraged synthetic equity or fixed-income investments, such as equity swaps, bond swaps, TRSs and contracts for differences.

> *Example 82:*
>
> Company A hedges its economic exposure against a portfolio of bonds with cash-settled TRSs entered into with Bank B. Under the TRSs, Company A pays Bank B any increase in the value of the bonds and any interest received, and Company A receives from Bank B any decrease in the value of the bonds and LIBOR-based interest payments.[210]

By applying the description of the term 'beneficial owner' used in the *2011 OECD Discussion Draft*, Company A could be regarded as passing on the 'beneficial ownership' of the bonds to Bank B under the TRSs, although the obligations under the swaps are independent of the ownership of the bonds.[211]

Because of the wide interpretation of the term 'beneficial owner', taxpayers and their advisers sharply criticised the *2011 OECD Discussion Draft*.[212] It was suggested that the OECD had established the 'beneficial ownership' criterion as a 'tax-avoidance fall-back clause' for tax authorities to tackle cross-border transactions in cases where general tax-avoidance clauses would not apply.[213]

In light of the arguments of the banking industry and other stakeholders, the OECD issued *Revised Proposals* in *2012*, which confirmed that the mere obligation to pass on the dividend received to another person would not deny 'beneficial ownership'.[214] In the *2012 Revised Proposals*, the Commentary on Article 10, paragraph 12.4. reads as follows:

> In these various examples [...] the recipient of the dividend is not the 'beneficial owner' because that recipient's right to use and enjoy the dividend is constrained by a contractual or legal obligation to pass on the payment received to another person. Such an obligation [...] may also be found to exist on the basis of facts and circumstances showing that, in substance, the recipient does not have the right to use and enjoy the dividend unconstrained by a contractual or legal obligation to pass on the payment received to another person. This type of obligation must be related to the payment received; it would therefore not include contractual or legal obligations unrelated to the payment received even if those obligations could effectively result in the recipient using the payment received to satisfy those

210. Hull (2006), at 515.
211. Herbert (2011).
212. Helmer (2012); *also* Collier (2011) at 701-702.
213. Helmer (2012). More differentiated: Collier (2011) at 701 who suggested that the tax authorities may cite the proposed wording selectively in support of substance-based interpretation of the term 'beneficial owner'.
214. OECD, *OECD Model Tax Convention: Revised Proposals Concerning the Meaning of 'beneficial owner' in Articles 10, 11 and 12* (2012), E. Para. 12.4. of the Commentary on Art. 10, paras 11-19.

> obligations. Examples of such unrelated obligations are those unrelated obligations that the recipient may have as a debtor or as a party to financial transactions.[215]

In 2013, the stakeholder comments on the *2012 Revised Proposals* were considered by the OECD Committee of Fiscal Affairs, Working Party 1.[216] The 2014 Update to the OECD Model Tax Convention contains further 'clarifications' of the term 'beneficial owner' in the new Commentary on Article 10, paragraphs 12.1 and 12.4. to 12.6.

In the author's view, it is not entirely clear whether the 'clarifications' in the wording of paragraph 12.4. were intended to change the meaning of the paragraph or not. Compared to the *2012 Revised Proposals*, there have been particular changes in the 2014 Update relating to the Commentary on Article 10, paragraph 12.4, sentence 3, namely:

> This type of obligation would not include contractual or legal obligations that are not dependent on the receipt of the payment and which the direct recipient has as a debtor or as a party to a financial transaction [...]. Where the recipient of a dividend does have the right to use and enjoy the dividend unconstrained by a contractual or legal obligation to pass on the payment received to another person, the recipient is the beneficial owner of that dividend.[217]

Hence, beneficial ownership can be passed to a party of a financial transaction (for example, a swap contract) if the transaction includes a *contractual or legal obligation* that is *dependent on the receipt of the dividend and that the direct recipient of the dividends* (for example the Danish Bank) has as a party to a financial transaction.

In the author's opinion, the meaning of paragraph 12.4, sentence 3 may have changed significantly compared to the version in the *2012 Revised Proposals,* as the phrase 'not dependent on the receipt of payment' may have a narrower meaning than the phrase 'unrelated to the payment received'.[218]

This may seem strange at first glance, but one needs to compare the complete wording of paragraph 12.4. of the *2012 Revised Proposals* with the wording of paragraph 12.4. in the 2014 Update to the OECD Model.

Under the *2012 Revised Proposals*, paragraph 12.4, one would be able to argue that beneficial ownership is not passed in cases where a derivatives transaction was a hedge of an exposure arising out of a share purchase as the *derivative contract* would constitute a *legal obligation* that is *unrelated to the dividends received*, even if the dividends where passed on to the party of the derivative. This is explicitly confirmed by the following sentences in the Commentary:

> it would therefore not include contractual or legal obligations unrelated to the payment received even if those obligations could effectively result in the recipient

215. 2012 Revised Proposals, Commentary on Art. 10, para. 12.4. (emphasis added).
216. *See* OECD, *2014 Update to the OECD Model Tax Convention* (OECD Publishing), Executive Summary, 2.
217. OECD Model (2014), Commentary on Art. 10, para. 12.4. (emphasis added).
218. *Other opinion* Vogel and Lehner (2015), Vor Arts 10-12, para. 19, who compare simply the terms 'related to' and 'be dependent on'.

> using the payment received to satisfy those obligations. Examples of such unrelated obligations are those unrelated obligations that the recipient may have as a debtor or as a party to financial transactions.[219]

This particular sentence stipulates that beneficial ownership in relation to the dividends is still accepted for the legal owner of the shares if the owner enters into a separate contract that is unrelated to receiving the dividends 'even if those obligations [under this separate contract] could effectively result in the recipient using the payment received to satisfy those obligations'.[220] Further, the *2012 Revised Proposals* explicitly give examples of such unrelated obligations, namely 'unrelated obligations that the recipient may have as a debtor or a party to financial transactions'.[221]

If one applied the *2012 Revised Proposals* to the *Swiss Swaps* case, one would have to conclude that even if all risks and rewards of the shares (including all risks and rewards in relation to the dividends) had been transferred, it could not necessarily be assumed that a transfer of beneficial ownership to the counterparties of the swaps had taken place. Instead, the TRSs would most likely be regarded as not imposing on the Danish Bank an obligation to pass on the dividends received from the Swiss shares. Thus, according to the wording of the *2012 Revised Proposals*, paragraph 12.4, beneficial ownership in relation to the dividends could be retained by the legal owner who received dividends and passed on those dividends to a third party under a swap agreement. As the transfer of 'economic ownership' via swaps may not be sufficient to assume the transfer of beneficial ownership according to the *2012 Revised Proposals*, one would have to further consider whether other factors (such as anti-avoidance considerations) could have led to a transfer of beneficial ownership.[222]

In contrast, under the 2014 Update to the Commentary on Article 10, paragraph 12.4, sentence 3, the conclusion of a TRS agreement, under which the exposure to the share price risk and the dividends are passed to a swap counterparty, may lead to a transfer of beneficial ownership of the dividends as the *obligations* of the short party under a standard TRS *are dependent* on the *receipt of the dividends* by the direct recipient.[223]

Under a standard TRS documented under ISDA, it is not the expected dividends that are passed on, but the dividend amounts that were actually paid out to the shareholders after the dividends were declared. If the dividends that are paid out are different from what the reasonable expectations of both parties were when entering

219. 2012 Revised Proposals, Commentary on Art. 10, para. 12.4. (emphasis added).
220. *Ibid.*
221. *Ibid.*
222. *Ibid.*, para. 12.5.
223. *Other opinion* Vogel and Lehner (2015), Vor Arts 10-12, para. 19, who suggest that the obligation to pass on the dividend has to relate to the received dividend as such. This obligation needs to legally oblige the direct recipient of the dividend to pass on *this payment* to another person. If a received payment was only used to fulfil another, independent obligation, which the recipient has as a party to a financial transaction, that obligation does not influence the beneficial ownership position of the recipient of the dividends.
The author does not agree that this interpretation can be easily derived from the new wording of Art. 10 para. 12.4. because one has to consider the complete text of para. 12.4.

into the TRS, the short party of the TRS will have to pay the realised, not the expected dividends.

Thus, for a TRS documented under standard ISDA terms, the obligations of the short party of the TRS (holder of the shares that passes on the dividend) may be dependent on the receipt of the actual dividend.

The 2014 Update of the OECD Model has widened the scope of the term beneficial owner in the Commentary to catch shareholdings where the economic exposure to the dividend and the share price risk was hedged with derivatives. Thus, the 2014 Update of the OECD Model and its Commentary can serve as a basis for tax authorities and tax courts to apply a wide definition of the term 'beneficial owner' and use the wide interpretation of the term as a means to counter transactions that are designed to avoid withholding taxes on interest or dividends, such as stock lending transactions over dividend dates, securities lending transactions involving tax-exempt bonds and TRS transactions.

The reference to the criterion of 'interdependence' by the Swiss Federal Supreme Court in the *Swiss Swaps* case shows that the new criterion of 'dependence' can be interpreted by domestic courts in such a way that a transfer of beneficial ownership in relation to dividends under a TRS may take place.

Based on the new wording, one can assume that the *obligations* of the short party under a TRS concluded under ISDA to pass on the dividends to the swap counterparties *can be regarded as dependent* on the actual receipt of the dividends by the direct recipient.

More generally, based on the new Commentary on Article 10, paragraph 12.4, derivatives transactions where dividends received are passed on to the derivatives counterparty could be regarded as transferring the beneficial ownership of the dividends from the legal holder of the shares to the derivatives counterparty that has obtained a synthetic exposure in the shares.[224]

In summary, the amendments to the Commentary on Article 10 of the OECD Model in 2014 have contributed to a new dimension of the 'beneficial ownership' criterion that would accept a transfer of beneficial ownership from the legal owner of the shares to a derivatives counterparty if all, or major risks of the underlying asset are synthetically transferred to the derivatives counterparty.

[b] The SMI Futures Case[225]

The analysis of the *Swiss Swaps* case was primarily concerned with legal questions relating to the transfer of beneficial ownership and the use of derivatives to pass on the dividends received. The analysis of the *SMI Futures* case goes beyond this question as

224. The Swiss Federal Supreme Court's decision in the *SMI Futures* case is another example where beneficial ownership is not attributed to the legal holder of the shares but is assumed to lie with the derivatives counterparties. *See* Swiss Federal Supreme Court, 2_C_895/2012 (*SMI Futures* case), para. 9.3.
225. The discussion has been previously published in more detail in the journal *Intertax*: Weidmann (2017), 229-253.

this case determines the legal boundaries of the taxation of cash-futures arbitrage transactions in Switzerland.

[i] The Facts of the Case

A bank resident in Denmark ('Danish Bank') applied to the Swiss tax authorities for a refund of withholding taxes for dividends received in 2006 and 2007. The dividends were paid by companies whose shares were listed on the SIX Swiss Exchange. The shares listed were constituents of the Swiss Market Index (SMI).[226] The Danish Bank was a 100% subsidiary of a Swedish financial institution.[227]

The Danish Bank claimed that it was the beneficial owner of dividends received from Swiss shares under the Switzerland/Denmark Double Taxation Convention (1973).[228]

The Swiss tax authorities denied the withholding tax refund in three cases concerning such claims for 2007 and asked for repayment of the already refunded withholding taxes in four cases.[229] The tax authorities argued that the Danish Bank was not the beneficial owner of the dividends under the Switzerland/Denmark Double Taxation Convention (1973).[230]

The Danish Bank entered into the following transactions:

(1) a sale of SMI futures to counterparties that were neither domiciled in Switzerland nor Denmark (short SMI futures position), and
(2) a same-day purchase of a basket of Swiss equities (composed as a weighted basket mirroring the equities contained in the SMI) with the same market value in Swiss Francs (CHF) compared to the disposal value of the SMI futures (long equities position).[231]

The SMI futures were sold on the EUREX exchange, whereas the Swiss equities were purchased on the electronic exchange virt-x.[232] The disposal of the SMI futures and the purchase of the shares were executed via *block crosses*[233] with two different international brokers.[234]

226. Swiss Federal Administrative Court (Bundesverwaltungsgericht) decision of 23 July 2012, A-1246/2011 (*SMI Futures* case), para. A.
227. *Ibid.*; *also* Federal Supreme Court, 2C_895/2012, para. 7.2.1.
228. *Ibid.*, para. A.
229. Federal Administrative Court, A-1246/2011, para. B.a.
230. Federal Supreme Court, 2C_895/2012, para. B.
231. Federal Administrative Court, A-1246/2011, para. 7.1; Federal Supreme Court, 2C_895/2012, para. 6.1. *See also* Baumgartner and Frick (2015), 4.
232. Federal Administrative Court, A-1246/2011, para. 7.1.
233. Block crosses, also known as block trades, are pre-arranged trades that are entered into pursuant to a prior understanding by two different exchange participants. In a block cross, the two parties agree on the number of futures contracts or the number of shares and the price prior to a trade, and the parties trade the pre-agreed number of contracts at the pre-agreed price via the exchange. The futures prices and the number of contracts of both parties are not randomly

The first international broker who executed the purchase and the later disposal of the shares ('Equities Broker') did not act as an agent but as a principal.[235] The second international broker who executed the SMI futures ('Futures Broker') only acted as an agent for the Danish Bank.[236]

It was not entirely clear from the facts of the case if the basket of Swiss equities was purchased as a hedge for the SMI futures or if the futures served as a hedge for the purchase of the share basket.

The Swiss Federal Administrative Court assumed in its reasoning that the SMI futures were hedged with a basket of Swiss equities.[237] In contrast, the Swiss Federal Supreme Court only acknowledged that the Danish Bank purchased a large number of Swiss equities, which were components of the SMI, and on the same day sold SMI futures for the same amount to counterparties who were neither resident in Denmark nor in Switzerland.[238]

The SMI futures were held from 19 February until 15 June 2007, with a *futures roll* being executed on 15 March 2007 (one day before maturity of the March futures contracts).[239] The Danish Bank held the SMI equity basket for exactly the same period as the SMI futures.[240]

The overall gain of the first tranche of the combined transaction equalled approximately 9% of the total dividends received.[241] The overall gain of the second tranche of the combined transaction between 15 March and 15 June 2007 equalled approximately 6.6% of the total dividends received.[242]

[ii] The Reasoning of the Federal Administrative Court

In the *SMI Futures* case, the question arose whether a refund of dividend withholding taxes under Article 10 of the Switzerland/Denmark Double Taxation Convention (1973) could be denied to the Danish Bank (being the physical holder of the shares

---

matched 'on exchange' but are matched between the two parties by the exchange. *See* Eurex, Block Trades, https://www.eurex.com/ex-en/trade/eurex-t7-entry-services/block-trades, accessed 2 January 2024.

234. Federal Administrative Court, A-1246/2011, paras B.d. and C.a; *also* Federal Supreme Court, 2C_895/2012, para. 8.1.2.
235. Federal Administrative Court, A-1246/2011, para. B.c; Federal Supreme Court, 2C_895/2012, para. 8.2.1.
236. Federal Administrative Court, A-1246/2011, para. B.d. Similarly, the Federal Supreme Court assumed that the international broker with whom the Danish Bank traded the SMI futures only acted as an agent, *see* Federal Supreme Court, 2C_895/2012, para. 8.2.1.
237. Federal Administrative Court, A-1246/2011, para. 7.1.
238. Federal Supreme Court, 2C_895/2012, para. 6.1. The Federal Supreme Court suggested in its reasoning that the SMI futures served as a hedge for the share baskets and dismissed the suggestion by the Danish Bank that the share baskets served as a hedge for the futures. *Compare also* Federal Supreme Court, 2C_895/2012, paras 8.4.1. and 8.4.2.
239. Federal Administrative Court, A-1246/2011, para. 7.1.; Federal Supreme Court, 2C_895/2012, para. 6.1.
240. *Ibid.*
241. Federal Administrative Court, A-1246/2011, para. 7.2; Federal Supreme Court, 2C_895/2012, para. 6.3.2.
242. *Ibid*, para. 6.2.3.

which were hedged with futures) because it was not regarded as the beneficial owner of the dividends received. The court further investigated whether the combined transaction constituted an abuse of the tax treaty. The Federal Administrative Court held that the Danish Bank was the beneficial owner of the dividends and, further, that no treaty abuse took place based on the following arguments:

First, the Federal Administrative Court suggested that beneficial ownership could not be denied just because the Danish Bank was a 100% subsidiary of the Swedish financial institution, as one could not assume a direct conduit structure.[243]

Second, the court investigated whether the Danish Bank had a factual obligation to pass on the dividends to the futures counterparties and to the Swedish parent company, which financed the share purchases, based on a 'substance-over-form' analysis.[244] It suggested that the Danish Bank was not obliged to pass on the dividends to its Swedish parent company, although the purchase of the shares was financed by the parent company. The interest payments, which the Danish Bank owed to the Swedish parent company, had to be paid notwithstanding whether the Danish Bank could generate dividends from the Swiss shares.[245]

Further, the court suggested that one could not assume a 'circular trade' concluded with the futures counterparties as the shares and futures were traded anonymously with two different brokers.[246] Lastly, the court held that no treaty abuse took place as the Danish Bank conducted an active business in Denmark.[247]

[iii] The Reasoning of the Federal Supreme Court

The Federal Supreme Court reversed the decision of the Federal Administrative Court. It held that the refund of Swiss dividend withholding taxes must be denied, and the refund amounts already paid by the Swiss tax authorities had to be repaid to them because the Danish Bank was not the beneficial owner of the dividends.[248]

The facts of the *SMI Futures* case were far more complicated than those of the *Swiss Swaps* case, as the dividends were not simply passed on to counterparties under total return swaps as manufactured dividends. Rather, part of the dividends received by the Danish Bank were included in the futures pricing. Nonetheless, the question remained whether the Danish Bank could maintain beneficial ownership of the dividends if:

(1) the share purchases were fully financed by the Swedish parent company, and
(2) the share baskets only served as a hedge for the SMI futures.[249]

243. Federal Administrative Court, A-1246/2011, para. 7.3.
244. *Ibid.*, para. 7.3.1.
245. *Ibid.*
246. *Ibid.*, para. 7.3.2.
247. *Ibid.*, paras 8.1-8.2.
248. Federal Supreme Court, 2C_895/2012, paras 10-11.
249. The Federal Supreme Court questioned whether the shares served as a hedge for the SMI futures position (as suggested by the Danish Bank) and followed in its reasoning the opinion of the Swiss tax authorities that the SMI futures served as a hedge of the Swiss share basket. *See* Federal Supreme Court, 2C_895/2012, paras 8.4.1. and 8.4.2.

The court focused its reasoning on three aspects.

First, the court asked whether the beneficial ownership criterion was implicitly contained in the Switzerland/Denmark Double Taxation Convention (1973). Parallel to the reasoning in the *Swiss Swaps* case,[250] the Federal Supreme Court held that the beneficial ownership criterion was implicitly contained in the Switzerland/Denmark Double Taxation Convention (1973).[251]

Second, the court asked whether the Danish Bank failed in its obligations to cooperate with the Swiss tax authorities and disclose information concerning the overall transaction and the identities of the counterparties. The court then investigated the legal consequences of such a failure.[252]

Third, like in the *Swiss Swaps* case, the main question the court needed to determine was whether there was an interdependence between obtaining the dividends and passing them on to the Swedish parent company and/or 'third party' counterparty banks.[253]

The author analyses the court's reasoning regarding the last two questions in more detail in the following:[254]

The decision of the Federal Supreme Court discussed whether the Danish Bank was obliged to provide information in respect of the transactions and cooperate with the tax authorities,[255] and it investigated the scope of this obligation.[256] In this respect, the court referred to a general principle of Swiss tax law that a taxpayer should not benefit from non-compliance to cooperate and provide information to the tax authorities.[257]

The Federal Supreme Court concluded that the Danish Bank failed in its obligation to provide information on the overall transaction and cooperate with the tax authorities.[258] In particular, the Danish Bank did not disclose to the Swiss tax authorities who the counterparties of the *Equities Broker* were[259] in respect of the purchase and disposal of the shares.[260] The Danish Bank only submitted that the counterparties of the equity transactions were eight counterparties resident in Sweden, the US and the Netherlands.[261]

The court regarded the disclosure of the identities of the *Equities Broker*'s counterparties as essential for determining if there was an obligation to pass on the

250. Swiss Federal Supreme Court, 2C_364/2012 and 2C_377/2012, paras 4-4.5.
251. Federal Supreme Court, 2C_895/2012, paras 3-3.2.
252. Federal Supreme Court, 2C_895/2012, paras 5.1-5.3. and 8.3.3-8.3.4.
253. *Compare* Baumgartner and Frick (2015), 4.
254. The authors will rely very close on the wording of the court's decision as no official translation of the case has been published.
255. Federal Supreme Court, 2C_895/2012, paras 5.1-5.2.1.
256. *Ibid.*, paras 5.2.1-5.3.
257. *Ibid.*, para. 5.3.
258. *Ibid.*, para. 8.3.3.
259. In the following, the author will call the 'Broker Y' who entered into the equities purchase and disposal with the Danish Bank and its (indirect) counterparties, the *Equities Broker.*
260. Federal Supreme Court, 2C_895/2012, para. 8.3.3.
261. *Ibid.*, para. 8.3.1.

dividends to the *Equities Broker* and further on to the *Equities Broker's* counterparties.[262]

The court suggested that the bank's failure to comply with the obligation to provide information and cooperate resulted in an information deficit concerning the facts of the case, which could not be remedied.[263] The court concluded that the Danish Bank should not benefit from this information deficit because the Danish Bank had caused this lack of information by interposing a broker as an intermediary counterparty.[264]

Hence, it was sufficient (in terms of the burden of proof) that the Swiss tax authorities provided coherent indications that the dividends had been passed on to the counterparties in the course of the share transactions.[265] Due to the information deficit, the Danish Bank could not provide equally convincing arguments and evidence which could explain the course of action of all parties in the transactions.[266]

Concerning the question of interdependence between obtaining the dividends and passing the dividends on to the Swedish parent company and the counterparties of the *Equities Broker*, the Federal Supreme Court referred to the decision in the *Swiss Swaps* case.[267]

The court suggested that it was important for the determination of beneficial ownership if the Danish Bank had the freedom to decide how to use the dividends, namely whether the Danish Bank had both legal ownership and economic control (in relation to the dividends).[268]

According to the court, it was important to consider the effectively exercised powers, not only in a legalistic sense but also in consideration of all economic circumstances ('substance-over-form').[269] The court relied on a definition of beneficial ownership developed by *Baumgartner*,[270] referred to in the *Swiss Swaps* case.

Citing this definition, the court suggested that beneficial ownership must be denied to a person if the dividends must be passed on because of legal obligations or factual limitations that already existed at the point of time of the dividend payments.[271] It further indicated that a factual limitation to enjoying these dividends can be assumed if there is an interdependence between obtaining the dividends and passing on the dividends, namely if:

(a) obtaining the income is dependent on the obligation to pass on the income (first dependence),

262. *Ibid.*, para. 8.3.3.
263. *Ibid.*, para. 8.3.4.
264. *Ibid.*, paras 8.3.3. and 8.3.4.
265. *Ibid.*, para. 8.3.3.
266. *Ibid.*
267. *Ibid.*, paras 3-3.2. For an analysis of the similar issues in the *Swiss Swaps* case, *see* Weidmann (2016), at 620.
268. Federal Supreme Court, 2C_895/2012, para. 4.1.
269. *Ibid.*
270. Baumgartner (2010) 130-150.
271. Federal Supreme Court, 2C_895/2012, para. 4.2; *compare also* Federal Supreme Court, 2C_364/2012 and 2C_377/12, para. 5.2.2.

(b) the obligation to pass on the income is dependent on obtaining the income (second dependence).[272]

In order to answer the question of interdependence, the Federal Supreme Court not only considered the question of the obligation to provide information but also the following questions:

(i) Did the Danish Bank retain only a small percentage of the dividends?

The Federal Supreme Court discussed in detail the economics of the transaction[273] and concluded that the Danish Bank retained a total of 9 % of the dividends in the combined transaction from 19 February to 15 March, which equalled approximately 0.04 % of the overall transaction volume (in relation to the short futures position).[274] Further, the court suggested that the Danish Bank retained a total of only 6.6 % of the dividends in the combined transaction from 15 March to 15 June, equalling 0.08 % of the transaction volume (in relation to the short futures position).[275]

The court concluded that the Danish Bank only retained a 'small percentage' of the dividends.[276] The court suggested that the retention of a small dividend percentage by the Danish Bank would not preclude the court from deciding that a transfer of beneficial ownership of the dividends had taken place.[277]

(ii) Did the Danish Bank pass on the dividends to the Swedish parent company by repaying the interest amounts owed because the parent company financed the purchase of the shares?

Referring to *Baumgartner's first dependence* criteria between obtaining the income and the obligation to pass on the income, the court indicated that it needed to determine whether the dividends were (partly) passed on by way of (increased) financing costs owed internally within the group.[278]

The Federal Supreme Court considered it detrimental that the Swedish parent company would not have received the full dividend withholding tax refund if it had held the shares directly. Instead, Switzerland would have retained a 15 % withholding tax under the Switzerland/Sweden Double Taxation Convention.[279]

The court questioned if the Danish Bank, as a subsidiary of the Swedish parent company, could act independently at all.[280] The court suggested that the Danish Bank

272. Federal Supreme Court, 2C_895/2012, para. 4.2; Federal Supreme Court, 2C_364/2012 and 2C_377/12, para. 5.2.2.; referencing to Baumgartner (2010), at 150. *Also* Baumgartner and Frick (2015), 4.
273. Federal Supreme Court, 2_895/2012, paras 6.1-6.2.3.
274. *Ibid.*, para. 6.2.3.
275. *Ibid.*, para. 6.2.3.
276. *Ibid.*, para. 6.3.
277. *Ibid.*
278. *Ibid.*, para. 7.
279. *Ibid.*, para. 7.2.1, 2nd paragraph.
280. *Ibid.*, para. 7.2.1, 1st paragraph. *Compare* Baumgartner and Frick (2015), at 4.

may have conducted major business transactions in favour of the Swedish parent company in order for it to benefit from a 0% withholding tax rate.[281]

Further, it pointed out that the Danish Bank admitted that the real financing costs for the purchase of the shares were substantially lower than the financing costs calculations provided to the Swiss tax authorities.[282] The court assumed that the amounts paid to the Swedish parent company, which were above the effective financing costs, were used to pass on parts of the dividends within the group or, rather, to the parent company.[283]

(iii) Did the Danish Bank pass on the dividends received by way of a non-market standard purchase and disposal prices of the shares?

The Federal Supreme Court considered whether the dividends were passed on in the course of the purchase and the disposal of the shares.[284]

The Federal Supreme Court maintained that it was unusual that the Danish Bank only used one broker for the purchase of the shares and one for the futures transactions and that the *Equities Broker* concluded both the purchase of the shares and their later disposal.[285]

Moreover, it is regarded as unusual that the *Equities Broker* did not act as a mere agent but as a principal.[286] The court further highlighted that the *Equities Broker* was neither resident in Denmark nor in Switzerland but in the UK, where it would have been subject to a residual withholding tax rate of 15% on dividends from Swiss shares.

The court concluded that the transactions between the Danish Bank and the *Equities Broker* should be regarded as a 'circular transaction' between known counterparties,[287] maintaining that it was important for the legal analysis that both parties had been regular business partners for many years.[288]

According to the court, the specific arrangement as a pre-agreed 'circular transaction' between known counterparties also had a direct effect on the pricing mechanism of the transaction.[289] Although the share transactions were formally concluded as *block trades*[290] on the exchange, it would be misleading to assume that the transactions were concluded 'on exchange' via a broker and that the purchase of the shares was based on market prices.[291]

Rather, the court suggested that the purchase and disposal of the shares via block trades could not be regarded as standardised and anonymised transactions for which

281. Federal Supreme Court, 2C_895/2012, para. 7.2.1.
282. *Ibid.*, para. 7.2.2.
283. Federal Supreme Court, 2C_895/2012, para. 7.2.2. *Compare* Baumgartner and Frick (2015), at 4.
284. Federal Supreme Court, 2C_895/2012, para. 8.
285. *Ibid.*
286. *Ibid.*
287. Federal Supreme Court, 2C_895/2012, para. 8.2.2. *Compare* Baumgartner and Frick (2015), at 4.
288. Federal Supreme Court, 2C_895/2012, para. 8.2.2.
289. *Ibid.*, para. 8.2.2.
290. For a description of a 'block trade', *see* above.
291. Federal Supreme Court, 2C_895/2012, para. 8.2.2.

the usual market mechanisms of the exchange applied. Instead, they were specifically arranged, individual transactions with pre-agreed pricing, which was negotiated between known counterparties. Those pre-agreed transactions allowed the Danish Bank to pass on the dividends to the *Equities Broker*, other than the portion of the dividends that was agreed to be retained by the bank.[292]

(iv) Did the Danish Bank only pass on those dividends which were actually received (second dependence)?

The court investigated whether also the *second dependence* was fulfilled, i.e., whether only those dividends were passed on to the counterparties (of the *Equities Broker*) which were actually received.[293] The court held that the overall transaction construct allowed the Danish Bank to obtain the dividends free of withholding tax in the course of very short-term circular transactions and to pass on the majority of those dividends to the previous and subsequent owners of the Swiss shares (i.e., the counterparties of the *Equities Broker*).[294]

According to the court, the lack of risk borne by the Danish Bank in the context of the overall transaction construct was consistent with its 'interposition' and a complex multi-party agreement within a closed circle of participants.[295]

That applied foremost to the share price risk of the Swiss shares, which was fully hedged with futures contracts by the Danish Bank.[296] Further, it also applied to the dividend risk, i.e., that no or only a part of the expected dividends was actually received by the Danish Bank.[297]

The court suggested that this 'second dependence' question could not be decided conclusively because the Danish Bank had declined to disclose the identities of the counterparties of the *Equities Broker* and the risk distribution between the parties. The court concurred with the argument advanced by the Swiss tax authorities that the Danish Bank only retained a very small portion of the dividends and that no company, applying commercial sense, would take high market risks if it only received a small portion of the dividend income.[298]

As the Danish Bank could not substantiate any significant risks permitting a different conclusion, the court concluded that the *second dependence* was fulfilled and that the Danish Bank was not the beneficial owner of the dividends received.[299]

292. *Ibid.*, para. 8.2.2.
293. *Ibid.*, para. 9.
294. *Ibid.*, para. 9.2.
295. *Ibid.*, para. 9.3.
296. *Ibid.*
297. *Ibid.*
298. *Ibid.*
299. *Ibid. Compare* Baumgartner and Frick (2015), 5.

[iv] Critical Analysis of the Federal Supreme Court's Decision in the SMI Futures Case

The author agrees with legal aspects decided by the Federal Supreme Court, in particular, in relation to the failure of the Danish Bank's obligation to cooperate and disclose information.

Banks entering into a cash-futures arbitrage via block crosses may often know the likely counterparties on the other side, even if the transactions are executed with a broker standing between the banks and acting as principal, simply because the counterparties may be seeking to hedge themselves in the opposite manner by entering into a long SMI futures position.

Based on several 'peculiarities' of the case, the court concluded that the whole transaction was different from a standardised and anonymised transaction conducted on the exchange.[300] It held that the predominant part of the dividends received by the Danish Bank was passed on by way of 'non-market standard' purchase and disposal prices of the shares, besides passing them on as financing costs to the Swedish parent. The court referred to the 'stepping stone conduit model' where the passing on of the income away from the resident state was not done by way of passing on the income but by way of passing on the expenses.[301]

The court based its assumption of 'non-market standard' purchase and disposal prices of the shares (which allowed a passing on of the dividends) on the following arguments:

(1) It regarded the transaction between the Danish Bank and the *Equities Broker*, acting as principal, as a 'circular transaction' and extended this circularity also to the counterparties of the *Equities Broker*.
(2) It affirmed the transaction scenario advanced by the Swiss tax authorities instead of the transaction scenario advanced by the Danish Bank, based on the argument that the non-disclosure of the identities of the *Equity Broker's* counterparties had to be held against the Danish Bank as it caused a lack of information for the court.
(3) It affirmed an overall transaction construct, which was different from the transaction steps suggested by the Danish Bank. Moreover, the court indicated what might have been the likely 'overall transaction construct'.

The court ruled that the passing on of the dividends by way of (increased) expenses was executed by the parties under circumstances which indicated a duty of the Danish Bank to pass on the dividends. Accordingly, the *first dependence* was fulfilled.[302]

The author agrees with the court's reasoning that a likely condition for the transaction of this size was that the parties of the transactions (the Danish Bank, the

300. *Ibid.*, paras 8-8.5.
301. Federal Supreme Court, 2C_895/2012, para. 8.5.
302. *Ibid.*, para. 8.5.

Equities Broker and the counterparties of the *Equities Broker*) would have known each other and that there was a likelihood that the parties had pre-agreed the pricing.[303]

The author also agrees that the non-disclosure of the identities of the counterparties of the *Equities Broker* caused uncertainty for the court, as it could not be certain whether the counterparties of the *Equities Broker* were the same as the counterparties of the Danish Bank in the futures contracts.[304]

In order to answer the question of whether the Danish Bank only passed on those dividends which were actually received (*second dependence*), one has to identify the risk/reward profile of the combined transaction and ask the following questions:

(a) Who bears the risks and rewards in relation to the share price?
(b) Who bears the risks and rewards in relation to the dividends, i.e., if the effectively distributed dividends do not equal the expected dividends?
(c) Who bears the credit risk in the futures transaction, i.e., the risk that no payment is made by the futures counterparties?

The court mentioned both the share price risk and the dividend payment risk but did not investigate whether the Danish Bank had borne the credit risk of the counterparties in relation to the SMI futures concluded 'on exchange' via block crosses with the various counterparties (with the *Futures Broker* acting only as an agent).[305]

With respect to this risk, one has to acknowledge that – unlike in the *Swiss Swaps* case – the Danish Bank did not have to bear the credit risk of its futures counterparties because the transactions were executed 'on exchange'. Even if the futures transactions were entered among known counterparties and executed via block crosses, the parties did not bear the credit risk of each other, but the exchange functioned as a counterparty. Thus, the Danish Bank only bore the default risk of the exchange but not the credit risk of the counterparties.

In respect of the share price risk, the court suggested that the Swiss share basket was fully hedged with the SMI futures.[306] The author agrees with this assumption from an economic point of view. Although index futures do not provide an exact hedge for single stocks, it is very likely that the SMI futures provided an exact hedge for the basket of SMI shares, assuming that the share basket mirrored the SMI both in its composition and the weighting of the shares in the index.

In the author's view, it would be irrelevant if the share basket was fully hedged with futures that were concluded among known counterparties or if the futures trades were executed anonymously on exchange. In both cases, the futures would provide a full hedge for the underlying share basket.

Concerning the economic impact of the *SMI Futures* case, the author believes that the decision of the Federal Supreme Court has put an end to cash-futures arbitrage, which is executed between known (or not disclosed) counterparties block crossing

303. *Ibid.*, para. 8.1.1.
304. *Ibid.*, para. 8.3.3.
305. *Ibid.*, para. 9.3.
306. *Ibid.*, para. 9.3.

their share transactions and/or futures on exchange. In the author's opinion, this will not only apply to cases where a double taxation convention is in place which provides a full refund of dividend withholding taxes, such as the now amended Switzerland/Denmark Double Taxation Convention, but also to cases where the counterparty is not a Danish Bank but a Swiss bank which also receives a full dividend withholding tax refund.

In this respect, one needs to see the *SMI Futures* case in conjunction with the domestic *Single Stock Futures* case, which is outlined below.

Both cases - taken together - may have put an end not only to cash-futures arbitrage using SMI futures as a hedge, which are executed via a block cross 'on exchange', but also to any form of cash-futures arbitrage which utilises OTC forwards that are agreed between known counterparties.

In light of both decided cases, one will have to assume that OTC forward transactions with a foreign counterparty, which is able to apply for a full dividend withholding tax refund under a treaty, as well as OTC forwards between a foreign bank and a domestic Swiss bank which receives a full refund, will be under the scrutiny of the Swiss tax authorities.

On the other hand, cash-futures arbitrage with anonymous third parties 'on exchange' without using the block cross facility of the exchange may still be considered as not transferring the beneficial ownership from the legal owner of the shares (and the recipient of the dividends) to the futures counterparty.

[c] The Single Stock Futures Case

The *Single Stock Futures* case[307] concerns the question of attributing beneficial ownership of the dividends under Swiss domestic law.

[i] Facts of the Case

A Swiss resident bank ('Swiss Bank') applied for a refund of Swiss withholding taxes on dividends received in 2006 to the Swiss Federal Tax Administration ('FTA').[308] The dividends were paid by Swiss companies which had their shares listed on the Swiss Exchange, the shares being constituents of the SMI.[309]

307. *Swiss Federal Supreme Court (Bundesgericht) decision of 2nd October 2015, 2C_383/2013 (Single Stock Futures* case).
For an analysis of the Federal Administrative Court's decision, *see also* Peter Hongler, 'New Swiss Court Decision on Hedged Equity Investments' (2013) 71(2) Tax Notes International, 155 (2013).
308. *Swiss Federal Administrative Court (Bundesverwaltungsgericht) decision of 13 March 2013, A-4794/2012 (Single Stock Futures* case*)*, (Federal Administrative Court, A-4794/2012), paras D. and E.
309. *Swiss Federal Administrative Court* (Bundesverwaltungsgericht) decision of 23 July 2012, A-1246/2011 (*SMI Futures* case), para. A.

The Swiss Bank entered into the following transactions:

(1) it purchased six different positions in Swiss shares from various counterparty banks, and
(2) simultaneously sold single stock futures[310] at the EUREX exchange[311] over these underlying shares to the same counterparties ('the Counterparties').[312]

The Counterparties were banks resident in the UK.[313] The shares purchases were bilaterally agreed OTC transactions.[314] The transactions were executed via international brokers, which were acting as agents. The Swiss Bank knew the identities of the Counterparties.[315]

The purchases of the Swiss shares were executed before the dividend record date[316] but after an announcement of the board of directors of the companies distributing the dividend in respect of the amount of the dividends to be distributed.[317] The single stock futures had a maturity shortly after the dividend due date.[318]

The single stock futures were executed 'on exchange' via *block crosses*,[319] meaning that the parties individually agreed to execute a certain amount of single stock futures at a pre-agreed price, with the trades being matched between the parties by the exchange.[320]

The futures were cash settled, with the payments being settled at the maturity of the contracts by the exchange.[321] The Swiss Bank sold the share positions

310. For a definition of the instrument, *see* Frank J. Fabozzi and Harry M. Markowitz, *The Theory and Practice of Investment Management: Asset Allocation, Valuation, Portfolio Construction, and Strategies* (2nd edn Wiley 2011) 368 (under the header: Single stock futures): 'A single stock futures (SSF) contract is an agreement between two parties to buy or sell shares of individual companies (as opposed to a stock index in the case of a stock index futures contract) at some time in the future with the terms agreed upon today. The value of traditional futures contracts is captured by SSFs as well because the agreement requires low capital commitment upfront in the form of an initial margin. Originally there were two key benefits to investors. These included that shorting was not constrained by the uptick rule or by complicated stock loans and a single long or short strategy in the underlying stock can be created.'
311. Federal Administrative Court, A-4794/2012, para. 3.2.
312. *Ibid.*, paras 3.1. and 3.3.
313. *Ibid.*, para. 3.1.
314. *Ibid.*, paras 3.1. and 3.6.1, confirming that the shares purchases were bilaterally agreed and executed via brokers acting as agents.
315. *Ibid.*, para. 3.1.
316. *Ibid.*, para. 3.3.
317. *Ibid.*, para. 3.1.
318. *Ibid.*, paras 3.1. and 3.3.
The court explained that the futures had a maturity equalling the next possible EUREX expiry date following the dividend due date.
Single stock futures at the EUREX have monthly expiry dates, *see* EUREX, Single Stock Futures (2023), 10, https://www.eurex.com/resource/blob/1252/1ddc50df36c1e5e0a00aeb03141bcea3/data/presentation_eurex-single-stock-futures.pdf, accessed 2 January 2024.
319. Federal Administrative Court, A-4794/2012, paras 3.2. and 3.3.
320. For a description of the term 'block cross', *see* above.
321. Federal Administrative Court, A-4797/2912, paras 3.1. and 3.5.1.

anonymously on exchange on the same day when the futures contracts matured (no block cross facility was used).[322]

The FTA denied the refund of the dividend withholding taxes on the basis that the Swiss Bank was not the beneficial owner of the dividends. In addition, the tax authorities suggested that the transactions constituted an 'abuse of law'.[323]

The six share and single stock futures transactions were illustrated in the reasoning of the Federal Administrative Court at the example of UBS shares and single stock futures.[324] The following table illustrates the positions in the combined transaction on 5-6 April 2006:

Long equity position on 5-6 April	CHF 501,934,640
Short single stock futures position 5-6 April	CHF 492,152,000
Gross dividends (ex-date 20 April)	CHF 11,040,000

The court did not mention the disposal price of the shares, nor did it determine at which market prices the single stock futures were closed. Nevertheless, the table above shows that the equity position in UBS shares was almost fully hedged with single stock futures.

The difference in price between the equity position and the single stock futures position (which were entered nearly simultaneously) can be explained by the total expected gross dividends of CHF 11,040,000, which were already announced by the board of directors of UBS to be CHF 3.20 per share on 22 March 2006. In the general meeting of UBS on 19 April 2006, this announcement by the board of directors was accepted by the shareholders. The dividends went ex-dividend on the 20 April 2006.

It is interesting to note that a dividend amount of CHF 9,782,640 was priced into the UBS single stock futures (leaving aside the financing costs of the transaction). This dividend amount equals approximately 88.6% of the gross dividends.[325] The FTA indicated that the Swiss Bank made a total profit of CHF 1,257,360 in the combined UBS shares and single stock futures transaction.[326]

If the UK bank had held the shares directly, it would have paid a 35% domestic withholding tax on the dividends, which would have been reduced under the UK/Switzerland Double Taxation Convention (1977) to a final withholding tax rate of

322. *Ibid.*, paras 3.1. and 3.5.1.
323. *Ibid.*, para. F; *also* Federal Supreme Court, 2C_383/2013, para. A.
324. Federal Administrative Court, A-4797/2912, paras 3.1.
325. The amount of the gross dividends was CHF 11,040,000.
326. Federal Administrative Court, A-4794/2012, para. 3.4.

One should note that the profit made by the Swiss Bank equalled approx. 11.4% of the total dividends. The profit of the Counterparties of the share and futures transactions only amounted to 3.6% of the dividends if one assumed that the Counterparties would have paid a final withholding tax rate of 15% under the UK/Switzerland Double Taxation Convention (1977). The 3.6% benefit would equal approx. CHF 400,000 in the UBS share/futures transaction.

15%.[327] Thus, the UK banks would have received net dividends, which amounted to 85% of the gross dividends.

[ii] Domestic Tax Law Background of the Case

Under Swiss domestic tax law, a domestic dividend withholding tax is levied on the dividends received from Swiss shares at a rate of 35%.[328] The tax has to be *deducted at source* by the company distributing the dividends.[329]

As the withholding tax is used as a means to secure taxation of these dividends and to avoid tax fraud or tax avoidance in a domestic context,[330] companies and banks resident in Switzerland will receive a full refund of dividend withholding taxes,[331] provided certain conditions are fulfilled.[332]

According to Article 21 (1) a) *Verrechnungssteuergesetz*[333] (VStG), a person (who is eligible according to Articles 22 to 28 VStG) has a right to receive a refund of withholding taxes on the dividends received if 'the person – on the due date of the claim[334] – has the "right of use of the asset" which generated the taxable income'.[335]

Domestic companies and partnerships have the right to receive a refund if they had – at maturity of the claim (dividend due date) – their seat in Switzerland.[336]

A refund of the dividend withholding taxes must be denied if the refund of the withholding tax 'would lead to an avoidance of withholding taxes'.[337]

Hence, the Swiss resident bank as the holder of the shares (and recipient of the dividends) will only receive a full refund of withholding taxes (and thus effectively pay 0% withholding taxes) under domestic law if:

(1) the Swiss Bank is the beneficial owner of the shares
(2) no abuse of law has taken place that led to an avoidance of tax.[338]

In contrast, most of the foreign banks that hold Swiss shares will have to pay a final 15% dividend withholding tax under a double taxation convention between their

327. Convention for the Avoidance of Double Taxation with respect to Taxes on Income (1977), as amended by the Protocols in 1981 and 2007, Art. 10, para. 2b).
328. Articles 1(1), 4(1) b), 13(1) a), 14(1) *Verrechnungssteuergesetz* (Law concerning withholding taxes).
329. Article 10(1), 14(1) VStG.
330. Federal Administrative Court, A-4794/2012, para. 2.2.
331. Article 24 (2) VStG.
332. Article 21(1) a) VStG and 21(2) VStG.
Compare Federal Administrative Court, A-4794/2012, para. 2.3.
333. *Law concerning withholding* taxes.
334. Shareholders who are registered as the owner of the shares on or before the dividend record date, will receive the dividend.
335. Federal Administrative Court, A-4794/2012, para. 2.3. 1st paragraph.
336. Article 24(2) VStG.
337. Article 21(2) VStG.
338. Article 21(1) a) and (2) VStG.

resident country and Switzerland, as the 35% domestic withholding tax will be reduced under a respective double taxation convention (partial refund of withholding tax).[339]

[iii] The Decision of the Federal Administrative Court

The Federal Administrative Court discussed the following questions:

(1) Was the Swiss Bank the beneficial owner of the Swiss dividends received?

The Federal Administrative Court maintained that Article 21(1) a) VStG had to be interpreted not in a legalistic sense, but it had a commercial meaning. According to the court, one needed to interpret the term 'right of use' of the asset which generated the income in an economic context instead of interpreting the term in a pure legalistic sense, referring to a previous decision of the Federal Administrative Court:[340]

> It is possible that the 'right of use' must be attributed to someone else than the (formal) legal owner of the assets, for example if the owner is contractually obliged to pass on the income of the asset to third parties even if no formal obligation to pass on the income exists but it can be derived from the circumstances as a whole that the use of the capital income does not remain with the legal owner.[341]

The Federal Administrative Court indicated that even if the Swiss Bank was the beneficial owner of the dividends according to Article 21(1) a) VStG, the exception of Article 21(3) VStG could lead to a different result in respect of the refund of withholding taxes if the special conditions of this paragraph were fulfilled.[342]

This was, in particular, the case if the right of refund of the withholding tax could not be relied upon 'the right of use of the asset' because it would lead to 'unnecessary intricateness or even to wrong results'.[343] The court states in this respect:

> The legal rights of an asset are usually transferred upon the conclusion of the contract. However, in case of a forward purchase (or futures contract) of a security, the party purchasing the security forward (long party) has a contractual claim against the party selling the security forward (short party) in respect of the income which is due between the conclusion of the contract and the settlement of the contract. Thus, the forward seller therefore pays a compensation payment to the forward buyer in respect of the income [...] According to Article 62 *Verrechnungssteuerverordnung* (regulation concerning withholding taxes) (hereinafter:

339. Under Art. 10(2) b of the UK/Switzerland Double Taxation Convention (1977), the 35% Swiss withholding tax rate is reduced to a 15% withholding tax rate on Swiss dividends. UK resident shareholders of Swiss can apply for a refund of 20% (difference between 35% and 15%) Swiss dividend withholding taxes according to Arts 1 to 3 of the *Verordnung zum schweizerisch-britischen Doppelbesteuerungsabkommen* (1975) – Regulation concerning the UK/Switzerland Double Taxation Convention (1977).
340. Federal Administrative Court, A-4794/2012, para. 2.6. Reference is made to the decision of the Swiss Federal Administrative Court of 30 October 2008, A-2163/2007, para. 3.3.
341. Federal Administrative Court, A-4794/2012, para. 2.6. 2nd paragraph, referring to a decision of the Swiss Federal Supreme Court of 8 July 2007, 2A.660/2006, para. 4.1. which concerned the rights to repurchase own shares.
342. Federal Administrative Court, A-4794/2012, para. 2.7.
343. *Ibid.*, para. 2.7. 1st paragraph.

VStV), the *right* to receive the withholding tax refund *is attributed to* the forward seller of the security, if – at the due date of the income – the seller owns both the security and the coupons, otherwise it is attributed to the third party who at the due date of the income, has the right of use of the security (which is to be delivered at maturity).[344]

The court ruled that Article 62 VStV only attributed the right of a withholding tax refund to the forward seller of the security, but it does not determine if the forward seller was the beneficial owner of the distributed dividends (or not) on the relevant date.[345]

(2) Did an *abuse of law* take place, resulting in a denial of the withholding tax refund?

A refund of withholding taxes could be denied based on the notion of *abuse of law* according to Article 21(2) VStG even if the prerequisites of Article 21(1) a) VStG applied, and the recipient of the dividends was the beneficial owner of the dividends.

The Federal Administrative Court suggested that a refund of withholding taxes could be denied:

(a) if the legal structure of the transaction seems unusual, improper or rather strange, in any case considering the economic circumstances unreasonable (objective criterion),
(b) if it can be assumed that the chosen legal structure was only chosen in order to save taxes which would have been due in case of a proper implementation of the transaction (subjective criterion), and
(c) if the chosen structure has, in fact, led to a significant saving of taxes provided the tax authorities accepted the structure (effective tax saving).[346]

Whether the criteria defined above are *cumulatively fulfilled* depends on the actual facts of the case.[347]

The Federal Administrative Court concurred with the reasoning of the FTA in the administrative appeal, which ruled that the transactions constituted an *abuse of law*. The overall transaction construct was structured in a way that the Swiss Bank neither had borne the dividend risk nor the share price risk and additionally, also not the credit risk of the counterparties.[348] The structure was 'absolutely inadequate', as the Swiss Bank was factually obliged to pass on the bigger part of the dividends by way of implied net dividend yields priced into the single stock futures.

The Federal Administrative Court indicated that the Swiss Bank did not execute the transactions anonymously on exchange but used the block cross facility of the exchange where bilaterally pre-agreed contracts were matched by the exchange. The court ruled that both transactions (share purchase and disposal of the single stock

344. *Ibid.*, 2nd paragraph.
345. *Ibid.*
346. Federal Administrative Court, A-4794/2012, para. 2.8.1.
347. *Ibid.*
348. *Ibid.*, para. 4.1.

futures), executed between known counterparties under the block cross facility, had to be regarded as an economic unity.[349]

The Swiss Bank purchased Swiss shares shortly before the dividend record date from the Counterparties and simultaneously sold them forward via single stock futures to the same Counterparties at a loss. The loss could only be covered as the Swiss Bank received the dividends, which were already announced by the board of directors. The Swiss Bank only entered into the transaction in order to make a profit,[350] which consisted of the spread between the (gross) dividends received and the implied (net) dividends priced into the futures. According to the court, the transaction made economic sense for the Swiss Bank as it could receive a – nearly riskless – profit of 0.26% on the invested capital in the course of two weeks.[351]

The court could not identify any economic motives of the Counterparties to enter into the transactions apart from the motive to avoid the Swiss dividend withholding tax.[352] According to the court, the Counterparties still maintained the full share price risk and additionally paid the Swiss Bank a fee for the riskless transaction.[353] The court disregarded the argument advanced by the Swiss Bank that the Counterparties entered into the transactions in order to generate liquidity.[354]

Further, the court indicated that the fee, which the Counterparties paid to the Swiss Bank, equalled an annualised interest rate of 6.5% on the capital provided by the Swiss Bank to the Counterparties (liquidity provision by purchasing the shares and selling single stock futures).[355] The court regarded a 6.5% annualised interest rate (compared to a Swiss reference interest rate of 1.15% to 1.3%) as excessive if the amount was only paid for the provision of the liquidity and affirmed that the main reason for paying such a fee was that the Swiss Bank entered into tax-motivated transactions with the Counterparties.[356]

The court ruled that the *objective criterion* of an *abuse of law* was fulfilled based on the following 'peculiarities' of the case:

(i) significant costs for the Counterparties to enter into the transaction;
(ii) necessary economic connection between the share and the futures transactions;

349. *Ibid.*, para. 4.3.
350. *Ibid.*
351. *Ibid.*, para. 4.4.
352. *Ibid.*
353. *Ibid.*
354. One should indeed consider that the sale of the asset and the purchase of a derivative instrument with the same underlying can generate liquidity and enable the counterparties to enter into leveraged equity investments. In order generate liquidity, the counterparties could sell the shares for, say, 100, thereby generating cash of 100, and simultaneously enter into a long derivatives position (here: single stock futures) for, say, an initial margin payment of 10, thereby generating excess liquidity of 90 which could, for example, be used to enter into further equity derivatives transactions. By doing so, the counterparties could obtain a synthetic equity position, which is 10 times larger than a physical investment into shares, thereby levering both its potential profits by 10, but also levering its potential losses.
355. Federal Administrative Court, A-4794/2012, para. 4.4.
356. *Ibid.*, para. 4.4.

(iii) the shares were purchased shortly before the dividend record date;
(iv) a short term of the single stock futures contracts;
(v) no other economic motives for the Counterparties to enter into the transactions apart from the motive to save Swiss dividend withholding taxes.[357]

Further, the parties would have achieved a tax saving in respect of Swiss dividend withholding taxes if these transactions were accepted by the tax authorities and the court (*effective tax saving*).[358] Hence, the second definition criterion of an abuse of law was also fulfilled.

Lastly, it could be assumed that the chosen legal structure was only chosen in order to save taxes, which would have been due in the case of a proper implementation of the transaction (*subjective criterion*).

The court affirmed that the aim to protect the tax base could not be achieved simply because the 35% withholding taxes were initially collected by the company distributing the dividends if the Swiss Bank would be able to receive a full refund of the dividend withholding tax.[359] The court regarded the *large fee* received by the Swiss Bank as an indicator that the Swiss Bank knew that the Counterparties only entered into the transactions because they wanted to save Swiss dividend withholding taxes.

According to the court, it was not for the court to prove that the Swiss Bank intended to avoid Swiss dividend withholding taxes. Rather, it was sufficient that the Swiss Bank significantly participated in the avoidance of dividend withholding taxes for the benefit of the Counterparties.[360] The court, therefore, concluded that the FTA – as the lower instance – rightfully assumed an abuse of law.

It reiterated that if the prerequisites of assuming an abuse of law were fulfilled, a (substitute) transaction would have to be assumed, which would have been the appropriate transaction construct in order to achieve the economic results aimed at by the parties of the transactions.[361]

The court objected to the proposition by the Swiss Bank that it should receive at least a 20% dividend withholding tax refund as the UK counterparties would have received at least this refund if they had held the Swiss shares directly and received the dividends.[362]

The court ruled that if the transactions had been executed in a proper way, the Swiss Bank would not have had a right to receive the refund, as it would not have bought the shares at all. Hence, the Swiss Bank's right to reclaim the dividend withholding taxes had been forfeited.

The court affirmed that it could not determine whether the Counterparties had a right to reclaim the 20% withholding taxes. The court indicated that no refund applications were submitted by the Counterparties. Further, it was not certain whether

357. *Ibid.*, 2nd paragraph.
358. *Ibid.*
359. *Ibid.*
360. *Ibid.*
361. *Ibid.*, para. 4.5.
362. *Ibid.*

the Counterparties were the beneficial owners of the shares or whether they entered into the transactions on behalf of other parties who would have been the beneficial owners of the shares.[363]

The Federal Administrative Court held that the dividend withholding tax refund to the Swiss Bank had to be denied as the Swiss Bank was not the beneficial owner of the dividends (Article 21(1) a) VStG), and additionally, because the refund had to be denied because abuse of law took place (Article 21(2) VStG).[364]

[iv] The Decision of the Swiss Federal Supreme Court

The Federal Supreme Court affirmed the decision of the Federal Administrative Court and ruled that the appeal by the Swiss Bank had to be dismissed.[365] The Federal Supreme Court identified *three characteristics of the transactions*, which were based on the reasoning of the Federal Administrative Court and regarded them as relevant for determining whether the Swiss Bank was the beneficial owner of the dividends,[366] namely:

(1) The transactions were executed shortly before the dividend record date and matured shortly after the dividend record date.[367]

The court indicated that this applied to the share transactions as the shares were purchased shortly before the dividend record date but after the board of directors announced the dividend amount. Simultaneously, the Swiss Bank sold single stock futures that matured after the dividend record date.[368]

(2) The transactions were inseparable and constituted an economic unity.[369]

Single stock futures are futures on the underlying shares. These underlying shares were forward sold to the Counterparties at a certain date with a pre-agreed futures price. The Counterparties purchased the same amount of single stock futures as they sold the underlying shares. Thus, one transaction was only executed because of the other transaction, and both transactions constituted an inseparable economic unity.[370]

(3) Both transactions were executed with the same UK counterparty banks, which were known to the Swiss Bank.[371]

The Swiss Bank knew the circumstances of the transactions and the identities of the Counterparties as the transactions were executed via a broker acting as an agent. The broker had disclosed the counterparties. The same counterparties, which sold the

363. *Ibid.*
364. *Ibid.*, para. 4.6.
365. Federal Supreme Court, 2C_383/2013, *see* Judgment, para. 1.
366. *Ibid.*, para. 5.2-5.3.
367. *Ibid.*, para. 5.2.1.
368. *Ibid.*
369. *Ibid.*, para. 5.2.2.
370. *Ibid.*
371. *Ibid.*, para. 5.2.3.

shares OTC to the Swiss Bank, simultaneously purchased single stock futures over the very same shares.[372]

The Federal Supreme Court concurred with the decision of the Federal Administrative Court and affirmed that the Swiss Bank was not the beneficial owner of the dividends, and thus, the refund could be denied.[373] According to the court, the Swiss Bank *was only interposed by the Counterparties* in order to obtain the benefit of a full withholding tax refund.[374]

The Federal Supreme Court indicated that the purchase of the shares and the simultaneous sale of the single stock futures over the very same shares had contradicting economic purposes and made no sense economically unless one considered the tax motive of the transaction.[375] Although the shares were sold by the Counterparties to the Swiss Bank, the purpose of the transaction was to pass on the majority of the dividends to the Counterparties as if they had been the legal owner of the shares. Further, the court held that it could be derived from the overall transaction construct that the parties of the share transactions wanted to achieve a full refund of Swiss dividend withholding taxes, which would not have been possible if the Counterparties had not sold the shares to the Swiss Bank.[376]

In contrast to the *SMI Futures* case, the Federal Supreme Court acknowledged that the parties could determine the difference between the share purchase price and the single stock futures price by bilaterally agreeing on the futures price in a block-crossed single-stock futures transaction.[377] According to the court, this allowed the parties to attribute the majority of the dividends to the Counterparties by way of pricing the dividends into single stock futures.[378]

The court held that the Swiss Bank, by entering into the combined share and single stock futures transaction, could advance a pre-payment of the dividends in the form of the dividends implied in the futures pricing to the Counterparties and later receive the real dividends upon distribution. Hence, the court indicated that the Swiss Bank's profit was not the dividend received but a mere 'fee' for entering into these combined share and single stock futures transactions.[379]

The Federal Supreme Court explained at the UBS share example that one needed to set off the loss on the combined shares and single stock futures transaction (CHF 9,782,640) against the gross dividends (65% net dividends received plus 35% withholding tax refund) of CHF 11,040,000, thus leading to a profit of CHF 1,257,300 for the Swiss Bank. The court reiterated that the transaction made only economic sense for the Swiss Bank if the loss under the combined share and single stock futures transaction was compensated by the net dividend yield received and, *in addition*, if a full withholding tax refund of 35% could be obtained by the Swiss Bank.

372. *Ibid.*
373. *Ibid.*, para. 5.3.
374. *Ibid.*
375. *Ibid.*
376. *Ibid.*
377. *Ibid.*, para. 5.3.1, 2nd paragraph.
378. *Ibid.*
379. *Ibid.*

The Federal Supreme Court further confirmed that the *aim* of the combined transaction was a full refund of the 35% withholding tax rate for the Swiss Bank.[380] It indicated that there were no economic motives for the Counterparties to enter into the transaction apart from avoiding a definitive dividend withholding tax of 15% on the gross dividends. If the Counterparties had held the shares directly, a 35% withholding tax on the dividends received would have been due. This withholding tax rate may have been reduced to a final source tax rate of 15% if the conditions for a refund had been fulfilled according to the UK/Switzerland Double Taxation Convention (1977).[381]

The Federal Supreme Court regarded it as detrimental that the Swiss Bank and its Counterparties entered into a combined share and single stock futures transaction with the aim of receiving a full withholding tax refund on Swiss dividends.[382] The Federal Supreme Court concluded that the Counterparties of the combined transactions had to bear the full share price risk and paid the Swiss Bank a fee for the nearly risk-free 'service' of avoiding the dividend withholding tax – with the Swiss Bank proposing to the FTA that it was the beneficial owner of the dividends.[383]

The Federal Supreme Court held that the Swiss Bank was the legal owner of the shares at the dividend record date but that it was *not* the beneficial owner of the dividends.[384] The court affirmed that not only the use of an agent, trustee or nominee could lead to a transfer of beneficial ownership but also a combined transaction where the share purchases were fully hedged with the sale of single stock futures.[385]

In particular, the court distinguished the *Single Stock Futures* case from other share disposals of a foreign counterparty shortly before the dividend date, where the expected dividend was partly priced into the share purchase contract.[386] It indicated that the mere share disposal before the dividend record date would not, in every case, constitute a shift of beneficial ownership of the dividends from the party purchasing the shares to the party selling the shares, although the expected dividends were partly priced into the share purchase price.[387]

Although the *Single Stock Futures* case concerns the refund of dividend withholding taxes under domestic law by a Swiss resident bank, the court additionally denied the Swiss Bank the beneficial ownership of the dividends because it regarded the *interdependence* criterion advocated by Baumgartner as fulfilled.[388]

380. *Ibid.*, para. 5.3.2, 1st paragraph.
381. *Ibid.*, 2nd paragraph.
382. Federal Supreme Court, 2C_383/2013, para. 5.3.3, 2nd paragraph.
383. *Ibid.*, para. 5.3.2, 3rd paragraph.
384. *Ibid.*, para. 5.3.3, 1st paragraph.
385. *Ibid.*, 3rd paragraph.
386. *Ibid.*, 2nd paragraph.
387. The court noted that 'special circumstances' have to be fulfilled in order to consider a change of beneficial ownership from the buyer of the shares to the former owner as the buyer would act as a trustee for the seller of the shares.
388. *Ibid.*, paras 4.2 and 5.4, referring to the concept of interdependence developed by Baumgartner and applied by the Swiss Federal Supreme Court in the *Swiss Swaps* case, *see* Federal Supreme Court, 2C_364/2012 and 2C_377/2012, para. 5.2.2.
Compare Baumgartner (2010), 130-150.

The Federal Supreme Court affirmed that the concept of *interdependence* in the context of beneficial ownership could also be applied in the context of the domestic law provision of Article 21(1) a) VStG.[389]

According to the concept of beneficial ownership applied by the Federal Supreme Court in the *Swiss Swaps* case, beneficial ownership must be denied to a person if the dividends have to be passed on because of legal obligations or factual limitations that exist already at the point of time of the payment of the dividends.[390]

According to the Federal Supreme Court, a factual limitation to enjoy the dividends can be assumed if there is an interdependence between obtaining the dividends and passing on the dividends, namely if:

(a) obtaining the income is dependent on the obligation to pass on the income (1st dependence), and
(b) the obligation to pass on the income is dependent on obtaining the income (2nd dependence).[391]

In the *Single Stock Futures* case, the Federal Supreme Court criticised that the Federal Administrative Court had not considered the concept of *interdependence* at all in order to determine if the Swiss Bank was the beneficial owner of the dividends received according to Swiss domestic law (Article 21(1) a) VStG).[392]

The court, however, concluded that based on the facts as determined by the Federal Administrative Court, one could assume that an *interdependence* between obtaining the dividends and passing on the dividends existed. The Swiss Bank was not the beneficial owner of the dividends, which the Federal Supreme Court based on the following reasoning:[393]

First, the Swiss Bank was obliged to pass on the majority of the dividends to the Counterparties.

Second, the combined share purchase/futures transaction was a complex overall transaction construct executed with known Counterparties who would not have entered into the transactions if the transaction did not have the purpose of passing on

389. Federal Supreme Court, 2C_383/2013, para. 4.2.
390. Federal Supreme Court, 2C_364/2012 and 2C_377/2012, para. 5.2.2; *compare also* Federal Supreme Court, 2C_895/2012, para. 4.2 and Federal Supreme Court, 2C_383/2013, para. 4.2.
391. Federal Supreme Court, 2C_383/2013, para. 4.2; *also* Federal Supreme Court, 2C_364/2012 and 2C_377/2012, para. 5.2.2 and Federal Supreme Court, 2C_895/2012, para. 4.2.
Baumgartner and Frick propose in a case summary: 'Such a factual limitation is given if the following characteristics exist (concept of interdependence):

(i) the realization of the (dividend) income depends on the duty to forward this (dividend) income (first dependency); and
(ii) the duty to forward this (dividend) income depends on the realization of this (dividend) income (second dependency.'

See Baumgartner and Frick (2015), 4.
392. Federal Supreme Court, 2C_383/2013, para. 5.4.
393. *Ibid.*, para. 5.4.

the majority of the dividends to the Counterparties and achieving a full refund of Swiss dividend withholding taxes.[394]

Third, it did not make any difference whether the dividends were passed on in the course of separate payments or whether the dividends were passed on by way of pre-payments of the expected dividends, being the market price difference between the share purchase prices and the bilaterally agreed single stock futures prices.[395] The court held that it was also irrelevant whether a payment in lieu of the real dividend was passed on or whether the majority of the expected dividends were forwarded to the Counterparties in the form of the dividends implied in the futures prices.[396]

Fourth, the Federal Supreme Court ruled that the *second dependence* was also fulfilled because the Swiss Bank needed to pass on only the dividend income, which was effectively received, meaning that the duty to pass on the dividends was dependent on the actual receipt of the dividends.[397] The Swiss Bank only entered into the transactions in order to receive a 'quasi-riskless' fee as it acted as the holder of the shares and recipient of the dividends, although it did not have to bear any share price risk.[398] The court concurred with the reasoning advanced by the Federal Administrative Court, which held that although only the expected dividends and not the realised dividends were priced into the futures, the dividend risk could be neglected as the shares were purchased only after the announcement of the dividend amount by the board of directors shortly before the dividend record date.[399]

The Federal Supreme Court did not consider whether an abuse of law took place according to Article 21(2) VStG as it already denied the Swiss Bank the beneficial ownership of the dividends.[400]

[v] Critical Discussion of the *Single Stock Futures* Case

The *Single Stock Futures* case was the most obvious case of withholding tax arbitrage cases among the three Swiss cases concerning this topic, and the facts were straightforward: The Swiss Bank knew the counterparties of the share purchases and the single stock futures transactions as the shares were initially purchased by the Swiss Bank in the course of bilaterally agreed OTC transactions, the single stock futures were block-crossed on exchange, and the counterparties of the share purchases were the same as the counterparties of the single stock futures.

In addition, the tax saving motive of the counterparties was obvious; the purpose of the combined transactions was a full refund of Swiss dividend withholding taxes

394. *Ibid.*, para. 5.4.1, 1st paragraph.
395. *Ibid.*, para. 5.4.1, 2nd paragraph.
396. *Ibid.*
397. *Ibid.*, para. 5.4.2, 1st paragraph.
398. *Ibid.*, 2nd and 3rd paragraphs.
399. *Ibid.*, 3rd paragraph.
400. *Ibid.*, para. 5.5.

instead of a payment of a 15% non-recoverable Swiss dividend withholding tax by the Counterparties under the UK/Switzerland Double Taxation Convention (1977).[401]

The reasoning of the Federal Supreme Court thoroughly considered the facts of the case, and it was in line with the economic reality, as the Federal Supreme Court acknowledged that the majority of the dividends were implied in the pricing of the single stock futures.[402]

The court was correct in assuming that the risk of not obtaining the expected dividend but instead receiving lower actual dividends was only a theoretical risk in the *Single Stock Futures* case. The shares were purchased shortly before the dividend date but after the proposal by the board of directors with respect to the dividend amount.[403] In contrast to the *SMI Futures* case, the Federal Supreme Court did not debate whether only a 'small part of the dividends' remained with the Swiss Bank and whether the majority of dividends were passed on to the Counterparties.[404]

The decision in the *Single Stock Futures* case shows that the criterion of 'retaining only a small part of the dividends' may not be a suitable criterion for determining whether beneficial ownership of the dividends has remained with the Swiss Bank, at least in cases applying the domestic law provision. In the *Single Stock Futures* case, it was obvious that the Swiss Bank obtained the majority of the arbitrage profit between the cash instrument and the derivatives. In the exemplary transactions over UBS shares, the Swiss Bank only passed on approximately 88.6% of the gross dividends by implying this amount in the single stock futures prices.

Assuming that the UK counterparty banks would have been subject to an irrecoverable Swiss dividend withholding tax of 15% after the application of the UK/Switzerland Double Tax Convention (1977), the combined transaction would have generated for the Counterparties an arbitrage profit of only 3.6%, whereas the Swiss Bank had received an arbitrage profit of approximately 11.4% if the transactions had been accepted by the Swiss tax authorities and the Swiss courts.

The Federal Supreme Court focused in its reasoning on two lines of argument that allowed the court to deny the Swiss Bank the refund of dividend withholding taxes:

First, it identified and highlighted three unusual characteristics of the combined transactions that were also outlined by the Federal Administrative Court and viewed them as decisive whether beneficial ownership of the dividends had been retained by the Swiss Bank or not, namely:

(1) The combined share purchases/futures transactions were executed shortly before the dividend date, with the settlement of the futures (and simultaneous

401. Article. 10(2) b) UK/Switzerland Double Taxation Convention (1977), as amended by the 2009 Protocol.

402. Federal Supreme Court, 2C_383/2013, para. 5.3.1.
In contrast, the Federal Supreme Court ruled in the *SMI Futures* case that the dividends were passed by way of non-standard purchase and disposal prices of the shares and did not consider that the implied dividend yield of the expected dividends is priced into a future, *see* Federal Supreme Court, 2C_895/2012, paras 8.2.1 and 8.5.

403. Federal Supreme Court, 2C_383/2013, para. 5.2.1.

404. Federal Supreme Court, 2C_895/2012, paras 6.2.3-6.3.

disposal of the shares) taking place shortly after the dividend payment date.[405]

(2) The transactions were inseparable and constituted an economic unity.[406]

(3) Both transactions were executed with the same counterparties' banks, which were known to the Swiss Bank.[407]

Second, the court denied the Swiss Bank beneficial ownership of the dividends because it considered that there was an *interdependence* between obtaining the dividends and passing them on.[408]

Unlike the Federal Administrative Court, the Federal Supreme Court did not consider whether an abuse of law occurred according to Article 21(2) VStG, and it did not examine whether the three definition criteria of an abuse of law, advocated by the Federal Administrative Court, were fulfilled.[409] By doing so, the Federal Supreme Court only relied on *objective criteria* to determine whether a transfer of beneficial ownership of the dividends had taken place from the owner of the shares to the derivatives counterparty. It also failed to focus in detail on the *subjective motives* of the Swiss Bank claiming the refund.[410]

In the author's view, the Federal Supreme Court's decision in the *Single Stock Futures* case may have caused significant uncertainties for Swiss Banks and their counterparties and clients which enter into hedged derivatives transactions as they might - under certain circumstances - also fall under the objective criteria advocated by the Federal Supreme Court, even if no subjective tax-saving motive was apparent.

Swiss Banks often act as prime brokers for their foreign prime brokerage clients (whether foreign companies, investment funds or other investment entities). The Swiss Banks often need to buy shares as a hedge for derivatives entered with their clients or counterparties, which invest synthetically into Swiss shares by way of derivatives. Swiss Banks facilitate leveraged synthetic equity investments of their clients, for example, by offering them contracts for differences, portfolio swaps, equity swaps and single stock futures.

The *Single Stock Futures* case might have had an impact on Swiss Banks acting as prime brokers and providing their clients with synthetic exposures to Swiss shares, even if those were entered into with the sole purpose of investing in the Swiss market in a leveraged form.

405. Federal Supreme Court, 2C_383/2013, para. 5.2.1.
406. *Ibid.*, para. 5.2.2.
407. *Ibid.*, para. 5.2.3.
408. *Ibid.*, paras 5.4-5.4.2.
409. Federal Supreme Court, 2C_383/2013, para. 5.5.
410. In contrast, the Federal Administrative Court considered the subjective motives in its reasoning by applying the abuse of law – test; *see* Federal Administrative Court, A-4794/2012, para. 4-4.5.

[d] *A Plc v. Federal Tax Administration*

In 2020, the Federal Supreme Court decided another beneficial ownership case, which provided further clarity on how far the Federal Supreme Court would go in denying treaty benefits in hedged derivatives transactions.[411] The author refers to a discussion of this case by *Danon* and *Malek*.[412]

§9.03 SOLUTIONS FOR THE TREATMENT OF DERIVATIVES IN CROSS-BORDER TRANSACTIONS

Derivatives may be used to mitigate dividend withholding taxes by shifting the economic risks and rewards of the dividends to the other party. Domestic tax systems have to act in order to prevent losses in their tax base.

If tax systems want to prevent withholding tax losses, they can either do so by narrowly defining the term 'beneficial owner' and disallowing the transfer of the risks and rewards of the dividends via derivatives transactions. Alternatively, they can apply the same (or no) corporate and withholding tax rates on dividends to both foreign and domestic market participants.

A further solution would be the introduction of withholding taxes on derivatives both on a domestic and tax treaty level in order to prevent withholding tax avoidance schemes that transfer the economic risks and rewards of assets or income to third parties via derivatives.

[A] Solution 1: Alternative Definition of 'Beneficial Owner' in Domestic Law and in the Tax Treaties

The approach of defining the term 'beneficial owner' narrowly seems to be difficult both on a domestic and international level.

At the domestic level, the *Single Stock Futures* case and its different outcome compared to the *Swiss Swaps* and *SMI Futures* cases show the general difficulty of the national courts to decide the attribution of income or assets based on the concept of beneficial ownership in transactions where derivatives are used to hedge the economic exposure of the overall transaction and to pass on income.

Likewise, at an international level, the current concept of beneficial ownership advocated by the OECD may not be able to reliably distinguish between common commercial hedging transactions that utilise derivatives and tax-avoidance schemes that are designed to reap withholding tax benefits by entering into hedged derivatives transactions.

411. Swiss Federal Supreme Court, *A Plc v. Federal Tax Administration* Case 2C_880/2018, 23 ILTR, 864, 867.
412. Robert Danon and Benjamin Malek, Commentary to: *A Plc v. Federal Tax Administration*, 23 ILTR, 864, 867-871.

In particular, the 2014 Update of the OECD Model Commentary and the amendments to paragraph 12.4, sentence 3, have, in the author's view, added further uncertainty on how to reliably distinguish between genuine commercial hedging transactions and dividend tax arbitrage.

The Spanish and Swiss cases show that *objective criteria* to define beneficial ownership need to be developed that allow distinguishing bona fide commercial transactions from tax-motivated transactions. These objective criteria will have to be supported by a second layer outside the specific definition of the term 'beneficial owner', namely efficient anti-avoidance rules, disclosure clauses and other measures with anti-avoidance effect.

Alternatively, one may resort to a *wide definition* of beneficial ownership that consists of both objective definitional criteria and a *subjective tax motive test* to tackle withholding tax avoidance schemes. If such a motive test is applied, this test should also be established based on objective criteria that distinguish tax avoidance schemes from other, evidently non-tax-motivated transactions.

In drafting successful criteria, the author believes that tax authorities would have to define in which cases all risks and rewards of an asset or an income stream have been transferred with the result that the asset or the income is attributed to the beneficial owner and where that is not the case.

[1] Objective Criteria to Determine Beneficial Ownership

When investigating the case of a common TRS, one needs to consider three economic risk factors that are characteristic of shares and determine whether each of the risk factors has been transferred under the TRS. A holder of shares is exposed to the following risks and rewards:

- the share price movement, i.e., the share price moves up or down after purchase;
- the dividend amount realised, i.e., the amount of dividend actually paid out;
- the amount realised by lending the shares out to third parties.

In the following, the author investigates whether all these risks and rewards are fully transferred under a TRS:

[a] Market Risk with Regard to the Share Price Movement

Under a TRS, the short party passes any upside movement in the price of the shares to the long party and receives any downside movement in the share price. Thus, the risks and rewards regarding the share price movement are transferred from the short party to the long party under a standard TRS.

[b] *Market Risk with Regard to the Dividends*

Under normal terms of a TRS, the parties will agree that the 'realised'[413] and not the 'expected' dividend[414] will be passed on by the short party of the TRS to the long party. This means that the risks and rewards regarding the dividend amounts are transferred from the short party to the long party under a standard TRS.[415]

> *Example 83:*
>
> Company A (short TRS party) enters into a TRS with Bank B (long TRS party) over the shares in Company C. It is assumed that Company A is resident in the same country where the underlying shares of Company C are issued and traded on the stock exchange and receives the dividends gross. Under the TRS, both Company A and Bank B agree that Company A will pass on the 'realised dividends' to Bank B. Both A and B expect a gross dividend of EUR 1 per share. Company C, however, declares only 50 cents per share due to a profit decline.[416] As both parties have agreed to pay 'realised dividends' under the swap, Company A will have to pass on only the 'realised dividends' of 50 cents per share to Bank B under the TRS.

Under a standard TRS, the pricing is not based on the expected dividends, i.e., the dividends that both parties assume when entering into the TRS, but on the dividend amounts that were actually paid out to the shareholders after the dividends were declared.

Thus, if the dividends that are paid out are different from what the parties' reasonable expectations were when entering into the TRS, the short party of the TRS will only ever have to pay the realised dividends and not the expected dividends. Thus, the risks and rewards with regard to the dividends are fully transferred from the short to the long TRS counterparty.

> *Example 84:*
>
> *Swiss Swaps* case
>
> One could question whether the Danish Bank was in any way exposed to the risk that the percentage of withholding tax reclaim under the treaty may have changed adversely due to a renegotiation of the treaty.

413. *Realised dividend* is the amount of gross dividend that is actually paid out by the company.
414. *Expected dividend* means the gross dividend amount, which both parties of the derivative expect the dividend-paying company to pay.
415. This is at least the case if 'realised' dividends are agreed under the terms of the TRS.
416. In exceptional circumstances, the dividend amount may also change between declared date of the dividend and dividend record date.

> As the Danish Bank would, however, have been able to terminate any TRS agreement under ISDA, clause 2D, if its dividend withholding tax reclaim rate had changed, the Danish Bank was not exposed to such a risk under the swaps.

[c] Market Risk with Regard to the Lending Amount Received

If professional market participants hold shares, it is very common for them to lend out the shares as they can generate an additional amount of income by lending out the shares to a third party, provided that there is a liquid lending market on these shares.

Thus, the amount of the lending fee received for lending out the shares is also a market risk factor with regard to the shares. Hence, the parties of a TRS will include in their pricing the additional amount, which the short party of the TRS can receive by lending out the shares that it holds as a hedge during the term of the swap.[417]

When both parties negotiate the terms of the TRS, the short TRS party will price into the TRS the lending fee that it will receive for the term of the TRS from a third party based on market quotes from third-party borrowers of shares, and it will agree the final price of the TRS based on a firm quote from this borrower and conclude the lending agreement at the same time when entering into the TRS agreement. As the lending fee is fixed during the term of the TRS, the short party has, in fact, also transferred the market risk with respect to the lending fee to the long party.

Thus, all three market risk positions with regard to the shares are commonly transferred under a standard TRS, independent of whether the TRS is entered into for tax-avoidance purposes or not. As a full transfer of risks and rewards has taken place, one can conclude based on objective criteria that beneficial ownership is commonly transferred under these swaps.

[B] Solution 2: Equalisation of Corporate and Withholding Tax Rates on Dividends

Domestic tax systems may decide to exempt both dividends and manufactured dividends received by domestic as well as foreign shareholders from (corporate and withholding) taxation and correspondingly disallow any form of withholding tax credit on both dividends as well as manufactured dividends and similar payments under derivatives.

The UK has opted for such an approach.[418] This alternative seems to be a robust solution as it does not allow for generating withholding tax credits in the first place. Hence, it should be carefully considered by the domestic tax legislator whether the

417. This amount is factored into the calculation of a TRS, as the long party to the TRS will want to be in the same economic position as if it held the shares, as the TRS is, in fact, a synthetic shareholding. If it held the shares directly, it could also have received the amount from lending out the shares.
418. Ch. 9 §9.01[C][1].

losses in tax revenues due to a tax exemption of dividends received by domestic shareholders and a corresponding withholding tax exemption on dividends received by foreign shareholders outweigh the benefits related to the prevention of withholding tax avoidance schemes.[419]

A further alternative would be to establish a taxation system that applies the same (corporate or withholding) tax rate to all dividends and manufactured dividends received by foreign and domestic market participants in the form of a non-refundable, non-creditable flat tax in order to avoid withholding tax avoidance and the inherent problem of attribution of income based on the criterion of beneficial ownership.[420] In the author's view, such a system would, however, only be effective if the tax on dividends and manufactured dividends was levied on all foreign and domestic market participants (including investment funds, public funds and all forms of pension funds), thereby preventing these entities from converting dividends that are subject to withholding tax into withholding tax-free dividends by way of stock loans, equity swaps or futures transactions.

However, most tax systems would not want to deny privileged taxpayers, such as pension funds, an exemption from withholding tax solely based on tax policy considerations.[421] Hence, such an alternative may not be fully effective in terms of preventing tax avoidance schemes as long as groups of taxpayers exist that enjoy a privileged withholding taxation on dividends, either based on domestic law or based on an exemption under a double tax treaty. Thus, only the approach that fully exempts dividends received by domestic and foreign shareholders and denies the withholding tax credit is able to comprehensively tackle withholding tax avoidance schemes.

[C] Solution 3: Application of a Withholding Tax on Derivatives

The third possibility to prevent withholding tax avoidance schemes relating to dividends and interest income might be the introduction of withholding tax provisions on derivatives in domestic tax legislation.

At a cross-border level, such an introduction may, however, be difficult as the current OECD Model only provides limited room for source states to apply withholding taxes on derivatives.[422] Under tax treaties following the OECD Model, income from derivatives is likely to be qualified as business income, capital gains or other income so that the taxing right is allocated to the resident state and not to the source state.

In order to receive a share of the tax on the income from derivatives relating to sources in their territory, source countries might be able to include certain derivatives

419. Complete exemption of dividends and manufactured dividends and disallowing any withholding tax credits may be an effective means to counter double reclaims of withholding taxes or reclaims of tax credits on both the dividends and the manufactured dividends.
420. The German approach is different as the withholding tax can be credited against any corporate tax liability. It has been shown in Ch. 9 §9.01[C][2] that the German system is prone to withholding tax arbitrage.
421. Tax legislators may want to protect pensioner's money from immediate taxation at the level of the pension fund.
422. OECD (2013b) 41.

into the definition of interest or dividends of bilaterally negotiated double taxation conventions. Most countries will, however, lack the negotiating power to do so.

In contrast, the UN Model stipulates that other income may be taxed in the source state. An imposition of withholding taxes on derivatives may be possible for the source state if the income received is qualified as other income and not as business income.

However, income from derivatives entered into by financial institutions in the ordinary course of their business will qualify as business income, so even the UN Model only provides limited scope for the source state to impose withholding tax on derivatives.

Hence, transactions that use derivatives to circumvent dividend or interest withholding taxes will, in many cases, be successful if neither solution 1 nor solution 2 is applied by the domestic tax legislator, as derivatives will generally not be caught by the withholding tax rules of the OECD or the UN Model.

As a more comprehensive solution, one might argue for the introduction of a new article on derivatives in the OECD and the UN Model that specifically deals with income from derivatives and provides clear rules for the attribution of the taxing rights between the source and the residence state.

Compared to unilaterally drafted tax legislation or bilaterally agreed conventions, a separate article on derivatives incorporated into the OECD or the UN Model may encourage countries to share the tax on income from derivatives. Such an article added to the Models could define derivatives for the purposes of the double tax treaty[423] and could allocate limited taxing rights to the source country. Indeed, a derivatives article incorporated into double tax treaties might provide countries where capital markets transactions are used for tax avoidance involving derivatives with an effective weapon to prevent an erosion of their tax base.[424] If the source country fears that withholding taxes on derivatives has an adverse effect on its capital markets, it could be free to abstain from levying withholding tax at a domestic level or may not include the derivatives article in its double tax treaties.

423. *See* Ch. 4 §4.06[B][6].

424. Nevertheless, a gross basis taxation of derivatives gains or income should be avoided, *see* Ch. 3 §3.06[A].

CHAPTER 10
Countering Tax Avoidance: Derivatives and Cryptoassets

There is no avoidance in delay.

— Aeschylus, *Agamemnon*

The following chapter contains predominantly a summary of the anti-avoidance legislation applying to derivatives in the UK and Germany. In the context of hybrid instruments and structured products, the BEPS Action 2 measures are briefly discussed.

Chapter 10 §10.04 discusses tax avoidance in the context of cryptoassets and crypto derivatives.

Beyond the discussion of tax avoidance and anti-avoidance rules in relation to derivatives and cryptoassets, the author will briefly analyse the rules of Pillar Two, which propose to introduce a minimum effective tax rate of 15% to certain multinational companies from 2024 onwards.

Chapter 10 is a mere kaleidoscope which provides a glimpse of the challenges that taxpayers and tax administrations alike may face in the context of domestic and cross-border derivatives transactions. A detailed discussion of the specific and general avoidance legislation applying to derivatives and cryptoassets would be a work of its own and, therefore, goes beyond the scope of this book.

§10.01 ANTI-AVOIDANCE LEGISLATION IN THE UK APPLYING TO DERIVATIVES

In the UK, the anti-avoidance legislation that applies to derivatives consists of three layers:

(1) specific anti-avoidance measures that are directly tailored to apply to derivative contracts;

(2) regime anti-avoidance rules that 'require adjustments to be made to counteract any [...] derivative-related tax advantages which would otherwise arise as a result of relevant avoidance arrangements';[1] and
(3) general anti-avoidance legislation.

The author suggests that the general rule of *lex specialis derogat legi generali* should also apply in the context of anti-avoidance rules so that the more specific rule has priority over the more general rule.

HMRC confirms in the Corporate Finance Manual CFM39570[2] that the relationship between the specific anti-avoidance rules applying to derivatives and the newly introduced regime anti-avoidance rules is as follows:

> in some cases, it may be possible that both a specific rule and the new regime anti-avoidance rule could apply to a set of arrangements, or a part of them. Where that is the case, the approach should be to consider the specific rule first; if that rule applies, it will not be appropriate to seek to apply the regime anti-avoidance rules as well to those arrangements, or that part of them, assuming that the tax advantage has already been negated. However, if the arrangements are aimed at exploiting or circumventing a specific anti-avoidance rule within Part 5 or Part 7, the regime rules would be capable of applying.[3]

[A] Specific Anti-avoidance Legislation Applying to Derivative Contracts

The anti-avoidance legislation applying to derivative contracts is incorporated into Chapter 11 of CTA 2009, Part 7.[4]

It contains – among others – specific anti-avoidance rules on:

(1) derivative contracts for unallowable purposes;[5]
(2) transfer pricing adjustments under Part 4 of TIOPA 2010[6] in relation to derivative contracts[7] and related foreign exchange gains and losses;[8]
(3) value-shifting transactions between connected companies using option contracts;[9]

1. *See* HMRC, CFM39560, referring to CTA 2009, s. 698B.
2. HMRC, CFM39570.
3. *Ibid.*
4. CTA 2009, s. 689; *see* HMRC, CFM56005.
5. CTA 2009, ss 690-692; *see* HMRC, CFM56010-CFM56040 which discuss in detail the HMRC's position on the 'unallowable purpose rule'.
6. CTA 2009, ss 693-695A; *see* HMRC, CFM56050-CFM56080.
7. CTA 2009, s. 693 applies the transfer pricing rules of TIOPA 2010, Part 4 to derivative contracts; *see* HMRC, CFM56050.
8. CTA 2009, s. 694; *see* CFM56060.
9. CTA 2009, s. 695 is applicable if option contracts are used between connected parties to transfer value from a UK company to a non-resident connected company ('company which is not chargeable to corporation tax in relation to the derivative contract'), for example by a non-exercise or only partial exercise of an option that is valuable, i.e., in the money, leading to a give-up or transfer of value to the connected non-resident company. CTA 2009, s. 695a was

(4) derivative contracts with non-UK residents;[10]
(5) amounts not fully recognised for accounting purposes; and
(6) debts arising from derecognition of derivative contracts.[11]

In addition, there are anti-avoidance rules 'dealing with tax avoidance arrangements'[12] that apply to:

(7) certain types of derivatives, such as the rules on arrangements in the context of currency derivative contracts;[13]
(8) the transfer of derivative contracts within groups for tax avoidance reasons;[14]
(9) risk transfer schemes;[15] and
(10) group mismatch schemes.[16]

In the following, the specific anti-avoidance rules applying to derivatives, such as the above-mentioned rules on derivative contracts for unallowable purposes, derivative contracts with non-UK residents and the rules on arrangements in the context of currency derivatives, are briefly summarised, among others.

Beyond what is discussed below, a discussion of specific anti-avoidance rules, such as those applying to the transfer of derivatives within groups and the group mismatch schemes, will not be part of this work.[17]

[1] Derivative Contracts for Unallowable Purposes

Under CTA 2009, sections 690 and 691, any debits[18] and any foreign exchange credits[19] 'will be left out of account for the purposes of the derivative contracts legislation and may not be brought into account for any other purposes'[20] if a derivative contract or a related contract (such as an 'acquisition, disposal, novation or variation of a derivative contract')[21] is entered into for an unallowable purpose.[22]

introduced by FA 2014 as an anti-avoidance measure applying to intra-group derivatives transactions, where payments are made under derivative contracts (typically a total return swap) that comprise all or a significant part of the profits of the paying group company or another company of the same group.

10. CTA 2009, ss 696-697.
11. CTA 2009, s. 698A.
12. CTA 2009, s. 689(2)(f).
13. CTA 2009, ss 606A-H.
14. CTA 2009, s. 629.
15. CTA 2010, Part 21A. The risk transfer scheme rules have already been outlined in the context of discussing post-tax hedging transactions, *see* Ch. 7 §7.04[B].
16. CTA 2010, Part 21B.
17. An overview of anti-avoidance rules on currency one-way bet schemes can be found in: HMRC, CFM63010-63100.
18. CTA 2009, s. 690(3).
19. CTA 2009, s. 690(2).
20. CTA 2009, s. 690(3), (5); *see* Bramwell et al. (2023), H.1.5.3.
21. Ghosh, Johnson and Miller (2022) [E8.5] (issue 28).

Bramwell et al. state:

> For accounting periods on or after 1 January 2016, where this provision applies, any debits and foreign exchange credits arising in respect of the contract that, on a just and reasonable basis, are attributable to the unallowable purpose will be left out of the account for the purposes of the derivative contract legislation and may not be brought into account for any other purposes.[23]

For accounting periods before 1 January 2016, those debits could be offset against any non-foreign exchange credits[24] that have arisen under the same contract[25] with the result that any losses under the derivative contract were ring-fenced.[26]

'Unallowable purpose' is defined as a purpose 'which is *not* amongst the business or other commercial purposes of the company'.[27] As the definition of 'unallowable purpose' is not a positive but a negative definition, one de facto defines an unallowable purpose by what it is not, i.e., not business or commercial purpose for that specific company entering into the derivative.

Ghosh, Johnson and Miller suggest that unallowable purposes are not only tax avoidance purposes but any other purpose which is not a business or commercial purpose and suggests that in practice, most cases of 'unallowable purposes' are those purposes that the legislation suggests in CTA 2009, section 691 as not being within a business or commercial purpose.[28]

A tax avoidance purpose is not regarded as a business or other commercial purpose of the company 'if it is the main purpose or one of the main purposes for which the company is party to the derivative contract or enters into a related transaction by reference to it (section 691(3))'.[29] Thus, if tax avoidance is one of the main purposes, the derivative is regarded as entered into or held for an unallowable purpose.[30]

The Special Commissioners considered in *Prudential plc v. HMRC* the unallowable purpose rule in relation to derivative contracts under the former FA 1994.[31] Although the foreign exchange rules of FA 1994 are now superseded, the decision in *Prudential plc v. HMRC* is also important with regard to the current rules of CTA 2009, sections 690 and 691 concerning derivative contracts for unallowable purposes, as these rules are very similar to the unallowable purpose rule for FX contracts under FA 1994.

---

22. CTA 2009, s. 690 (1)-(3). *See* Southern (2017) para. 13.57; Ghosh, Johnson and Miller (2022), [E8.42] (issue 28).
23. Bramwell et al. (2023), H1.5.3.
24. Before that calculation, debits could be offset against any foreign exchange credits, resulting possibly in an accumulated net loss (CTA 2009, s. 692(2)) that would be ring-fenced, i.e., it was only eligible for relief against any accumulated non-foreign exchange losses on that contract.
25. CTA 2009, s. 692. *See* Bramwell et al. (2023), H1.5.3.
26. Ghosh, Johnson and Miller (2022), [E8.41] and [E8.45].
27. CTA 2009, s. 691(1).
28. Ghosh, Johnson and Miller (2022), [E8.21] and [E8.22].
29. *Ibid.*, [E8.22].
30. Haworth and Hollis (2010) 29; Ghosh, Johnson and Miller (2022), [E8.23]; *Simon's Taxes*, vol. 5, Issue 176, June 2023, D1.8111.
31. *Prudential plc v. HMRC* [2007] UKSPC SPC00636.

Example 85:

Facts of the case:
Prudential entered into two currency swaps with third-party banks to hedge their foreign exchange exposure on two loans until 2011. The swaps were priced at a rate in favour of Prudential plc. Thus, in order to adjust the swap pricing to arm's length terms, Prudential made an upfront payment to the banks under the swaps and sought a deduction for the whole upfront payment in 2002.

Special Commissioners (SpC):
Although the swaps had the purpose of hedging Prudential's currency exposure on two loans, the *SpC* held that the main purpose or one of the main purposes for entering into the swaps was to obtain a tax deduction for the upfront payment and thus, one of the main purposes was tax avoidance. Hence, the *SpC* decided that the swaps were entered into for an unallowable purpose and decided against the taxpayer. The High Court and the Court of Appeal upheld the decision.[32]

Because there had been no clear commercial purpose for entering into two currency swaps, the Special Commissioners regarded the swaps as entered for the purpose of tax avoidance, which constituted an unallowable purpose under the foreign exchange rules of FA 1994.

Southern criticises the definitions of 'tax avoidance purpose' and 'tax advantage' used in the anti-avoidance provisions on derivative contracts as 'entirely circular'.[33] They would only serve as an instrument for HMRC 'to tax a transaction on a different basis than that which would apply if the ordinary rules applied, but whose effects can be suspended by invoking the notion of "tax avoidance"'.[34]

The author agrees with *Southern*. The circularity of the provisions can be shown by the example of CTA 2009, section 691. The provision of section 691(5) refers to a *tax avoidance purpose* that is defined as 'any purpose which consists of securing a tax advantage for the company or any other person'.[35]

The term 'tax advantage' is, however, defined as: '(a) a relief from tax or increased relief from tax, (b) a repayment of tax or increased repayment of tax, (c) the avoidance or reduction of a charge to tax or an assessment to tax, or (d) the avoidance of a possible assessment to tax'.[36]

Hence, a tax advantage is, in fact, defined as any tax saving 'which would otherwise be payable if there were no tax avoidance arrangements'.[37]

HMRC confirms that the 'unallowable purpose rules' for derivatives may overlap with the regime anti-avoidance rules and proposes that in such a case, 'the general approach should be that, where avoidance is aimed at exploiting or sidestepping

32. *Prudential plc v. HMRC* [2009] EWCA Civ 622.
33. Southern (2017) para. 13.56.
34. *Ibid.*
35. CTA 2009, s. 691(5).
36. CTA 2009, s. 691(6) referring to CTA 2010, s. 1139(2).
37. Southern (2017) para. 13.56.

provisions of Part 5 or Part 7, the counteraction should be taken under the rules in S455B or S698B that are intended to protect those regimes'.[38]

That effectively means that it would not be the unallowable purpose rules that would apply but the more general regime anti-avoidance rules. HMRC acknowledges that the unallowable purposes rules of CTA 2009, section 690:

> have a wider scope than [...] S698B, in that their application is not limited to [...] derivative-related tax advantages defined in terms of [...] Part 7 credits and debits. They draw on the much more general definition of a tax advantage in CTA2010/S1139 and do not include any equivalent provisions to [...] S698C(4), requiring consideration of the principles or policy objectives behind relevant legislation.[39]

[2] Non-arm's Length Derivative Contracts

As the derivative contracts legislation does not contain anti-avoidance provisions that concern cases where a company enters into a derivative or related contract on non-arm's length terms, those cases are dealt with in Part 4 of TIOPA 2010, which are the general transfer pricing rules. As previously said, they are not further discussed in the context of this work.

[3] Value Shifting to Connected Companies with Option Contracts

If a company allows an in-the-money option to lapse or only partially exercises an in-the-money option 'and allows the balance of the option to expire and in either case, as a result, there is a transfer of value to the connected company which is not within the charge to the derivative contracts legislation in respect to the contract' an anti-avoidance provision applies, CTA 2009, section 695.[40] In this instance, the 'option holder is required to include the premium that it paid to enter into the option, or in the case of an option which is partially exercised, the proportion of the premium which is attributable to the unexercised portion of the option in calculating its derivative contracts profits'.[41]

[4] Derivative Contracts with Non-residents

The anti-avoidance rule of CTA 2009, section 696 potentially applies to derivative contracts of UK companies with non-resident counterparties if the contract is entered into or maintained by the UK company[42] and if it is a derivative contract that 'makes provision for notional interest payments'.[43]

38. HMRC, CFM39570.
39. *Ibid.*
40. Bramwell et al. (2023), H1.5.4.
41. *Ibid.*, H1.5.5.
42. CTA 2009, s. 696(1).
43. CTA 2009, s. 696(2).

A payment qualifies as a notional interest payment if the derivative contract specifies the notional principal amount, the rate of interest and the period for which the interest is calculated,[44] provided that 'the value of the rate is the same at all times as that of the specified rate of interest'.[45]

Hence, the provision catches principally plain vanilla fixed and floating rate interest rate swaps[46] as well as cross-currency swaps, as payments would be 'calculated by applying an interest to the notional currencies which are the subject of a swap'.[47] If CTA 2009, section 696 applies, any credits or debits will not be included in the accounts of the UK company as *relevant debits* for the purposes of CTA 2009, Part 7.[48]

The purpose of this provision is to disallow payments made by UK resident companies to non-resident companies under these interest rate derivatives for UK tax purposes if the same payments would also be disallowed if the payment had been an interest payment on a loan.[49]

However, as CTA 2009, section 697 provides for certain exceptions, the anti-avoidance rule of CTA 2009, section 696 does not apply if the UK company is a bank, building society, a financial trader or clearing house, acting as principal and which enters into the derivative contract for the purposes of a trade or part of a trade.[50]

Likewise, section 696 does not apply if the non-resident counterparty - acting as principal - holds the contract solely for the purposes of a trade that is carried on in the UK through a branch or agency.[51]

In addition, the rule is not applied if the non-UK resident counterparty to the derivative is resident in a country with which the UK has a double tax treaty, provided that the treaty has an interest article.[52] Thus, in many cases, CTA 2009, section 696 will not apply to interest rate derivatives and instead, mainly transactions with non-treaty tax havens are caught under the provision.[53]

[5] Amounts Not Fully Recognised for Accounting Purposes

CTA 2009, section 599A applies in cases where amounts are not fully recognised in the accounts in accordance with generally accepted accounting practice.[54]

44. CTA 2009, s. 696(4)(a).
45. CTA 2009, s. 696(4)(c). It is sufficient that payments are calculated *mainly*, not exclusively by reference to a particular interest rate; *see* CTA 2009, s. 696(4)(b).
46. Floating rate interest swaps are within the provision if the payments are calculated with reference to standard interest rates, such as SOFR, SONIA, EURIBOR or the overnight repo rate. *See* HMRC, CFM56090.
47. Ghosh, Johnson and Miller (2022), [E8.120].
48. *Ibid.*, [E8.118]; *compare* CTA 2009, s. 696(2) and (3).
49. HMRC, CFM56090.
50. CTA 2009, s. 697(1). *See also* Bramwell et al. (2023), H1.5.6.
51. CTA 2009, s. 697(2). *See* Ghosh, Johnson and Miller (2022), [E8.155].
52. CTA 2009, s. 697(3). *See* HMRC, CFM56090; Ghosh, Johnson and Miller (2022), [E8.156].
53. HMRC, CFM56090.
54. HMRC, CFM56116. *See* Southern (2017) para. 13.60.

HMRC states that:

> An act of derecognition may also give rise to a debit in one of the accounting statements in CTA09/S597 – the profit and loss account or income statement, the statement of total recognised gains and losses or statement of changes in equity, or any other statement of items taken into account in computing the company's profits and losses. In some instances, the act of derecognition may result in an amount being debited in the company's balance sheet.[55]

Ghosh, Johnson and Miller explain that:

> CTA 2009, s 599A was HMRC's response to a series of schemes designed to shelter taxable income. Most of the planning revolved around matching amounts in such a way that they did not need to be recognised for accounting purposes. Since amounts did not go through the accounts, the rules that might otherwise have prevented deduction for some of the offsetting amounts never *applied.*[56]

Ghosh, Johnson and Miller provide an example for those tax transactions where a company issues preference shares 'whose rights are crafted so they pay out amounts exactly equal to those amounts, and the company 'puts the arrangements together so as to ensure that the income on the [...] derivative and the shares qualify for either some form of off-balance sheet treatment (e.g., if using Old UK GAAP) or hedging treatment which insurance that the income on the [...] derivative does not hit the P&L'.[57]

CTA 2009, section 599A ensures that 'unrecognised amounts are treated as arising in the accounts; thus, there is then a debit in the accounts which the normal rules could disapply'.[58] CTA 2009, sections 599A, 599B[59] and 698A provide that gains from derivatives are fully brought into account for tax purposes, even if those gains are not fully recognised, derecognised or offset for the purposes of GAAP,[60] for example, by an equal and opposite dividend payment.[61]

[6] Debts Arising from Derecognition of Derivative Contracts

CTA 2009, section 698A 'also applies to arrangements seeking a derecognition treatment'.[62] The function of CTA 2009, section 698A is to deny a deduction 'for such a debit where the company is party to tax avoidance arrangements and continues to be party to the derivative contract after its derecognition'.[63] The rule has the same function as CTA 2009, section 455A, which applies to loan relationships.[64]

55. HMRC, CFM56116.
56. Ghosh, Johnson and Miller (2022*)*, [E8.163] (issue 28).
57. *Ibid.*
58. *Ibid.*
59. As amended by FA 2011, Sch. 4.
60. Ghosh, Johnson and Miller (2022), [E8.163]-[E8.169].
61. HMRC, CFM56110-CFM56116.
62. Ghosh, Johnson and Miller (2022), [E8.168] (issue 28).
63. HMRC, CFM56116.
64. Bramwell et al. (2023), H1.5.9.

[B] Provisions Concerning the Counteracting of Avoidance Arrangements (Regime Anti-avoidance Rules)

CTA 2009, section 698B-D are regime anti-avoidance rules. CTA 2009, section 698B-D contain provisions concerning the counteracting of avoidance arrangements where derivative transactions are involved and where a derivative-related tax advantage exists 'by making of such adjustments as are just and reasonable in relation to the debits and credits to be brought into account for the purposes of the derivative contract legislation'.[65] They were introduced by Finance No. 2 Act 2015.[66]

CTA 2009, section 698C(2) defines arrangements as including any arrangement, understanding, scheme, transaction or series of transactions (whether or not legally enforceable). 'Arrangements are relevant avoidance arrangements if their main purpose, or one of their main purposes, is to enable a company to obtain a derivative-related tax advantage.'[67]

CTA 2009, section 698C(5) states that:

> a company will obtain a derivative-related tax advantage if—
>
> (a) it brings into account a debit to which it would not otherwise be entitled,
> (b) it brings into account a debit which exceeds that to which it would otherwise be entitled,
> (c) it avoids having to bring a credit into account,
> (d) the amount of any credit brought into account by the company is less than it would otherwise be, or
> (e) it brings a debit or credit into account earlier or later than it otherwise would.[68]

CTA 2009, section 698C(6) confirms that '[i]n subsection (5), references to bringing a debit or credit into account are references to bringing a debit or credit into account for the purposes of' the derivative contracts legislation'.[69]

CTA 2009, section 698C(4) states that:

> arrangements are not 'relevant avoidance arrangements' if the obtaining of any derivative-related tax advantages that would (in the absence of section 698B) arise from them can reasonably be regarded as consistent with any principles on which the provisions of this Part that are relevant to the arrangements are based (whether expressed or implied) and the policy objectives of those provisions.[70]

CFM39580 specifically sets out whether and how the regime anti-avoidance rules 'might apply to a particular set of facts and proposes that the following questions have to be answered:[71]

---

65. CTA 2009, ss 698B-698D. *See* Bramwell et al. (2023), H1.5.10.
66. HMRC, CFM39510.
67. Bramwell et al. (2023), H1.5.10.
68. CTA 2009, s. 698C(5).
69. *See also* Bramwell et al. (2023), H1.5.10.
70. CTA 2009, s. 698C(4).
71. Whereas CTA 2009, s. 698B-D are designed to apply to derivative contracts, CTA 2009, s. 455B-D deal as a quasi-parallel provision with loan relationships, and thus might apply to hybrid instruments, such as convertible and exchangeable bonds, and structures products in a narrow

- Are there "arrangements" and what is their scope?
- Does a [...] derivative-related tax advantage arise as a result of the arrangements?
- Was obtaining the tax advantage a main purpose of the arrangements?
- Does the tax advantage arise as a result of a provision in [...] Part 7 that was intended to apply in the way which the arrangements envisage?'[72]

HMRC maintains that those questions can only be answered 'considering the specific facts of a case, established by careful examination of the evidence available'[73] and that generic indicators may not always provide a solution. For example, in the majority of commercial cases, the facts will be straightforward, HMRC highlights,[74] but there may be cases that 'give rise to material uncertainty'.[75]

CTA 2009, section 698(D)(1) contains examples where the exclusion is not applicable, meaning they are not relevant avoidance arrangements for the purposes of obtaining any derivative-related tax advantage, such as:

(a) the elimination or reduction, for purposes of corporation tax, of profits of a company arising from any of its derivative contracts, where for economic purposes profits, or greater profits, arise to the company from that contract;
(b) the creation or increase, for purposes of corporation tax, of a loss or expense arising from a derivative contract, where for economic purposes, no loss or expense, or a smaller loss or expense, arises from that contract;
(c) preventing or delaying the recognition as an item of profit or loss of an amount that would, apart from the arrangements, be recognised in the company's accounts as an item of profit or loss or be so recognised earlier;
(d) ensuring that a derivative contract is treated for accounting purposes in a way in which it would not have been treated in the absence of some other transaction forming part of the arrangements;
(e) enabling a company to bring into account a debit in respect of an exchange loss in circumstances where a corresponding exchange gain would not give rise to a credit or would give rise to a credit of a smaller amount;
(f) enabling a company to bring into account a debit in respect of a fair value loss in circumstances where a corresponding fair value gain would not give rise to a credit or would give rise to a credit of a smaller amount.[76]

HMRC discusses in CFM39580 ten examples where the regime anti-avoidance rules may or may not apply.[77] Examples 1, 2, 4, 5, 8, 9 and 10 outlined by CFM39580 are likely to apply only to loan relationships within CTA 2009, Part 5. Examples 3, 6 and 7 may apply to derivative contracts.

Example 3 applies to those arrangements that 'may have the effect of artificially changing the nature of an amount in accounts so that it either is, or is not, recognised

sense, i.e., those which have a loan relationship as a debt instrument with a derivative overlay, i.e., one or more embedded derivatives.

72. HMRC, CFM39580.
73. *Ibid.*
74. *Ibid.*
75. *Ibid.*
76. CTA 2009, s. 698D(1); *see* Bramwell et al. (2023), H1.5.10.
77. HMRC, CFM39580.

as an item of "profit or loss", as opposed to an item of "other comprehensive income", for example'.[78] HMRC states that if those 'arrangements have a main purpose of increasing or decreasing amounts recognised as items of profit or loss so that the [...] Part 7 credits or debits derived from them are affected, then the regime anti-avoidance rules are likely to apply'.[79]

Example 6 includes 'timing effects within the scope of [...] derivatives-related tax advantages'[80] and Example 7 applies where companies enter into transactions 'aimed at circumventing other elements of [...] the derivative contract regime'.[81]

[C] Hybrid Mismatch and Hybrid Capital Instrument Rules

The UK tax law contains legislation dealing with hybrid mismatches in TIOPA 2010, Part 6A, sections 259A-259E, as introduced by FA 2016, Schedule 10, which implemented BEPS Action 2, and the hybrid capital instruments rules of FA 2019, Schedule 20 and CTA 2009, sections 320B, 420A and 475C.[82]

Southern states that the hybrid mismatch rules of TIOPA 2010, Part 6A 'can apply to deny a company within the charge of corporation tax relief for interest payable on a loan relationship in the circumstances set out in TIOPA 2010, Part 6A',[83] whereas the hybrid capital instruments rules 'allow companies, principally banks and insurance companies, to treat instruments as equity but obtain a tax deduction for interest paid in respect to them, thereby achieving the alchemist's gold of tax-deductible equity'.[84]

Before briefly discussing those rules, the author outlines BEPS Action 2 and analyses if BEPS Action 2 may apply to hybrid instruments and structured products within the meaning of Chapter 8 of this work.

[1] BEPS Action 2: Hybrid Mismatch Arrangements

Cross-border qualification conflicts that occur directly or indirectly due to the use of hybrid instruments may be solved in the context of domestic tax legislation or at the level of tax treaties. A unilateral approach could either involve the introduction of domestic tax legislation which disallows dividend exemption or withholding tax credits in the country where payments are received from hybrid instruments or, alternatively, a denial of the tax deduction for the payments under the hybrid instrument in the country of the payer.

At the level of double tax treaties, *switch-over clauses* may prevent payments from hybrid instruments from being qualified as deductible interest in the state of the issuer but as tax-exempt dividends in the state of the holder. Under such a clause, the

78. *Ibid.*
79. *Ibid.*
80. *Ibid.*
81. *Ibid.*
82. Southern, Supplement (2020), para. 4.1.
83. *Ibid.*
84. *Ibid.*

exemption method would be disallowed in case of a treaty qualification conflict, and the credit method would apply.

The OECD has discussed and proposed solutions on how to deal with 'hybrid instruments' and 'hybrid entities' in a 2012 report,[85] two public discussion drafts,[86] and a 2015 final report.[87]

Further, the *Code of Conduct Group* (Business Taxation) of the European Union suggested in a report that if payments under a hybrid instrument are qualified as tax-deductible expenses for the debtor, payments received by the creditor of the hybrid instrument should not qualify as tax exempt under a participation exemption in the country of residence of the creditor.[88] Based on this report, the European Commission published a proposal that suggested the amendment of the Parent-Subsidiary Directive in such a way that the participation exemption would not apply to profit distributions that were deductible by the subsidiary.[89] This proposal was implemented as Council Directive 2014/86/EU.[90]

The following briefly summarises the proposed recommendations by the OECD in relation to 'hybrid financial instruments' in the context of BEPS Action 2 and then asks if those recommendations would also apply to 'hybrid instruments' as defined in Chapter 8 of this work.

The OECD Report on BEPS Action 2: 2015 Final Report contains recommendations on domestic law in Part I and recommendations on treaty issues in Part II.[91]

With regard to domestic law issues, the OECD proposed several hybrid financial instrument rules that allow neutralising the effect of hybrid financial instruments. The domestic rules are contained in Chapters 1 to 8 of the report.[92] It also suggests an order of responses to how domestic tax legislation should react to hybrid mismatches arising under hybrid financial instruments.[93]

Primarily, according to the recommendations, jurisdictions should deny a deduction for any payment made under a financial instrument to the extent that the payee does not include the payment as ordinary income under the laws of any jurisdiction.[94] Only as a secondary or 'defence' rule, the state of residence that provides a tax exemption for dividends and qualifies any periodical payments under hybrid financial instruments as dividends for domestic tax purposes should deny such a tax exemption

85. OECD, *Hybrid Mismatch Arrangements: Tax Policy and Compliance Issues* (OECD Publishing, 2012).
86. OECD, *BEPS Action 2: Neutralise the effects of hybrid mismatch arrangements (Recommendations for Domestic Laws)*, Public Discussion Draft 2014; OECD, *BEPS Action 2: Neutralise the effects of hybrid mismatch arrangements (Treaty issues)* (Public Discussion Draft, 2014).
87. OECD, Neutralising the Effects of Hybrid Mismatch Arrangements, OECD/G20 BEPS Project, Action 2 (OECD Publishing October 2015).
88. *See* Report of the Code of Conduct Group of 25 May 2010 (doc.10033/10, FISC 47) para. 31.
89. COM(2013) 814 final of 25 November 2013, Proposal for a Council Directive amending Directive 2011/96 EU on the common system of taxation applicable in the case of parent companies and subsidiaries of different Member States.
90. Council Directive 2014/86/EU *O.J.* July 2014, L 219, vol. 57.
91. OECD (2015) Action 2.
92. *Ibid.*, paras 23-92.
93. *Ibid.*, paras 23-44.
94. *Ibid.*, Part 1, Ch. 1, 23, Recommendation 1 1(a).

if those dividends were tax deductible in the state of the payer, and instead, tax it as ordinary income.[95]

Recommendation 1 determines that the rule only applies to 'a payment under a financial instrument that results in a hybrid mismatch'[96] and defines a financial instrument as 'any arrangement that is taxed under the rules for taxing debt, equity or derivatives under the laws of both the payee and payer jurisdictions and includes a hybrid transfer'.[97]

In the BEPS Action 2 Final Report, the OECD suggests on treaty issues that countries should either avoid the exemption method in their tax treaties as a means to counter hybrid mismatches or at least introduce Article 23A paragraph 4 of the OECD Model.[98]

The BEPS Action 2 Final Report applies to *hybrid mismatch arrangements* that include both mismatches arising due to the design of the entity being a *hybrid entity* or the design of the instrument as a *hybrid instrument.*[99]

The Final Report states:

> Some arrangements exploit differences between the transparency or opacity of an entity for tax purposes (hybrid entities) and others involve the use of hybrid instruments, which generally involve a conflict in the characterisation of the instrument (and hence the tax treatment of the payments made under it). Hybrid instruments and entities can also be embedded in a wider arrangement or group structure to produce indirect D/NI [Deduction/non-inclusion] outcomes.[100]

The BEPS Action 2 Final Report does not provide explicit guidance on whether convertible or exchangeable bonds are intended to fall under the term 'hybrid financial instrument'.

The term 'hybrid financial instruments' used in the Final Report has a very wide meaning. The term hybrid financial instrument term, for example, includes collateralised loan repos,[101] share lending repos,[102] and bond lending repos.[103]

The BEPS Action 2 Final Report defines a financial instrument as 'any arrangement that is taxed under the rules for taxing debt, equity or derivatives under the laws of both the payee and payer jurisdictions and includes a hybrid transfer'.[104]

95. *Ibid.*, Part 1, Ch. 1, 20 and 23, Recommendation 1 1(b).
96. *Ibid.*, Recommendation 1 1.
97. *Ibid.*, Recommendation 1 2.(a).
98. *Ibid.*, paras 442-444.
99. *Ibid.*, 18.
100. *Ibid.*
101. *Ibid.*, 38.
102. *Ibid.*, 39.
103. *Ibid.*, 37.
104. *Ibid.*, 23.

Hybrid transfer is defined as including:

> any arrangement to transfer a financial instrument entered into by a taxpayer with another person where:
>
> (i) the taxpayer is the owner of the transferred asset and the rights of the counterparty in respect of that asset are treated as obligations of the taxpayer; and
> (ii) under the laws of the counterparty jurisdiction, the counterparty is the owner of the transferred asset and the rights of the taxpayer in respect of that asset are treated as obligations of the counterparty.
>
> Ownership of an asset for these purposes includes any rules that result in the taxpayer being taxed as the owner of the corresponding cash flows from the asset.[105]

The BEPS Action 2 Final Report maintains that the 'hybrid financial instrument rule focuses on whether the payment is expected to give rise to a mismatch in tax outcomes and whether that mismatch is attributable to differences in the way the instrument is taxed under the laws of the payer and payee jurisdictions'.[106]

The term 'hybrid instrument' used in this work only applies to certain 'non-linear derivative instruments' that have a legal and economic character between debt and equity because they contain features of both debt and equity,[107] such as convertible and exchangeable bonds.[108]

In the author's opinion, convertible bonds would fall under the term 'hybrid financial instrument' as defined in the BEPS Action 2 Final Report if the coupon payments under a convertible note are treated as interest in the payer's jurisdiction and as tax-free dividends in the jurisdiction of the recipient.

For example, in the *Alesco* case,[109] the tax effect primarily occurred because the non-interest-paying convertible note was bifurcated into a debt and equity component for accounting and tax purposes in New Zealand. Thus, Alesco NZ was treated for both accounting and tax purposes as paying interest to Alesco Australia under the note, which was calculated on the debt component of the convertible note.[110] In contrast, the Australian tax authorities did not request bifurcation of the convertible note but treated it as 100% equity for tax purposes in Australia.[111]

Thus, the notional interest payments under the note to Alesco Australia were neither subject to non-resident withholding tax nor income tax in Australia, as Alesco Australia was not treated as earning interest on the note for tax purposes. The New Zealand court, however, denied the tax benefits intended to be achieved by the

105. *Ibid.*
106. *Ibid.*, para. 25.
107. Thuronyi (2001a) 271; Southern (2007) para. 1.36.
108. *See* Ch. 8 §8.03.
109. *Alesco New Zealand Ltd and others v. Commissioner of Inland Revenue* CA53/2012 [2013] NZCA 40.
110. *Ibid.*, para. 13.
111. *Ibid.*

arrangement as it regarded the structure as a tax avoidance arrangement under New Zealand law.[112]

The *Alesco* case shows that some domestic tax legislators have already implemented domestic tax legislation that is able to target hybrid mismatch arrangements. The zero-coupon convertible note in the *Alesco* case would qualify as a hybrid mismatch arrangement under BEPS Action 2 (domestic laws).

Under domestic New Zealand law, the New Zealand court could solve the hybrid mismatch based on the notion of tax avoidance and New Zealand, as the country of the debtor of the note, denied the interest deduction for the notional interest payments.

Thus, the *Alesco* case is a good example of Recommendation (a) contained in the BEPS Action 2 Final Report, as the country of the debtor of the convertible note solves the qualification conflict by denying a tax deduction for (notional) interest.

A convertible or exchangeable bond may qualify as a structured arrangement within the meaning of the BEPS Action 2 Final Report, which defines those as 'any arrangement where the hybrid mismatch is priced into the terms of the arrangement or the facts and circumstances (including the terms) of the arrangement indicate that it has been designed to produce a hybrid mismatch'.[113]

The Final Report states, in particular, that:

> Facts and circumstances that indicate that an arrangement has been designed to produce a hybrid mismatch include any of the following:
>
> (a) an arrangement that is designed, or is part of a plan, to create a hybrid mismatch;
> (b) an arrangement that incorporates a term, step or transaction used in order to create a hybrid mismatch;
> (c) an arrangement that is marketed, in whole or in part, as a tax-advantaged product where some or all of the tax advantage derives from the hybrid mismatch;
> (d) an arrangement that is primarily marketed to taxpayers in a jurisdiction where the hybrid mismatch arises;
> (e) an arrangement that contains features that alter the terms under the arrangement, including the return, in the event that the hybrid mismatch is no longer available; or
> (f) an arrangement that would produce a negative return absent the hybrid mismatch.[114]

The proposed definition of a structured arrangement tries to capture these transactions with a list of 'objective, readily identifiable indicators'.[115]

In the author's opinion, these indicators will not be sufficient to distinguish between genuine commercial activities and tax transactions.

Under indicator (a), it might be difficult for the tax authorities to prove that the arrangement was developed to exploit differences in the tax treatment. Also, regarding

112. *Ibid.*, paras 72 and 117.
113. OECD (2015), Action 2, Ch. 10, Recommendation 10, 105.
114. *Ibid.*
115. *Ibid.*, 106.

(c), it may be difficult to validate if the arrangement has been marketed as a 'tax-advantaged product' because structured transactions often include motives other than saving tax. Further, the marketing material is likely to include no hint of the product being tax advantaged.

Qualification conflicts may also occur in the case of hybrid instruments if one country bifurcates convertible and exchangeable bonds under their accounting rules and follows this bifurcation also for tax purposes, whereas the other country treats the convertible (or exchangeable) bond as one integrated equity instrument for tax purposes.

One should, however, always consider that not all transactions that result in a tax advantage for the holder and/or the issuer of a financial instrument are part of a structured arrangement between the parties. The tax advantage could simply occur because the parties sought the most favourable tax outcome independently from each other.

Example 86:

Company A, resident in country X, wants to raise new capital in the market and issue a convertible bond to the market. The tax legislation in country X follows the IAS 39 accounting treatment for tax purposes (bifurcation into a bond and an equity option) and allows a deduction of the increased notional interest payments for the issuer.

Some of the holders of the convertible bonds are tax residents of country Y. Country Y does not follow IAS 39 for tax purposes and treats the convertible bonds as non-bifurcated equity instruments for tax purposes. The payments under the convertible bond qualify as tax-free dividends in that country.

Some of the bondholders are residents of country Z. Country Z bifurcates the convertible bond also for tax purposes, and thus, some of the payments under the convertible (related to the 'debt part' of the convertible) are treated as taxable interest, whereas payments that are attributed to the equity option under the accounting rules are treated as tax-free dividends.

Could one really argue that those bondholders who are tax residents of country Y and subject to favourable taxation on their coupon payments should be treated as a party to a structured arrangement?

In the author's view, the BEPS Action 2 Final Report should have contained an explicit recommendation and examples of whether and to what extent convertible and exchangeable bonds are included in the scope of the report in order to avoid any uncertainties regarding the application of the BEPS Action 2 to convertible and exchangeable bonds.

[2] The UK Hybrid Mismatch Rules

From 1 January 2017 onwards, the hybrid mismatch rules have substituted the arbitrage rules.[116] The hybrid mismatch rules of TIOPA 2010, Part 6A apply to a wide range of hybrid mismatch arrangements. They are designed 'for the purposes of counteracting certain cases that it is reasonable to suppose would otherwise give rise to (a) a deduction/non-inclusion mismatch, or (b) a double deduction mismatch'.[117]

HMRC's International Manual (INTM) deals extensively with the hybrid mismatch arrangements in INTM550000-561700, which is referred to for details.[118]

TIOPA 2010, section 259N says a 'financial instrument' means:

(a) *an arrangement* profits or deficits arising from which would, on the assumption that the person to whom they arise is within the charge to corporation tax, fall to be brought into account for corporation tax purposes in accordance with Part 5 or 6 of CTA 2009 (loan relationships and relationships treated as loan relationships);
(b) *a contract* profits or losses arising from which would, on the assumption that the person to whom they arise is within the charge to corporation tax, fall to be brought into account for corporation tax purposes in accordance with Part 7 of CTA 2009 (derivative contracts);
(c) *a type 1, type 2 or type 3 finance arrangement* for the purposes of Chapter 2 of Part 16 of CTA 2010 (factoring of income, etc.: finance arrangements);
(d) *a share* forming part of a company's issued share capital or any arrangement that provides a person with economic rights corresponding to those provided by holding such a share; or
(e) *anything else* that is a financial instrument.[119]

This definition is very wide and does not only apply to loan relationships and derivative contracts but also to a wide range of other financial instruments, including those as defined for UK GAAP purposes.[120]

TIOPA 2010, section 259B says:

'tax' means certain taxes on income and includes foreign tax etc.
(1) In this Part, 'tax' means –
  (a) income tax,
  (b) the charge to corporation tax on income,
  (c) diverted profits tax,
  (d) the CFC charge,
  (e) foreign tax, or
  (f) a foreign CFC charge.[121]

116. TIOPA 2010 'Pt. 6 omitted (with effect in relation to accounting periods beginning on or after 1.1.2017 in accordance with Sch. 10 para. 22 of the amending Act) by virtue of Finance Act 2016 (c. 24), Sch. 10 para. 15; and ss. 257, 257 so far as continuing to have effect are amended (with effect in accordance with Sch. 15 para. 44 of the amending Act) by Finance (No. 2) Act 2017 (c. 32), Sch. 15 paras. 41, 42', *see* TIOPA 2010, Part 6, F1, Textual Amendments.
117. TIOPA 2010, s. 259A(1).
118. HMRC, International Manual (9 April 2016, updated 4 July 2023), INTM550000.
119. TIOPA 2010, s. 259N.
120. HMRC, INTM550600, para. 4.5.
121. TIOPA 2010, s. 259B.

Withholding taxes are specifically excluded under TIOPA, section 259B(3A).[122]

TIOPA 2010, section 259A(2) addresses the deduction/non-inclusion mismatch. The legislation states that:

> A deduction/non-inclusion mismatch arises where an amount is deductible from a person's income –
>
> (a) without a corresponding amount of ordinary income arising to another person, or
> (b) where an amount of ordinary income does arise to a person but is under taxed.[123]

TIOPA 2010, section 259A(3) concerns the double deduction mismatch and defines that:

> A double deduction mismatch arises where –
>
> (a) an amount is deductible from more than one person's income, or
> (b) an amount is deductible from a person's income for the purposes of more than one tax.[124]

Southern sums those two subsections up as follows and states that hybrid mismatch arrangements are:

> arrangements which give rise to a deduction for one party in one jurisdiction without a corresponding charge in the other party in another jurisdiction, because the instrument is classified for tax purposes as debt in the payer's jurisdiction and equity in the payee's jurisdiction. Alternatively, both parties may claim a deduction for the same economic expenditure.[125]

This statement is confirmed by TIOPA 2010, section 259A(1), which refers to the hybrid mismatch rules as having the purpose of only 'counteracting certain cases that it is reasonable to suppose would *otherwise* give rise to (a) a deduction/non-inclusion mismatch, or (b) a double deduction mismatch'.[126] Hence, it is necessary to understand 'how the receipt is taxed in a foreign jurisdiction'[127] so as '[t]o know where there is a mismatch'.[128]

Southern rightfully observes that the term 'otherwise' means 'if the hybrid mismatch rules had not been enacted'.[129]

Thus, the rules only apply if 'the payer is in one jurisdiction and the payee in a different jurisdiction, provided that one of the jurisdictions is the UK'[130] and

122. HMRC, INTM550520; *see* TIOPA, s. 259B(3A)
123. TIOPA 2010, s. 259A(2).
124. TIOPA 2010, s. 259A(3).
125. Southern, Supplement (2020), para. 4.2.
126. TIOPA 2010, s. 259A(1).
127. Southern, Supplement (2020), para. 4.8.
128. *Ibid.*
129. *Ibid.*
130. *Ibid.*, para. 4.10.

(1) 'the payer and payee [are] related or within the same control group'[131] as defined in TIOPA 2010, section 259NB, or
(2) where 'the financial instrument, or an arrangement connected with it, is a "structured arrangement" if it is reasonable to suppose that –

  (a) the financial instrument, or arrangement, is designed to secure a hybrid or otherwise impermissible deduction/non-inclusion mismatch, or
  (b) the terms of the financial instrument or arrangement share the economic benefit of the mismatch between the parties to the instrument or arrangement or otherwise reflect the fact that the mismatch is expected to arise'.[132]

Other carve-outs of the hybrid mismatch rules concern regulatory capital securities[133] as initially defined by Taxation of Regulatory Capital Securities Regulations 2013 (SI 2013/3209) as amended by SI 2015/2056 (until 31 December 2018).[134]

From 2020, Statutory Instrument 2019/1345 ensures that any exemption meets the criteria set out in Article 9(4)(b) of ATAD, which is the EU Anti-Tax Avoidance Directive (ATAD I)[135] that sets out minimum standards for various anti-avoidance measures.[136] ATAD was amended by EU Directive 2017/952 (ATAD II), which contains more detailed rules in relation to hybrid mismatches.[137]

In summary, the author believes that the UK Hybrid Mismatch Rules of TIOPA, Part 6A, have a limited application range compared to what would have been possible under BEPS Action 2. However, TIOPA Part 6 A 'extend more widely so that some Chapters derive from Action 2, while others have a different origin'.[138]

[3] The Hybrid Capital Instruments Rules

The hybrid capital instruments rules can be found in CTA 2009, sections 320B, 420A and 475C,[139] and apply to loan relationships that are regarded as 'hybrid capital instruments'. The rules were introduced by FA 2019, Schedule 20 and apply to all

131. *Ibid.* Compare for the meaning of control group: HMRC, INTM550610.
132. TIOPA 2010, s. 259CA (7).
133. HMRC, INTM551060.
134. *Ibid.*
135. Council Directive (EU) 2016/1164 of 12 July 2016 laying down rules against tax avoidance practices that directly affect the functioning of the internal market, *OJ L 193,* 19.7.2016, 1-14.
136. HMRC, INTM551065. HMRC states in INTM551065 that the 'Regulations operate by a simple cross-reference to the detailed conditions set out in Art. 9(4)(b) of the Directive. This approach was considered to be more straightforward than transposing those conditions into UK law.' Again, this means that those rules also apply after Brexit, compare Statutory Instrument 2022/1144, The Hybrid and Other Mismatches (Financial Instruments: Excluded Instruments) (Amendment) Regulations 2022, https://www.legislation.gov.uk/uksi/2022/1144/contents/made, accessed 18 July 2023.
137. Council Directive (EU) 2017/952 of 29 May 2017 amending Directive (EU) 2016/1164 as regards hybrid mismatches with third countries, *OJ L 144, 7.6.2017, 1-11.*
138. Southern, Supplement (2020) para. 4.20 sets out in detail which recommendations of Action 2 have been incorporated in TIOPA 2010, Part 6A.
139. FA 2019, Sch. 20: Taxation of hybrid capital instruments.

companies from 1 January 2019.[140] FA 2019 revoked the old Regulatory Capital Securities Regulations (SI 2013/3209) and the Taxation of Regulatory Capital Securities (Amendment) Regulations 2015 (SI 2015/2056),[141] which applied only to banks and insurance companies. The Regulatory Capital Securities Regulations were revoked based on the perception of those regulations as possible state aid.[142] HMRC states that the policy intention of the new hybrid capital instruments rules is 'to provide coupon deductibility for commercial hybrid capital instruments that are, in essence, genuine debt instruments'.[143]

The new rules contain three sections:

(1) CTA 2009, section 475C defines hybrid capital instruments for tax purposes;[144]
(2) CTA 2009, section 420 deals with the amount payable in respect of hybrid capital instruments;[145] and
(3) CTA 2009 defines the amounts recognised in equity.[146]

Southern sums up the function of the hybrid capital instruments rules as ensuring the deductibility of coupons for convertible bonds.[147] CTA 2009, section 475C defines 'the circumstances in which a loan relationship can be classified as a "hybrid financial instrument" at the option of the issuer'.[148] It should be noted, however, that 'only loan relationships within the scope of CTA 2009, sections 302-303, 479-480 and 585'[149] are able to qualify as hybrid capital instruments.

CTA 2009, section 475C determines that a loan relationship is only a hybrid capital instrument if it meets the following conditions:

(a) the issuer of the loan relationship is entitled to defer or cancel interest payments,[150]
(b) the loan relationship has no other significant equity features,[151] and
(c) the issuer has 'made an irrevocable election into the new rules within six months of issue, or on or before 30 September 2019 where the instrument was issued before 31 December 2018'.[152]

140. FA 2019, Sch. 20, s 10.
141. FA 2019, Sch. 20, s. 1(1) and (2).
142. Southern, Supplement (2020) para. 4.50.
143. HMRC, CFM37840.
144. *Ibid.*
145. CTA 2009, s. 420A.
146. CTA 2009, s. 320B.
147. Southern, Supplement (2020) para. 4.52.
148. *Ibid.*
149. *Ibid.*
150. CTA 2009, s. 475C(1)(a).
151. CTA 2009, s. 475C(1)(b).
152. HMRC, CFM37840; *see* CTA 2009, s. 475C(1)(c), (8).

[a] The Issuer of the Loan Relationship Is Entitled to Defer or Cancel Interest Payments

CTA 2009, section 475C(1)(a) requires a hybrid capital instrument within the meaning of the section to contain a feature where the issuer of the debt instrument is entitled to either defer or cancel interest payments in the accounting period.[153]

HMRC states that those are instruments where the issuer has the discretion to defer (or cancel) interest payments at any time will meet this criterion.[154] However, those debt instruments which have the following features would not qualify for an election under the rules, such as instruments that:

- only allow the issuer to defer or cancel interest payments when the issuer makes a loss;
- only allow the issuer to defer or cancel interest payments after a certain number of years;
- require the issuer to defer or cancel interest payments when it has insufficient distributable reserves; or
- requires the issuer to defer or cancel interest payments when certain regulatory requirements are not met.[155]

[b] The Loan Relationship Has No Other Significant Equity Features

CTA 2009, section 475C (2) to (5) defines when the debt instrument has no other significant equity features. This is the case according to CTA 2009, section 475C(2) if:

> under the loan relationship—
>
> (a) there are neither voting rights in the debtor (ignoring insignificant voting rights in the debtor)[156] nor a right to exercise a dominant influence over the debtor,[157]
> (b) any provision for altering the amount of the debt is limited to write-down or conversion events in qualifying cases,[158] and
> (c) any provision for the creditor to receive anything other than interest or repayment of the debt is limited to conversion events in qualifying cases.[159]

HMRC states:

> A loan relationship will only qualify as an HCI[160] if it has no significant equity features throughout the accounting period. Where a loan relationship is amended

153. HMRC, CFM37840.
154. *Ibid.*
155. *Ibid.*
156. CTA 2009, s. 475C(2)(a) 1st alternative.
157. CTA 2009, s. 475C(2)(a) 2nd alternative; *see* HMRC, CFM37840.
158. CTA 2009, s. 475C(2)(b).
159. CTA 2009, s. 475C(2)(c); *see* HMRC, CFM37840.
160. HMRC abbreviates the term hybrid capital instruments with HCI. The author has chosen not to use this still quite unfamiliar abbreviation.

early in an accounting period so it no longer has any significant equity features, it cannot qualify as an HCI until the next accounting period.[161]

A conversion event within the meaning of CTA 2009, section 475C(2)(b) and (c) is defined in CTA 2009, section 475C(5). According to this provision, a conversion event means (1) the conversion of the loan relationship into ordinary shares capital of the issuer, or (2) the conversion of the loan relationship into shares which form part of the parent company of the issuer,[162] i.e., the bond can be converted into shares of the parent company.

That means that the hybrid capital instruments rules apply to convertible bonds (as defined in Chapter 8 of this work) and also to some exchangeable bonds[163] if the debt is exchanged into the shares of the parent company.

A write-down event is when a 'reduction of the debt may be permanent or temporary provided that, where the reduction is temporary, any subsequent write-back cannot increase the debt beyond its original amount.[164] Qualifying cases are defined in CTA 2009, section 475C(6), and include cases where:

(1) there is a material risk of the issuer becoming unable to pay its debts as they fall due,[165] i.e., the issuer has liquidity issues;
(2) the value of the issuer's assets is less than the amount of its liabilities, taking into account contingent and prospective liabilities,[166] i.e., the issuer has solvency issues; or
(3) there is a need to comply with a regulatory or other legal requirement.[167]

HMRC states that 'regulatory and other legal requirements can include overseas requirements such as those of an overseas regulator, where these apply to the debtor. Whether a provision is made to comply with a regulatory or other legal requirement needs to be considered on a case-by-case basis'.[168]

[c] *The Issuer Has Made an 'Irrevocable Election into the New Rules Within Six Months of Issue of the Debt Instrument'*

CTA 2009, section 475C(8) defines when an election is irrevocable. CTA 2009, section 475C(9) contains a main purpose test which renders the election as having no effect if 'the main purpose of, or one of the main purposes of, the arrangements is to secure a

161. HMRC, CFM37840.
162. CTA 2009, s. 475C(5).
163. Ch. 8 §8.03 defines exchangeable bonds as 'corporate bonds that can be converted into a pre-determined number of shares in a company other than the issuer's company at certain times during its life'.
164. HMRC, CFM37840.
165. CTA 2009, s. 475C(6)(a).
166. CTA 2009, s. 475C(6)(b).
167. CTA 2009, s. 475C(6)(c).
168. HMRC, CFM37840.

tax advantage for the company or any other person'.[169] HMRC states that it will take into account the following considerations when applying the test, namely:

- Whether a tax avoidance purpose is the main, or one of the main, purposes is ultimately a question of fact which depends on all the circumstances of the particular case.
- In line with HMRC's general approach in this area, HMRC will not give clearance covering the application of the anti-avoidance rule. [...].
- Companies have a choice between debt and equity in raising funds. If they choose a debt instrument and it includes permitted coupon waiver/deferral features or write-down/conversion features (whether to qualify as regulatory capital/MREL[170] or for another commercial purpose), then the inclusion of those features would not normally in itself indicate a tax purpose.
- If a company issues hybrid debt to protect or enhance its credit rating in respect of more senior debt instruments, this would not normally indicate a tax purpose.[171]

[D] UK General Anti-avoidance Legislation Applying to Derivatives

The general anti-avoidance legislation serves as an additional layer for HMRC to counter tax avoidance schemes that utilise derivatives. It mainly consists of the disclosure rules, the Code of Practice on Taxation for Banks and the General Anti-Abuse Rule (GAAR). In the same way, the Corporate Interest Restriction (CIR) rules are general anti-avoidance rules.

The UK has introduced general anti-avoidance measures, such as the CIR, in addition to the already existing rules on loss relief, transfer pricing and controlled foreign companies.[172] A discussion of those rules alone would be a work of its own and, thus, is not part of this book.[173] Further, the global minimum effective tax rate rules, as proposed to be introduced in the UK as the multinational and domestic top-up tax from 1 January 2024, can be viewed as a kind of general anti-avoidance regime. They are briefly discussed below.

[1] The Disclosure Rules

The UK has implemented three different disclosure regimes, two for value-added tax (VAT) and other indirect taxes and one for direct taxes, namely the VAT disclosure

169. CTA 2009, s. 475C(9); *see* HMRC, CFM37840.
170. The abbreviation stands for: minimum requirement on own funds and eligible liabilities.
171. HMRC, CFM37840.
172. Because controlled foreign companies are treated as UK resident companies for applying the CFC rules, TIOPA 2010, s. 371SD, any profits or losses under derivative contracts arising to CFCs, will be subject to CTA 2009, Part 7 'in the same way and to the same extent as if they were UK companies', *see* Ghosh, Johnson and Miller (2022), [E9.2] (issue 28).
173. The author refers to the excellent work of Southern, which discusses those more general anti-avoidance measures in great detail: David Southern, Supplement to the 10th Edition to Taxation of Loan Relationships and Derivatives Contracts, 2020.

regime (VADR), the Disclosure of Tax Avoidance Schemes: VAT and other indirect taxes (DASVOIT), and the Direct taxes (including Apprenticeship Levy), Stamp Duty Land Tax, Inheritance Tax and National Insurance contributions (DOTAS) regime.[174] In addition, the regulations for UK Mandatory Disclosure Rules, also known as The International Tax Enforcement (Disclosable Arrangements) Regulations 2023 (SI 38/2023), came into force on 28 March 2023.[175]

[a] Mandatory Disclosure Rules (MDR)

The rules 'replaced the existing DAC6 regulations,[176] which were repealed at the same time'.[177] SI 38/2023 outlines in section 3 that the regulations apply:

> where an intermediary with respect to a CRS[178] avoidance arrangement or opaque offshore structure –
>
> (a) either –
>   (i) makes that CRS avoidance arrangement or opaque offshore structure available for implementation, or
>   (ii) provides relevant services in respect of that CRS avoidance arrangement or opaque offshore structure,
>   through a branch or office located in the United Kingdom,
>
> (b) is resident in the United Kingdom,
> (c) has its place of management in the United Kingdom, or
> (d) is incorporated in the United Kingdom.[179]

174. HMRC, Guidance: Disclosure of tax avoidance schemes (2014, updated 8 July 2022), https://www.gov.uk/guidance/disclosure-of-tax-avoidance-schemes-overview, accessed 20 July 2023.
175. The International Tax Enforcement (Disclosable Arrangements) Regulations 2023 (SI 38/2023), s. 1.
176. 'DAC6' is the name for the EU Council Directive 2011/16 in relation to cross-border tax arrangements which aims at transparency and fairness in taxation.
    DAC6 'applies to cross-border tax arrangements, which meet one or more specified characteristics (hallmarks), and which concern either more than one EU country or an EU country and a non-EU country. It mandates a reporting obligation for these tax arrangements if in scope no matter whether the arrangement is justified according to national law', *see* Council Directive 2011/16/EU of 15 February 2011 on administrative cooperation in the field of taxation and repealing Directive 77/799/EEC (*OJ L 64, 11.3.2011*, 1, *compare* PWC, DAC6, The EU Directive on cross-border tax arrangements, https://www.pwc.com/gx/en/services/tax/tax-policy-administration/dac6-eu-directive-on-cross-border-tax-arrangements.html, accessed 20 July 2023.
    See also the recent amendment of DAC6: Council Directive (EU) 2018/822 of 25 May 2018 amending Directive 2011/16/EU as regards mandatory automatic exchange of information in the field of taxation in relation to reportable cross-border arrangements, ST/7160/2018/INIT, *OJ L 139, 5.6.2018, 1-13.*
177. Sharon Baynham, UK Mandatory Disclosure Rules are published (23 January 2023), KPMG, https://kpmg.com/uk/en/home/insights/2023/01/tmd-uk-mandatory-disclosure-rules-regulations-are-published.html, accessed 20 July 2023.
178. Common Reporting Standard.
179. SI 38/2023, s. 3.

[b] Disclosure Rules Applying to Direct Taxes

The disclosure rules applying to direct taxes were first introduced by FA 2004, Part 7, sections 306-319, with effect from 1 August 2004,[180] and only applied to certain anti-avoidance schemes in the area of employment income and in the context of financial products.[181] Two years later, the rules were extended to apply to all tax arrangements relating to income tax, corporation tax[182] and capital gains tax.[183]

Guidance on the disclosure of tax avoidance schemes has been regularly published by HMRC.[184] Under the disclosure rules, a 'tax arrangement' qualifies as a 'notifiable arrangement' if:

(1) it enables or might be expected to enable any person to obtain a tax advantage;[185]
(2) where the 'tax advantage is, or might be expected to be, the main benefit or one of the main benefits of the arrangement';[186] and
(3) the arrangement falls within any description ('hallmarks')[187] prescribed by the Treasury in the relevant regulations.[188]

A disclosure must be either made by a 'promoter'[189] of the 'notifiable arrangement', by an introducer of the scheme[190] or by the scheme user, i.e., the client entering into the scheme under certain conditions,[191] for example, by a person entering or implementing the scheme, if no promoter exists (so-called in-house schemes).[192]

Promoters must disclose the scheme to the Revenue within five days of a trigger event; such an event is either: (1) making a firm approach to another person with a view to making the scheme available for implementation, (2) making a scheme available for implementation or (3) becoming aware of a transaction forming part of the

180. FA 2004, s. 319(1).
181. HMRC, 'Disclosure of tax and NICs avoidance schemes: Summary of the disclosure rules' (*HMRC Anti-Avoidance Group*, 2013) – on file with the author.
182. FA 2004, s. 318.
183. HMRC, *Summary of the disclosure rules* (2013); HMRC, *Guidance: Disclosure of Tax Avoidance Schemes* (2012) Ch. 2.3.1 and 6.2.
184. This work refers to the guidance updated on 16 June 2022, *see* HMRC, *Guidance: Disclosure of Tax Avoidance Schemes: guidance*. The laws covered by the guidance can be found in 1.3.1. of the guidance.
185. FA 2004, s. 306(1)(b).
186. FA 2004, s. 306(1)(c); *see* HMRC, *Summary of the disclosure rules* (2013).
187. *Ibid.*
188. FA 2004, s. 306(1)(a).
189. FA 2004, s. 307 (1).
190. FA 2004, s. 307(1A), as amended by FA 2010, Sch. 17.
191. FA 2004, s. 309(1) determines the disclosure obligations of scheme users in cases where a non-UK resident promoter does not disclose the scheme. FA 2004, s. 310 prescribes the disclosure obligation of clients in cases where the promoter has no duty to disclose the scheme, for example because he is covered by the legal professional privilege (s. 314).
192. FA 2004, s. 310. *See* HMRC, *Guidance: Disclosure of Tax Avoidance Schemes*, 3.11.

scheme.[193] 'In-house' schemes with no promoter must be disclosed within thirty days of being implemented.

Various Treasury regulations prescribe certain 'hallmarks' that indicate to HMRC that the taxpayer may have entered or intends to enter into a tax avoidance scheme.[194] 'Some of these are designed to capture new and innovative arrangements. Others are designed to capture areas of specific concern. These may include schemes that are well known or commonly used.'[195]

The 'hallmarks' are not exclusive, and the absence of a hallmark does not indicate that the arrangement is acceptable to HMRC. If there is a 'notifiable arrangement' under the definitions above, upon disclosure, HMRC will issue an eight-digit reference number to the promoter for the disclosed scheme, which the promoter must provide to each client that enters into the scheme.[196]

[2] The UK GAAR

The Finance Act 2013[197] introduced a so-called General Anti-Abuse Rule[198] with the aim to 'strengthen HM Revenue & Customs' (HMRC's) anti-avoidance strategy and help HMRC tackle abusive avoidance'.[199]

[a] The Basic Design of the GAAR

FA 2013, section 206 does not define precisely what is meant by a *General Anti-Abuse Rule*, but FA 2013, section 206 (1) and (2) merely states:

> (1) This Part has effect for the *purpose of counteracting tax advantages* arising from *tax arrangements* that are *abusive.*[200]
> (2) The rules of this Part are *collectively to be known as 'the general anti-abuse rule'*.[201]
>
> Thus, the GAAR of FA 2013, sections 206-215, is, by design, a set of *principles-based* rules rather than rules based on abstract definitional criteria.[202] FA 2013 defines tax arrangements as *abusive* 'if they are arrangements the entering into or carrying out of which cannot *reasonably* be regarded as a *reasonable* course

193. FA 2004, s. 308(1) and (3). *See* SI 2012/1836, regs 5(4), (5) and 2(3); HMRC, *Guidance: Disclosure of Tax Avoidance Schemes*, 12.2 and 12.3.1-12.3.3.
194. The various 'hallmarks' are prescribed in: Tax Avoidance Schemes (Prescribed Descriptions of Arrangements) Regulations 2006 (SI 2006/1543 as subsequently amended), Regs 6-17.
For details of the hallmarks: HMRC *Guidance: Disclosure of Tax Avoidance Schemes*, 5.-5.9.12.
195. *Ibid.*, 5.1.
196. HMRC, *Summary of the Disclosure Rules* (2013).
197. The GAAR was introduced in the Finance Act 2013 on 17 July 2013 by receiving royal assent.
198. FA 2013, Part 5, ss 206-215.
199. HMRC, *Tax Avoidance: General Anti-Abuse Rule* (2014), https://www.gov.uk/government/publications/tax-avoidance-general-anti-abuse-rules, accessed 15 April 2013 (old 2014 GAAR guidance).
200. FA 2013, s. 206(1), emphasis added.
201. FA 2013, s. 206(2).
202. In contrast, the German GAAR is based on abstract definitional criteria.

> of action in relation to the relevant tax provisions, having regard to all the circumstances [...]'.[203]

This *double reasonableness test* has, by design, a narrow application.[204] For the GAAR to apply, the judge:

> is required to consider the range of reasonable views that could be held in relation to the arrangements. This means that the arrangement would not be regarded as abusive, and hence the GAAR will not apply if the judge considers in all the circumstances that the arrangements could reasonably be regarded as a reasonable course of action, even if the particular judge does not himself or herself regard it as a reasonable course of action.[205]

Thus, if the judge regards the tax arrangement as not reasonable, they may, however, still decide that the GAAR will not apply if it can be said that a reasonable view can be held to the contrary that the arrangements are a reasonable course of action.[206] 'If something can reasonably be regarded as reasonable tax planning, then it is not caught.'[207]

[b] Procedural Requirements for HMRC to Apply the GAAR

The counteraction of HMRC under the GAAR follows certain procedural requirements. First, the counteraction must be notified to the taxpayer by a designated HMRC officer.[208] The taxpayer can then make written representations in response to the notice for which they have forty-five days from the beginning of the day on which the notice is given.[209] FA 2013, Schedule 43, section 4A(1)-(9) deals with corrective action by taxpayers, and FA 2013, Schedule 43, section 4A(1) states that 'if the taxpayer takes the relevant corrective action before the beginning of the closed period mentioned in section 209(8), the matter is not to be referred to the GAAR Advisory Panel'.[210]

If the representations are made by the taxpayer, they will be considered by the designated HMRC officer in their decision on whether to proceed with the counteraction.[211] If the HMRC officer decides to proceed, the tax arrangement must be presented to an Advisory Panel established by the Commissioners for HMRC for its opinion.[212]

Only after considering the opinion of the Advisory Panel, will HMRC decide on the counteraction,[213] and the adjustments made must be on a just and reasonable basis.[214] The counteraction can be taken in various forms.[215] Before any court or

203. FA 2013, s. 207(2) – emphasis added.
204. HMRC, GAAR Guidance (2021), B2.1.
205. *Ibid.*, C5 10.2.
206. Economic Affairs Committee, *First Report, The Draft Finance Bill 2013* (2013) Ch. 3, para. 64.
207. *Ibid.*, para. 67.
208. FA 2013, Sch. 43, ss 2 and 3(1).
209. FA 2013, Sch. 43 s. 4(1).
210. FA 2013, Sch. 43, s. 4A(1).
211. FA 2013, Sch. 43, ss 4 and 6(1).
212. FA 2013, Sch. 43, s. 6(2).
213. FA 2013, Sch. 43, s. 12.
214. FA 2013, s. 209(2).

tribunal, HMRC must show (burden of proof) that 'there are tax arrangements that are abusive, and that the adjustments made to counteract the tax advantages arising from the arrangements are just and reasonable'.[216]

[c] Critical Analysis of the UK GAAR

The GAAR is – in theory – narrower than GAARs in some other countries[217] as it targets only 'abusive tax avoidance arrangements'[218] and not 'the centre ground of responsible tax planning'.[219]

Freedman states that the UK GAAR was deliberately designed as an 'anti-abuse rule' and not an 'anti-avoidance rule' as '"avoidance" in the extended sense in which that word is now being used in the media and political discussion is almost impossible to define so as to give a viable operational rule. The UK GAAR, therefore, covers a defined area of egregious abuse and not everything that might be described as avoidance in recent popular discourse'.[220]

Similarly, HMRC acknowledged in the consultation draft that 'a "broad spectrum" general anti-avoidance rule would not be beneficial for the UK [...] as it risks compromising the certainty that is vital to provide the confidence to do business in the UK'.[221]

After the *Aaronson* Report,[222] the business community thought that the UK GAAR should generally not apply to those arrangements that, although tax avoidance, cannot be regarded as abusive as the decisions made with respect to a specific transaction or set of transactions were reasonable in a commercial (non-tax) sense.[223]

However, after the consultation document on the GAAR,[224] the guidance notes[225] and the draft legislation[226] were published by HMRC, the business community became more critical towards the introduction of the GAAR as it was now regarded as an

215. HMRC, *Overview of Legislation in Draft* (11 December 2012), A192, https://assets.publishing.service.gov.uk/media/5a7a3781ed915d1a6421be1e/fb2013_overview_of_legislation_in_draft.pdf, accessed 1 January 2024.
216. FA 2013, s. 211(1).
217. Countries like Canada and Germany have 'general anti-avoidance rules' which in theory are targeted not only at highly abusive schemes but also more generally at 'tax avoidance schemes'. *See* Ernst & Young, *GAAR Rising, Mapping Tax Enforcement's Evolution* (2013).
218. HMRC, *A General Anti-Abuse Rule, Consultation Document* (2012) Ch. 1.7. and 2.1.
219. Graham Aaronson, GAAR Study: A Study to Consider Whether a General Anti-avoidance Rule Should Be Introduced into the UK Tax System (2011) Ch. 1.7. (vi); *see* HMRC, *GAAR – consultation document* (2012) Ch. 2.4.
220. Judith Freedman, General Anti-Avoidance Rules (GAARs) – A Key Element of Tax Systems in the Post-BEPS Tax World? The UK GAAR, Legal Research Paper Series (24 April 2016), https://papers.ssrn.com/sol3/papers.cfm?abstract_id=2769554, accessed 21 July 2023.
221. HMRC, *GAAR – consultation document* (2012), Ch. 1.6.
222. Aaronson (2011).
223. Jaimie Kaffash, 'The GAAR report: was it worth it?' AccountancyAge, http://www.accountancyage.com/aa/analysis/2127165/gaar-report-worth, accessed 17 April 2023.
224. HMRC, *GAAR – consultation document* (2012).
225. HMRC, *HMRC's GAAR Guidance – consultation drafts, Part–A-C (scope, examples, procedure)* (2012).
226. HMRC, *General Anti-Abuse Rule – draft legislation* (2012).

instrument to erode the protection of the taxpayer.[227] In this context, various features of the GAAR and the process towards the GAAR have been criticised as being detrimental to business activity and taxpayers' certainty in the UK.

Fast forward, the *2021 GAAR Guidance*[228] states that:

> [t]he primary policy objective of the GAAR is to deter taxpayers from entering into abusive arrangements, and to deter would-be promoters from promoting such arrangements. There may be tax avoidance arrangements that are challenged by HMRC using other parts of the tax code, but if they are not abusive, they are not within the scope of the GAAR.[229]

The world has changed within the last ten years with the introduction of various general anti-avoidance measures not only at the domestic[230] but also at EU and multinational level.[231] The UK GAAR – although the UK was late in introducing a GAAR compared to other countries which had a GAAR already for many years in their tax legislation – has some attractive features and clarity that led to the UK GAAR being somewhat a model for the GAAR introduced by the EU's ATAD, as *Freedman* observed.[232]

Ten years have passed since the introduction of the UK GAAR by FA 2013. HMRC's latest GAAR Guidance is from 16 July 2021.[233]

The GAAR applies in addition to the specific anti-avoidance rules on derivative contracts, the disclosure rules and other anti-avoidance measures,[234] such as the Code of Practice on Taxation for Banks.[235] This means that the specific anti-avoidance rules, disclosure rules and other measures will still be applied, with the GAAR being a general fall-back provision for HMRC in case the more specific anti-avoidance rules do not apply.[236] This allows HMRC to counter tax avoidance with a broader rule in addition to the anti-avoidance rules that counter prescriptively certain avoidance schemes already known to HMRC.

In the author's view, most cases of tax avoidance schemes that use derivatives transactions as a means to achieve the tax benefit will also, in the future, be caught by specific anti-avoidance rules applying to derivatives rather than the GAAR. In addition

227. For example: Ernst & Young (2013) 9.
228. The latest GAAR Guidance is HMRC, General anti-abuse rule (GAAR) guidance, (Approved by the GAAR Advisory Panel with effect from 16 July 2021), Parts A, B and C, and General anti-abuse rule (GAAR) guidance, (Approved by the GAAR Advisory Panel with effect from 11 September 2020), Parts D – Examples.
229. HMRC, General anti-abuse rule (GAAR) guidance (2021), B3.1.
230. Various countries have introduced GAARs dealing with abuses of national since the introduction of the UK GAAR in 2013.
231. '[T]he GAAR introduced via the MLI amending bilateral treaties around the world', *see* Juliana Cubillos González and Irma Johanna Mosquera Valderrama in: Mukesh Butani and Tarun Jain (eds), *General Anti-Avoidance Rules: The Final Tax Frontier?, Indian and International Tax Perspectives* (Thomson Reuters 2021), Ch. 44, 978.
232. Judith Freedman, 'The UK General Anti-Avoidance Rule: Transplants and Lessons' (2019) 73(6/7) Bulletin for International Taxation 332-338 DOI: 10.59403/2ezp67n.
233. HMRC, GAAR Guidance (2021).
234. HMRC, *Overview of Legislation in Draft*, A191.
235. HMRC, *Code of Practice on Taxation for Banks* (2009).
236. HMRC, *GAAR – draft legislation*, s. 7(1)-(3).

to the GAAR, the disclosure rules help HMRC identify new tax avoidance schemes quickly. Thus, the GAAR only has a limited scope of application in the context of transactions that utilise derivative contracts, as most transactions would be caught by existing anti-avoidance rules.

The fear by critics of the GAAR was in 2013 that the GAAR may, over time, not only be used by HMRC to apply to abusive tax schemes but may also be extended in its application to deal with non-abusive anti-avoidance schemes.

Gillard stated that 'the use of a reasonableness test and the reliance on guidance also means that there is a significant risk of mission creep in the future [...]. Once the legislation has been enacted, the scope of the GAAR could easily be expanded by HMRC without scrutiny by Parliament'.[237]

HMRC instead reacted more specifically. For example, the regime anti-avoidance rules of CTA 2009, section 698B-D were introduced which apply to derivative transactions. Those rules are designed to close the gap between specific anti-avoidance rules applying to derivative contracts and the GAAR. Thus, instead of extending the scope of the GAAR, the legislator enacted regime anti-avoidance rules, which provide HMRC with an additional tool to counter avoidance schemes that utilise or concern derivative transactions. So, the GAAR has not moved to the 'centre ground of tax planning', but the regime anti-avoidance rules applying to derivatives function as 'mini-GAARs' instead.[238]

[3] Pillar Two

The following subsection contains a brief summary of the Pillar Two rules that were introduced by the Finance (No. 2) Act 2023.[239] The rules 'apply to large multinational enterprises for accounting periods beginning on or after 31 December 2023'.[240]

To sum up its policy background, as part of the OECD/G20's BEPS project, the OECD/G20 released the Global Anti-Base Erosion Model Rules (GloBE rules), commonly referred to as *Pillar Two*.[241] Those rules are designed to reform international corporate tax rules beyond the OECD/G20's fifteen BEPS Actions.[242] Pillar Two aims to

237. Gilleard (2012) citing John Overs of *Berwin Leighton Paisner*.
238. CTA 2009, ss 698B, 698C and 698D.
239. Finance (No. 2) Act 2023 of 20 July 2023.
240. EY, UK passes Finance (No. 2) Act 2023 introducing OECD Pillar Two measures, Tax News Update (July 2023), https://taxnews.ey.com/news/2023-1243-uk-passes-finance-no2-act-2023-introducing-oecd-pillar-two-measures, accessed 1 January 2024.
241. OECD (2021), *Tax Challenges Arising from the Digitalisation of the Economy – Global Anti-Base Erosion Model Rules (Pillar Two): Inclusive Framework on BEPS*, OECD, Paris, https://www.oecd.org/tax/beps/tax-challenges-arising-from-the-digitalisation-of-the- economy-global-anti-base-erosion-model-rules-pillar-two.htm, accessed 1 August 2023.
242. Allen & Overy, 20 Questions on Pillar Two and the GloBE rules, 3 April 2023, https://www.allenovery.com/en-gb/global/news-and-insights/publications/20-questions-on-pillar-two-and-the-globe-rules, accessed 1 August 2023.

introduce a global minimum corporation tax rate in the participating countries.[243] The aim of Pillar Two is to hinder the opportunity for base erosion and profit shifting.[244]

The Pillar Two rules do not function on an entity basis but on a jurisdiction basis. The aim of the Pillar Two rules is to deter multinationals from shifting their profits to low-income tax countries. Under Pillar Two, those multinationals with more than EUR 750 million in annual revenue must pay a minimum effective tax rate (ETR) of 15% on income arising in each jurisdiction where they operate.[245] The tax is, therefore, calculated at the group level, not at a single company level. In that respect, Pillar Two functions differently than corporation or income tax. The OECD has released a total of three administrative guidances to Pillar Two, the latest in December 2023.[246]

The Spring Budget 2023 not only increased the main corporation tax rate from 19% to 25% for the financial year 2024,[247] save for small businesses with annual profits of GBP 50,000 or less.[248] The Spring Budget 2023 'also confirmed the introduction of the new multinational top-up tax to be levied on UK parent companies in a multinational enterprise group'.[249]

Finance (No. 2) Act 2023 outlines the mechanics of the multinational top-up tax in Part 3.[250] Finance (No. 2) Act 2023 also introduces a domestic top-up tax in Part 4 'to make provision for a qualified domestic minimum top-up tax within the meaning of the

243. PWC, 'Pillar Two', https://www.pwc.com/us/en/services/tax/multinationals/pillar-two-model-for-data-and-reporting.html, accessed 15 March 2023.
244. See for example, the proposed introduction of minimum taxation rules in the EU: European Council, Council of the European Union, 'International taxation: Council reaches agreement on a minimum level of taxation for largest corporations' (12 December 2022), https://www.consilium.europa.eu/en/press/press-releases/2022/12/12/international-taxation-council-reaches-agreement-on-a-minimum-level-of-taxation-for-largest-corporations/, accessed 15 March 2023.
245. PWC, Pillar Two Model Rules, Private companies take note: Pillar Two Guide for US Multinational Enterprises, 22 August 2023, https://www.pwc.com/us/en/services/trust-solutions/private-company-services/library/pillar-two-guide.html, accessed 3 January 2024.
246. OECD (2023), *Tax Challenges Arising from the Digitalisation of the Economy – Administrative Guidance on the Global Anti-Base Erosion Model Rules (Pillar Two)*, February 2023, OECD/G20 Inclusive Framework on BEPS, https://www.oecd.org/tax/beps/agreed-administrative-guidance-for-the-pillar-two-globe-rules.pdf, accessed 1 January 2024; OECD (2023), *Tax Challenges Arising from the Digitalisation of the Economy – Administrative Guidance on the Global Anti-Base Erosion Model Rules (Pillar Two)*, July 2023, OECD/G20 Inclusive Framework on BEPS, https://www.oecd.org/tax/beps/administrative-guidance-global-anti-base-erosion-rules-pillar-two-july-2023.pdf, accessed 1 January 2024; OECD (2023), *Tax Challenges Arising from the Digitalisation of the Economy – Administrative Guidance on the Global Anti-Base Erosion Model Rules (Pillar Two), December 2023*, OECD/G20 Inclusive Framework on BEPS, http://www.oecd.org/tax/beps/administrative-guidance-global-anti- base-erosion-rules-pillar-two-december-2023.pdf, accessed 1 January 2024.
247. 2023 Spring Budget, Ch. 3, para. 3.68. This is confirmed in the Finance (No. 2) Act 2023, s. 5(1) and (2).
248. Finance (No. 2) Act 2023, s. 6(1).
249. BDO Global, United Kingdom – Spring budget includes Pillar Two and transfer pricing documentation announcements, 17 March 2023, https://www.bdo.global/en-gb/insights/tax/international-tax/united-kingdom-spring-budget-includes-pillar-two-and-transfer-pricing-documentation-announcements, accessed 15 April 2023.
250. Finance (No. 2) Act 2023, Part 3, ss 121-264.

Pillar Two rules'.[251] HMRC released two draft guidance documents on both the multinational and domestic top-up tax in June[252] and December 2023.[253]

Multinational Top-up Tax (MTT) will be charged where a UK parent member holds an interest in entities in another jurisdiction, and the group's profits arising in that jurisdiction are taxed below the minimum 15% rate; the amount brought to charge will be required to achieve a 15% minimum rate.[254] No additional tax will arise in respect of jurisdictions where the group's profits are taxed at 15% or more.[255]

Domestic Top-up Tax (DTT) 'applies the rules of multinational top-up tax to the UK operations of groups and certain entities, to ensure that UK entities will be taxed at the minimum rate'.[256] In the Autumn Statement 2022, the UK announced the introduction of an undertaxed profits rule (UTPR), functioning as a backstop within the GloBE rules, for accounting periods beginning on or after 31 December 2024.[257]

[E] Case Law Concerning Derivative Arrangements

The following subsection outlines various UK cases where derivative transactions and avoidance arrangements involving derivative arrangements were under scrutiny by HMRC. The topics of those cases are only briefly mentioned below.[258]

[1] Griffin (Inspector of Taxes) v. Citibank Investments Ltd [2000] STC 1010

The case concerned the relationship between derivative transactions and lending transactions. The case concerned an equity call and put options combination, a so-called equity box structure[259] over the FTSE 100 Index. HMRC claimed that the arrangement was producing a return equivalent to a zero-coupon bond, thereby taxable as income on an accruals basis, whereas the taxpayer proposed that the equity index option combination was a gain on qualifying options and subject to capital gains tax. The High Court held that the transactions were commercial derivative transactions

251. Finance (No. 2) Act 2023, s. 265(1).
252. HMRC, Multinational top-up tax draft guidance manual, 15 June 2023, https://assets.publishing.service.gov.uk/government/uploads/system/uploads/attachment_data/file/1163051/Multinational-top-up-tax-draft-guidance.pdf, accessed 3 January 2024.
253. HMRC, Open Consultation, Draft guidance on Multinational Top-up Tax and Domestic Top-up Tax, 21 December 2023, https://www.gov.uk/government/consultations/draft-guidance-on-multinational-top-up-tax-and-domestic-top-up-tax, accessed 1 January 2024.
254. *Ibid.*
255. BDO Global, United Kingdom – Spring budget includes Pillar Two and transfer pricing documentation announcements, 17 March 2023, emphasis added.
256. HMRC, Multinational Top-up Tax and Domestic Top-up Tax (December 2023).
257. Gov.UK, Multinational top-up tax: undertaxed profits rule and other amendments, Policy paper, updated 27 September 2023, https://www.gov.uk/government/publications/multinational-top-up-tax-adoption-of-the-undertaxed-profits-rule-and-other-amendments/multinational-top-up-tax-undertaxed-profits-rule-and-other-amendments, accessed 1 December 2023.
258. A summary of the facts and the decisions can be found in: Southern (2017), Ch. 17.
259. Southern (2017), para. 17.3.

and that the Ramsey principle did not apply, holding that it was 'a legitimate choice between investment options having regard to his own fiscal and financial position'.[260]

[2] HSBC Life (UK) Ltd v. Stubbs [2002] STC (SCD) 9

The case concerns the question of whether equity derivatives bought by insurance companies in order to back guaranteed investment bonds which were sold to various investors were to be taxed under TCGA 1992 as capital gains or if they were subject to the FA 1996 loan relationship legislation. As *Southern* notes, 'the policy of the financial instruments legislation in FA 1994 and the loan relationship legislation in FA 1996, was to bring into income taxation profits on debt and debt-based products while leaving gains on shares and equity-linked instruments within the capital gains tax rules'.[261] In *HSBC Life (UK) Ltd v. Stubbs*, the Special Commissioner held that transactions from financial futures were not profits from loan relationships and, therefore, not be taxed under the loan relationship rules on an accruals basis, but instead, the realisation basis had to apply under the capital gains rules.[262] The decision shows that although taxpayers may utilise the benefits of the put-call parity by replicating the economic outcome of a zero-coupon bond, the actual legal substance of the instruments, here, derivatives, has to be respected.

[3] IRC v. Scottish Provident Institution [2004] UKHL 52

The case concerned an option combination where Scottish Provident, an insurance company, wrote a call option on UK gilts (call option holder and counterparty: Citibank) and received an option premium of GBP 30 million, and at the same time, bought a call option on UK gilts for which it paid GBP 10 million. Both options were exercisable on the same date. The tax result would have been as follows: under FA 1994, section 147A, the option premium received by an insurance company was not taxable, whereas the option premium paid was tax deductible, resulting in an aggregate tax-deductible loss of GBP 20 million for tax purposes although one option was hedged economically by the opposite option. Consequently, the question the court had to answer was whether both options had to be seen as a single transaction or separately. The Special Commissioners held that the option premium received by the insurance company was part of a composite transaction.[263]

[4] HBOS Treasury Services Plc v. R&C Commissioners [2010] SFTD 134

The case concerned a fixed-for-floating interest rate swap and was extensively discussed in Chapter 6 §6.01[B][2] of this work.[264] In this case, the bank held an interest

260. *Griffin (Inspector of Taxes) v. Citibank Investments Ltd* [2000] STC 1010, 1039 (Judge Patten).
261. Southern (2017), para. 17.12.
262. *Ibid.*
263. *Ibid.*, paras 17.26-17.27.
264. Ch. 6 §6.01[B][2].

rate swap, which it novated in order to achieve a tax benefit. 'The Tribunal held that there was a tax avoidance scheme, aimed at avoiding the tax which would have been payable [...] by turning an income receipt into a capital receipt.'[265]

[5] Abbey National Treasury Services Plc v. R&C Commissioners [2015] SFTD 929

This case concerned gross paying in-the-money interest rate swaps where a group treasury company issued tracker shares so that its parent company would be entitled 'to receive dividends equivalent to the cash flows on the swaps'.[266] The Tribunal held that the debt element under the swap was not a tax-deductible debt but a de facto non-deductible dividend payment.[267]

[6] Bristol & West Plc v. R&C Commissioners [2016] STC 1491

The case concerned intra-group transfers of derivative contracts, being 'in the money interest rate swaps novated from one group company to another'[268] against consideration.

[7] Greene King Plc v. R&C Commissioners [2016] EWCA Civ 782

The case concerns 'a scheme to secure asymmetric tax treatment in a group'.[269]

[8] Union Castle Main Steamship Company Ltd v. R&C Commissioners [2016] UKFTT 0256 (TC)

Again, this is an arrangement within a group that seeks to 'turn taxable profit on derivatives into tax-free capital gains'.[270]

§10.02 ANTI-AVOIDANCE LEGISLATION IN GERMANY APPLYING TO DERIVATIVES

Apart from the ring-fencing rule for derivatives losses, no specific anti-avoidance rules applying explicitly to derivatives have been enacted. Anti-avoidance rules on the limitation of interest deduction (debt cap provisions), rules on the limitation of losses in the context of tax deferral models, the re-qualification of income under section 20(1) No. 7 Income Tax Act (ITA) and treaty switch-over clauses may however also apply to derivatives transactions. In addition, the anti-treaty shopping rule of section 50d(3)

265. Southern (2017), para. 17.30.
266. *Ibid.*, para. 17.35.
267. *Ibid.*, paras 17.35-17.37.
268. *Ibid.*, para. 17.42.
269. *Ibid.*, para. 17.56.
270. *Ibid.*, para. 17.58.

ITA may apply to certain derivative transactions. Further, the EU ATAD Implementation Law came into force on 1 July 2021, thus including a new anti-hybrid rule, amending the existing CFC legislation, providing an amendment of the cross-border assets transfer and exit tax rules to allow 'a deferred payment of any tax relating to a deemed gain from an exit event'.[271]

[A] Specific Anti-avoidance Legislation Applying to Derivatives

The following subsection contains a brief summary of specific anti-avoidance legislation applying to derivative contracts held by companies.

[1] The Derivatives Loss Ring-Fencing Rule

Under the loss ring-fencing rules of section 15(4) sentence 3 to 5 ITA, certain losses from derivatives cannot be offset against other income of the company[272] but can only be offset against gains from other derivatives transactions.[273]

The loss ring-fencing rule of section 15(4) ITA does not apply if the derivatives transactions belong to the regular course of the business of a bank, credit institution, financial services company or financial company. In addition, the loss ring-fencing provision does not apply to all business taxpayers if the derivative was used to hedge business activities that are 'part of the regular course of the taxpayer's business'.[274]

Both carve-outs of section 15(4) sentence 4 ITA do not apply, and the derivatives losses are ring-fenced if the derivative is used to hedge equity positions that would qualify as tax-exempt for the taxpayer.[275]

[2] Ring-Fencing of Losses from Tax Deferral Models

Section 15b ITA determines that losses from tax deferral models are ring-fenced and cannot be offset against any other business income,[276] but only against income generated by the taxpayer in subsequent assessment periods from the very same tax deferral model.[277]

For the rules to apply, an intention to generate a tax advantage is necessary that has to be in the form of negative income and is based on a model structure.[278] Such a model structure is assumed by the legislation if the taxpayer is provided with a

271. EY, Tax News Update, Germany agrees on draft ATAD Implementation Law (26 March 2021), https://globaltaxnews.ey.com/news/2021-5355-german-government-agrees-on-draft-atad-implementation-law, accessed 19 July 2023.
272. The loss ring-fencing provision applies by reference also to companies, although it is contained in the Income Tax Act, *see* ss 8(1) CTA, 15(4) sent. 3 ITA.
273. For a more detailed description of the rules, *see also* Ch. 4 §4.03[C][2], Ch. 6 §6.03 and §6.04.
274. Sections 8(1) CTA, 15(4) sent. 4 ITA.
275. For details, *see also* Ch. 6 §6.04.
276. The provision also applies to companies, s. 8(1) CTA.
277. Section 15b(1) sent. 1 ITA.
278. Section 15b(2) sent. 1 ITA.

pre-arranged concept in which the taxpayer – by investing in the model – is provided with the opportunity to generate losses that can be used by the taxpayer to offset other items of income.[279]

This anti-avoidance rule predominantly applies to certain media or new energy funds, where the generation of losses is certain at the outset. Tax-avoidance schemes involving derivatives, where it is usually uncertain at the outset if the transactions generate gains or losses, will generally not be caught by the provisions of section 15b ITA.

[3] Re-qualification of Income on the Basis of Section 20(1) No. 7 ITA

Section 20(1) No. 7 ITA provides that any capital claims that provide a capital guarantee, i.e., the repayment of capital, will be treated as interest.

Based on section 20(1) No. 7 ITA, the Federal Fiscal Court re-qualified a JPY cash deposit that was fully hedged by an FX swap as interest income with the argument that the income constituted a capital claim on a combined basis.[280] Although the decision was made with regard to investment income received by a private individual, the courts might apply the decision also in the context of combined derivatives transactions entered into by companies. They might argue that certain combinations of derivatives and/or financial instruments constitute a capital guarantee for the investor. As a result, they might regard both the losses from one leg of the transaction and the gains from the other leg of the transaction as a combined, fully taxable investment providing a capital guarantee instead of allowing a tax-exempt gain to occur on one leg of the transaction, and tax-deductible losses on the other.
However, the provision may not apply if it is not certain whether the investor incurs a pre-tax loss or a pre-tax gain from the combined investment made. In those cases, a re-qualification on the basis of section 20(1) No. 7 ITA may not be possible.

[4] Treaty Switch-Over Clauses

In the context of cross-border transactions, some German tax treaties may apply switch-over clauses with regard to income from hybrid instruments.[281]

For example, the US/Germany Double Taxation Convention (2008) applies a switch-over clause in Article 23(4), where a change from the exemption method to the credit method is agreed upon in cases of qualification conflicts.[282] If the income, for

279. Section 15b(2) sent. 2 ITA.
280. BFH, decision of 19 April 2005, VIII R 80/02.
281. Domestically, from 1 January 2014 onwards, the amended s. 8b(1) sent. 2 CTA now denies the 95% corporate tax exemption for dividends and similar distributions in cases where the payments are treated as tax deductible for the payee company. In addition, a treaty override may apply under s. 8b(1) sent. 3 CTA and the tax exemption may be disallowed. *See* Ch. 10 §10.01[E].
282. The qualification conflicts are defined as occurring either due to the treaty rules leading to double non-taxation (Art. 23(4)(b) 1st alt.), the US domestic tax law leading to double non-taxation (Art. 23(4)(b) 2nd alt.), or other cases of double non-taxation (Art. 23(4)(c)).

example, from a profit participating loan or convertible bond, is classified as a dividend under domestic German tax law[283] but as interest income in the other country, the exemption method under the treaty would be disallowed, and instead, the credit method would apply.[284]

[5] Anti-treaty Shopping Rule of Section 50d(3) ITA

Section 50d(3) ITA was designed as a specific anti-avoidance rule directed against purely tax-motivated arrangements which were set up for 'treaty shopping' or 'Directive-shopping' purposes which are conducted by conduit companies.[285]

Schoenfeld and Erdem explain that section 50d(3) ITA is structured in a way that it prevents any relief of withholding taxes if two indications of abuse are cumulatively given, which - seen in their entirety - allow the assumption to be made that there is tax avoidance and an abuse of the law.[286] *Schoenfeld and Erdem* also discuss in detail the relationship between section 50d(3) ITA and the general EU anti-avoidance rule, as confirmed for direct taxation in the Danish cases,[287] and conclude that the EU anti-avoidance rule should be *lex specialis* in relation to section 50d(3) ITA.[288]

The Federal Fiscal Court has recently confirmed that the general anti-avoidance rule of section 42 General Tax Act (GTA) is also applicable even if the *lex specialis* rule of section 50d(3) ITA does not apply to the specific facts of a case.[289] That means that the specific treaty-shopping rule of section 50d(3) ITA can apply alongside section 42 GTA.[290]

[B] Anti-Hybrid Mismatch Rules: EU ATAD Implementation

Germany implemented the EU Anti-Tax Avoidance Directives 2016/1164 (ATAD I) and 2017/952 (ATAD II) as a Member State.[291] ATAD I and II contain the anti-avoidance measures concerning:

- Article 4: Interest Limitation Rules
- Article 5: Exit Taxation Rules

283. Section 43(1) ITA.
284. Laukkanen (2007) 385 referring to: Friedhelm Jacob, 'German Tax Treatment of Hybrid Financial Instruments in Cross-Border Transactions' (August/September 2000) Bulletin for International Fiscal Documentation 442, 451.
285. Jens Schoenfeld and Elias Erdem, Anti-Treaty-Shopping und EU-Recht, Die Neufassung des § 50d Abs. 3 EStG durch das AbzStEntModG, 1st edn, ottoschmidt 2022, § 50d Abs. 3 EStG, II., para. 7. The book gives an excellent and in-depth summary of the law applicable.
286. Schoenfeld and Erdem (2022).
287. T Danmark and others, CJEU decision of 26 February 2019 - C-116/16, ECLI:EU:C:2019:135, and N Luxembourg and others, CJEU decision of 26 February 2019, - C115/16, ECLI: EU:C:2019:134.
288. Schoenfeld and Erdem (2022), I., para. 25.
289. BFH, decision of 17 November 2020, I R 2018, BStBl II 2021, 580, paras 21, 26.
290. Schoenfeld and Erdem (2022). VI., B, para. 597.
291. Deloitte, Actions Implementation by Country, Action 2 - Hybrids (2017), https://www2.deloitte.com/content/dam/Deloitte/global/Documents/Tax/dttl-tax-beps-action-2-hybrids-implementation-matrix.pdf, accessed 18 July 2023.

- Article 6: General Anti-Abuse Rules (GAAR)
- Articles 7 & 8: Controlled Foreign Company (CFC) Rules
- Article 9: Anti-Hybrid Mismatch Rules.

ATAD II states in Article 9 that:

> [r]ules on hybrid mismatches should address mismatch situations which result from double deductions, from conflict in the characterisation of financial instruments, payments and entities, or from the allocation of payments. Since hybrid mismatches could lead to a double deduction or to a deduction without inclusion, it is necessary to lay down rules whereby the Member State concerned either denies the deduction of a payment, expenses or losses or requires the taxpayer to include the payment in its taxable income, as appropriate. However, those rules apply only to deductible payments and should not affect the general features of a tax system, whether it is a classical or an imputation system.[292]

ATAD I and II set minimum standards for anti-avoidance measures that concern hybrid mismatches involving taxpayers in the EU[293] and third countries.[294]

On 30 June 2021, Germany published the EU ATAD Implementation Law,[295] which also included new anti-hybrid rules (*Betriebsausgabenabzug bei Besteuerungsinkongruenzen*), which are contained in a new section 4K ITA.[296] The law came into force on 1 July 2021.[297] 'The new anti-hybrid rules focus on a potential whole or partial denial of deductibility for expenses in Germany to the extent the resulting earnings are not taxed or are low taxed due to a hybrid mismatch or that deductions are taken twice (Deduction/Non-Inclusions, Double-Deductions, Imported Mismatches).'[298]

The rules apply retroactively to expenses accruing after 31 December 2019.[299] The rules are based on the ATAD I and II wording but 'do not cover cases where the foreign non- or low taxation is not triggered by a hybrid mismatch, but due to the general rules applied in the recipient jurisdiction'.[300]

The rules apply along the lines of ATAD I and II to:

(1) financing transactions where, due to a mismatch of either instrument qualification or asset attribution, the income is subject to no or lower taxation at the recipient level than without the mismatch;[301]

292. Council Directive (EU) 2017/952 of 29 May 2017.
293. ATAD I.
294. ATAD II.
295. *Gesetz zur Umsetzung der Anti-Steuervermeidungsrichtlinie (ATAD-Umsetzungsgesetz – ATADUmsG)* of 25 June 2021.
296. EY, Germany enacts EU ATAD Implementation Law including anti-hybrid rules (15 July 2021), https://www.ey.com/en_gl/tax-alerts/germany-enacts-eu-atad-implementation-law-including-anti-hybrid-rules, accessed 18 July 2023.
297. *Ibid.*
298. *Ibid.*
299. Section 52(8c) ITA.
300. EY, Tax News Update, Germany agrees on draft ATAD Implementation Law (26 March 2021), https://globaltaxnews.ey.com/news/2021-5355-german-government-agrees-on-draft-atad-implementation-law, accessed 19 July 2023.
301. *Ibid.*

(2) any deduction/no inclusion scenarios where the absence of an inclusion as taxable income is due to a mismatch in the qualification of the paying entity;
(3) reverse hybrids;
(4) any double deduction scenario; and
(5) imported mismatch scenarios.[302]

Thus, those rules also apply to convertible and exchangeable bonds within the meaning of 'hybrid instruments' in Chapter 8 of this work.

The proposal of the EU's ATAD III aims at tackling shell companies and proposes to introduce a 'minimum substance test'.[303] Although ATAD III was supposed to come into force on 1 January 2024,[304] its implementation was delayed, with the Directive's technical aspects being refined and clarified.[305]

[C] The General Anti-avoidance Rule Applying to Derivatives

In addition to the specific anti-avoidance rules, a GAAR laid down in section 42 GTA[306] may apply to tax avoidance schemes that utilise derivatives. Section 42 GTA is a rule based on abstract definitional criteria that have to be fulfilled in order for the GAAR to apply. It will only apply if:

- there is an abuse of legal planning possibilities;[307]
- no special anti-avoidance rule applies in the context of the transaction, which would supersede the GAAR;[308]
- the taxpayer cannot demonstrate considerable bona fide commercial or other non-tax reasons for entering into the transaction.[309]

The abuse of legal planning possibilities is given if the taxpayer has chosen a legal structure that is inappropriate to achieve the commercial goal of the transaction and that leads – compared to an appropriate legal structure – to a tax benefit that was not designed to apply by the legislation in question.[310] The tax benefit needs to arise to the taxpayer or a third party.

302. *Ibid.*, for a detailed summary of all applicable cases.
303. Deloitte, ATAD III (Shell Companies), https://www2.deloitte.com/dl/en/pages/legal/articles/atad-III-investment-management-newsletter.html, accessed 19 July 2023.
304. Deloitte, ATAD III (Shell Companies).
305. Council of the European Union, Draft Ecofin report to the European Council on tax issues, 16100/23, FISC 275 ECOFIN 1294 (30 November 2023), https://data.consilium.europa.eu/doc/document/ST-16100-2023-INIT/en/pdf, accessed 1 January 2024.
306. *Abgabenordnung*, here referred to as General Tax Act (GTA).
307. Section 42(1) sent. 1 GTA.
308. Section 42(1) sent. 2 GTA.
309. Section 42(2) sent. 2 GTA.
310. Section 42(2) sent. 1 GTA.

The 'inappropriate legal structure' is defined by the Federal Fiscal Court as any legal structure that:

- is inappropriate to achieve the specific commercial goal of the transaction,
- is entered to achieve a tax benefit, and
- can neither be justified by considerable bona fide commercial nor other non-tax reasons.[311]

A legal structure is regarded as inappropriate if reasonable third parties would not have chosen to achieve the specific commercial benefit compared to the actual economic aim pursued by the taxpayer.[312] Considerable non-tax reasons will be dismissed if the structure is predominantly chosen for tax reasons.[313] The GAAR is, by design, a very broad rule that targets not only abusive structures but also any structure that could be regarded as inappropriate because it achieves a tax benefit which was not intended by the legislator to apply.

One would expect the GAAR to be frequently applied to tax planning schemes in Germany. However, in the past, the Federal Fiscal Court has often denied the application of section 42 GTA.[314] Hence, the GAAR, in practice, mainly applies to cases where no considerable non-fiscal motive can be provided for the transaction by the taxpayer. In summary, section 42 GTA has a narrow application, but in many cases, other provisions will serve as anti-avoidance provisions under German law.

[D] Pillar Two

In the EU, the global minimum Effective Tax Rate (ETR) will apply to multinational groups with consolidated revenue over EUR 750 million. If such entities satisfy the revenue threshold and have income arising in low-tax jurisdictions, they will be subject to an ETR of 15%. *Council Directive (EU) 2022/2523 of 14 December 2022 on ensuring a global minimum level of taxation for multinational enterprise groups and large-scale*

311. BFH, decision of 3 February 1993 – I B 90/92, BFHE 170, 197, BStBl II 1993, 426 and BFH, decision of 19 August 1999 – I R 77/96, BStBl II 2001, 43.
312. BFH, decision of 17 January 1991 – IV R 132/85, BFHE 163, 449, BStBl II 1991, 607; BFH, decision of 16 January 1992 – V R 1/91, BFHE 167, 215, BStBl II 1992, 541; BFH, decision of 21 January 1999 – IV R 96/96, BStBl II 2002, 771.
313. Bundestags-Drucksache 16/6290, 81.
314. For example: BFH, decision of 25 August 2009, IX R 60/07, http://lexetius.com/2009, 2964 where it was held that the un-hedged disposal and repurchase of the same shares at the same day, but for a different price at the stock exchange did not constitute an inappropriate legal structure to obtain a speculative loss that could be offset against other speculative gains of the taxpayer. *See also* BFH, decision of 15 December 1999, I R 29/97, BStBl II 2000, 527 (decision confirmed that dividend stripping did not constitute abuse under s. 42 GTA as the provision of s. 50c ITA was *lex specialis* and in the case at hand did not apply). BFH, decision of 19 January 2000, I R 94/97, DB 2000, 651 (investment in Dublin Dock IFSC companies does not constitute abuse); BFH, decision of 19 August 1999 – I R 77/96, BStBl II 2001, 43 (distribution of dividends and re-contribution of capital not regarded as abusive).

domestic groups in the Union[315] required EU Member States to introduce the Pillar Two rules by 31 December 2023 with some generous transition rules.[316] As explained above, Pillar Two functions as a separate layer of taxation and takes a jurisdictional approach towards minimum taxation.

§10.03 COMPARISON OF THE EFFECTIVENESS OF ANTI-AVOIDANCE LEGISLATION IN THE UK AND GERMANY

The problem of tax avoidance schemes that utilise derivatives has been a significant one in both countries for many years. In the author's view, UK tax authorities were able to employ a more balanced and long-term approach towards those schemes as HMRC aimed to better understand the economic properties and the legal design of complex derivatives transactions. As a result, highly targeted anti-avoidance legislation, disclosure rules and codes of conduct for banks were enacted that allowed HMRC to deal with existing tax avoidance opportunities effectively. In particular, the UK approach that did not levy withholding taxes on dividends and manufactured dividends, and correspondingly did not provide any withholding tax credits proved a robust solution against tax avoidance schemes utilising withholding tax credits.

In the last few years, the German tax legislator has also enacted effective tax legislation and anti-avoidance rules that deal with derivatives and other complex financial instruments, partly due to the EU initiatives leading to EU Directives that required Member States to implement some of the rules contained in the OECD's BEPS Action plan, such as the ATAD Directives. Still, the new anti-avoidance rules have not been tested yet to see if they are efficient in preventing tax avoidance schemes that utilise newly emerged derivatives, such as crypto derivatives and ESG derivatives.

§10.04 TAX AVOIDANCE AND CRYPTOASSETS

[A] The UK

[1] Cryptocurrencies and Impairment Losses

In the context of cryptoassets, the author mentioned in Chapter 5 §5.05[A][2] the accounting treatment of impairment losses stemming from cryptocurrencies. The author outlined in Chapter 6 §6.08 how relatively easy it is to generate impairment

315. Council Directive (EU) 2022/2523 of 14 December 2022 on ensuring a global minimum level of taxation for multinational enterprise groups and large-scale domestic groups in the Union, ST/8778/2022/INIT *OJ L 328, 22.12.2022,* 1–58.

316. EU member states have the option to defer the implementation of the Income Inclusion Rule (IRR) and the Undertaxed Profits Rule (UTPR) until 31 December 2029 in case of a maximum of twelve ultimate parent entities (UPE) resident in their country. Estonia, Latvia, Lithuania, Slovakia and Malta have deferred the implementation of the IRR and UTPR. *See* KPMG, BEPS 2.0: state of play (3 January 2024), 9-10, https://assets.kpmg.com/content/dam/kpmg/xx/pdf/2023/04/beps-2-0-state-of-play-april-2023.pdf, accessed 4 January 2024.

losses on cryptoassets investments for tax purposes, which can be used to offset other (non-cryptoasset) gains, thereby de facto allowing a tax deferral of those gains.

The following discussion concerns UK resident companies and the tax treatment of impairment losses, which are accounted for under FRS 102, Section 18 or IAS 38 in order to showcase the potential use of cryptoasset transactions for tax avoidance purposes.

[a] Cost Model

To reiterate, if UK companies apply the cost model to account for cryptocurrencies under FRS 102, Section 18 or IAS 38, any movements below cost can be recognised as impairment losses – even if those losses occur during the financial year.[317] However, any appreciation in value is not recognised in the financial accounts until the cryptocurrency is disposed of.

'If companies hold different cryptocurrencies, and there is not an active market for all cryptocurrencies held, [that means the company also holds an illiquid cryptocurrency] those assets should be measured using the cost model'[318] because the same measurement model is used for all assets in an asset class.[319]

It should be noted that no amortisation takes place due to the infinite life of cryptocurrencies,[320] but only regular testing for impairment, which can also happen during the accounting year, i.e., at any point in time throughout the year when the cryptocurrency has depreciated in value.[321]

Thus, entities may recognise impairment losses whenever the cryptocurrency depreciates in value. At this point in time of depreciation, impairment is tested, and those impairment losses are recognised in the financial accounts.

However, if the cryptocurrency subsequently appreciates in value, cost accounting prohibits a 'write-up' to the higher value of the cryptocurrency, thus leaving the position at the lower value, although the cryptocurrency is de facto more valuable according to its market price.[322]

[b] Taxation Follows the Financial Accounts

The tax accounts follow the financial accounts so that those impairment losses can be used to offset against cryptocurrency or non-cryptocurrency gains, thereby de facto allowing a tax deferral of those gains.[323]

In this respect, it should be noted that the UK tax legislation does not contain specifically designed anti-avoidance legislation applying to cryptoassets.

317. Southern and Weidmann (2023), 68, 84-85.
318. *Ibid.*, 85.
319. Ch. 6 §6.08.
320. Ch. 5 §5.05[A][2].
321. IAS 38, para 108(b).
322. Southern and Weidmann (2023), 68, 93.
323. *Ibid.*

The author believes tax administrations need to deal with the phenomenon of the tax deductibility of impairment losses, which can be recognised in the financial and tax accounts in case of falling cryptocurrency prices, whereas any appreciations in value are not recognised until the disposal of the cryptocurrencies. The author understands that this disparity in the treatment of gains and losses can easily lead to taxpayers utilising this mismatch in order to defer the taxation of any (cryptocurrency and non-cryptocurrency) gains by utilising the impairment losses to absorb the gains.

The author refers to *Example 87* as well as to the several examples provided in the article by *Southern and the author*, which show how impairment losses are recognised and treated in the tax accounts.[324]

Example 87

based on Southern and Weidmann (2023)[325]

A Ltd. buys Ethereum (ETH) for GBP 500 during the financial year ending 31 December 2021. The position has a market value of GBP 1,000 on 31 December 2021. For tax purposes, no recognition of the increase in the value of the cryptocurrency takes place on 31 December 2021.

In the next financial year, A Ltd. buys further ETH for GBP 1,000. On 31 December 2022, A Ltd.'s holdings of cryptocurrency were valued at GBP 200 (for each of the two positions). An impairment loss was recognised for tax purposes.

Year-end	Income	Balance sheet	Revaluation reserve	SOCIE[326]	Tax
31 December 2021	0	500	500	500	0
31 December 2022	(1,100)[327]	(1,100)	(500)	(1,600)	(1,100)

324. *Ibid.*, 68, 89-94.
325. *Ibid.*
326. Statement of changes in equity.
327. The first part of the position was in accounts for GBP 500 (no write-up to GBP 1000 end of 2021) and depreciates to GBP 200 on 31 December 2022, thus generating a loss of GBP 300 (GBP 500 - GBP 200 = GBP 300). The second part of the position (purchased in 2022 for GBP 1000) drops in value to GBP 200, thus generating a loss of GBP 800 which is recognised as an impairment loss for accounting and tax purposes. Thus, the overall loss which shows in the income is GBP 1,100 in total and will also be recognised for tax purposes as an impairment loss, although the cryptocurrency has not been disposed of in 2022.

[2] Tax Avoidance and Crypto Derivatives

Crypto derivatives tend to fall outside the scope of specific anti-avoidance legislation in the context of the UK's *derivative contracts regime*, as those anti-avoidance rules are often specifically tailored to derivatives over certain underlyings.

Hence, the author proposes to *broaden* the existing *definition of derivatives for tax purposes* in the derivative contracts regime so that it can also apply to crypto derivatives. The author suggests that this legislative step would allow the existing derivatives anti-avoidance rules to also capture crypto derivatives. Thus, if the issue is addressed at the level of the definition of derivatives, there is no need to introduce new anti-avoidance legislation specifically tailored to crypto derivatives as the existing anti-avoidance legislation, particularly the regime anti-avoidance rules, can apply to crypto derivatives.

[B] Germany

[1] Tax Avoidance and Cryptoassets

The German legislator has not introduced specific anti-avoidance rules applying to cryptoassets. The author believes that some of the more general tax avoidance rules may, however, also apply to cryptoassets.

[2] Tax Avoidance and Crypto Derivatives

The definition of derivatives for tax purposes in the German tax legislation is abstract-prescriptive. Thus, crypto derivatives may fall under that definition. However, it is uncertain if specific anti-avoidance legislation, such as the derivative ring-fencing rule, would also apply to crypto derivatives.[328]

[3] EU Reporting Requirements for Cryptoassets

The EU has introduced new reporting requirements and an automatic exchange of information on revenues from cryptoassets and on advance tax rulings concerning cryptoassets.[329] The author believes that this exchange of information will help to shed light on a world of alternative financial transactions which operate on a peer-to-peer basis outside the traditional financial system with the consequence that cryptoasset gains are often underreported by taxpayers. The new tax transparency rules will apply to 'all service providers facilitating transactions in cryptoassets for customers resident

328. *See* Ch. 7 § 7.06.
329. Council Directive amending Directive 2011/16/EU on administrative cooperation in the field of taxation, 10215.23, FISC 115, ECOFIN 566, 18 September 2023.

in the EU'.[330] They are contained in an update to the directive on administrative cooperation (DAC8).[331]

The new reporting requirements are in line with the OECD's *Crypto-Asset Reporting Framework*[332] and 'will improve member states' ability to detect and counter tax fraud, tax evasion, and tax avoidance'.[333] The author, however, believes that tax reporting requirements alone will not solve the issues relating to the taxation of cryptoassets stemming from their accounting treatment.

§10.05 SOLUTIONS TO PROBLEM 7: TACKLING TAX AVOIDANCE EFFECTIVELY

If tax legislators seek to limit tax avoidance schemes that utilise derivatives or cryptoassets, they need to introduce targeted and general tax avoidance legislation. They should also seek to align their existing tax legislation with new developments in the context of derivatives and cryptoassets. For example, legislators should design new legislation that applies to cryptoassets, and they should also ensure that the existing derivatives legislation is capable of capturing newly emerged derivatives, such as crypto derivatives and ESG derivatives, or alternatively, implement new rules for those instruments. Furthermore, tax legislators need to take into account the more general trends in domestic and international taxation and evaluate those developments with respect to their efficiency in applying to derivatives and cryptoassets.

The true difficulty in designing anti-avoidance rules that limit the use of tax avoidance schemes is to find the right balance between achieving maximum effectiveness of the rules while generating as few obstacles as possible that may deter sound commercial activity.

On the one hand, if general or targeted tax avoidance rules concerning derivatives or cryptoassets are too lax, not properly applied, or simply poorly designed, a tax system may suffer significant revenue losses due to taxpayers utilising tax avoidance schemes. Schemes involving derivatives are often built on the *possibility of economic replication* of derivatives and other financial instruments, which can facilitate a change of the legal character of an income stream or capital gain or loss without a change of the economic character of the transaction with the aim to achieve the most favourable tax result.

330. Council Directive amending Directive 2011/16/EU on administrative cooperation in the field of taxation (DAC8) of 18 October 2023, 10215/23, Limite, Fisc 115 Ecofin 566; *compare also* KPMG, EU: New directive on tax transparency rules for service providers facilitating cryptoasset transactions (17 October 2023), https://kpmg.com/us/en/home/insights/2023/10/tnf-eu-new-directive-on-tax-transparency-rules-for-service-providers-facilitating-cryptoasset-transactions.html, accessed 20 October 2023.

331. Council Directive amending Directive 2011/16/EU on administrative cooperation in the field of taxation.

332. OECD (2022), Crypto-Asset Reporting Framework and Amendments to the Common Reporting Standard, OECD, Paris, https://www.oecd.org/tax/exchange-of-tax-information/crypto-asset-reporting-framework-and-amendments-to- the-common-reporting-standard.htm, accessed 20 October 2023.

333. KPMG, EU: New directive on tax transparency rules.

On the other hand, if the tax avoidance rules are too extensive or the general tax environment of a country is too burdensome (either by: (1) catching genuine commercial activities, (2) creating legal uncertainty, (3) introducing tax compliance provisions that are too burdensome for smaller taxpayers to follow, or (4) overtaxing certain regular business activity due to punitive taxation), the business environment of a country or a specific industry may suffer as a result and investors may be deterred from investing into businesses of this country.

Overtaxation of certain business activities due to special taxation rules belongs to the area of restrictive government taxation measures, which may have a similar or a more substantial effect than anti-avoidance rules because they may deter businesses and specific industries from functioning properly. Alternatively, overtaxation may effectively deny investors from deciding in favour of certain investment opportunities.

For example, in Germany, the investment into a foreign alternative investment fund was subject to penalty taxation under section 6 Investment Tax Act (old version) if certain, very strict reporting and publication requirements were not fulfilled by the fund so that investing into the fund became unattractive because of overtaxation. The Court of Justice of the European Union (CJEU) ruled that the penalty taxation of the Investment Tax Act limited the free movement of capital and thus contradicted Article 63 Treaty on the Functioning of the European Union (TFEU).[334] Germany, therefore, revised the Investment Tax Act in the wake of the CJEU decision, with the new rules applying from 1 January 2018.[335]

The author proposes that any legislation in relation to the taxation of derivatives or cryptoassets which aims to tackle problems concerning structured finance transactions should ideally not hinder taxpayers in utilising the commercial function of derivatives, such as the use of derivatives for hedging, (non-tax) business arbitrage opportunities, speculation and leveraged financing and investing. Thus, anti-avoidance legislation that is targeted only at derivatives avoidance schemes will allow countries to foster the competitiveness of commercial and investment activity.

The solutions proposed by the author apply to traditional derivatives. The same considerations should also apply to newly emerged crypto derivatives and ESG derivatives. The author also makes suggestions for cryptoassets.

[A] Improvement of the General Design of the Tax System

Tax legislators should consider the issues discussed below when designing their tax system in order to achieve acceptable domestic and cross-border solutions for the taxation of derivatives and cryptoassets. In the author's view, they need to find a

334. Judgment of the Court (First Chamber) of 9 October 2014, van Caster and van Caster (Case C-326/12), http://curia.europa.eu/juris/document/document.jsf?text=&docid=158426&pageIndex=0&doclang=EN&mode=lst&dir=&occ=first&part=1&cid=467959, accessed 13 May 2023.
335. Deloitte tax@hand, Taxation of investment fund income revised, 21 May 2018, https://www.taxathand.com/article/9698/Germany/2018/Taxation-of-investment-fund-income-revised-#!, accessed 18 July 2023.

balance between tight enough anti-avoidance measures and restrictive deduction rules, on the one hand, and the smooth functioning of the countries' businesses, on the other.

[1] Specific Taxation Rules Versus the Application of General Taxation Rules

In relation to derivatives, both the implementation of a special taxation regime as well as the application of the general taxation rules, constitute workable solutions for a tax system to deal with the taxation issues arising in the context of derivatives.[336]

However, if properly designed, taxation regimes that are tailored to apply specifically to derivatives will, in the author's view, provide fewer opportunities for tax avoidance[337] compared to tax systems that apply the general taxation rules to derivatives (and at the same time privilege capital over income, and/or equity over debt).

In any case, both approaches would need to be assisted by specific anti-avoidance rules that target derivatives transactions, which allow the conversion of one category of (fully taxable) income (or gains) into another category of income (or gains) which is subject to preferential tax treatment.

Existing derivative contract regimes should be regularly tested to see if they can also cater for novel derivatives, such as crypto derivatives and the various forms of ESG derivatives. In this respect, the author believes that abstract-prescriptive definitions applying derivatives are more suitable to counter tax avoidance schemes as those definitions may more easily capture any new derivative forms and types that the capital markets may devise.

In respect of cryptoassets, the author proposes that tax legislators should introduce a special taxation regime to deal with this newly emerged asset class comprehensively.

In the same way, legislators should carefully think about how they tax carbon credits – and respective derivatives – based on the accounting treatment of those intangible assets and the challenges that the treatment of impairment losses in the IFRS (or UK GAAP) financial accounts may cause for the tax treatment of carbon credits and their derivatives.[338]

[2] Accounting and Taxation Alignment as a Way to Counter Tax Avoidance?

As analysed in Chapter 6 §6.05[A], the alignment of accounting and taxation rules may not necessarily lead to a reduction of tax avoidance opportunities as the accounting rules are not designed to achieve a coherent taxation system with the aim of preventing

336. *See* Ch. 5 §5.06[A], §5.06[B] and §5.06[C].
337. *See* Ch. 5 §5.06[C][3].
338. The author will publish a book on the regulatory, accounting and tax treatment of ESG investments in the near future which has a special focus on carbon credits and ESG derivatives.

tax avoidance. Further, if a tax system applies the fair value accounting method to the taxation of derivatives but taxes some or all other financial assets or liabilities on an accruals basis or even a cash basis, opportunities for tax avoidance schemes are likely to arise. For example, tax deferral schemes may exploit the timing differences in recognition and try to tax gains generated on one leg of the transaction as late as possible and unrealised losses arising on the other leg of the transaction as early as possible.

Thus, the alignment of accounting and taxation rules and the application of the fair value accounting method to derivatives, but not to other financial instruments and assets, may not constitute an appropriate solution to prevent the implementation of tax avoidance schemes by taxpayers.[339]

The same applies to cryptoassets. An alignment of accounting standards and taxation rules applying to cryptoassets may not be desirable as those instruments are treated as infinite-life intangible assets for accounting purposes. The current applicable accounting standards (IFRS, UK GAAP and German GAAP) do not prescribe fair value accounting for cryptoassets.

If the tax rules follow the accounts, impairment losses may be used by corporate taxpayers who invest in those cryptoassets to defer their tax liabilities by offsetting those impairment losses against other gains. Hence, anti-avoidance rules are desirable which do not permit a deduction for tax purposes of non-realised cryptoasset impairment losses, i.e., before the cryptoassets are sold.

[3] Hedging Approaches and Tax Avoidance

In Chapter 7 §7.05[A] and [B], the author analysed how tax systems should deal with different hedging approaches and post-tax hedging schemes in order to prevent the utilisation of tax avoidance schemes. Tax systems should aim to achieve tax-neutral outcomes for the hedged instrument and the hedge (gains taxable/losses deductible), both in cases where derivatives are used for hedging purposes and also where other financial instruments are used to hedge derivatives (vertical tax neutrality).[340]

Differences in the taxation of different assets, for example, different tax rates applying to equity and debt instruments, will inevitably lead to tax avoidance opportunities in the area of post-tax hedging schemes. Tax legislators should seek to abolish the difference in the taxation of equity and debt (horizontal tax neutrality), or they have to enact anti-avoidance legislation in order to prevent tax avoidance schemes that utilise the different taxation rules.

Liquid cryptoassets like Bitcoin and Ethereum and their respective derivatives will fulfil the criterion of hedge effectiveness in a hedging relationship between those instruments. Hedged cryptoasset positions over less liquid cryptoassets, as shown in Chapter 7 §7.06[B], *Examples 58* and *59*, do not qualify for hedge accounting. In those examples which discussed hedged *Dogecoin* transactions, the author explained how

339. For further details, *see* Ch. 6 §6.05[B].
340. *See* Ch. 10 §10.01[D], Table (OECD).

easily hedged cryptoasset positions can be used to generate a one-sided tax deduction. Thus, tax legislators need to determine how they enable tax-efficient hedged cryptoasset positions while, at the same time, preventing tax avoidance opportunities in hedged cryptoasset transactions that generate a one-sided tax deduction.

[4] Hybrid Instruments and Tax Avoidance

Hybrid instruments should not be bifurcated but require an integrated treatment for tax purposes.[341] An integration approach for tax purposes should be applied symmetrically for holders and issuers of hybrid instruments. Thus, the issuer should be able to deduct only the lower coupon on the convertible or exchangeable bonds (but not an increased coupon due to a bifurcation of the hybrid instrument), whereas the holder should only be taxed on the lower coupon.

If the issuer of the hybrid instrument is treated differently than the holder, as is the case under German GAAP, tax avoidance opportunities are likely to arise. Whereas the issuer of the convertible bond will be able to obtain an increased tax deduction on a coupon of a comparable straight bond (because the convertible bond will be bifurcated for the issuer both in the financial and the tax accounts according to the majority view in the literature),[342] the holder of the convertible bond will only pay tax on the lower coupon of the convertible bond. Further, if the bond is converted into shares, any equity capital gains on disposal of the shares will be 95% tax-free for corporate tax purposes. Thus, companies may structure their tax affairs in an efficient way by issuing a convertible bond that is purchased by a subsidiary or group company, thereby profiting from the different tax treatment of the coupons for the issuer and the holder of the convertible bond in combination with the tax exemption for equity capital gains in case of a conversion of the convertible bond into shares. The hybrid mismatch rules of ATAD have, however, put, to a certain extent, an end to those kinds of tax avoidance schemes.

[5] Structured Products and Tax Avoidance

In Chapter 8 §8.08, the author suggested that structured products provide less room for tax avoidance if the single elements of structured products are taxed according to the same rules as the combined structured products. If the single elements and the structured products are taxed differently based on the categories of debt, equity and derivatives, the tax legislator may provide for a bifurcation of structured products for tax purposes in the tax legislation in order to avoid tax avoidance opportunities between the different categories of income. 'False friends' have to be distinguished from genuine structured products and may have to be treated according to an

341. *See* Ch. 8 §8.08.
342. *See* Ch. 8 §8.06[B][2][b].

integration approach for tax purposes as a measure to prevent tax avoidance schemes.[343]

Further, crypto structured products may lead to further tax avoidance opportunities due to a mismatch in the accounting and tax treatment of crypto derivatives and crypto structured products and the underlying cryptoassets. Similar considerations may apply to ESG derivatives and ESG-linked structured products. The author believes that tax systems would profit from those instruments accounted for and taxed as one instrument as a bifurcation of those instruments opens further room for tax avoidance schemes due to the qualification of cryptoassets and verified carbon credits as intangible assets and the tax treatment of impairment losses.

Thus, crypto and ESG-linked structured products (with underlying carbon credits) should be taxed as one - non-bifurcated - instrument in order to prevent tax avoidance opportunities that may arise if those instruments are bifurcated, *see* Chapters 8 §8.09[C] and 8.10 [E][2].

[6] Hybrid Instruments and Qualification Conflicts in Cross-Border Transactions

Cross-border qualification conflicts that occur directly or indirectly due to the use of hybrid instruments may be solved in the context of domestic tax legislation or at the level of tax treaties.[344] A unilateral approach could either involve the introduction of domestic tax legislation which disallows dividend exemption or withholding tax credits in the country where payments are received from hybrid instruments or, alternatively, a denial of the tax deduction for the payments under the hybrid instrument in the country of the payer.

Switch-over clauses in double tax treaties may prevent payments arising from hybrid instruments from being qualified as deductible interest in the state of the issuer and, at the same time, as tax-exempt dividends in the state of the holder of the instrument. Under such a clause, the exemption method would be disallowed in case of a treaty qualification conflict, and the credit method would apply.

The OECD's Action Plan 2 on hybrid mismatches has successfully proposed solutions on how to deal with 'hybrid instruments' and 'hybrid entities', and both the UK and Germany have implemented those rules in their national law by following the proposals of the ATAD I and II Directives.

Further, the Code of Conduct Group (Business Taxation) of the European Union suggested in a report that if payments under a hybrid instrument are qualified as tax-deductible expenses for the debtor, payments received by the creditor of the hybrid instrument should not qualify as tax-exempt under a participation exemption in the country of residence of the creditor.[345] Based on this report, the European Commission published a proposal that suggested the amendment of the Parent-Subsidiary Directive

343. *See* Ch. 8 §8.08.
344. In OECD (2013c) 30, several anti-avoidance strategies are summarised as Action 2 that may neutralise the effects of these qualification conflicts.
345. *See* Report of the Code of Conduct Group of 25 May 2010 (doc.10033/10, FISC 47) para. 31.

in such a way that the participation exemption would not apply to profit distributions that were deductible by the subsidiary.[346] This proposal was implemented as Council Directive 2014/86/EU.[347]

[B] Improving the Design of Anti-avoidance Legislation and Similar Measures

When tax systems seek to prevent tax avoidance efficiently but at the same time want to foster the greatest possible freedom in using derivatives and cryptoassets for a wide range of commercial activities, fundamental tax policy questions have to be answered.

First, tax systems have to decide which kind of anti-avoidance approaches they want to implement and consider their benefits and threats.

Second, any specific anti-avoidance rules should be evaluated not only based on their potential effectiveness but also based on their potential deterrence of proper commercial activity.

Third, after implementation, anti-avoidance rules should be subject to evaluation and monitoring as to whether they are effective and whether and how they might deter commercial activity.

Fourth, tax administrations should evaluate if informal meetings with taxpayers, voluntary disclosure encouragement and codes of conduct for banks will reduce the scale of avoidance schemes used by taxpayers or if those measures take away the focus of the tax authorities from large schemes that are not disclosed in favour of minor schemes that were disclosed voluntarily.

When implementing anti-avoidance rules in order to tackle specific tax avoidance problems, tax systems will normally face the following choices:

(1) the introduction of specific or regime anti-avoidance rules versus the application of general anti-avoidance rules, or both;
(2) the introduction of disclosure rules versus the application of general anti-avoidance rules;
(3) the introduction of principles-based legislation to tackle specific tax avoidance problems versus maintaining the formal approach in tax law design; and
(4) the implementation of broader rules that tackle the overall tax behaviour of certain taxpayers.

[1] Introduction of Specific or General Anti-avoidance Rules

In the author's view, anti-avoidance rules that apply to specific derivatives and cryptoasset transactions will generally be more effective in tackling tax avoidance than

346. COM(2013) 814 final of 25 November 2013, Proposal for a Council Directive amending Directive 2011/96 EU on the common system of taxation applicable in the case of parent companies and subsidiaries of different Member States.
347. Council Directive 2014/86/EU *O.J.* July 2014, L 219, vol. 57.

the application of a GAAR. For example, although a GAAR has existed in Germany for many years, it was only of limited use when countering sophisticated tax avoidance schemes.[348] If a GAAR exists in the legislation for some time, it is easier to predict from existing case law whether the courts are likely to apply the rule or not. Thus, tax scheme designers can, in many cases, easily structure around a GAAR.

If a tax system decides in favour of a GAAR, the following considerations should be made in order to counter tax avoidance but, at the same time, ensure that genuine commercial activity is not hindered:

First, a GAAR should not be the only rule to counter abusive tax schemes that utilise derivatives. It also needs to be accompanied by a set of specific anti-avoidance rules which deal with most cases of avoidance known by the tax authorities.

Second, a GAAR should be designed as a preventive means to tackle clearly abusive tax schemes. If such a GAAR is only restricted to abusive schemes, such a provision may not create unnecessary uncertainty for taxpayers.

Third, the tax authorities should have a legislative mechanism, for example by way of Statutory Instruments (as in the UK), which allows them to quickly enact new specific anti-avoidance rules. This ensures that tax authorities will not lag behind for too long when new avoidance schemes become known to them.

Fourth, the author believes that the introduction of a regime anti-avoidance rule may indeed provide an effective tool to close the gap between overly specific anti-avoidance rules and an overly wide GAAR. Technically, the introduction of those rules into the UK derivative contracts regime could be seen as additional 'mini-GAARs' that apply to the avoidance schemes that involve derivatives.

Regime anti-avoidance rules can act as mop-up provisions that catch all those avoidance schemes which potentially fall within the gap between specific anti-avoidance rules and the GAAR. The concern one may, however, raise is that those rules again create more uncertainty for the taxpayer to determine if they apply or not. In light of the global policy trends of tackling any form of tax avoidance, the uncertainty for taxpayers may be a necessary disadvantage that tax administrations will accept in order to tackle tax avoidance successfully.

[2] Implementation of Disclosure Rules

Disclosure rules are an important measure to complement targeted anti-avoidance legislation as they work in more than one direction compared to traditional anti-avoidance measures.

First, they allow the Revenue to get to know new anti-avoidance schemes without the need to guess new schemes that taxpayers may come up with. As the tax authorities do not have to wait until an anti-avoidance scheme becomes common market knowledge but receive the description of the scheme directly from the promoter or designer, they can react more swiftly with specific anti-avoidance rules, and thus, they may avoid successful schemes being broadly marketed to taxpayers.

348. *See* Ch. 10 §10.03[B].

Second, disclosure rules also have a preventive anti-avoidance effect as they may deter taxpayers upfront from entering into these schemes because they do not want to be known by the tax authorities as someone who is willing to enter into tax avoidance as part of their regular business activity. Taxpayers may also fear that other commercial activities and the respective tax returns will be scrutinised more closely by the Revenue once they are known by the tax authorities as users of disclosed tax avoidance schemes.

Third, disclosure rules may deter the tax scheme designers themselves from coming up with new avoidance schemes in a jurisdiction where disclosure rules have been enacted. It may become commercially less attractive to design new schemes for a particular jurisdiction if the scheme has to be disclosed and thus can be marketed only for a short period of time until the tax authorities close down the scheme. Instead, tax scheme designers may focus on jurisdictions that have no disclosure rules in place where a scheme can be marketed potentially much longer to customers before the tax authorities receive knowledge of the scheme.

Lastly, disclosure rules allow the tax authorities valuable insight into how tax avoidance schemes are structured and thus may provide them with a better understanding over time of how these schemes can be tackled successfully. Disclosure rules may also foster coherence of both general taxation rules as well as tax rules on derivatives, as they allow the tax authorities to see more clearly where weaknesses and inconsistencies of the tax rules exist.

With respect to the UK disclosure rules, it seems to the author that the 'learning curve' of HMRC has increased since they were exposed to hundreds of successful tax avoidance schemes and thus became more familiar with the general techniques and understood more clearly the cases where a weak design of the tax rules led to tax avoidance.

In summary, the author, therefore, suggests that the implementation of disclosure rules and reporting requirements - if properly designed - will be an appropriate anti-avoidance solution with a high probability of success in tackling derivatives and cryptoasset tax avoidance schemes.[349]

For example, the reporting of cryptoasset positions under the new EU Council Directive will help identify taxpayers who have large holdings in cryptoassets and those who use advanced tax rulings in relation to cryptoassets.[350] The author believes that those new reporting requirements, although they are not strictly speaking disclosure rules, will help tax administrations to identify those taxpayers who may utilise cryptoassets for tax avoidance purposes.

---

349. House of Commons, *Tax avoidance: tackling marketed avoidance schemes*, 10.

The success of the UK disclosure rules has been confirmed in the author's view, as the report stated that ninety-three changes to the tax law were made as a result of information from the disclosure rules, and it is anticipated that 46% of overall tax avoidance is captured by the rules. The rules have captured almost half of the total tax avoidance schemes and additionally may also have deterred many taxpayers from entering into these schemes.

350. *See* Chapter 10 §10.04[C].

[3] *The Principles-Based, the Purposive and the Formal Approach in the Application of Tax Rules*

When considering the terminology, one has to distinguish between the formal approach, the principles-based approach, the purposive approach and the in-betweens, such as the 'coherent principles approach'.[351] These approaches will also play a role in the interpretation of the tax legislation.[352]

Although more recent approaches in designing tax law, such as the purposive approach and the coherent principles approach, may not in themselves be regarded as anti-avoidance measures when dealing with tax avoidance,[353] tax administrations have to consider if these approaches should be used as effective means to prevent tax avoidance schemes in the context of derivatives instead of a formal approach to designing tax law. The author believes that tax administrations also have to decide which approach they apply in designing new tax rules in the context of the newly emerged cryptoassets and crypto derivatives.

Further, one has to consider if these approaches can be regarded as 'good tax policy' or if they create unnecessary uncertainty for taxpayers.[354]

[a] *The Formal Approach*

The formal or rule-based approach[355] in designing tax law regards rules as the only source to determine whether and under which conditions a certain fact pattern will lead to a charge to tax or a relief. Under this approach, the tax rules, including the operating provisions, will be detailed and precise[356] and will give the taxpayer relative certainty as to whether the tax provision will apply or not.

Often, the formal approach to tax law is applied by countries where no formal written constitution exists that entails broader or 'higher' principles in the form of written basic constitutional rights that the taxpayer may use against the tax authorities in court.

For example, the UK has traditionally applied the formal approach in tax law. The UK does not have a formally written (in the sense of *codified*) constitution that is contained in one document.[357] 'The essentials of the United Kingdom's constitution are

351. Pinder (2005) 77.
352. Freedman (2010) 721-727 advocates making a clear distinction between a 'principles-based approach', a 'purposive approach' and a 'coherent principles approach'.
353. Freedman (2010) 727.
354. In favour of a purposive or 'principles-based approach' to counter tax avoidance in the area of financial products: Richard Thomas, 'Principles-based approach to financial products avoidance' (The Centre of Business Taxation (CBT) Summer Conference, 20 and 21 June 2008, Saïd Business School, Oxford).
355. David Haworth, 'Section 48 and Schedule 24: Disguised Interest' (2009) BTR 570, 570.
356. John Avery Jones, 'Tax Law: Rules or Principles?' (1996) BTR 580, 581 and 584 DOI: 10.1111/j.1475-5890.1996.tb00494.x.
357. *Memorandum by Professor John McEldowney, University of Warwick* (submitted to the House of Lords Select Committee on the Constitution, Ninth Report, 2003) paras 2.1-2.4.

the sovereignty of parliament and the rule of law.'[358] Thus, the legislation passed by Parliament is the supreme and final source of law,[359] even if the fundamental rights of the taxpayer are overruled.[360]

[b] *The Principles-Based Approach*

A principles-based approach in tax law is one that commonly entails more than one layer of legislation.[361] Usually, there is a constitution or some form of higher level treaty (e.g., the German Constitution, called *Grundgesetz*, or the Treaty on European Union (TEU), including its preamble) that establishes general principles, such as 'equality, proportionality, legal certainty and protection of legitimate expectations, fundamental rights and effectiveness'.[362] Then, there is a second layer of legislation that entails all the operating provisions of general law, including the tax law.[363]

The higher-level 'constitutional principles' have, in the author's view, two directions. First, they *limit* what the (tax) legislator can enact, i.e., they determine the general borders of the tax legislation. If those borders are crossed in tax law, in many countries, ultimately the court of the highest instance (e.g., the German constitutional court or the CJEU) has to decide if the tax legislation is still in line with the general principles, including the various freedoms that taxpayers may call for their protection.[364] Thus, these principles and fundamental rights limit the tax legislator and determine the borders of possible tax legislation rather than conferring specific rights on the legislator.

Second, these constitutional principles can be used in interpreting the tax legislation.[365] Thus, one can determine the possible legislative intent by considering these principles.

358. *Ibid.*, para. 2.5.
359. The Supremacy of European law has been granted by Parliament (European Communities Act 1972).
360. Eric Barendt, 'Is There a United Kingdom Constitution' (1997) 17 Oxford Journal of Legal Studies 137, 142 DOI: 10.1093/ojls/17.1.137. By incorporating the European Convention on Human Rights into UK law through the Human Rights Act 1998, some protective rights have been granted to the UK citizens.
361. The author will use the term 'principles-based approach' for the approach that was suggested by *Avery Jones* as 'a modified proposal' in his article: Avery Jones (1996) 593-594; *Freedman* also used the term 'principles-based approach' to refer to the approach first suggested for the UK by *Avery Jones*; *see* Freedman (2010) 719-721.
362. Freedman (2010) 721.
363. Avery Jones (1996) 593.
364. In the case of a formal constitution, in some countries, the lower court itself can determine whether the law is in line with the constitution or not and may determine that the secondary law is void because it contradicts the constitution. In other countries, not the lower courts but only the constitutional court can decide that the tax law is void because it contradicts broader constitutional rights and principles. The lower courts can only refer the law on which the case is based to the constitutional court and request a decision on whether the law is unconstitutional or not. In Germany, when deciding that the constitutional law contradicts the constitution, the constitutional court can either rule that the secondary law is void for the past or only for the future or require the legislator to change the law for the future, allowing further application of the law until then.
365. Avery Jones (1996) 593; Freedman (2010) 721.

[c] *The Purposive Approach*

A purpose-based or purposive clause is one where 'the purpose statement in purposive legislation is not itself a charging (or relieving) provision. It is simply a statement giving a purpose to the other provisions of the legislation to which it relates'.[366]

Purpose statements that are not part of a charging or relieving provision have been used in the UK tax legislation to deal with repo transactions.[367]

With regard to an HMRC consultation on the modernisation of the loan relationships and derivative contracts rules, it seems to the author that a purposive approach has been proposed by suggesting that 'it is intended to *articulate more clearly* the purpose and scope of the regime, and in particular, to clarify the role to be played by a company's financial statements in identifying and qualifying taxable amounts'.[368]

HMRC proposes that:

> The legislation should unequivocally set out the purpose of the regime and the subject matter within this scope. This might be expressed as:
>
> > To tax or relieve, as the case may be, profits, gains and losses of a company on its loan relationships and derivative contracts.[369]

If the purpose becomes part of the legislation as proposed above, this clause can, in the author's view, only be regarded as a purposive clause without being itself a charging provision, as the simple window-dressing sentence 'to tax or relieve' will be too unspecific to convert a non-operative purpose clause into an operative clause containing a charging provision.

[d] *The Coherent Principles Approach*

The coherent principles approach is one that applies principles in the tax legislation. Those principles are, however, not located in the higher-level legislation, like a constitution, but are part of the tax legislation.[370] In contrast to the purposive approach, the principle will usually be part of the operating charging or relieving provision, albeit it will only state the very general outcome and 'will be cut down by the further provisions'.[371]

The Australian Taxation of Financial Arrangements (TOFA) rules contain a comprehensive set of principles and rules for the taxation of gains and losses from

366. Brian Drummond and Philip Marwood, 'Purposive Drafting in the Finance Bill 2007' (2007) BTR 350, 352.
367. FA 2007, Sch. 13, para. 1.
368. HMRC, *Consultation on corporate debt and derivative contracts taxation* (2013) para. 1.5.
369. *Ibid.*, para. 3.4.
370. Often the term 'principles-based approach' has been used to describe the approach that is here described as the 'coherent principles approach'. *See* Graeme S. Cooper, 'Legislating Principles as a Remedy for Tax Complexity' (2010) BTR 334, 335.
371. Freedman (2010) 725.

financial arrangements[372] and apply such a 'coherent principles approach', which aims to produce law expressed in such principles. A *principle* in this context:

- is an operative legislative rule;
- specifies the outcome rather than the mechanism that achieves it; and
- expresses the outcome at the highest possible level rather than itemising a list of outcomes for every conceivable case.[373]

The UK has drafted anti-avoidance rules on disguised interest[374] based on a coherent principles approach.[375]

[e] Evaluation of the Approaches as Possible Solutions to Counter Tax Avoidance Schemes

[i] Evaluation of the Purposive Approach

It has been brought forward in favour of a purposive approach to the drafting of tax legislation that:

> the volume of [...] legislation and explanatory notes could be significantly reduced. [...] Overall the combination of the (albeit reduced) detail which would remain in the legislation and the explicitly stated purpose of each provision has the potential to give taxpayers an appropriate level of certainty.[376]

The author disagrees with this analysis. First, the general argument one can bring forward against the purposive approach is that – although it is an express statement of legislative intention – it is usually not part of the operative rules that define the charge to tax and thus cannot be used to override operative provisions, but only as an interpretative means to fill the gaps.

Freedman points out that: '[i]f the provision is not operative, then its relationship with the detailed provisions that follow is very unclear. It is unlikely to be taken to override the clear words of an operative provision in the statute'.[377]

Hayworth confirms that:

> the courts have thus far held that the second type of purpose clause, which stands alone [...] does not impose a separate condition for the imposition of tax, instead it is to be used as an *interpretative tool* [emphasis added], but only in situations

372. Australian Treasury Exposure Draft: Tax Laws Amendment (Taxation of Financial Arrangements) Bill 2008, Explanatory Material, Ch. 1.19.
    See also Stephen Southon, 'Chapter E2: Taxation of Derivatives: Australia' in Steven Conlon and Vincent Aquilino (eds), *Principles of Financial Derivatives, US and International Taxation* (Thomson Reuters/WG&L 2011) E2.02[11].
373. Pinder (2005) 78.
374. FA 2009, s. 48 and Sch. 24.
375. *See* Haworth (2009) 572-573.
376. Brian Drummond, 'A Purposive Approach to the Drafting of Tax Legislation' [2006] BTR 669, 675.
377. Freedman (2010) 723.

> where there is ambiguity or difficulty in applying the operative provisions to which they related [citing: Page *(Inspector of Taxes) v. Lowther* [1993] STC 799 (CA)].[378]

Second, as the taxpayer does not know what the tax charge is, based on non-operative purposive rules, these rules do not foster certainty but are likely to create uncertainty for the taxpayer.

Third, the purposive approach will lead to an imbalance of the traditional separation of powers between legislator, executive and judiciary. It is the role of the judges to decide which interpretation method they apply when deciding what the law in the respective case is. The purpose of the legislation can justifiably be considered by judges as a means to interpret the law.[379] The purposive approach contradicts the autonomy of judges as it both limits their interpretative task and the decision on which interpretational route - the literal, the purposive or any other - they may take in their case.

Thus, the purposive approach is, in the author's view, not an appropriate means of drafting tax legislation, given its shortcomings.

[ii] Evaluation of the Principles-Based Approach

A principles-based approach - as defined in Chapter 10 §10.05[B][3][b] - can be designed as an approach that fully applies the rule of law. If the higher (constitutional) principles such as equality, legality, proportionality and fundamental rights are used to interpret the secondary law, or if the secondary law contradicts these higher principles, the taxpayer can rely on these principles and claim in court that the secondary law is invalid because it contradicts the higher principles incorporated in the constitution.[380]

Again, in those cases, it will be up to the judges to determine whether the secondary rules that were drafted by the legislator are in line with the higher principles or not[381] and how these rules have to be interpreted in the light of the constitution in cases where there is room for interpretation.

This principles-based approach, as understood in the pure sense, will, however, not be a means for the tax authorities to tackle cases of anti-avoidance as the higher principles can only be used by the taxpayer to protect against the unconstitutionality of secondary law. Tax authorities may not argue a case against the taxpayer based on these higher constitutional principles ('Grundrechte'), as these principles should protect the citizens, but not the authorities.

378. Haworth (2009) 572.
379. As applied by Lord Hoffmann in: *Barclays Mercantile Business Finance Ltd v. Mawson* (Inspector of Taxes) [2004] UKHL 51.
380. *See* Ch. 10 §10.05[B][3][b].
381. *Compare* Ch. 10 §10.05[B][3][b]. The secondary legislation will normally become unconstitutional (and void) based on the decision of a country's constitutional court (or in some countries the lower courts). In Germany, the unconstitutionality of secondary legislation will be determined by the Constitutional Court (*Bundesverfassungsgericht*). Other courts are, however, able to refer the case to the Constitutional Court directly if they regard the secondary law as contradicting to the constitution.

[iii] Evaluation of the Coherent Principles Approach

Based on the idea that higher principles such as equality, legality, proportionality and fundamental freedoms are designed to protect taxpayers, the author opposes the notion of the coherent principles approach as applied in the TOFA rules and the UK's disguised interest rules.

When applying the coherent principles approach, tax authorities use the mechanism that higher principles may override more detailed legislative provisions as general protection from gaps in the legislation. Principles will, however, not be used in favour of the taxpayer but against the taxpayer to fill gaps and be applied to cases that the legislator has not thought of in the more detailed legislation.

But how can these principles that were designed by the very legislator who designed the detailed rules (that are entailed in the same taxation act) be said to override these other more detailed rules?

The author doubts that this is an appropriate approach in designing tax legislation if those principles in the tax law are not based on 'higher' general principles of law or constitutional principles but are, in fact, only there to state in more or less express words that it is the intention of the draftsman not to get 'cheated' with tax avoidance schemes that use the letter of the law to fall outside the scope of the rules.

In the author's view, coherent tax legislation cannot be achieved if new principles are invented and designed to be 'operating provisions' simply in order to ensure that everything is taxed and relieved according to what the legislator intends to be taxed and relieved.

Rather, tax legislation should apply the rule of law and tax and relieve everything that is expressly stated in the legislation. The coherent principles approach may lead to considerable uncertainty for the taxpayer and may foster carelessly drafted tax legislation, as it could be easily assumed by the draftsmen that the principles will catch everything which they have not foreseen.

Tax avoidance schemes should be countered with anti-avoidance rules and/or disclosure rules. In the author's view, a coherent principles approach is not a justifiable means to counter tax avoidance as it allows tax authorities to undermine the rule of law by referring to artificial new principles that are neither based on 'higher principles' of law nor are they founded in the constitution.

Thus, the author proposes that an approach based on principles will only honour the rule of law if the principles overriding the detailed tax legislation are part of a higher law, for example, a constitution that may override and nullify secondary law.

If principles, even if they are embedded in a basic charging or relieving provision, become part of the same level of law as the more detailed rules, a justification that these principles can override the more detailed rules is, in the author's view, hard to give, as these principles become normal rules and thus cease to exist as higher principles.

[iv] Evaluation of the Formal Approach

In the author's view, a formal or rule-based approach (possibly combined with a principles-based approach that is based on constitutional principles in countries where a formal written constitution exists) will provide certainty for the taxpayer. When a formal approach in designing tax law is applied, the taxpayer will know if the rules will apply or not simply by looking at the rules in question, provided they are properly drafted.

From a general viewpoint, this approach will also ensure that the rule of law is applied.[382] One may, however, argue against the formal approach that it may not be the most effective approach in the prevention of tax avoidance schemes as it may leave gaps in the legislation.

The author, however, argues that if a tax system establishes highly specific anti-avoidance rules, possibly combined with a GAAR,[383] which are backed up by effective disclosure rules, these measures will be sufficient to deal with tax avoidance in the area of derivatives and also cryptoassets. In such a legislative environment, the formal approach can be used to create maximum certainty for the taxpayer by upholding the rule of law, as the various anti-avoidance rules and disclosure rules will provide sufficient means to counter tax avoidance schemes.

[v] Proposed Solution

In summary, the author proposes that neither a purposive approach nor a coherent principles approach constitutes solutions in combating effectively tax avoidance schemes that utilise derivatives or cryptoassets without compromising the rule of law and a minimum of certainty for the taxpayer. Thus, these approaches should be avoided. A formal approach in designing tax law should be applied, which is combined with specific anti-avoidance rules, possibly accompanied by regime anti-avoidance rules, a GAAR and disclosure rules.[384]

[4] Implementing Broader Rules That Tackle the Overall Tax Behaviour of Certain Taxpayers

It remains to be seen if tax avoidance schemes employed by large multinationals can be countered with a more generic approach, such as the introduction of a global minimum

382. Southern suggests that 'certainty is a component of the rule of law. It embodies the fundamental principle of legality to which the tax system should confirm'. *See* Southern (2017) para. 1.3.
383. *Freedman* prefers as a short-term remedy a GAAR compared to a tax regime that needs to implement a 'coherent principles approach' or a purposive approach across the tax legislation. *See* Judith Freedman, 'GAAR as a Process and the Process of Discussing the GAAR' (2012) BTR 22, 26.
384. In countries where a formal, written constitution exists that can override secondary law, constitutional principles may be claimed in court by the taxpayer to override the formal law in cases where these principles protect the taxpayer's position.

ETR as envisaged by Pillar Two.[385] Pillar Two was designed by the OECD/G20 and specifically encouraged by high-tax countries like France and Germany with the backing of other EU members.[386]

Pillar Two measures are not targeted at specific financial transactions. Rather, they aim to deter multinationals from engaging in tax-efficient structuring either through entities established in low-corporate tax countries or the utilisation of specific tax exemptions and incentives given by some jurisdictions in developed nations, such as, for example, patent box regimes in the UK[387] and Switzerland, but also the various tax incentives provided to US-resident multinationals.

It remains to be seen how effective Pillar Two will be in practice as countries like the US and China are not likely to implement Pillar Two in its OECD version, thus somehow putting the two largest world economies on a different footing compared to those countries who aim to implement Pillar Two. The author maintains that the Pillar Two rules have substantial weaknesses, which the designers of those rules have not sufficiently addressed.

First, a weakness of the Pillar Two rules is that the taxable profit can be managed by multinationals.

Second, certain safe harbours, such as the taxation of investment funds and pension funds, are carved out of Pillar Two and thus provide scope for structuring around Pillar Two.

Third, those rules are only targeted to apply to large corporations that have the most financial power to circumvent those rules by employing a lot of money and talent from accounting and solicitor firms to find loopholes.

Fourth, Pillar Two significantly increases the compliance burden for developing countries, which are often not equipped and financially supported to implement those complex rules and tax monitoring and reporting processes required by Pillar Two.

Lastly, developing countries and small countries with lower tax rates might not be willing to put the utmost effort into the execution of those rules as the benefit of Pillar Two for those countries seems rather limited. On the contrary, the implementation of Pillar Two may be detrimental to their tax base as a significant part of the GDP of such developing, low-tax nations is based on attracting multinationals through favourable tax legislation. Hence, significant push-back against the Pillar Two rules,

385. OECD (2021).

386. Robert Goulder, 'Expectations for 2024: Pillar 1 Finds an Off-Ramp' (2023) 111 Tax Notes International, 1819.It is interesting to note that the EU, through their representatives in the OECD in Paris, pushes developing nations to implement Pillar Two swiftly. However, the implementation and ongoing administration costs will be significant. At the same time, the EU, however, allows Member States under the Council Directive (EU) 2022/2523 of 14 December 2022 to ensure a global minimum level of taxation for multinational enterprise groups and large-scale domestic groups in the Union (Pillar Two Directive) to delay the introduction of Pillar Two income inclusion rule (IIR) and the undertaxed payment rule (UTPR) for up to six consecutive years. As of December 2023, five EU countries have delayed the implementation of those rules; see Grant Thornton, Five EU countries to postpone Pillar 2 (December 2023) https://www.lexology.com/library/detail.aspx?g=c550cddc-13e0-46f0-8d21-04ee75cbde29, accessed 29 December 2023.

387. Allen & Overy, 20 Questions on Pillar Two and the GloBe rules.

which are said to benefit predominantly developed, high-tax nations, comes from the UN,[388] some African countries, Southern American and Asian countries,[389] in short, the developing world or 'Global South'. Similarly, academics criticise the Pillar Two rules not only for their one-sided preference for developed, high-tax nations but also for their clash with existing international investment agreements.[390]

388. *Compare* KPMG, UN Resolution on International Tax Cooperation https://assets.kpmg.com/content/dam/kpmg/xx/pdf/2023/10/un-resolution-international-tax-cooperation-web.pdf, accessed 1 November 2023; Sarah Paez, UN General Assembly Adopts International Tax Cooperation Resolution, Tax Notes Today International (TNTI) December 2023, 246-6, DOC 2023-37225.
389. Stephanie Soong, 'ASEAN Investment Ministers Call for Global Minimum Tax Review' (2023) 111 Tax Notes International, 1151.
390. Peter Hongler et al., 'UTPR – Potential Conflicts with International Law' (2023) 111 Tax Notes International,141; Błażej Kuźniacki, 'Pillar 2 and International Investment Agreements: "QD-MTT Payable" Seals anInternationally Wrongful Act' (2023) 111 Tax Notes International, 159.

CHAPTER 11
Conclusion

A conclusion is simply the place where you got tired of thinking.

— Dan Chaon, *Stay Awake: Stories*

§11.01 FINAL THOUGHTS

In this work, the author has delved into the complex realm of taxation issues associated with derivatives and cryptoassets. The research entailed a thorough analysis of the taxation models adopted by the UK and Germany to address the challenges posed by those instruments. In the context of beneficial ownership and derivatives, the author also analysed several cases from Spain and Switzerland.

Recent issues arising in the context of the taxation of cryptoassets, crypto derivatives and ESG derivatives, as well as related structured products, have been discussed throughout the chapters of this work.

Following an assessment of the advantages and disadvantages of the tax legislation applying to derivatives and cryptoassets in the UK and Germany, the author suggested solutions in each chapter that she considers appropriate, coherent and effective to deal with the taxation problems. In Chapter 10 of this work, the author re-examined those solutions concerning their effectiveness in tackling tax avoidance schemes that employ derivatives, structured products, hybrid instruments or cryptoassets.

In this concluding chapter, the author summarises how the solutions proposed in this work allow the establishment of a coherent corporate taxation framework for derivatives and cryptoassets.

§11.02 PROBLEMS IDENTIFIED IN THE TAXATION OF DERIVATIVES AND CRYPTOASSETS

In Chapter 3 of this work, the author identified seven problems that she regards as important in the context of taxing derivatives and cryptoassets – both at the national and international level.

They are:

(1) the definition of derivatives for tax purposes in the domestic tax legislation and the application of the definition to newly emerged derivatives, such as crypto derivatives and ESG derivatives;
(2) the application of a special taxation regime versus applying the general taxation rules when taxing derivatives and cryptoassets, and the influence of the distinction between income and capital and equity and debt on the taxation of derivatives;
(3) the question of alignment of accounting standards and taxation rules and the application of fair value accounting when taxing derivatives and cryptoassets;
(4) tax-efficient hedging, the application of different hedging approaches and hedge accounting rules for tax purposes and the taxation of post-tax hedging transactions;
(5) bifurcation versus integration approaches applying to structured products and hybrid instruments for tax purposes, including crypto structured products and ESG-linked structured products;
(6) the application of withholding taxes to derivatives and the beneficial ownership concept in the context of derivatives transactions;
(7) design of effective specific anti-avoidance measures, regime anti-avoidance rules and GAARs applying to derivatives, and the need for a design of anti-avoidance legislation applying to cryptoassets and the newly emerged crypto derivatives, ESG derivatives, and related structured products.

§11.03 SUMMARY OF SOLUTIONS ADOPTED BY THE UK AND GERMANY AND SOLUTIONS PROPOSED BY THE AUTHOR REGARDING THE TAXATION PROBLEMS POSED BY DERIVATIVES AND CRYPTOASSETS

Tax legislators need to act at various levels in order to tackle the problems posed by derivatives and cryptoassets comprehensively and successfully.

First and foremost, domestic tax legislators have to deal coherently with the taxation issues arising in the context of domestic derivative and cryptoasset transactions.

Second, national legislation has to deal with the taxation problems that arise if those instruments are used in cross-border transactions.

Third, solutions for the taxation of those complex cross-border transactions may only be found at an international level, either in the context of bilateral tax treaties or at a multilateral level in the context of the OECD and the UN.

From a tax policy perspective, coherent taxation rules on derivatives and cryptoassets should ensure uninhibited access to the derivatives and cryptoassets markets for taxpayers, promote a level playing field for all market participants, and, at the same time, prevent loopholes in the tax system that encourage taxpayers to enter into tax avoidance schemes.

[A] Problem 1 and Its Solution

[1] Definitions of Derivatives in the UK and German Tax Legislation

The UK has adopted an advanced approach in defining derivatives for corporate tax purposes by implementing a three-step test in the tax legislation to determine if an instrument qualifies as a 'derivative contract'.[1]

Nevertheless, the existing definition under CTA 2009, Part 7 may not cater for all newly emerging derivatives, such as crypto and ESG derivatives, as the types of derivatives and the underlyings are only dealt with by way of enumeration instead of defining the scope of the term 'derivative contract' with the help of abstract definitional criteria.

The second weakness of the definition contained in CTA 2009, Part 7 is the definitional method that allows defining the term by way of exceptions and counter-exceptions entailed in the 'accounting test' and the 'excluded underlying subject matter test' to narrow down the scope of the definition. Thus, no clear concept arises as to what constitutes a derivative contract for tax purposes.

Although problems with the definition of derivative contracts under CTA 2009, Part 7 exist and have become more imminent in the context of crypto derivatives and ESG derivatives, the UK legislator may have adopted a more sophisticated approach in defining derivatives for tax purposes compared to the German legislator.

The German tax legislation applying to derivatives borrows the term 'derivative contract' ('Termingeschäft') from capital markets law without defining the term in the corporate tax legislation itself.[2] This approach has created significant uncertainty concerning the scope of the term 'derivative contract' as it is unclear whether the term has the same meaning as in capital markets law or an independent meaning for tax purposes. In particular, it remains open to interpretation whether losses from physically settled derivatives will be subject to the loss ring-fencing rule applying to business and corporate taxpayers or not.[3] Therefore, it is imperative from a systematic point of view that the German tax legislator defines derivatives comprehensively in the corporate tax legislation in order to allow a determination of its exact scope.

1. *See* Ch. 4 §4.03[A][2][a] to §4.03[A][2][c].
2. *See* Ch. 4 §4.03[C][1] and §4.03[C][2].
3. *See* Ch. 4 §4.03[C][2].

[2] *Solution to Problem 1: Abstract Definition of Derivatives in the Domestic Tax Legislation*

An abstract and comprehensive definition of derivatives in the domestic tax legislation would allow the capture of newly emerging derivatives, like, for example, crypto derivatives and ESG derivatives, without an adjustment of existing tax legislation to new instruments and, therefore, would help tax legislators respond more swiftly to tax avoidance schemes that utilise those instruments.

The author has, therefore, proposed the following abstract definitional criteria to define derivatives for tax purposes in Chapter 4 §4.06[B][5]:

A financial instrument qualifies as a derivative if:

(1) its value depends on the value of one or more independent underlying variables,
(2) its payoff is deterministically dependent on stochastic variables, i.e., the payoff depends in an uncertain way on the value of the underlying variable, but the payoff function as such is pre-defined,
(3) it has some future date at which it will mature, and
(4) it is at any time during the term of the financial instrument possible to replicate the sum of its payoffs by following a trading strategy using the underlying asset(s), cash or other derivative(s).

This definition could be incorporated in the national tax legislation but could also serve as a basis for a definition that is included in a new article on derivatives in the OECD and UN model tax conventions.

[B] Problem 2 and Its Solution

[1] *Solution to Problem 2: Introduction of a Different Set of Taxation Rules Instead of Complete Alignment of Accounting and Taxation Rules*

The UK has increasingly aligned the accounting standards and the taxation rules applying to derivatives.[4] The derivative contracts regime relies on accounting standards as a basis for taxation. Fair value accounting methods are accepted to be applied to derivatives held by corporate taxpayers.[5] With the introduction of fair value accounting for tax purposes, the recognition of gains and losses has moved away from realisation as a trigger for recognising income towards a tax system that recognises gains and losses independently from any realisation event.

4. Ch. 5 §5.02[D].
5. Exceptions to fair value accounting of derivatives for tax purposes also exist if the Disregard Regulations are applied, *see* Ch. 7 §7.03[A][2].

The German tax legislation regards German GAAP as a starting point for taxing business income, and German GAAP is also applicable for tax purposes unless the tax legislation provides for special rules. German GAAP remains the only financial accounting basis for the determination of the tax base.[6] As German GAAP does not contain comprehensive rules regarding the accounting treatment of financial instruments and derivatives, the general accounting principles – in the form of principles of proper bookkeeping (*Grundsätze ordnungsgemäßer Buchführung*) – will be applied to derivatives.[7] Hence, derivatives held by corporate taxpayers are not accounted for at fair value but on an accrual basis and the prudence and realisation principles are applied.[8]

The author concluded that the alignment of accounting standards and tax rules may not be the right answer to the question of how tax legislators should deal with the problem of derivatives in tax law.[9]

In the author's opinion, there is a substantial risk that the alignment of accounting standards and tax rules may provide taxpayers with an opportunity for tax avoidance, as accounting rules are not designed to avoid the erosion of the tax base.

Instead of aiming for a complete alignment of accounting and taxation rules, legislators may want to introduce a completely different set of taxation rules for derivatives. By doing so, the taxation of derivatives can be based on tax rules that are specifically tailored to the needs of the tax system instead of accounting rules, including the timing of when to tax these instruments.

The second question that had to be answered in this work is which approaches are the most appropriate to measure the value of derivatives for tax purposes and which approaches are able to determine an appropriate point of time at which gains and losses of these instruments are recognised for tax purposes.

The author suggested that the UK approach that uses the fair value basis to determine when derivatives income and losses are recognised for tax purposes is, in her view, not a very suitable approach for corporate taxpayers (except for banks and similar financial institutions) as it does not promote the principle of realisation, which is essential for tax purposes because of the ability-to-pay principle.[10]

The author further argued that the fair value accounting method may not constitute an appropriate method to tax derivatives because the taxation of unrealised gains contradicts the ability-to-pay principle.[11] When this method is applied to recognise profits for tax purposes, taxpayers may be forced to sell their assets before they intended because they have to pay taxes on unrealised gains. Hence, the author has proposed that an amortised cost basis will be more appropriate to determine the value and point in time at which derivatives should be recognised for tax purposes. As

6. Ch. 5 §5.03[A].
7. Ch. 5 §5.03[B].
8. Only with regard to derivatives held in the trading book of a credit institution or bank, some of the special accounting rules requiring a modified fair value approach will also apply for tax purposes; *see* Ch. 6 §6.03[B].
9. Ch. 5 §5.05[A].
10. Ch. 5 §5.04.
11. Ch. 5 §5.05[B].

an alternative, the tax legislator could introduce a new tax realisation principle in the tax legislation, as *Freedman* has suggested.[12]

In the context of trading books of banks, the fair value accounting method applying to derivatives may constitute an acceptable method for determining the point of time when derivatives gains and losses are recognised for tax purposes. Banks can sell and buy back derivatives quickly as they have privileged access to capital markets and short-term lending facilities and thereby, they may realise derivatives gains and losses arising in their trading books at each balance sheet date.[13] The author acknowledged that on a global level, tax authorities increasingly lean towards solutions that either allow or prescribe the fair value accounting approach also for the taxation of derivatives held by or entered into by corporate taxpayers – and not only for banks and other financial institutions.

The author proposed that solutions in the context of cryptoassets may look different compared to those applying to derivatives. For cryptoassets, a simple 'follow the accounts' approach may create tax avoidance opportunities if the historical cost method is applied to cryptoassets as they are qualified as indefinite-life intangible assets with no amortisation for accounting purposes. Applying this accounting treatment also to the tax accounts enables taxpayers to utilise unrealised impairment losses from cryptoasset impairment losses. A viable solution proposed by the author may indeed be the switch from a historical cost accounting method of cryptoassets (as currently applied under IFRS 9 and UK GAAP) to a fair value measurement of cryptoassets.

[C] Problem 3 and Its Solution

[1] The Influence of the Distinction Between Income and Capital, and Between Equity and Debt on the UK and German Taxation of Derivatives

The UK has incorporated in CTA 2009 a special taxation regime that applies to most derivatives.[14] In contrast, Germany applies the general corporate taxation rules to derivatives and has enacted only one provision in the general tax law that specifically deals with derivatives losses.[15]

Whereas the income and capital divide has been largely abolished in the corporate tax rules applying to derivatives in both the UK and Germany, different taxation rules for equity and debt are still in existence in both countries, albeit on a different scale.

12. Freedman (2004a) 85.
13. Based on these considerations, the author has proposed in Ch. 5 §5.05[B] that the realisation principle and the ability-to-pay principle cannot be regarded as significant arguments against the introduction of the fair value accounting method when taxing gains and losses from derivatives arising in the trading books of banks.
14. Ch. 6 §6.01.
15. Ch. 6 §6.03.

The UK corporate tax law still privileges certain equity derivatives over other derivative contracts. In those cases, the distinction between equity and debt will usually result in a timing difference in the context of the recognition of the income.[16]

The German corporate tax rules still privilege equity compared to debt with an almost full tax exemption of equity capital gains and non-portfolio dividends. These rules also apply to physically settled derivatives.

In the author's view, the UK's 'special regime approach' will pose fewer opportunities for tax avoidance compared to the German 'integrative approach',[17] which applies the general taxation rules to derivatives and, at the same time, significantly privileges equity over debt.

[2] Solution to Problem 3: A Special Taxation Regime Applying to Derivatives and Cryptoassets

Although both the 'special regime approach' and the 'integrative approach' may, in theory, achieve consistent taxation results when taxing derivatives, coherence in the latter approach can only be ensured if the general tax system subjects income to the same taxation rules as capital gains. At the same time, the general tax system would need to abolish the privilege of equity over debt in the domestic tax legislation as far as possible in order to avoid the utilisation of tax avoidance schemes in a domestic context and qualification conflicts in cross-border scenarios.

As many domestic tax systems will, however, privilege equity in some way compared to debt or capital gains over income, it will be easier for tax legislators to achieve coherent taxation results by implementing a special regime for derivatives in the tax legislation. But even in a special regime applying to derivatives, tax avoidance may occur if equity is privileged over debt, as economic replication may enable taxpayers to convert non-privileged derivatives gains into equity capital gains.

Thus, tax legislators who implement a special taxation regime for derivatives but want to privilege equity capital gains for tax policy reasons need to implement anti-avoidance rules that prevent the tax-motivated conversion of non-privileged derivatives gains into privileged equity capital gains. Alternatively, they may consider abolishing or minimising the privilege for equity capital gains as far as possible.

Further, if dividends received by corporate taxpayers are preferentially taxed in order to avoid economic double taxation of the dividends, anti-avoidance rules, including CFC rules, may also have to apply to tax avoidance schemes that generate derivatives gains in low-tax jurisdictions and distribute them as dividends that are tax-exempt in the resident country of the corporate shareholder.

In the context of cryptoassets, a separate taxation regime applying to this new asset class is desirable. Crypto derivatives should be captured either by such a new regime or should fall within the existing derivative contracts regime, potentially by

16. Ch. 6 §6.02.
17. For a definition of the terms, *see* Ch. 6, Introduction.

extending the existing definition of a derivative contract also to those instruments. The same is desirable for ESG derivatives.

[D] Problem 4 and Its Solutions

[1] Solutions in the UK and Germany: Tax-Efficient Hedging and Post-tax Hedging Approaches

Both the UK and Germany have generous provisions that allow hedging transactions to be effective for tax purposes, although the approaches to achieving tax-efficient hedging are quite different.

The UK tax legislator has allowed a deviation from the financial accounts for the tax treatment of hedges that involve derivatives when a company accounts under IFRS 9, IAS 39 or FRS 102, Sections 11 and 12. This deviation allows the avoidance of unnecessary P&L volatility for tax purposes that would otherwise be caused by mandatory fair value accounting during the term of the hedge.[18]

In contrast, German tax legislation follows the hedging provisions in the financial accounts, as the single company financial accounts have to be drawn in accordance with German GAAP. No significant problems arise when applying these financial hedge accounting rules in German tax accounts, as the hedging provisions under German GAAP are generous.[19]

With respect to hedging symmetry, the UK approach is, however, much more sophisticated than the German approach. The UK acknowledges that it is essential that commercial hedging transactions are treated on a tax-neutral basis by symmetrically taxing the hedged item and the hedge.[20]

In contrast, Germany applies loss ring-fencing provisions to derivatives[21] that can lead to a mismatch of the pre-tax and the post-tax hedging position, as the final post-tax hedging result is, in certain cases, not tax neutral.[22]

Whereas the UK has enacted measures to counter post-tax hedging schemes in order to prevent tax avoidance and risk-shifting from the taxpayer to the Revenue,[23] German tax rules do not provide specific anti-avoidance approaches which target those tax avoidance schemes that let the state effectively participate in the market risk of the transaction by way of underhedging or overhedging.[24]

18. Ch. 7 §7.03[A][2].
19. Ch. 7 §7.03[B][2].
20. Ch. 7 §7.04[B].
21. Ch. 5 §5.03 and §5.04.
22. Ch. 7 §7.04[C].
23. Ch. 7 §7.04[B].
24. Ch. 7 §7.04[C].

[2] *Solutions to Problem 4: Tax-Efficient Hedging Provisions and the Implementation of Anti-avoidance Legislation*

The author has concluded that applying IFRS 9 (or old IAS 39 under the accounting choice of UK GAAP) in the single company accounts poses significant problems in the context of hedging transactions for tax purposes. Either the tax legislator can follow IFRS 9/IAS 39 with the consequence of possibly significant P&L volatility due to restrictive hedging provisions under IFRS 9/IAS 39, or the tax legislator has to deviate from the provisions of IFRS 9/IAS 39 for tax purposes with the consequence of complex tax legislation which has to provide criteria under which hedge accounting for tax purposes is permitted.[25]

Thus, tax legislators may find it easier to deal with derivatives hedging transactions if the taxation of hedging transactions relies on the local accounting rules, provided these hedge accounting rules are comprehensive in their scope and respect the principle of realisation.

If no local accounting principles are implemented that permit tax-neutral hedging, tax legislators should aim for an extra set of tax-neutral hedging rules that ensure that the hedge is as effective on an after-tax basis as it is on a pre-tax basis.[26] Tax hedging provisions that enable taxpayers to hedge their positions so that they are tax-neutral on a post-tax basis may, however, also be used for tax avoidance purposes. Hence, tax systems should monitor hedging transactions closely and, in case of potential abuse, may want to allow only certain hedging transactions or portfolios to be effective for tax purposes.

Although *macro hedges* of derivatives portfolios do have some economic merit, tax policymakers should not apply or extend existing macro hedge accounting approaches of whole portfolios (that include different underlying risks) to the tax hedging provisions because of the potential tax avoidance risk.[27]

When favourable hedging provisions are used to shift economic risk from the taxpayer to the state, tax legislators can counter these post-tax hedging schemes by abolishing general mismatches in the taxation of different items of income or by introducing targeted anti-avoidance rules.[28] At the same time, the legislator may want to establish rules that determine under what conditions legitimate post-tax hedging approaches are permissible in order to achieve a competitive tax system that does not increase hedging costs for taxpayers due to tax inefficiencies in the hedging rules.

25. Ch. 7 §7.05[A].
26. Neighbour (2001) para. 16.
27. Ch. 7 §7.05[A].
28. Ch. 7 §7.05[B].

[E] Problem 5 and Its Solution

[1] The UK and German Solutions for Taxing Structured Products and Hybrid Instruments

The UK tax law deviates in some cases from the bifurcation rules of IFRS 9 and FRS 102, Sections 11 and 12. Despite the bifurcation rules in the tax law being codified properly and in detail, they are quite arbitrary in their application as they depend only on the characterisation of the host contract as a loan relationship or a non-loan relationship. Although an integration approach is applied under IFRS 9 and FRS 102, Sections 11 and 12 to most financial assets that entail embedded derivatives,[29] bifurcation is still an issue for tax purposes for issuers of structured products and hybrid instruments, as financial liabilities are bifurcated under IFRS 9 as well as under FRS 102, Sections 11 and 12.

The German approach towards bifurcation in the tax accounts is somewhat incoherent, and no clear picture arises. The reason for this incoherence is that there are no specific rules in German accounting or tax law that determine whether these instruments should be bifurcated or not.[30] Both for tax and accounting purposes, the reliance on general accounting principles of orderly accounting creates uncertainty as it is not clear which general accounting rule will take priority over the other.[31] Thus, the accounting literature and the tax literature come to different conclusions regarding bifurcation and integration, although their conclusions are based on the same German GAAP.[32]

[2] Solution to Problem 5: Striking the Balance Between Integration and Bifurcation for Tax Purposes

The following steps would, in the author's view, contribute to a coherent approach towards bifurcation and integration for tax purposes:

(1) A tax system should develop a special taxation regime for structured products and hybrid instruments that applies a differentiated integration and bifurcation approach to the various instruments. Such an approach would not necessarily follow the accounting rules as accounting rules are not formulated to prevent the erosion of the tax base. Thus, accounting rules may legitimately bifurcate or integrate structured products and hybrid instruments according to different criteria compared to tax law.

(2) A bifurcation or integration approach for tax purposes should be determined separately for 'structured products' and 'hybrid instruments'.

29. Ch. 8 §8.05[C] and §8.07.
30. An exception is s. 272(2) No. 2 CLA that applies to issuers of convertible bonds and bond cum warrants.
31. Ch. 8 §8.06[B].
32. Ch. 8 §8.06[A][1], §8.06[B][1] and §8.06[B][2].

(3) Hybrid instruments should not be bifurcated for tax purposes as they are economically inseparable.[33] Instead, an integration approach is an appropriate solution for tax purposes as it mirrors the economic reality of these instruments[34] and may also prevent tax avoidance schemes.[35]

(4) If the tax legislator wants to minimise tax avoidance opportunities and already taxes equity, debt and derivatives according to the same rules, it should apply an integration approach to genuine structured products, as no benefit exists to tax structured products any different than their separate elements.

(5) Only if a tax legislator preferentially taxes equity and equity derivatives compared to debt should a bifurcation approach be applied to structured products. Structured products that contain different constituents of debt, equity and/or derivatives would have to be bifurcated, and the single constituents would have to be taxed according to the rules of the single instruments in order to allow taxation according to the different asset classes.

(6) Even if a bifurcation approach is applied to some structured products for tax purposes, specific anti-avoidance approaches should apply to:
   (a) legally separable combinations of instruments (taxed as single instruments),
   (b) 'false friend put-call parity combinations' (integration),[36] and
   (c) combinations of derivatives (integration only if the combinations are taxed the same way as their constituents).[37]

(7) Tax legislators need to adapt their existing tax rules to ensure that they also capture crypto structured products and ESG-linked structured products.

[F] Problem 6 and Its Solutions

[1] Solutions Adopted by the UK and Germany to Deal with Cross-Border Derivatives Transactions

[a] Withholding Tax Regimes Applying to Derivatives

In the UK, payments under derivative contracts falling within CTA 2009, Part 7 will be excluded from withholding taxes, and even derivatives falling outside the derivative contracts regime will, in many cases, not be subject to withholding taxes.[38]

In the context of manufactured dividends received under equity swaps, total return swaps, or dividend swaps, the application of withholding taxes based on the old

33. Ch. 8 §8.03 and §8.04.
34. Ch. 8 §8.08.
35. Ch. 10 §10.05[A][4].
36. *See* Ch. 8 §8.01[B][1].
37. Ch. 8 §8.08.
38. Ch. 9 §9.01[A].

UK MOD rules was less certain.[39] Rules were introduced in FA 2013 to counter tax avoidance schemes that utilised tax credits under the complex MOD rules.[40] Under those new rules, manufactured payments are generally not subject to withholding tax and thus do not give entitlement to a tax credit.[41] There are good arguments for adopting such an approach, as only a complete abolition of tax credits for MODs will significantly reduce tax avoidance opportunities in that area.[42]

Under the German tax rules, no withholding tax is levied on derivatives income and received option premiums.[43] As no withholding tax was levied on payments under dividend swaps, equity swaps, price swaps and total return swaps (no matter whether dividends or manufactured dividends were paid under these instruments or rolled up in the pricing), tax avoidance schemes aimed at reducing withholding taxes on German dividends received by foreign shareholders. To counter those schemes, Germany introduced a 15% corporate tax rate on portfolio dividends and tackled those transactions successfully by introducing anti-avoidance legislation.

[b] The Beneficial Ownership Concept in Cross-Border Transactions

In relation to the concept of beneficial ownership, the UK has moved from a purely domestic understanding of beneficial ownership to the term having an 'international meaning' when interpreting double tax treaties.[44] In contrast, the authors of the leading German treaty commentary suggest that concerning dividends, the term *Nutzungsberechtigter* ('beneficial owner') used in the treaty has a similar meaning as the term 'shareholder' used in domestic tax law.[45]

[2] Solutions to Problem 6: Adjustment of Withholding Tax Provisions, Amendment of the 'Beneficial Owner' Definition or Introduction of a New Definition of Derivatives at Tax Treaty Level

There are, in principle, three possible solutions to deal with the problem of withholding tax avoidance schemes in the context of cross-border derivatives transactions.

If tax systems want to prevent tax avoidance in the context of dividends and interest but at the same time not hinder genuine commercial hedging transactions, they can do so by carefully defining the term 'beneficial owner' in their domestic law and using a wide interpretation of the concept of beneficial owner in a tax treaty context, as developed in the *Swiss Swaps* case and further refined in the *SMI Futures* case.

39. Ch. 9 §9.01[C][1].
40. HMRC, *Corporation tax and income tax: changes to rules for manufactured payments* (2012). In addition, anti-avoidance legislation was introduced in FA 2012, *see* Ch. 9 §9.01[C][1].
41. HMRC, CFM74440.
42. Ch. 9 §9.01[C][1] and §9.03[B].
43. Ch. 9 §9.01[B].
44. Ch. 9 §9.02[A][1].
45. Ch. 9 §9.02[A][2].

As a second solution, domestic tax systems could apply no withholding tax on dividends and manufactured dividends received by foreign and domestic market participants. That solution is highly effective as it abolishes the incentive for dividend withholding tax avoidance. Some countries, however, shy away from this solution as it leads to a complete loss of dividend withholding taxes for the domestic tax system.[46] The author prefers this approach as a robust solution for any tax system to prevent any form of dividend withholding tax schemes.

A further possible solution is the introduction of withholding taxes on derivatives both on a domestic and tax treaty level in order to prevent tax avoidance schemes that transfer the economic risks and rewards of assets or income to third parties via derivatives. As withholding taxes on derivatives are difficult to apply under the existing treaty network, such a solution would, however, be the most radical of all. It might, however, be considered as a long-term policy concept that provides a solution to tax derivatives at the level of double tax treaties, for example, in the form of a new article on derivatives designed in the OECD and UN model.

[G] Problem 7 and Its Solutions

[1] The UK and German Solutions in Tackling Tax Avoidance

Compared to the German tax authorities, the UK tax authorities could better balance the need for general tax certainty for the taxpayer against the need for effective anti-avoidance measures.

On the one hand, the UK allowed businesses to maintain their competitiveness by establishing a highly developed legal and administrative tax framework. In addition, the general design of the tax system was improved, and comprehensive rules on the taxation of derivatives were established.

On the other hand, tax avoidance schemes were systematically tackled by introducing specific anti-avoidance rules applying to derivatives and related transactions and by establishing and constantly improving the comprehensive disclosure regime. Existing tax legislation was constantly fine-tuned to close loopholes, which existed, for example, due to differences in taxation of equity and debt and derivatives. New regime anti-avoidance rules that were incorporated into the derivative contracts regime support the general GAAP in tackling not only abusive tax schemes but also transactions motivated by tax avoidance.

Unfortunately, the UK has not yet implemented robust anti-avoidance rules to counter avoidance in the context of cryptoasset- and crypto derivatives transactions. The author believes that this step will be taken in the near future.

For a long time, the German tax authorities have lagged behind in efficiently tackling tax avoidance schemes that utilise derivatives. Although more general anti-avoidance rules, such as rules on the limitation of interest deduction, the limitation of losses in the context of tax deferral models, CFC rules and treaty 'switch-over

46. Ch. 9 §9.03[B].

clauses',[47] applied to derivatives transactions, no specific anti-avoidance or disclosure rules (apart from the derivatives loss ring-fencing provision) existed that allowed the targeting of tax avoidance schemes that utilise derivatives. Furthermore, the German GAAR has proved largely ineffective in relation to derivatives tax avoidance.[48] However, new legislation which was introduced in the context of the ATAD Directives now targets tax avoidance schemes that utilise derivatives and hybrid instruments. Further, legislation targeting abusive dividend tax avoidance schemes was introduced to shut down those schemes.

[2] Solutions to Problem 7: Improving the General Design of the Tax System and Introducing Effective Anti-avoidance Legislation

If tax legislators seek to limit tax avoidance schemes that use either 'traditional' derivatives or cryptoassets and related derivatives, a comprehensive approach is necessary that improves both the general design of the tax system and introduces targeted tax avoidance legislation.

Possible approaches that limit tax avoidance schemes relating to derivatives or cryptoassets, such as introducing a special taxation regime for derivatives and cryptoassets, de-aligning the accounting rules and tax law, improving the tax hedging provisions, applying integration approaches instead of allowing the bifurcation of structured products, implementing 'switch-over clauses' in double tax treaties and other measures such as a robust beneficial ownership definition have been summarised in Chapter 10 §10.05[A][1] to §10.05[A][7].

In addition, specific anti-avoidance rules need to be implemented as a further layer to tackle tax avoidance schemes that involve derivatives, cryptoassets and newly emerged derivatives, such as crypto derivatives and ESG derivatives. The author has suggested that targeted anti-avoidance rules, which target specific derivatives transactions and cryptoasset transfers and holdings, will generally be more effective in tackling tax avoidance than a GAAR.[49] The author also acknowledged that regime anti-avoidance rules may be an effective tool for tax administrations. Furthermore, disclosure rules should be implemented in order to improve the learning curve of the tax authorities quickly.

The author further argued that neither the purposive approach nor a coherent principles approach constitute appropriate solutions in combating tax avoidance schemes that utilise derivatives without compromising the rule of law.[50] Thus, these approaches should be avoided, and a formal approach in designing tax law should be kept, combined with efficient specific and regime anti-avoidance rules and disclosure rules.

47. Ch. 10 §10.03[A].
48. Ch. 10 §10.03[B].
49. Ch. 10 §10.05[B][1].
50. Ch. 10 §10.05[B][3][e].

§11.04 OUTLOOK

Derivatives are complex financial instruments, and tax administrations should establish a clear and comprehensive framework for taxing them. The rules applying to derivatives should strike a balance between not impeding commercial activities involving derivatives and preventing tax avoidance schemes from utilising them.

The financial landscape continues to transform with the widespread use of cryptoassets – not only by individuals but also by corporate investors. Whenever a new asset class emerges, tax rules need to adapt as the traditional rules may not fit those newly emerged instruments and, thus, lead to tax avoidance opportunities.

Three decades ago, domestic legislators implemented anti-avoidance rules targeting those schemes in response to taxpayers using derivatives for tax avoidance. Today, tax legislators must rapidly devise coherent solutions for taxing cryptoassets, crypto derivatives and crypto structured products. Likewise, tax legislators need to address the emergence of ESG derivatives, ESG-linked structured products and carbon credits (as underlying assets of new financial instruments) as they are set to play a pivotal role in the rapidly evolving realm of investments and finance.

Failing to address those taxation challenges could lead to taxpayers applying previously utilised tax avoidance methods to these newly emerging instruments, just as they did when derivatives gained widespread popularity.

Bibliography

Aaronson (2011):

Aaronson G, *GAAR Study: A Study to Consider Whether a General Anti-avoidance Rule Should Be Introduced into the UK Tax System* (2011).

Abrahamson (2020):

Abrahamson J, *International Taxation of Banking* (Series on International Taxation Wolters Kluwer, 2020).

ACCA (2013):

ACCA, Cash Accounting – The Pros and Cons, July 2013, https://www.accaglobal.com/gb/en/technical-activities/technical-resources-search/2013/july/cash-accounting.html, accessed 1 November 2023.

ACCA (2022):

ACCA, Technical factsheet, Accounting for cryptocurrencies (September 2022) https://www.accaglobal.com/uk/en/technical-activities/technical-resources-search/2022/september/tf-accounting-for-cryptocurrencies.html, accessed 1 August 2023.

ACCA, Accounting for Cryptocurrencies:

ACCA, Accounting for Cryptocurrencies, https://www.accaglobal.com/in/en/student/exam-support-resources/professional-exams-study-resources/strategic-business-reporting/technical-articles/cryptocurrencies.html, accessed 1 August 2023.

ACCA, Financial Instrument:

ACCA, What Is a Financial Instrument? – Part 2, https://www.accaglobal.com/gb/en/student/exam-support-resources/fundamentals-exams-study-resources/f7/technical-articles/financial-instrument-part2.html, accessed 2 May 2023.

Adejumo (2022):

Adejumo O, Public companies holding Bitcoin face impairment losses amid market crash, Cryptoslate, 4 July 2022, https://cryptoslate.com/public-companies-holding-bitcoin-face-impairment-losses-amid-market-crash/, accessed February 2023.

Alexander (2022):

Alexander C, The Guardian, https://www.theguardian.com/commentisfree/2022/nov/23/ftx-binance-crypto-market, 23 November 2022, accessed 24 July 2023.

Allen & Overy (2023):

Allen & Overy, 20 Questions on Pillar Two and the GloBe rules, April 2023, https://www.allenovery.com/en-gb/global/news-and-insights/publications/20-questions-on-pillar-two-and-the-globe-rules, accessed 1 August 2023.

Ali (2023):

Ali AM, 'Convertible Bond Pricing Model', http://www.yieldcurve.com/Mktsoftware/excelCB.htm accessed 12 February 2023.

Ananda (2022):

Ananda N, Bloomberg Professional Services, 'How to Analyze, Create, and Risk-Manage ESG-Linked Structured Products' (29 May 2022), https://www.bloomberg.com/professional/blog/how-to-analyze-create-and-risk-manage-esg-linked-structured-products/, accessed 25 May 2023.

Anzinger (2012):

Anzinger H, 'Übergang des wirtschaftlichen Eigentums an girosammelverwahrten Aktien im System der Kapitalertragsteuer' Recht der Finanzinstrumente 2012 394.

Arndt (2023):

Arndt C, Bitcoin & Co: BFH rules crypto profits are taxable! What do crypto investors need to know now?, Acconsis (2023), https://www.acconsis.de/en/bitcoin-co-bfh-rules-crypto-profits-are-taxable-what-do-crypto-investors-need-to-know-now/, accessed 1 October 2023.

ASB, Amendment to FRS 25 (IAS 32):

ASB, Amendment to FRS 25 (IAS 32) 'Financial Instruments: Presentation', Classification of Rights Issues (2010).

ASSB, Digital Currency:

ASSB, Digital Currency – A case for standard setting activity, https://www.aasb.gov.au/admin/file/content102/c3/AASB_ASAF_DigitalCurrency.pdf, page 12, accessed 28 August 2022.

Assmann and Schneider (2012):

Assmann H-D and Schneider U, *Wertpapierhandelsgesetz Kommentar* (6th edn, Verlag Dr Otto Schmidt 2012).

Atlantic Council (2023):

Atlantic Council, Central Bank Cryptocurrency tracker, https://www.atlanticcouncil.org/cbdctracker/, accessed 2 August 2023.

Australian Treasury Exposure Draft:

Australian Treasury Exposure Draft: Tax Laws Amendment (Taxation of Financial Arrangements) Bill 2008, Explanatory Material

Avery Jones (1996):

Avery Jones J, 'Tax Law: Rules or Principles?' (1996) BTR 580.

Avi-Yonah (2000):

Avi-Yonah R, 'Commentary (Response to Article by H. David Rosenbloom)' (2000) 53 Tax Law Review 167.

Baker (2012):

Baker P, *Double Tax Conventions: A Manual on the Model Tax Convention on Income and on Capital*, looseleaf (3rd edition 2001, Release 23 December 2012, Sweet & Maxwell).

Baker (2019):

Baker P, Editor's Note in: A. SÀRL v Federal Tax Administration (beneficial ownership) Case 2C_209/2017, 22 ITLR 435.

Banfield (2023):

Banfield L, Linklaters, Derivatives and Structured Products Legal Outlook 2023, https://www.linklaters.com/en/insights/publications/legal-outlook/2023/derivatives-and-structured-products, accessed 28 December 2023.

Barckow (2004):

Barckow A, *Die Bilanzierung von derivaten Finanzinstrumenten und Sicherungsgeschäften* (IDW-Verlag 2004).

Barendt (1997):

Barendt E, 'Is there a United Kingdom Constitution' (1997) 17 Oxford Journal of Legal Studies 137.

Barth (2022):

Barth ME, Accounting Standards: The "too difficult box" – the big accounting issue, August 2022, https://www.tandfonline.com/doi/full/10.1080/00014788.2022.2079757, accessed 14 August 2023.

Bartsch, Gabler Wirtschaftslexikon (2023):

Bartsch M, 'Gabler Wirtschaftslexikon, Stichwort: wirtschaftlichen Eigentum' (*Gabler Verlag*) https://wirtschaftslexikon.gabler.de/definition/wirtschaftliches-eigentum-50246/version-162966, accessed 5 August 2023.

Basar (2023):

Basar S, NDFs could boost institutional crypto use, *Marketsmedia newsletter*, https://www.marketsmedia.com/ndfs-could-boost-institutional-crypto-use/, accessed 1 August 2023.

BAT (2023):

BAT, 'Delivering Transformation' Combined Performance and ESG Summary (2023), https://docs.publicnow.com/viewDoc?hash_primary=A80FFDEB57CEC9FE68700F643978CB1487232384, accessed 12 August 2023

Baumgartner (2010):

Baumgartner B, *Das Konzept des beneficial owner im internationalen Steuerrecht der Schweiz: Unter besonderer Berücksichtigung der Weiterleitung von abkommensbegünstigten Dividenden- und Zinseinkünften*, PhD dissertation, Schriften zum Steuerrecht, volume 21 (Schulthess Verlag, 2010), 130-150.

Baumgartner and Frick (2015):

Baumgartner, B and Frick G, 'Written Judgements on Swiss Supreme Court Decisions on Denial of Withholding Tax Refund for Danish Banks' (*Loyens&Loeff*, 18 November 2015) https://www.loyensloeff.com/insights/news--events/news/written-judgements-on-swiss-supreme-court-decisions-on-denial-of-withholding-tax-refund-for-danish-banks/, accessed 16 October 2023.

Baynham (2023):

Baynham S, UK Mandatory Disclosure Rules are published (23 January 2023), KPMG, https://kpmg.com/uk/en/home/insights/2023/01/tmd-uk-mandatory-disclosure-rules-regulations-are-published.html, accessed 20 July 2023.

BBC (2022):

BBC, Bitcoin cash machines ordered to shut down in UK, 11 March 2022, https://www.bbc.com/news/technology-60709209, accessed 10 July 2023.

BDO Global (2023):

BDO Global, United Kingdom – Spring Budget Includes Pillar Two and Transfer Pricing Documentation Announcements, 17 March 2023, https://www.bdo.global/en-gb/insights/tax/international-tax/united-kingdom-spring-budget-includes-pillar-two-and-transfer-pricing-documentation-announcements, accessed 15 April 2023.

Becker (2022):

Becker S, Risk.net, Crypto Structured Products Come of Age (8 November 2022), https://www.risk.net/our-take/7955057/crypto-structured-products-come-of-age, accessed 29 May 2023.

Benatti and Napolitano (2018):

Benatti N and Napolitano F, European Central Bank, Irving Fisher Committee on Central Bank Statistics, Ninth IFC Conference on 'Are post-crisis statistical initiatives completed?' Basel, 30-31 August 2018, *An insight into the derivatives trading of firms in the euro area*, https://www.bis.org/ifc/publ/ifcb49_20.pdf, accessed 3 August 2023.

Bhattacharya and Fabozzi (1997):

Bhattacharya A and Fabozzi F, 'Interest-rate swaps' in Fabozzi F (ed.), *Handbook of Fixed Income Securities* (5th edn, Irwin Professional Publishing 1997).

Binance, Crypto Futures and Options (2023):

Binance, Crypto Futures and Options: What Are the Similarities and Differences? (4 January 2023), https://www.binance.com/en/blog/futures/crypto-futures-and-options-what-are-the-similarities-and-differences-421499824684902074, accessed 12 August 2023.

Binance, Ether Futures:

Binance, Ether Futures, A Beginner's Guide to Trading Ethereum Futures, https://www.binance.com/en/e/ether_futures, accessed 12 August 2023.

Binance, NFT Derivatives (2022):

Binance, Binance Blog, Everything You Need To Know About NFT Derivatives, 8 December 2022, https://www.binance.com/en/blog/nft/everything-you-need-to-know-about-nft-derivatives-8218050223473231524, accessed 12 August 2023.

Bitcoin, White paper (2023):

Bitcoin.com, Bitcoin White paper, Satoshi's archive. https://www.bitcoin.com/satoshi-archive/whitepaper/, accessed 1 December 2023.

Bitnomial, Bitcoin US Dollar Futures:

Bitnomial, Bitcoin US Dollar Futures, https://bitnomial.com/products/bitcoin-us-dollar-futures, accessed 11 August 2023).

Black (1976):

Black F, 'The Pricing of Commodity Contracts' (1976) Journal of Financial Economics 167.

Black and Scholes (1973):

Black F and Scholes M, 'The Pricing of Options and Corporate Liabilities' 81 (1973) Journal of Political Economy 637.

Blödtner, Bilke and Heining (2009):

Blödtner W, Bilke K and Heining R, *Lehrbuch Buchführung und Bilanzsteuerrecht* (8th edn, nwb Verlag 2009).

Bloomberg Intelligence (2021):

Bloomberg Intelligence, Game on! ESG debt issuance passes $ 3 trillion with record speed, 21 June 2021, https://www.bloomberg.com/professional/blog/game-on-esg-debt-issuance-passes-3-trillion-with-record-speed/, accessed 26 May 2023.

Bloomberg Law (2021):

Bloomberg Law (6 May 2021), Goldman Offers New Bitcoin Derivatives to Wall Street Investors, https://news.bloomberglaw.com/banking-law/goldman-offers-new-bitcoin-derivatives-to-wall-street-investors, accessed 11 July 2023.

Böcking and Gros (2007):

Böcking H-J and Gros M, 'IFRS und die Zukunft der steuerlichen Gewinnermittlung' DStR 2007, 2339.

Bode in *Blümich* (2013) § 15 EStG:

Bode W, '§ 15 EStG' in Heuermann B and Brandis P (eds), Blümich, EStG, KStG GewStG Kommentar (2013).

Boerse Frankfurt, ETC Group Physical Bitcoin (2023):

Boerse Frankfurt, ETC Group Physical Bitcoin, https://www.boerse-frankfurt.de/en/etf/de000a27z304-etc-issuance-gmbh-0-000, accessed 29 May 2023.

Boerse Stuttgart, BTCetc Bitcoin Exchange Traded Crypto:

Boerse Stuttgart, BTCetc Bitcoin Exchange Traded Crypto (BTCE), https://www.boerse-stuttgart.de/de-de/produkte/etps/etns/stuttgart/a27z30-btcetc-bitcoin-exchange-traded-crypto-btce, accessed 29 May 2023.

Boerse Stuttgart, Using ETNs to Invest in Bitcoin:

Boerse Stuttgart, Using ETNs to Invest in Bitcoin, Dollars, etc. https://www.boerse-stuttgart.de/en/products/etps/etns/, accessed 29 May 2023.

Bradley (2023):

Bradley I, EY, *How Taxes on Cryptocurrencies and digital assets will soon take shape*, https://www.ey.com/en_gl/tax/how-taxes-on-cryptocurrencies-and-digital-assets-will-soon-take-shape, accessed 20 July 2023.

Bramwell et al. (2023):

Bramwell R et al., *Taxation of Companies and Company Reconstructions*, vol. 2 (9th edn, Sweet & Maxwell 2009, with updates through Release 41, January 2023), further eds cited: 8th (2002).

Brandis/Heuermann (2023):

Brandis P and Heuermann B, Ertragsteuerrecht, Kommentar, Looseleaf, Vahlen 166th edn, 2023.

Buchholz and Weis (2002):

Buchholz R and Weis B, 'Maßgeblichkeitsprinzip ade? Zur inhaltlichen Vereinbarkeit der Gewinnermittlung nach IAS und EStG (Teil 1)' DStR 2002 512.

Buciek *in Blümich* (2013) § 5 EStG:

Buciek K, '§ 5 EStG' in Brandis P and Heuermann B (eds), Blümich, EStG, KStG GewStG Kommentar (120th edn, 2013).

Business Wire (2021):

Business Wire, A Berkshire Hathaway Company, *Bitnominal Launches Margined, Physically Settled Bitcoin futures in the US* (15 November 2021) https://www.businesswire.com/news/home/20211115005890/en/Bitnomial-Launches-Margined-Physically-Settled-Bitcoin-Futures-in-the-US, accessed 23 February 2023.

Busin and Vock (2002):

Busin C and Vock ME, 'Abkommensberechtigung von ausländischen Holdingesellschaften' (2002) Der Schweizer Treuhänder 6-7/02 624.

Busse von Colbe and Seeberg (1999):

Busse von Colbe W and Seeberg T, *Vereinbarkeit internationaler Konzernrechnungslegung mit handelsrechtlichen Grundsätzen* (Empfehlungen des Arbeitskreises 'Externe Unternehmensrechnung' der Schmalenbach-Gesellschaft – Deutsche Gesellschaft für Betriebswirtschaft e.V. 1999).

Bybit, Crypto Structured Products (2022):

Bybit, Crypto Structured Products: Maximising Yields During Choppy Markets (27 July 2022) https://learn.bybit.com/bybit-shark-fin/crypto-structured-products/, accessed 29 May 2023.

Caudevilla (2022):

Caudevilla O, China Daily, China's digital yuan can leverage the Road Initiative, 12 August 2022, https://www.chinadaily.com.cn/a/202208/12/WS62f9a7d1a310fd2b29e722e9.html, accessed 16 August 2023.

Chandrasekera (2022):

Chandrasekera S, Bitcoin's Accounting Treatment Is Depressing MicroStrategy's Bottom Line, June 2022, https://www.forbes.com/sites/shehanchandrasekera/2022/06/01/bitcoins-accounting-treatment-is-artificially-degrading-microstrategys-bottom-line/?sh=d9dd55233e11, accessed 28 February 2023.

Choudhry (2006):

Choudhry M, *An Introduction to Bond Markets* (3rd edn, John Wiley & Sons 2006).

Clutton (2012):

Clutton O, 'Practical implications of a GAAR' Financial Director http://www.financialdirector.co.uk/financial-director/analysis/2178678/practical-implications-gaar, accessed 10 June 2013.

CME Group, Bitcoin Futures:

CME Group, Bitcoin Futures, https://www.cmegroup.com/markets/cryptocurrencies/bitcoin/bitcoin.contractSpecs.html, accessed 11 August 2023.

CME Group, Get to know options on Bitcoin futures:

CME Group, Get to know options on Bitcoin futures, https://www.cmegroup.com/education/courses/introduction-to-bitcoin/get-to-know-options-on-bitcoin-futures.html, accessed 11 January 2023.

CME Group, Weather Products:

CME Group, Weather Products, https://www.cmegroup.com/trading/weather/, accessed 8 May 2023.

CNBC Interview Buffett (2019):

CNBC, Interview Warren Buffett, February 2019, https://www.youtube.com/watch?v=m4vDTAelhCM, accessed 23 July 2023.

CNBC Interview Buffett (2020):

CNBC, Interview Warren Buffett, February 2020, https://www.youtube.com/watch?v=d6yqrwOZVjY, accessed 4 January 2024.

Coinbase (2023):

Coinbase, What is mining? https://www.coinbase.com/learn/crypto-basics/what-is-mining, accessed 14 July 2023.

Coingecko, Top Derivative Exchanges:

Coingecko, Top Derivative Exchanges Ranked by Open Interest & Trade Volume, https://www.coingecko.com/en/exchanges/derivatives, accessed 11 January 2024.

Collier (2011):

Collier R, 'Clarity, Opacity and Beneficial Ownership' (2011) 6 BTR, 684-703.

Collier (2014):

Collier R, Derivatives & Financial Instruments (DFI) 2014, IBFD, 247-252.

Collier and Andrus (2019):

Collier R and Andrus J, *Transfer Pricing and the Arm's Length Principle After BEPS* (Oxford University Press, 2019).

Conlon & Aquilino: Derivatives:

Conlon & Aquilino: *Principles of Financial Derivatives: U.S. & International Taxation* (WG&L, Thomson Reuters), Looseleaf, issue: March 2022, further eds cited: 2011.

Conrad (2022):

Conrad J, 'China's Digital Yuan Works Just Like Cash – With Added Surveillance', 8 November 2022, *Wired*, https://www.wired.com/story/chinas-digital-yuan-ecny-works-just-like-cash-surveillance/, accessed 8 March 2023.

Cooper (2010):

Cooper GS, 'Legislating Principles as a Remedy for Tax Complexity' (2010) 4 BTR 334-360.

Coroner-I Navigate (2023):

Coroner-I Navigate, Differences between FRS 102, IAS 39 and IFRS 9, https://library.croneri.co.uk/cch_uk/nuk102-02/ufs11-9-1a, accessed 2 May 2023.

Council of the EU, European Green Bonds:

Council of the EU, *European Green Bonds: Council adopts new regulation to promote sustainable finance, Press release*, 24 October 2023, https://www.consilium.europa.eu/en/press/press-releases/2023/10/24/european-green-bonds-council-adopts-new-regulation-to-promote-sustainable-finance/, accessed 1 December 2023.

Cox (2023):

Cox B, Zerocap, Introducing Crypto Structured Products with Investment Grade Credit Ratings (17 March 2023) https://zerocap.com/insights/articles/zerocap-partners-with-marex/, accessed 29 August 2023.

Crawley (2021):

Crawley J, *Coindesk*, 2021, https://www.coindesk.com/markets/2021/07/26/tulip-bulb-crypto-has-no-inherent-worth-man-group-ceo-says/, accessed 28 July 2023.

Crowe (2021):

Crowe, Accounting for cryptocurrencies in financial statements, 1 June 2021, https://www.crowe.com/my/insights/how-should-cryptocurrencies--be-accounted--for-in-the--financial-statements, accessed 1 August 2023.

Cryptoresearch (2021):

Cryptoresearch, Structured Products for Digital Assets, (3 March 2021) https://cryptoresearch.report/crypto-research/structured-products-for-digital-assets/, accessed 29 May 2023

Cullinane (2005):

Cullinane J, 'IAS – what's it all about (Part 2)' (2005) Tax Adviser 10.

Dahm and Hamacher (2008):

Dahm J and Hamacher R, 'Termingeschäfte und Abgeltungsteuer' DStR 2008 1910.

Daily Mail (2021):

Daily Mail (2021): Daily Mail, 1 October 2021, Crypto traders should be warned 'abandon all hope', NatWest's boss declares, as he praises China for 'banning the damned stuff', https://www.dailymail.co.uk/news/article-10047803/NatWest-boss-Sir-Howard-Davies-applauds-China-banning-practice-crypto-trading.html, accessed 11 August 2023.

Danon and Malek (2020):

Danon R and Malek B, *Commentary to A Plc v Federal Tax Administration*, 23 ILTR, 864, 867-871.

David and Buffin (2021):

Davis D and Buffin J, The Frontier Line, The how and why of ESG derivatives, Issue 182, September 2021, https://www.frontieradvisors.com.au, accessed 14 August 2023.

Deloitte (2005):

Deloitte, 2005 Special Edition: *Amendment to IAS 39 and IFRS 4 – Financial Guarantee Contracts* (2005) http://www.iasplus.com/de/binary/iasplus/0512guarantees.pdf, accessed 1 August 2023.

Deloitte (2012a):

Deloitte, *International Tax, United Kingdom Highlights 2012* – on file with the author.

Deloitte (2012b):

Deloitte, 'IFRS 9 Classification and Measurement Are You Lost?' http://www.iasplus.com/en/publications/uk/other/ifrs-9-classification-and-measurement-2014-are-you-lost, accessed 20 October 2023.

Deloitte (2013):

Deloitte, 'Portfolio Revaluation Approach through OCI' (25 July 2013) http://www.iasplus.com/en/meeting-notes/iasb/2013/july/macro-hedging, accessed 16 October 2023.

Deloitte (2014a):

Deloitte, 'IFRS 9 – Financial Instruments' http://www.iasplus.com/en/standards/ifrs/ifrs9, accessed 11 May 2023.

Deloitte (2014b):

Deloitte, *Germany Tax Alert: Upper house of parliament proposes new anti-hybrid rule and other measures* (7 November 2014) https://www2.deloitte.com/content/dam/Deloitte/global/Documents/Tax/dttl-tax-alert-germany-071114.pdf, accessed 13 May 2023.

Deloitte (2015):

Deloitte, A Closer Look 'Basic/Non-basic Classification under FRS 102 (June 2015), 7, https://www.iasplus.com/en-gb/publications/uk/closer-look/2015/a-closer-look-basic-non-basic-frs-102, accessed 3 August 2023.

Deloitte (2016):

Deloitte, IFRS 9: Financial Instruments – high level summary (April 2016), https://www2.deloitte.com/content/dam/Deloitte/lu/Documents/audit/lu-IFRS-9.pdf, accessed 15 February 2023.

Deloitte (2017):

Deloitte, Actions Implementation by Country, Action 2 – Hybrids (2017), https://www2.deloitte.com/content/dam/Deloitte/global/Documents/Tax/dttl-tax-beps-action-2-hybrids-implementation-matrix.pdf, accessed 18 July 2023.

Deloitte, Accounting and Financial Implications of ESG Initiatives:

Deloitte, Accounting and financial implications of ESG initiatives, https://www2.deloitte.com/us/en/pages/audit/articles/hu-accounting-reporting-esg.html, accessed 27 May 2023.

Deloitte, Accounting and Reporting Considerations for Environmental Credits:

Deloitte, Accounting and Reporting Considerations for Environmental Credits (updated May 2023), https://dart.deloitte.com/USDART/home/publications/deloitte/accounting-spotlight/2022/environmental-credits, accessed 1 October 2023.

Deloitte, ATAD III:

Deloitte, ATAD III (Shell Companies), https://www2.deloitte.com/dl/en/pages/legal/articles/atad-III-investment-management-newsletter.html, accessed 19 July 2023.

Deloitte, Financial Instruments – Macro Hedge Accounting:

Deloitte, 'Financial Instruments – Macro Hedge Accounting', http://www.iasplus.com/en/projects/major/macro-hedge-accounting, accessed 16 October 2023.

Deloitte, FRS 102:

Deloitte, FRS 102, https://www.iasplus.com/en-gb/standards/uk-gaap/frs102, accessed 1 August 2023.

Deloitte, IAS 39:

Deloitte, IAS 39 – Financial Instruments: Recognition and Measurement, https://www.iasplus.com/en/standards/ias/ias39, accessed 2 May 2023.

Deloitte, IFRS 9:

Deloitte, IFRS 9 – Financial Instruments, Hedge Accounting, https://www.iasplus.com/en-gb/standards/ifrs-en-gb/ifrs9, accessed 1 October 2023.

Deloitte tax@hand, Taxation of investment fund income:

Deloitte tax@hand, Taxation of investment fund income revised, 21 May 2018, https://www.taxathand.com/article/9698/Germany/2018/Taxation-of-investment-fund-income-revised-#!, accessed 18 July 2023.

Delp (1999):

Delp U, 'Erste Anwendungs- und Zweifelsfragen bei der Besteuerung von Termingeschäften privater Personen nach dem SEG 1999/2000/2002' INF 1999 584.

Delta Exchange, Crypto Options:

Delta Exchange, *Home of Crypto Options*, https://www.delta.exchange, accessed 5 July 2023.

Desax and Busenhart (2012):

Desax M and Busenhart M, 'Swiss Tribunal Rules on Ownership and Treaty Abuse Issues Regarding Total Return Swaps' (2012) 6 Tax Notes International, vol. 66, 557-564.

Deutsche Boerse Group (2021):

Deutsche Boerse Group, EUREX announces launch of Bitcoin ETN futures (20 August 2021), https://deutsche-boerse.com/dbg-en/media/press-releases/Eurex-announces-launch-of-Bitcoin-ETN-futures-2713576, accessed 30 May 2023.

Deutsche Bundesbank (2022):

Deutsche Bundesbank, Press Release, *Foreign exchange trading and derivatives transactions in Germany see significant growth in activity*, 27 October 2022, https://www.bundesbank.de/en/press/press-releases/foreign-exchange-trading-and-derivatives-transactions-in-germany-see-significant-growth-in-activity-899262, accessed 3 July 2023.

Deutscher Bundestag (Finanzausschuss) (2012):

Deutscher Bundestag (Finanzausschuss), *Wirtschaft und Banken begrüßen Steuerfreistellung bestimmter Dividenden* (2012), https://webarchiv.bundestag.de/archive/2013/0920/presse/hib/2012_11/2012_525/01.html, accessed 1 October 2023.

Dötsch et al. (2009):

Dötsch E et al., *Körperschaftsteuer* (15th edn, Schäfer-Poeschel Verlag 2009).

Dreyer and Herrmann (2001):

Dreyer G and Herrmann H, 'Die Besteuerung von Aktien-, Wandel- und Umtauschanleihen' BB 2001, 705.

Drummond (2006):

Drummond B, 'A Purposive Approach to the Drafting of Tax Legislation' (2006) BTR 669.

Drummond and Marwood (2007):

Drummond B and Marwood P, 'Purposive Drafting in the Finance Bill 2007' (2007) BTR 350.

Dunne (2022):

Dunne E, 'China Doles Out Free Digital Yuan During New Year to Boost Adoption' (updated 6 February 2023) *inside bitcoins*, https://insidebitcoins.com/news/china-doles-out-free-digital-yuan-during-new-year-to-boost-adoption, accessed March 2023.

Eccles and Mirchandani (2022):

Eccles R and Mirchandani B, We Need Universal ESG Accounting Standards, Harvard Business Review, 15 February 2022, https://hbr.org/2022/02/we-need-universal-esg-accounting-standards, accessed 27 May 2023.

Economic Affairs Committee (2013):

Economic Affairs Committee, *First Report, The Draft Finance Bill 2013* (2013).

Edgar (2000a):

Edgar T, *The Income Tax Treatment of Financial Instruments: Theory and Practice* (Canadian Tax Foundation 2000).

Edgar (2000b):

Edgar T, 'The Taxation of Financial Arrangements (TOFA) Proposals: A Modest and Defensible Agenda of Reform' (2000) 23 UNSW Law Journal 288.

EFRAG, Accounting for Crypto-Assets (2022):

EFRAG, 'Recommendations and Feedback Statement on Accounting for Crypto-Assets (Liabilities)' (April 2022), https://www.efrag.org/News/Project-585/EFRAGs-Recommendations-and-Feedback-Statement-on-Accounting-for-Crypto-Assets-Liabilities-, accessed 1 October 2023.

Eller, Gruber and Reif (1999):

Eller R, Gruber W and Reif M, *Kreditrisikomodelle und Kreditderivate* (1999).

Eom, Helwege and Huang (2004):

Eom YH, Helwege J and Huang J-Z, 'Structural Models of Corporate Bond Pricing: An Empirical Analysis' (2004) Vol. 17, No. 2 The Review of Financial Studies 499-544, https://doi.org/10.1093/rfs/hhg053, accessed 1 October 2023.

Ernst & Young (2013):

Ernst & Young, *GAAR Rising, Mapping Tax Enforcement's Evolution* (2013), http://sataxguide.co.za/wp-content/uploads/2015/03/GAAR-rising-Mapping-tax-enforcement's-evolution-February-2013.pdf, accessed 1 January 2024.

ESG Investing (2021):

ESG Investing, NYSE launches new sustainable asset class, 15 September 2021, https://www.esginvesting.co.uk/2021/09/nyse-launches-new-sustainable-asset-class/, accessed 15 June 2023.

Ettlich in Blümich (2013) § 36 EStG:

Ettlich R, '§ 36 EStG' in Brandis P and Heuermann (eds), Blümich, EStG, KStG GewStG Kommentar (120th edn, 2013).

EUREX, Block Trades:

EUREX, Block Trades, https://www.eurex.com/ex-en/trade/eurex-t7-entry-services/block-trades, accessed 2 January 2024.

EUREX, Single Stock Futures:

EUREX, Single Stock Futures (November 2023), 10, https://www.eurex.com/resource/blob/1252/1ddc50df36c1e5e0a00aeb03141bcea3/data/presentation_eurex-single-stock-futures.pdf, accessed 2 January 2024.

EY, Cryptoassets (2021):

EY, 'Applying IFRS, Accounting by holders of cryptoassets' (updated October 2021), https://www.ey.com/en_gl/ifrs-technical-resources/accounting-by-holders-of-crypto-assets-updated-october-2021, accessed 1 March 2023.

EY, Crypto derivatives (2022):

EY, Crypto derivatives are becoming a major digital asset class (2022), 1, https://assets.ey.com/content/dam/ey-sites/ey-com/en_us/topics/financial-services/ey-crypto-derivatives-pov_final4.pdf?download, accessed 11 July 2023.

EY, Germany enacts EU ATAD:

EY, Germany enacts EU ATAD Implementation Law including anti-hybrid rules (15 July 2021), https://www.ey.com/en_gl/tax-alerts/germany-enacts-eu-atad-implementation-law-including-anti-hybrid-rules, accessed 18 July 2023.

EY, ATAD Implementation Law (2021):

EY, Tax News Update, Germany agrees on draft ATAD Implementation Law (26 March 2021), https://globaltaxnews.ey.com/news/2021-5355-german-government-agrees-on-draft-atad-implementation-law, accessed 19 July 2023.

EY, Finance (No.2) Act 2023 (2023):

EY, UK passes Finance (No.2) Act 2023 introducing OECD Pillar Two measures, Tax News Update (July 2023), https://taxnews.ey.com/news/2023-1243-uk-passes-finance-no2-act-2023-introducing-oecd-pillar-two-measures, accessed 1 January 2024.

Fabozzi (1997):

Fabozzi F, *The Handbook of Fixed Income Securities* (Irwin Professional Publishing 1997).

Fabozzi et al. (2002):

Fabozzi F et al., *Foundation of Financial Markets and Institutions* (3rd edn, Pearson 2002).

Fabozzi and Markowitz (2011):

Fabozzi FJ and Markowitz HM, *The Theory and Practice of Investment Management: Asset Allocation, Valuation, Portfolio Construction, and Strategies*, 2nd edn Wiley, 2011.

Fama (1970):

Fama E, 'Efficient Capital Markets: A Review of Theory and Empirical Work' (1970) The Journal of Finance 383.

Feyerabend in Erle/Sauter, § 15 EStG:

Feyerabend H-J, '§ 15 EStG' in Erle B and Sauter T (eds), *Heidelberger Kommentar zum Körperschaftsteuergesetz* (3rd edn, C.F. Müller 2010).

Feyerabend (2009):

Feyerabend H-J (ed.) *Besteuerung privater Kapitalanlagen* (C.H.Beck 2009).

Fichtenbaum (2001):

Fichtenbaum M, 'Corporate Applications of Derivatives' in Fabozzi FJ (ed.), *The Use of Derivatives in Tax Planning* (John Wiley & Sons 2001).

Finnis (1980):

Finnis J, Natural Law and Natural Rights (Oxford University Press 1980).

Forbes (2022):

Forbes, What Really Happened to LUNA Crypto? (20 September 2022), https://www.forbes.com/sites/qai/2022/09/20/what-really-happened-to-luna-crypto/?sh=2c2428d14ff1, accessed 1 July 2023.

Francis, Frost and Whittaker (1999):

Francis JC, Frost J and Whittaker JG, *The Handbook of Credit Derivatives* (McGraw Hill 1999).

Frankenfield (2023):

Frankenfield J, Investopia, Cryptocurrency Explained with Pros and Cons for Investment, (updated 4 February 2023), https://www.investopedia.com/terms/c/cryptocurrency.asp, accessed 30 August 2023.

Fraser and Oliver (2007):

Fraser R and Oliver JDB, 'Beneficial Ownership: HMRC's Draft Guidance on Interpretation of the Indofood Decision' (2007) BTR 39.

Freedman (1995):

Freedman J, 'Defining Taxable Profits in a Changing Accounting Environment' (1995) BTR 434.

Freedman (1996):

Freedman J, 'The Role of Realisation: Accounting, Company Law and Taxation' in Series ICS (ed.), *The Influence of Corporate Tax Law and Accounting Principles in Determining Taxable Income*, vol. 21b (1996).

Freedman (2004a):

Freedman J, 'Aligning Taxable Profits and Accounting Profits: Accounting Standards, Legislators and Judges' (2004) 2 eJournal of Tax Research 71, http://classic.austlii.edu.au/au/journals/eJlTaxR/2004/4.html, accessed 8 July. 2023.

Freedman (2004b):

Freedman J, 'Accounting Standards: A Panacea?' (2004) The Tax Journal, 18 October 2014, 9.

Freedman (2010):

Freedman J, 'Improving (Not Perfecting) Tax Legislation: Rules and Principles Revisited' (2010) 6 BTR 717.

Freedman (2012):

Freedman J, 'GAAR as a Process and the Process of Discussing the GAAR' (2012) BTR 22.

Freedman (2016):

Freedman J, 'General Anti-Avoidance Rules (GAARs) – A Key Element of Tax Systems in the Post-BEPS Tax World? The UK GAAR', Legal Research Paper Series (24 April 2016), https://papers.ssrn.com/sol3/papers.cfm?abstract_id=2769554, accessed 21 July 2023.

Freedman (2019):

Judith Freedman, 'The UK General Anti-Avoidance Rule: Transplants and Lessons', (2019) 73(6/7) Bulletin for International Taxation 332-338.

Fuller (2012):

Fuller C, 'CBI: GAAR Gives Too Much Power to Taxman' Accountancy Age http://www.accountancyage.com/aa/news/2205957/cbi-gaar-gives-too-much-power-to-taxman, accessed 11 June 2023.

Gammie (2013):

Gammie, M, 'Moral Taxation, Immoral Avoidance – What Role for the Law?' (2013) BTR 577.

Cubillos González and Mosquera Valderrama (2021):

Cubillos González J and Mosquera Valderrama I in: General Anti-Avoidance Rules: The Final Tax Frontier? Indian and International Tax Perspectives (Mukesh Butani and Turun Jain, eds), Thomson Reuters, 2021, Chapter 44, 978.

Geman (1999):

Geman H, *Insurance and Weather Derivatives: From Exotic Options to Exotic Underlyings* (Risk Books 1999).

Geurts (2001):

Geurts M, 'Steuerliche Behandlung von Kreditderivaten' DB 2001 1163.

Geurts (2002):

Geurts M, 'Besteuerung von Finanzderivaten im Privatvermögen' DB 2002 110.

Geurts (2007):

Geurts M, 'Die neue Abgeltungsteuer - das Ende einer steuerinduzierten Kapitalanlage?' DStZ 2007 341.

Geurts in Bordewin/ Brandt, § 20 EStG:

Geurts M, '§ 20 EStG' in Bordewin A and Brandt J (eds), *Einkommensteuergesetz, Kommentar* (C.F. Müller 2009).

Ghosh, Johnson and Miller (2022):

Ghosh, Johnson and Miller on the Taxation of Corporate Debt and Derivatives (Tolley, LexisNexis 2009, looseleaf with updates through issue 28, December 2022).

Gilleard (2012):

Gilleard M, 'UK GAAR Reaction Reveals Serious Constitutional Problems' International Tax Review, http://www.internationaltaxreview.com/Article/3090626/UK-GAAR-reaction-reveals-serious-constitutional-problems.html accessed 11 June 2013.

Glenk in Blümich (2010) § 23 EStG:

Glenk H, '§ 23 EStG' in Heuermann B (ed.), *Blümich, EStG, KStG, GewStG* (108th edn, Verlag Franz Vahlen München 2010).

Google Finance: Bitcoin (2023):

Google Finance, https://www.google.com/finance/quote/BTC-USD, accessed 28 July 2023.

Gosch (2009):

Gosch D (ed.) *Körperschaftsteuergesetz: KStG* (2nd edn, C.H. Beck 2009).

Goulder (2023):

Goulder R, 'Expectations for 2024: Pillar 1 Finds an Off-Ramp' (2023) 111 Tax Notes International, 1819.

Gov.UK, Multinational top-up tax:

Gov.UK, Multinational top-up tax: undertaxed profits rule and other amendments, Policy paper, updated 27 September 2023, https://www.gov.uk/government/publications/multinational-top-up-tax-adoption-of-the-undertaxed-profits-rule-and-other-amendments/multinational-top-up-tax-undertaxed-profits-rule-and-other-amendments, accessed 1 October 2023.

Grant Thornton (2018):

Grant Thornton, IFRS Viewpoint, Accounting for cryptocurrencies - the basics, 2018, https://www.grantthornton.global/globalassets/1.-member-firms/global/insig

hts/article-pdfs/ifrs/ifrs-viewpoint-9---accounting-for-cryptocurrencies--the-basics.pdf, 4, accessed 3 October 2023.

Grant Thornton (2023):

Grant Thornton, Five EU countries to postpone Pillar 2 (December 2023), https://www.lexology.com/library/detail.aspx?g=c550cddc-13e0-46f0-8d21-04ee75cbde29, accessed 29 December 2023.

Greenberg and James (2012):

Greenberg D and James M, 'GAAR Proposals Could Be Unconstitutional' Accountancy Age http://www.accountancyage.com/aa/feature/2219190/gaar-proposals-could-be-unconstitutional, accessed 11 June 2013.

Greenhouse Gas Protocol, Corporate Value Chain:

Greenhouse Gas Protocol, Corporate Value Chain (Scope 3) Accounting and Reporting Standard, https://ghgprotocol.org/sites/default/files/standards/Corporate-Value-Chain-Accounting-Reporing-Standard_041613_2.pdf, accessed 27 May 2023.

Hahn (2007):

Hahn T, 'Bilanzierung und Besteuerung von Wandelanleihen' (GRIN Verlag, 2007).

Haisch (2010):

Haisch M, 'Derivatebesteuerung im Privatvermögen ab 2009' (Richard Boorberg Verlag 2010).

Haisch and Helios (2011):

Haisch M and Helios M, *Rechtshandbuch Finanzinstrumente* (C.H. Beck 2011).

Harari et al. (2023):

Harari D et al., Rising Cost of Living in the UK, House of Commons Library, 24 November 2023, https://researchbriefings.files.parliament.uk/documents/CBP-9428/CBP-9428.pdf, accessed 6 December 2023.

Harenberg in H/H/R (2003) § 23:

Harenberg F, '§ 23' in Herrmann C, Heuer G and Raupach A (eds), *Einkommensteuer- und Körperschaftsteuergesetz Kommentar* (21st edn, Verlag Dr. Otto Schmidt 2003).

Harenberg in H/H/R (2013) § 20:

Harenberg F, '§ 20' in Herrmann C, Heuer G and Raupach A (eds), *Einkommensteuer- und Körperschaftsteuergesetz Kommentar* (Verlag Dr. Otto Schmidt 2013).

Hatjantonas (2012):

Hatjantonas F, 'The Draft GAAR: The "Double Reasonableness" Test' Tax Journal, August 2012.

Haug (2007):

Haug EG, *Derivatives, Models on Models* (John Wiley & Sons Ltd 2007).

Häuselmann (2000):

Häuselmann H, 'Wandelanleihen in der Handels- und Steuerbilanz des Emittenten' BB 2000 139.

Häuselmann (2005):

Häuselmann H, *Die steuerbilanzielle Erfassung von Finanzinstrumenten* (10th edn, Freshfields Bruckhaus Deringer 2005).

Häuselmann and Wagner (2002a):

Häuselmann H and Wagner S, 'Steuerbilanzielle Erfassung aktienbezogener Anleihen: Options-, Wandel-, Umtausch- und Aktienanleihen' BB 2002 2431.

Häuselmann and Wagner (2002b):

Häuselmann H and Wagner S, 'Grenzen der Einbeziehung von Aktienderivaten in das Halbeinkünfteverfahren' BB 2002 2170.

Häuselmann and Wiesenbart (1990):

Häuselmann H and Wiesenbart T, 'Fragen zur bilanzsteuerlichen Behandlung von Geschäften an der Deutschen Terminbörse (DTB)' DB 1990 641.

Haworth (2009):

Haworth D, 'Section 48 and Schedule 24: disguised interest' (2009) BTR 570.

Haworth and Hollis (2010):

Haworth D and Hollis J, 'IFRS and Derivatives Taxation' (March/April 2010) Derivatives and Financial Instruments (DFI), 23.

Helmer (2012):

Helmer G, 'Beneficial Ownership – A Looming Disaster?' PWC, 2012 – on file with the author.

Henisz, Koller and Nuttall (2019):

Henisz W, Koller T and Nuttall R, Five Ways that ESG creates value, 14 November 2019, McKinsey Quarterly, https://www.mckinsey.com/capabilities/strategy-and-corporate-finance/our-insights/five-ways-that-esg-creates-value, accessed 16 June 2023.

Herbert (2011):

Herbert M, 'HSBC – Comments on Discussion Draft – Clarification of the Meaning of "Beneficial Ownership" in the OECD Model Tax Convention', http://www.oecd.org/tax/treaties/48413959.pdf, accessed 2 October 2023.

Herzig (2006):

Herzig N, 'Steuerliche Gewinnermittung und handelsrechtliche Rechnungslegung' IStR 2006 557.

Hoheisel (2020):

Hoheisel M, in: Littmann/Bitz/Pust, Das Einkommensteuerrecht, EStG § 23 Abs 1 Nr 2 EStG, 2. Andere Wirtschaftgueter, paragraph 82, (issue 142, April 2020).

Homburger (2015):

Homburger, Supreme Court Denies Refunds of Swiss Withholding Tax Arbitrage Cases, Bulletin May 6, 2015 – on file with the author.

Hongler (2013):

Hongler P, 'New Swiss Court Decision on Hedged Equity Investments' (2013) 71 Tax Notes International, 155.

Hongler et al. (2023):

Hongler P et al., 'UTPR – Potential Conflicts with International Law' (2023) 111 Tax Notes International, 141.

Hougan and Lavant (2021):

Hougan M and Lavant D, CTA Research Foundation, *Cryptoassets, The Guide to Bitcoin, Blockchain and Cryptocurrency for Investment Professionals* (2021) 2.

House of Commons and House of Lords Parliamentary Commission on Banking Standards (2013):

House of Commons and House of Lords *Parliamentary Commission on Banking Standards, Changing Banking for Good—Volume I: Summary, and Conclusions and Recommendations*, 12 June 2013, HL Paper 27-I of session 2013–14, 8–13, https://publications.parliament.uk/pa/jt201314/jtselect/jtpcbs/27/27.pdf, accessed 1 November 2023.

Howcroft (2022):

Howcroft E, Crypto derivatives volumes surge to $3.12 trillion in July – CryptoCompare, Reuters (12 September 2023), https://www.reuters.com/technology/crypto-derivatives-volumes-surge-312-trillion-july-cryptocompare-2022-08-11/, accessed 6 February 2024.

Hudson (2010):

Hudson A, 'Chapter D1: Taxation of Derivatives: The United Kingdom' in Conlon S and Aquilino V (eds), *Principles of Financial Derivatives, US and International Taxation* (Thomson Reuters/WG&L 2010).

Huld (2022):

Huld A, "China Launches Digital Yuan App – All You Need to Know" (22 September 2022) *China Briefing from Dezan Shira & Associates*, https://www.china-briefing

.com/news/china-launches-digital-yuan-app-what-you-need-to-know/, accessed 1 August 2023.

Hull (1997):

Hull J, *Introduction to Futures and Options Markets* (Prentice Hall 1997).

Hull J (2018):

Hull J, *Options, Futures and Other Derivatives* (10th edn, Pearson, 2018), further eds cited: 6th (2006).

Hull and Basu (2022):

Hull J and Basu S, *Options, Futures and Other Derivatives* (11th edn, Pearson, 2022).

Hwang and Weidmann (2019):

Hwang S and Weidmann O, *General Report: Investment Funds*, International Fiscal Association, 2019 London Congress in: Cahiers de Droit fiscal international, volume 104.

ICE (2023):

ICE, All Products, All Futures, Options, OTC Products & Physicals, https://www.theice.com/products/?filter=renewable%20energy%20certificate%20futures, accessed 13 April 2023.

Indeed (2022):

Indeed, A guide to accounting standards (UK GAAP and IFRS), (updated 7 December 2022), https://uk.indeed.com/career-advice/career-development/accounting-standards, accessed 17 February 2023.

Ingersoll (1997):

Ingersoll J, *Theory of Financial Decision Making* (Rowman & Littlefield 1987).

Intemann in H/H/R (2013) § 15:

Intemann J, '§ 15' in Herrmann C, Heuer G and Raupach A (eds), *Einkommensteuer- und Körperschaftsteuergesetz, Kommentar* (Verlag Dr Otto Schmidt 2013).

International Capital Market Association (2023):

International Capital Market Association (ICMA) Green Bond Principles,' https://www.icmagroup.org/assets/documents/Regulatory/Green-Bonds/Green-Bonds-Principles-June-2018-270520.pdf, accessed 12 April 2023.

investDEFI, Driving the Evolution of Crypto Investing:

investDEFI, Driving the Evolution of Crypto Investing, https://www.investdefy.com, accessed 29 May 2023.

Investopedia, Non-fungible Tokens:

Investopedia, What are Non-fungible Tokens?, https://www.investopedia.com/non-fungible-tokens-nft-5115211, accessed 12 February 2023.

Jacob (2000):

Jacob F, 'German Tax Treatment of Hybrid Financial Instruments in Cross-Border Transactions' (August/September 2000) Bulletin for International Fiscal Documentation 442.

Jacobs, Endres and Spengel (2011):

Jacobs O, Endres D & Spengel C (eds), *Internationale Unternehmensbesteuerung* (7th edn, C.H. Beck 2011).

Jacobs-Soyka in Littmann/Bitz/Pust (2009), § 23:

Jacobs-Soyka J, '§ 23' in Littmann E, Bitz H and Pust H (eds), *EStG – Das Einkommensteuerrecht* (82nd edn, Schäffer-Pöschel 2009).

James (2009):

James S, 'The Relationship Between Accounting and Taxation', Paper 02/2009, https://core.ac.uk/download/pdf/12824388.pdf, accessed 14 January 2023.

Jimenez (2013):

Jimenez AM, 'Beneficial Ownership as an Attribution-of-Income Rule in Spain: Source and Residence Country Perspectives in: Beneficial Ownership: Recent Trends' (IBFD 2013) 199ff.

Kaffash:

Kaffash J, 'The GAAR Report: Was It Worth It?' AccountancyAge, November 2011, http://www.accountancyage.com/aa/analysis/2127165/gaar-report-worth, accessed 17 April 2023.

Kelly, Farrelly et al. (2021):

Kelly R, Farrelly G et al., ESG derivatives: a look at their use and regulation (2021), https://www.matheson.com/insights/detail/esg-derivatives-a-look-at-their-use-and-regulation, accessed 28 July 2023.

Kharpal and Browne (2022):

Kharpal A and Browne R, "From $250,000 to $10,000 price calls: How market watchers got it wrong with bitcoin in 2022" (23 December 2022), *CNBC*, https://www.cnbc.com/2022/12/23/bitcoin-price-calls-in-2022-how-the-market-got-it-wrong.html, accessed 9 August 2023.

Kilius (1989):

Kilius, 'The Concept of "Beneficial Ownership" of Items of Income under German Tax Treaties' Intertax No. 8/9 (1989) 340.

Kindleberger (2005):

Kindleberger C, *Manias, Panics and Crashes, A History of Financial Crises* (5th edn, John Wiley 2005).

Kleinbard (2003):

Kleinbard E, 'Taxing Convertible Debt: A Layman's Perspective' (2003) 56 SMU Law Review 453.

Kleinbard (2005):

Kleinbard E, 'Designing an Income Tax on Capital' (Conference on Taxing Capital Income, Brookings Institution, Washington, 23 September 2005), https://www.taxpolicycenter.org/sites/default/files/legacy/newsevents/kleinbard_v2.pdf, accessed 1 August 2023.

Koelbel et al. (2021):

Koelbel J et al., How disclosing transition and physical climate risks affect credit default swaps (8 April 2021), https://www.unpri.org/pri-blog/how-disclosing-transition-and-physical-climate-risks-affects-credit-default-swaps/7418.article, accessed 13 April 2023.

KPMG (2004):

KPMG, *Financial Instruments Accounting* (2004) – on file with the author.

KPMG, BEPS 2.0:

KPMG, BEPS 2.0: state of play (3 January 2024), 9-10, https://assets.kpmg.com/content/dam/kpmg/xx/pdf/2023/04/beps-2-0-state-of-play-april-2023.pdf, accessed 4 January 2024.

KPMG, Carbon offsets and credits:

KPMG, Carbon offsets and credits under IFRS® Accounting Standards (March 2023), https://kpmg.com/us/en/articles/2023/carbon-offsets-credits-ifrs-accounting-standards.html, accessed 2 October 2023.

KPMG, EU: New directive on tax transparency rules:

KPMG, EU: New directive on tax transparency rules for service providers facilitating cryptoasset transactions (17 October 2023), https://kpmg.com/us/en/home/insights/2023/10/tnf-eu-new-directive-on-tax-transparency-rules-for-service-providers-facilitating-cryptoasset-transactions.html, accessed 20 October 2023.

KPMG, Germany (2021):

KPMG, Germany: Legislation transposing ATAD measures (exit taxation, CFC rules, hybrid mismatches) (30 June 2021), https://kpmg.com/us/en/home/insights/2021/06/tnf-germany-legislation-transposing-atad-measures-exit-taxation-cfc-rules-hybrid-mismatches.html, accessed 24 March 2023.

KPMG, Get Ready for Global Sustainability Standards:

KPMG, Get Ready for Global Sustainability Standards (18 May 2023), https://kpmg.com/au/en/home/insights/2022/04/issb-sustainability-reporting-disclosures-guide.html, accessed 25 May 2023.

KPMG, IFRS announce new ESG reporting standard:

KPMG, IFRS announce new ESG reporting standard, 2021, https://kpmg.com/dp/en/home/insights/2021/10/ifrs-announce-new-esg-reporting-standard.html, accessed 27 May 2023.

Kußmaul and Klein (2001):

Kußmaul H and Klein N, 'Überlegungen zum Maßgeblichkeitsprinzip in Kontext jüngerer nationaler sowie internationaler Entwicklungen' DStR 2001 546.

Kuźniacki (2023):

Kuźniacki B, 'Pillar 2 and International Investment Agreements: "QDMTT Payable" Seals an Internationally Wrongful Act' (2023) 111 Tax Notes International, 159.

Lapienyte (2023):

Lapienyte J, investDEFY launches Equal Weighted Metaverse + Web 3.0 NFT index for investors, cybernews, https://cybernews.com/news/investdefy-launches-equal-weighted-metaverse-web-3-0-nft-index-for-investors/, accessed 1 October 2023.

Lardner et al. (2023):

Lardner G et al., Demystifying jurisdiction and ownership of crypto assets, IFLR 2023, https://www.iflr.com/article/2c5v0ti3bg7v249x1yneo/demystifying-jurisdiction-and-ownership-of-crypto-assets, accessed 18 October 2023.

Lang (2021):

Lang M, *Introduction to the Law of Double Taxation Conventions* (IBFD, 3rd edn 2021).

Lang, Storck and Petruzzi (2016):

Lang M, Storck A and Petruzzi R, *Transfer Pricing in a Post-BEPS World* (EUCOTAX Series on European Taxation, Wolters Kluwer, 2016), volume 50.

Laukkanen (2007):

Laukkanen A, *Taxation of Investment Derivatives*, vol. 13, Doctoral Series (IBFD 2007).

Lee and Repetto (2010):

Lee I and Repetto E, *Structured Products* (Dimensional Fund Advisors, 2010).

Linklaters, ESG Legal Outlook 2023:

Linklaters, ESG Legal Outlook 2023, 7, https://lpscdn.linklaters.com/-/media/digital-marketing-image-library/files/01_insights/publications/legal-outlook/2023/linklaters_esg-legal-outlook-2023.ashx?rev = bbb9e054-d57b-4cc7-aaf1-565cf9a2b9cc&extension = pdf&hash = B0956C799EF9661F42F6463E880EA5F9, accessed 28 May 2023.

Lindberg in Blümich (2013) § 43 EStG:

Lindberg K, '§ 43 EStG' in Heuermann B and Brandis P (eds), Blümich, EStG, KStG, GewStG, Kommentar (120th edn, 2013).

Lindsay (2005):

Lindsay J, 'Derivative Contracts' in Brown A (ed.), *CCH British Tax Reporter, Taxation of Companies*, vol. 7 (Wolters Kluwer (UK) Limited 2005).

Lindsay (2006a):

Lindsay J, 'Convertibles and Exchangeables, Part 1: The Position for Issuers' (2006) Tax Journal 11.

Lindsay (2006b):

Lindsay J, 'Convertibles and Exchangeables, Part 2: The Position for Investors' (2006) Tax Journal 13.

LucaNet, White paper (2023):

LucaNet, White paper, 'Key differences between IFRS and UK GAAP' (2022) https://www.icaew.com/-/media/corporate/files/insights/sponsored-content/key-differences-between-uk-gaap-and-ifrs-uk.ashx?la = en, accessed 1 March 2023.

Market Risk Advisory Committee of the US Commodity Futures Trading Commission (2020):

Market Risk Advisory Committee of the US Commodity Futures Trading Commission, Managing climate risk in the U.S. financial system, Report of the Climate-Related Subcommittee (2020), https://www.cftc.gov/sites/default/files/2020-09/9-9-20%20Report%20of%20the%20Subcommittee%20on%20Climate-Related%20Market%20Risk%20-%20Managing%20Climate%20Risk%20in%20the%20U.S.%20Financial%20System%20for%20posting.pdf, accessed 8 February 2024.

Martínez Laguna (2019):

Martínez Laguna F D, *Hybrid Financial Instruments, Double Non-taxation and Linking Rules* (Series on International Taxation, Wolters Kluwer 2019).

Matteotti (2012):

Matteotti R, 'Beneficial Ownership Switzerland' (Beneficial Ownership conference, Vienna, 18–19 May 2012).

Maulshagen and Maulshagen (2000):

Maulshagen A and Maulshagen O, 'Rechtliche und bilanzielle Behandlung von Swapgeschäften' BB 2000 243.

Maulshagen, Trepte and Walterscheidt (2008):

Maulshagen O, Trepte F and Walterscheidt S, *Derivative Finanzinstrumente in Industrieunternehmen* (4th edn, Fachverlag Moderne Wirtschaft 2008).

Maxwell (2014):

Maxwell F, 'Thousands of Derivatives Users Not Ready for Emir Reporting' Risk Magazine, http://www.risk.net/risk-magazine/news/2326624/thousands-of-derivatives-users-not-ready-for-emir-reporting accessed 4 August 2023.

McKenna (2022):

McKenna F, *Taxes are a wild card for public companies holding crypto*, 22 February 2022, https://finance.yahoo.com/news/taxes-wild-card-public-companies-145853836.html, accessed 28 February 2023.

Mendiratta et al. (2021):

Mendiratta R et al., How ESG Affected Corporate Credit Risk and Performance, Journal of Impact & ESG, vol. 2, issue 2, https://www.msci.com/documents/10199/19248715/Foundations-of-ESG-Investing-in-Corporate-Bonds-How-ESG-Affects-Corporate-Credit-Risk-and-Performance + (002).pdf, accessed 13 April 2023.

Meriam Webster Dictionary, greenwashing:

Merriam Webster Dictionary, definition of greenwashing, Merriam Webster Dictionary, definition of greenwashing, https://www.merriam-webster.com/dictionary/greenwashing, accessed 12 April 2023.

Merton (1973):

Merton R, 'Theory of Rational Option Pricing' (1973) 4 Bell Journal of Economics and Management Science 141.

MicroStrategy, Q2 2022 Financial Results (2022a):

MicroStrategy, Q2 Financial Results, 17, https://assets.contentstack.io/v3/assets/bltb564490bc5201f31/blt877d68364545d726/6541023a20567d001b090c87/Q2-2022_microstrategy-earnings-presentation_(1).pdf, accessed 28 February 2024.

Microstrategy, Q 4 2022 Financial Results (2022b):

MicroStrategy, Q 4 2022 Financial Results (2 February 2023), 15 https://assets.contentstack.io/v3/assets/bltb564490bc5201f31/bltb01b5df34532ba81/654a3b67e965d6040a3dd779/Q4-2022_microstrategy-earnings-presentation_(2).pdf, accessed 21 February 2024.

Miller (2001):

Miller D, 'Overview of the Taxation of Credit Derivatives' in Fabozzi F (ed.), *The Use of Derivatives in Tax Planning* (John Wiley & Sons, 2001).

Moddermann (2022):

Modderman G, Cointelegraph, Bitcoin as a payment method, 5 June 2022, https://cointelegraph.com/explained/who-accepts-bitcoin-as-payment, accessed 11 July 2023.

MSCI, ESG Indexes (2023):

MSCI, 30 years ESG indexes, https://www.msci.com/our-solutions/indexes/esg-indexes, accessed 12 April 2023.

MSCI, MSCI Screened Indexes (2023):

MSCI, MSCI Screened Indexes, https://www.msci.com/our-solutions/indexes/esg-screened-indexes, accessed 12 April 2023.

Mujkanovic (2018):

Mujkanovic R, NWB Experten Blog, Bilanzierung von Kryptowaehrungen nach HGB, 14 September 2018, https://www.nwb-experten-blog.de/bilanzierung-von-kryptowaehrungen-nach-hgb/, accessed 6 March 2023.

Muyldermans, De Haen and Jeunen (2002):

Muyldermans J, De Haen K and Jeunen T, 'Tax Treatment of Index Participation Units' (2002) Derivatives and Financial Instruments 2.

Nakamoto (2008):

Nakamoto S, *Bitcoin: A Peer-to-Peer Electronic Cash System*, 2008, satoshin@gmx.com, www.bitcoin.org, https://bitcoin.org/bitcoin.pdf, accessed 7 July 2023.

Natenberg (1994):

Natenberg S, *Option Volatility and Pricing* (McGraw-Hill 1994).

Neftci (2000):

Neftci S, *An Introduction to the Mathematics of Financial Derivatives* (3rd edn, Academic Press 2013).

Neighbour (1997):

Neighbour J, 'Innovative Financial Instruments Challenge the Global Tax System' (1997) Tax Notes International 931.

Neighbour (1998):

Neighbour J, 'The Taxation of Global Trading of Financial Instruments' (1998) Tax Notes International 1269.

Neighbour (2001):

Neighbour J, *Taxing Financial Innovation in a Global Economy* (in: Report of the Ad Hoc Group of Experts on International Co-operation in Tax Matters, UNPAN Conference Documents, 2001).

Neske (2005):

Neske C, 'Grundformen von Kreditderivaten' in Burghof H-P et al. (eds), *Kreditderivate* (2nd edn, Schäffer-Poeschel 2005).

Newman, Milgate and Eatwell (1992):

Newman P, Milgate M and Eatwell J (eds), *The New Palgrave Dictionary of Money and Finance* (Macmillan 1992).

New York Times (2022):

New York Times, 11 November 2022, Embattled Cryptoexchange FTX files for Bankruptcy, https://www.nytimes.com/2022/11/11/business/ftx-bankruptcy.html, accessed 11 January 2023.

Nguyen (2007):

Nguyen T, *Bilanzielle Abbildung von Finanzderivaten und Sicherungsgeschäften* (Herbert Utz Verlag 2007).

Niedling (2012):

Niedling D, 'Neuregelung des Kapitalertagsteuerabzugs durch das OGAW-IV-UmsG – erste Bestandsaufnahme und Problemfelder in der Praxis' Recht der Finanzinstrumente 2012, 43.

Nijenhuis (2011):

Nijenhuis E, 'New Tax Issues Arising from the Dodd-Frank Act and Related Changes to Market Practice for Derivatives' Columbia Journal of Tax Law, Vol. 2, No. 1 (2011) 1 .

Nobes (2004):

Nobes C, *A Conceptual Framework for the Taxable Income of Businesses, and How to Apply it under IFRS* (2004), http://citeseerx.ist.psu.edu/viewdoc/download;jsessionid=09E0A28B67755EF186BB905093E9D4F2?doi=10.1.1.193.1111&rep=rep1&type=pdf, accessed 13 May 2023.

Nguyen T, 'Differences Between Amortizations and Accruals':

Nguyen T, 'Differences Between Amortizations and Accruals' Chron. – on file with the author.

O'Neill (2015):

O'Neill D, OMNIPRO, FRS 102 Summary – Section 18 – Intangible Assets other than goodwill (18 December 2015), https://frs102.com/blog/2015/12/18/frs-102-summary-section-18-intangible-assets-other-than-goodwill/, accessed 23 February 2023.

OpenSea (2023):

OpenSea, *Discover, collect, and sell extraordinary NFTs*, https://opensea.io, accessed 21 July 2023.

Paez (2023):

Paez S, UN General Assembly Adopts International Tax Cooperation Resolution, Tax Notes Today International (TNTI) December 2023, 246-6, DOC 2023-37225.

PAIR (2020):

PAIR, Artificial Intelligence in Asset Allocation, Derivatives Pricing and Risk Management (2020), https://pairlabs.ai/en/portfolio-item/artificial-intelligence-in-asset

-allocation-derivatives-pricing-and-risk-management-p-en/, accessed 17 July 2023.

Parada (2018):

Parada L, *Double Non-Taxation and the Use of Hybrid Entities, An Alternative Approach in the New Era of BEPS* (Series on International Taxation, Wolters Kluwer, 2018).

Philipowski (2004):

Philipowski R, 'Verfall wertlos gewordener Kauf- und Verkaufsoptionen' DStR 2004 978.

Philipowski (2007):

Philipowski R, 'Werbungskosten bei fehlgeschlagenen Termingeschäften' DStR 2007 1615.

Pinder (2005):

Pinder G, 'The Coherent Principles Approach to Tax Law Design' Economic Round-Up, (Autumn 2005) 75–90, 75, Greg Pinder, 'The Coherent Principles Approach to Tax Law Design' (2005) Economic Round-up, 75–90, https://treasury.gov.au/publication/economic-roundup-autumn-2005/the-coherent-principles-approach-to-tax-law-design, accessed 2 January 2023.

Pinsent Masons (2013):

Pinsent Masons, Out-law.com, 'Proposed EU Financial Transaction Tax Not Legal, Say EU Lawyers' (10 September 2013) http://www.out-law.com/en/articles/2013/september/proposed-eu-financial-transaction-tax-not-legal-say-eu-lawyers/ accessed 20 September 2013.

Prasad (2021):

Prasad E, *Five Myths about Cryptocurrency*, OP-ED, Brookings, 24 May 2021, https://www.brookings.edu/opinions/five-myths-about-cryptocurrency/, accessed 4 July 2023.

PRI – Principles for Responsible Investments:

PRI – Principles for Responsible Investments, ESG incorporation in securitised products: challenges ahead (May 2021), https://www.unpri.org/fixed-income/esg-incorporation-in-securitised-products-the-challenges-ahead/7462.article, accessed 25 May 2023.

Prinz (2003):

Prinz U, 'Reform der deutschen Rechnungslegung – Gedanken und Anregungen an den Gesetzgeber zur Umsetzung der Mitgliedstaatenwahlrechte der IAS/IFRS-Verordnung aus Praktikersicht' DStR 2003 1359.

PWC (2014):

PWC, IFRS 9 – Expected credit losses (13 August 2014), https://www.pwc.nl/nl/banken/assets/documents/in-depth-ifrs9-expected-credit-losses.pdf, accessed 14 March 2023.

PWC (2017):

PWC, IFRS 9, Financial Instruments, Understanding the basics (2017), https://www.studocu.com/id/document/universitas-indonesia/economics/ifrs-9-understanding-the-basics/4238425, accessed 9 February 2024.

PWC (2021a):

PWC, 2.4.2. Accounting for forward contracts and options to acquire real estate (13 December 2021, updated 1 February 2023), https://viewpoint.pwc.com/dt/ca/en/pwc/industry/industry_INT/industry_INT/real_estate__1_INT/Applying-IFRS-for-the-real-est/2_Acquisition_or_construction_of_real_estate/2_4_Asset_acquisitions_measurement_at_initial_recognition/2_4_2_Accounting_for_forward_contracts_and_options_to_acquire_real_estate.html, accessed 15 March 2023.

PWC (2021b):

PWC, Crypto assets, August 2021, 3-5, https://viewpoint.pwc.com/dt/us/en/pwc/accounting_guides/crypto-assets-guide/assets/crypto9202021.pdf, accessed 29 May 2023.

PWC (2022):

PWC, UK GAAP Illustrative financial statements, For 2021 Year ends, January 2022, https://viewpoint.pwc.com/dt/uk/en/pwc/ilustrative_financia/assets/UK_illustrative_accounts_year_ended_31_December_2021_FRS_102_0222.pdf, accessed 6 May 2023.

PWC, Cryptographic assets and related transactions (2019):

PWC, Cryptographic assets and related transactions: accounting considerations under IFRS, December 2019, https://www.pwc.com/gx/en/audit-services/ifrs/ publications/ifrs-16/cryptographic-assets-related-transactions-accounting-considerations-ifrs-pwc-in-depth.pdf, accessed 8 July 2023.

PWC, DAC6:

PWC, DAC6, The EU Directive on cross-border tax arrangements, https://www.pwc.com/gx/en/services/tax/tax-policy-administration/dac6-eu-directive-on-cross-border-tax-arrangements.html, accessed 20 July 2023.

PWC, Hedge effectiveness criterion (2019):

PWC, Hedge effectiveness criterion, 13 October 2019, https://viewpoint.pwc.com/dt/us/en/pwc/accounting_guides/ifrs_and_us_gaap_sim/ifrs_and_us_gaap_sim_US/chapter_11_derivativ_US/118hedge_effectivene_US.html, accessed 25 April 2023.

PWC, Latest News from the Standardsetters and Regulators:

PWC, Latest News from the Standardsetters and Regulators (23 May 2023), https://viewpoint.pwc.com/dt/gx/en/pwc/esg/external/esg-external/global-sustainability/global-pwc-sustainability-reporting-newsletter-may-2023/latest-news-from-the-standard-setters-and-regulators.html, accessed 27 May 2023

PWC, Pillar Two:

PWC, 'Pillar Two', https://www.pwc.com/us/en/services/tax/multinationals/pillar-two-model-for-data-and-reporting.html, accessed 15 March 2023.

PWC, Pillar Two Guide (2023):

PWC, Pillar Two Model Rules, Private companies take note: Pillar Two Guide for US Multinational Enterprises, 22 August 2023, https://www.pwc.com/us/en/services/trust-solutions/private-company-services/library/pillar-two-guide.html, accessed 3 January 2024.

Ratschow in Blümich (2013) § 20 EStG:

Ratschow E, '§ 20 EStG' in Heuermann B and Brandis P (eds), Blümich, EStG, KStG GewStG Kommentar (2013).

Rau (2006):

Rau S, 'Zur steuerbilanziellen Behandlung von Aktienanleihen' DStR 2006, 627.

Redson (2005–2006):

Redson A, *University of London LL.M. Handout, Loan Relationships* (2005–2006) - on file with the author.

Reedsmith Client Alerts (2020):

Reedsmith Client Alerts, First German Tax Court decision on the qualification of Bitcoins (2020), https://www.reedsmith.com/en/perspectives/2020/02/first-german-tax-court-decision-on-qualification-of-bitcoins, accessed 1 September 2023.

Reich (2007):

Reich Y, 'International Arbitrage Transactions Involving Creditable Taxes' (2007) Taxes - The Tax Magazine, 53.

Reiner (2002):

Reiner G, *Derivative Finanzinstrumente im Recht*, (Deutsches, Europäisches und Vergleichendes Wirtschaftsrecht, Band 24, Nomos, 2002), https://www.nomos-elibrary.de/10.5771/9783845287164/derivative-finanzinstrumente-im-recht, accessed 14 January 2023.

Reislhuber and Bacmeister (2010):

Reislhuber A and Bacmeister F, 'Weitere ausgewählte Aspekte des neuen BMF - Anwendungsschreibens zur Abgeltungsteuer' DStR 2010 684.

Rengers in Blümich (2013) § 8b KStG:

Rengers J, '§ 8b KStG' in Heuermann B and Brandis P (eds), Blümich, EStG, KStG GewStG Kommentar (120th edn, 2013).

Rigby (2023):

Rigby, Where is vaping banned? Countries with strict e-cig laws, https://vapoholic.co.uk/2022/02/11/where-is-vaping-banned-countries-with-strictest-e-cig-laws/, accessed 14 June 2023.

Rohit (2022):

Rohit KVN, After Bitcoin, Tesla now accepts Dogecoin cryptocurrency for merchandise purchase, 22 January 2022, Deccanherald, https://www.deccanherald.com/business/technology/after-bitcoin-tesla-now-accepts-dogecoin-cryptocurrency-for-merchandise-purchase-1071023.html, accessed 20 July 2023.

Romer (2011):

Romer P, 'Process, Responsibility, and Myron's Law', Chapter 12 in: In the Wake of the Crisis: Leading Economists Reassess Economic Policy, Olivier J. Blanchard, David Romer, A. Michael Spence and Joseph E. Stiglitz (eds) Cambridge: MIT Press, 2012, 111, 112.

Root (2023):

Root A, Tesla Got Added to an ESG Index. But Oil and Tobacco Firms Scored Higher, Barron's, 1 June 2023, https://www.barrons.com/articles/tesla-chevron-stock-sp500-esg-score-index-bf95e0fe, accessed 13 February 2024.

Rose and Glorius-Rose (2000):

Rose G and Glorius-Rose C, 'Missbrauchsrechtsprechung des BFH in Bewegung' DB 2000 1633.

Rosenbloom (2000):

Rosenbloom D, International Tax Arbitrage, (2000) 53 Tax Law Review, 137.

Rubinstein (1999a):

Rubinstein M, *Rubinstein on Derivatives* (Risk Books 1999).

Rubinstein (1999b):

Rubinstein M, *Derivatives: A PowerPlus Picture Book* vol. 1 (In-The-Money 1999).

Rudolph (1999):

Rudolph B, *Derivative Finanzinstrumente* (Schäffer-Poeschel Verlag 1999).

Rudolph and Schäfer (2010):

Rudolph B and Schäfer K, *Derivative Finanzmarktinstrumente: Eine anwendungsbezogene Einführung* (2nd edn, Springer 2010).

Sadiq, Sawyer and McCredie (2019):

Sadiq K, Sawyer A and McCredie B, *Tax Design and Administration in a Post-BEPS Era: A Study of Key Reform Measures in 18 Jurisdictions* (Fiscal Publications 2019).

Schaber et al. (2010):

Schaber M et al., *Handbuch strukturierte Finanzinstrumente, HGB – IFRS* (2nd edn, IDW Verlag 2010).

Scharpf and Luz (2000):

Scharpf P and Luz G, *Risikomanagement, Bilanzierung und Aufsicht von Finanzderivaten* (2nd edn, Schäffer-Poeschel Verlag 2000); further edn referred to 1st edn (1999).

Scharpf and Schaber (2009):

Scharpf P and Schaber M, *Handbuch Bankbilanz* (3rd edn, IDW Verlag 2009).

Scheffler (2011):

Scheffler W, *Besteuerung von Unternehmen II, Steuerbilanz* (7th edn, C.F. Müller Verlag 2011).

Schizer (2004):

Schizer D, 'Balance in the Taxation of Derivative Securities: An Agenda for Reform' (2004) Columbia Law and Economics Working paper No. 247.

Schmid and Renner (2005):

Schmid H and Renner G, 'Bilanzielle und steuerliche Behandlung einer Kaufoption (long call)' DStR 2005 815.

Schmidt, EStG (2012):

Weber-Grellet H (ed.) *Schmidt Einkommensteuergesetz Kommentar* (31st edn, C.H-.Beck 2012).

Schmidt (2023):

Schmidt J, 'Accruals Accounting' (updated 4 January 2023) Corporate Finance Institute, https://corporatefinanceinstitute.com/resources/accounting/accrual-accounting-guide/, accessed 16 February 2023.

Schmittmann and Welper (2001):

Schmittmann P and Welper A, 'Voraussetzungen der Verlustausgleichsbeschränkung bei Termingeschäften im Betriebsvermögen' DStR 2001 1783.

Schmitz and Huthmann (2012):

Schmitz F and Huthmann A, *Bilanzierung von Finanzinstrumenten, IAS/IFRS und BilMoG* (Gabler 2012).

Schoenfeld and Erdem (2022):

Schoenfeld J and Erdem E, Anti-Treaty-Shopping und EU-Recht, Die Neufassung des § 50d Abs. 3 EStG durch das AbzStEntModG, (ottoschmidt 2022).

Schön (2002):

Schön W, 'Arbeitskreis Bilanzrecht der Hochschullehrer Rechtswissenschaft' BB 2002 2379.

Schön (2004):

Schön W, 'International Accounting Standards – a "Starting Point" for a Common European Tax Base?' *European Taxation, Vol. 44, No. 10, 2004, 426-440*, https://papers.ssrn.com/sol3/papers.cfm?abstract_id=1603758, accessed 1 February 2024.

Schön (2005):

Schön W, *Steuerliche Maßgeblichkeit in Deutschland und Europa* (Verlag Dr Otto Schmid 2005).

Schön et al. (2014):

Schön W et al., 'Debt and Equity in Domestic and International Tax Law – A Comparative Policy Analysis' (2014) BTR 146.

Schreiber in Blümich (2006) § 5 EStG:

Schreiber J, '§ 5 EStG' in Heuermann B (ed.), Blümich, EStG, KStG, GewStG, Kommentar (91st edn, Verlag Franz Vahlen 2006).

Schumacher (2000):

Schumacher A, 'Die Besteuerung von Compound Instruments beim Privatanleger am Beispiel von Reverse Convertibles' DStR 2000 416.

Schumacher (2001):

Schumacher A, 'Nochmals: Besteuerung von Hochzins- und Umtauschanleihen' DStR 2001 1021.

Schwark (2000):

Schwark E, 'Ist die Aktienanleihe ein Börsentermingeschäft?' WM 2000 1973.

Seneca, Dialogs and Essays:

Seneca L A, Dialogs and Essays, On the Happy Life, To Gallio, Neeland Media, 2021.

Senior (2022):

Senior T, *The Best Steam Skins*, 2022, https://www.pcgamer.com/the-best-steam-skins/, accessed 20 July 2023.

Sharecast (2023):

Sharecast, What does China's Digital Yuan mean for Bitcoin?, https://www.sharecast.com/promoted/cryptocurrencies/what-does-chinas-digital-yuan-mean-for-bitcoin.html, accessed 7 February 2023.

Sheppard (2006a):

Sheppard L, 'New Analysis: Global Dealing Regulations and the Hedge Fund Model' (2006) Tax Notes International 945.

Sheppard (2006b):

Sheppard L, 'New Analysis: Banks' Foreign Tax Credit Arbitrage' (2006) Tax Notes International 193.

Sibarium (2023):

Sibarium A, How Tobacco Companies are crushing ESG ratings, The Washington Free Beacon, 13 June 2023, https://freebeacon.com/latest-news/how-tobacco-companies-are-crushing-esg-ratings/, accessed 1 August 2023.

Simon's Taxes (2022):

Simon's Taxes, vol. 5 (Lexis Nexis UK, 2008, Looseleaf) (Issue 171, December 2022).

Singh (2021):

Singh A, NDTV, Can cryptocurrency Be converted into Cash? 31 October 2021, https://www.ndtv.com/business/can-cryptocurrency-be-converted-into-cash-read-on-to-find-out-2594499, accessed 17 July 2023.

Société Générale (2019):

Société Générale, Enel Electrifies Sustainability Market With Inaugural Green-Linked Bond And Swap (2019), https://wholesale.banking.societegenerale.com/en/news-insights/clients-successes/clients-successes-details/news/enel-electrifies-sustainability-market-with-inaugural-green-linked-bond-and-swap/, accessed 2 September 2023.

Soong (2023):

Soong S, 'ASEAN Investment Ministers Call for Global Minimum Tax Review' (2023), 111 Tax Notes International, 1151.

Southern (2017):

Southern D, *Taxation of Loan Relationships and Derivative Contracts* (10th edn, Bloomsbury 2017); further eds referred to: 6th (2002), 7th (2004), 8th (2007) and 9th (2012).

Southern, Supplement (2020):

Southern D, Taxation of Loan Relationships and Derivative Contracts, Supplement to the 10th Edition (Bloomsbury Professional 2020).

Southern (2023):

Southern D, The Taxation of Redeemable Preference Shares, FCTC Digest, 14th edn, 2023, 66, https://www.fieldtax.com/wp-content/uploads/2023/09/FCTC-Digest-14th-Edition-March-2023.pdf, accessed 1 November 2023.

Southern and Weidmann (2023):

Southern D and Weidmann O, 'Cryptotaxation: A Guide to a Brave New World', British Tax Review 2023, Issue 1, 68-96.

Southon (2011):

Southon S, 'Chapter E2: Taxation of Derivatives: Australia' in Conlon S and Aquilino V (eds), *Principles of Financial Derivatives, US and International Taxation* (WG&L 2011).

Spengel (2003):

Spengel C, 'International Accounting Standards und Unternehmensbesteuerung in der Europäischen Union (Teil 1)' IStR 2003 29.

Statista (2023):

Statista, Bitcoin price per day from April 2013 to February 2023, https://www.statista.com/statistics/326707/bitcoin-price-index/, accessed 18 February 2023.

Steinberg (2001):

Steinberg LR, 'Using OTC Equity Derivatives for High-Net-Worth Individuals' in Fabozzi FJ (ed.), *The Use of Derivatives in Tax Planning* (Wiley 2001).

Steinherr (1998):

Steinherr A, *Derivatives, The Wild Beast of Finance* (Wiley 1998).

Stobbe in H/H/R (2013) § 5:

Stobbe T, '§ 5' in Herrmann C, Heuer G and Raupach A (eds), *Einkommensteuer- und Körperschaftsteuergesetz Kommentar* (Verlag Dr Otto Schmidt KG 2013).

Stobbe (2021):

Stobbe S, Bitcoin & Co, Kryptowährungen im externen Rechnungswesen, (Westermann 2021), https://www.westermann.de/landing/schmolke-deitermann/bitcoin#p394643, accessed 6 March 2023.

Strnad (1994):

Strnad J, 'Taxing New Financial Products: A Conceptual Framework' (1994) 46 Stanford Law Review 569.

Strnad (2003):

Strnad J, 'Taxing Convertible Debt' (2003) 56 SMU Law Review 399.

Stuhrmann in Blümich (2010) § 15 EStG:

Stuhrmann G, '§ 15 EStG' in Heuermann B (ed.), *Blümich, EStG, KStG GewStG Kommentar* (Vahlen 2010).

Stuhrmann in Blümich (2010) § 20 EStG:

Stuhrmann G, '§ 20 EStG' in Heuermann B (ed.), *Blümich, EStG, KStG GewStG Kommentar* (Vahlen 2010).

S&P Global (2023):

S&P Global, S&P Global Inc. ESG Score, https://www.spglobal.com/esg/scores/results?cid=4574287, accessed 12 June 2023.

Tappen and Wehe (2022):

Tappen F and Wehe S, Bilanzierung von Kryptoassets, IWW Institute (1 July 2022), https://www.iww.de/pstr/schwerpunktthema/kryptowaehrungen-bilanzierung-von-kryptoassets-f146883, accessed 1 October 2023.

Teiss (2022):

Teiss M, NFT Collections Explained (Dexterlab 2022), https://dexterlab.com/nft-derivatives/, accessed 1 September 2023.

Teller (2023):

Teller A, CoinTax, 'The Essential Guide to Crypto Tax in Germany' (23 February 2023), https://tokentax.co/blog/crypto-taxes-in-germany, accessed 21 April 2023.

Theophilou (2022):

Theophilou, 'Deconstructing Pillar Two—Impact on Multinational Enterprises' Bloomberg Tax, 2022, https://news.bloombergtax.com/daily-tax-report-international/deconstructing-pillar-two-impact-on-multinational-enterprises, accessed 30 July 2023.

Thomas (2008):

Thomas R, 'Principles-Based Approach to Financial Products Avoidance' (CBT Summer Conference, 20 and 21 June 2008, Saïd Business School, Oxford) - on file with the author.

Thuronyi (2001a):

Thuronyi V, 'Taxation of New Financial Instruments' (2001) 24 Tax Notes International 261.

Thuronyi (2001b):

Thuronyi V, *International Tax Aspects of New Financial Instruments* (in: Report of the Ad Hoc Group of Experts on International Cooperation in Tax Matters, UNPAN conference documents, 2001), https://digitallibrary.un.org/record/44676, accessed 1 February 2024.

Thuronyi (2001c):

Thuronyi V, *Taxation of New Financial Instruments* (in: Report of the Ad Hoc Group of Experts on International Cooperation in Tax Matters; UNPAN conference documents, 2001), https://digitallibrary.un.org/record/453791, accessed 1 February 2024.

Tolley's CGT 2022-23:

Tolley's Capital Gains Tax 2022-23 (Tolley Publishing, 2022).

Trofi Group (2022):

Trofi Group, What Are Crypto Structured Products (4 May 2022), https://blog.trofi.group/what-are-crypto-structured-products-1c3f648f163f, accessed 29 May 2023.

UK.Gov, Correspondence:

UK.Gov, Correspondence, UK accounting and audit framework from 1 January 2021, https://www.gov.uk/government/publications/uk-accounting-and-audit-framework-from-1-january-2021, accessed 23 February 2023.

Vallada (2014):

Vallada F, *Beneficial Ownership under Articles 10, 11 and 12 of the 2014 OECD Model Convention* in *The OECD-Model-Convention and Its Update 2014*, 25, 32-35 (Michael Lang et al. eds, Linde 2014).

Vann (1998):

Vann R, 'Chapter 18, International Aspects of Income Tax' in Thuronyi V (ed.), *Tax Law Design and Drafting*, vol. 2 (International Monetary Fund 1998).

Vann (2003):

Vann R, 'Reflections on Business Profits and the Arm's Length Principle' in Arnold B, Sasseville J and Zolt E (eds), *The Taxation of Business Profits under Tax Treaties* (Canadian Tax Foundation 2003).

Vann (2012):

Vann R, 'Beneficial Ownership: OECD 2011 Draft and History' (Beneficial Ownership conference, Vienna, 18–19 May 2012).

Vermeulen (2021):

Vermeulen D-S, Managing Climate Risk with CME Weather Futures and Options (20 January 2021), https://www.cmegroup.com/education/articles-and-reports/managing-climate-risk-with-cme-group-weather-futures-and-options.html, accessed 8 May 2023.

Vidal (2018):

Vidal P, Refinitiv, 'IFRS 9 Hedge Accounting: A Financial Opportunity for Corporate Treasuries' (24 May 2018) – on file with the author.

Vogel and Lehner (2008):

Vogel K and Lehner M (eds), *Doppelbesteuerungsabkommen* (5th edn, C.H.Beck 2008).

Vogel and Lehner (2015):

Vogel K & Lehner M, *Doppelbesteuerungsabkommen, Kommentar* (6th edn, C.H.Beck 2015).

Volatility calculator (2023):

Volatility calculator, https://vlab.stern.nyu.edu/volatility/VOL.BTCUSD%3AFOREX-R.GARCH, accessed 2 July 2023.

Wales and Wales (2012):

Wales CJ and Wales CP, *Structures, Processes and Governance in Tax Policy-Making: an Initial Report* (Oxford University, Centre for Business Taxation, 2012).

Wappenschmidt (2022).

Wappenschmidt W, Bloomberg Professional Services, ESG Structured Products Rise to Meet Investor Demands (29 May 2022), https://www.bloomberg.com/professional/blog/esg-structured-products-rise-to-meet-investor-demand/?bbgsum-page=DG-WS-PROF-BLOG-POST-137418&tactic-page=630365, accessed 25 May 2023.

Warren (1993):

Warren A, 'Financial Contract Innovation and Income Tax Policy' (1993) 107 Harvard Law Review 460.

Wassermeyer (2014):

Wassermeyer F, *Doppelbesteuerung, Kommentar zu allen deutschen Doppelbesteuerungsabkommen* vol. 1 (Loose leaf, C.H. Beck Verlag 2014), Art. 10 OECD-MA, Eigene Kommentierung (125th issue)

Wassermeyer (2022):

Wassermeyer F (ed.), *Doppelbesteuerung, Kommentar zu allen deutschen Doppelbesteuerungsabkommen*, vol. 1 (Looseleaf, 89th edn, C.H. Beck Verlag, August 2022) Art. 11 Zinsen, Eigene Kommentierung, (158th issue).

Weisbach (2005):

Weisbach D, 'Colloquium on Financial Instruments: Tax Responses to Financial Contract Innovation' (2005) 50 Tax Law Review 491.

Weidmann (2015):

Weidmann O, *Taxation of Derivatives* (Wolters Kluwer 2015).

Weidmann (2016):

Weidmann O, 'Beneficial Ownership and Derivatives: An Analysis of the Decision of the Swiss Federal Supreme Court Concerning Total Return Swaps' 44 Intertax 8&9 (2016), 620-641.

Weidmann (2017):

Weidmann O, 'Beneficial Ownership and Derivatives: Has the Swiss Federal Supreme Court Decision in the SMI Futures Case Put an End to Cash-Futures Arbitrage?' 45 Intertax 3, (2017), 229-253.

Wendt (1999):

Wendt M, 'Steuerentlastungsgesetz 1999/2000/2002: Änderungen bei betrieblichen und privaten Veräußerungsgeschäften' FR 1999, 333.

Wendt in H/H/R, Steuerreform I (2001) § 15:

Wendt M, '§ 15' in Herrmann C, Heuer G and Raupach A (eds), *Einkommen-und Körperschaftsteuergesetz, Steuerreform I* (Verlag Dr Otto Schmidt 2001).

Wendt et al. in H/H/R, Steuerreform I (2001) § 6:

Wendt M et al., '§ 6' in Herrmann C, Heuer G and Raupach A (eds), *Einkommen-und Körperschaftsteuergesetz, Steuerreform I* (Verlag Dr. Otto Schmidt 2001).

Wendt in H/H/R (2010) § 15:

Wendt M, '§ 15' in Herrmann C, Heuer G and Raupach A (eds), *Raupach Einkommen- und Körperschaftsteuergesetz Kommentar* (Verlag Dr Otto Schmidt 2010).

Whaley (2006):

Whaley R, *Derivatives: Markets, Valuation, and Risk Management* (John Wiley & Sons, Inc. 2006).

Wheeler (2020):

Wheeler J, *The Aftermath of BEPS* (IBFD 2020).

Whittington (2004):

Whittington G, 'Accounting Standards as a Basis for Taxation: The Case Against' (Tax law workshop on accounting principles and taxable profits, Queen's College, Cambridge, 16 January 2004).

Wiese and Dammer (1999):

Wiese G and Dammer T, 'Zusammengesetzte Finanzinstrumente der AG' DStR 1999 867.

Wiesenbart (2011):

Wiesenbart T, 'Internationale Steuerfragen bei derivativen Finanzinstrumenten' Recht der Finanzinstrumente 2011, 106.

Wigmore (2018):

Wigmore I, Bitcoin Address, July 2018, https://www.techtarget.com/whatis/definition/Bitcoin-address, accessed 1 August 2023.

Wilmott (2000):

Wilmott P, *Derivatives* (Wiley 2000).

Witt in H/H/R (2022) § 15:

Witt S, '§ 15' in Herrmann C, Heuer G and Raupach A (eds), *Einkommensteuer - und Körperschaftsteuergesetz, Kommentar* (Verlag Dr Otto Schmidt 2022), further edition referred to: 2013.

Wittgenstein (1922):

Wittgenstein L, *Tractatus Logico-Philosphicus* (Ogden C tr, Kegan Paul, Trench, Trubner & Co Ltd 1922).

Wohlfahrt and Brause (1998):

Wohlfahrt J and Brause C, 'Strukturierte Wertpapiergeschäfte als Termingeschäfte?' WM 1998 1859.

Worldbank (2015):

Worldbank, What are green bonds?, 1 December 2015, https://documents1.worldbank.org/curated/en/400251468187810398/pdf/99662-REVISED-WB-Green-Bond-Box393208B-PUBLIC.pdf, accessed 12 April 2023.

Woywode (2006):

Woywode U, 'Die abkommensrechtliche Einordnung von Einkünften aus Swapverträgen' IStR 2006 368.

YieldApp (2023):

YieldApp, An Introduction to Crypto Structured Products: Variable Risk Return Profiles, Blog, https://yield.app/blog/intro-crypto-structured-products#:~:text=Structured%20products%20are%20investment%20products,the%20return%20profile%20in%20the, accessed 30 May 2023.

Zelinsky (1997):

Zelinsky EA, 'For Realization: Income Taxation, Sectoral Accretionism, and the Virtue of Attainable Virtues' (1997) 19 Cardozo Law Review 861.

Table of Cases and Decisions

European Union

Commission v. Germany C-284/09 [2011] ECR I-09879, Ch. 6 §6.04, Ch. 9 §9.01[C][2]

van Caster and van Caster C-326/12, Judgement of the Court (First Chamber) of 9 October 2014 (ECLI:EU:C:2014:2269), Ch. 10 §10.04

T Danmark and others, CJEU decision of 26 February 2019, C-116/16, ECLI: EU:C:2019:135, Ch. 10 §10.02[A][5]

N Luxembourg and others, CJEU decision of 26 February 2019, C115/16, ECLI: EU:C:2019:134, Ch. 10 §10.02[A][5]

Netherlands

Hoge Raad (Dutch Supreme Court), No. 28 638 of 4 April 1994, BNB 1994/ 217, cited in Du Toit, Beneficial Ownership of Royalties in Bilateral Treaties, 151ff., Ch. 9 §9.02[A]

New Zealand

Alesco New Zealand Ltd and others v. Commissioner of Inland Revenue CA53/2012 [2013] NZCA 40, Ch. 10 §10.01[C][1]

Germany

Federal Fiscal Court

BFH, decision of 21 February 1973, I R 106/71, BFHE 109, 22, BStBl II 1973, 460, Ch. 8 §8.06[B][2][b]

BFH, decision of 5 March 1981, IV R 94/78, BStBl II 1981, 658, Ch. 5 §5.03[B]

BFH, decision of 8 December 1981, VIII R 125/79, BStBl II 1982, 618, Ch. 4 §4.06[B][4]

BFH, decision of 17 January 1991, IV R 132/85, BFHE 163, 449, BStBl II 1991, 607, Ch. 10 §10.02[C]

BFH, decision of 4 July 1991, IV R 29/88, BStBl II 1992, 76, Ch. 5 §5.03[B]

BFH, decision of 12 September 1991, III R 233/90, BStBl II 1992, 182, Ch. 9 §9.02[C]

BFH, decision of 16 January 1992, V R 1/91, BFHE 167, 215, BStBl II 1992, 541, Ch. 10 §10.02[C]

BFH, decision of 3 February 1993, I B 90/92, BFHE 170, 197, BStBl II 1993, 426, Ch. 10 §10.02[C]

BFH, decision of 19 February 1997, IX R 1/96, BStBl II 1997, 399, Ch. §5.03[B]

BFH, decision of 23 June 1997, GrS 2/93, BStBl II 1997, 735, Ch. 5 §5.03[B]

BFH, decision of 1 October 1997, X R 91/94, BStBl II 1998, 203, Ch. 9 §9.02[C]

BFH, decision of 21 January 1999, IV R 96/96, BStBl II 2002, 771, Ch. 10 §10.02[C]

BFH, decision of 19 August 1999, I R 77/96, BStBl II 2001, 43, Ch. 10 §10.02[C]

BFH, decision of 15 December 1999, I R 29/97, BStBl II 2000, 527, Ch. 10 §10.02[C]

BFH, decision of 19 January 2000, I R 94/97, BStBl II 2001, 222, DB 2000, 651, Ch. 10 §10.02[C]

BFH, decision of 18 December 2002, I R 17/02, BStBl II 2004, 126, BB 2003, 1006, Ch. 6 §6.06[C][2][b][i](A)(2)(aa)(1), §6.06[C][2][b][i](A)(2)(cc), §6.06[C][2][b][i](B)(1)

BFH, decision of 19 April 2005, VIII R 80/02, Ch. 10 §10.02[A][3]

BFH, decision of 30 November 2005, I R 26/04, BFH/NV 2006, 616, DStRE 2006, 385, Ch. 8 §8.06[B][2][b]

BFH, decision of 19 December 2006, IX R 33/04, BFH/NV 2007, 1097, Ch. 9 A9.02[C]

BFH, decision of 17 April 2007, IX R 40/06, BStBl II 2007, 608, DStR 2007, 1075, Ch. 6 §6.06[C][2][b][i](A)(2)(aa)(1), §6.06 [C][2][b][i](B)(2)(aa)

BFH, decision of 3 May 2007, VI R 36/05, BStBl II 2007, 647, DStR 2007, 1158, Ch. 6 §6.06[C][2][b][i](A)(2)(aa)(1)

BFH, decision of 26 September 2007, I R 58/06, BStBl II 2009, 294, Ch. 6 §6.06[C][2][a]

BFH, decision of 11 October 2007, IV R 52/04, BStBl II 2009, 705, WPg 2008, 216, Ch. 6 §6.06[C][2][b][i](B)(1)

BFH, decision of 19 December 2007, IX R 11/06, BStBl II 2008, 519, DStR 2008, 968, Ch. 6 §6.06[C][2][b][i](A)(2)(aa)(1)

BFH, decision of 9 October 2008, IX R 69/07, BFH/NV 2009, 152, Ch. 6 §6.06[C][2][b][i](A)(2)(aa)(1)

BFH, decision of 25 August 2009, IX R 60/07, BStBl II 2009, 999, Ch. 10 §10.02[C]

BFH, decision of 6 March 2013, I R 18/12, DB 2013, 1274, Ch. 6 §6.06[C][2][b][i](A)(2)(aa)(1), §6.06[C][2][b][i](B)(2)(cc)[ii]

BFH decision of 12 January 2016, IX R 48/14, BStBl 2016 II, 456, Ch. 6 §6.06[C][2][b][i](A)(2)(aa)(1)

BFH decision of 6 July 2016, I R 25/14, BStBl II, 124, Ch. 4 §4.03[C][2], Ch. 6 §6.06[C][2][b][i](A)(2)(aa)(1)

BFH decision of 24 October 2017, VIII R 35/15, BStBl II 2018, 189, Ch. 6 §6.06[C][2][b][i](A)(2)(aa)(1)

BFH, decision of 20 November 2018, VIII R 37/15 BStBl 2019 II S. 507, Ch. 4 §4.03[C][2], Ch. 6 §6.06[C][2][b][i](A)(2)(aa)(1)

BFH, decision of 17 November 2020, I R 2018, BStBl II 2021, 580, Ch. 10 §10.02[A][5]

BFH, decision of 17 January 2023, Az. IX R 15/20, Ch. 6 §6.06[A]

BFH decision of 14 February 2023, IX R 3/22, ECLI:DE:BFH:2023:U.140223.IXR3.22.0, Ch. 5 §5.05[C]

Lower Fiscal Courts (Finanzgerichte)

FG Baden-Württemberg, decision of 5 June 2003, 14 K 190/02, EFG 2004, 907, Ch. 6 §6.06[C][2][b][i](A)(2)(aa)(1)

FG Berlin-Brandenburg, 20 June 2019, 13 V 13100/19, Ch. 5 §5.05[C]

FG Münster, decision of 7 December 2005, 10 K 5715/04, EFG 2006, 669, Ch. 6 §6.06[C][2][b][i](A)(2)(aa)(1)

FG Rheinland-Pfalz, decision of 19 May 2005, 4 K 1678/02, DStRE 2005, 1326, Ch. 6 §6.06[C][2][b][i](A)(2)(aa)(1)

Niedersächsisches FG, decision of 12 September 2007, 2 K 252/05, DStRE 2008, 473, Ch. 6 §6.06[C][2][b][i](A)(2)(aa)(1)

Finanzgericht Koeln, decision of 18 December 2018, 8K 3086/16, Ch. 6 §6.06[C][2][a]

Finanzgericht Baden Wuertemberg (FG BaWue), decision of 22 July 2019, 10K 1157/17, Ch. 6 §6.06[C][2][a]

Spain

Goldman Sachs case I Audiencia Nacional of 25 November 2010, rec no. 389/2007, cited in Jimenez, Beneficial Ownership as an Attribution-of-Income Rule in Spain: Source and Residence Country Perspectives in: Beneficial Ownership: Recent Trends (IBFD 2013) 199ff, Ch. 9 §9.02[E][1]

Goldman Sachs case II Audiencia Nacional of 23 February 2012, rec no. 182/2009, cited in Jimenez, Beneficial Ownership as an Attribution-of-Income Rule in Spain: Source and Residence Country Perspectives in: Beneficial Ownership: Recent Trends (IBFD 2013) 199ff, Ch. 9 §9.02[E][1]

Switzerland

Swiss Federal Administrative Tribunal (Bundesverwaltungsgericht) decision of 7 March 2012, A-6537/2010; also cited as: 'Re Swiss Swaps Case I/A, A-6537/2010' (2012) 14 ITLR 638, Ch. 9 §9.02[E][2], §9.02[E][2][a][i], §9.02[E][2][c]

Swiss Federal Administrative Tribunal (Bundesverwaltungsgericht) decision of 23 July 2012, A-1246/2011, Ch. 9 §9.02[E][2], §9.02[E][2][b], §9.02[E][2][c]

Swiss Federal Administrative Tribunal (Bundesverwaltungsgericht) decision of 13 March 2013, A-4794/2012, Ch. 9 §9.02[E][2][c]

Swiss Federal Supreme Court (Bundesgericht) decision of 5th May 2015, 2C_364/2012 and 2C_377/2012 (Swiss Swaps Case), Re Swiss Swaps Case I/A in 18 ITLR, 138, Ch. 3 §3.06[B], Ch. 9 §9.02[E][2][a][ii], Ch. 9 §9.02[E][2][b]

Swiss Federal Supreme Court (Bundesgericht) decision of 2 October 2015, 2C_383/2013 (Single Stock Futures Case), Ch. 3 §3.06[B], Ch. 9 §9.02[E][2][c]

Swiss Federal Supreme Court (Bundesgericht) decision of 5 May 2015, 2C_895/*2012* (SMI Futures Case), Ch. 3 §3.06[B]

Swiss Federal Supreme Court, 2C_880/2018, decision of 19 May 2020, *A Plc v. Swiss Tax Administration* in 23 ITLR, 864, Ch. 3 §3.06[B]

United Kingdom

Abbey National Treasury Services Plc v. R&C Commissioners [2015] SFTD 929, Ch. 10 §10.01[E][5]

Barclays Mercantile Business Finance Ltd v. Mawson (Inspector of Taxes) [2004] UKHL 51, Ch. 10 §10.04[B][3][e][i]

Beswick v. Beswick [1968] AC 58, Ch. 4 §4.03[A][2]

Bristol & West plc v. R&C Commissioners [2016] STC 1491, Ch.10 §10.01[E][6]

CIR v. Livingston [1926] 11 TC 538, Ch. 6 §6.05[B][2][a]

City Index Ltd v. Leslie [1991] 3 All ER 180, Ch. 4 §4.03[A][2][a][iii]

Cooper v. Stubbs 2 KB [1925] 753, Ch. 4 §4.06[B][4]

DCC Holdings v. HMRC [2010] STC 80 (CA), Ch. 6 §6.05[B][2][b]

Gallagher v. Jones [1993] STC 537, Ch. 6 §6.05[B][2][b]

Glenboig Union Fireclay Co Ltd v. IRC (1922) 12 TC 427 (HL), Ch. 6 §6.02

Greene King plc v. R7C Commissioners [2016] EWCA Civ 782, Ch. 10 §10.01[E][7]

Griffin (Inspector of Taxes) v. Citibank Investments Ltd [2000] STC 1010, Ch. 10 §10.01[E][1]

HBOS Treasury Services plc v. HMRC [2009] UKFTT 261 (TC), [2010] SFTD 134, Ch. 6 §6.05[B][2][b], §6.05[B][2][c], §10.01[E][4]

Herbert Smith v. Honour (Inspector of Taxes) [2000] STC 173, Ch. 5 §5.02[B][4]

HMRC v. DCC Holdings (UK) Limited [2010] UKSC 58, [2011] STC 326, Ch. 6 §6.05[B][2][b], Ch. 9 §9.02[E]

HSBC Life (UK) Ltd v. Stubbs [2002] STC (SCD) 9, Ch. 10 §10.01[E][2]

Indofood v. JPMorgan Chase Bank N.A. [2006] EWCA Civ 158, Ch. 9 §9.02[D][1]

IRC v. John Lewis Properties plc [2003] STC 117 (CA), Ch. 6 §6.02

IRC v. Scottish Provident Institution [2004] UKHL 52, Ch. 10 §10.01[E][3]

J Sainsbury plc v. O'Connor (Inspector of Taxes) [1991] STC 318, Ch. 9 §9.02[B]

Marson v. Morton and Others [1986] 59 TC 381, Ch. 6 §6.05[B][2][a]

Morgan Grenfell Ltd v. Welwyn Hatfield District Council [1995] 1 All ER 1, Ch. 6 §6.05[B][2][a]

Prudential plc v. HMRC [2007] UKSPC SPC00636, Ch.6 §6.05[B][1]

Prudential plc v. HMRC [2009] EWCA Civ 622, Ch. 6 §6.05[B][1], Ch. 10 §10.01[A][1]

Ransom v. Higgs [1974] 50 TC 1, Ch. 6 §6.05[B][2][a]

Rutledge v. IRC [1929] 14 TC 490, Ch. 6 §6.05[B][2][a]

Trustees of the British Telecom Pension Schemes v. Clark (Inspector of Taxes) [2000] STC 222, Ch. 6 §6.05[B][2][a]

Union Castle Main Steamship Company Ltd v. R&C Commissioners [2016] UKFTT 0256 (TC), Ch. 10 §10.01[E][8]

United States of America

Bank of New York Mellon Corporation Inc (as successor in interest to the Bank of New York Company) v. Commissioner of Internal Revenue United States Tax Court, 140 TC No. 2, decision of 11 February 2013, Ch. 9 §9.02[E][2][a][i]

Thor Power Tools Company v. Commissioner of Internal Revenue 439 US 522 (1979), Ch. 4 §4.05

Table of Double Taxation Conventions, OECD and UN Model Conventions and Other OECD and UN Materials

Double Taxation Conventions

US/Germany treaty (2008):

Convention between the United States of America and the Federal Republic of Germany for the Avoidance of Double Taxation and the Prevention of Fiscal Evasion with Respect to Taxes on Income and Capital and to Certain Other Taxes (2008), Ch. 9 §9.01[C][2], Ch. 10 §10.02[A][4]

Switzerland/Denmark treaty (1973):

Abkommen der Schweizerischen Eidgenossenschaft und dem Königreich Dänemark zur Vermeidung der Doppelbesteuerung auf dem Gebiete der Steuern vom Einkommen und vom Vermögen (1973), Ch. 9 §9.02[E][2][a][i], §9.02[E][2][a][ii], §9.02[E][2][b]

UK/Spain treaty (1976):

Convention between the United Kingdom of Great Britain and the Northern Ireland and Spain for the Avoidance of Double Taxation and the Prevention of Fiscal Evasion with respect of Taxes on Income and on Capital (1976), Ch. 9. §9.02[E][1]

US/UK treaty (2003):

Convention Between the Government of the United Kingdom of Great Britain and Northern Ireland and the Government of the United States of America for the Avoidance of Double Taxation and the Prevention of Fiscal Evasion with Respect to Taxes on Income and on Capital Gains (2003), Ch. 9 §9.02[E]

Model Conventions

OECD Model (2010):

OECD Model Tax Convention on Income and on Capital, Condensed version (July 2010, OECD Publishing), Introduction

OECD Model (2014):

OECD Model Tax Convention on Income and on Capital, Condensed version (July 2014, OECD Publishing), Ch. 9 §9.02[D], §9.02[D][3], §9.02[E][2][a][ii]

2014 Update to the OECD Model:

The 2014 Update to the OECD Model Tax Convention (July 2014, OECD Publishing), Ch. 9 §9.02[D][3], §9.02[E][2], §9.02[E][2][a][ii], §9.03[A]

OECD Model (2017):

OECD Model Tax Convention on Income and on Capital, Condensed version (November 2017, OECD Publishing), Introduction, Ch. 3 §3.06, §3.06[B], §3.06[C], Ch. 4 §4.06[D], Ch. 6 §6.08[C][2], Ch. 9 §9.02[A], §9.02[D][2], §9.02[D][3], §9.03[C], §11.03[B], §11.03[F][2]

UN Model (2011):

United Nations Model Double Taxation Convention between Developed and Developing Countries (2011, United Nations), Ch. 1 §1.02, Ch. 3 §3.01, Ch. 4 §4.06[D], Ch. 9 §9.03[C], Ch. 11 §11.03[A][2], §11.03[B], §11.03[F][2]

Other OECD Materials

OECD (1994):

OECD, *Taxation of New Financial Instruments* (OECD Publishing, 1994), Ch. 1 §1.02, Ch. 3 §3.06[C]

OECD (1998):

OECD, *The Taxation of Global Trading of Financial Instruments* (OECD Publishing, 1998), Ch. 1 §1.02

OECD (2001):

OECD, *Innovative Financial Transactions: Tax Policy Implications (A Report by the Special Sessions on Innovative Financial Transactions of the OECD)* (Ad Hoc Group of Experts on International Cooperation in Tax Matters, UNPAN conference documents, 2001), Ch. 1 §1.02, Ch. 2 §2.01[A], §2.02[A], §2.02[A][1], §2.02[A][2], §2.02[B], Ch. 3 §3.01, §3.02[A], §3.03[A]-§3.03[C], §3.04, §3.05[B], §3.06, §3.06[A], §3.06[B], §3.07, Ch. 4 §4.04[B], §4.05, §4.06[D], Ch. 5 §5.01, Ch. 5 §5.08[A], Ch. 6 §6.08[A], §6.08[C][3], Ch. 7 §7.01, §7.02[A], §7.04[A], §7.05[A], Ch. 8 §8.04, §8.08, Ch. 9 §9.02[D][3]

OECD (2008):

OECD, *Report on the Attribution of Profits to Permanent Establishments* (OECD Centre for Tax Policy and Administration, 2008), Ch. 1 §1.02

OECD (2010):

OECD, *2010 Report on the Attribution of Profits to Permanent Establishments* (Centre for Tax Policy and Administration, 2010), Preface, Ch. 1 §1.02

2011 OECD Discussion Draft:

OECD, *Clarification of the meaning of 'beneficial owner' in the OECD model tax convention, discussion draft* (2011), https://web-archive.oecd.org/2012-06-14/96897-47643872.pdf, accessed 30 October 2023, Ch. 9 §9.02[D][3], 9 §9.02[E][2][a][ii]

OECD (2012):

OECD, *Hybrid Mismatch Arrangements: Tax Policy and Compliance Issues* (OECD Publishing, 2012), https://www.oecd.org/ctp/aggressive/hybrid-mismatch-arrangements-tax-policy-and-compliance-issues.pdf, accessed 1 November 2023, Ch. 10 §10.01[C][1]

OECD, 2012 Revised Proposals:

OECD, *OECD Model Tax Convention: Revised Proposals Concerning the Meaning of 'beneficial owner' in Articles 10, 11 and 12* (2012), https://web-archive.oecd.org/2012-10-30/214157-Beneficialownership.pdf, accessed 1 November 2023, Ch. 9 §9.02[D], §9.02[D][3], §9.02[E][2][a][ii]

OECD (2013a):

OECD, *Aggressive Tax Planning based on After-Tax Hedging* (2013), https://www.oecd.org/ctp/aggressive/after_tax_hedging_report.pdf, accessed 15 August 2023, Ch. 1 §1.02, Ch. 3 §3.04, §7.04[C]

OECD (2013b):

OECD, *Addressing Base Erosion and Profit Shifting* (OECD Publishing, Paris, 2013), https://read.oecd-ilibrary.org/taxation/addressing-base-erosion-and-profit-shifting_9789264192744-en#, accessed 1 October 2023, Ch. 3 §3.06[A], §3.06[B]

OECD (2013c):

OECD, *Action Plan on Base Erosion and Profit Shifting* (2013), http://www.oecd.org/ctp/BEPSActionPlan.pdf, accessed 25 July 2023, Ch. 4 §4.06[D]

OECD, BEPS Action 2 (Domestic laws):

OECD, *BEPS Action 2: Neutralise the effects of hybrid mismatch arrangements (Recommendations for Domestic Laws)*, Public Discussion Draft 2014, Ch. 10 §10.01[C][1]

OECD, BEPS Action 2 (Treaty Issues):

OECD, *BEPS Action 2: Neutralise the effects of hybrid mismatch arrangements (Treaty issues)*, Public Discussion Draft 2014, Ch. 10 §10.01[C][1]

OECD (2015), Action 2:

OECD, Neutralising the Effects of Hybrid Mismatch Arrangements, OECD/G20 BEPS Project, Action 2 – 2015 Final Report (OECD Publishing October 2015), Ch. 10 §10.01[C][1]

OECD (2015), Action 4:

OECD, Limiting Base Erosion Involving Interest Deductions and Other Financial Payments, Action 4 – 2015 Final Report, Introduction, Ch. 3 §3.03[C]

OECD (2016):

OECD, Limiting Base Erosion Involving Interest Deductions and Other Financial Payments, Action 4 – 2016 Update, Inclusive Framework on BEPS, Introduction Ch. 1 §1.02, Ch. 3 §3.03[C]

OECD (2021):

OECD (2021), Tax Challenges Arising from the Digitalisation of the Economy – Global Anti-Base Erosion Model Rules (Pillar Two): Inclusive Framework on BEPS, https://www.oecd.org/tax/beps/tax-challenges-arising-from-the-digitalisation-of-the- economy-global-anti-base-erosion-model-rules-pillar-two.htm, accessed 1 August 2023, Ch. 10 §10.01[E], §10.04[B][4]

OECD (2022):

OECD, Crypto-Asset Reporting Framework and Amendment to the Common Reporting Standard (2022), https://www.oecd.org/tax/exchange-of-tax-information/crypto-asset-reporting-framework-and-amendments-to-the-common-reporting-standard.pdf, accessed 20 October 2023, Ch. 1 §1.02, Ch. 10 §10.04[C]

OECD, Administrative Guidance Pillar Two (February 2023):

OECD (2023), *Tax Challenges Arising from the Digitalisation of the Economy – Administrative Guidance on the Global Anti-Base Erosion Model Rules (Pillar Two)*, February 2023, OECD/G20 Inclusive Framework on BEPS, https://www.oecd.org/tax/beps/agreed-administrative-guidance-for-the-pillar-two-globe-rule s.pdf, accessed 1 January 2024, Ch. 10 §10.01[E]

OECD, Administrative Guidance Pillar Two (July 2023):

OECD (2023), *Tax Challenges Arising from the Digitalisation of the Economy – Administrative Guidance on the Global Anti-Base Erosion Model Rules (Pillar Two)*, July 2023, OECD/G20 Inclusive Framework on BEPS, https://www.oecd.org/tax/beps/administrative-guidance-global-anti-base-erosion-rules-pillar-two-july-2023.pdf, accessed 1 January 2024, Ch. 10 §10.01[E]

OECD, Administrative Guidance Pillar Two (December 2023):

OECD (2023), *Tax Challenges Arising from the Digitalisation of the Economy – Administrative Guidance on the Global Anti-Base Erosion Model Rules (Pillar Two)*, December 2023, OECD/G20 Inclusive Framework on BEPS, http://www.oecd.org/tax/beps/administrative-guidance-global-anti-base-erosion-rules-pillar-two-december-2023.pdf, accessed 1 January 2024, Ch. 10 §10.01[E]

Other UN Materials

UN, Scaling Finance for sustainable development goals:

UN, Scaling Finance for sustainable development goals, 26, https://globalcompact.no/app/uploads/2020/01/Scaling-SDG-Finance.pdf, accessed 12 April 2023, Ch. 4 §4.06[C][4][c]

UN, Interntional Tax Cooperation:

UN, Advanced unedited version of a report on Resolution 77/22 titled 'Promotion of inclusive and effective international tax cooperation at the United Nations (August 2023), Ch. 10 §10.04[B][4]

Table of Financial Accounting Standards and Other Materials

International Financial Reporting Standards

IFRS/IAS/ IFRS S 1 and 2

IAS 32:

IAS 32, Financial Instruments: Presentation (IASB, Standard 2021 Issued), Ch. 4 §4.06[C][3], §5.02[A], Ch. 5 §5.05[A]

IAS 39:

IAS 39, Financial Instruments: Recognition and Measurement (IASB, Standard 2022 Issued), Ch. 5 § 5.02[A], Ch. 7 § 7.03[A][1]

IAS 39 (2009):

IAS 39, Financial Instruments: Recognition and Measurement (IASB, Standard 2009 Issued), Ch. 5 §5.02[B][2], Ch. 7 §7.03[A][1][a], Ch. 8 §8.05[B][1]

IFRS 9 (2010):

IFRS 9 (2010), Financial Instruments (IASB, IFRS Foundation Publications, 2011), Ch. 8 §8.05[C][1]

IFRS 9:

IFRS 9, Financial Instruments (IASB, Standard 2023 Issued), Ch. 5 §5.02[A]

ISSB, IFRS S 1:

ISSB, IFRS S 1 General Requirements for Disclosure of Sustainability-related Financial Information, June 2023, Ch. 5 §5.07

ISSB, IFRS S 2:

ISSB IFRS S 2, Climate-related Disclosures, June 2023, Ch. 5 §5.07

IASB, IFRS 9 (Current stage):

Selected Publications by the IASB and IFRS Foundation

IASB, IFRS 9 Financial Instruments (replacement of IAS 39) http://www.ifrs.org/Current-Projects/IASB-Projects/Financial-Instruments-A-Replacement-of-IAS-39-Financial-Instruments-Recognitio/Pages/Financial-Instruments-Replacement-of-IAS-39.aspx, accessed 16 October 2023, Ch. 7 §7.01

IASB, IFRS 9, Phase I:

IASB, IFRS 9: Financial Instruments; Phase I: Classification and measurement (2010), http://www.ifrs.org/Current-Projects/IASB-Projects/Financial-Instruments-A-Replacement-of-IAS-39-Financial-Instruments-Recognitio/Phase-I-Classification-and-measurement/Pages/Phase-I-Classification-and-measurement.aspx, accessed 17 October 2023, Ch. 8 §8.05[C]

IASB, IFRS 9 Project Summary:

IASB, IFRS 9 Financial Instruments (Project Summary, July 2014), http://www.ifrs.org/Current-Projects/IASB-Projects/Financial-Instruments-A-Replacement-of-IAS-39-Financial-Instruments-Recognitio/Documents/IFRS-9-Project-Summary-July-2014.pdf, accessed 10 May 2023, Ch. 8 §8.05[C]

IASB, Accounting for macro hedging:

IASB, Financial instruments: Accounting for macro hedging (2013), https://www.ifrs.org/content/dam/ifrs/meetings/2013/may/iasb/accounting-for-macro-hedging/ap4a-income-statement-balance-sheet-presentation.pdf, accessed 16 October 2023, Ch. 7 §7.01

IASB, Climate-related matters (2020):

IASB, Effects of climate-related matters on financial statements (November 2020), https://www.ifrs.org/content/dam/ifrs/supporting-implementation/documents/effects-of-climate-related-matters-on-financial-statements.pdf, accessed 1 June 2023, Ch. 5 §5.07

IASB, Climate-related matters (2023):

IASB, Effects of climate-related matters on financial statements (Republished July 2023), https://www.ifrs.org/content/dam/ifrs/supporting-implementation/documents/effects-of-climate-related-matters-on-financial-statements.pdf, accessed 25 July 2023, Ch. 5 §5.07

IASB, Dynamic Risk Management (2023):

IASB, Dynamic Risk Management (2023), https://www.ifrs.org/projects/work-plan/dynamic-risk-management/#current-stage, accessed 1 December 2023.

IASB, Macro hedging (2010):

IASB, Financial Instruments (Replacement of IAS 39), Hedge Accounting, Macro hedge accounting - the economic objective (Staff paper, November 2010) – on file with the author, Ch. 7 §7.01

IASB, Macro Hedging (2012):

IASB, Accounting for Macro Hedging, Risks other than interest rate (Staff Paper, December 2012), http://www.ifrs.org/Meetings/MeetingDocs/IASB/2012/December/4-Macro-1212.pdf, accessed 16 October 2023, Ch. 7 §7.01

IASB, Macro Hedging – Discussion Paper (2014):

IASB, Discussion Paper DP/2014/1, Accounting for Dynamic Risk Management: a Portfolio Revaluation Approach to Macro Hedging (April 2014), https://www.ifrs.org/content/dam/ifrs/project/dynamic-risk-management/discussion-paper/published-documents/dp-accounting for dynamic-risk-management.pdf, accessed 13 May 2023, Ch. 7 §7.01

IFRS, Disclosures–Transfers of Financial Assets:

IFRS, *Disclosures–Transfers of Financial Assets* (Amendments to IFRS 7 *Financial Instruments: Disclosures*), https://www.ifrs.org/projects/completed-projects/2010/disclosures-transfers-of-financial-assets-amendments-to-ifrs-7/, accessed 9 March 2023, Ch. 5 §5.02[A], Ch. 7 §7.03[A][1]

IFRS Foundation, Conceptual Framework:

IFRS Foundation, Conceptual Framework for Financial Reporting, issued September 2010, revised March 2018, DOI: 10.1002/9781119207917.ch1, accessed 1 December 2023, Ch. 5 §5.01, §5.08[A]

IFRS Interpretations Committee Meeting:

IFRS Interpretations Committee Meeting, Holding of Cryptocurrencies, Agenda Decision to finalise, June 2019, https://www.ifrs.org/content/dam/ifrs/meetings/2019/june/ifric/ap12-holdings-of-cryptocurrencies.pdf, accessed 9 May 2022, p. 1, Ch. 5 §5.05[A][1]

IFRIC Update March 2019, Holding of Cryptocurrencies:

IFRIC Update March 2019, Holding of Cryptocurrencies, Agenda Paper 4, https://www.ifrs.org/news-and-events/updates/ifric/2019/ifric-update-march-2019/#1, accessed 6 July 2023, Ch. 5 §5.05[A]

UK Financial Reporting Standards

Amendment to FRS 25 (IAS 32):

ASB, *Amendment to FRS 25 (IAS 32) 'Financial Instruments: Presentation', Classification of Rights Issues* (2010), http://www.frc.org.uk/Our-Work/Publications/ASB/Amendment-to-FRS-25-(IAS-32)-Financial-Instruments.aspx, accessed 21 June 2013, Ch. 5 §5.02[A]

FRS 4:

FRS 4: Capital Instruments (ASB, 1994), Ch. 8 §8.05[A]

FRS 18:

FRS 18: *Accounting Policies* (ASB, 2000), Ch. 5 §5.01

FRS 25:

FRS 25 (IAS 32) *Financial Instruments: Presentation* (ASB, as amended in 2010), Ch. 4 §4.06[C], Ch. 5 §5.02[A], §5.05[A]

FRS 26:

FRS 26 (IAS 39) *Financial Instruments: Recognition and Measurement* (ASB, as amended in 2009), Ch. 5 §5.02[A], §5.02[B], §5.02[B][2], Ch. 8 §8.05

FRS 100:

FRS 100 *Application of Financial Reporting Requirements* (FRC, November 2022), Ch. 4 §4.03[A][2], Ch. 5 §5.02[A]

FRS 101:

FRS 101, *Reduced Disclosure Framework, Disclosure exemptions from EU-adopted IFRS for qualifying entities* (January 2022), Ch. 4 §4.03[A][2], Ch. 5 §5.02[A], §5.02[B]

FRS 102:

FRS 102, *The Financial Reporting Standard applicable in the UK and Republic of Ireland* (January 2022), cited previous editions: FRS 102 (2013), Ch.5 §5.02[A], §5.02[B], Ch. 8 §8.05

FRSSE:

FRSSE, Financial Reporting Standard for Smaller Entities (FRC, 2015), Ch. 5 §5.02[A]

Other publications to the UK Financial Reporting Standards

FRC, FRS 102, Factsheet 4:

FRC, FRS 102, Factsheet 4, Financial Instruments, https://www.frc.org.uk/getattachment/f790644d-4802-459a-816a-b57df46c92b6/FS-04-FRS-102-Financial-Instruments-(Dec-2018).pdf, accessed 1 May 2023, Ch. 5 §5.02[B], §5.02[C]

FRC, FRS Factsheet 1:

FRC, FRS Factsheet 1, Triennial Review 2017 Amendments, 5 https://www.frc.org.uk/getattachment/fad30eea-aa8f-4961-beda-a7d8128e3165/FS-01-FRS-102-Triennial-Review-2017-(Dec-2018).pdf, accessed 1 August 2023, Ch. 5 §5.02[B]

FRC, Significant Differences between FRS 102 and IFRS:

FRC, Significant Differences between FRS 102 and IFRS for SMEs Standard, https://www.frc.org.uk/accountants/accounting-and-reporting-policy/uk-accounting-standards/significant-differences-between-frs-102-and-the-if#section-12, accessed 1 May 2023, Ch. 8 §8.05[D]

FRC and BEIS (2020):

FRC and BEIS, 'Accounting and Corporate Reporting after the end of the Transition Period' (November 2020), https://assets.publishing.service.gov.uk/government/uploads/system/uploads/attachment_data/file/937294/Letter_to_the_accounting_sector_preparing_for_1_January_2021.pdf, accessed 22 February 2023, Ch. 5 §5.02[A]

ICAEW, FRS 18:

ICAEW, FRS 18: Accounting Policies, https://www.icaew.com/library/subject-gateways/accounting-standards/uk-frs/frs-18, accessed 9 March 2023, Ch. 5 §5.01

ICAEW, FRS 100:

ICAEW, *FRS 100 Application of Financial Reporting Requirements*, https://www.icaew.com/technical/financial-reporting/uk-gaap/frs-100-application-of-financial-reporting-requirements, accessed 8 July 2023, Ch. 4 §4.03[A][2]

ICAEW, FRS 101:

ICAEW, *FRS 101 Reduced Disclosure Framework*, https://www.icaew.com/technical/financial-reporting/uk-gaap/frs-101-reduced-disclosure-framework, accessed 8 July 2023, Ch. 4 §4.03[A][2]

ICAEW, FRS 102:

ICAEW, *FRS 102 The Financial Reporting Standard applicable in the UK and Republic of Ireland*, https://www.icaew.com/technical/financial-reporting/uk-gaap/frs-102-the-financial-reporting-standard, accessed 8 July 2023, Ch. 4 §4.03[A][2]

ICAEW, Old UK GAAP:

ICAEW, Old UK GAAP – The Financial Reporting Standard for Smaller Entities (FRSSE), https://www.icaew.com/technical/financial-reporting/uk-gaap/old-uk-gaap-standards/financial-reporting-standard-for-smaller-entities-frsse, accessed 23 February 2023, Ch. 5 §5.02[A]

ICAEW, Technical Advisory Service:

ICAEW, Technical Advisory Service, Fixed Asset Investments under FRS 102, https://www.icaew.com/-/media/corporate/files/helpsheets/technical/fixed-asset-investments-under-frs-102.ashx, accessed 2 May 2023, Ch. 5 §5.02[B]

UK.Gov, Correspondence (2021):

UK.Gov, Correspondence, UK accounting and audit framework from 1 January 2021, https://www.gov.uk/government/publications/uk-accounting-and-audit-framework-from-1-january-2021, accessed 23 February 2023, Ch. 5 §5.02[A]

German Accounting Standards: IDW Publications on German GAAP

IDW (1995):

IDW, BFA 2/1995, *Bilanzierung von Optionsgeschäften* (1995) WPg 1995, 421, Ch. 6 §6.06[C][2][b][i](A)(1)

IDW (2001):

IDW, RH BFA 1.003, *Rechnungslegungshinweis: Zur Bilanzierung strukturierter Produkte* (2001) WPg 2001 916, Ch. 8 §8.06[A][1]

IDW (2002):

IDW, RS BFA 1, *Bilanzierung von Kreditderivaten* (4 December 2001) WPg 2002, 195ff, Ch. 4 §A4.06[C]

IDW (2006):

IDW, *Entwurf einer Neufassung der IDW Stellungnahmen zur Rechnungslegung: Einzelfragen zum Übergang von wirtschaftlichem Eigentum und zur Gewinnrealisierung nach HGB, IDW ERS HFA 13 n.F.* (29 November 2006) WPg Supplement 1/2007, 69ff, Ch. 9 §9.02[C]

IDW (2008):

IDW, RS HFA 22, *Zur einheitlichen und getrennten handelsrechtlichen Bilanzierung strukturierter Finanzinstrumente* (2 September 2008) WPg Supplement 4/2008, 41ff, FN-IDW 10/2008, 455ff, Ch. 8 §8.06[A][1], §8.06[A][2][b]

IDW (2009):

IDW, *Comment on IDW ERS HFA 13 n.F. by IDW* (26 /27 November 2009), http://www.idw.de/idw/portal/d302224, accessed 7 March 2013, Ch. 9 §9.02[C]

IDW (2011a):

IDW, RS HFA 35, *Handelsrechtliche Bilanzierung von Bewertungseinheiten* (10 June 2011) WPg Supplement 3/2011, 59 ff., FN-IDW 7/2011, 445 ff, Ch. 7 §7.01

IDW (2011b):

IDW, RS BFA 6, *Handelsrechtliche Bilanzierung von Optionsgeschäften bei Instituten* (18 August 2011) WPg Supplement 4/2011, 50ff, FN-IDW 10/2011, 656ff, Ch. 6 §6.06[C][2][b]

IDW, *WP-Handbuch 2012*:

IDW, *WP-Handbuch 2012, Anhang 3, Die fachlichen Verlautbarungen des IDW* (2012) 3009, Ch. 8 §8.06[A][1]

US Accounting Standards: Publications by the FASB

FASB, Exposure Draft (2023):

FASB, Exposure Draft, Intangibles - Goodwill and Other - Crypto Assets, Accounting for and Disclosure of Crypto Assets (23 March 2023), https://fasb.org/page/ShowPdf?path = Prop%20ASU—Intangibles—Goodwill%20and%20Other—Crypto%20Assets%20(Subtopic%20350-60)—Accounting%20for%20and%20Disclosure%20of%20Crypto%20Assets.pdf&title = Proposed%20Accounting%20Standards%20Update—Intangibles—Goodwill%20and%20Other—Crypto%20Assets%20(Subtopic%20350-60), accessed 29 May 2023, Ch. 5 §5.05[D][1]

FASB, Invitation to comment:

FASB, Invitation to comment, 24 June 2021, https://fasb.org/page/ShowPdf?path = ITC—Agenda_Consultation.pdf&title = INVITATION%20TO%20COMMENT—AGENDA%20CONSULTATION, accessed 1 October 2023, Ch. 5 §5.06

FASB, May 11, 2022 Board Meeting:

FASB, Minutes of the May 11, 2022 Board Meeting on Exchange Traded Digital Assets, https://www.fasb.org/Page/ShowPdf?path = CRYPTO-bmin-20220511.pdf&title = May%2011,%202022%20Board%20Meeting%20Minutes—Accounting%20for%20Exchange—Traded%20Digital%20Assets%20and%20Commodities, accessed 1 December 2023, Ch. 5 §5.05[D][1]

FASB, September 6, 2023 Board Meeting:

FASB, Minutes of the September 6, 2023 Board Meeting on Accounting for and Disclosure of Crypto Assets, 14 September 2023, https://fasb.org/Page/ShowPdf?path = CRYPTO-MIN-20230906.pdf&title = September%206,%202023%20Board%20Meeting%20Minutes—Accounting%20for%20and%20Disclosure%20of%20Crypto%20Assets, accessed 1 November 2023, Ch. 5 §5.05[D][1], §5.06[A][1]

FASB, Tentative Board Decisions (2022):

FASB, Tentative Board Decisions, 12 October 2022, https://fasb.org/page/PageContent?pageId = /news_and_meetings/past-meetings/10-12-22.html, accessed 1 August 2023, Ch. 5 §5.05[D][1], §5.06[A][1]

FASB, Tentative Board Decisions (2023):

FASB, Accounting for and Disclosure of Crypto Assets, Tentative Board Decisions to Date, 1 February 2023, https://fasb.org/page/PageContent?pageId = /news_and_meetings/past-meetings/02-01-23.html, accessed 4 December 2023, Ch. 5 §5.05[D][1]

Table of ISDA and BCBS Documents

ISDA Definitions and Annexes

ISDA, 2014 ISDA Credit Derivatives Definitions:

ISDA, 2014 ISDA Credit Derivatives Definitions, Ch. 4 §4.06[C][2]

ISDA, 2022 ISDA Verified Carbon Credit Transaction Definitions:

ISDA, 2022 ISDA Verified Carbon Credit Transaction Definitions, Ch. 8 §8.08[B][3]

ISDA, ISDA Digital Assets Derivatives Definitions:

ISDA, ISDA Digital Assets Derivatives Definitions (2023), Ch. 7 §7.06[B][1][a][i]

ISDA, US Renewable Energy Certificate Annex:

ISDA, US Renewable Energy Certificate Annex, Ch. 2 §2.01[D]

ISDA Comment Letters, White Papers and Other Publications

ISDA, Crypto-asset Risk and Hedging Analysis (2022):

ISDA, Crypto-asset Risk and Hedging Analysis (2022), 3, https://www.isda.org/a/pMWgE/Crypto-asset-Risks-and-Hedging-Analysis.pdf, accessed 18 August 2023, Ch. 6. §6.05[B], Ch. 7 §7.06, §7.06[A], §7.06[B][1][a], §7.06[B][1][b], §7.06[B][1][c]

ISDA, Digital Assets (2022):

ISDA, Accounting for Digital Assets, Key considerations (May 2022) https://www.isda.org/a/88VgE/Accounting-for-Digital-Assets-Key-Considerations.pdf, accessed 20 August 2023, Ch. 5 §5.05[D][1], Ch. 7 §7.06[A], Ch. 8 §8.08[B][3]

ISDA, Digital Asset Derivatives (2023):

ISDA, Bringing Legal Certainty to Digital Asset Derivatives, derivatiViews, informal comments by ISDA CEO Scott O'Malia, 30 January 2023, https://www.isda.org/2023/01/30/bringing-legal-certainty-to-digital-asset-derivatives/, accessed 25 December 2023, Ch. 7 §7.06[B][1][a][i]

ISDA, Letter to the FASB (2021):

ISDA, Letter to the FASB, Request: Investors accounting for crypto assets (7 June 2021), https://www.isda.org/a/3SEgE/Agenda-Request-Investors-accounting-for-crypto-assets.pdf, accessed 6 August 2023, Ch. 5. §5.05[D], §5.06

ISDA, Overview of ESG-related Derivatives (2021):

ISDA, Overview of ESG-related Derivatives Products and Transactions, January 2021, https://www.isda.org/a/qRpTE/Overview-of-ESG-related-Derivatives-Products-and-Transactions.pdf, accessed 23 July 2023, Ch. 2 §2.01[D], Ch. 4 §4.06[C][4]

ISDA Future Leader in Derivatives, Sustainability-linked derivatives (2022):

ISDA Future Leader in Derivatives, Sustainability-linked derivatives: Where to begin, White paper, (May 2022), https://www.isda.org/a/ZfVgE/Sustainability-linked-Derivatives-Where-to-Begin.pdf, accessed 25 December 2023, Ch. 4 §4.06[C][4]

ISDA et al., Joint Trade Associations Comment Letter:

ISDA et al., Joint Trade Associations Comment Letter, Re Comments in Response to the Consultative Document on Prudential Treatment of Cryptoasset Exposures, September 20, 2021, https://www.isda.org/a/OBggE/Joint-Trades-Comment-Letter-Prudential-Treatment-of-Cryptoasset-Exposures.pdf, accessed 21 December 2023, Ch. 7 §7.06[A]

BCBS Consultative Documents and Standards

BCBS, 2021 BCBS Consultative Document:

BCBS, 2021 Consultative Document, Prudential treatment of cryptoasset exposures' (September 2021), https://www.bis.org/bcbs/publ/d519.pdf, accessed 20 August 2023, Ch. 6 §6.05[B][3][a], Ch. 7 §7.06[A]

BCBS, 2023 Consultative Document:

BCBS, Consultative Document, Cryptoassets standards amendments (14 December 2023), https://www.bis.org/bcbs/publ/d567.pdf, accessed 26 December 2023, Ch. 7 §7.06[A]

BCBS, Prudential Treatment of Cryptoasset Exposures (2022):

BCBS, Prudential Treatment of Cryptoasset Exposures (December 2022), https://www.bis.org/bcbs/publ/d545.pdf, accessed 26 December 2023, Ch. 7 §7.06[A]

BCBS, SCO60 Cryptoasset Standard:

BCBS, SCO60 – Cryptoasset exposures (December 2022), https://www.bis.org/basel_framework/chapter/SCO/60.htm?tldate=20230521&inforce=20250101&published=20221216, accessed 26 December 2023, Ch. 7 §7.06[A], [B]

BCBS, Second consultation (2022):

BCBS, Second consultation on the prudential treatment of cryptoasset exposures' (June 2022), https://www.bis.org/bcbs/publ/d533.pdf, accessed 20 August 2023,Ch. 7 §7.06[A]

Table of National Legislation and EU Materials

Australia

Taxation of Financial Arrangement Rules (TOFA) in: Income Tax Assessment Act 1997, Ch. 4 §4.04[A], Ch. 10 §10.05[B][3][d]

Germany

Abgabenordnung - General Tax Act (GTA), Ch. 9 §9.02[C], Ch. 10 §10.02[A]

Einkommensteuergesetz - Income Tax Act (ITA), Ch. 4 §4.03[C][1], §4.03[C][2], §4.03[D], Ch. 5 § 5.03[A], § 5.03[B], Ch. 6 §6.03, §6.04, §6.06[A], §6.06[C][2][a], §6.06[C][2][b], Ch. 7 §7.03[B][2], §7.04[C], §7.04[C][2], Ch. 8 §8.06[B][2][a], Ch. 9 §9.01[B], §9.01[C][2], §9.01[D][2], Ch. 10 §10.02[A][1]-[5]

Einkommensteuergesetz (2008) - Income Tax Act 2008 (ITA 2008), Ch. 4 §4.03[C][1], §4.03[C][2], Ch. 6 §6.06[C][2][b](aa)

Gesetz zur Modernisierung des Bilanzrechts - Accounting Law Modernisation Act, Ch. 5 §5.03[A], §5.03[B], Ch. 7 §7.03[B][1], §7.06[C][1]

Gesetz zur Umsetzung des EuGH-Urteils vom 20. Oktober 2011 in der Rechtssache C-284/09 - Legislation implementing the ECJ decision of 20 October 2011 C-284/09, Ch. 6 §6.06[A]

Gewerbesteuergesetz - Trade Tax Act (TTA), Ch. 6 §6.04, §6.06[A]

Gesetz zur Umsetzung der Anti-Steuervermeidungsrichtlinie (ATAD-Umsetzungsgesetz – ATADUmsG) vom 30. Juni 2021– ATAD Implementation Law, Ch. 10 §10.02[B]

Handelsgesetzbuch - Commercial Law Act (CLA), Ch. 5 §5.03[A], §5.03[B], Ch. 6 §6.04, §6.06[B], §6.06[C][2], Ch. 7 §7.03[B][1], §7.06[C][1], Ch. 8 §8.06[A][1], [2], §8.06[B][1], [2], §8.07, Ch. 11 §11.03[E][1]

Körperschaftsteuergesetz - Corporation Tax Act (CTA), Ch. 4 §4.03[C][2], Ch. 5 §5.03[A], Ch. 6 §6.03, §6.04, §6.06[A], §6.06[C], §6.07[C], Ch. 8 §8.06[B][1], Ch. 9 §9.01[B], §9.01[C][2], Ch. 10 §10.02[A][1]

Kreditwesengesetz - Banking Act, Ch. 6 §6.04

Wertpapierhandelsgesetz - Securities Trading Act (STA), Ch. 4 §4.03[C][1], §4.03[D]

United Kingdom

Companies Act 2006, Ch. 5 §5.02[A]

Corporation Tax Act 2009, Ch. 1 §1.02, Ch. 4 §4.03[A], §4.06[C], Ch. 5 §5.01, §5.02[B], §5.02[D], Ch. 6 §6.01, §6.02, §6.03, §6.05[A], [B], §6.05[B], §6.06[A], §6.07[B], Ch. 7 §7.03[A], Ch. 8 §8.05[D], §8.05[F][1], §8.07, §8.08[B], Ch. 9 §9.01[A], §9.01[C], Ch. 10 §10.01[A]-[D], Ch. 11 §11.03[A][1], §11.03[B][1]

Corporation Tax Act 2010, Ch. 5 §5.02[D], Ch. 6 §6.02, §6.05[A], §6.05[B], Ch. 7 §7.04[B], §7.04[D], Ch. 8 §8.05[F], Ch. 9 §9.01[C], Ch. 10 §10.01[A]

Finance Act 1993, Ch. 6 §6.05[B][1]

Finance Act 1994, Ch. 6 §6.05[B][1], Ch. 10 §10.01[A], §10.01[E]

Finance Act 1996, Ch. 6 §6.05[B][1], Ch. 10 §10.01[E]

Finance Act 2002, Ch. 4 §4.03[A][2], Ch. 6 §6.02, §6.05[B]

Finance Act 2004, Ch. 4 §4.03[A][2][c], Ch. 5 §5.02[B], §5.02[D], Ch. 6 §6.05[B], Ch. 9 §9.01[C], Ch. 10 §10.01[D]

Finance Act 2005, Ch. 4 §4.03[A], Ch. 6 §6.05[B]

Finance Act 2007, Ch. 10 §10.01[D][1], §10.04[B][3][c]

Finance Act 2008, Ch. 10 §10.01[D][1]

Finance Act 2009, Ch. 4 §4.03[A][2], Ch. 10 §10.04[B][3][d]

Finance Act 2010, Ch. 10 §10.01[D][1]

Finance Act 2012, Ch. 9 §9.01[C][1], Ch. 11 §11.03[F][1]

Finance Bill 2013, Ch. 10 § 10.01[D][2][a]

Finance Act 2013, Ch. 6 §6.05[B][2][e], Ch. 9 §9.01[C][1], Ch. 10 §10.01[D][2], Ch. 11 §11.03[F][1][a]

Finance Bill 2014, Ch.10 §10.01[A]

Finance Bill 2015, Ch. 7 §7.03[A][2], Ch. 10 §10.01[D][1]

Finance Act 2016, Introduction, Ch. 10 §10.01[C]

Finance (No. 2) Act 2017, Introduction

Finance Act 2018, Introduction

Finance Act 2019, Ch. 4 §4.03[A][1], Ch. 6 §6.01, §6.02, Ch. 10 §10.01[C]

Finance (No. 2) Bill 2023, Ch. 10 §10.01[E], §10.02[D]

Finance (No. 2) Act 2023, Ch. 10 §10.01[D]

Financial Services and Markets Act 2000, Ch. 4 §4.03[A][2][a][iii], §4.06[B][4]

Income and Corporation Taxes Act 1988, Ch. 5 §5.02[D], Ch. 6 §6.06[B][2][a]

Income Tax (Earnings and Pensions) Act 2003, Ch. 6 §6.05

Income Tax (Trading and Other Income) Act 2005, Ch. 4 §4.03[A][1]

Income Tax Act 2007, Ch. 9 §9.01[A], §9.01[C][1]

Taxation (International and Other Provisions) Act 2010, Ch. 6 §6.02, §6.05[A], Ch. 10 §10.01[A], §10.01[A][2], §10.01[C], §10.01[C][2], §10.01[D]

Taxation of Chargeable Gains Act 1992, Ch. 4 §4.03[A][1], §4.06[B][4], §4.06[C][3][b], Ch. 6 §6.01, §6.02, §6.05[A], §6.05[B][1], §6.05[B][2], §6.05[B][3][b], Ch. 8 §8.05[F][2], Ch. 10 §10.01[E][1][b]

United States of America

Dodd-Frank Act, Ch. 4 §4.06[A]

Internal Revenue Code, Ch. 3 §3.04

EU Directives, Regulations and Other EU Documents

Council Directives

Council Directive 2011/16/EU of 15 February 2011 on administrative cooperation in the field of taxation and repealing Directive 77/799/EEC (*OJ L 64, 11.3.2011*, 1 (DAC6), Ch. 10 §10.01[D][1]

Proposal for a Council Directive amending Directive 2011/96 EU on the common system of taxation applicable in the case of parent companies and subsidiaries of different Member States (COM(2013) 814 final), Ch. 10 §10.01[C][1], §10.04[A][6]

Council Directive 2014/86/EU of 8 July 2014 amending Directive 2011/96/EU on the common system of taxation applicable in the case of parent companies and subsidiaries of different Member States, *O.J.* L 219, vol. 57, 40f, Ch. 10 §10.01[C][1], §10.04[A][6]

Council Directive (EU) 2016/1164 of 12 July 2016, *Laying down rules against tax avoidance practices that directly affect the functioning of the internal market (*EU Anti-Tax Avoidance Directives 2016/1164 (ATAD I)), Introduction, Ch. 3 §3.03[C], Ch. 10 §10.01[C][2], §10.01[D], §10.02[B], Ch. 11 §11.03[G]

Council Directive (EU) 2017/952 of 29 May 2017 amending Directive (EU) 2016/1164 as regards hybrid mismatches with third countries, *OJ L 144, 7.6.2017, 1-11. (*EU Anti-Tax Avoidance Directives 2017/952 (ATAD II)), Introduction, Ch. 10 §10.01[C][2], Ch. 10 §10.02[B]

Council Directive (EU) 2022/2464 of the European Parliament and of the Council of 14 December 2022 amending Regulation (EU) No 537/2014, Directive 2004/109/EC, Directive 2006/43/EC and Directive 2013/34/EU, as regards corporate sustainability reporting – Corporate Sustainability Reporting Directive (CSRD), *OJ L 322, 16.12.2022, 15–80*, Ch. 8 §8.10[B]

Council Directive amending Directive 2011/16/EU on administrative cooperation in the field of taxation (DAC8) of 18 September 2023, 10215/23, LIMITE, FISC 115 ECOFIN 566 (DAC8), Ch. 10 §10.04[C]

Regulations

Regulation (EC) No. 1606/2002 of the European Parliament and of the Council of 19 July 2002 on the application of international accounting standards, Ch. 5 §5.02[A], §5.02[D]

Regulation (EU) 2019/2088 on sustainability-related disclosure in the financial services sector (SFDR) – Sustainable Finance Disclosures Regulation (SFDR), Ch. 8 §8.10[B]

Regulation (EU) 2020/852 of the European Parliament and of the Council of 18 June 2020 on the establishment of a framework to facilitate sustainable investment, and amending Regulation (EU) 2019/2088 *OJ L 198, 22.6.2020*, 13–43 (EU Taxonomy Regulation), Ch. 8 §8.10[B]

Regulation of the European Parliament and of the Council on European Green Bonds and optional disclosures for bonds marketed as environmentally sustainable and for sustainability-linked bonds, 2021/0191 (COD), Ch. 8 §8.10[B]

Other Documents

Report of the Code of Conduct Group of 25 May 2010 (doc.10033/10, FISC 47), Ch. 10 §10.04[A][6]

Treaty on the Functioning of the European Union of 26 October 2012, Ch. 10 §10.04

European Commission, Debt-equity bias reduction allowance (DEBRA), 11 May 2022, https://ec.europa.eu/info/law/better-regulation/have-your-say/initiatives/12995-Debt-equity-biasreduction-allowance-DEBRA-_en, accessed 2 July 2023, Ch. 3 §3.03[C]

Council of the European Union, Draft Ecofin report to the European Council on tax issues, 16100/23, FISC 275 ECOFIN 1294 (30 November 2023), https://data.consilium.europa.eu/doc/document/ST-16100-2023-INIT/en/pdf, accessed 1 January 2024, Ch. 10 §10.02[B]

Table of Statutory Instruments, Legislative Material and Other Official Documents

Germany

Legislative Materials

BT - Drucksache 14/443 (3 March 1999), Dritter Bericht des Finanzausschusses zu dem Gesetzentwurf der Fraktionen SPD und BÜNDNIS 90/DIE GRÜNEN – Drucksache 14/23 – Entwurf eines Steuerentlastungsgesetzes 1999/2000/2002, Ch. 4 §4.03[C][1], §4.03[C][2], §4.03[D], Ch. 6 §6.06[C][2][a]

BR-Drucksache 220/07 (30 March 2007), Gesetzesentwurf der Bundesregierung, Entwurf eines Unternehmensteuerreformgesetzes 2008, Ch. 4 §4.03[C][1]

BT - Drucksache 16/6290 (4 September 2007), Gesetzesentwurf der Bundesregierung, Entwurf eines Jahressteuergesetzes 2008, Ch. 10 §10.02[C]

BR - Drucksache 344/08 (23 May 2008), Gesetzentwurf der Bundesregierung, Entwurf eines Gesetzes zur Modernisierung des Bilanzrechts (Bilanzrechtsmodernisierungsgesetz - BilMoG), Ch. 7 §7.01, §7.03[B][1], §7.06[C][1], §7.06[C][2]

BT - Drucksache 17/2823 (27 August 2010), Unterrichtung der Bundesregierung zum Entwurf eines Jahressteuergesetzes 2010 –Drucksache 17/2249, Stellungsnahme des Bundesrates und Gegenäußerung der Bundesregierung, Ch. 4 §4.03[C][2]

'Coalition Agreement between CDU/CSU and SPD' (11 November 2005), https://webarchiv.bundestag.de/archive/2008/0416/aktuell/archiv/2005/koalition/vertrag_en.pdf, accessed 25 October 2023, Ch. 5 §5.04

Statutory Instruments (Letter Rulings of the Federal Ministry of Finance)

BMF, Schreiben vom 27. November 2001, Einkommensteuerliche Behandlung von Termingeschäften im Bereich der privaten Vermögensverwaltung (IV C 3 - S 2256 - 265/01 BStBl I 2001, 986), Ch. 6 §6.06[C][2][b], Ch.8 §8.01[B][3]

BMF, Schreiben betr. steuerbilanzielle Behandlung von Optionsprämien beim Stillhalter vom 12. Januar 2004 (IV A 6 - S 2133 - 17/03, BStBl I 2004, 192), Ch. 6 §6.06[C][2][b]

BMF, Schreiben vom 23. September 2005, Verlustabzugsbeschränkung nach § 15 Abs. 4 Satz 3 EStG (IV B 2 - S 2119 – 7/05, DStR 2005, 1900), Ch. 4 §4.03[C][2], Ch. 6 §6.06[C]

BMF, Schreiben vom 12. Februar 2007 (IV B 2 - S 2119 -10-5 - unpublished), Ch. 4 §4.03[C][2]

BMF, Maßgeblichkeit der handelsrechtlichen Grundsätze ordnungsgemäßer Buchführung für die steuerliche Gewinnermittlung vom 12. März 2010 (IV C 6 – S 2133/09/10001), Ch. 5 §5.03[A]

BMF, Schreiben betr. Eindämmung der Normenflut; BMF-Schreiben, die bis zum 31. Dezember 2009 ergangen sind. (Verwaltungsanweisung vom 23. April 2010 – IV A 6 - O 1000/09/10095, BStBl I 2010, 391ff), Ch. 4 §4.03[C][2]

BMF, Schreiben vom 25. August 2010, Steuerliche Gewinnermittlung bei der Bildung von Bewertungseinheiten (IVC 6 - S 2133/07/10001, Der Betrieb 2010, 2024), Ch. 5 §5.03[B], Ch. 7 §7.03[B][2], §7.06[C][2]

BMF, Schreiben vom 9. Oktober 2012, Einzelfragen zur Abgeltungsteuer (IV C 1 - S2252/10/10013), Ch. 4 §4.03[C][1]

BMR, Schreiben vom 18. Januar 2016, Einzelfragen zur Abgeltungsteuer, Neuveroeffentlichung des BMF-Schreibens, (IV C 1 – S 2252/08/10004:017), paras 22 and 36, https://www.bzst.de/SharedDocs/BMF/DE/Downloads/bmf_Schreiben_20160118_Einzelfragen_Abgeltungsteuer.html, accessed 9 January 2023, Ch. 4 §4.03[C][1], Ch. 4 §4.03[C][2], before Ch. 6 §6.01

BMF, Schreiben vom 3 Juni 2021, IV C 1 - S 2252/19/10003:002 BStBl 2021 I S. 723, Einzelfragen zur Abgeltungsteuer; Ergänzung des BMF-Schreibens vom 18. Januar 2016 (BStBl 2016 I S. 85), https://datenbank.nwb.de/Dokument/857870/, accessed 15 July 2023, before Ch. 6 §6.01

United Kingdom

Statutory Instruments

Finance Act 2002, Schedule 26, Part 2 and 9 (Amendment No. 2) Order 2004, SI 2004/3270, Ch. 4 §4.03[A][2][c], Ch. 6 §6.05[B][1]

Finance Act 2002, Schedule 26 (Parts 2 and 9) (Amendment No. 3) Order 2005, SI 2005/3440, Ch. 6 §6.05[B][1]

Finance Act 2002, Schedule 26, Part 2 and 9 (Amendment) Order 2005, SI 2005/646, Ch. 4 §4.03[A][2][c], Ch. 6 §6.05[B][1]

Finance Act 2002, Schedule 26, Parts 2 and 9 (Amendment No. 2) Order 2005, SI 2005/2082, Ch. 4 §4.03[A][2][c], Ch. 6 §6.05[B][1]

Financial Services and Markets Act 2000 (Regulated Activities) Order 2001, SI 2001/544, Ch. 4 §4.03[A][2][a][iii]

Income Tax (Manufactured Overseas Dividends) Regulations 1993, SI 1993/2004, Ch. 9 §9.01[C][1]

Insurance Companies (Corporation Tax Acts) (Miscellaneous Amendments) Order 2006, SI 2006/3270, Ch. 6 §6.05[B][1], §6.05[B][2]

Loan Relationships and Derivative Contracts (Disregard and Bringing into Account of Profits and Losses) Regulations 2004, SI 2004/3256, Ch. 6 §6.05[B][1], §6.05[B][2][d], Ch. 7 §7.03[A][2], §7.04[B], §7.06[B][2][b]

Tax Avoidance Schemes (Information) Regulations 2012, SI 2012/1836, Ch. 10 §10.01[D][1]

Tax Avoidance Schemes (Prescribed Descriptions of Arrangements) Regulations 2006, SI 2006/1543, Ch. 10 §10.01[D][1]

The Taxation of Regulatory Capital Securities Regulations 2013, SI 2013/3209, Ch. 8 §8.05[F], Ch. 10 §10.01[C][2], §10.01[C][3]

The Hybrid and Other Mismatches (Financial Instruments: Excluded Instruments) (Amendment) Regulations 2022, SI 2022/1144, https://www.legislation.gov.uk/uksi/2022/1144/contents/made, accessed 18 July 2023, Ch. 10 §10.01[C][3]

Other Official Materials

Economic Affairs Committee, First Report, The Draft Finance Bill 2013 (2013), http://www.publications.parliament.uk/pa/ld201213/ldselect/ldeconaf/139/13902.htm, accessed 1 August 2023, Ch. 10 §10.01[D][2][a]

House of Commons (Committee of Public Accounts), Tax avoidance: tackling marketed avoidance schemes (29th Report of Session 2012-13, 2013), http://www.

publications.parliament.uk/pa/cm201213/cmselect/cmpubacc/788/788.pdf, accessed 14 June 2023, Ch. 10 §10.04[B][2]

House of Commons and House of Lords, Oral evidence taken before the Parliamentary Commission on Banking Standards, Tuesday 5 February 2013, Antony Jenkins and Sir David Walker, Barclays (Transcript), http://www.publications.parliament.uk/pa/jt201213/jtselect/jtpcbs/c606-xxxii/c60601.pdf accessed 11 March 2023, Ch. 6 §6.05[B][1]

House of Lords (Select Committee on the Constitution), Memorandum by Professor John McEldowney, University of Warwick (submitted to the House of Lords Select Committee on the Constitution, Ninth Report, 2003), https://publications.parliament.uk/pa/ld200203/ldselect/ldconst/168/16809.htm, accessed 1 June 2023, Ch. 10 §10.04[B][3][a]

Royal Commission, Final Report on the Taxation of Profits and Income (Cmd 9474, 1955), Ch. 6 §6.05[B][2][a]

HMRC Manuals

HMRC, BIM:

HMRC, Business Income Manual (2013), updated September 2023, Ch. 4 §4.06[B][4], §4.06[C][3][b]

HMRC, CFM:

HMRC, Corporate Finance Manual (2016), updated 1 November 2023, Ch. 4 §4.03[A][2][a][i], §4.03[A][2][a][iii], Ch. 5 §5.01, §5.06[A][1][a], Ch. 5 §5.06[A][2], Ch. 6 §6.02, Ch. 10 §10.01[C][3]

HMRC, CG:

HMRC, Capital Gains Manual (2016), updated 5 October 2023, Ch. 4 §4.03[A][1]

HMRC, CRYPTO:

HMRC, Crypotassets Manual (2021), updated 21 August 2023, Ch. 4 §4.06[C][3][b], Ch. 6 §6.05[B][3][a]

HMRC, CTM:

HMRC, Company Taxation Manual (2016), updated 14 July 2023, Ch. 6 §6.02, Ch. 7 §7.04[B]

HMRC, IHTM:

HMRC, Inheritance Tax Manual (2016), updated 16 June 2023, Ch. 9. §9.02[A], §9.02[E]

HMRC, INTM:

HMRC, International Manual (2016), updated 25 July 2023), Ch. 10 §10.01[C][2]

HMRC Documents and Consultation Documents

HMRC, Accounting Standards (2006):

HMRC, Accounting Standards – the UK tax implications (2006) – on file with the author, Ch. 5 §5.02[A]

HMRC, Code of Practice on Taxation for Banks:

HMRC, Code of Practice on Taxation for Banks (5 December 2013), https://www.gov.uk/government/publications/code-practice-taxation-banks/code-of-practice-on-taxation-for-banks, accessed 1 August 2023, Ch. 9 §9.01[C][1], §10.01[D][2][c]

HMRC, Consultation, Corporation tax reform (2003):

HMRC, Corporation tax reform - A consultation document (LNB News 13 August 2003), on file with the author, Ch. 6 §6.05[B][1]

HMRC, Consultation, General Anti-Abuse Rule (2012):

HMRC, A General Anti-Abuse Rule, Consultation document (2012), Ch. 10 §10.01[D][2][c]

HMRC, Consultation, Manufactured Payments (2012):

HMRC, Proposed Changes to Tax Rules on Manufactured Payments, Consultation Document (27 March 2012), https://www.yumpu.com/en/document/view/13781224/proposed-changes-to-tax-rules-on-manufactured-payments/3, accessed 29 May 2023, Ch. 9 §9.01[A]

HMRC, Corporation Tax Act, Explanatory Notes (2009)

HMRC, Corporation Tax Act, Explanatory Notes (2009), https://www.legislation.gov.uk/ukpga/2009/4/notes/contents accessed 3 July 2023, Ch. 4 §4.03[A][2]

HMRC, Disclosure of tax and NICs avoidance schemes:

HMRC, 'Disclosure of tax and NICs avoidance schemes: Summary of the disclosure rules' (HMRC Anti-Avoidance Group, 2013) – on file with the author, Ch. 10 §10.01[D][1][b]

HMRC, Disregard Regulations:

HMRC, Corporation Tax: Disregard Regulations for derivative contracts, Business tax - guidance (2015), updated 30 October 2015, https://www.gov.uk/guidance/corporation-tax-disregard-regulations-for-derivative-contracts, accessed 1 August 2023, Ch. 7 §7.03[A][2]

HMRC, General Anti-Abuse Rule – draft legislation:

HMRC, General Anti-Abuse Rule – draft legislation (2012), https://assets.publishing.service.gov.uk/government/uploads/system/uploads/attachment_data/file/179262/general_anti_abuse_rule.pdf.pdf, accessed 3 August 2023, Ch. 10 §10.01[D][2][a]

HMRC Guidance: Disclosure of tax avoidance schemes (2014):

HMRC, Guidance: Disclosure of tax avoidance schemes (2014), updated 8 July 2022, https://www.gov.uk/guidance/disclosure-of-tax-avoidance-schemes-overview, accessed 20 July 2023, Ch. 10 §10.01[D][1]

HMRC, Guidance: Tax avoidance (2021):

HMRC, Guidance, Tax avoidance: general anti-abuse rule guidance – latest version (2021), Ch. 10 §10.01[D][2][c]

HMRC, HMRC's GAAR Guidance (Approved by the Advisory Panel with effect from 15 April 2013), https://assets.publishing.service.gov.uk/government/uploads/system/uploads/attachment_data/file/396179/gaar-part-abc.pdf accessed 16 July 2023, Ch. 10 §10.01[D][2][c]

HMRC, HMRC's GAAR Guidance:

HMRC, HMRC's GAAR Guidance – consultation drafts, Part A – C (scope, examples, procedure) (2012), Ch. 10 §10.01[D][2][c]

HMRC, International Accounting Standards:

HMRC, International Accounting Standards, Comparison Document, https://webarchive.nationalarchives.gov.uk/ukgwa/20130129110402/http://www.hm-treasury.gov.uk/d/comparison_document.pdf, accessed 15 February 2023, Ch. 8 §8.05[B][2]

HMRC, Manufactured Overseas Dividends: Anti-avoidance, draft legislation and draft explanatory note (15 September 2011), https://webarchive.nationalarchives.gov.uk/ukgwa/20140109143644/http://www.hmrc.gov.uk/budget-updates/march2011/mod-tech-note.pdf, accessed 13 July 2023, Ch. 9 §9.01[C][1]

HMRC, Manufactured payments:

HMRC, Corporation tax and income tax: changes to rules for manufactured payments (2012), https://assets.publishing.service.gov.uk/government/uploads/system/uploads/attachment_data/file/179263/manufactured_payments.pdf.pdf, accessed 13 July 2023, Ch. 9 §9.01[A], §9.01[C][1], Ch. 11 §11.03[F][1][a]

HMRC, Modernising the taxation of corporate debt and derivative contracts, Consultation:

HMRC, Modernising the taxation of corporate debt and derivative contracts, Consultation Document (6 June 2013), https://assets.publishing.service.gov.uk/government/uploads/system/uploads/attachment_data/file/205432/2013_06_05_Condoc_FINAL_FOR_PUBLICATION.pdf, accessed 13 July 2023, Ch. 4 §4.03[A][3], Ch. 5 §5.08[A], Ch. 7 §7.03[A][2], Ch. 10 §10.04[B][3][c]

HMRC, Modernising the Taxation of Corporate Debt and Derivative Contracts (Technical Note):

HMRC, Modernising the Taxation of Corporate Debt and Derivative Contracts, Technical Note (8 April 2014), https://webarchive.nationalarchives.gov.uk/ukgwa/

20140109143644/http://www.hmrc.gov.uk/news/tech-note-corp-debt.pdf, accessed 24 January 2023, Ch. 7 §7.03[A][2]

HMRC, Multinational top-up tax (June 2023):

HMRC, Closed consultation, Draft guidance: multinational top-up tax and domestic top-up tax, 15 June 2023, https://www.gov.uk/government/consultations/draft-guidance-multinational-top-up-tax-and-domestic-top-up-tax, accessed 3 October 2023, Ch. 10 §10.01[D][3]

HMRC, Multinational Top-up Tax and Domestic Top-up Tax (December 2023):

HMRC, Open Consultation, Draft guidance on Multinational Top-up Tax and Domestic Top-up Tax, 21 December 2023, https://www.gov.uk/government/consulta tions/draft-guidance-on-multinational-top-up-tax-and-domestic-top-up-tax, accessed 1 January 2024, Ch. 10 §10.01[D][3].

HMRC Overview of Disregard Regulations (2015):

HMRC, Overview of Disregard Regulations (27 March 2015), https://www.gov.uk/government/publications/corporation-tax-hedging-derivative-contracts-and-dis regard-regulations/overview-of-disregard-regulations, accessed 18 April 2023, Ch. 7 §7.03[A][2][a][i]

HMR, Overview of Legislation in Draft:

HMRC, *Overview of Legislation in Draft* (11 December 2012), https://assets.publishing .service.gov.uk/media/5a7a3781ed915d1a6421be1e/fb2013_overview_of_legis lation_in_draft.pdf, accessed 1 January 2024, Ch. 10 §10.01[D][2][b]

HMRC, Strengthening the Tax Avoidance Disclosure Regimes:

HMRC, Strengthening the Tax Avoidance Disclosure Regimes, Consultation Document (31 July 2014), https://assets.publishing.service.gov.uk/government/uploads/system/uploads/attachment_data/file/339105/DOTAS-VADR_consultation_201 4.pdf, accessed 13 July 2023, Ch. 10 §10.01[D][1]

HMRC, Tax Law Rewrite:

HMRC, Tax Law Rewrite (2011), https://webarchive.nationalarchives.gov.uk/ukgwa /20140206160137/http://www.hmrc.gov.uk/rewrite/index.htm, accessed 8 January 2023, Ch. 4 §4.03[A][3]

HMRC, Technical Note on overhedging and underhedging:

HMRC, Technical Note on overhedging and underhedging (2009), https://webarchive .nationalarchives.gov.uk/ukgwa/20091103043120/http://www.hmrc.gov.uk/drafts/over-underhedging.htm, accessed 12 August 2023, Ch. 7 §7.04[A]

Inland Revenue, Technical Note exchange gains and losses:

Inland Revenue, Technical Note on tax legislation for exchange gains and losses, derivative financial instruments, and corporate and government debt (8 November 2000) – on file with the author, Ch. 6 §6.05[B][1]

Index

Accounting method

accounting on a cash basis — Ch. 5 §5.01, Ch. 10 §10.05[A][2]

accruals accounting — Ch. 3 §3.02, §3.05[B], Ch. 5 §5.01, §5.02[B], §5.08[B], Ch. 6 §6.05[B][1], §6.06[C][2][c][i], Ch. 7 §7.03[A][1], Ch. 10 §10.01[E][1], [2], §10.05[A][2]

amortised cost basis — Ch. 5 §5.01, §5.02[B][1]-[4], §5.02[C][1], [2], §5.08[B], Ch. 6 §6.05[B][2][d], Ch. 7 §7.03[A][1], [2], Ch. 8 §8.05[C][2], §8.05[D][1], §8.05[F][2], Ch. 11 §11.03[C][1]

fair value accounting — Ch. 1 §1.03, Ch. 3 §3.02, Ch. 5 §5.01-§5.06, §5.08, Ch. 6 §6.02[B], §6.05[B], §6.06, §6.08[B], Ch. 7 §7.03[A][1], [2], §7.06[A], §7.06[B][2], Ch. 8 §8.05[F][2], §8.09[C], Ch. 10 §10.05[A][2], Ch. 11 §11.02, §11.03[B][1], §11.03[D][1]

realisation basis — Ch. 3 §3.05[B], Ch. 5 §5.01, §5.02, Ch. 6 §6.02, §6.05[B][1], Ch. 10 §10.01[E][2]

Alignment of accounting standards and taxation rules

Ability-to-pay (principle), and — Ch. 4 §4.05, Ch. 5 §5.02[D], §5.04, §5.08[B], Ch. 11 §11.03[B][1]

Anti-tax Avoidance Directive (ATAD)	Ch. 1 §1.03, Ch. 3 §3.03[C], Ch. 7 §7.04[C], Ch. 10 §10.01[C][2], §10.01[D][2], §10.02[B], §10.05[A][4], [6]
Base Erosion and Profit Shifting (BEPS)	
BEPS Action 2	Ch. 1 §1.02, Ch. 10 §10.01[C], §10.01[C][1], [2], §10.05[A]
BEPS Action 4	Ch. 1 §1.02, Ch. 3 §3.03[C]
Bifurcation	
hybrid instruments, and	Ch. 1 §1.03, Ch. 3 §3.01, §3.05[A], [B], §3.06[C], §3.07, Ch. 6 §6.09[C][1], [2], Ch. 8 §8.03-§8.08, Ch. 10 §10.01[C], §10.02[A][4], [6], §10.05[A][4], [6], Ch. 11 §11.02, §11.03[E][1], [2], §10.03[G][1]
LEGO® principle	Ch. 8 §8.02, §8.04
structured products, and	Ch. 1 §1.01-§1.03, Ch. 2 §2.01[A], [D], Ch. 3 §3.03[B], §3.05[A], [B], Ch. 4 §4.03[C], §4.06[C][2], Ch. 5 §5.07, Ch. 6 §6.09[C][1], [2], Ch. 8 §8.01-§8.10, Ch. 9 §9.01[B], Ch. 10 §10.01[C], §10.05[A], Ch. 11 §11.01, §11.02, §11.03[E][1], [2], §11.03[G][2]
Block cross	Ch. 9 §9.02[E][2][b], [c]
Convertible bond	
bifurcation, and	Ch. 8 §8.04, §8.05[B][1], §8.05[E][1], [2], §8.05[D], [1], [2], §8.05[F][2], §8.06[A][1], §8.06[B][1], [2], §8.07, Ch. 9 §9.01[B], Ch. 10 §10.01[C][1], §10.05[A][4]
definition	Ch. 8 §8.03
integration, and	Ch. 8 §8.05[D], [E], §8.06[A][1], §8.06[B][2], §8.07, §8.08[A], Ch. 10 §10.04[A][4]
qualification as hybrid instrument	Ch. 8 §8.03
Credit derivatives	
definition	Ch. 2 §2.01[B], Ch. 4 §4.03[C][1], §4.06[C][2]

general	Ch. 2 §2.01[B], Ch. 4 §4.03[C][1], §4.06[C][2], §4.06[D][4][d]
recovery rate	Ch. 4 §4.06[C][2]
Cross-border derivatives transaction	Ch. 1 §1.03, Ch. 3 §3.06, §3.07, Ch. 4 §4.03[B], §4.06[D], Ch. 6 §6.05[B], Ch. 10 §10.02[A], §10.02[A][4], [6], Ch. 11 §11.03[F][1], [2]
Crypto derivatives	
accounting, and	Ch 5. §5.06
tax avoidance, and	Ch. 10 §10.04[A][2], §10.04[B][2]
taxation, and	Ch. 6 §6.05[B][3], §6.08
types	Ch. 2 §2.01[C], Ch. 4 §4.01, §4.06[C][3], Ch. 6 §6.05[B][3][a]
Crypto structured products	
accounting, and	Ch. 8 §8.09[B], Ch. 11 §11.02
definition	Ch. 8 §8.09[A]
taxation, and	Ch. 8 §8.09[C], Ch. 10 §10.05[A][5], Ch. 11 §11.03[E][2], §11.04
types	Ch. 8 §8.09[A]
Cryptoassets/cryptocurrencies	
accounting, and	Ch. 5 §5.05
definition	Ch. 2 §2.01[C], Ch. 4 §4.06[C][3]
hedge accounting, and	Ch. 7 §7.03[B][1], §7.06, Ch. 10 §10.05[A][3]
reporting requirement, and	Ch. 1 §1.02, Ch. 6 §6.05[B][3][a], §6.08[C], Ch. 10 §10.04[B][3], §10.05[B][2]
tax avoidance, and	Ch. 10 §10.04
taxation, and	Ch. 6 §6.05[B][3][a], §6.08, §6.09, Ch. 7 §7.06, Ch. 8 §8.09, Ch. 10 §10.04
types	Ch. 2 §2.01[C], Ch. 4 §4.06[C][3]
Defining derivatives, approach to	
abstract or abstract-prescriptive approach	Ch. 4 §4.02, §4.03[B], §4.03[D], §4.04[B], §4.06[A], §4.06[B][5], Ch. 8 §8.04, Ch. 10 §10.01[D][2][a], §10.02[C], §10.04[B][2], §10.05[A][1], Ch. 11 §11.03[A][1], §11.03[B][2]

'borrowing from other legislation' approach — Ch. 4 §4.02, §4.03[A][1][c], §4.03[D]
economic definition approach — Ch. 4 §4.02, §4.04[A], §4.06[B][1]
enumerative approach — Ch. 4 §4.02, §4.03[B], §4.03[D], §4.04[B], §4.06

Derivative contracts legislation, UK
accounting test — Ch. 4 §4.03[A][2], §4.03[B], Ch. 6 §6.02, §6.05[B][3][b], Ch. 9 §9.01[A], Ch. 11 §11.03[A][1]
relevant contract — Ch. 4 §4.03[A][1]-[3], Ch. 5 §5.06[A][2], Ch. 6 §6.02, §6.05[B][1], §6.05[B][3][b], [c], Ch. 8 §8.05[F][1][b], §8.05[F][2][a], Ch. 9 §9.01[A]
underlying subject matter test — Ch. 4 §4.03[A][3], §4.03[B], Ch. 6 §6.02, §6.05[B][1], [3], Ch. 8 §8.05[F][2][a], Ch. 11 §11.03[A][1]

Derivative, derivative contract
cash-settled derivative, cash settlement — Ch. 3 §3.03[C], Ch. 4 §4.03[A][1]-[3], §4.03[C][1], [2], Ch. 5 §5.06[A], Ch. 6 §6.03, §6.04, §6.05[B][2], §6.06[C][2][a], [b], §6.07[C], §6.09[B], [C]
commodity derivative — Ch. 4 §2.01[B], §4.03[A][2], Ch. 7 §7.03[A][2], §7.06[B][2][b]
contingent claims — Ch. 2 §2.01, Ch. 4 §4.06[B][1], [3]
contract for differences (CFD) — Ch. 4 §4.01, §4.03[A][1], §4.03[A][1][c], §4.03[B], [C], Ch. 6 §6.05[B][2][e], [f], §6.05[B][3][a], Ch. 8 §8.05[F][2][a]
credit derivative — Ch. 1 §1.03, Ch. 2 §2.01[B], §2.01[D], Ch. 4 §4.03[C][1], §4.06[C][2]
currency derivative/ FX derivative — Ch. 2 §2.01[B], Ch. 4 §4.06[C][4][c], Ch. 6 §6.05[B][1], §6.05[B][2][d], Ch. 7 §7.03[A][2][a], Ch. 10 §10.01[A]
deterministic dependence, and — Ch. 4 §4.06[B][2]

embedded derivative — Ch. 1 §1.03, Ch. 4 §4.03[A], [B], Ch. 5 §5.02[B], §5.06, §5.07, Ch. 6 §6.02, §6.05[B], §6.05[B][1], §6.05[B][2][f], §6.05[B][3], Ch. 8 §8.05[B][1], [2], §8.05[C][1], §8.05[D][1], §8.05 [D][2][b], §8.05[D][3], [4], §8.05[F][1][b], §8.05[F][2][a], §8.09[A]-[C], §8.10[D][2], [3], §8.10[E][1][a], [b], Ch. 11 §11.03[E][1]

equity derivative — Ch. 2 §2.01[B], Ch. 3 §3.03[C], Ch. 4 §4.03[A][3], Ch. 5 §5.02[C][2], Ch. 6 §6.02, §6.02[C][2], §6.05[B][1], §6.05[B][2][a], [d], [f], §6.05[B][3][b], §6.06[C][2][b], §6.07[A], [C], §6.09[B], [C], Ch. 8 §8.05[F][2][a], Ch. 10 §10.01[E][2], Ch. 11 §11.03[C][1], [2], §11.03[E][2]

fixed income or interest rate derivative — Ch. 2 §2.01[B], Ch. 7 §7.03[A][2], Ch. 8 §8.06[A][1][a], Ch. 10 §10.01[A][4]

New Financial Instruments (NFI), and — Ch. 4 §4.04[B], §4.06[A], Ch. 11 §11.04

over-the-counter (OTC) — Ch. 2 §2.01[A], Ch. 3 §3.06[B], Ch. 4 §4.03[A][1], §4.06[C][2]-[4], Ch. 6 §6.05[B][1], §6.06[C][2][a], Ch. 7 §7.06[B][1][c], §7.06[C][2], Ch. 9 §9.02[E][2][a]

physically settled derivative, physical settlement — Ch. 4 §4.03[A][1][c], §4.03[C][1], [2], Ch. 5 §5.06[A][1], §5.06[C], §6.04, §6.06[C][2][a], §6.07[C], §6.09[C][1], [2], Ch. 7 §7.06[B][1], Ch. 11 §11.03[A], §11.03[C][1]

stochastic variables, and — Ch. 4 §4.06[B][2], [5], §4.06[C][3], Ch. 11 §11.03[B][2]

weather derivative — Ch. 2 §2.01[D], Ch. 4 §4.06[B][4], §4.06[C][4][a], [b]

Designing tax law, approach to

coherent principles approach — Ch. 4 §4.02, §4.04[A], Ch. 10 §10.05[B][3], §10.05[B][3][d], §10.05[B][3][e][iii], §10.05[B][2][e][v], Ch. 11 §11.03[G][2]

formal approach	Ch. 10 §10.05[B], §10.05[B][3][a], §10.05[B][3][e][iv], §10.05[B][3][e][v], Ch. 11 §11.03[G][2]
principles-based approach	Ch. 4 §4.02, Ch. 10 §10.01[D][2][a], §10.05[B][3], §10.05[B][3][b], §10.05[B][3][e][ii], [iv]
purposive approach	Ch. 10 §10.05[B][3][c], §10.05[B][3][e][i], §10.05[B][3][e][v], §10.05[B][4], Ch. 11 §11.03[G][2]
Disregard Regulations	Ch. 6 §6.05[B][2][d], Ch. 7 §7.03[2], §7.03[2][a], §7.03[C], §7.06[B][2][b], Ch. 11 §11.03[B][1]
Efficient-market hypothesis	Ch. 7 §7.04[B]
ESG derivatives	
accounting, and	Ch. 5 §5.07
definition	Ch. 2 §2.01[D], Ch. 4 §4.03[D], §4.04[B], §4.06[C][4]
types	Ch. 4 §4.06[C][4]
ESG-linked structured products	
accounting, and	Ch. 8 §8.10[D]
definition	Ch. 8 §8.10[A]
regulation, and	Ch. 8 §8.10[B]
taxation, and	Ch. 8 §8.10[E]
types	Ch. 8 §8.10[C]
Exchangeable bond	
bifurcation, and	Ch. 8 §8.05[C][2], §8.05[D][3], §8.05[E], §8.05[F][1][b][iv], [v], §8.05[F][2][a][ii], §8.06[A][2][a], [b], §8.06[B][2][b], §8.07, Ch. 10 §10.01[C][1], §10.05[A][4]
definition	Ch. 8 §8.03
integration, and	Ch. 8 §8.04, §8.05[A], §8.05[C][2], §8.05[D][3], §8.05[E], §8.05[F][1][a], §8.05[F][2][a][ii], §8.06[A][2][a], [b], §8.06[B][2][a], [b], §8.07, Ch. 10 §10.01[C][1], §10.05[A][4]
Forward contract, forward	
definition	Ch. 2 §2.01[A], Ch. 4 §4.03[A][1][a], §4.06[C][3], §4.06[D][4][a], Ch. 5 §5.02[C][3][e], §5.06[A][1][a][ii]

forward purchase	Ch. 2 §2.01[A], Ch. 5 §5.02[C][3][e], Ch. 9 §9.02[E][2][c][iii]
forward sale	Ch. 2 §2.01[A]
replication, and	Ch. 2 §2.02[A], §2.02[A][1]
Futures contract, future(s)	
accounting treatment, and	Ch. 5 §5.02[B][1], §5.02[C][1], [3], §5.02[D][3][e], §5.03[B], §5.06[A][1], Ch. 7 §7.01, §7.03[A][1], §7.06[B][1][a], [b], §7.06[C][2], Ch. 8 §8.09[A]
definition	Ch. 2 §2.01[A], §2.01[D], §2.02[A], Ch. §4.03[A][1][a], §4.03[A][3], §4.03[B], §4.03[C][1]
hedging, and	Ch. 7 §7.01, §7.03[A][1], §7.06[B][2][b], §7.06[C][2], Ch. 8 §8.05[F][2]
withholding tax, and	Ch. 9 §9.01[A], [B], §9.01[E][2][b], [c], §9.03[A], [B], Ch. 11 §11.03[F][2]
General Anti-Abuse Rule, General Anti-Avoidance Rule (GAAR)	
double reasonableness test	Ch. 10 §10.01[D][2][a]
general	Ch. 3 §3.07, Ch. 10 §10.01[D][2], §10.02[A][5], §10.02[B], [C], §10.05[B][1], §10.05[B][3][e][iv], Ch. 11 §11.02, §11.03[G][1], [2]
German Generally Accepted Accounting Principles (German GAAP)	
authoritative principle (*Grundsatz der Maßgeblichkeit*)	Ch. 5 §5.03[A], §5.04, Ch. 8 §8.06[B][1], §8.06[B][2][b], Ch. 9 §9.02[C]
general principles of orderly accounting (*Grundsätze ordnungsgemäßer Buchführung*)	Ch. 5 §5.03[A], [B], Ch. 8 §8.06[A], §8.06[B][1], §8.06[B][2][b], Ch. 11 §11.03[B][1], §11.03[E][1]
historical cost principle	Ch. 5 §5.03[B], §5.08[B], Ch. 11 §11.03[B][1]
imparity principle	Ch. 5 §5.03[B], Ch. 7 §7.03[B][1], §7.06[C][1]

item-per-item valuation	Ch. 5 §5.03[B], Ch. 8 §8.06[A], §8.06[A][1], §8.06[B][1]
modified fair value method	Ch. 5 §5.03[B], Ch. 11 §11.03[B][1]
pending transactions	Ch. 5 §5.03[B], Ch. 6 §6.06[C][2][c], Ch. 7 §7.03[B][1]
prudence principle	Ch. 5 §5.03[B], §5.08[A], Ch. 11 §11.03[C][1]
realisation principle	Ch. 5 §5.03[B], Ch. 10 §10.03[B][1]
Hedge accounting	
anticipatory hedge	Ch. 7 §7.03[A][2][a], §7.03[B][1], §7.03[C], §7.06[B][2][b], §7.06[C][1]
cash flow hedge	Ch. 5 §5.02[1], Ch. 7 §7.03[A][1][a]-[c], §7.03[A][2], §7.03[B][1], §7.06[B][1][a], §7.06[C][1]
fair value hedge	Ch. 5 §5.01, §5.02[C][1], Ch. 7 §7.03[A][1][a][iv], §7.03[A][1][b], [c], §7.03[A][1][c][iii], §7.03[A][2][a][ii], §7.03[B][1], §7.06[B][1][a][ii], §7.06[B][2][b]
hedge effectiveness	Ch. 2 §2.02[B], Ch. 3 §3.04, Ch. 6 §6.05[B][1][a], Ch. 7 §7.03[A][1][a], [c] §7.03[A][2], §7.03[B][1], §7.03[C], §7.05[A], §7.06[B][1][a]-[c], §7.06[B][2][a], [b], §7.06[C][1], [2], Ch. 10 §10.05[A][3]
Hedging	
dynamic hedging	Ch. 2 §2.02[B], §2.02[C], Ch. 7 §7.04[A], Ch. 8 §8.04
hedging portfolio	Ch. 2 §2.02[B], Ch. 7 §7.01
macro hedge, macro hedging	Ch. 7 §7.01, §7.03[B][1], [2], §7.05[A], §7.06[C][1], [2], Ch. 11 §11.03[D][2]
micro hedging	Ch. 7 §7.01, §7.03[A][1], §7.03[B][2], §7.05[A], §7.06[C][2]
overhedging	Ch. 6 §6.06[C][2][a], Ch. 7 §7.04[A], §7.04[B], §7.04[C], §7.04[D], §7.05[B], Ch. 10 §10.01[D], Ch. 11 §11.03[D][1]
portfolio hedge, portfolio hedging	Ch. 7 §7.01, §7.03[A][1][b], §7.03[B][1], §7.05[A], §7.06[C][1], [2]

post-tax hedging, after-tax hedging	Ch. 3 §3.04, Ch. 7 §7.02, §7.02[B], §7.04[A], §7.04[B], §7.04[C], §7.04[D], §7.05, §7.05[B], Ch. 10 §10.01[D], §10.01[A], §10.05[A][3], Ch. 11 §11.02, §11.03[D][1], §11.03[D][2]
static hedging	Ch. 2 §2.02[B]
underhedging	Ch. 7 §7.01, §7.04[A], §7.04[B], §7.04[C], §7.04[D], §7.05[B], Ch. 11 §11.03[D][1]
Hybrid capital instruments	Ch. 10 §10.01[C][3]
Hybrid instruments	
bifurcation, and	Ch. 1 §1.03, Ch. 3, §3.05, §3.05[B], Ch. 6 §6.09[C][2], Ch. 8 §8.04, §8.05[B][1], [2], §8.05[C][1], [2], §8.05[D], §8.05[D][1], [2], §8.05[D][2][b], §8.05[E], §8.05[F][1][b], §8.05[F][1][b][ii], [iv], [v], §8.05[F][2][a][ii], §8.06[A], §8.06[A][1], §8.06[A][2][a], [b], §8.06[B][2][a], [b], §8.07, §8.08, §8.08[A], Ch. 10 §10.01[C][1], §10.05[A][4], Ch. 11 §11.02, §11.03[E][1], [2], §11.03[G][2]
definition	Ch. 8 §8.03
integration, and	Ch. 3, §3.05, §3.05[B], Ch. 6 §6.09[C][2], Ch. 8 §8.04, §8.05[A], §8.05[B][1], [2], §8.05[C][1], [2], §8.05[D][1], [2], §8.05[E], §8.05[F][1][a], §8.05[F][1][a][v], §8.05[F][2][a][ii], §8.06[A][2][a], [b], §8.06[B][2][a], [b], §8.07, §8.08, Ch. 10 §10.05[A][4], Ch. 11 §11.02, §11.03[E][1], [2], §11.03[G][2]
qualification conflict, and	Ch. 3 §3.06[A], §3.06[C], §3.07, Ch. 10 §10.01[C][1], §10.02[A][4], Ch. 11 §11.03[C][2]
Hybrid mismatch rules	Ch. 1 §1.02, §1.03, Ch. 7, §7.04[C], Ch. 10 §10.01[C][1], [2], §10.02[B], §10.04[A][4], [6]

Integrative approach Ch. 6 §6.03, §6.07[A], §6.09[A]-[C], §6.09[C][1], [3], Ch. 8 §8.05[C][2], Ch. 11 §11.03[C][1], [2]

International Accounting Standards (IAS)

IAS 32 Ch. 4 §4.06[C][3][a], Ch. 5 §5.02[A], §5.02[B][3], §5.05[A][1][a], Ch. 6, §6.05[B][3][b], Ch. 8 §8.05, §8.05[B][1], §8.05[C][2], §8.05[D][3], [5], §8.05[E], §8.05[F][2][a][ii], §8.06[A][1]

IAS 39 Ch. 4 §4.03[A][2], §4.05, Ch. 5 §5.02[A], §5.02[B], §5.02[B][2], [4], §5.02[C], §5.02[C][2], §5.02[D], §5.06[A][2], §5.08[B], Ch. 6 §6.01, §6.05[B][1], Ch. 7 §7.03[A][1], §7.03[A][2], §7.03[B][1], §7.03[C], §7.06[B][1], §7.06[B][1][b], [c], §7.06[2][a], [b], §7.06[C][1], Ch. 8 §8.05, §8.05[B][1], [2], §8.05[C][2], §8.05[D][1], [2], §8.05[D][2][b], §8.05[D][3], §8.05[E], §8.05[F][1][b][iv], §8.05[F][2][a][i], [ii], §8.10[E][1][a], Ch. 10 §10.01[C][1], Ch. 11 §11.03[D][1], [2]

International Financial Reporting Standards

IFRS 9 Ch. 4 §4.01, §4.03[A][2], §4.05, §4.06[C][3][a], Ch. 5 §5.01, §5.02[A], [B], §5.02[B][3], [4], §5.02[C][3], §5.02[D], §5.05[A][1][a], §5.06[A][1][a], [b], §5.06[A][2], §5.07, §5.08, §5.08[B], Ch. 6 §6.02, §6.05[B][3][a], [b], Ch. 7 §7.03[A][1], §7.03[A][1][c], §7.03[C], §7.06[B][1][c], §7.06[B][2][a], [b], Ch. 8 §8.05, §8.05[C][1], [2], §8.05[D][1][a], §8.05[D][5], §8.05[E], [F], §8.07, §8.09[B], §8.10[D][3], §8.10[E][1][a], [b], Ch. 11 §11.03[B][1], §11.03[D][1], [2], §11.03[E][1]

ISDA

documented under — Ch. 2 §2.01[D], Ch. 4 §4.03[A][1][a], §4.06[C][2], §4.06[C][4][c]-[f], Ch. 7 §7.04[B], Ch. 8 §8.10[C], Ch. 9 §9.02[D][3], §9.02[E][2][a][v], Ch. 10 §10.04[A][6]

Loan relationships — Ch. 4 §4.03, Ch. 5 §5.01, Ch. 6 §6.01, §6.02, §6.05[B][1], §6.05[B][2][a], [c], Ch. 8 §8.05[D][2][b], §8.05[F][1][a], [b], §8.05[F][2][a][i], §8.07, §8.09[C][1], §8.10[E][1][a], Ch. 10 §10.01[A][6], §10.01[B], §10.01[C], §10.01[C][2], [3], §10.01[C][3][a], [b], §10.01[E][2], §10.05[B][3][c], §10.03[E][1]

Manufactured dividends — Ch. 3 §3.06[A], Ch. 6 §6.06[C][2][c], Ch. 9 §9.01[C][1], §9.02[C][2], §9.02[E], §9.02[E][2][a], [b], §9.03[B], Ch. 11 §11.03[F][1][a], §11.03[F][2]

Manufactured overseas dividends (MODs) — Ch. 9 §9.01[C][1], Ch. 11 §11.03[F][1][a]

Non-structured financial instrument

definition — Ch. 3 §3.05, §3.05[A], Ch. 8 §8.01[A], §8.06[A][1]

Option contract, option

American option — Ch. 2 §2.01[A]

call option, call — Ch. 2 §2.01[A], [B], §2.02[A][1], §2.02[B], Ch. 4 §4.03[C][1], Ch. 6 §6.05[B][2][a], [e], §6.06[C][2][b][i], Ch. 7 §7.03[A][1][b], Ch. 8 §8.01[A], §8.01[B][1], [3], §8.02, §8.04, §8.05[C][2], [4], §8.06[A][2][a], Ch. 9 §9.02[C], Ch. 10 §10.01[E][3]

cap — Ch. 2 §2.01[A]

collar — Ch. 2 §2.01[A], Ch. 3 §3.04, Ch. 4 §4.06[C][4][a], Ch. 7 §7.03[A][1][a], Ch. 8 §8.01[B][3]

definition — Ch. 2 §2.01[A], Ch. 4 §4.02, §4.03[A][1][b], §4.03[C][1], §4.04[A], §4.06[C], §4.06[C][2]-[4]

equity option — Ch. 2 §2.02[C], Ch. 6 §6.02, §6.05[B][2][d], §6.05[B][2][f][i], [ii], §6.06[2][b][i], Ch. 7 §7.01, §7.05[A], Ch. 8 §8.04, §8.05[B][1], §8.05[C][2], Ch. 9 §9.02[B], Ch. 10 §10.01[C][1]

European option — Ch. 2 §2.01[A], Ch. 4 §4.06[C][4][a]

floor — Ch. 2 §2.01[A]

put option, put — Ch. 2 §2.01[A], §2.02[A][1], Ch. 3 §3.04, Ch. 4 §4.06[C][4][a], Ch. 6 §6.06[C][2][b][i], Ch. 8 §8.01[A], §8.01[B][1], [4], §8.02, §8.05[E][4], §8.06[A][1][a], §8.09[A], Ch. 10 §10.01[E][1]

Ownership

beneficial ownership — Ch. 1 §1.03, Ch. 3 §3.06, §3.06[B], Ch. 9 §9.02, §9.02[A], [B], [D], [E], §9.02[E][1], [2], §9.03[A], [B], Ch. 11 §11.02, §11.03[F][1][b], §11.03[G][2]

economic ownership — Ch. 3 §3.06[B], Ch. 9 §9.02[C], [D], §9.02[E][3]

Pillar Two

Germany, and — Ch. 10 §10.02[D], §10.05[B][4]

UK, and — Ch. 10 §10.01[D][3], §10.05[B][4]

Put-call parity

basic building blocks — Ch. 4 §4.04[B], Ch. 8 §8.01[A], §8.01[B][1], §8.04

general — Ch. 2 §2.02[A][1], Ch. 3 §3.03[B], §3.03[C], §3.05[B], Ch. 6 §6.08[C][3], Ch. 8 §8.01[A], §8.01[B][1], §8.04, §8.05[E][4], §8.08[B][2], Ch. 10 §10.01[E][2], Ch. 11 §11.03[E][2]

Qualification conflicts — Ch. 3 §3.06, §3.06[A], §3.06[C], §3.07, Ch. 6 §6.08[C][1], Ch. 10 §10.01[C][1], §10.02[A][4], §10.05[A][6], Ch.11 §11.03[C][2]

Replication

dynamic replication — Ch. 2 §2.02[A], §2.02[A][2], §2.02[B], Ch. 8 §8.04

economic replication	Ch. 2 §2.02[A], Ch. 3 §3.03[C], Ch. 6 §6.09[B], Ch. 10 §10.05, Ch. 11 §11.03[C][2]
static replication	Ch. 2 §2.02[A], §2.02[A][1], §2.02[B], Ch. 3 §3.03[B], Ch. 8 §8.04 §8.05[E]
synthetic replication	Ch. 2 §2.02[A][1], Ch. 3 §3.05
Reverse convertible bond	
general	Ch. 8 §8.01[B][4], §8.05[E][4], [5], §8.06[A][1][a]
Ring-fenced (derivatives) losses	Ch. 3 §3.04, §3.07, Ch. 4 §4.03[C][2], §4.03[D], Ch. 6 §6.04, §6.06[C][2][a], §6.06[C][2][b], [c], §6.07[C], Ch. 7, §7.04[B], §7.06[C][2], Ch. 8 §8.09[C][1], §8.10[E][2], Ch. 10 §10.01[A][1], §10.02[A][1], [2]
Risk transfer scheme	Ch. 3 §3.07, Ch. 6 §6.05, Ch. 7 §7.04[B], §7.05, §7.05[B], Ch. 10 §10.01
SOCIE	Ch. 5 §5.02[B]
Special regime approach	Ch. 6 §6.01, §6.05[B][1], §6.07[A], §6.09[B], §6.09[C][2], [3], Ch. 11 §11.03[C][1], [2]
Specific anti-avoidance rule/targeted anti-avoidance rule	Ch. 3 §3.07, Ch. 6 §6.05[B], §6.05[B][1], Ch. 7 §7.04[C], §7.05[B], Ch. 10 §10.01, §10.01[A], §10.01[D][2][c], §10.02, §10.02[A][1], [5], §10.02[C], §10.04[A][2], §10.04[B][1], [2], §10.05[B], §10.05[B][1], Ch. 11 §11.02, §11.03[D][1], §11.03[E][2], §11.03[G][1], [2]
STRGL	Ch. 6 §6.05[B][2][d]
Structured products	
bifurcation, and	Ch. 3 §3.05, §3.05[A], [B], Ch. 4 §4.03[A][3], Ch. 6 §6.02, §6.09[C][2], Ch. 8 §8.02, §8.05[B]-[F], §8.06[A][1], [2], §8.06[B][1], §8.07, §8.08[B][1], §8.09[B], §8.10[D][2], [3], §8.10[E][1], [2], Ch 10, §10.01[C][1], §10.05[A][5], Ch. 11 §11.03[E][2], §11.03[G][2]

combinations of derivatives, and	Ch. 3 §3.03[B], Ch. 8 §8.08[B][2]
definition	Ch. 3 §3.05[A], Ch. 8 §8.01[A], §8.01[B][1]-[4], §8.01[C], §8.09[A], §8.10[A]
false friends, and	Ch. 8 §8.01[B][1]-[3], §8.05[E][4], §8.08[B][2], Ch. 10 §10.05[A][5]
integration, and	Ch. 3 §3.05, §3.05[A], Ch. 6 §6.09[C][2], Ch. 8 §8.05, §8.05[C][1], [2], §8.05[D], [E], §8.06[A][1], §8.06[B][1], §8.07, §8.08, §8.08[B][2], §8.09[B], §8.10[D][3], Ch. 10 §10.05[A][5], Ch. 11 §11.02, §11.03[E][1], §11.03[E][2]
legally inseparable combinations	Ch. 8 §8.01[A], §8.01[B][2]-[4], §8.02, §8.06[B][1], §8.09[B], §8.10[A]
Swap	
definition	Ch. 2 §2.01[A], §2.01[D], Ch. 4 §4.03[A][1][a], [c], §4.04[A], §4.05, §4.06[C][1]-[3], §4.06[C][4][b], [c]
dividend swap	Ch. 3 §3.06[A], Ch. 4 §4.06[B][1], §4.06[C][1], §4.06[D], Ch. 9 §9.01[C][1], [2], Ch. 11 §11.03[F][1][a]
equity swap	Ch. 3 §3.06[B], Ch. 4 §4.03[A][1][a], §4.03[B], §4.06[D], Ch. 6 §6.05[B][2][f][ii], §6.06[C][2][c], Ch. 8 §8.01, Ch. 9 §9.01[C][1], [2], §9.02[D][3], §9.02[E][2][a][iv], §9.02[E][2][c][v], Ch. 11 §11.03[F][1][a]
interest rate swap	Ch. 2 §2.01[D], Ch. 3 §3.06[A], [B], Ch. 4 §4.06[C][1], §4.06[C][4], Ch. 5 §5.02[C][1], Ch. 6 §6.05[B][2][a], Ch. 7 §7.01, §7.03[A][1][b], Ch. 8 §8.01, Ch. 9 §9.01[A], Ch. 10 §10.01[A][4], §10.01[E][4]-[6]
total return equity swap	Ch. 4 §4.03[A][2][a][i], §4.03[A][3]

total return swap — Ch. 3 §3.06[B], Ch. 4 §4.06[C][2], Ch. 6 §6.05[B][2][e], §6.06[C][2][c][i], Ch. 7 §7.04[B], Ch. 9 §9.01[C][1], §9.02[C], §9.03[D][3], §9.03[E][2][a][ii], [iii], §9.03[E][2][b][iii]

Switch-over clause — Ch. 10 §10.01[C][1], §10.02, §10.02[A][4], §10.05[A][6], Ch. 11 §11.03[G][1], [2]

Tax Law Rewrite — Ch. 4 §4.03[A], [B]

Taxation of Financial Arrangement Rules (TOFA)

generally — Ch. 4 §4.04[A], Ch. 10 §10.04[B][3][d], §10.04[B][3][e][iii]

UK Financial Reporting Standards

FRS 100 — Ch. 5 §5.02[A]

FRS 101 — Ch. 5 §5.02[A], §5.03[B][3], Ch. 7 §7.03[A][2][a][i]

FRS 102 — Ch. 4 §4.03[A][1][c], §4.03[A][2], §4.06[C][3], Ch. 5 §5.02[A], [B], §5.02[B][1], [4], §5.02[C], §5.02[C][1], §5.02[D], §5.05[B][1], [2], §5.06[A][1], Ch. 6 §6.02, §6.05[B][3][a], §6.08[A], Ch. 7 §7.02[A][2][a][i], §7.03[A][2], §7.03[C], §7.06[B][1][a], §7.06[B][2][a], [b], Ch. 8 §8.05, §8.05[D][1], [2], §8.05[D][2][a], §8.05[D][3]-[5], §8.05[F][2], §8.07, §8.09[B], §8.10[D][3], §8.10[E][1][a], [b], Ch. 10 §10.04[A][1][a], Ch. 11 §11.03[D][1], §11.03[E][1]

UK Generally Accepted Accounting Practice (UK GAAP)

generally — Ch. 4 §4.03[A], §4.03[A][1], Ch. 5 §5.02[A], [B], §5.02[C][2], §5.02[D], §5.05[B][1], Ch. 6 §6.05[B][1], Ch. 7 §7.03[A][1], §7.03[A][1][a][i], [ii], §7.06[B], Ch. 8 §8.05, §8.05[A], §8.05[F][1][a], [b], §8.07, Ch. 10 §10.01[C], §10.05[A][1], [2], Ch. 11 §11.03[B][1], §11.03[D][2] old UK GAAP — Ch. 5 §5.02[A], §5.05[A], Ch. 6 §6.05[B][1], Ch. 7 §7.03[A][1], [2], §7.03[A][a][i], [ii], §7.06[B][2][b], Ch. 8 §8.05, §8.05[A], §8.05[F][2][a][i], [ii], §8.07, Ch. 10 §10.01[A][5]

Underlying

underlying asset — Ch. 1 §1.03, Ch. 2 §2.01[A], [B], §2.02[A], §2.02[A][1], [2], §2.02[C], [D], Ch. 4 §4.03[C][1], [2], §4.06[B][1], [3], [4], §4.06[B][5], §4.06[C], §4.06[C][2], §4.06[C][3], §4.06[C][3][a], §4.06[C][4], Ch. 5 §5.02[C][3][a], §5.06, §5.06[A], §5.06[A][1][a][i], §5.06[A][1][b], §5.06[C], Ch. 6 §6.06[C][1], §6.06[C][2][a], Ch. 7 §7.06[B][1][b], Ch. 8 §8.01[A], §8.01[B][1], §8.09, §8.09[A], §8.10[A], [B], Ch. 9 §9.02[E][2][a][i], Ch. 11 §11.03[A][2], §11.04

underlying parameter — Ch. 4 §4.03[C][1], §4.06[B][1]

underlying variable — Ch. 2 §2.01, §2.01[A]-[D], §2.02[A], [B], §2.02[C], [D], Ch. 4 §4.03[A][2], §4.03[C][1], [2], §4.03[D], §4.05, §4.06[B][1], [2], [4], [5], §4.06[C][1]-[4], Ch. 5 §5.02[B][1], [3], §5.02[C][3], [4], §5.02[C][4][e], §5.05[A][1][a], §5.06[A][1][b], Ch. 6 §6.05[B], §6.05[B][3][a], Ch. 7 §7.01, Ch. 8 §8.06[A][1][a], Ch. 11 §11.03[B][2]

Valuation, of options

Black-Scholes model/ Black-Scholes formula — Ch. 2 §2.02[C], Ch. 7 §7.01, Ch. 8 §8.02

intrinsic value — Ch. 2 §2.02[C], Ch. 7 §7.03[A][1][a][ii], §7.06[B][1][a][i]

time value — Ch. 2 §2.02[C], Ch. 7 §7.03[A][1][a][ii], §7.06[B][1][a][i]

Withholding tax

derivatives, and Ch. 3 §3.05[B], §3.06, §3.06[A], [B], §3.07, Ch. 5 §5.08[A], Ch. 6 §6.06[A], §6.09[C][2], Ch. 9 §9.01, §9.01[A], [B], §9.01[C][1], [2], §9.02[D][3], §9.03[E], §9.02[E][2][a]-[c], §9.03, §9.03[A], §9.03[A][1][b], §9.03[B], [C], Ch. 10 §10.01[C][1], [2], §10.02[A][5], §10.03, §10.05[A][6], Ch. 11 §11.02, §11.03[F][1][a], §11.03[F][2]

SERIES ON INTERNATIONAL TAXATION

1. Alberto Xavier, *The Taxation of Foreign Investment in Brazil,* 1980 (ISBN 90-200-0582-0).
2. Hugh J. Ault & Albert J. Rädler, *The German Corporation Tax Law with 1980 Amendments,* 1981 (ISBN 90-200-0642-8).
3. Paul R. McDaniel & Hugh J. Ault, *Introduction to United States International Taxation,* 1981 (ISBN 90-6544-004-6).
4. Albert J. Rädler, *German Transfer Pricing/Prix de Transfer en Allemagne,* 1984 (ISBN 90-6544-143-3).
5. Paul R. McDaniel & Stanley S. Surrey, *International Aspects of Tax Expenditures: A Comparative Study,* 1985 (ISBN 90-654-4163-8).
6. Kees van Raad, *Nondiscrimination in International Tax Law,* 1986 (ISBN 90-6544-266-9).
7. Sijbren Cnossen (ed.), *Tax Coordination in the European Community,* 1987 (ISBN 90-6544-272-3).
8. Ben Terra, *Sales Taxation. The Case of Value Added Tax in the European Community,* 1989 (ISBN 90-6544-381-9).
9. Rutsel S.J. Martha, *The Jurisdiction to Tax in International Law: Theory and Practice of Legislative Fiscal Jurisdiction,* 1989 (ISBN 90-654-4416-5).
10. Paul R. McDaniel & Hugh J. Ault, *Introduction to United States International Taxation* (3rd revised edition), 1989 (ISBN 90-6544-423-8).
11. Manuel Pires, *International Juridicial Double Taxation of Income,* 1989 (ISBN 90-6544-426-2).
12. A.H.M. Daniels, *Issues in International Partnership Taxation,* 1991 (ISBN 90-654-4577-3).
13. Arvid A. Skaar, *Permanent Establishment: Erosion of a Tax Treaty Principle,* 1992 (ISBN 90-6544-594-3).
14. Cyrille David & Geerten M.M. Michielse (eds), *Tax Treatment of Financial Instruments,* 1996 (ISBN 90-654-4666-4).
15. Herbert H. Alpert & Kees van Raad (eds), *Essays on International Taxation,* 1993 (ISBN 90-654-4781-4).
16. Wolfgang Gassner, Michael Lang & Eduard Lechner (eds), *Tax Treaties and EC Law,* 1997 (ISBN 90-411-0680-4).
17. Glória Teixeira, *Taxing Corporate Profits in the EU,* 1997 (ISBN 90-411-0703-7).
18. Michael Lang et al. (eds), *Multilateral Tax Treaties,* 1998 (ISBN 90-411-0704-5).
19. Stef van Weeghel, *The Improper Use of Tax Treaties,* 1998 (ISBN 90-411-0737-1).

20. Klaus Vogel (ed.), *Interpretation of Tax Law and Treaties and Transfer Pricing in Japan and Germany*, 1998 (ISBN 90-411-9655-2).
21. Bertil Wiman (ed.), *International Studies in Taxation: Law and Economics; Liber Amicorum Leif Mutén*, 1999 (ISBN 90-411-9692-7).
22. Alfonso J. Martín Jiménez, *Towards Corporate Tax Harmonization in the European Community*, 1999 (ISBN 90-411-9690-0).
23. Ramon J. Jeffery, *The Impact of State Sovereignty on Global Trade and International Taxation*, 1999 (ISBN 90-411-9703-6).
24. A.J. Easson, *Taxation of Foreign Direct Investment*, 1999 (ISBN 90-411-9741-9).
25. Marjaana Helminen, *The Dividend Concept in International Tax Law: Dividend Payments Between Corporate Entities*, 1999 (ISBN 90-411-9765-6).
26. Paul Kirchhof, Moris Lehner, Kees van Raad, Arndt Raupach & Michael-Rodi (eds), *International and Comparative Taxation: Essays in Honour of Klaus Vogel*, 2002 (ISBN 90-411-9841-5).
27. Krister Andersson, Peter Melz & Christer Silfverberg (eds), *Liber Amicorum Sven-Olof Lodin*, 2001 (ISBN 90-411-9850-4).
28. Juan Martín Jovanovich, *Customs Valuation and Transfer Pricing: Is It Possible to Harmonize Customs and Tax Rules?*, Second Edition, 2018 (ISBN 978-90-411-6134-5).
29. Stefano Simontacchi, *Taxation of Capital Gains under the OECD Model Convention: With Special Regard to Immovable Property*, 2007 (ISBN 978-90-411-2549-1).
30. Michael Lang, Josef Schuch, & Claus Staringer (eds), *Tax Treaty Law and EC Law*, 2007 (ISBN 978-90-411-2629-0).
31. Duncan Bentley, *Taxpayers' Rights: Theory Origin and Implementation*, 2007 (ISBN 978-90-411-2650-4).
32. Sergio André Rocha, *Interpretation of Double Taxation Conventions: General Theory and Brazilian Perspective*, 2008 (ISBN 978-90-411-2822-5).
33. Robert F. van Brederode, *Systems of General Sales Taxation: Theory, Policy and Practice*, 2009 (ISBN 978-90-411-2832-4).
34. John G. Head & Richard Krever (eds), *Tax Reform in the 21st Century: A Volume in Memory of Richard Musgrave*, 2009 (ISBN 978-90-411-2829-4).
35. Jens Wittendorff, *Transfer Pricing and the Arm's Length Principle in International Tax Law*, 2010 (ISBN 978-90-411-3270-3).
36. Marjaana Helminen, *The International Tax Law Concept of Dividend*, Second Edition, 2017 (ISBN 978-90-411-8394-1).
37. Robert F. van Brederode (ed.), *Immovable Property under VAT: A Comparative Global Analysis*, 2011 (ISBN 978-90-411-3126-3).
38. Dennis Weber & Stef van Weeghel, *The 2010 OECD Updates: Model Tax Convention & Transfer Pricing Guidelines - A Critical Review*, 2011 (ISBN 978-90-411-3812-5).
39. Yariv Brauner & Martin James McMahon, Jr. (eds), *The Proper Tax Base: Structural Fairness from an International and Comparative Perspective— Essays in Honour of Paul McDaniel*, 2012 (ISBN 978-90-411-3286-4).
40. Robert F. van Brederode (ed.), *Science, Technology and Taxation*, 2012 (ISBN 978-90-411-3125-6).

41. Oskar Henkow, *The VAT/GST Treatment of Public Bodies*, 2013 (ISBN 978-90-411-4663-2).
42. Jean Schaffner, *How Fixed Is a Permanent Establishment?*, 2013 (ISBN 978-90-411-4662-5).
43. Miguel Correia, *Taxation of Corporate Groups*, 2013 (ISBN 978-90-411-4841-4).
44. Veronika Daurer, *Tax Treaties and Developing Countries*, 2014 (ISBN 978-90-411-4982-4).
45. Claire Micheau, *State Aid, Subsidy and Tax Incentives under EU and WTO Law*, 2014 (ISBN 978-90-411-4555-0).
46. Robert F. van Brederode & Richard Krever (eds), *Legal Interpretation of Tax Law*, 2014 (ISBN 978-90-411-4945-9).
47. Radhakishan Rawal, *Taxation of Cross-border Services*, 2014 (ISBN 978-90-411-4947-3).
48. João Dácio Rolim, *Proportionality and Fair Taxation*, 2014 (ISBN 978-90-411-5838-3).
49. Paulo Rosenblatt, *General Anti-avoidance Rules for Major Developing Countries*, 2015 (ISBN 978-90-411-5839-0).
50. Gaspar Lopes Dias V.S., *Tax Arbitrage through Cross-Border Financial Engineering*, 2015 (ISBN 978-90-411-5875-8).
51. Geerten M.M. Michielse & Victor Thuronyi (eds), *Tax Design Issues Worldwide*, 2015 (ISBN 978-90-411-5610-5).
52. Oktavia Weidmann, *Taxation of Derivatives and Cryptoassets*, Second Edition, 2024 (ISBN 978-94-035-2383-5).
53. Chris Evans, Richard Krever & Peter Mellor (eds), *Tax Simplification*, 2015 (ISBN 978-90-411-5976-2).
54. Reuven Avi-Yonah & Joel Slemrod (eds), *Taxation and Migration*, 2015 (ISBN 978-90-411-6136-9).
55. Alexander Bosman, *Other Income under Tax Treaties: An Analysis of Article 21 of the OECD Model Convention*, 2015 (ISBN 978-90-411-6610-4).
56. John Abrahamson, *International Taxation of Manufacturing and Distribution*, 2016 (ISBN 978-90-411-6664-7).
57. Frederik Boulogne, *Shortcomings in the EU Merger Directive*, 2016 (ISBN 978-90-411-6713-2).
58. Angelika Meindl-Ringler, *Beneficial Ownership in International Tax Law*, 2016 (ISBN 978-90-411-6833-7).
59. Andreas Waltrich, *Cross-Border Taxation of Permanent Establishments: An International Comparison*, 2016 (ISBN 978-90-411-6832-0).
60. Sergio André Rocha & Allison Christians (eds), *Tax Sovereignty in the BEPS Era*, 2017 (ISBN 978-90-411-6707-1).
61. Peter Antony Wilson, *BRICS and International Tax Law*, 2018 (ISBN 978-90-411-9435-0).
62. Louise Otis, Brigitte Alepin & Blanca Moreno-Dodson (eds), *Winning the Tax Wars: Tax Competition and Cooperation*, 2018 (ISBN 978-90-411-9460-2).

63. Marta Castelon, *International Taxation of Income from Services under Double Taxation Conventions: Development, Practice and Policy*, 2018 (ISBN 978-90-411-9594-4).
64. D.M. Broekhuijsen, *A Multilateral Tax Treaty: Designing an Instrument to Modernise International Tax Law*, 2018 (ISBN 978-90-411-9872-3).
65. John Abrahamson, *International Taxation of Energy Production and Distribution*, 2018 (ISBN 978-90-411-9101-4).
66. Leopoldo Parada, *Double Non-taxation and the Use of Hybrid Entities: An Alternative Approach in the New Era of BEPS*, 2018 (ISBN 978-90-411-9991-1).
67. Richard Snoeij, *International Tax Aspects of Sovereign Wealth Investors: A Source State Perspective*, 2018 (ISBN 978-90-411-9431-2).
68. Aleksandra Bal, *Taxation, Virtual Currency and Blockchain*, 2019 (ISBN 978-94-035-0103-1).
69. Werner Haslehner, Georg Kofler, Katerina Pantazatou & Alexander Rust (eds), *Tax and the Digital Economy: Challenges and Proposals for Reform*, 2019 (ISBN 978-94-035-0361-5).
70. Eva Escribano, *Jurisdiction to Tax Corporate Income Pursuant to the Presumptive Benefit Principle: A Critical Analysis of Structural Paradigms Underlying Corporate Income Taxation and Proposals for Reform*, 2019 (ISBN 978-94-035-0640-1).
71. Jérôme Monsenego & Jan Bjuvberg (eds), *International Taxation in a Changing Landscape: Liber Amicorum in Honour of Bertil Wiman*, 2019 (ISBN 978-90-411-9234-9).
72. Kasper Dziurdź, *Non-discrimination in Tax Treaty Law and World Trade Law: The Impact of Formal, Substantive and Subjective Approaches*, 2019 (ISBN 978-94-035-0904-4).
73. Félix Daniel Martínez Laguna, *Hybrid Financial Instruments, Double Nontaxation and Linking Rules*, 2019 (ISBN 978-94-035-1074-3).
74. Jan Gooijer, *Tax Treaty Residence of Entities*, 2019 (ISBN 978-94-035-1301-0).
75. John Abrahamson, *International Taxation of Banking*, 2020 (ISBN 978-94-035-1094-1).
76. Richard Krever & François Vaillancourt (eds), *The Allocation of Multinational Business Income: Reassessing the Formulary Apportionment Option*, 2020 (ISBN 978-94-035-0614-2).
77. Ajit Kumar Singh, *Exploring the Nexus Doctrine in International Tax Law*, 2021 (ISBN 978-94-035-3363-6).
78. Galya Savir, *Regulation and Tax in Space*, 2021 (ISBN 978-94-035-3393-3).
79. Rita Julien, *Credit Method Compatibility and Constraints under EU Law: An Analysis of the Case Law of the CJEU*, 2022 (ISBN 978-94-035-2363-7).
80. Sergio André Rocha & Allison Christians (eds), *A Multilateral Convention for Tax: From Theory to Implementation*, 2022 (ISBN 978-90-411-9428-2).
81. Brigitte Alepin, Lyne Latulippe & Louise Otis (eds), *Coordination and Cooperation: Tax Policy in the 21st Century*, 2022 (ISBN 978-94-035-3740-5).
82. Chunyang Zhang, *The Role of Tax Law in Mergers and Acquisitions: A Chinese Perspective*, 2022 (ISBN 978-94-035-3741-2).

83. Florian Navisotschnigg, *Substance in International Tax Law: DEMPE Approach, Substantial Activity Requirement and Beneficial Ownership*, 2022 (ISBN 978-94-035-4895-1).
84. Mees Vergouwen, *The Effect of Directives Within the Area of Direct Taxation on the Interpretation and Application of Tax Treaties*, 2023 (ISBN 978-94-035-0907-5).
85. Rachna Matabudul, *Tax Treaty Dispute Resolution: Lessons from the Law of the Sea*, 2023 (ISBN 978-94-035-3407-7).

www.ingramcontent.com/pod-product-compliance
Lightning Source LLC
Chambersburg PA
CBHW071234230926
51849CB00001B/103
9789403523835